Building Distributed Applications
with Visual Basic .NET

Dan Fox
Quilogy, Inc.

201 West 103rd St., Indianapolis, Indiana, 46290 USA

Building Distributed Applications with Visual Basic .NET

Copyright © 2002 by Sams Publishing

International Standard Book Number: 0-672-32130-0

Library of Congress Catalog Card Number: 00-111343

Printed in the United States of America

First Printing: November 2001

04   03   02   01   4   3   2   1

Trademarks

Warning and Disclaimer

ASSOCIATE PUBLISHER
Linda Engelman

ACQUISITIONS EDITOR
Sondra Scott

DEVELOPMENT EDITOR
Shannon Leuma

MANAGING EDITOR
Charlotte Clapp

PROJECT EDITOR
Elizabeth Finney

COPY EDITORS
Geneil Breeze
Michael Henry

INDEXER
Erika Millen

PROOFREADER
Plan-it Publishing

TECHNICAL EDITORS
Phil Syme
Dan Suceava

TEAM COORDINATOR
Chris Feathers

MEDIA DEVELOPER
Dan Scherf

INTERIOR DESIGNER
Anne Jones

COVER DESIGNER
Aren Howell

Contents at a Glance

Table of Contents

Foreword

The shift to .NET technologies is underway, bringing with it exciting opportunities that only distributed computing makes possible. This I know to be true, having experienced the awesome power of .NET technologies at work each day where our award-winning internal systems run on the .NET platform.

As Chief Technology Officer at Quilogy, a provider of business solutions through digital consulting, advanced hosting, and technical education, I have worked closely with Dan Fox over the past several years learning, experimenting with, and applying new Microsoft technologies to our own organization. For only by testing and building proven solutions for ourselves can we be sure to provide our customers with the best, most effective solutions. Our work over the past year to incorporate .NET strategies has been especially rewarding.

Dan's demonstrated mastery of .NET technologies at Quilogy as well as his previous professional experiences building large-scale systems for a major oil company, extensive knowledge of database and object-oriented systems, as well as numerous Microsoft certifications make him uniquely qualified to write this book. Additionally, this year marks the 10th anniversary of Visual Basic, which makes this book's publication particularly meaningful. As we have found for ourselves, the best way for professional VB developers to enter into the .NET sphere is through Visual Basic .NET.

As the leading language used by corporate developers to build solutions, VB with its new .NET qualities now can address even more of the needs and concerns of business developers, which makes understanding it at this time so crucial. Part of the great news about .NET is that you can move into it and still leverage your existing skills because of its multilanguage support. As the book shows, there are some concepts and techniques you'll need to learn, but they'll build on those you already have, so you can start to take advantage of all the new features and capabilities that .NET has to offer.

Rather than restating Microsoft's documentation, Dan explains the course of an application's development and offers wide-ranging insight as he delves into the whys, such as why VB .NET is important, and the hows, such as how VB .NET fits into the general scheme. Additionally, numerous code examples clearly illustrate key points and complement the book's easy readability. Dan is a sought-after instructor and speaker at such major events as TechEd and Developer Days. He is also a regular contributor to several print and online magazines including *Visual Basic Programmers Journal*, *SQL Server* Magazine, InformIT, and *Advisor* journals. His exemplary teaching methods, engaging speaking voice, and comprehensive knowledge shine through in this book.

Currently as Technical Director, Dan is charged with helping me select technologies, set application architecture, identify successful design patterns, and educate staff on emerging technologies. Since taking on this important position in the company, he has been instrumental in the development of Quilogy's breakthrough system for building portal solutions called Quilogy Accelerator (QA). Using the code to Quilogy's own intranet as a .NET accelerator, QA facilitates the process of creating portal and intranet solutions faster and less expensively than either buying or building from scratch.

As we have found with QA and you will find as you apply .NET strategies to your own business practices, .NET is changing the face of technological business solutions in extraordinarily exciting new directions.

Alan Groh
CTO Quilogy

About the Author

Dan Fox is Technical Director for Quilogy in Overland Park, Kansas. Quilogy (www.quilogy.com) is a leading Microsoft Gold Certified Partner and Solution Provider with more than 450 consultants nationwide in 16 cities. Quilogy provides digital consulting and technical education services to a wide range of clients and specializes in building solutions on the Microsoft platform. As a Certified Technical Education Center, Quilogy teaches the range of Microsoft Official Curriculum (MOC) courses and specializes in building solutions and teaching courses using both .NET development and .NET Enterprise Servers.

Dan is a Microsoft Certified Solutions Developer, Systems Engineer, and Trainer who has been a consultant, instructor, and managing consultant on a variety of projects. In his role as a Technical Director, Dan provides technical guidance to Quilogy's consultants and customers.

Before joining Quilogy in 1995, Dan worked for Chevron in Houston, Texas, and the National Association of Insurance Commissioners in Kansas City, Missouri. Dan earned his B.S. in Computer Science from Iowa State University in 1991.

Dan has been a frequent contributor to the *Visual Basic Programmer's Journal* and has written numerous articles for *SQL Server* magazine, *Advisor* journals, and InformIT.com. He authored the book *Pure Visual Basic* from Sams and coauthored a book on the Visual Basic 6 Distributed Exam (70-175) for Certification Insider Press. He has spoken at TechEd and several Developer Days conferences and Microsoft events.

Dan lives in Shawnee, Kansas, with his lovely wife, Beth, and two young daughters, Laura and Anna. Besides earning the nickname "Dan.NET" from his family, Dan spends his time reading, enjoying movies, and as always, rooting for the Cubs.

About the Technical Reviewers

Dan Suceava is currently a Senior Programmer for Vitrix, Inc., a time-and-attendance software company located in Tempe, Arizona. He has been developing desktop and n-tiered applications in Visual Basic since 1996. He currently has completed working on an ASP solution that offers time keeping over the Web to other businesses. He holds a Master's Degree in Computer Science from Arizona State University.

Phil Syme has been programming with C++ and Visual Basic since the release of Windows 3.1. He helped create several enterprise-scale projects developed for Fortune 100 companies that used Microsoft technologies. Phil has coauthored two articles published in IEEE symposiums. Currently, Phil is writing two books with Peter Aitken, called *Sams Teach Yourself Internet Programming with C# in 21 Days* and *Sams Teach Yourself Internet Programming with VB .Net in 21 Days*.

Eric Wilson has been developing business applications for eCommerce, Internet, and LAN-based solutions since 1994. Eric is certified in a variety of Microsoft solutions and has achieved the following status with Microsoft: MCSE (Microsoft Certified Systems Engineer), MCSD (Microsoft Certified Solutions Developer), MCT (Microsoft Certified Trainer), MCP (Microsoft Certified Professional), and MCP + I (Microsoft Certified Professional + Internet). Currently, Eric is the President and CEO of Web Basix, Inc., located in RTP (Research Triangle Park), North Carolina, focusing on enterprise level application development and developer training.

Dedication

To my daughters, Laura and Anna, who are always a reminder of God's blessings.

Acknowledgments

First, I'd to thank the Senior Acquisitions Editor on this project at Sams, Sondra Scott. From our initial contact, she has been an encouragement and a great person to work with. She made sure that each step in the process went smoothly and provided excellent feedback early in the process in the form of reviews. In addition, I'd like to thank Shannon Leuma, the Development Editor, who was ever vigilant to keep me on schedule, make sure that the content was well organized, and made many suggestions that served to make this a better book.

Of course, the two key elements of any technical book such as this, the actual written word and the code, were greatly improved by the copyediting skills of Mike Henry and Geneil Breeze, and the technical reviews of Phil Syme, Dan Suceava, and Eric Wilson. The five of them made sure that the book was readable and contained accurate information, something that was difficult given the fact that the reviewers had to work with multiple beta versions of the product for most of the development cycle.

As you can tell from the cover and forward, this book was a team effort by Quilogy, the company for which I work. President and CEO Randy Schilling and Chief Technology Officer Alan Groh's encouragement and investment in the project was instrumental to making it a success. Because the book was developed so early in the product life cycle, their willingness to give me the resources to develop a book of this scope, including both the time and travel to Redmond, contributed greatly to the quality of the final result. Throughout the process, Quilogy consultants and instructors reviewed the content and provided helpful advice and suggestions. To all these talented people, I'm certainly indebted, particularly, Tim Vanover, Dave Wanta, Jason Wisener, Sue Van Gels, Adrian Anttila, and Cathey Barrett.

In addition, the scope and purpose of the book was shaped and honed through excellent reviews by Ari Bixhorn, VB Product Manager at Microsoft; Steve Hoag, Senior Technical Writer for VB User Education at Microsoft; Kyle Lutes, Assistant Professor at the Computer Technology Department of Purdue University; Richard Nelson, Senior Software Architect at Intuitive Manufacturing Systems; Lars Powers, Vice President/Solution Development at Acclarant, Inc.; Mike Snell, Chief Software Architect at Acclarant, Inc.; and Larry Wall, Team Leader Microsoft Group at Synapse Technology. Thanks to all of you for your help.

And so, as is true of any book, this one was truly a team effort. That being said, any errors are only mine, so feel free to e-mail me at `dfox@quilogy.com` with corrections and suggestions.

Finally and most importantly, I couldn't have embarked on this project without the loving support of my wife, Beth, and daughters, Laura and Anna. Beth's continuous encouragement and patience during this project made it much easier to accomplish, and my girls as always provided the balance that keeps my technological pursuits in perspective.

Tell Us What You Think!

As the reader of this book, *you* are our most important critic and commentator. We value your opinion and want to know what we're doing right, what we could do better, what areas you'd like to see us publish in, and any other words of wisdom you're willing to pass our way.

As an Associate Publisher for Sams Publishing, I welcome your comments. You can fax, e-mail, or write me directly to let me know what you did or didn't like about this book—as well as what we can do to make our books stronger.

Please note that I cannot help you with technical problems related to the topic of this book, and that due to the high volume of mail I receive, I might not be able to reply to every message.

When you write, please be sure to include this book's title and author as well as your name and phone or fax number. I will carefully review your comments and share them with the author and editors who worked on the book.

Fax: 317-581-4770

E-mail: feedback@samspublishing.com

Mail: Linda Engelman
         Associate Publisher
         Sams Publishing
         201 West 103rd Street
         Indianapolis, IN 46290 USA

Introduction

Congratulations on stepping into the world of .NET! As you no doubt know by now, for many developers, this is a big step. .NET in general and VB .NET in particular introduce new technology and new ways of performing familiar tasks that require attention to both conceptual and practical issues when designing and developing software.

This introduction explains the focus, layout, illustrative style, sample application, Web site, and intended audience of the book.

The Book's Focus

Not all software is created equal. The architecture and techniques you use when designing and building a forms-based application, for example, are not the same as for building a Web-based application. Because many different types of applications require different approaches, and thus will use VB .NET in different ways, this book focuses on building distributed applications.

By "building" distributed applications, I'm referring to the design and construction of the software. To that end, this book focuses both on architectural issues and implementation by explaining how a certain aspect of VB .NET fits into the bigger picture, and how it can or should be used in a distributed application in addition to the details of the syntax. By distributed applications, I mean those applications that employ a Web architecture and typically are constructed in logical services or tiers (presentation, business logic, data access). As a result, for example, developing forms-based applications using the Windows Forms package is beyond the scope of this book, whereas almost a quarter of the book is devoted to building presentation services using both Web Forms and Web Services.

As mentioned, distributed applications also include building business logic and data access services. Therefore, some of the largest chapters deal with integrating VB .NET with Component Services and using ADO.NET and XML. Many readers might be familiar with this architecture as Windows DNA although that marketing term refers to the previous generation of technology including VB 6.0 and COM. Indeed, this book can be thought of as a collection of techniques for building updated Windows DNA applications with VB .NET.

In addition, I've placed some emphasis on building server-based applications as well and have included coverage on Windows service applications and employing the networking APIs in .NET. I've included these topics because they often are employed as simply an additional interface to a distributed application and are needed to create robust back ends for data exchange or data loading.

The Book's Layout

To walk you through the conceptual and practical issues, this book is comprised of three sections that will facilitate understanding of not only the how but also the why of building distributed applications.

Part I: .NET Concepts

Part I, ".NET Concepts," provides an overview of the key concepts that developers need to be aware of when undertaking projects using VB .NET. The section begins with Chapter 1, "The Microsoft .NET Architecture," which not only introduces the platform but also dives right into the substrate of VB .NET, the common-language runtime (CLR) upon which everything in the product is built. The CLR is indeed the revolutionary aspect of VB .NET, and, as you'll see, when put in proper context, VB .NET can simply be thought of as a tool used to build applications for the CLR, referred to as managed applications.

Although a good deal of technical information is found in Chapter 1, my intent is not to scare off anyone. However, I think it is crucial to gain at least a surface level understanding of the CLR because it helps make sense of many of the other concepts in VB .NET such as those discussed in Chapter 4, "Object-Oriented Features," and Chapter 5, "Packaging, Deployment, and Security." In addition, Part I covers the changes and new features in both Visual Studio .NET in Chapter 2, "The Development Environment," and the VB language itself in Chapter 3, "VB .NET Language Features." Finally, the section closes with Chapter 6, "Error Handling and Debugging," which discusses how error handling and debugging have been improved in this version of the product.

Part II: Enterprise Techniques

Part II, "Enterprise Techniques," is the core of the book and is comprised of five chapters that discuss each of the services layers (presentation, business, data access) in a distributed application in reverse order. The section begins with Chapter 7, "Accessing Data with ADO.NET," which examines how the ADO.NET programming model enables you to more easily build loosely coupled applications while taking advantage of XML.

This chapter, and the others in the section, provide examples from a sample application that implements a simple student registration site for the company I work for, Quilogy. Quilogy (www.quilogy.com) is a digital consulting firm that offers technical education at training centers around the country. To that end, students need to be able to query our course schedule, register for class, review their transcript, and so on from our public Web site. The sample application implements these features using VB .NET and is provided, along with the underlying database schema, on the companion Web site (www.samspublishing.com). The application uses SQL Server 2000 on the back end, so although ADO.NET supports accessing other providers, the examples in this section and throughout the book will focus on SQL Server.

Chapter 8, "Building Components," discusses how components are built in VB .NET. The chapter also looks at legacy DLLs to ensure that your existing code can be used in .NET. Finally, a discussion on how components in VB .NET applications can be shared with .NET Remoting is presented, which, like its precursor DCOM, often comes in handy when the subsystems in a distributed application need to communicate across process and machine boundaries. Chapter 9, "Accessing Component Services," logically follows by discussing how business and data access logic in VB .NET components can be integrated with Windows 2000 Component Services. This allows your VB .NET components to take advantage of the object pooling, just-in-time activation, transactional control, and other features VB developers routinely implement in distributed applications. In addition, this chapter shows how components built in VB .NET can interoperate with classic COM components.

Part II is rounded out with Chapter 10, "Building Web Forms" and Chapter 11, "Building Web Services," which cover the aspects of the presentation services layer necessary to build a Web-based application. In large part, Chapter 10 covers the architecture and features of ASP.NET and how they differ from ASP and then discusses in detail the Web Forms programming model using the UI of the Quilogy sample application for illustration. Chapter 11 introduces a second type of interface that VB .NET can produce by discussing Web Services. Because Web Services are a new concept to many developers, this chapter provides a foundation by exploring the underlying technologies involved and how they are implemented in VB .NET.

Part III: Integration

The last section of the book, Part III, "Integration," is comprised of a collection of topics that allow VB .NET developers to extend their code. Chapter 12, "Accessing System Services," covers I/O concepts, creating multithreaded applications, and a brief introduction to using cryptography. Chapter 13, "Implementing Services," walks through creating Windows Services in VB .NET as well as using scheduling, the event log, performance counters, and network communication. Finally, Chapter 14, "Integrating with the Enterprise," examines three topics that allow VB .NET developers to extend their reach to data sources other than relational databases by using the XML classes, message queuing, and integrating with Active Directory.

As you might be aware, VB .NET largely gains its functionality from the class libraries that all the Visual Studio .NET languages can take advantage of, which I'll refer to as the Services Framework. As such, you'll notice that only Chapters 2, 3, and 4 actually discuss issues particular to VB .NET. Most of the rest of the book is simply an explication of how the classes of the Services Framework can be used within the VB .NET language. This realization is key to understanding VB .NET as a product and its role in Visual Studio .NET. In this way, VB .NET can be thought of as a tool used to integrate the prebuilt components of the Services Framework into a specific solution. Thinking of VB .NET this way should come as no surprise to existing VB developers because the strength of previous versions of VB also was integrating prebuilt and custom components.

The Book's Illustrative Style, Sample Application, and Web Site

Typically, each chapter or major section begins with an explanatory paragraph or two that attempts to put the topic under discussion in the proper context. For example, when discussing ADO.NET, the first question many developers have is how it interoperates with ADO 2.x and how knowledge of ADO will be leveraged when programming data access in VB .NET. With the context set, the discussion moves into explaining the relevant syntax and APIs that enable you to take advantage of the feature. In many cases, the explanation of the syntax is illustrated using code snippets as well as tables and figures that explicate the syntax, list the methods of a particular class, for example, or show a hierarchy that illustrates how the class fits into the bigger picture. Finally, in most cases, a functional example is presented in one or more code listings that illustrate techniques in context. This is used as a springboard to point out interesting aspects of the feature and alternative techniques.

Along the way, the text is peppered with explanatory notes, cautions, and sidebars that point out related issues or point you to places elsewhere in the book or external to it where additional information can be found. For example, several notes refer to background information from my previous book, *Pure Visual Basic*. Because no single book can cover a topic as big as VB .NET and the .NET Framework, notes are often used to delineate the boundaries of the book by giving you hints as to how a particular technique could be extended or alternatively implemented.

To be sure, this style requires some discipline on the part of the reader because many of the details and alternatives are embedded in the explanatory paragraphs, and the reader must refer back to the code listings frequently to follow the discussion. However, I've also tried to limit the amount of information to that immediately relevant to building applications and so, for example, not all the overloaded signatures of each method are explained along with the myriad arguments supported. That kind of information is better presented and should be found in the excellent online help that ships with the product.

The other key implication of the style I've employed is that it is definitely not a tutorial. Readers attempting to type in the code exactly as presented in the book will have trouble because in many cases the code shows only the relevant portion of a larger concept that will not execute by itself. In addition, in many cases, the code is analogous to pseudo code and is designed to show how a particular API can be used but does not implement all the details.

The approach I recommend when reading the book is to read the entire section, tracking with the code listings and snippets, and then perusing the online documentation or other sources for any additional information before developing your own samples in your own problem domain using the listings as a starting point. To help you in this endeavor, as mentioned earlier, the code listings, along with the complete Quilogy sample application discussed in Chapters 7 through 11, can be found on the Sams Web site at www.samspublishing.com. To remind you of this as you read, each chapter introduction includes the following note:

> **NOTE**
>
> All code listings and supplemental material for this chapter can be found on the book's Web site at www.samspublishing.com.

In addition, when using the listings, it should be noted that because in VB .NET the act of referencing external libraries usually entails placing an Imports statement at the beginning of your code file, many of the code listings and examples contain shaded Imports statements at the beginning. These are shaded because they wouldn't appear in actual code in that location but are required to produce the code found in the listing or example.

This book intentionally is heavy on code listings and short on figures. I believe that developers can learn more quickly by viewing the code of others rather than through a tutorial or a simple discussion. I tried to restrict the use of figures to those required to place a concept in context or, for example, to give you an idea of where in the VS .NET UI to look for a particular feature. The screen shots should not be used as a tutorial, and as you work with VS .NET, the particulars of your solution will mean that the screens you see might differ.

I've also focused primarily on how you implement features using code rather than the graphical designers and wizards included in VS .NET. This too is intentional because I believe that to develop a firm foundation you need to understand what's happening at the code level and by nature, graphical interactions and wizards don't translate well to this medium.

The Book's Audience

As you read the book, you might notice that I had a primary and a secondary audience in mind. Existing corporate VB developers are the primary audience. As a result, the book is primarily written from the perspective of a developer comfortable with the syntax of VB 6.0 who is building Windows DNA applications today. In fact, the prototypical reader I pictured in my mind is the typical student who attends one of Quilogy's Microsoft Official Curriculum (MOC) courses on VB. Typically, these developers have been using VB for some time and are building

COM components to house their data access and business logic and employing Microsoft Transaction Server or Component Services. They are also versed in ADO and ASP development and are just beginning to use XML. For these developers, the primary challenge when moving to VB .NET is the object-oriented nature of the Services Framework and the additional language syntax used to implement these features. As such, Chapters 3 and 4 will be especially useful.

The secondary audience is the ASP developer who typically has less formal training and specializes in Web development. For these developers, the challenge is to move from building two-tiered Web applications to a multitiered architecture, as described in Chapter 7. In addition, the richness of the VB .NET language, as opposed to VBScript or JScript, will require an adjustment.

Finally, the many classes in the Services Framework that allow you to easily use system services will open up a new world of possibilities. I've tried to highlight the portions of the Services Framework (especially in Part III) that will be the most useful.

I wrote this book because I think that the underlying technology of the platform and the direction Microsoft has chosen with VB .NET make it ideally suited to developing distributed applications. However, the paradigm shift associated with the platform and the sheer size of the product will make it difficult for some VB developers to get a handle on how to use VB .NET. In the end, this book provides a bit of a roadmap and a survey of VB .NET and the Services Framework and how it can be used to build distributed applications.

So what are you waiting for? Let's get started by exploring the foundation of VB .NET: the Microsoft .NET architecture.

Dan Fox

Shawnee, Kansas
August 2001

.NET Concepts

PART

I

IN THIS PART

The Microsoft .NET Architecture

IN THIS CHAPTER

As you are no doubt already aware, Visual Basic .NET (VB .NET) is far more than simply a new release of Visual Basic. VB .NET is actually a piece in the larger puzzle of Microsoft's .NET architecture. This architecture encompasses not only a new release of Visual Studio (Visual Studio .NET), which includes a suite of languages and a common platform on which all the Visual Studio languages run referred to as the .NET Framework, but also new releases of server products such as SQL Server 2000, BizTalk Server 2000, and Application Center Server 2000, collectively referred to as .NET Enterprise Servers.

A Storm Coming?

In addition to the .NET development and server story, Microsoft has disclosed preliminary plans for building and hosting a set of Web-based services under the name .NET My Services (formerly codenamed Hailstorm). Briefly, these services will be built using technology in the .NET Framework and will allow users the ability to share and consume personal information anywhere on any device. The core of the initiative is to integrate disparate silos of information such as tasks, contacts, inbox, schedule, notifications, and favorites, among others, into a single secure Web-based information store accessible via standard Internet protocols.

Currently, Passport, Microsoft's authentication service, is the only publicly available piece of this vision that is referred to both as Building Block Services and Foundation Services. Passport integration in ASP.NET will be discussed in Chapter 10, "Building Web Forms" while more information on .NET My Services can be found at `http://www.microsoft.com/myservices/default.asp`.

Together, all these new tools are designed to help developers build modern, robust, distributed applications. To help you understand how VB .NET fits into the architecture, this chapter will discuss the platform and its implications for VB developers. Although this is a large chapter with a lot of technical material, the differences in the fundamental architecture between previous versions of VB and VB .NET are significant. So significant, in fact, that you need to immediately get a baseline for how these changes have been implemented and what they mean to the larger picture of the .NET Framework and Visual Studio .NET.

NOTE

All code listings and supplemental material for this chapter can be found on the book's Web site at `samspublishing.com`.

A New Platform

For corporate developers, application development has gone through several major shifts in the last decade. As we started the 1990s, we were already immersed in the shift from developing character-based monolithic mainframe applications to two-tier client/server applications on PC-based hardware and operating systems utilizing ODBC-compliant relational databases and graphical user interfaces (GUIs). At nearly the same time, we began to see the adoption of object-oriented programming (OOP) concepts such as encapsulation, inheritance, polymorphism, and reusable components into development tools such as PowerBuilder and Visual Basic. With a subsequent move to distributed computing relying on n-tier architectures and component-based programming, by early 1997, many of these tools and technologies were relatively mature, widely distributed, and entrenched in the corporate developer community.

From the perspective of a corporate developer utilizing Microsoft products, this produced an architecture in which a Visual Studio client application written in VB or Microsoft Foundation Classes (MFC) communicated with COM components running in Microsoft Transaction Server (MTS) using the DCOM protocol. The components themselves accessed a relational database such as SQL Server or Oracle using an ODBC driver or, later, an OLEDB provider. By utilizing the object context, MTS gave developers the ability to handle transactions across these heterogeneous databases using XA (a subset of services from the X/Open Distributed Transaction Processing (DTP)) and centralized object destruction and creation.

Of course, the largest change had reached critical mass by 1997 with the widespread adoption of the Internet, HTML, and now XML. Although Microsoft released a new development tool, Visual InterDev (VID), and a programming model for Web development, Active Server Pages (ASP), both of these were largely additions to the existing architecture that provided integration with existing components and relational databases, but did not alter the way development was done in the core Visual Studio languages Visual Basic and Visual C++. In addition, the programming model and visual design tools provided in VID and ASP were not nearly as robust as those in the more mature products. Attempts to integrate Web programming into VB, such as the inclusion of ActiveX documents, DHTML applications, and Web classes, only illustrated the point that at their core, the flagship development tools were ill-suited for life in a Web world. One of the main reasons for this is that the tools relied on technology—such as the Win32 API, COM, and DCOM—that was developed in the early 1990s when desktop computing was central and when persistently connected clients in an insulated LAN environment were the norm.

Developing applications for which the Internet is the platform requires a different mindset—a mindset that moves from thinking of writing software for only internal consumption to one in which all users of the Internet are your potential customers. And this requires different technology that is up to the task of incorporating support for the loosely coupled nature of clients and servers, a new security model, and the integration of industry standard HTTP and XML as ubiquitous protocols. I don't know about you, but if all this could be packaged within a modern object-oriented framework that provides maximum reusability and developer productivity, it sounds like a platform I'd like to use.

And so, at its core, the .NET Framework and Visual Studio .NET (which I'll refer to together as simply .NET) are tools designed to take advantage of the Internet as the major platform for application development. At the highest level, the goals for the initial release were to produce a development environment:

- Where the Internet and Internet standards are second nature
- Where distributed Web applications are easy to build
- That combines the power of object-oriented programming and relieves the burdens of complicated versioning and deployment

In the remainder of this section and chapter, I'll talk specifically about what .NET is and discover how Visual Basic .NET fits in.

What .NET Is and Is Not

In the months leading up to the release of Visual Studio .NET (VS .NET), there has been much speculation and confusion about exactly what .NET is and what it is not. To set the stage for the rest of this chapter—and indeed for the entire book—I want to cover a few points along those lines.

First and foremost, the .NET Framework and VS .NET are not evolutionary upgrades to the Visual Studio 6.0 (VS 6.0) product set. In almost all respects, they are revolutionary in that they offer a fundamentally different programming model based on the Common Language Runtime (CLR) that all the development tools share. The mere fact that I refer to the .NET Framework apart from VS .NET indicates that these are two separate products, where VS .NET is dependent on the .NET Framework. However the reverse is not true. This new model requires new thinking on the part of developers because not only has syntax changed in their chosen .NET language, but the fundamental structure and runtime behavior of programs might be quite different in .NET.

Second, .NET is not a Microsoft version of Java. Although .NET borrows a little from the Java playbook in terms of using ideas such as just-in-time compilation and garbage collection, its strength will probably not lie in the fact that it can be platform independent. However, as you'll see, the architecture of .NET makes it possible to port the CLR to various platforms so that your applications could, in the future, be compiled once and run anywhere. In fact, .NET's greatest strength is its language independence. As was the strength of classic COM, being able to write code that interoperates well with code written in another language is typically more important than being able to run the same binary on various platforms. In addition, the amount of integration possible in .NET far exceeds that provided by COM and extends all the way to cross-language inheritance.

In any case, Microsoft's vision for platform independence relies on industry standards such as Simple Object Access Protocol (SOAP), an XML-based protocol, to make cross-platform calls and interact with services exposed over the Web (also known as XML Web Services). Companies throughout the industry from IBM to Sun are supporting the SOAP standard now in the hands of the W3C (http://www.w3.org/TR/SOAP/), and so its inclusion in .NET moves us forward to the time when applications built on differing platforms will be able to communicate seamlessly.

> **NOTE**
>
> For a look at a variety of Web Services built on various platforms, see www.xmethods.net.

On the other side of the fence, .NET is a new platform for developing distributed Web applications. .NET mainstreams the concept of Web Services as programmable application components accessible via standard Web protocols. The .NET Framework includes hundreds of prebuilt classes that encapsulate these Web standards and protocols to provide a great foundation for building both interactive Web applications and Web Services, as I'll discuss in Chapters 10, "Building Web Forms," and 11, "Building Web Services."

.NET also provides a new model for building and sharing components. As you're probably aware, the reliance of classic COM components on registry entries, Globally Unique Identifiers (GUIDs), v-tables, and IUnknown makes distributing and invoking those components across the network using DCOM sometimes tricky. In .NET, all those concepts go away and are replaced by a simpler mechanism that allows remoting of components across the network, easy deployment, and side-by-side versioning of components on the same machine. You will explore many of these concepts in Chapters 5, "Packaging, Deployment, and Security," and 8, "Building Components."

Finally, .NET is a Rapid Application Development (RAD) tool for distributed applications. The inclusion of the Server Explorer window in the VS. NET IDE (covered in Chapter 2, "The Development Environment"), the .NET Framework classes for manipulating data through ADO.NET (covered in Chapter 7, "Accessing Data with ADO.NET"), and integrating with both low-level system services such as threading (covered in Chapter 12, "Accessing System Services") and high-level services such as messaging and Active Directory (covered in Chapter 14, "Integrating with the Enterprise") make it a high-productivity environment.

VB's Place in .NET

Visual Basic as a development tool has gone through several major revisions over the years. Particularly, the releases of VB 3.0, 4.0, and 5.0 provided significant enhancements that enabled VB to access databases, act as a COM client, and create ActiveX controls and COM components. However, with the release of Visual Basic .NET (VB .NET), VB has undergone its biggest change by far in its now ten-year history.

Perhaps the key point to remember with VB .NET is that it is now a first-class citizen within VS .NET. What this means is that VB .NET has full access to the IDE, services, and features within the .NET Framework and is not limited by a "glass ceiling." Because of this fact, in theory, almost all code written in other VS .NET languages such as Visual C# (VC#), JScript, and Visual C++ (VC++) with managed extensions will be able to be translated to VB .NET with identical performance.

NOTE

The phrase *in theory* in the previous paragraph refers to the fact that compilers, as well as the .NET Framework, play a role in performance. Even if the VB .NET language contains syntactical equivalents for all VC# constructs, the VB .NET compiler would still have to produce intermediate language code (as discussed later) identical to that produced by the VC# compiler in order for two applications to perform identically. This is unlikely, and so in certain circumstances a language built on the .NET Framework might outperform another language when executing similar operations. However, these small differences will also tend to even out in the scope of an entire application.

In the initial release of VS .NET, VC++ will be the only language through which you can create code that does not use the CLR at all. VC# will allow you to write code blocks that do not use the CLR and so in both cases, when using these features, all bets on performance are off.

Entire books have been written on how to extend VB to implement specific features (and break through the "glass ceiling") of the Win32 API, such as threading, callbacks, and writing NT services. (I know because I've written one of them.) However, with VB .NET, all these features are transparent and accessible through a set of class libraries that ship with VS .NET, called the .NET Framework classes or the *Services Framework*. Using the Services Framework in your applications allows VB .NET to support the RAD model that VB developers have come to expect.

> **NOTE**
>
> Throughout this book I'll use the term *Services Framework* to refer to the entire collection of over a thousand classes that ship with Visual Studio .NET, both those that implement support for the various programming models such as Web Forms and Web Services, and the lower-level classes that implement network communication, IO, threading, and so on. Some authors will refer to the entire collection as simply the .NET Framework, .NET Frameworks, or Base Class Libraries (BCL). Although I seldom use the term, I reserve BCL for the lower-level classes upon which the higher-level programming models are built.

The second point to consider is that VB .NET not only encompasses the functionality of previous versions of VB to create form-based applications and components, it also can be used to create Web applications using a robust event-driven programming model. In other words, the functionality of the forms package and ASP have been abstracted into application programming models and exposed to all the .NET programming languages through reusable framework classes.

> **NOTE**
>
> As a result of the inclusion of the Web-based programming into the Services Framework, developers who in the past used Visual InterDev as their primary tool will likely be migrating to VB .NET. For developers, moving from a language such as VBScript, which did not support types other than `Variant` and lacked support for more sophisticated features like classes and events, to the robust .NET languages might at first seem daunting. For those developers I say, bear with me. Much of the information in this chapter is crucial for getting the big picture. That being said, those developers will find more of the information for which they are looking, and can move through the book using a faster track, by concentrating on Chapters 2, 3, 4, 7, 10, and 11.

In addition, many of the intrinsic functions and statements have been abstracted into the Services Framework and the CLR, the result being that VB .NET actually contains fewer keywords than previous versions. A picture of how these parts fit together can be seen in Figure 1.1.

> **NOTE**
>
> VB .NET is a Common Language Specification (CLS)–compliant language and so it can take advantage of the CLR. There is a more complete discussion of the CLS later in this chapter.

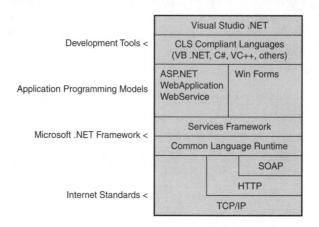

FIGURE 1.1

The .NET architecture. Much of the functionality of previous versions of VB has been abstracted into the application programming models and Services Framework.

Taken together, you can infer that VB .NET is different from previous versions of VB because it is now only one of many languages that take advantage of the services provided by the .NET Framework. This is great for VB developers because they can now access all the features .NET provides without paying the price of increased complexity, kludgy workarounds, and degraded performance.

In the remainder of this chapter, I'll drill down on the foundation of Figure 1.1 and discuss the key concepts behind the CLR and the Services Framework.

Common Language Runtime Architecture

At the core of .NET is certainly the CLR. Simply put, the CLR provides the environment in which all code compiled in VB .NET (and other compliant languages) executes. Although my goal in discussing the CLR is not to delve into the low-level details, which has been done in other publications, the CLR is so important that all VB .NET developers should have at least a rudimentary understanding of how it works and its key features.

> **NOTE**
>
> See Jeffery Richter's series of articles on the MSDN Web site (msdn.microsoft.com) for more details on the CLR.

As was true with VB 6.0 and COM, developers creating distributed applications could get by with developing their applications without any appreciation for the internals of COM. However, extending that knowledge just a little bit allows you to create applications that take full advantage of what the CLR provides.

Goals of the CLR

To create a new platform for distributed Web application development, Microsoft needed to develop a common architecture on which to base this platform. As mentioned previously, the current way most VB developers develop distributed applications is by integrating ASP, VB, MTS, COM+, and Win32 API calls, all of which have different programming semantics and their own idiosyncrasies in the ways they perform basic functions such as error handling, dealing with return values, passing arguments, handling data types, and memory management. And so it became apparent that if a new platform was going to be developed, it needed to unify these programming models under a central architecture. This is what the CLR is and does.

At the highest level, then, the CLR was designed to implement the following four goals:

- Simplify application development
- Provide a robust and secure execution environment
- Support multiple programming languages
- Simplify deployment and management

To deliver on these goals, the designers of the CLR had to address the issue of application interoperability. In the past, two pieces of software often communicated using COM, which relied on a common binary standard that both pieces of software implemented so that they could safely invoke methods on each other's objects. Although this provided a level of integration, both pieces of software still needed to implement the plumbing (interfaces and `AddRef` and `Release` code) and rely on the operating system's COM Library (OLE32.DLL and STDOLE.DLL among others) and registry for support. And even though VB hid these details quite nicely from developers, these two pieces of software could not directly interact, for example, to extend each other's objects through implementation inheritance.

> **NOTE**
>
> COM does support the notion of interface inheritance so that one object can implement another's interfaces (which defines the required method and property signatures including the method names, arguments, and return values, if any). This allows you to write polymorphic code and could also be done in VB 6.0 (see Chapter 15 of my book, *Pure Visual Basic*, Sams Publishing, August 1999, for a more in-depth discussion). However, this technique does not allow the actual code inside the object to be reused. *Implementation inheritance* means that one object can be derived from another and that when the derived object is executed, the code from the parent will also run if desired. This leads to greater code reuse, although there are pitfalls as well. We'll look more closely at these features as they've been added to VB .NET in Chapter 4, "Object-Oriented Features."

The CLR provides the common substrate within which all the software runs so that objects can directly interact, and so that all the plumbing code is eliminated from both the components themselves and the operating system. For example, in the COM world, components were responsible for the in-memory layout of their objects into v-table structures so that the appropriate methods could be located at runtime. Now, however, this responsibility has been relieved from the components and is handled by the CLR.

Because all VB .NET code is run by the CLR, it can provide services like those listed here:

- **Different compilation models**—As I'll discuss shortly, the abstraction of the CLR from the development languages allows the runtime to determine when an application is compiled.

- **Automatic lifetime management**—Because all objects—and everything is ultimately an object in .NET—are managed by the CLR, it can monitor when those objects are created and used, and when they are no longer needed. As a result, it will use a garbage collection (GC) algorithm to free resources as necessary. This means that you can no longer have stray pointers and that circular references will be resolved. In fact, you are no longer responsible for freeing resources (setting an object to Nothing, for example) at all. This is great news, but it changes the way you will design your code, for example, because Terminate events are no longer supported. I'll cover this topic in more detail both in this chapter and in Chapter 3, "VB .NET Language Features."

- **Code correctness and type-safety**—VB developers have always taken for granted that in many cases they could assign a variable of one type to another and VB would automatically convert it for them. By default, however, the CLR strictly enforces type safety so that developers can't make arbitrary references to memory locations and make unsafe casts—things that VB developers typically don't care about, but that happen frequently in VC++ and are exploited by hackers. What it means to VB .NET developers is that there is a new default behavior and more levels of type safety that can be used. I'll cover this in detail in Chapter 3.

- **Simplified deployment**—Because the CLR eliminates the plumbing required for components to communicate, it also reduces the installation and deployment burden for developers. By eliminating registration (for the most part, as you'll see in Chapter 5.) and allowing features such as side-by-side execution both on the same machine and even within the same process, some .NET applications can be deployed simply by copying directories (referred to as *XCOPY deployment*).

- **Evidence-based security**—This new platform also requires a new security model. In the past, security models typically relied on the credentials of the user running the code. However, in distributed applications where code can be downloaded from the Internet and executed, the code itself needs to be trusted. The .NET security model is not simply a rehashing of the Microsoft Authenticode technology used for signing and encrypting ActiveX controls; it is a new model based on evidence provided by both the code as well as the user (through operating system accounts or roles) and is policy-based. In addition, the security model can be accessed both declaratively and imperatively inside your code. I will discuss this in more detail in Chapter 5.

- **Common exception handling**—As mentioned previously, the varying programming models used by corporate developers all handle errors in different ways. COM uses HRESULTs, the Win32 API uses function return values with a second call to retrieve the error, ASP uses inline error handling, and VB uses error trapping within a module. The CLR includes structured exception handling, which allows isolation of the error code and works well across language boundaries. I'll discuss how VB .NET implements this feature in Chapter 6, "Error Handling and Debugging."

These features of the CLR allow languages to work together and leverage common tools such as the debugger and profiler so that cross-language and even cross-machine debugging (covered in Chapter 6) are simplified. This results in a greater freedom to use the language of your choice without sacrifice. This is, once again, good news for VB .NET developers.

And finally, as implied earlier and discussed in the following sections, the all-encompassing nature of the CLR gives it the nature of a Hardware Abstraction Layer (HAL) and makes it possible to write code that might not require recompilation as you move it to a new platform. Initially, Microsoft is planning to port the CLR to its family of operating systems including Windows 98, Windows Me, Windows NT 4.0, Windows 2000, Windows XP, 64-bit Windows, and even Windows CE in a package called the .NET Compact Framework. In the future, other non-Microsoft operating systems might also be included.

Managed Versus Unmanaged Code

All code that executes outside the CLR—meaning code written for previous versions of VB as well as calls to the Win32 API, calls to classic COM and COM+ components, and calls to third-party ActiveX controls—is referred to as *unmanaged code*. There is a sharp distinction between unmanaged code and the managed code produced to run in the CLR. *Managed code* is structured so that the CLR can augment it with its services. Requirements for managed code include the ability for the CLR to

- Locate the metadata for a particular method given an address
- Walk the call stack
- Handle exceptions
- Store and retrieve security information

For example, to walk the call stack, the CLR uses a specific API to understand the layout of stack frames produced by a particular compiler vendor. As a result, the compiler must provide an implementation of this API either in the just-in-time compiler (discussed later) or in the managed code itself.

NOTE

As mentioned previously, only VC++ can produce unmanaged code. The default mode for VC++ is to create unmanaged code, and so the product is referred to as "Visual C++ with managed extensions." However, VC# will also allow you to write unmanaged code within a method by using the unsafe modifier. As a result, a VC# developer can use pointers and override the GC algorithm in certain cases to keep it from freeing resources using a technique called *pinning*. As implied by its name, the unsafe modifier can allow developers to override the features of the CLR noted in the "Automatic lifetime management" bullet point earlier and therefore create stray pointers and unresolved circular references. Note, however, that this unmanaged code will run only if the code is trusted by the CLR security model.

VB .NET produces only managed code and so must use the interoperability features of .NET (referred to simply as "interop") to access any form of unmanaged code. We'll take a look at how this is accomplished in Chapter 9, "Accessing Component Services."

One of the ramifications of this for VB .NET developers is that upgrading VB 6.0 projects to VB .NET (covered in Chapter 3) means that the interop services will be relied upon heavily, which adds a layer of complexity and slows performance. For these and other reasons, VB .NET developers will need to be very careful when deciding what and when to upgrade.

Death of COM?

With all these changes, what does this mean for COM? Well, the good news is that because VB hid many of the complexities of COM from developers, changing the infrastructure should not inconvenience most developers. In addition, doing away with the headaches of GUIDs and the registry, the single-version-per-machine scheme that it implied, as well as dealing with compatibility settings, are all a good thing. Is COM dead? Yes, in terms of its infrastructure.

However, many corporate VB developers have a good understanding of COM and take advantage of interface-based programming in their designs. These developers can still use the same techniques in their designs, while they can also augment them with implementation inheritance. Is COM dead? No, in terms of the concept of sharing and reusing code.

In any case, many of us will have to coexist in both worlds for some time to come. For example, one of the most common scenarios will be that newly developed managed code (perhaps a new ASP.NET UI or Web Service) will need to call previously deployed COM+ components written in VB 6.0. For this to work, VB .NET developers will need to be aware of both the old and new worlds and how they interoperate (as I'll discuss in Chapter 9). In fact, it might be argued that some new VB .NET developers will need a short course on classic COM to implement scenarios like the one mentioned.

Common Language Specification

As mentioned previously, VB .NET is only one of several languages Microsoft is creating to target the CLR. However, the CLR makes it possible for other language vendors to create compilers that target it as well. To assist in this process, Microsoft has published the Common Language Specification (CLS). Simply put, the CLS is published on msdn.microsoft.com and defines a set of rules that the vendors must live by if they want their languages to work with the CLR. Most of these rules have to do with how languages expose type information (including primitive types such as integers, strings, and complex types such as arrays, enumerations, and objects) and special features such as exception handling, attributes, and interfaces.

NOTE

Strictly speaking, the CLS binds vendors to rules only for types that are made public and accessible outside a particular assembly. Assemblies will be covered in more detail at the end of this chapter.

In fact, the CLS dictates a subset of what the CLR provides for languages to be compatible. Individual vendors can then implement more of the functionality if they desire. The CLS defines three levels for compatibility:

- **consumers**—Languages that use the CLR but do not extend it
- **extenders**—Languages that use the CLR and extend it by adding additional data types
- **frameworks**—Languages that implement libraries used by a wide range of programming languages and tools

As of this time, many vendors have indicated their willingness to create compilers for languages such as Pascal, Smalltalk, LISP, FORTRAN, Perl, and over 20 others. In fact, Microsoft has even produced a version of Java (J# .NET) that targets the CLR as a part of its JUMP (Java User Migration Path) program.

To assist in this effort, Microsoft and Hewlett Packard jointly submitted the CLS, CLR (referred to as the Common Language Infrastructure), and the C# language specification to the international industry standards body ECMA. See msdn.microsoft.com/net/ecma and www.ecma.ch for more details.

> **NOTE**
>
> Obviously, this book is geared towards existing VB and ASP developers, and as such, I am definitely of the opinion that these developers will be much more productive much sooner using VB .NET than VC# due to the syntax similarities. In addition, VB .NET preserves much of what was good about BASIC to begin with, namely a more readable and hence understandable syntax. VC# was designed with C++ and Java developers in mind and so will be the natural path to .NET for those developers. That being said, VC# is in many respects more like VB .NET than C++, and so many VB developers will have no trouble reading and understanding the syntax.

CLR Internals

To help you get a feel for how the CLR works, I'll use an inside-out approach by first discussing what happens on a binary level and then moving up to a single application level, cross-application level, and finally to the cross-machine and deployment level. I'll begin the discussion by focusing on how code is compiled and executed for the CLR.

MSIL

As with any executable today, the code you write in VB .NET eventually must execute as native CPU instructions for the processor on which the code will be run. However, although unmanaged compilers create these native CPU instructions directly, and interpreters such as

ASP create instructions on the fly that map to CPU instructions, the managed compilers written for the CLR, which include VB .NET, create a higher level, machine-independent set of instructions referred to as Microsoft Intermediate Language (MSIL). The MSIL instructions are then stored in a portable executable (PE) file with a .DLL or .EXE extension based on the Microsoft Portable Executable format, which itself extends the Common Object File Format (COFF) commonly used for executable content. These files are referred to as *modules* in .NET (not to be confused with VB modules as discussed in Chapter 2). MSIL is eventually loaded by the CLR and compiled to native instructions and executed.

To view the MSIL created by the VB .NET compiler, you can use the IL Disassembler utility (ILDasm.exe) that ships with .NET. This graphical utility lets you view each method in your program, along with its associated MSIL, by double-clicking on the method. Figure 1.2 shows ILDasm opened up on a method called AddOrder in a class called Orders.

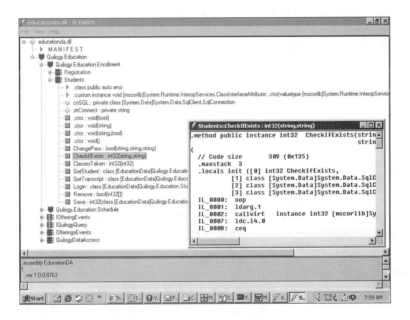

FIGURE 1.2

The IL Disassembler. This graphical utility lets you view the MSIL created for your VB .NET code. Note that the instructions begin with IL_0000 in the foreground window.

This basic architecture and its implications should be familiar to VB developers. First, it means that VB. NET binaries are not native code but a form of intermediate code as was true for most of VB's history. The big difference is that MSIL is a much lower level set of instructions than the interpreted code produced in previous versions of VB. Although you might be thinking that the fight for adding native compilation to VB was in vain and that this is a giant step backwards in terms of performance, there are benefits to using this approach, as will be discussed later in this chapter. Second, it means that the .NET Framework must be installed on each machine that executes VB .NET code. Yes, a runtime distribution is required for operating systems on which the runtime is not preinstalled (which is all of them at this point, even the newly released Windows XP).

On the other hand, the use of MSIL is what makes it possible for VB .NET developers to take advantage of all the services of the CLR discussed previously, such as garbage collection, type safety, structured exception handling, security, integrated cross-language development, and cross-language debugging. In addition, using MSIL will enable VB .NET code to run without recompilation on new platforms, such as 64-bit Windows, by providing a hardware abstraction layer.

At this time, operating systems don't know how to begin executing programs written in MSIL, so each managed executable contains an unmanaged entry point that the operating system's loader calls. This small stub simply jumps to the _CorExeMain function in the CLR engine contained in MSCorEE.dll. After the CLR has been initialized, this function continues execution of the MSIL instructions from within the managed code. This implies that each process loads its own copy of the CLR and that only one copy of the CLR is loaded per process. The bulk of the core services in the CLR, such as the base classes for the Common Type System discussed later, are contained in the MSCorLib.dll, which each managed binary also references.

JIT Compilation

Perhaps the biggest issue and perceived drawback to using MSIL and managed code is performance. Obviously, adding another layer of abstraction also adds a performance hit as the MSIL is compiled to native code. Fortunately, .NET uses some optimization techniques to try and offset this potential problem.

Caution

Another drawback is that in its current form, MSIL can be disassembled as shown in Figure 1.2. This allows "reverse-engineers" to study the instructions for your source code and duplicate it, thereby risking intellectual property. However, it should be noted that any code (natively compiled or not) is in danger of reverse engineering if the binary is accessible.

By default, the CLR uses just-in-time (JIT) compilation at runtime to compile the MSIL. It does this as opposed to compiling the entire application at load time so that the initialization time is reduced, and because applications typically do not end up calling all their code. The component of the CLR that performs this run-time compilation is often referred to as the JITer. Note that the JITer and the CLR communicate via a standard interface so that JITers can be produced by other vendors for specific platforms.

For example, when a managed application is executed, it is loaded by the CLR using its class loader (technically a part of the Virtual Execution System or VES), which has the responsibility for first allocating memory for the code to be loaded, resolving access to other managed code, and conducting basic consistency checks. When these checks are complete, the class loader creates a stub for each method implementation that is loaded. As the methods are actually called in the course of program execution, the JITer is used to compile the MSIL into native code that then replaces the stub. On subsequent invocations of the method, the native code will run without intervention by the JITer.

In addition, the JITer also supports a code verification stage that might take place during compilation. This algorithm uses input from the class loader and the CLR base class library to make certain that the code about to run is type-safe. This means that the method implements the correct signatures and that any incoming values to the method have the correct signature. If the code passes the type-safe verification, it is ensured to access only those memory locations it is authorized to access. Note that administrators might create a security policy that allows code to bypass this verification step because some code might be designed not to be type-safe and because some languages do not produce verifiably type-safe code.

> **NOTE**
>
> Microsoft had talked of shipping two JIT compilers: the normal compiler and an economy version. The basic difference is that the economy version uses fewer resources (that is, memory footprint and CPU cycles) during the compilation, but produces less optimized code. As a result, the economy compiler would be useful for platforms such as Windows CE devices, in which the cost of compilation outweighs the performance benefit from fully optimized code. The economy compiler would also be easier to implement because it uses a straight instruction-for-instruction substitution rather than a full method and data flow analysis. However, the economy compiler did not make it into version 1 of the .NET Framework.

However, even with this architecture, the execution of your applications when they are first loaded will be slowed. To prevent this, the CLR also ships with a command-line PreJIT compiler (CLR Native Image Generator or ngen.exe) that you can use to precompile your application to native code and persist it on disk at installation time. By doing this, your applications will load much faster although the one-time cost at installation will be increased. The mechanics of doing this are covered in more detail in Chapter 5.

To summarize, refer to Figure 1.3, which outlines the process of compilation and execution of your VB .NET application. Note that your code is first compiled into MSIL at development time and then compiled into native CPU instructions at either install time, prior to it (PreJIT), or at run-time (JITer).

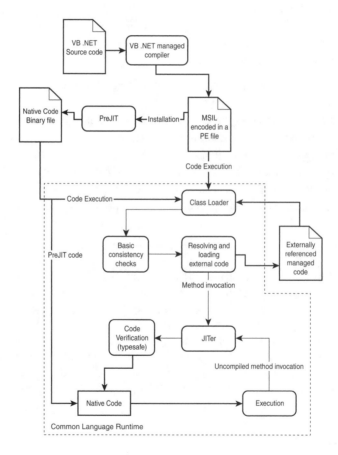

Figure 1.3

A simplified view of the .NET execution environment. The default mode of the CLR uses a JITer that compiles each method to native code as it is invoked.

Although using JIT definitely has its costs, there are several scenarios in which JIT might actually improve performance. For example, by its very nature, both PreJIT and a JITer know more about the runtime execution environment than developers who compile their application at their development workstation far removed from the machine that eventually runs their code. As a result, JIT provides the opportunity to include install-time and run-time optimizations; for example, creating native instructions optimized for the particular CPU (Pentium 4 versus AMD) and generating efficient code for variables that are not used or that always contain specific values.

Secondly, the use of JIT means that developers can also expect performance improvements as new JIT compilers are installed on the machines running their code. In other words, you won't have to recompile your code to take advantage of new processor improvements that are added to JIT compilers. However, it remains to be seen how this will affect support centers that in the future might have to deal with various JIT compilers.

Common Type System

One of the reasons the CLR was designed was so that languages could more fully interoperate. Historically, this has been complicated because languages often have very different notions about how to fundamentally structure data. A typical example is the difference between VB and the Win32 API in terms of strings and structures. For example, in the case of strings, VB internally represented them in a form referred to as BSTR, whereas in the Win32 API, they were encoded as an LPSTR. This difference meant that VB developers had to be wary of passing strings from VB to the Win32 API and had to make sure that the proper calling conventions were used.

In .NET these differences go away because all data types are implemented by the Common Type System (CTS), which governs the types supported by the CLR, including how they are defined, referenced, and used, and how they interact with each other. Note that the types defined by the CTS are a superset of what is contained in the CLS. Therefore, not all languages will support all the available types. At the highest level, all types, including both intrinsic data types such as integers and strings and user-defined types such as classes, are derived from an object in the CLR found in the Services Framework (MSCorLib.dll) called Object. This class is located within the System namespace and is therefore referred to with dot-notation as System.Object.

NOTE

As I'll discuss later, the Services Framework is organized hierarchically into namespaces that are used to group classes as well as other namespaces. The System namespace contains the core implementations of classes used by the CLR.

Object includes virtual, or instance, methods to perform comparison, to create a string representation of the object, to clean up in the garbage collection process, to return the type of the object, and to quickly create a hash value for the object.

NOTE

Hash tables have long been used by C and Perl developers as a quick means of storing and retrieving values, similar to a collection but with some limitations and better performance. The CLR implements a System.Collections.Hashtable class that uses the GetHashCode method from System.Object to generate the key value that is placed in the hash table. The Hashtable class then exposes methods such as Contains and ContainsKey for finding the key.

In the CTS, all data types (also simply referred to as *types*) are ultimately derived from System.Object. At the highest level, all types can be broken down into what are called value types and reference types. A diagram of how the types are organized can be seen in Figure 1.4.

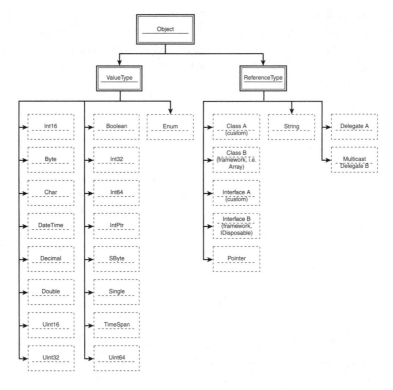

FIGURE 1.4

Common Type System. This diagram shows how the CTS is organized. All types are derived from System.Object.

Value Types

Value types are those types that can be described by a series of bits, are typically passed by value within applications, and are used by the CLR to implement many of the intrinsic data types supported by modern programming languages.

In the CTS, value types are inherited from System.ValueType. Although they are derived from System.Object, the value types intrinsic to the CLR do not consume the overhead of traditional object instances and are stored efficiently. This is because unlike object instances, value types are allocated in a thread's stack and not on the garbage-collected heap, which requires the calculation of pointers to access. For example, the value types in Table 1.1 are typically implemented as primitive data types in a programming language but are actually implemented by the CTS.

TABLE 1.1   CTS Value Types

Data Type	Description
System.Boolean	Represents True or False
System.Byte	Unsigned 8-bit integer
System.Char	A Unicode 16-bit character
System.DateTime	Stores date and time information from 1/1/0100 12:00:00AM in 100-nanosecond tick intervals
System.Decimal	Represents positive and negative values with up to 28 significant digits
System.Double	IEEE 64-bit float
System.Int16	Signed 16-bit integer
System.Int32	Signed 32-bit integer
System.Int64	Signed 64-bit integer
System.IntPtr	Signed integer, native size
System.SByte	Signed 8-bit integer
System.Single	IEEE 32-bit float
System.TimeSpan	Represents a time interval
System.UInt16	Unsigned 16-bit integer
System.UInt32	Unsigned 32-bit integer
System.UInt64	Unsigned 64-bit integer

Keep in mind that each language might not implement the types in Table 1.1 and will not necessarily use the same identifiers for each one. For example, VB.NET does not support unsigned integers as native types. In Chapter 3, I'll discuss the mapping of these CTS types to the types exposed in VB .NET.

Value types also have several behaviors that you might expect including

- Default initialization to zero
- Copy by value, in which assigning one variable dimensioned as a value type to another simply copies the value rather than the address of the value. As a result, two or more value types cannot refer to the same physical memory address.

In addition to using the intrinsic types, the CTS also supports creating your own value types that derive from System.ValueType. You might want to do this if you want to create your own simple data types that are typically passed by value and that you'll reuse in a series of custom applications. For example, you might create a value type for a batting average that is used to store a baseball player's average and include your own methods for additional calculations.

It should be noted that each time a variable dimensioned as a value type is passed to a method that accepts an argument of type System.Object, the CLR uses what is called the *boxed* type of the variable to create an addressable memory location on the heap for the variable. In other words, the CLR creates a second representation of the variable (a process referred to as *boxing*) so that it can be treated as an object and passed by reference since by definition, a value type is simply a sequence of bits. When the variable is eventually updated, it is said to be *unboxed*. The nice aspect of this behavior is that it provides a unified view of the type system and makes it possible to write polymorphic code that simply accepts arguments of type System.Object, but can be used on any value types in addition to actual objects. This is analogous to creating procedures in VB that accepts Variant arguments so they can work on both simple data types, arrays, or even class objects.

Although some languages will include special syntax for when you refer to the boxed type versus the unboxed type such as VC++, in VB .NET you don't have to worry about explicitly boxing and unboxing your code.

NOTE

In some circumstances, you might get small performance improvements if you explicitly cast your value types to objects before passing them to a method.

Enumerations

The CTS also implements enumerations (enums) as value types. All enums are derived from System.Enum. As in VB 6.0, each enum provides a set of named constants (fields) that map to one of the integer data types (Int16, Int32, or Int64) in the CTS. Enums cannot define their own methods, implement interfaces, or properties and events. VB .NET fully supports enums, as I'll discuss in Chapter 4.

Reference Types

The second type of variable structure that the CTS supports is called a *reference type*. As you would expect, a reference type is derived from System.Object and is always referenced by its memory location rather than the actual data that comprises it. In other words, when a reference type is created, memory is allocated on the heap and the address is returned and stored in a variable. Unlike value types, reference types are automatically garbage collected by the CLR, as will be discussed shortly.

> **NOTE**
>
> The subsystem of the CLR that deals with the manipulation of reference types is sometimes referred to as the *Virtual Object System (VOS)*. Note that the inclusion of an object system in the runtime is a unique feature of the CLR and is what gives it much of its power.

Because reference types refer to the memory address of a variable, two variables can point to the same underlying object. By default, reference types default to NULL (or Nothing) until they are initialized. In the CLR, the only primitive data type implemented as a reference type is System.String. Other uses for reference types include the implementation of classes, interfaces and pointers, and delegates.

Classes

Classes are perhaps the fundamental construct in the CTS and are used for just about any kind of programming endeavor in a managed application, which includes

- Access to all the system services, such as messaging and data access (ADO.NET) as provided by the Services Framework
- The implementation of the forms package using Windows Forms
- The implementation of Web sites and Web services using ASP.NET
- The implementation of custom code for business logic
- The implementation of custom code derived from the Services Framework

Suffice it to say that all of the code you write in VB .NET will be in the context of a class. In that respect, VB .NET is not the same procedural language with some object-oriented syntax; it is now a fully object-oriented language.

As you might expect, classes in the CTS can contain methods, fields, properties, and events, much like classes in VB 6.0. However, they are much more powerful. As a result, VB has added many keywords that allow it to take advantage of the features of classes in the CTS. Some of these features include

- Implementation inheritance from a single base class (multiple inheritance is not supported)
- The ability to create abstract base classes that cannot be instantiated
- The ability to define parameterized constructors on the class that can be called when the class is instantiated
- The ability to implement one or more interfaces
- Public and private classes
- Overridden methods that are replacements for methods in the base class
- Overloaded methods that have the same method name but different arguments
- Static methods that are shared among all instances of a class and can be called prior to instantiation
- Synchronized methods that allow only one thread of execution within the method at any one time
- Methods that are accessible only from within the class and classes that inherit from it

In Chapter 4, I'll cover the language enhancements to VB .NET that make it possible to access these features of classes implemented by the CTS.

Interfaces and Pointers

As in VB 6.0, VB .NET supports interfaces, although they are implemented as the reference type interface. Interfaces simply define the signatures of methods, fields, properties, and events in the interface that includes the specification for the names, arguments, and return values. Classes that implement the interface can provide an implementation for the methods of the interface using syntax very similar to that found in VB 6.0, where the Implements keyword was used to implement COM interfaces. Interfaces cannot contain constructors and all the members must be public.

As in VB 6.0, interfaces are very useful for creating polymorphic code because a class may implement one or more interfaces and then be passed to a method that queries on the interface and calls its methods. However, because interfaces are supported in the CTS, VB .NET exposes them as first-class citizens that are defined with their own syntax and can be included in the same source code file as classes that implement them. However, the CLR, unlike COM, also supports creating classes without first defining an interface. When VB developers previously created COM components, they relied on the VB compiler to create a default COM interface for their class, thereby hiding this requirement.

In some respects, interfaces serve the same purpose as abstract base classes. The difference is that an abstract base class can include functionality within its methods that can be reused by classes that inherit from it. Interfaces, by definition, have no implementation.

> **TIP**
>
> Because VB.NET now supports both interfaces and abstract base classes, and both can be used for polymorphism, which one should you use? A good rule of thumb is to use abstract base classes when there is generic code from which all the derived classes can benefit and when the derived classes follow the "is a" relationship. In other words, an abstract base class for Person with a derived class of Employee follows this rule because "employee is a person." However, interfaces should be used when the class that implements the interface will use the same calling semantics but not the same implementation. For example, an interface called IQuery that includes a GetByID method could be implemented by both an Order class and an Employee class.

The CTS supports a pointer type as a reference type, which is the value of a machine address that contains some data. Pointer types cannot be used as if they were objects and, in fact, as in previous versions of VB, VB .NET does not support syntax to deal with pointers.

Delegates

The CTS also supports a concept called *delegates*. Delegates can be thought of as an object-oriented way to create a function pointer. Each delegate forwards calls to a method on some object instance when the delegate is instantiated. However, because they are implemented as part of CLR, they are type-safe and always point to valid objects (unlike function pointers in C++).

The closest equivalent in VB 6.0 to using delegates as function pointers was found in the AddressOf keyword that developers used to define callback routines when dealing with the Win32 API; for example, when using the system timer. In the CTS, delegates are used to implement callbacks. You can also define your own delegates to set up your own callback schemes, but they also form the basis for all event handling in the CLR. For example, delegates are used in the Windows Forms classes to implement the typical event handlers you would expect for controls and windows.

Delegates are well suited for events because they can be used to provide the communication from the source of the event, such as a control on a form, to the receiver of the event, such as code within the form. When dealing with events, you can think of delegates as the runtime linking mechanism between an event source and an event receiver.

The CLR supports two delegate classes: System.Delegate and System.MulticastDelegate, from which all delegates are derived. As you might expect, MulticastDelegate supports a list of methods (referred to as the *invocation list*) that are called when the delegate is invoked, whereas Delegate supports only one.

The basic process in using a delegate is to dimension it, instantiate it at runtime with the method(s) it is to invoke in its constructor, and then to call the delegate, which will in turn call the methods in its invocation list. Of course, in many instances, the Services Framework or the language you are working with abstracts these underlying steps in the language constructs or in higher-level classes such as controls and forms. However, as mentioned previously, you can take advantage of delegates at the lowest level to create your own notification architecture.

Garbage Collection

As mentioned previously, one of the benefits that the CLR offers is automatic lifetime management for objects. This feature is implemented by a garbage collection (GC) algorithm that cleans up data on the managed heap. Basically, each time an object is instantiated, the CLR tries to allocate space on the heap for the object. If no space is available, it runs its GC algorithm to try and determine which objects can no longer be referenced and then compacts the heap before allocating the new memory. As a result, you no longer need to set your object references to Nothing in order for their memory to be reclaimed.

> **NOTE**
>
> The process of allocating space on the heap (when there is room and no GC is required) is very fast. For example, the time needed to create 100,000 small objects in VB .NET is more than four times faster than creating the same objects in VB 6.0. When the heap is full, this process will take longer because GC must occur at this time. As a result, creating designs that require the use of many small objects is not prohibitive in terms of performance as it was in VB 6. In this way, the CLR assists developers in designing more purely object-oriented applications.

Of course, by allowing the CLR to manage the lifetime of your objects, by definition it does not allow *deterministic finalization*. This means that you cannot write code that will run immediately when the object is set to Nothing because the runtime determines when your object instances are actually deallocated. In other words, the CLR does not allow you to use Terminate events in VB and destructors in VC++. Keep in mind that for the purposes of this discussion, a destructor in VB is the Terminate event.

The way in which the CLR deallocates object instances is through a process called *finalization*. Internally, when an object is instantiated, the CLR looks to see whether the class has overridden (created an implementation of) the `Finalize` method of `System.Object`. If so, it places a pointer to the `Finalize` method in a separate data structure. Later, when the GC determines that the object instance is no longer reachable, a thread controlled by the GC runs the `Finalize` methods for each of these objects and then removes them from the heap. For the CLR, it is much more efficient if your classes do not implement a `Finalize` method because the overhead described here could be avoided. However, in many cases, you'll want to write code to clean up resources you've acquired, such as database connections and file handles.

However, the main problem with nondeterministic finalization is that, by default, you have no control over when the finalization actually occurs and in what order your objects are deallocated. Obviously, this is a problem that must be addressed and that will affect the way in which you write your VB .NET code.

As I'll show in Chapter 4, in these cases, you can implement your own destructor by implementing an interface called `IDisposable` that contains a method called `Dispose`. A client application can then call this method to clean up your object. This method should then call the `Finalize` method to clean up your resources and instruct the GC not to finalize this object because it has already been done.

To programmatically affect the behavior of the GC, in this case and in others, the `System` namespace includes a static or shared class called `GC`. It contains methods to force garbage collection such as `Collect` and to suppress the finalization of an object such as `SuppressFinalize`, as would be used in the case described earlier.

The CLR also supports a concept known as *weak references*. These are used when you want, for example, to place object instances into a collection for future reference. However, you do not want for the instances to stay alive simply because they are in the collection. By creating the object variable as a weak reference, the GC will deallocate the instance when all normal (also called strong) references are gone. A *strong reference* is simply one created using the `New` keyword in the typical way. To create a weak reference, you use the wrapper class `System.WeakReference` and pass the variable with the strong reference in the constructor. You can then subsequently re-create a strong reference from the weak one, if necessary, using the `CType` function.

The final concept that affects the GC is *resurrection*. Simply put, resurrection allows an object instance from within its `Finalize` method to create a new reference to itself in another variable. At this point, the GC cannot deallocate it, so the instance is said to be resurrected. When the resurrected instance is finally garbage collected, the GC will not by default call the object's `Finalize` method a second time. To ensure that it is called, you can call the GC's `ReRegisterForFinalize` method and pass it a reference to the object from within `Finalize`. Although resurrection is possible, there are few if any cases in which you would actually want to implement it.

Component Metadata

As VB 6.0 developers, you're probably familiar with the concept of using the References dialog from the Project menu to reference a component, coding against it using IntelliSense, and using the Object Browser to view its method and property signatures. Until now, I haven't discussed how or where this information exists in .NET, although Figure 1.3 certainly implies that one VB .NET application can, for example, reference and make use of classes declared in another application. In fact, using the System namespace and its classes is just such an example of referencing code from MSCorLib.dll.

The answer is that all the information that VB 6.0 developers found in type libraries, IDL, and the use of Regsvr32 is incorporated directly in the PE file (module) that contains the classes to be used in the same way that type libraries are automatically compiled into an unmanaged VB 6.0 COM component. This data, which includes declarations, implementations, and references specific to the module, is referred to as *component metadata*. This technique allows managed code to be self-describing.

Tools such as VS .NET provide a References dialog that allows you to select the managed code to reference. This process reads the metadata from the component so that VS .NET can provide IntelliSense and early binding.

> **NOTE**
>
> As you'll see, the selection of code in this process actually occurs at a higher level called an *assembly* (described later), and not for individual modules.

Keep in mind that selecting the component and using its metadata during development does not affect the deployment of the application. Even though at design-time you add a reference to a local component, at run-time you can configure your application to find the component across the network or across the Internet.

> **NOTE**
>
> Not surprisingly, the System namespace also contains classes—Reflection and Reflection.Emit—that you can use to inspect metadata at run-time in order to dynamically instantiate objects and to actually emit metadata to a PE file, respectively. Most corporate developers will not utilize these classes, so they are beyond the scope of this book. For more information, review the .NET SDK samples on Reflection.Emit and Reflection.

Run-time Components

The two main run-time components of the CLR with which VB .NET developers need to be familiar are *assemblies* and *application domains*. As you'll see, both have big implications for how VB .NET developers construct, package, and execute their applications.

Assemblies

A proper understanding of assemblies is critical for developing VB .NET applications. First and foremost, all MSIL code executed by the CLR must exist in an assembly, which therefore can be thought of as a versionable, self-describing, and reusable building block for a .NET application. .NET applications are made up of one or more assemblies. More specifically, an assembly is a collection of one or more modules (.dlls, .exes, resource files such as bitmaps) that form a security boundary, are the smallest unit of deployment and versioning, and form the boundary for types. In other words, a class (type) that you declare in an assembly is different from all other types even if its name is the same as a type from a different assembly. The rules associated with assemblies are also what allow the CLR to enable side-by-side execution where multiple versions of the same assembly can be run both on the same machine and even within the same process. These rules and the process used to load assemblies are the key to ending "DLL Hell," where the installation of a new version of a component breaks existing applications. However, before getting ahead of ourselves, let's look at the manifest.

Manifest

For the assembly to be self-describing, it must contain some metadata that specifies information on all items in the assembly, the items that can be accessible outside the assembly, and a collection of references to other assemblies. This data is referred to as the *manifest* and contains the following information.

- A string name for the assembly.
- Version information in four parts and referenced as `major version.minor version.revision number.build number`. The CLR uses the version number to determine which assembly to load at runtime.
- Shared name information. This includes a public key and a hash of the file containing the manifest signed with a private key. Creating a shared name (also referred to as *strong name*) is optional, but is used for tighter security and guarantees name uniqueness. In some cases, such as when you want more than one application to use the assembly on the same machine (referred to as a global assembly), you must create a strong name.
- Culture (locale), processor, and operating systems supported.
- A list of all files in the assembly using relative pathing. This implies that all files in the assembly must be in the same directory or subdirectory as the manifest.

- A list of other assemblies that are referenced within this assembly including the name, some metadata (such as version and culture), and the public key if the assembly is shared.

In the simple case where the assembly consists of a single binary file (module), the manifest is compiled into the PE file by the VB .NET compiler. You'll notice in Figure 1.2 that ILDasm allows you to view the manifest information. In assemblies that contain more than one file, the manifest can be stored in one of the files or in a separate file using the Assembly Linker (AL.exe) command-line utility.

In addition to the required information in a manifest, developers can also include information such as the company, description, title, trademark, and copyright. This information must be specified by the developer using attributes and is provided automatically in VS .NET through the inclusion of an AssemblyInfo.vb file in the project.

Attributes

As will be discussed in Chapter 2, attributes are new to VB developers and are simply additional information that decorate methods, classes, modules, or the assembly. The CLR and compilers use attributes to make decisions at compile and run-time regarding the behavior of the code. Attributes allow developers to declaratively ensure that their code is used in a particular way. For example, an attribute can decorate a class that will use COM+ services to specify that the class requires the creation of a new transaction. Another example is the attribute that is used at the assembly level to specify the file that contains the key pair used to create a strong name.

Versioning

As mentioned earlier, assemblies are the smallest unit of versioning in the CLR and have a four-part numbering structure called the *compatibility version number*. Assemblies can also contain a text string that is used for documentation purposes and that contains the textual description of the version. This information is created automatically by VS .NET, but can also be specified using an assembly attribute called `AssemblyVersion` from the `System.Reflection` namespace.

The compatibility number is used by the CLR when making decisions about whether to load the assembly when it is referenced by another assembly. Note, however, that this is done only when the assembly has been created with a strong name and is therefore intended for sharing. Assemblies that are compiled without a strong name are referred to as *private assemblies* and must be distributed in the application directory.

For example, assume that assembly A uses a class from shared assembly B. At compile time, the manifest of assembly A contains a reference to the compatibility number of assembly B. At run-time, the CLR goes through several steps, discussed later, to find assembly B. When the CLR finds assembly B, it compares its major and minor versions with those in the manifest. If they differ, the assembly by definition is incompatible and the CLR will not use it. If they are the same, the CLR checks the revision number. If the revision numbers differ, the assembly might be compatible but by default the CLR will use it anyway.

CAUTION

In the case where the revision and build numbers have changed, the CLR does not guarantee that the newer revision is backward-compatible. That is why it "might be compatible." Note that this is different from the COM specification where a component was loaded only if the interfaces it implemented had not changed. This self-versioning scheme ensured backward-compatibility but did not allow side-by-side execution.

The build number is often referred to as the Quick Fix Engineering (QFE) number and will always be seen as compatible by the CLR. This allows developers to create quick fixes to assemblies without requiring dependent assemblies to be recompiled.

The scenario described in this section assumes the default versioning policy but this can be changed by the presence of configuration files.

Configuration Files

During the process of loading an assembly, the CLR can use information found in configuration files to assist it. The application configuration file is identified by having the same name as the application except with a .config extension or for Web applications be specified in the Web.config configuration file. This XML file contains a root element called <configuration> and child elements <runtime>, <assemblyBinding>, <dependentAssembly>, <publisherPolicy> and <probing>. Perhaps the best method to illustrate the use of an application configuration file is through an example.

TIP

Note that all elements, attributes, and values in the configuration files are case sensitive.

Let's assume that, as in the previous scenario, the CLR is attempting to load the shared assembly B. However, assembly A has an A.config file in its application directory. The file might look as shown in Listing 1.1.

LISTING 1.1   A sample application configuration file used by the CLR to make decisions about how to load assemblies at run-time.

```
<configuration>
   <runtime>
      <assemblyBinding xmlns="urn:schemas-microsoft-com:asm.v1">
         <probing privatePath="bin;bin2 "/>
         <publisherPolicy apply="yes"/>

         <dependentAssembly>
            <assemblyIdentity name="B"
                              publickeytoken="32ab4ba45e0a69a1"
                              culture="en-us" />
            <bindingRedirect oldVersion="*"
                             newVersion="5.3.1.1"/>
            <codeBase version="5.3.1.1"
                      href="http://www.quilogy.com/bin/b.dll"/>
         </dependentAssembly>
      </assemblyBinding>
   </runtime>
</configuration>
```

In this example, the configuration file first specifies in the `<probing>` tag several relative paths that should also be used when searching for assemblies using `privatePath`.

In the `<assemblyBinding>` tag, the `<publisherPolicy>` element is used to specify whether the application must run only with the original versions of other assemblies with which it was tested and compiled. If `apply` is set to "no" all other policies in the file and any configuration information specified by the publisher is ignored. The default mode is "yes," which means that the other information specified in the `<assemblyBinding>` tag will be used.

The `<assemblyBinding>` tag includes a `<dependentAssembly>` element that includes child elements that specify how to handle reference to the assembly identified in the `<assemblyIdentity>` element. In this case all references to assembly B should be redirected per the `<bindingRedirect>` element to use version 5.3.1.1 as noted in the `newVersion` attribute. Other attributes specify the `publickeytoken` (which is a hash of the public key) for the shared assembly B and the `oldVersion`, which should be redirected (in this case, all of them *).

The <dependentAssembly> tag includes a <codeBase> element that specifies a new location from which to download assembly B. This location will be tried before any other attempts are made.

At a higher level the CLR will also examine a publisher policy file if one exists and the <publisherPolicy> is set to "yes." This file might be distributed by a publisher along with a shared component and can be used to redirect the assembly reference to a new version. If used by the CLR, information in this file overrides that found in the application configuration file.

Administrators can also specify configuration information by placing binding information in the Machine.config file in the Config directory of the root directory where the runtime is installed (typically *<windows directory>*\Microsoft.NET\Framework*<version>*\CONFIG>). This file can contain all the same tags as in the application and publisher configuration files but will, of course, override any other settings.

> **NOTE**
>
> As discussed in Chapter 5, the .NET Admin tool can be used to create both application and administrator settings.

The Assembly Load Process

To summarize the information from the previous sections, let's run through the process that the CLR uses to locate an assembly at run-time. The process begins when the class loader attempts to resolve an assembly reference (referred to as initiating a bind).

Applying Version Policy

First, the class loader must resolve which version of the assembly to load. To do this, it looks for the presence of an application configuration file and specifically for the <assemblyBinding> and <publisherPolicy> tags. If the apply attribute is set to "no", the class loader will ignore the <bindingRedirect> tag and attempt to load the assembly with the version found in the calling assembly. If the <bindingRedirect> tag exists, it compares this information, such as the version to bind to, with the compatibility number stored in the assembly reference. Together this information is used to construct the compatibility number for which the class loader is looking. Remember that this step is skipped entirely if the reference is to a private assembly (one without a strong name).

Locating the Assembly

With the compatibility number resolved, the class loader now needs to find the actual file. It does this by using information from the publisher and application configuration file, searching application directories, and using the Global Assembly Cache (GAC).

First, if a `<codeBase>` is found in the config file, it uses the information to attempt to download the assembly and make sure that it can be loaded by checking its version, culture, and public key as specified in the tag. Note that if the download fails, the process ends at this point and an exception is thrown. In other words, if a codebase hint is specified, it is the only way the assembly can be loaded.

A second interesting behavior the class loader supports is that it remembers the codebase for the assembly. So, for example, if assembly A is downloaded and refers to assembly B, which must be subsequently loaded, the class loader will look at the URL from which it retrieved assembly A to find assembly B. In this case, however, if assembly B is not found in that location, the rest of the process described later continues.

If the hint is not present, the class loader proceeds to use a process called *probing*. Probing begins by searching for files in the application directory with the name of assembly and extensions of .exe, .dll, or .mcl. It then moves on to the directories relative to the application directory specified in the application configuration file's `<probing>` tag. The class loader also takes into consideration the culture of the assembly and automatically searches within subdirectories for the culture. For example, if the culture (locale) of assembly B is Deutsch (de), the class loader looks for a subdirectory de under each directory it eventually searches.

Note that probing is used to find both private and shared assemblies and that for private assemblies, if the assembly is not found at this point, an exception is thrown. However, for shared assemblies (those with a public key) the class loader also looks in the Global Assembly Cache (GAC). The GAC is a storage area under *<windows directory>*\ assembly that is used to store shared assemblies that can be used by more than one application on a particular machine. .NET ships with a command-line utility (GACUtil.exe), Windows shell extensions, and the .NET Admin tool that allow you to place your assembly in the GAC. Although the GAC is analogous to registering components in the registry, the GAC can store multiple versions of the same assembly and is very tightly coupled so that the contents of the GAC are always synchronized with the registration information.

For shared assemblies, then, the class loader looks in the GAC to see whether a version exists with a higher build and/or revision number and to consult a publisher policy file if one exists. If so, the version from the GAC is loaded even if the assembly was previously found during probing. This ensures that assemblies in the GAC have higher priority. If a match is found in the GAC, the assembly will be loaded.

Administrator Policy

Finally, the Machine.config file is consulted for any possible version redirection. If one is encountered, the class loader does not go through the entire probing process again but simply looks for the assembly in the GAC. If it is found, the assembly is loaded.

Security

To accommodate modern distributed applications, security in the .NET world is more complex. We'll explore many of these issues in Chapter 5, but for now the key point is that security information—such as the permissions the assembly needs to run—is compiled into the assembly manifest. This is referred to as *code-based security*. At run-time, the CLR uses this information in conjunction with security policies set by the administrator to determine whether the code should be allowed to run.

Secondly, a shared assembly is verified at load time to ensure that it has not been altered since it was compiled. It can do this by comparing the hash value of the file stored in the manifest with a hash performed at load time of the actual file. If the two do not match, the assembly file is not loaded. In addition, the CLR validates the assembly's signature by using the public key.

Considerations for Development

What does all of this mean? For one thing, it means the VB. NET developers must have a firm grasp of assembly concepts when determining how to architect their applications.

For example, because assemblies are the fundamental unit of versioning, you'll want to group modules and classes together that must be versioned together. Second, because assemblies dictate the scope of classes (types), you'll want to group classes together that must all share a common class but that you do not want to expose to the rest of the world. Third, because security information is stored in the assembly manifest, you'll want to group code together that has the same security requirements into an assembly. And finally, for all these reasons, assemblies are the fundamental unit of code reuse in .NET, so you'll want to group code together that will be shared amongst applications in an assembly.

Application Domains

The final concept—and the highest level explored in this section—is that of *application domains*. Application domains (or *app domains*), as the name implies, are boundaries created by the CLR in which applications run. App domains are isolated from each other, for example, by providing a security boundary between domains, providing fault tolerance where one app domain cannot bring down another, and making sure that code loaded in one app domain cannot directly access code in a second app domain.

App domains do not map directly to Win32 processes but can be thought of as lightweight Win32 processes that don't incur the overhead of context switches and other operating system overhead. Many app domains can coexist in the same process created by a runtime host. Note that this architecture is much different than was the case historically, when separate processes were used as the fundamental boundary between applications. Several of the advantages to app domains include the fact that applications can be stopped and started without taking down the entire process, and that the code from an assembly that is used by multiple app domains in the same process must be loaded only once.

However, app domains are also not analogous to threads because many different threads can run the code in a single application domain (in the case of a managed COM+ component) or the same thread can run code in several application domains (in the case of a Web server).

> **NOTE**
>
> The responsibilities of the runtime host include loading the CLR, creating the app domains, and loading the user code within the app domain. Runtime hosts include ASP.NET and Internet Explorer, among others. In fact, you can write your own runtime host using the unmanaged APIs that ship with the .NET Framework and are described in the online documentation.

The way the CLR uses application domains in the two most common scenarios is as follows. For console, services, and Windows Forms applications, by default a single app domain is created for each application in separate Win32 processes. For Web applications, each Web site is created within its own app domain inside the Web server process.

Note that individual applications can programmatically spawn new app domains. The System namespace supports an AppDomain class that allows developers to programmatically create and manipulate domains. For example, an application that instantiates an object can request to have it loaded in a separate app domain for isolation. In this case, a proxy and stub arrangement analogous to that found in classic COM is used to facilitate communication. These concepts collectively are called *.NET remoting* and will be discussed in Chapter 8.

Class Libraries

Much of the discussion in this chapter has referred to the System namespace and classes within it. In this section, I'll formally introduce the concepts of namespaces and the Services Framework and their implications for VB. NET developers.

Namespaces

VB developers who are familiar with dot notation should have no trouble envisioning the concept of a namespace. Basically, .NET uses namespaces in two ways:

- To organize (scope) code within and among assemblies into collections of functionality
- To expose that organizational unit to other applications so that they can "import" it at design time

Each assembly can contain multiple namespaces, and each namespace can contain multiple classes or even other namespaces. Therefore, the AsymmetricAlgorithm class nested within the

Cryptography namespace nested within the Security namespace within the System name-space and found in the system assembly is denoted as

System.Security.Cryptography.AsymmetricAlgorithm

Each project you create in VS .NET will automatically have a default or global namespace that is the same as the project name and, ultimately, the assembly name. However, you can create your own namespace hierarchy as you see fit. In addition, you can also create nested name-spaces that span assemblies as is done in the Services Framework. For example, you can create an assembly that contains the Quilogy namespace that exposes some high-level classes and then subsequently create a namespace in a different assembly called Quilogy.Utils. When a client program references both assemblies, the namespaces will be grouped together by IntelliSense. However, in this case, you'll need to be sure that you don't create name collisions by creating a class called Utils in the original Quilogy assembly.

> **NOTE**
>
> Many of the chapters in the book (especially those in Part II) will use examples from a distributed application that the company I work for, Quilogy (www.quilogy.com) could implement using .NET. Quilogy is a services company that offers digital consulting, managed hosting, and technical education. Many of the examples relate to a Web application for handling student enrollment in our technical education courses.

It should also be pointed out that there is nothing to prevent name collisions between name-spaces created by different companies. For example, two companies called Smith Brothers could create SmithBros namespaces. When the assemblies are used together in a client pro-gram, there is currently no way to disambiguate the reference. As a result, you should try to specify as unique a name as possible for your namespaces, perhaps starting with your com-pany's Web site address.

Services Framework

As discussed previously, the goals of .NET include a simplified and unified programming model. One of the ways this has been accomplished is with the inclusion in .NET of the Services Framework.

The Services Framework contains namespaces developed by Microsoft that encapsulate the core functionality of the CLR and often-used system services. In fact, much of this book is about showing you techniques used with the classes of the Services Framework. To give you a short introduction to the kinds of functionality supported, Table 1.2 lists the key namespaces found in the Services Framework and how they fit into this book.

TABLE 1.2   Services Framework namespaces. These namespaces are explored in more detail throughout this book.

Namespace	Description	Chapter(s) Discussed in
`Microsoft.VisualBasic`	Contains VB specific keywords	Throughout
`System.Security`	Used to implement declarative (using attributes) and imperative (within the method code) security within code	5, 8
`System.Diagnostics`	Used to perform system monitoring; that is, processes, performance monitor, and the Event Log	6, 12, 13, 14
`System.Data`	Used to communicate with data providers	7
`Microsoft.Win32`	Used to interface with the Win32 API.	8
`System.EnterpriseServices`	Used to create components for use in COM+	9
`System.Runtime. InteropServices`	Used to interact with COM and the Win32 API	8,9
`System.Runtime.Remoting`	Used to communicate with other managed applications	8
`System.Web.UI`	Used to create interfaces for Web applications	10
`System.Web.Services`	Used to create Web services	11
`System.IO`	Used to interact with the file system	12
`System.Threading`	Used to create and manage multiple threads of execution	12
`System.Security. Cryptography`	Used to encrypt and decrypt programmatically	12
`System.Timers`	Used to set up and monitor system timers	13

Namespace	Description	Chapter(s) Discussed in
System.Net	Used to communicate with Web protocols	13
System.XML	Used to load and manipulate XML documents programmatically	14
System.Messaging	Used to interact with Microsoft Message Queue	14
System.DirectoryServices	Used to interact with directory services	14

Obviously, the Services Framework is large, containing over 80 high level namespaces and over 1,200 classes, and no single book can explore all of its aspects. That's why this book is focused on those aspects of the Framework used to build distributed business systems in VB .NET by giving you techniques you can reuse.

However, one of the key benefits of the Services Framework for organizations is that they can provide language-independent training on the framework for their developers working in any of the CLR-supported languages. In addition, the Services Framework contains common programming patterns and conventions that not only unify the framework from a programmer's perspective, but act as a template for the design of custom class libraries.

Summary

Obviously, building distributed applications in VB .NET is, in many respects, going to be a whole new ballgame. As a result, this chapter tried to provide a firm foundation by taking you through both the reasons for the changes and a first look at how the internals work. Hopefully, you'll be better able to put in context the chapters that follow.

To begin, we'll look at the changes to Visual Studio .NET and particularly the IDE that will assist you in building great distributed applications. To that end, let's get started.

The Development Environment

IN THIS CHAPTER

As mentioned in Chapter 1, "The Microsoft .NET Architecture," one of the goals of the .NET initiative is to unify the various programming models developers have used to build a complete solution. This unification also is extended to the integrated development environment (IDE), Visual Studio .NET. The unification of the Visual C++, Visual Basic, and Visual Interdev/Visual J++ development environments means that all developers on the Microsoft platform have access to the same sets of tools—for example, the integrated debugger and macro facilities—thereby leveling the playing field. In addition, a single environment should make training and team development within your organization simpler, as well.

The IDE that served as the basis for the VS .NET IDE was the Visual Interdev/Visual J++ IDE that shipped with Visual Studio 6.0. As you'll see, it has been extended to include a variety of new features that VB .NET developers can take advantage of while retaining a familiar feel for VB developers.

NOTE

Incidentally, VS .NET itself is an example of an application that combines both managed and unmanaged code. The core of VS .NET was written in unmanaged code, but many of the new features discussed in this chapter were written in managed VC# .NET.

This chapter takes a quick tour of the IDE and is designed to get the VB developer up to speed quickly to begin using VB .NET productively.

NOTE

All code listings and supplemental material for this chapter can be found on the book's Web site at www.samspublishing.com.

A New IDE

One of the first things you'll notice when executing VS .NET, because it appears first, is the Start page. This page is "home base" for VS .NET and is used to review and open projects, as well as act as a conduit for information from Microsoft. For example, the links on the left side of the page include an Online Community link, which provides a list of Web resources including newsgroups; a Headlines link, which displays the current headlines from msdn.microsoft.com; a Search Online link, which allows you to search the MSDN online library; and a Downloads link, which provides links to additional Web releases and public betas that can be downloaded.

> **NOTE**
>
> In addition, look for Microsoft to offer links to third-party services from the Start page as well. For example, the Web Hosting link provides information about hosting ASP.NET applications with various application service providers. From here, you can find more information or set up a relationship with one of the preferred hosting vendors.

However, the most important link on the Start page is the My Profile link. This page allows you to customize the keyboard scheme, window layout, and help filter and combine these settings in a custom profile. In addition, predefined profiles that match the various Visual Studio developers (Visual Basic, Visual C++, Visual Interdev, and so on) are available. As a starting point, I'm sure many VB developers will choose the Visual Basic profile as they become familiar with the IDE.

Finally, the At Startup option also can be used to control whether the Start page is even shown, or whether VS .NET automatically loads the last project or displays an open project dialog.

The remainder of this section discusses creating and managing projects using the various features of the IDE including the IDE windows, supported file types, referencing other projects, and using macros and add-ins.

Projects and Solutions

At the highest level, VS .NET works in the context of *solutions*. Simply put, a solution is a container for projects and files that VS .NET creates automatically when a project is created. Solutions allow you to work easily on multiple related projects within the same instance of the IDE. In addition, you can set options that affect all the projects and build all the projects with a single mouse click using the Build menu in the order specified in the Project, Project Build Order menu option.

> **TIP**
>
> The Project Build Order menu option only appears if you have multiple projects in your solution.

Additionally, solutions can be used to manage files related to the projects, but not actually contained in them. For example, you can add readme files to the solution so that you can edit and work with them from within the IDE. A solution typically is comprised of both a .sln file for storing the project references and build configuration, and a .suo file for storing IDE configuration settings.

> **NOTE**
>
> A solution is analogous to a group (.vbg) in previous versions of VB.

Creating a Project

The first step in creating a project is to click on File, New Project. The resulting dialog contains Project Types on the left and various templates within each type on the right. The project templates allow you to create projects that support the two primary programming models in .NET—Windows Forms and ASP.NET—in addition to ancillary project types. Table 2.1 lists the basic templates in the Visual Basic Project folder that ship with the professional version of VS .NET.

TABLE 2.1   VB .NET Project Templates

Template	Description
Windows Application	Used to build forms-based applications using Windows Forms. Creates a single default form derived from `System.Windows.Forms.Form`. This template is beyond the scope of this book.
Class Library	Used to build classes, such as data access and business logic classes, with no visual interface, as we will discuss in Chapter 7, "Accessing Data with ADO.NET," and Chapter 8, "Building Components." Creates a single public class.
Windows Control Library	Used to build visual controls for Windows Forms applications. Creates a `UserControl` derived from `System.Windows.Forms.UserControl`. This is beyond the scope of this book.
ASP.NET Web Application	Used to build ASP.NET applications that rely on Web Forms, as discussed in Chapter 10, "Building Web Forms." Accepts a project name and location used to build the IIS virtual directory, as in VID 6.0. Includes a default form, Global.asax, and Web.config files.
ASP.NET Web Service	Used to build ASP.NET Web services, as discussed in Chapter 11, "Building Web Services." Accepts a project name and location used to build the IIS virtual directory, as in VID 6.0. Includes a default Web Service, Global.asax, and Web.config files.

TABLE 2.1   Continued

Template	Description
Web Control Library	Used to build ASP.NET server controls for reuse across ASP.NET applications, as discussed in Chapter 10. Provides a template control derived from `System.Web.UI.WebControls.WebControl`.
Console Application	Used to build applications that can be run at the command prompt and used frequently for building utilities and testing. Many examples throughout the book use this project template.
Windows Service	Used to build Windows Service applications, discussed in Chapter 13, "Implementing Services." Creates a template service derived from `System.ServiceProcess.ServiceBase`.
Empty Projects	You can create both empty local projects and empty Web projects. This might be useful when moving projects from one machine to another so that you don't have to delete the template files created for each project.

NOTE

Note that Visual Studio .NET Enterprise Developer and Visual Studio Studio .NET Enterprise Architect ship with additional templates. For example, under the Other Project node in the list of project types are Enterprise Template Projects including the Visual Basic Distributed Application template. These enterprise templates provide architectural guidance, access to application and database modeling features, and definition of policies connected to a solution. They allow an organization to customize the IDE, among other things. Many organizations will want to use these features; however, this book will focus on only those templates and features found in the professional edition.

The dialog also contains options as to whether the new project will be created in the existing solution or a new one. The default is to create a new solution in which the project lives in the directory shown in the dialog.

TIP

Additional projects also can be added to the solution by using the Add Project option on the File menu, rather than New Project.

As mentioned, one advantage to using solutions is to be able to work with multiple projects simultaneously, so that, as in VB 6.0, one project can reference code from another. This behavior typically is used to create test harness projects for unit testing your assemblies.

Now You Can Build for the Web

Now that the capabilities of Visual Interdev (VID) have been subsumed in the .NET Framework and exposed to any language that uses the Common Language Runtime (CLR), VB developers are for the first time able to directly create Web applications. Keep in mind that for ASP.NET projects that include both Web Forms applications and Web Service applications, the actual source files are placed under the control of the Web server (typically in a virtual directory with the same name as the project under the `Inetinfo\wwwroot` directory), whereas the solution file (.sln) is placed on the local machine.

This location can be changed when building a Web project through the New Project dialog. This should come as no surprise to developers familiar with VID. In this way, individual developers can either develop their pages and components on their own machine and subsequently copy them to a development server or, more likely, work directly from a development server. As with previous versions of Visual Studio, VS .NET supports source code control by integrating with Visual SourceSafe or other source code control providers. In fact, a version of Visual SourceSafe ships with the Enterprise versions of VS .NET and can be used in both the enterprise and professional editions simply by right-clicking on the solution or project name and choosing Add Solution to Source Control.

You'll also find options that control how VS .NET works with files under source code control in the Tools, Options menu item. The general options include four settings: Visual SourceSafe, Team Development, Independent Developer, and Custom. Basically, each setting affects how and when items are checked in and out. For example, when using the Independent Developer option, all files in the solution are checked out when the solution is opened. In addition, source code control providers can hook into this dialog to provide custom settings—for example, to allow you to enter the authentication information for the source code control system.

The other point to note about Web projects, in particular, is that when a Web project is created on the local machine, VS .NET now automatically uses file share access, rather than the FrontPage server extensions to improve reliability and performance. If the project is hosted on a remote server and a file share is available, it can be configured by right-clicking on the project and selecting Properties or using the Project, Properties menu option. The resulting dialog includes a host of configuration settings, and under Web Settings, allows you to change to FrontPage server extensions and configure the file share. The default Web access method can be set in the Project, Web Settings pane of the Options dialog invoked from the Tools, Options menu.

Web projects also can be taken offline by clicking on the Work Offline option on the Project, Web Project menu. Taking a project offline copies its files to a directory under the directory shown in the Options dialog in the Web Settings panel. You then can edit the files locally and subsequently compare and synchronize them with the Web server using options under the Project, Web Project menu.

Finally, unlike other types of projects, Web projects can be copied using the Copy Project menu option on the Project menu or the toolbar button on the Solution Explorer window. The resulting dialog allows you to specify a destination project folder and copy all files or a subset of them using either the FrontPage or file share Web access method.

In addition to the project templates shown in Table 2.1, VS .NET includes a series of setup and deployment project templates, as well. These will be discussed in Chapter 5, "Packaging, Deployment, and Security."

When the project is created, its definition is stored in a .vbproj file in the appropriate directory. As you might expect, this file is simply an XML file that contains the project information.

IDE Windows

After the project type has been selected and loaded, you can work with the project using the various windows discussed in this section. Figure 2.1 shows the primary windows.

Solution Explorer

Once inside a project, the main window used for navigating the project is the Solution Explorer. Typically situated in the upper right-hand corner of the screen, it contains three views: File (default) view, Class view, and Resource view.

The default view includes the files and directories that comprise the project, in addition to the additional project references including both local and Web references. Obviously, from here, you can edit the various files in the project in both Design and Code views by double-clicking on them or highlighting the appropriate file and using the toolbar buttons on the window.

TIP

To view files that are typically hidden in the File view, you can click the Show All Files button in the toolbar. This is useful, for example, for viewing the compiled and referenced assembly files in the `bin` directory in addition to providing direct access to the code behind files used with ASP.NET pages, as we will discuss in Chapter 10.

2

THE
DEVELOPMENT
ENVIRONMENT

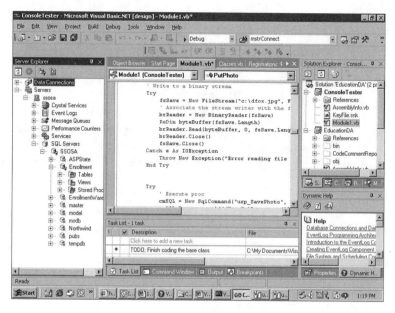

FIGURE 2.1

The primary windows used in VS .NET.

As mentioned, the Solution Explorer also supports Class and Resource views, which can be accessed using the View menu. The Class view presents a hierarchical view of the projects, namespaces, classes, and members in the solution, and allows you to group them or sort them alphabetically, by type and by access level. By double-clicking on any node in the tree, the code editor window displays the definition. Obviously, this can be an efficient way to traverse your code and can take the place of using the drop-downs on the top of the code editor as is traditionally done, because the Class view displays the entire project rather than a single class.

The Resource view displays the resource files included in the project and hierarchically shows the types and the resources within each file.

Properties

As in VB 6.0, the Properties dialog displays the properties associated with whatever object is currently highlighted in the Solution Explorer, visual designer, or code editor window. It appears in the lower right-hand corner of the screen with the dynamic help window, but as with the other windows, it can be undocked and moved to another location. Obviously, properties that are not disabled can be set at design time simply by clicking on the property and directly changing its value. Some properties also provide special property editors that allow you to graphically set the property, such as the color editor used with properties, as in BackColor.

Toolbox

The Toolbox window displays on the left-hand side of the screen and, when using the Visual Studio Developer profile, it is set to auto-hide and only appears when you place your cursor over the small preview window or use the View, Toolbox menu.

When the toolbox is displayed, it is comprised of a series of tabs. In addition to the General and Clipboard Ring tabs, which always are there, which tabs appear and which components are enabled depend on the type of project you're working on, what is selected in the development environment, and whether an Enterprise Template policy is in effect.

> **TIP**
>
> The Toolbox goes away when you move your cursor off it or click elsewhere in the IDE. To keep it open, turn off Auto Hide using the thumbtack icon or the menu option on the Window menu when the Toolbox has the focus. This applies to all other windows, as well.

As with previous versions of VB, you can drag and drop items from the Toolbox onto a designer surface, such as a Web Form. However, note that the Toolbox also contains tabs that include inherently nonvisual components, such as event logs and performance monitor counters. These types of components can be dragged onto the designer and automatically generate the template code to use the component within the .vb file.

To customize the Toolbox, you can right-click on it and add a tab, sort, add and delete components on a tab, show all the available tabs, and rename tabs. The Customize Toolbox dialog, that is invoked by right-clicking on the Toolbox and choosing Customize Toolbox, displays both classic COM components, as well as .NET components installed on the current machine. The Reset button allows you to restore the contents of the Toolbox to the state it was when VS .NET was first launched.

One interesting functionality of the Toolbox that was not available in VB 6.0 is the capability to store text (fragments) on any of the tabs by simply highlighting the text in the code editor and dragging and dropping it onto the tab. You then can rename the item and subsequently drag it into other pages. This simple form of reuse can be handy for frequently used programming constructs such as loops and conditional logic.

Code Editor

The majority of time a developer spends with the IDE is spent in the code editor. Luckily, the editor in VS .NET contains the same powerful features that VB developers are used to, in addition to several new features.

The first point to note is that, as in VB, the code editor typically is invoked only after the graphical designer has been opened. For example, by default, when you double-click on a file in the Solution Explorer, its designer is loaded and the Web page, form, or component designer is displayed. In some instances, the designers themselves contain more than one view. For example, when editing a Web Form, the designer supports both a graphical view and an HTML view accessed through tabs found at the bottom of the view. Both views affect the visual interface, so they are logically a part of the designer. However, the code that executes behind the form then can be accessed by double-clicking on the designer, using the context menu, or as noted earlier, using the toolbar button in the Solution Explorer window.

TIP

When editing a Web page in HTML view, the code editor window also contains two buttons in the upper right-hand corner. These can be used to toggle between Full HTML view and Script Only view so that you can edit only the server- and client-side script blocks in your code.

After the code editor is opened, it contains the familiar drop-downs at the top used to create handlers for events. The drop-down on the left displays the current class and any class-level variables declared using the `WithEvents` keyword. On the right, you'll find the events exposed for the currently selected object. In addition, the drop-down on the left contains the Overrides and Base Class Events items. The former is used to show a list of the methods on the left that can be overridden from the base class if one exists, whereas the latter shows a list of events that can be handled. By selecting one of these, a new method definition that uses the `Overrides` keyword (which will be discussed in Chapter 4, "Object-Oriented Features") or an event handler using the `Handles` keyword is created.

Notice that in both drop-downs, small icons are placed in front of the objects and members to indicate the access level (explained in Chapter 4) and type of the object or member, as shown in Figure 2.2.

FIGURE 2.2

The icons displayed in the code editor drop-downs.

In Figure 2.2, protected members, such as `Page_Init` are specified with a key, private members, such as `IntializeComponent` include a padlock, and public members simply have a cube.

One of the more visible new features of the code editor includes the outlining capability that uses the concepts of *regions*. To define a region, you can use the `#Region` and `#End Region` declarations to wrap a section of code. This region then can be collapsed and expanded to more easily navigate the code. The Outlining menu options on the Edit menu or accessed through the context menu also can be used to collapse and expand the regions.

Although VB developers always have been accustomed to a certain level of code reformatting in terms of keyword capitalization and text highlighting, the code editor now supports two levels of automatic indentation (block and smart) and the capability to insert spaces, as well as tabs. These options and others (such as line numbering) that affect the editor can be found in the Options dialog invoked from the Tools, Options menu in the Text Editor, Basic panel.

As in VB 6.0, full IntelliSense also is supported by default, including listing of members, parameter information, quick information, and statement completion. It can be explicitly invoked using the Edit, IntelliSense menu. IntelliSense defaults also can be set in the Text Editor, Basic panel.

> **NOTE**
>
> One feature that VB .NET developers wanted to be included, but that didn't make it into the released product, is XML comments. By placing comments in predefined XML tags, they can be included by the compiler into metadata that is subsequently displayed by IntelliSense and the Object Browser when the component is used. Although this is a great feature, it adds to the size of the code and reduces readability, so look for Microsoft to take a different approach in a future release.

Server Explorer

Perhaps the most interesting new window in the IDE is the Server Explorer. It appears in the same location as the Toolbox and behaves in the same manner in terms of its autohide setting. The concept behind the Server Explorer is to give graphical access to components that developers need to interact with, either on their machine or, more likely, on a server. In this way, the Server Explorer is definitely geared toward the middle-tier developer who needs to programmatically access reporting, message queues, event logs, performance counters, services, and SQL Server databases.

For example, to use the Server Explorer, simply click on View, Server Explorer, and the window appears. By default, the window shows the current machine, but can be used to access additional machines by right-clicking on the Servers node in the tree view and selecting Add Server. By drilling down into the server of interest, you can inspect the various components and then drag and drop one onto a designer surface. For developers building middle-tier components, this can be done by adding a new component to the project, which creates a class derived from `System.ComponentModel.Component`. This class allows the component to expose the Component Designer surface where components can be dragged and dropped. By dragging a component onto the surface, a visual representation of it appears on the designer while code is added to the class.

To illustrate the code created during this process, Figure 2.3 shows the Component Designer just after a SQL Server stored procedure called `usp_GetStudent` has been dropped onto the surface. Because the component is nonvisual only, an icon appears on the surface analogous to using the Internet or Mail controls that shipped with VB 6.0.

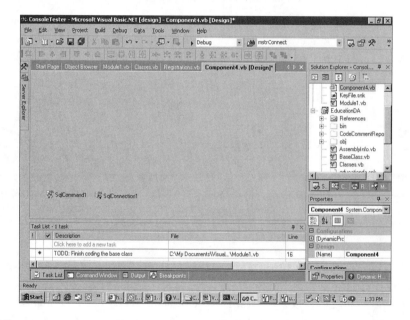

FIGURE 2.3

The Component Designer surface after dragging and dropping a component.

However, behind the scenes, two members were added to the class, and the `InitializeComponent` method was created to initialize objects that correspond with the components that were dropped. All the code is contained in a region that is collapsed by default. The results can be seen in Listing 2.1.

LISTING 2.1 Autogenerated Code. This code is generated by the Server Explorer to execute a SQL Server stored procedure.

```
#Region " Component Designer generated code "

  Public Sub New(ByVal Container As System.ComponentModel.IContainer)
      MyClass.New()

      'Required for Windows.Forms Class Composition Designer support
      Container.Add(Me)
  End Sub

Friend WithEvents SqlConnection1 As System.Data.SqlClient.SqlConnection
Friend WithEvents SqlCommand1 As System.Data.SqlClient.SqlCommand

  <System.Diagnostics.DebuggerStepThrough()> _
  Private Sub InitializeComponent()
      Me.SqlConnection1 = New System.Data.SqlClient.SqlConnection()
      Me.SqlCommand1 = New System.Data.SqlClient.SqlCommand()
      '
      'SqlConnection1
      '
      Me.SqlConnection1.ConnectionString = "data source=SSOSA;" & _
        "initial catalog=Enrollment;integrated security=SSPI;persist sec" & _
        "urity info=True;workstation id=SSOSA;packet size=4096"
      '
      'SqlCommand1
      '
      Me.SqlCommand1.CommandText = "dbo.usp_GetStudent"
      Me.SqlCommand1.CommandType = System.Data.CommandType.StoredProcedure
      Me.SqlCommand1.Connection = Me.SqlConnection1
      Me.SqlCommand1.Parameters.Add(New System.Data.SqlClient.SqlParameter( _
        "@RETURN_VALUE", System.Data.SqlDbType.Int, 4, _
        System.Data.ParameterDirection.ReturnValue, True, CType(10, Byte), _
        CType(0, Byte), "", System.Data.DataRowVersion.Current, Nothing))
      Me.SqlCommand1.Parameters.Add(New System.Data.SqlClient.SqlParameter( _
        "@StudentID", System.Data.SqlDbType.Int, 4, _
        System.Data.ParameterDirection.Input, True, CType(10, Byte), _
        CType(0, Byte), "", System.Data.DataRowVersion.Current, Nothing))
  End Sub

#End Region
```

In Listing 2.1, because executing a stored procedure requires a connection to a database, two objects, an ADO.NET SqlConnection and SqlCommand, are created. (We will discuss this in

2

more detail in Chapter 7.) You can graphically change the names of these components and their properties using the Properties window, and the corresponding code will be rewritten.

Although using the Server Explorer in this manner can speed up the development process, it also is good for learning how to use some of the Services Framework. In many instances, you might not want to inherit from Component, so the code generated here can simply be copied and used elsewhere. Also notice that the generated code is somewhat verbose because it fully qualifies all the called objects using their namespaces, rather than using the Imports statement.

> **TIP**
>
> If you intend to use code generated by the Server Explorer, you should not modify the generated code because VS .NET uses it to display the appropriate information in the Properties window and the Component Designer.

Document Outline

When developing HTML, it often comes in handy to view a hierarchical representation of the HTML contained on the page. The Document Outline window is a holdover from the VID/VJ++ IDE and displays a nested, hierarchical view of the elements and scripts on a Web page when either in Design or HTML view. The window is invoked from the View, Other Windows menu and can be used to navigate through the page when in HTML Outline view or to add a client-side script when in Script Outline view. Both views are accessible from the toolbar within the window. By double-clicking on an element, it is highlighted in the code editor.

Object Browser

VB developers should be familiar with the Object Browser window accessible through the View, Other Windows menu. As in VB 6.0, by default, it contains three panes and displays classes and their members for the active project, in addition to projects they reference. At the highest level, each assembly is displayed with its child namespaces followed by the interfaces and classes they support in the left-hand pane. The members and their signatures are displayed in the right-hand pane, whereas links to the online help are found in the bottom pane.

> **TIP**
>
> The Object Browser can be used to copy the fully qualified name of a particular member to the Clipboard by right-clicking on it and selecting Copy.

The Object Browser actually contains two browse modes. In addition to displaying information on the active project, you also can select Selected Components from the drop-down and use the Customize button to add components that are not referenced in the project. Although the list of objects changes with each project you click on in the Solution Explorer when in active project mode, the list of references remains the same and is saved when VS .NET closes when in Selected Components mode.

Unlike other windows, such as the Toolbox and Server Explorer, the Object Browser window is not set to dockable by default. Thus, it displays in the list of windows accessible through tabs, along with the Start page and code editor windows. As is the case for all windows, by right-clicking on the tab for the window or the title bar, the dockable option can be set to allow the window to be docked.

Task List

Like the Document Outline, the Task List window originated in the VID/VJ++ IDE, and can be used to track the development tasks you must complete. In addition, it can be used to display compilation errors and warnings. In this way, the Task List often includes a combination of user-defined and system-defined messages.

> **NOTE**
>
> The dockable Task List window also displays the Command, Output, and Breakpoints windows accessed using the tabs on the bottom of the window. We will discuss this in more detail in Chapter 6, "Error Handling and Debugging."

The left-hand columns of the Task List display the priority along with an icon that shows the type of message displayed in the description. The full list of types can be found in the online help. To add a new task, simply click on the first entry in the list and enter the data. User-defined tasks also allow you to mark when they are complete by using the check box. The tasks themselves then can be filtered by type and status, in addition to being sorted using the context menu invoked when you right-click on the window.

One of the more interesting uses of the Task List window is to annotate your code with comments that are automatically loaded as tasks. When the task is clicked on, the code window is opened and the commented line is navigated to. This feature is controlled through the Options dialog in the Environment, Task List pane. In this pane, you can add, modify, and delete tokens that you use as the prefixes for comments. By default, HACK, TODO, UNDONE, and UnresolvedMergeConflict tokens are defined. Although you cannot delete the TODO token because it is used by various classes in the framework, you can add your own tokens to, for example, highlight a particular algorithm for other developers.

For example, by creating a custom token called QUILOGY and creating a comment prefixed with the token and a colon, the description will be added to the Task List, as shown in the following code:

```
'QUILOGY: Authentication code
FormsAuthentication.SetAuthCookie(txtEmail.Text, False)

' Authenticated so send them to requested URL
If InStr(FormsAuthentication.GetRedirectUrl(txtEmail.Text, False), _
   "default.aspx") > 0 Then
     Response().Redirect("\QuilogyEducation\QEducation.aspx")
Else
     FormsAuthentication.RedirectFromLoginPage(txtEmail.Text, False)
End If
```

Dynamic Help

The final major window in the IDE in Figure 2.1 is the Dynamic Help window. The objective of this window is to display context-sensitive help topics based on the current area or task you are working with in the IDE. The list of topics is displayed based on the relative weight and is broken down into categories, such as Help, Actions, Miscellaneous, and Samples.

> **NOTE**
>
> The list of topics shown in this window is not affected by the help filter you can specify on the Start page.

You can customize which categories and topics, in addition to how many links are displayed in the window by using the Environment, Dynamic Help panel in the Options dialog.

When you click on a link, it is displayed directly within the IDE in a separate window. Although some developers might find this feature useful because it displays context-sensitive help, the sheer amount of screen real estate it entails, coupled with the fact that the help window tends to get lost, means that many developers will opt for opening the help standalone using the icon in the Microsoft Visual Studio .NET program group.

Supported File Types

Depending on which type of project you're currently in, the choices for items you can create or add will be filtered. However, taken as a whole, the most important items can be broken down into four basic categories: generic project items, Windows Forms items, ASP.NET project items, and auxiliary project items, all of which are discussed next.

Generic Project Items

After the project has been created, you can add new items to the project by right-clicking on the project in the Solution Explorer and choosing from the menu or using the Project menu. The items shown in Table 2.2 are those that can be added to any project. Typically, these items are used as the basis for reusable components and utility code used in the project.

TABLE 2.2   Generic Project Items

Item	Description
Class	Creates a file with a .vb extension and adds it to the project. Within the file, it defines a generic `Class`. Used for creating your own classes (that is, business logic or data access classes).
Module	Creates a file with a .vb extension, adds it to the project, and includes a `Module` declaration. As in VB 6.0, modules are used for utility functions and global data. Basically, a module is implemented as a class that contains only shared members and that is not createable. Any code within the same namespace as the module can access its members without qualification. This is not to be confused with CLR modules, which were discussed in Chapter 1.
Component class	Creates a file with a .vb extension and adds it to the project with a `Class` declaration derived from `System.ComponentModel.Component`. Allows visual design of components using the Server Explorer window.
Transactional component	Creates a file with a .vb extension and adds it to the project with a `Class` declaration that derives from `System.EnterpriseServices.ServicedComponent`. Can be used as the basis for business logic and data access components that use COM+ services such as transactions.
Code file	Creates an empty file with a .vb extension.
DataSet	Creates a file with a .xsd extension that allows you to graphically design an XSD schema for a `System.Data.DataSet` class. Exposes an autogenerated .vb file that represents a strongly typed `DataSet`.
XML file, XML schema, XSLT	Used to create files of these types to be contained in the project.

Windows Forms

When creating a form-based application, which is beyond the scope of this book, you can add Windows Forms, forms inherited from an existing form (referred to as an inherited form), user controls, inherited user controls, and custom controls.

ASP.NET Project Items

When building ASP.NET applications, you can add the project items found in Table 2.3.

TABLE 2.3 ASP.NET Project Items

Item	Description
Web Form	Creates a file with a .aspx extension and an associated .vb file that contains the page logic referred to as the "code-behind file." The class in the .vb file derives from `System.Web.UI.Page`. Used as the basis for the user interface in a Web application.
Web Service	Creates a file with a .asmx extension and an associated .vb file that contains the service logic in a class derived from `System.Web.Services.WebService`. Defines the interface of a Web Service.
HTML page	Creates a generic .html file.
Frameset	Creates an HTML file that defines a frameset tag based on a selection dialog.
Style sheet	Creates a cascading style sheet with a .css extension. Can be edited with a graphical editor built in to VS .NET.
Web custom control	Creates a .vb file that contains a class derived from `System.Web.UI.WebControls.WebControl`. Used for building ASP.NET server controls.
Web user control	Creates a file with a .ascx extension and an associated .vb file used to create a reusable control that can be graphically edited.
Global application class	Creates a Global.asax file and associated .vb file that contains a class called `Global` that inherits from `System.Web.HttpApplication`. This class defines `Application` and `Session` events for an ASP.NET application.

Auxiliary Project Items

Auxiliary project items are those that might be added to different types of projects and provide support services, as shown in Table 2.4.

TABLE 2.4 Auxiliary Project Items

Item	Description
Windows Service	Creates a file with a .vb extension that contains a class derived from `System.ServiceProcess.ServiceBase` used to implement a Windows service. Also references the appropriate assembly.
COM class	Creates a file with a .vb extension that contains a class signature and the appropriate attributes and GUIDs to build a component accessible from classic COM clients.
Crystal report	Automatically references the Crystal reports assemblies and invokes the Crystal Report Gallery to build a new report with a .rpt extension to add to the project.
Installer class	Creates a file with a .vb extension that contains a class derived from `System.Configuration.Install.Installer` used to install server-based resources, such as performance counters and event logs. Also references the appropriate assembly.
Assembly resource file	Creates a file with a .resx extension used to house resources used for localization.
Assembly information file	Creates a .vb file that contains standard assembly-level attributes used to specify general information about the assembly, such as the title, description, and version.
Application configuration file	Creates an app.config file in the project used to store configuration information as discussed in Chapter 1.
JScript, VBScript, Windows Script host	Creates empty files with .js, .vb, and .wsf extensions, respectively.

Setting Project References

Of course, one of the primary strengths of VB always has been the integration of external code in the form of COM components and controls. In VB .NET, as in any managed language, external code is housed in assemblies that can be referenced from within VS .NET.

By invoking the References dialog from the Project, Add Reference menu, or right-clicking on references in the Solution Explorer window, the references dialog is displayed, as shown in Figure 2.4.

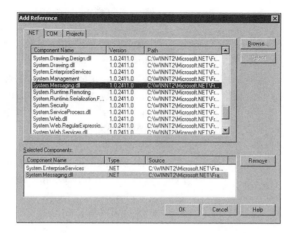

Figure 2.4
The References dialog allows you to reference assemblies external to your project.

NOTE

You also can add Web references using the Add Web Reference menu option. This is used to refer to Web Services and will be covered in detail in Chapter 11.

By referencing an assembly, you are including information about it in the manifest of your assembly, including the specific version you are referencing.

NOTE

As mentioned in Chapter 1 and expounded on in Chapter 5, assemblies can either be private or shared. Private assemblies are those that do not have a strong name and as a result are deployed in the application directory. To that end, VS .NET automatically copies private assemblies to the application directory. This behavior can be controlled on a per-assembly basis by changing the Copy Local property in the properties window to `False`. Note, however, that changing Copy Local to `False` causes an exception to be thrown at runtime if classes from that assembly are loaded by your application and not found.

Obviously, referenced assemblies then will appear in the Object Browser, and you can program against any of its public types. Because assemblies contain a hierarchy of namespaces, some of which are nested several levels, referencing a class from an assembly can require a lengthy statement. For example, if an assembly that contains data access classes for Quilogy is referenced, the required code for accessing the Students class is as follows:

```
Dim oEnroll As Quilogy.Education.Enrollment.Students
```

Because typing code like this, even with Intellisense, is unwieldy and hurts readability, you can use the Imports statement to reference a namespace to allow the names of types to be used without qualification. For example, the same declaration also could be made like so:

```
Imports Quilogy.Education.Enrollment
Dim oStud As Students
```

Each code file (.vb) can contain multiple Imports statements that must appear at the top of the file directly after the Option statements, such as Option Strict and Option Explicit.

> **NOTE**
>
> The scope of the names referenced in the Imports statement includes the namespaces declared within the file. In other words, Imports statements do not span source files.

Because it is certainly possible to reference assemblies that contain types with the same name, it is sometimes necessary to use an alias to refer to a specific namespace. For example, if both a client and the Quilogy.Education.Enrollment namespace contained a Students class, the two could be differentiated in the following manner:

```
Imports QEnroll = Quilogy.Education.Enrollment

Dim oMyStud As Students
Dim oStud As QEnroll.Students
```

Note that the alias is defined by setting the alias name equal to the name of the namespace.

Macros and Add-Ins

As you would expect, the VS .NET IDE also exposes a COM automation model (formerly known as the extensibility model) that allows you to write code that extends and enhances the IDE. Using the automation model, you can create developer tools that increase your productivity or assist other developers. The programming interface to the automation model can be used either through macros or add-ins.

Macros

In the past, VB developers did not have access to macros, although conceptually they are the same as the macros you might be familiar with in products, such as Microsoft Excel. As in those products, macros can be recorded in VS .NET using the macro recorder on the Tools, Macros menu. The resulting code is contained in a module accessible by viewing the Macro Explorer window from the Tools, Macros menu. The window appears as an additional pane in the Solution Explorer window and can be used to edit, delete, run, and add new macros. For example, by right-clicking on the macro and selecting Edit, the macro IDE opens to allow editing.

> **NOTE**
>
> Macros are compiled automatically, so you do not have to explicitly compile them in the macro editor. Simply saving your changes causes the macro to be recompiled the next time it is executed. If the macros you develop contain intellectual property that you want to distribute and conceal from third parties, consider implementing the macro as an Add-In, as discussed in the next section.

Typically, macros are used by a single developer to automate a common set of keystrokes, or to interject code into the code editor window that would otherwise require more complex manipulation. Macros are saved in the \VSMacros directory under the path found in the Options dialog in the Environment, Projects and Solutions panel. Macros can be stored as either binary or text files controlled through the StorageFormat property in the Properties window. Saving the macro as a binary file enables you to share it more easily, whereas saving it as text allows you to manipulate it outside VS .NET.

> **TIP**
>
> Macros can include event handling code that runs automatically when the macro is opened, although not when VS .NET is opened. Because this presents a potential security concern, event handling can be disabled for all macros using the DefaultSecurity property in the Properties window when the highest level node in the Macro Explorer is selected. In addition, event handling can be disabled for specific collections of macros in the same way.

Although a discussion of the automation object model is beyond the scope of this book, the code in Listing 2.2 illustrates what can be done with a macro.

2

TIP

As with any macro recorder, you can use it to explore the automation object model by recording a number of the actions you typically perform with VS .NET and then reviewing the generated code. You then can use this code as the basis for new macros.

LISTING 2.2   Creating a Macro. This listing shows the code to create a macro that inserts a new region around the highlighted text.

```
Imports EnvDTE
Imports System.Diagnostics
Imports Microsoft.VisualBasic.ControlChars

Public Module Module1

    Public Sub CreateRegion()
        Dim selection As TextSelection
        Dim startPt As EditPoint
        Dim endPt As EditPoint
        Dim regionName As String

        ' Prompt for the name of the region
        regionName = InputBox("Enter the name of the Region", _
          "Region", "New Region")

        ' Get the active selection
        selection = DTE.ActiveDocument.Selection()

        ' Get the start and end points of the selection
        startPt = selection.TopPoint.CreateEditPoint()
        endPt = selection.BottomPoint.CreateEditPoint

        ' Create an undo context in case of an error
        DTE.UndoContext.Open("Create Region")
        Try
            startPt.StartOfLine()
            startPt.Insert("#Region """ & regionName & """" & vbCrLf)
            endPt.StartOfLine()
            endPt.LineDown(1)
            endPt.Insert("#End Region" & vbCrLf)
        Finally
            ' Commit the change
```

LISTING 2.2 Continued

```
            DTE.UndoContext.Close()
        End Try
    End Sub

End Module
```

Listing 2.2 contains the complete code for a macro created by right-clicking on MyMacros in the Macro Explorer window and choosing New Macro. After renaming the Sub procedure, the code in the procedure was created to automatically create a collapsible region around any text currently highlighted in the code editor window.

In Listing 2.2, the automation model is exposed through an assembly called EnvDTE and is imported using the Imports statement. After prompting for the name of the region using the InputBox function, the active selection is retrieved in a TextSelection object using the Selection method of the ActiveDocument object within the highest level object in the automation model, DTE (Development Tools Extensibility).

The beginning and ending points for the TextSelection then are retrieved by using the TopPoint and BottomPoint properties. The capability to insert text at these points in the window is accomplished by creating edit points on each using the CreateEditPoint method.

To make sure that errors that occur while editing the code can be undone, the Open method of the UndoContext object is invoked. Basically, this is analogous to beginning a transaction within the IDE, and if an exception is thrown, all changes will be undone. The actual editing of the code occurs in the Try block (discussed in Chapter 6). The StartOfLine method moves the insertion point to the beginning of the line indicated in the EditPoint, in this case the starting point of the TextSelection, and then text is inserted using the Insert method. Similarly, the #End Region statement is inserted at the end of the selection. The Finally block then issues the Close of the UndoContext to commit the changes.

To use this macro, you can highlight a block of code and then double-click the macro in the Macro Explorer window. The result is a new region that contains the highlighted code.

NOTE

For more information on the automation object model, see the online documentation.

Add-Ins

The second way to extend the IDE is through the use of add-ins. Although VB developers should be familiar with the concept because VB 6.0 exposed an Add-In model, the programmatic interface is not the same. Add-ins are useful for encapsulating code that you want to distribute throughout an organization or to third parties. Typically, corporate developers have more use for macros than for add-ins, so a complete discussion of the topic is beyond the scope of this book.

In a nutshell, the best way to create an add-in and make sure that it is registered is to use the Visual Studio .NET Add-In project template found in the Other Projects, Extensibility Projects folder when creating a new project. The resulting project contains a class called `Connect` that includes stubs for the various methods you typically would implement for the add-in. In addition, it registers the add-in and provides additional instructions. The template also creates a Windows Installer project for packing the add-in with the appropriate dependencies.

After the add-in is registered, it can be loaded through the Add-In Manager dialog accessible from the Tools menu.

Using Attributes

One of the concepts introduced in the CLR, that will be new to many VB developers, is that of *attributes*. Basically, attributes are declarative structures that are placed at the assembly, interface, structure, class, or member level, and are typically used to instruct the compiler or components of the CLR—such as the security system—how to treat the entity on which the attribute is placed.

The syntax for using attributes in VB .NET is to enclose the attributes in < > symbols separated by commas directly before the declaration of the entity on which the attribute should take effect. In addition, each attribute can be placed on a separate line for readability. For example, attributes used by the RegAsm utility that registers a managed assembly as a COM class called `GuidAttribute` and `ProgIdAttribute` can be placed on a class declaration like so:

```
<GuidAttribute("A2AD3270-9BB3-4CBA-8206-C87CAA33F562"), _
 ProgIdAttribute("MyAddin1.Connect")> _
Public Class Connect
```

Attributes can contain constructors, as shown here, in addition to other public properties. To set a property not found in the constructor, use the `:=` operator like so:

```
<ConstructionEnabled(True, Default:="c:\logfile=da.log")> _
Public Class DataAccess
```

In this example, the constructor accepts a `Boolean` that enables Component Services object construction, and populates an additional `Default` property that can be set to a string that specifies the location of a log file, for example.

In addition to simply using attributes exposed by the framework, you can create your own attributes to specify custom metadata. For example, if you were designing a set of framework classes to be widely distributed, you could create a custom attribute to encapsulate information about reference documentation.

To create a custom attribute, you simply need to create a new class that derives from System.Attribute. Listing 2.3 illustrates creating a custom attribute called DocumentationAttribute to include documentation information.

> **NOTE**
>
> It is customary to add the suffix "Attribute" to the name of the attribute; however, clients that use the attribute needn't include this part of the name.

LISTING 2.3 Creating a Custom Attribute. This class implements a custom attribute for documentation purposes.

```
<AttributeUsage(AttributeTargets.Class Or _
  AttributeTargets.Interface Or AttributeTargets.Enum Or _
  AttributeTargets.Struct)> _
Public Class DocumentationAttribute : Inherits Attribute

    Private strUrl As String
    Private strAuthor As String

    Public Sub New(ByVal url As String)
       Me.strUrl = url
    End Sub

    Public Property Author() As String
     Get
        Return strAuthor
     End Get
     Set(ByVal Value As String)
       strAuthor = Value
     End Set
    End Property

    Public ReadOnly Property Url() As String
     Get
       Return strUrl
     End Get
    End Property

End Class
```

In Listing 2.3, even before the class is declared, it too uses an attribute called `AttributeUsage` to control on which types of entities the attribute can be placed. In this case, the `Or` operator is used with constants from the `AttributeTargets` enumeration to indicate that the `DocumentationAttribute` can be placed on a class, interface, enumerated type, or structure only.

> **TIP**
>
> To allow an attribute to be placed anywhere, you can use `AttributeTargets.All`. The `AttributeUsageAttribute` also exposes an `AllowMultiple` Boolean property that indicates whether multiple instances of the attribute can be placed on the same entity.

Also notice that this attribute contains two properties, `Author` and `Url`, and that `Url` is passed to the constructor and is required.

Users of the attribute then can decorate their classes with the `DocumentationAttribute` as follows:

```
<Documentation("http://www.quilogy.com/qa/dataaccess.aspx", _
  Author:="Dan Fox")> _
Public Class QuilogyDataAccess
```

As noted previously, "Attribute" can be omitted from the declaration, and because the `Author` property is not found in the constructor, it can be added to the declaration using the `:=` assignment operator.

At runtime, a client of the class that declared the attribute can read the attribute information using the `GetCustomAttributes` method of the `Type` object. For example, the following code uses the `GetType` function to return the `Type` object for `QuilogyDataAccess` from the previous code example:

```
Dim type As Type = GetType(QuilogyDataAccess)
Dim arr() As Object
Dim att As Attribute

arr = type.GetCustomAttributes(False)
For Each att In arr
    If TypeOf att Is DocumentationAttribute Then
        Dim da As DocumentationAttribute = _
          CType(arr(0), DocumentationAttribute)
        Console.WriteLine("Url = " & da.Url & "Author = " & da.Author)
    End If
Next
```

It then retrieves an array of custom attributes using the `GetCustomAttributes` method and walks through the array looking for the `DocumentationAttribute` using the `TypeOf` statement. When found, it converts the `Object` to the `DocumentationAttribute` type so that its properties, `Url` and `Author`, can be queried.

Command-Line Compilation

Although most developers typically use the VS .NET IDE to build their projects, VB .NET also ships with a command-line compiler, VBC.exe. This can come in handy for automating compilation through batch files, and it contains a complete set of switches to do everything that the VS .NET build option does.

> **TIP**
>
> A convenient way to use the command-line compiler is to open the Visual Studio .NET command prompt from the Visual Studio .NET Tools folder installed in the Visual Studio .NET program group. The command window opens with the appropriate paths set to access the command-line compilers.

For example, the following command line compiles all the .vb files in the current directory into a library assembly (/t:target) called EducationData.dll (/out). In addition, debugging information is included (/debug), and no logo information is displayed (/nologo), whereas the `/r` option references the MyCustom.dll assembly in a manner analogous to setting a project reference in VS .NET.

```
vbc /target:library /out:EducatiobData.dll /nologo /debug /r:MyCustom.dll *.vb
```

The command-line compiler additionally can create standalone modules using the `/target:module` option that later can be compiled into multifile assemblies that can include modules produced in other languages.

As shown in the previous code example, using the command-line compiler entails setting all the appropriate options for the project, such as references contained in the .vbproj file created by VS .NET when a project is created. To take advantage of the .vbproj file and still perform a command-line compile, you can use devenv.exe, the VS .NET IDE, from the command line.

For example, to compile a particular project from within a solution, you could use the following command line:

```
devenv DataAccess.sln /build debug /project EducationDA.vbproj
```

In this case, the `EducationDA` project from the `DataAccess` solution will be built using the `debug` configuration. The output written to the console is identical to that typically found in the Output Window within VS .NET.

Summary

This chapter provided a quick tour of the VS .NET IDE to get you up to speed on how it is organized and some of its features. Obviously, detailed information on the various options is best accessed by using the online documentation and especially the dynamic help window as you use the various features of the IDE.

Now that the stage is set, it's time to begin exploring the particular changes and features of the VB .NET language that will be used in building applications with VB .NET. This is precisely the subject of the next two chapters.

VB .NET Language Features

IN THIS CHAPTER

As is obvious by now, VB .NET and VS .NET contain significant changes from previous versions of VB in terms of the runtime architecture and the features of the development environment itself. In addition, the VB .NET language has been changed in accordance with the design goals to modernize and simplify the language, reduce programming errors, and provide full access to the Common Language Runtime (CLR) and Services Framework. Although some of these changes have produced much discussion in the VB community, my personal view is that this is good because it tightens the language and therefore makes it a better tool for development.

As a result of these changes, the language has actually been simplified in several respects by removing duplicate or confusing constructs, removing functionality now supported by the Services Framework, and taking away some of the idiosyncratic behavior particular to BASIC. In this chapter, we'll walk through the details of these changes as they related to both the structure of the language and the functional changes that might require you to think differently when coding in VB .NET. In addition, we'll explore the compatibility features that assist in transitioning code from VB 6.0 to VB .NET including using the Upgrade Wizard. However, it should be noted that some of the modernizing features that require more in-depth treatment, such as changes to classes, inheritance, explicit interface declaration, structured exception handling, and free threading, will be handled in Chapter 4, "Object-Oriented Features," Chapter 6, "Error Handling and Debugging," and Chapter 12, "Accessing System Services."

> **NOTE**
>
> All code listings and supplemental material for this chapter can be found on the book's Web site at www.samspublishing.com.

Keyword Changes

Unlike previous versions of VB, VB .NET runs within the context of the CLR and, as a result, must adhere to the rules of any Common Language Specification (CLS) compliant language. It shouldn't be surprising to learn that, as a result, the language itself is contained in an assembly with the namespace Microsoft.VisualBasic. When you choose to create a project in VS .NET with VB .NET, this assembly automatically is referenced, and its classes and methods can be referred to without using dot notation because they are declared with a special attribute making them global. This means that you don't have to be concerned with the class structure of the Microsoft.VisualBasic namespace, although the online documentation breaks it down for you. For the purposes of this chapter, we'll treat all the members of the classes contained in the Microsoft.VisualBasic namespace as peers and intrinsic keywords.

To begin, consider Table 3.1, which shows the keywords removed from VB .NET available in previous versions. Contrast this table with the keywords added to the language in Table 3.2.

TABLE 3.1 Obsolete Keywords, Functions, and Statements in VB .NET

Keyword, Function or Statement	Disposition
`Array`	Function formerly used to populate an array with arguments. Now the { } can be used in the declaration of the array.
`As Any`	Formerly used with the `Declare` statement. Now VB .NET supports overloading declares so that explicit data types must be used.
`Atn, Sgn, Sqr`	Replaced by the `System.Math` namespace.
`Calendar`	Replaced by the `System.Globalization` namespace.
`Circle, Line`	Replaced by the `System.Drawing` namespace.
`Currency`	Replaced by the `Decimal` data type.
`Date`	Still supported as a data type (mapping to `System.DateTime`) but is no longer a function returning a 4-byte date value. Use the `Today` property of the `System.DateTime` structure to return the day in the 8-byte CLR format.
`Debug.Assert, Debug.Print`	Replaced by methods in the `System.Diagnostics` namespace.
`DefBool, DefInt, DefStr`, and so on	Formerly used to specify data types for implicit declarations. No longer supported.
`DoEvents`	Replaced by a method in the `System.WinForms.Application` class.
`Empty, Null, IsEmpty, IsNull`	Formerly used for uninitialized variables and those that don't contain data. Now both conditions are handled by `Nothing`. Statements to check for these conditions also have been removed. Database nulls can be tested for using the `IsDBNull` function or against the `System.DBNull.Value` property.
`Eqv, Imp`	Bitwise operators replaced by the equals (=) operator and using `Not` and `Or` in conjunction (A `Imp` B) = ((`Not` A) `Or` B).

TABLE 3.1   Continued

Keyword, Function or Statement	Disposition
GoSub	Formerly used to branch to a line label and return later. No longer supported.
On..GoSub, On..Goto	Formerly used to conditionally branch to a line label. Should use `Select Case` or `Switch` instead.
IsMissing	Formerly used to determine whether a value was supplied for an `Optional` parameter. Now all optional parameters must have default values.
IsObject	Formerly used to determine whether a variable referenced an object. Replaced with `IsReference`.
Let, Set	Formerly, `Set` was used to indicate that an object reference was being assigned (`Let` was the default). Because default properties no longer are supported unless they accept parameters, these statements have been removed.
LSet, RSet	Replaced by `PadRight` and `PadLeft` methods of the `System.String` class, although still supported. However, `LSet` was also formerly used to copy user-defined types (UDTs). This use is no longer supported.
PSet, Scale	Formerly used to manipulate the color of a point and the coordinate system on forms and controls. No longer supported. Equivalent functionality exists in `System.Drawing`.
MsgBox	Still supported, but recommended use is the `System.WinForms.MessageBox` class.
Option Base	Formerly used to define the lower bound of arrays. Now all arrays are zero bound, so it is no longer supported.
Option Private Module	Formerly used to declare an entire module as private to the project. Now each module can be marked as private using the `Private` keyword.
Randomize, Rnd, Round	Replaced by the `System.Random` class and the `Round` method of the `System.Math` class. `Rnd` and `Randomize` still exist in the `Microsoft.VisualBasic` namespace, however.
String	Replaced by the overloaded constructor of the `String` class used for initialization.

TABLE 3.1   Continued

Keyword, Function or Statement	Disposition
String Functions	VB functions that returned strings by appending the $ have now been replaced by overloaded methods. Their counterparts that return `Variants` have been replaced with overloads that return `Object`.
Time	Replaced by the `TimeOfDay` property of the `System.DateTime` structure. Note that the `Date` data type is no longer represented as `Double` but rather as a `DateTime` structure.
Type	Replaced by the `Structure` statement.
VarType	Formerly used to determine the type of a `Variant`. Although it still exists, it should be replaced by the `GetTypeCode` method of the specific data types.
Variant	Formerly used to hold any type of data. Replaced with `System.Object` as the universal data type.
Wend	Formerly used in `While...Wend` loops. Now replaced with `While...End While`.

TABLE 3.2   New Keywords, Functions, and Statements in VB .NET

Class	Disposition
IsArray	Function used to determine whether an object is an array.
Choose	Function used to select and return a value from a list of arguments based on an index.
Short, CShort	New data type representing a 16-bit integer equivalent to `Integer` in VB 6.0. `CShort` converts from another data type to `Short`.
IsDBNull	Function that determines whether an expression evaluates to `System.DBNull`. Not the same as `Nothing` or a null string (`""`).
TimeOfDay	Statement that sets or returns the current system time.
GetException	Function that returns the `Exception` object used in the `Err` object. Provides a mapping from the `Err` object to exceptions.

TABLE 3.2 Continued

Class	Disposition
`Try...Catch...Finally, Throw`	Statements used to perform structured exception handling.
`GetType, CType, Convert`	Function used to return the `Type` of the argument and System classes to convert to a different type.
`Option Strict On|Off`	Statement used to ensure type-safe code at compile time when turned on. Default in VS .NET is `On`.
`^=, *=, /=, \=, +=, -=, &=`	Operators used to perform the operation in the first part of the expression and assign the result to the variable.
`AndAlso, OrElse`	Logical operators used for short-circuit comparisons.
`Delegate`	Statement used to declare a delegate (covered in Chapter 4).
`Imports`	Statement that imports namespace names from referenced assemblies.
`AddHandler, RemoveHandler`	Dynamically adds and removes event handlers.
`Inherits, Overloads, Overrides, NotInheritable, MustInherit, NotOverridable, Overridable`	Keywords used with classes, as discussed in Chapter 4.
`Interface`	Statement used to define an interface, as discussed in Chapter 4.
`Protected, Shadows, Shared, ReadOnly, WriteOnly`	Access attributes for a class, method, or property, as discussed in Chapter 4.
`MyBase`	Object used to access the base class from within a class, as discussed in Chapter 4.
`MyClass`	Object used to access the current class.
`Namespace`	Used to define a boundary for classes.
`Structure`	Statement that replaces UDTs.
`SyncLock..End SyncLock`	Statements that ensure that a block of code is not executed concurrently by multiple threads. Discussed in Chapter 12.
`IsReference`	Function that determines whether the given variable is a valid reference to an object.
`DirectCast`	Function used to more strictly convert to a different type

You'll notice that in most instances for keywords removed from the language, an equivalent functionality exists in the Services Framework. In addition, many of the new keywords are related to the object-oriented features of VB .NET provided by the CLR. However, taken as a whole, you can see that the language has not become more complex through the addition of scores of keywords.

Functional Changes

In addition to the syntactical changes, VB .NET behaves differently from previous versions in several respects. This section details the most significant of those changes.

Declarations

Several of the most obvious and productivity-enhancing changes in the language are related to dimensioning and instantiating variables.

As you might be aware through painful experience, in prior versions, a declaration like so

```
Dim x,y,z As Integer
```

did not result in three `Integer` variables. In fact, the first two variables were declared as `Variant`, which wastes memory and has the potential of causing type conversion problems down the road. In VB .NET, multiple declarations work as expected, and so the same declaration will result in three `Integer` variables. In addition, VB .NET supports the capability to use the declaration

```
Dim z
```

when the `Option Strict` statement is set to `Off`. In this case, rather than result in a `Variant`, the variable z is of type `System.Object`. Also note that unlike in previous versions, `Option Explicit` is defaulted to `On` so that variables cannot be used without first declaring them.

VB .NET also supports parameterized constructors so that objects can be initialized during the declaration. This, coupled with support for initialization during declaration, allows VB .NET to support the following types of syntax:

```
Dim dtAaron As New DateTime(1974, 4, 8)
Dim strName As String = "Hank Aaron"
Dim arTheropods() As String = {"Tyrannosaur", "Allosaurus", "Deinonychus"}
```

In this example, the `dtAaron` variable is declared as a `DateTime` structure and instantiated with arguments passed to the constructor specifying the day Hank Aaron hit his 715th homerun. This is shorthand for the statement:

```
Dim dtAaron As DateTime = New DateTime(1974, 4, 8)
```

In the second example, VB .NET takes care of calling the constructor for the `String` variable to allow developers to work with strings in a familiar fashion. The third example shows how to initialize an array of strings during declaration.

> **TIP**
>
> Although the constants you would expect (those prefixed with "vb") exist within the `Microsoft.VisualBasic` namespace, they also are exposed through enumerated types. Because the methods of the namespace expect the enumerated types, it is recommended that you use them rather than the constants.

Object Creation

Two other changes from the behavior of previous versions of VB are related to the creation of objects using the `New` operator. In previous versions the statement

```
Dim dino As New Dinosaur
```

would result in the compiler actually wrapping each line of code that referenced `dino` with a check to see whether the variable was `Nothing`. If so, the object was instantiated. In VB .NET, implicit object creation is not supported, and so the object is instantiated when the `Dim` statement is encountered. As a result, if you're going to use the `New` operator in a declaration, you'll want to place the declaration within the procedure in a place you know the variable will be used. In other words, it is more efficient if you defer dimensioning variables that might end up not being used, as long as possible.

In addition, in VB 6.0, the `New` operator actually used an internal algorithm that was more efficient to instantiate classes within the same project. In VB .NET, the CLR creates and manages all object instances, and so there is no difference when `New` is used with classes in the local assembly versus a remote assembly.

Finally, the `CreateObject` function, although still supported, will only be used to create a COM object. All managed classes are instantiated with the `New` keyword.

Operators

As shown in Table 3.2, VB .NET adds support for new operators. Perhaps the most significant from a keystroke-saving perspective are the operators that perform their operation and assign the result to the variable. For example, in VB 6.0, to concatenate a string on two lines, you would do the following:

```
Dim strMessage As String

strMessage = "This is a message that will be pretty long,"
strMessage = strMessage & " so I'll break it up a little."
```

In VB .NET, this can be compacted to the following:

```
strMessage = "This is a message that will be pretty long,"
strMessage &= " so I'll break it up a little."
```

In addition to concatenation, addition, subtraction, multiplication, division, and exponentiation are supported using this compacted syntax.

VB .NET also does not support default properties, and so the statement

```
Text1 = strName
```

does not assign the string variable `strName` to the `Text` property of the `Text1` object. As a result, you must explicitly use the property. The good news is that this means the `Set` and `Let` statements, which caused a good deal of confusion, are no longer required or supported. The one exception to default properties is in the case where the property accepts a parameter. In this instance, you can mark the property as the default so that working with objects that support collections through properties such as `Item` is simplified.

Operators evaluation in expressions also can be short-circuited in VB .NET so that a procedure like the one that follows can be more efficient:

```
Sub Insert(ByVal value As Integer, ByVal sortedArr() As Integer)
  Dim intIndex, intIndxSrch As Integer
  Dim intArrCount As Integer = sortedArr.Length

  'Scan for entry less than one to be inserted
  While intIndxSrch < intArrCount AndAlso value > sortedArr(intIndxSrch)
    intIndxSrch += 1
  End While

  'Make room for new value --- move remaining items up
End Sub
```

In this example, the `Insert` procedure inserts a new value in a sorted array. Note that the `While` loop contains the new `AndAlso` operator with two expressions. Using short-circuit evaluation, the second condition, which is the more expensive of the two, will not be executed if the first condition returns `False`. In the past, you needed to place these conditions on separate lines to gain this efficiency. Short-circuiting also is implemented with the new `OrElse` operator when the first expression evaluates to `True`.

> **NOTE**
>
> Although it was originally planned that the And, Or, Not, and Xor operators would only perform logical and not bitwise operations, feedback from the VB community ensured that these retain both functionalities and precedence rules as in VB 6.0.

Although not documented in VB 6.0, some developers became accustomed to using the VarPtr, VarPtrArray, VarPtrStringArray, ObjPtr, and StrPtr operators to return the memory addresses of variables of these data types. This was particularly useful when calling some Win32 API functions. These keywords are no longer supported in VB .NET.

Closely related to operators is the behavior of null values. In VB 6.0, null propagation was supported where adding or concatenating a value to Null, or a Variant that contained Null, always produced a null value. In VB .NET, Null has been replaced with Nothing, Variant with Object, and null propagation is not supported. As a result, the following behavior occurs in VB .NET when Option Strict is set to Off:

```
Dim x As Object
Dim i As Integer

i = 4
x = Nothing
i = i + x  ' i still equals 4
```

The Null keyword has been replaced with the System.DBNull class, and checking for nulls returned from databases can be done using the IsDBNull function. The equivalent syntax used in VB 6.0, where an empty string ("") concatenated to a null from a database produced an empty string, is still supported as well.

The absence of both variants and null values implies that functions that once accepted variants and possibly returned null values, such as Mid, Oct, Right, RTrim, Space, Str, Time, Trim, LTrim, UCase, and LCase, among others, now simply return their associated data types. As mentioned in Table 3.1, VB 6.0 also contained companion functions appended with $ (i.e. Trim$) that returned String values. These also have been replaced with overloaded methods that return a String.

Data Types

As discussed in Chapter 1, "The Microsoft .NET Architecture," all data types in VB .NET derive from System.Object and are therefore a part of the Common Type System (CTS) used by the CLR. VB .NET supports keywords that map to the CTS types shown in Table 1.1. This mapping is shown in Table 3.3.

TABLE 3.3 Data Type Mappings in VB .NET

VB .NET Data Type (with type character)	CTS Type
Boolean	System.Boolean
Byte	System.Byte

TABLE 3.3 Continued

VB .NET Data Type (with type character)	CTS Type
Char (new)	System.Char
Decimal (@) (new)	System.Decimal
Double (#)	System.Double
Integer (%)	System.Int32
Long (&)	System.Int64
Short (new)	System.Int16
Single (!)	System.Single
String ($)	System.String

As in VB 6.0, the type character can be used to automatically dimension a variable by appending it to the declaration. For example,

```
Dim z%
```

ensures that z is an Integer. However, because type characters make the code less readable, they are not recommended.

In addition, several of the data types include special characters (literal type characters) that can be used with literal values to force their representation to the appropriate type. These include C (Char), D (Decimal), R (Double), I (Integer), L (Long), S (Short), and F (Single). In other words, the statement

```
Dim b As Object

b = "T"C
```

forces the variable b to the type Char.

One of the most interesting aspects of Table 3.3, though, is the representation of integers. In VB 6.0, the Integer data type was 16 bits, and so the range was from -32,768 to 32,768. However, with the inclusion of Short to fill that spot, Integer is now a 32-bit value that is equivalent to the Long data type in VB 6.0. In turn, Long is now 64 bits with a range from ±9,223,372,036,854,775,808. Although this is desired because it brings VB .NET inline with other modern programming languages and applications, such as SQL Server, keep in mind that if you're porting existing code or rewriting code from VB 6.0 you'll want to change the data types as appropriate.

3

VB .NET LANGUAGE FEATURES

The internal representation of several data types in the CLR also is different from previous versions of VB. For example, the `Boolean` data type in VB 6.0 equated to -1 for `True` and 0 for `False`. Now, the more standard 0 for `False` and 1 for `True` is used by the runtime. However, to maintain backwards compatibility when working in VB .NET, the older -1 and 0 will be used. Keep in mind, though, that converting a `Boolean` to a CTS type such as `System.Int32`, or passing a `Boolean` to another managed language, will convert the result back to a 1 for `True` and 0 for `False`. Also, as mentioned in Table 3.3, the `Date` data type is no longer represented as a `Double`; it is mapped to `System.DateTime`, and implicit conversion between the two is no longer supported. Explicit conversion, however, can be accomplished by using the `ToDouble` and `FromOADate` methods of the `DateTime` class.

Of course, as should be obvious by now, the universal data type in previous versions of VB, the `Variant`, has been replaced with `Object`. The `Object` keyword used in VB 6.0 to refer to a late bound object has been subsumed into this definition.

Finally, as shown in Table 3.1 the `Currency` data type is no longer supported in VB .NET and has been replaced with the `Decimal` data type.

Arrays

There are several important changes in VB .NET with regards to arrays. First, the lower bound of an array can no longer be set using the `Option Base` statement. As a result, the syntax

```
Dim s(0 to 10) As String
```

no longer is supported because all arrays are zero bound.

> **NOTE**
>
> The designers of VB .NET originally planned that the array declaration would specify the number of elements and not the upper bound. In other words, the declaration
>
> ```
> Dim s(10) As String
> ```
>
> would produce an array of 10 elements with indices from 0 through 9. However, this changed shortly before the beta 2 was released based on feedback from the VB community.

Also in VB .NET, by default, all arrays are variable-sized arrays, so they all can be resized using the `ReDim` statement. However, the `ReDim` statement cannot be used in place of the `Dim` statement to dimension an array as in VB 6.0.

In addition, as seen previously, an array can be populated in the declaration using the { } brackets like so:

```
Dim sosaHomers() As Short = {66, 63, 50, 64}
```

This syntax replaces the Array function formerly used to populate an array with arguments passed to the function. VB .NET still supports multidimensional arrays; however, the number of dimensions (referred to as the *rank*) must be set in the Dim statement. For example, the code

```
Dim arPlayers(,) As String
ReDim arPlayers(1, 3)

arPlayers(0, 0) = "Pitcher"
arPlayers(0, 1) = "Catcher"
arPlayers(0, 2) = "1B"
arPlayers(0, 3) = "2B"

arPlayers(1, 0) = "Roger Clemens"
arPlayers(1, 1) = "Mike Piazza"
arPlayers(1, 2) = "Mark McGwire"
arPlayers(1, 3) = "Eric Young"
```

works in VB .NET because the comma in the Dim statement denotes that there are two dimensions to the array. The same declaration without the comma works in VB 6.0. As in VB 6.0, VB .NET also allows you to change the upper bound of the last dimension in the array while preserving the contents of the array, and so the statement

```
ReDim Preserve arPlayers(1, 4)
```

immediately after the preceding code example successfully adds another element to the second dimension. The Preserve keyword ensures that the data is preserved.

3

VB .NET
LANGUAGE
FEATURES

> **TIP**
>
> As in VB 6.0, if you don't know the rank the array will have at development time, then dimension the array simply As Array or As Object.

VB .NET also still supports ragged arrays or arrays of arrays, which, like multidimensional arrays, allow you to store tabular type data but allow a varying number of elements. For example, the code in Listing 3.1 shows how you would create a ragged array by dimensioning the array As Object and then placing arrays inside it.

LISTING 3.1 Creating Ragged Arrays in VB .NET. To create a ragged array use the Object type.

```
Dim a As Object
Dim b(0) As String
Dim c(1) As String
Dim obj As Object
Dim obj1 As Object

ReDim a(2)

' Fill the inner arrays
c(0) = "c1"
c(1) = "c2"
b(0) = "b1"

' Set the elements of the outer array
a(0) = b
a(1) = c
a(2) = "Third element"

' Traverse the contents of the array
For Each obj In a
    If IsArray(obj) Then
        For Each obj1 In obj
            Console.WriteLine(obj1.ToString)
        Next
    Else
        Console.WriteLine(obj.ToString)
    End If
Next
```

Note that Option Strict must be set to Off for this code to compile because late binding is occurring in the array referenced as a. Although this works in VB .NET, you might want to stick with multidimensional arrays because ragged arrays are not CLS compliant, and passing such an array to managed code written in another language might not work.

Many of these changes are made possible by the fact that all arrays in VB .NET are ultimately derived from System.Array. This class supports several shared methods that can be used to manipulate arrays as well as instance methods that can return data on a particular array. As you would expect, because System.Array is a reference type, assigning a variable to an existing array creates a reference to the array rather than a copy of it. To get a copy, you can use the Clone method of the Array class.

> **TIP**
>
> Shared methods can be called on a class without first instantiating an object from the class. This allows the class to contain various helper functions that can be used in a variety of situations. Conversely, instance methods are those that work on the current instance of the class.

For example, the declaration of the `arPlayers` array in VB .NET is actually translated to this:

```
Dim arPlayers As Array

arPlayers = Array.CreateInstance(GetType(String), 2, 4)
```

Note that the sizes of the dimensions as specified in the last two arguments to the `CreateInstance` method are set to 2 and 4, rather than 1 and 3 as you might expect. This is the case because arrays in the CLR typically are declared using the size of a dimension rather than the upper bound.

Even if the array is created in standard VB .NET syntax, all the `Array` methods and properties are available, the most important of which are shown in Table 3.4.

TABLE 3.4 Array Class Members

Member	Description
BinarySearch	Shared method that searches a one-dimensional array for a specific element
Clear	Shared method that sets a range of the array to zero or `Nothing`
Copy	Shared method that copies a section of one array to another array
CreateInstance	Shared method that initializes a new instance of the `Array` class
IndexOf	Shared method that returns the index of the first occurrence of a given value in a one-dimensional array
LastIndexOf	Shared method that returns the last index of the first occurrence of a given value in a one-dimensional array
Reverse	Shared method that reverses the order of elements in a one-dimensional array
Sort	Shared method that sorts the elements of a one-dimensional array
IsFixedSize	Instance property that returns `True` if the array is fixed size
IsReadOnly	Instance property that returns whether the array is read-only
IsSynchronized	Instance property that returns whether access to the array is thread-safe

TABLE 3.4   Continued

Member	Description
Length	Instance property that returns the total number of elements in all dimensions of the array
Rank	Instance property that returns the number of dimensions
SyncRoot	Instance property that returns an object that can be used to synchronize access to the array
Clone	Instance method that creates a copy of the array
CopyTo	Instance method that copies all or part of a one-dimensional array to another array
GetLength	Instance method that returns the number of elements from a specified dimension of the array
GetLowerBound	Instance method that returns the lower bound of a specified dimension of the array
GetUpperBound	Instance method that returns the upper bound of a specified dimension of the array
GetValue	Instance method that returns the specified values in the one-dimensional array
SetValue	Instance method that sets the specified values in the one-dimensional array
Initialize	Instance method that initializes every element of a value-type array if it has a constructor

To illustrate the use of the Array class, consider the procedure in Listing 3.2 used to find a specific item in an array.

LISTING 3.2   Using the Array Class. This method exercises some of the functionality of the Array class to sort and search the array.

```
Function FindVal(ByVal value As Object, ByRef arr As Array) As Integer
  Dim intIndex As Integer

  If Not IsArray(Arr) Then
    Throw New ArgumentException( _
      "Argument is not an array or array has no elements")
    Return -1
  End If

  Try
```

LISTING 3.2 Continued

```
    ' Sort the array
    Array.Sort(arr)
    ' Do a search
    intIndex = Array.BinarySearch(arr, value)
  Catch e As Exception
    Throw New Exception( _
      "There was an error working with the array: " & e.Message)
    Return -1
  End Try

  ' Negative if not found
  If intIndex < 0 Then
    Return -1
  Else
    Return intIndex
  End If

End Function
```

In this example, note that the FindVal procedure accepts an argument declared As Object to search for in the array, along with the array, and returns the index at which the value was found. The new IsArray function is used to determine whether the array has been initialized. If so, the array is first sorted using the Sort method and then a binary search is performed using BinarySearch. The return value from BinarySearch will be negative if the value is not found. Note that by definition, the BinarySearch method is case sensitive. In this case, the method returns the index of the element if the value is found, and a -1 if not. Since the array is passed to the method by reference, the array will be sorted when the method returns and the index will point to the new position of the value within the sorted array.

> **NOTE**
>
> Many of the methods of the Array class work only with one-dimensional arrays. If you attempt to call these methods on multidimensional arrays, exceptions will be thrown. To work with, sort, and search multidimensional arrays, you'll need to employ your own techniques. Some of these can be found in Chapter 24 of my book *Pure Visual Basic*.

Alternatives to Arrays

Although arrays in VB .NET are easily mapped to the System.Array type, they are not always ideal for manipulating data within your application. To provide more choice and flexibility in working with collections of data, the Services Framework includes the `System.Collections` and `System.Collections.Specialized` namespaces. In fact, using these prebuilt collections can offload some of the array manipulation code you would normally write and can greatly improve performance—for example, when needing random access to an in-memory collection of data.

You can think of these namespaces as containing prebuilt data structures for handling data. For example, the `System.Collections` namespace contains the `SortedList` class that can be used to store a collection of values and associated keys. As the name implies, the data added to the collection is sorted automatically by the key, and the class contains various methods to access the data either by the key, index, or value. The following code illustrates the use of the `SortedList` class to store a collection of names:

```
Dim employees As New SortedList()
Dim i As Integer

employees.Add(3322, "Steve Lake")
employees.Add(6743, "Jody Davis")
employees.Add(1233, "George Mitterwald")
employees.Add(1341, "Tim Hosey")

For i = 0 To employees.Count - 1
  Console.WriteLine("{0}:{1}", _
    employees.GetByIndex(i).ToString, employees.GetKey(i).ToString)
Next
```

When the `For` loop is executed, the names are printed in order by their key value.

> **NOTE**
>
> Many of the collection classes include constructors that accept the initial capacity of the collection. Although the capacity of the collection is increased automatically as required through reallocation, this can be used to increase performance when you know ahead of time how many members the collection will contain. In the `ArrayList` and `SortedList` classes, the `TrimToSize` method can subsequently be called to minimize a lists memory overhead.

Although explicating all the classes and their members is beyond the scope of this book, the other types of collections, their descriptions, and uses can be seen in Table 3.5.

TABLE 3.5 Collection Classes in the `System.Collections` and `System.Collections.Specialized` Namespaces

Class	Description	Use
ArrayList	Implements an array that is dynamically sized and able to be sorted	When you need to access the values by index
BitArray	Manages a compact array of bit values represented as true (1) or false (0)	When you need to track a series of switches
Hashtable	Implements a collection of values and associated keys where the key is hashed	When you need to quickly access a value by the key for large collections
HybridDictionary	Implements a `ListDictionary` when the collection is small and dynamically switches to a `HashTable` as the collection grows for performance reasons	
ListDictionary	Implements a linked-list of key-value pairs	When you have fewer than 10 values and need access to them by the key
NameValueCollection	Implements a sorted collection of `String` keys and values	When you need access to the values by the hash code of the key or the index
Queue	Implements a first-in, first-out collection of objects	When you need to access the values in FIFO order
SortedList	Implements a collection of key-value pairs sorted by the key	When you need to access the values in order by the key
Stack	Implements a last-in, first-out collection objects	When you need to access the values in LIFO order

3

VB .NET
LANGUAGE
FEATURES

TABLE 3.5   Continued

Class	Description	Use
StringCollection	Implements a collection of strings	When you need to store strings and access them by index
StringDictionary	Implements a hashtable where the key and value are both strings	When you need to access a large collection of strings by key

The only disadvantage to using most of the collection classes, except the last two shown in Table 3.5, is that they only accept keys and values of type Object. As a result, you'll need to convert the values to the appropriate type when retrieving them from the collection.

Structures

In VB 6.0, data could be grouped together in a user-defined type (UDT) using the Type statement. The UDT then could be instantiated and populated using dot notation and used as a return value from a function or as an argument to a procedure. Further, all the members of the type were public, and the type could only contain fields—no methods, properties, or events.

In VB .NET, the UDT has been replaced with the Structure. A Structure is much more powerful than a UDT. It can contain fields, methods, properties, events, enumerations, and even implement interfaces. In fact, a Structure can be thought of as simply a lightweight class. The primary difference is that a Structure is always a value type as discussed in Chapter 1, and is therefore always copied when used in an assignment statement or passed by value to a procedure. In addition, structures do not support inheritance, and you needn't use the New operator with structures because it is called implicitly in the declaration. However, structures can support constructors, as discussed in Chapter 4. As an example, consider the structure declaration shown in Listing 3.3.

Note that this structure encapsulates information about a baseball player. It contains public fields to represent the attributes of an offensive player—such as the number of hits (H), doubles (D), triples (T), homeruns (HR), and so on—as would be supported in a VB 6.0 Type. In addition, however, it contains public properties to expose the batting average (AVG) and slugging percentage (SLUG) along with a method to calculate the number of runs created (RunsCreated). Finally, the structure contains an enumerated type used to specify the player's position.

LISTING 3.3   Player Structure in VB .NET. Note that it looks much like a class.

```
Structure Player
  Public Sub New(ByVal playerName As String)
    Name = playerName
  End Sub
```

LISTING 3.3   Continued

```vb
Public Enum pPosition
  C = 2
  P = 1
  First = 3
  Second = 4
  Third = 5
  Shortstop = 6
  Left = 7
  Center = 8
  Right = 9
End Enum

Public Name As String
Public H As Integer
Public D As Integer
Public T As Integer
Public HR As Integer
Public BB As Integer
Public AB As Integer
Public SB As Integer
Public Position As pPosition

Public ReadOnly Property AVG() As Double
  Get
    Return H / AB
  End Get
End Property

Public ReadOnly Property SLUG() As Double
  Get
    Return (H + D + (2 * T) + (3 * HR)) / AB
  End Get
End Property

Public Function RunsCreated(ByVal useSB As Boolean) As Double
  If useSB Then
    Return ((H + BB) * (H + D + (2 * T) + (3 * HR) _
      + (0.7 * SB))) / (AB + BB)
  Else
    Return ((H + BB) * (H + D + (2 * T) + (3 * HR))) / (AB + BB)
  End If
End Function

End Structure
```

A user of this structure might use the following code to represent the statistics from Sammy Sosa's 2000 season:

```
Dim sPlayer As Player

With sPlayer
    .Name = "Sammy Sosa"
    .AB = 604
    .H = 193
    .D = 38
    .T = 1
    .HR = 50
    .BB = 91
    .SB = 7
    .Position = Player.pPosition.Right
End With

Console.WriteLine(Math.Round(sPlayer.AVG, 3).ToString)
Console.WriteLine(Math.Round(sPlayer.SLUG, 3).ToString)
Console.WriteLine(Math.Round(sPlayer.RunsCreated(True), 1).ToString)
```

Because the structure contains a constructor (the `New` procedure), an alternate declaration would be

```
Dim sPlayer As New Player("Sammy Sosa")
```

Conversion

As mentioned in Chapter 1, one of goals of the CLR is to provide a type-safe runtime environment. This means that by default, the CLR will enforce type-safety at compile time by not allowing an object of one type to be assigned to an object of a different type. This behavior is much different from VB 6.0, where type coercion happened implicitly, and VB developers didn't have to worry about statements like the following:

```
Dim s as String
s = 50
```

In this case, VB 6.0 implicitly converted the 50 to a string and made the assignment. In VB .NET, this same code will not compile unless the `Option Strict` statement is used and set to `Off`. This statement turns off the type-checking feature of the compiler, and then attempts to cast from one type to the other at runtime. In many instances, VB developers feel more comfortable turning off this option although it increases the likelihood of exceptions at runtime.

To perform explicit conversions, you can use the conversion functions (`CStr`, `CBool`, `CDate`, `Cint`, and so on), the `CType` and `DirectCase` functions, or methods of the `System.Convert` class. The CType function takes the expression to be converted and the type to convert to as parameters. For example, to convert the literal 50 to a string, you would use the following syntax:

```
s = CType(50, String)
```

The second argument can be used to explicitly pass a type, as in the preceding example, or you can use the GetType function to extract the type. You'll notice throughout the book that some listings have Option Strict set to Off for ease of coding and to make reading the code for VB developers more natural. The DirectCase function works in much the same way, although is more strict in that it only allows the conversion if the type parsed to it is exactly the same as the type being converted.

However, an easier approach is to use the System.Convert class, which contains seventeen To methods that convert to all of the system data types. In addition, each method supports myriads of overloads to convert from any of the types. Therefore, the previous code example could be rewritten:

```
s = Convert.ToString(50)
```

In addition, because all types are ultimately derived from System.Object, you can call the ToString method of any variable to convert it to a String. Calling ToString on a complex type, such as a structure or class, by default simply returns the type name as a string. However, if you define your own classes as described in Chapter 4, you can override the ToString method and return a string representation of your object.

Strings

Like arrays, strings in VB.NET are derived from a base class, in this case System.String, that contains both shared and instance members that allow you to manipulate the string. Table 3.6 shows the important members. Keep in mind that VB .NET also contains string functions in the Microsoft.VisualBasic.Strings module that wrap some of these methods or provide slightly altered functionality. Which technique you use is really a matter of personal preference. Existing VB developers will find the VB .NET functions more familiar, whereas developers new to the Microsoft product set, or coming from ASP, should use the Services Framework for the sake of uniformity among languages.

TABLE 3.6 String Class Members

Member	Description
Clone	Instance method that returns a new String with the same value
Compare	Shared method that compares two strings and returns an Integer specifying the result

TABLE 3.6 Continued

Member	Description
CompareOrdinal	Shared method that compares two strings and returns an Integer specifying the result without taking into account the language or culture
CompareTo	Instance method that compares this instance with a given object
Copy	Shared method that creates a new instance of a String with the same value as the specified string
CopyTo	Instance method that copies a portion of the string to a character array
Concat	Shared method that creates a new String from one or more strings or objects
Empty	Shared constant representing an empty string
EndsWith	Instance method that determines whether a given string matches the end of this string
Equals	Both a shared and instance method that determines whether two strings have the same value
Format	Shared method used to format the string with the given format specification
IndexOf	Instance method that returns the index of the first occurrence of a string within this string
Insert	Instance method that inserts the given string at a given position within this string
Join	Shared method that concatenates a given separator between each element in a given array
LastIndexOf	Instance method that returns the last occurrence of a given string within this string
PadLeft, PadRight	Instance methods that align the current string with spaces or a specified character for a specified length
Remove	Instance method that deletes the specified number of characters from this instance of the string at the specified location
Replace	Instance method that replaces all occurrences of a specified string with the given string
Split	Instance method that splits the string into an array of strings based on a separator

TABLE 3.6 Continued

Member	Description
StartsWith	Instance method that determines whether this string is prefixed with a given string
Substring	Instance method that retrieves a substring from the string
ToCharArray	Instance method that copies the characters of the string to a character array
ToLower, ToUpper	Instance methods that return a copy of the string in lower- or uppercase
Trim, TrimEnd, TrimStart	Instance methods that remove spaces or a set of characters from the string

However, even though System.String is a reference type, the contents of a string are immutable, and all the methods that work on a string actually return a new instance of a string in the modified form. For example, to trim a string, the code

```
Dim s As String

s = "    Some spaces"
s = Trim(s)
```

actually results in a new string being created and assigned the same variable s. Immutability also affects assignment statements, and so the code

```
Dim s As String
Dim y As String

s = "Hello"
y = s
s = "New value"
```

does not change the value of y because y is actually a different string.

Because working with strings in this way can be inefficient for large strings, the Services Framework also contains the StringBuilder class in the System.Text namespace. This class can be used to build strings that can be directly modified perhaps by removing, replacing, or inserting characters, without creating a new string with each modification. For example, if you were to write code that read multiple text files and appended the text from each file to a string, it would be more efficient to use a StringBuilder so that the string could be modified directly,

3

**VB .NET
LANGUAGE
FEATURES**

rather than creating a new string with each iteration of the loop. An analogous example is the following code:

```
Imports System.Text
Dim sbText As New StringBuilder()
Dim i As Integer

sbText.EnsureCapacity(600)

For i = 1 To 50
    sbText.Append("more…")
Next
```

In this example, the `StringBuilder` object is instantiated, and its `EnsureCapacity` method is called to make sure that enough space can be allocated to hold the result. The loop then appends the text to the string. Remember that because the `StringBuilder` object is not actually a string, you need to use the `ToString` method to convert it to a string for other uses.

> **NOTE**
>
> The `StringBuilder` class also is used to allocate string buffers that are filled by unmanaged DLL functions, as is frequently the case with the Win32 API.

VB .NET also does not support fixed-length strings, and so the code that would allocate a 30-character fixed-length string in VB 6.0

```
Dim s As String * 30
```

does not compile in VB.NET. The length of a string in VB .NET is determined by its contents only.

Because a string derives from a base class, you would think that you might be able to use a constructor for a string as in

```
Dim s As New String("E.D. Cope")
```

However, the `String` class does not support a constructor that accepts a string. An array of `System.Char` can be passed to the constructor like so:

```
Dim arrChar() As Char
arrChar = CType("O. Marsh", Char())
Dim strPaleo As New String(arrChar)
```

However, if you were going to do this, you would be better off using the initialization technique described earlier in the chapter because it would be more efficient. You would want to use the constructor when initializing a string with a repeated series of characters. The following code initializes a string to 50 spaces:

```
Dim s As New String(Convert.ToChar(" "), 50)
```

Finally, as shown in Table 3.6, the `String` class contains several versions of the `Compare` and `Equals` methods that you can use to perform both case-sensitive (the default) and case insensitive comparisons on strings. As in VB 6.0, string comparisons also can be done with the standard operators (=, <>, <, >, >=, <=) using either a binary or text comparison depending on the setting of `Option Compare`.

Block Scope

In previous versions of VB, variables could be declared at various scopes that included local (procedure), module, class, and global. Although VB .NET retains these scoping rules, it adds a lower level of scoping called the *block level*.

Block level scoping allows a developer to dimension a variable inside any block statement in VB .NET. These include looping constructs such as the `For` and `While` loops, `If Then` statements, and `Try Catch` statements, among others. If a variable is declared inside a block, the variables can be accessed only inside that block. For example, in the following code, the variable j is only accessible while in the `If Then` statement:

```
Dim i As Integer

If i = 3 Then
    Dim j As Integer
    j = 2
End If

j = 3 ' Causes a compiler error
```

In this case, the compiler stops you from referencing j outside the block. In addition, the compiler does not let you dimension a variable also called j with local scope. However, a j variable at the module or global level is allowed, although when executing the block, the block variable will be referenced, as you would expect.

Basically, the addition of block scope means that developers can more easily hide data and use it only where appropriate. It is good programming practice to declare variables at the lowest scope available and only raise them to a higher scope when absolutely necessary. This promotes reusability by creating fewer dependencies in your code.

> **NOTE**
>
> Variables in block scope are not deallocated when the block is exited. Block-scoped variables live for the entirety of the procedure they are declared in. When entering the same block several times in the same invocation of the procedure, you might need to initialize the variable.

Procedures

There are several subtle changes in the way VB .NET procedures and functions behave. The following list notes these changes:

- Perhaps the most important is the change in the default parameter passing mechanism. In VB 6.0, if you did not specify how a parameter was to be passed, it was always passed by reference (ByRef). In VB .NET, this has changed to by-value (ByVal) because many developers didn't take the time to explicitly use the ByVal keyword. Passing parameters by-value protects them from changes inside the procedure, and therefore is safer.

> **TIP**
>
> Although ByVal is now the default, you still should specify it explicitly for readability. In fact, VS .NET does this automatically.

- In VB 6.0, if you passed the property of an object into a procedure using ByRef, the property was not changed as expected when the procedure ended. This has been corrected in VB .NET, where ByRef arguments work as expected with properties.
- ParamArray parameters in VB 6.0 were always passed ByRef whereas in VB .NET they are passed ByVal, and the elements of the array must be declared as Object.
- Arguments marked as Optional in VB 6.0 did not require a default value, whereas in VB .NET, default values are required. This requirement makes the IsMissing keyword obsolete, so it has been removed.
- Returning data from functions also has changed in VB .NET with the inclusion of the Return keyword. This keyword can be used, rather than setting the return value equal to the name of the function. This makes the code both easier to read and write.

- The way procedures can be called also has changed. In previous versions of VB, the capability to call a `Sub` procedure without using parentheses caused a good deal of confusion. In VB .NET, the `Call` keyword is retained although it is optional, but all procedures that accept arguments must be called with parentheses. If the procedure does not accept arguments, the parentheses are optional, although VS .NET includes them for you anyway. As a result the statement

```
MsgBox "Done with process", vbOK, "Dinosaurs"
```

in VB.NET would now be

```
MsgBox("Done with process", MsgBoxStyle.OKOnly, "Dinosaurs")
```

- At the procedure declaration level, new access modifiers can be used, covered in Chapter 4.

- The `GoSub` statement is no longer supported. Although this has caused much discussion in the VB community, it is probably for the best because developers often can write code that is difficult to maintain with `GoSub`.

- A procedure can no longer be marked as `Static` to automatically make all its local variables static (to retain their values between invocations of the procedure). Now, each variable that is to be static must be declared with the `Static` keyword.

Using the Compatibility Class

With the core language assembly, VB .NET ships with types that allow you to write code that is more compatible with VB 6.0. This includes classes, interfaces, structures, constants, and enumerated types that are used in VB 6.0.

Primarily, these include types that facilitate the communication between VB 6.0 controls, such as CheckBox and ListBox with classes in the Windows Forms namespace. In addition they include types that are useful for working with the ADO Data Control (ADOC) and implementing data binding. As a result they are not particularly interesting for devleopers of distributed applications.

That being the case, it is not recommended that you use these types in your applications.

Upgrading from VB 6.0

Although it is recommended that you not use the compatibility classes directly, the VB 6.0 Upgrade Wizard might use them when upgrading projects from VB 6.0 to VB .NET. Before upgrading a previous project to VB .NET, you must decide whether you should.

Basically, this question must be answered on a project-by-project basis, but for most projects the answer will be no. The reasons for this are as follows:

- As evidenced by this chapter, many changes have been made to the structure of the language, and although the Upgrade Wizard makes some automatic corrections for these, it likely will not address all of them. In fact, Microsoft recommends several coding practices that should be employed in existing VB 6.0 projects for the upgrade to proceed more smoothly (`http://msdn.microsoft.com/library/default.asp?URL=/library/techart/vb6tovbdotnet.htm`). Because not all VB 6.0 projects follow these guidelines, there will be plenty of places where you need to change the code. This also will entail extensive testing, which, in the final analysis, might be more effort than is warranted given the reasons listed here.

- VB .NET and the Services Framework present totally new ways of dealing with certain scenarios. For example, ADO.NET exposes a new disconnected programming model for database applications that is different from the classic ADO model. When you upgrade a VB 6.0 project, the Upgrade Wizard does not convert your code to ADO.NET, rather it uses a translation layer (COM Interop, discussed in Chapter 9, "Accessing Component Services") to broker calls between managed code and classic COM components such as ADO. In addition, new project types such as the Windows Service application allow you to write applications in a different way. An upgraded NT service project that relies on a third-party ActiveX control or the Win32 API will not take advantage of the inherent integration. As a result, you won't get the benefits of the Services Framework by upgrading your VB 6.0 project.

- As a follow-on to the previous point, the Web Services model, perhaps the most important concept in .NET (discussed in Chapter 11, "Building Web Services"), will not automatically be integrated into your project. The design and implementation of Web Services likely will require redesign and implementation of your solutions.

- As discussed in Chapters 4 and 6 particularly, VB .NET contains entirely new language constructs, such as implementation inheritance and structured exception handling. The Upgrade Wizard will not add these powerful features to your code. That is a task for subsequent development.

- Although the .NET platform is a new and interesting way to develop applications, existing VB 6.0 applications will be supported and will run just fine on Windows operating systems. In fact, VB 6.0 and VS .NET can coexist peacefully on the same machine.

- As a corollary to the previous point, if your applications follow a multitiered architecture where the data access and business services are decoupled from the user interface, you can take a piecemeal approach and recode the user interface in ASP.NET to take advantage of its features while using COM Interop to call existing COM components that perform business logic and data access. In this way, the application needn't be reworked from the ground up, and other applications that rely on your middleware will continue to function.

- In any case, the Upgrade Wizard cannot upgrade certain types of projects in VB 6.0 (and yes, the project must have been previously saved in VB 6.0). For example, DHTML applications, data binding with DAO and RDO, and ActiveX document projects will not be upgraded, whereas WebClasses will require significant modification.

So what is the recommendation? Probably only the simplest of applications, such as utility applications, are suited for a simple upgrade, compile, and run. Any project that interoperates with other COM components and external DLLs will require significant work that is tantamount to a rewrite. As a result, I would use the Upgrade Wizard simply as a starting point and more of a check on syntactical changes. For example, you might run the Upgrade Wizard on your data access COM component to see how the ADOMD library is referenced and accessed in VB .NET. However, then you need to do the work of integrating new language features and Services Framework classes as appropriate.

Using the Upgrade Wizard

To run the wizard, you simply need to open the VB 6.0 project files (.vbp) in VB .NET and follow the wizard steps. The wizard analyzes your code and performs certain automatic translations—for example, from `Long` to `Integer` and `Variant` to `Object`. In addition, it places various warnings and errors as comments in the code. These are places you'll need to concentrate on. To summarize the upgrade, an HTML file is added to the project, which shows each error and provides additional information.

To illustrate the upgrade process, consider an ActiveX DLL project created in VB 6.0 called `SearchSortUtils`. This project contains a single class module called `Algorithms` that implements `BubbleSort`, `ShellSort`, and `BinSearch` (binary search) methods that work on zero-based multidimensional arrays. This project was run through the Upgrade Wizard, and Figure 3.1 shows the resulting upgrade report.

> **NOTE**
>
> The `SearchSortUtils` VB 6.0 project files can be downloaded from the companion Web site.

As you'll notice from the report, 0 errors and 57 warnings were issued in a project that comprised less than 275 lines in VB 6.0. The 57 warnings were primarily related to the fact that the wizard could not find a default property on variables that were of type `Variant` and converted to `Object`.

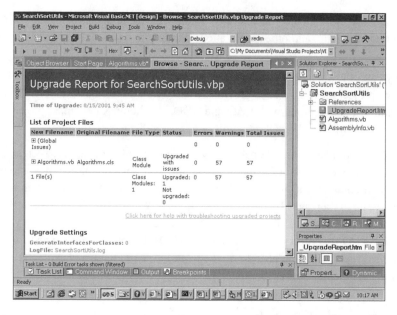

FIGURE 3.1

This HTML document shows that 57 issues were found when upgrading the SearchSortUtils *project.*

> **NOTE**
>
> The Upgrade Wizard can resolve parameterless default properties for classes that are referenced, but it cannot do so for objects that are late-bound, hence the warnings discussed previously.

Because this is a simple project that does not contain any references to COM components, ActiveX controls, or other external code, the project was immediately able to be compiled and run in VB .NET. However, to make the code more VB .NET friendly, and to illustrate the kinds of changes you'll make to your own code, the following changes were made:

- The wizard changed references from Variant to Object. Because this class used Variant to refer to arrays, Object was changed to Array.

- The methods were changed to shared methods so that a client does not have to create an instance of the class to use its methods.

- Because VarType is obsolete, the references to the VarType function were changed to the GetType function and the GetType method of the variable being inspected.

- The function return syntax was changed to use the Return statement rather than the name of the function.

- Overloaded signatures were created for each of the methods rather than Optional arguments.

Listing 3.4 shows the completely upgraded project with the preceding changes.

LISTING 3.4   Upgraded Utility Project. This listing shows the syntax of the upgraded SearchSortUtil project.

```
Option Strict Off
Option Explicit On

Public Class Algorithms

    ' Searching and sorting algorithms for zero-based
    ' variant two dimensional arrays where the first
    ' dimension is the columns and the second is the rows

    '******************************************************************
    Public Overloads Shared Sub BubbleSort(ByRef varArray As Array)
        Call BubbleSort(varArray, False, 0)
    End Sub

    Public Overloads Shared Sub BubbleSort(ByRef varArray As Array, _
        ByVal flDescending As Boolean)
        Call BubbleSort(varArray, flDescending, 0)
    End Sub

    Public Overloads Shared Sub BubbleSort(ByRef varArray As Array, _
        ByVal flDescending As Boolean, ByVal pIndex As Short)

        Dim i As Integer
        Dim j As Integer
        Dim lngUB As Integer
        Dim lngLB As Integer
        Dim lngUB1 As Integer
        Dim lngLB1 As Integer
        Dim z As Integer
        Dim varArrTemp As Object

        ' Cache the bounds
        lngUB = UBound(varArray, 2)
        lngLB = LBound(varArray, 2)
```

LISTING 3.4 Continued

```
lngUB1 = UBound(varArray, 1)
lngLB1 = LBound(varArray, 1)

' If the optional index is 0 then set it to the
' lower bound (sort by first column)
If pIndex = 0 Then
  pIndex = LBound(varArray, 1)
End If

' Loop through the array using the second
' dimension of the array (the rows)
For i = lngLB To lngUB
  For j = lngLB To lngUB - 1 - i
    ' Compare the items in the array
    If CompMe(varArray(pIndex, j), _
      varArray(pIndex, j + 1), flDescending) Then
      ReDim varArrTemp(UBound(varArray, 1), 0)

      ' If the first item is larger then swap them
      For z = lngLB1 To lngUB1
        varArrTemp(z, 0) = varArray(z, j)
      Next z
      For z = lngLB1 To lngUB1
        varArray(z, j) = varArray(z, j + 1)
      Next z
      For z = lngLB1 To lngUB1
        varArray(z, j + 1) = varArrTemp(z, 0)
      Next z
    End If
  Next j
Next i

End Sub


'******************************************************************
Public Overloads Shared Sub ShellSort(ByRef varArray As Array)
  Call ShellSort(varArray, False, 0)
End Sub

Public Overloads Shared Sub ShellSort(ByRef varArray As Array, _
  ByVal flDescending As Boolean)
  Call ShellSort(varArray, flDescending, 0)
End Sub
```

LISTING 3.4 Continued

```
Public Overloads Shared Sub ShellSort(ByRef varArray As Array, _
  ByVal flDescending As Boolean, ByVal pIndex As Short)

  Dim i As Integer
  Dim lngPos As Integer
  Dim varTemp As Object
  Dim lngLB As Integer
  Dim lngUB As Integer
  Dim lngSkip As Integer
  Dim flDone As Boolean
  Dim z As Integer
  Dim varArrTemp As Object


  ' If the optional index is 0 then set it to the
  ' lower bound (sort by first column)
  If pIndex = 0 Then
    pIndex = LBound(varArray, 1)
  End If

  ' Cache the lower and upper bounds
  lngLB = LBound(varArray, 2)
  lngUB = UBound(varArray, 2)

  ' Assign the skip count
  Do
    lngSkip = (3 * lngSkip) + 1
  Loop Until lngSkip > lngUB

  Do
    ' Decrement the skip each time through the loop
    lngSkip = lngSkip / 3

    ' Check the remainder of the array
    For i = lngSkip + 1 To lngUB
      ' Pick up the current value
      varTemp = varArray(pIndex, i)
      ReDim varArrTemp(UBound(varArray, 1), 0)

      For z = LBound(varArray, 1) To UBound(varArray, 1)
        varArrTemp(z, 0) = varArray(z, i)
      Next z
      lngPos = i
```

LISTING 3.4   Continued

```vbnet
      ' If we've reached the beginning then increment the
      ' skip count but signal that this is the last pass
      If lngSkip = 0 Then
        lngSkip = 1
        flDone = True
      End If
      ' Check to see if the preceding element is larger
      Do While CompMe(varArray(pIndex, lngPos - lngSkip), _
        varTemp, flDescending)
        ' If so then slide it in
        For z = LBound(varArray, 1) To UBound(varArray, 1)
          varArray(z, lngPos) = varArray(z, lngPos - lngSkip)
        Next z
        lngPos = lngPos - lngSkip
        If lngPos <= lngSkip Then Exit Do
      Loop
      ' Put the current value back down
      For z = 0 To UBound(varArray, 1)
        varArray(z, lngPos) = varArrTemp(z, 0)
      Next z
    Next i

  Loop Until lngSkip = lngLB Or flDone

End Sub

'*********************************************************************
Private Shared Function CompMe(ByVal pArg1 As Object, _
 ByVal pArg2 As Object, ByVal pDesc As Boolean, _
 Optional ByRef pEqual As Boolean = False) As Boolean

  ' If descending then do a less than compare
  If pDesc Then
    ' If equality is specified then use an equal sign
    Select Case pEqual
      Case True
        ' Check if its a string to do a string compare
        If pArg1.GetType Is GetType(System.String) Then
          If UCase(pArg1) <= UCase(pArg2) Then
            Return True
          End If
        Else
          If pArg1 <= pArg2 Then
            Return True
```

LISTING 3.4   Continued

```
            End If
          End If
        Case False
          ' If not specified then do a < compare
          If pArg1.GetType Is GetType(System.String) Then
            If StrComp(pArg1, pArg2, CompareMethod.Text) = -1 Then
              Return True
            End If
          Else
            If pArg1 < pArg2 Then
              Return True
            End If
          End If
      End Select
    Else
      ' If ascending doing a greater than compare
      Select Case pEqual
        Case True
          ' Check if its a string first
          If pArg1.GetType Is GetType(System.String) Then
            If UCase(pArg1) >= UCase(pArg2) Then
              Return True
            End If
          Else
            If pArg1 >= pArg2 Then
              Return True
            End If
          End If
        Case False
          ' Check if its a string
          If pArg1.GetType Is GetType(System.String) Then
            If StrComp(pArg1, pArg2, CompareMethod.Text) = 1 Then
              Return True
            End If
          Else
            If pArg1 > pArg2 Then
              Return True
            End If
          End If
      End Select
    End If

    Return False

End Function
```

LISTING 3.4 Continued

```
'*****************************************************************
Public Overloads Shared Function BinSearch(ByRef varArray As Array, _
  ByVal varSearch As Object, ByVal pIndex As Short) As Integer
  Call BinSearch(varArray, varSearch, pIndex, False)
End Function

Public Overloads Shared Function BinSearch(ByRef varArray As Array, _
  ByVal varSearch As Object, ByVal pIndex As Short, _
  ByVal flPartial As Boolean) As Integer

  Dim lngLow As Integer
  Dim lngUpper As Integer
  Dim lngPos As Integer

  ' Set the upper and lower bounds of the array
  lngLow = LBound(varArray, 2)
  lngUpper = UBound(varArray, 2)

  Do While True
    ' Divide the array to search
    lngPos = (lngLow + lngUpper) / 2

    ' Look for a match
    If flPartial Then
      ' If partial is specified then do a comparison
      ' on the substring since it should be a string
      If StrComp(Mid(varArray(pIndex, lngPos), 1, Len(varSearch)), _
        varSearch, CompareMethod.Text) = 0 Then
        ' If we've found it then get out
        Return lngPos
      End If
    Else
      ' Check to see if its a string
      If varSearch.GetType Is GetType(System.String) Then
        If StrComp(varArray(pIndex, lngPos), varSearch, _
          CompareMethod.Text) = 0 Then
          ' If we've found it then get out
          Return lngPos
        End If
      Else
        If varArray(pIndex, lngPos) = varSearch Then
          ' If we've found it then get out
          Return lngPos
        End If
      End If
```

LISTING **3.4**   Continued

```
         End If
      End If
      ' Check to see if its the last value to be checked
      If lngUpper = lngLow + 1 Then
         lngLow = lngUpper
      Else
         ' If we get to the lowest position then it's not there
         If lngPos = lngLow Then
            Return -1
         Else
            ' Determine whether to look in the upper or
            ' lower half of the array
            If varSearch.GetType Is GetType(System.String) Then
               If StrComp(varArray(pIndex, lngPos), varSearch, _
                  CompareMethod.Text) = 1 Then
                  lngUpper = lngPos
               Else
                  lngLow = lngPos
               End If
            Else
               If varArray(pIndex, lngPos) > varSearch Then
                  lngUpper = lngPos
               Else
                  lngLow = lngPos
               End If
            End If
         End If
      End If
   Loop

   End Function
End Class
```

3

Summary

This chapter discussed the primary changes to the structure and functionality of the VB .NET language. Although the changes are not insignificant, VB developers will find the vast majority of the syntax is the same, and what has changed makes the language simpler and more powerful.

With the syntactical changes out of the way, the next chapter focuses on perhaps the most important change to the VB .NET language with the inclusion of advanced object-oriented features.

Object-Oriented Features

IN THIS CHAPTER

One of the biggest .NET concepts that existing corporate VB developers and those moving from ASP need to get a handle on is the thoroughly object-oriented nature of VB .NET. Despite the addition of class modules in VB 4.0 and the enhanced ability to create COM components in VB 5.0 and 6.0, VB remained primarily a procedural language, and many developers continue to use it as such. This is not to say that you couldn't use some object-oriented techniques with VB 6.0 (see Chapter 15 of my book *Pure Visual Basic* for more information). However, what OO features you could use were derived from COM and were therefore limited, and the VB language itself did not contain the keywords necessary to enable a truly OO implementation.

In VB .NET, this changes with the inclusion of keywords that directly support OO features implemented by the common language runtime. VB .NET derives these features from the CTS that, as discussed in Chapter 1, "The Microsoft .NET Architecture," uses `System.Object` as the ancestor or root of all types in VS .NET. As a result, VB cannot help but be object-oriented to the core, and because the CLR uses the concept of classes to expose functionality, VB .NET developers, unlike in previous versions, cannot avoid the use of classes. Finally, the architecture of the Services Framework mandates that developers use inheritance and polymorphism (which I will discuss later in the chapter) to take advantage of its services effectively. In other words, to take advantage of the power of the CTS to be productive and to use system services provided by the Services Framework, a good understanding of OO is required.

The addition of OO features in VB .NET is both a good and bad phenomenon. First, it is positive because the language is more powerful and as a result you can express more sophisticated designs in your solutions. And for developers like me who have always appreciated VB, this increased power also gives it a more professional air and serves to extend the population of developers who use it. However, this increase in power also comes with responsibility. Designing solutions that use inheritance, polymorphism, and encapsulation requires more discipline and knowledge on the part of the developer. For that reason, developers with formal computer science backgrounds or those willing to learn these concepts will probably feel the most comfortable with the changes. Not to worry, though, VB .NET extends the language in many ways that will feel quite natural so that everyone can exploit these features.

In this chapter, I'll discuss the features of VB .NET that allow it to be a fully OO language.

OO Terminology

Before moving to the language syntax, let's formally define the key OO concepts and terms that will be used in this chapter beginning with encapsulation, polymorphism, and inheritance.

Encapsulation

Encapsulation means that an object can hide its internal data structures from consumers of the object. Therefore, all of the object's internal data is manipulated through members (methods, properties, events, fields) of the object, rather than through direct references.

The primary benefits of encapsulation are maintainability and reusability. Code that takes advantage of encapsulation is more maintainable because consumers of the code work with the object through its public members. With a fully encapsulated object, for example, code outside the object cannot directly change a variable declared inside the object. By shutting off this direct access, fewer bugs are introduced because consumers of the object cannot inadvertently change the state of an object at run-time.

Abstracting the internal data of the object from consumers also leads to greater reusability. This follows because encapsulation leads to fewer dependencies between the consumer and the class and fewer dependencies is a prerequisite for creating reusable software.

Polymorphism

The second characteristic of OO systems is *polymorphism*. This concept is defined as the ability to write code that treats objects as if they were the same when in fact they are different. In other words, polymorphism allows you to write code that is generic across a set of objects that provide the same public members. Underneath the covers, each object might be implemented differently. However, as far as the consumer is concerned, each object looks the same and can be treated as such. In VB .NET, polymorphism can be created using both classes and interfaces.

The benefits of polymorphism revolve around the central fact that consumers of objects do not have to be aware of how the object performs its work, only that it does so through a specific set of members. This makes writing code that uses objects simpler by allowing the code to treat the object as if it were a black box, which leads to increased maintainability. Along the same lines, polymorphism allows you to write less code because each individual object does not have to be dealt with separately. Finally, polymorphism lends itself to writing code that can be reused because it will not be specific to a particular object.

Inheritance

The final OO concept is inheritance. *Inheritance* allows objects to share their interfaces (the definition of their members) and/or implementation in a hierarchy. For example, Tyrannosaurus and Velociraptor objects might be derived or inherited from a more generic Theropod object. All three objects share a basic set of members and, possibly, behaviors, such as carnivorousness, although the descendant objects might also include additional members or override members of Theropod. Inheritance allows objects to become more specific further down the hierarchy by adding additional members. In a nutshell, inheritance allows objects to reuse features (either their definition or their code) of other objects to which they are naturally related. The primary benefit of inheritance is, thus, reuse.

Obviously, inheritance and polymorphism are closely related, and, in fact, inheritance is what makes polymorphism possible in OO designs. It is always the case that objects that are in an inheritance relationship can be treated polymorphically. For example, if the `Velociraptor` object is inherited from the `Theropod` object, any consumer that is designed to work with `Theropod` objects will also work with `Velociraptor` objects.

VB .NET developers can benefit from inheritance in two ways: through interface inheritance and implementation inheritance. *Interface inheritance* allows only the definition of the object to be reused, whereas *implementation inheritance* allows the actual code written for the ancestor object (and its ancestors all the way down the line) to be reused. Which one to use is a design decision as mentioned in Chapter 1 and discussed more fully in this chapter.

> **NOTE**
>
> If developers wanted to use a form of implementation inheritance in previous versions of VB, they had to design classes to take advantage of the concepts of *containment* and *delegation*. Basically, these concepts mean that a class accessible by a consumer will *contain* a private instance of a second class and *delegate* its services to the consumer through its own interface. Containment and delegation are familiar terms (along with aggregation) to COM programmers.

More OO Terms

Familiarity with the following OO terms will be useful in this discussion.

- *Class*—The fundamental unit of code reuse. Implemented with the `Class` statement in VB .NET. Classes can be inherited from and nested, and can contain members.

- *Base class*—A class that serves as the ancestor for an inherited class, although this usually means the direct ancestor. VB .NET uses the `MyBase` keyword to refer to the direct ancestor. As a group, the ancestors are referred to as the *base classes*. The base class at the top of the hierarchy is referred to as the *concrete base class*.

- *Abstract base class*—A base class that cannot be instantiated at run-time and serves only as the template for derived classes. In VB .NET, this is accomplished using the `MustInherit` keyword.

- *Interface*—A well-defined collection of members along with their signatures. Interfaces provide no implementation. They are created in VB .NET with the `Interface` keyword.

- *Members*—The methods, properties, events, and fields that make up an interface or class definition.

- *Methods*—Named blocks of code within a class that can accept arguments and might return a value. VB .NET supports both `Sub` methods that do not return a value and `Function` methods that do.

- *Properties*—Data exposed by a class and manipulated through code that runs when the property is set to a value or retrieved. In VB .NET, property creation is unified in a single `Property` statement.

- *Fields*—Data exposed by a class directly to the consumer. A field represents a data location and therefore, its access is not abstracted. Fields are created in VB .NET using public variables within a class.

- *Events*—Notifications fired by a class and captured by a consumer. In VB .NET, the `Event` and `RaiseEvent` statements are used to declare and raise events in addition to the use of delegates.

- *Overloading*—There are two forms of overloading. The first is that a class can contain multiple definitions of the same method, each with different arguments (signatures). The consumer can then choose which method to call. The second is that derived classes can overload methods in a base class to alter the signature of the method. VB .NET uses the concepts of optional parameters, parameter arrays (paramarrays), and the `Overloads` keyword to implement both forms.

- *Overriding*—Overriding a method means that a derived class can implement its own functionality for a method or property. VB .NET uses the `Overrides`, `Overridable`, `NotOverridable`, and `MustOverride` keywords to specify how methods and properties might or might not be overridden.

- *Static member*—A member that is exposed by the base class, is not allowed to be overridden in a descendant, is available to all instances of the class, and is available even before the instance is created. This is also referred to as a shared member and is implemented with the `Shared` keyword.

- *Virtual member*—The opposite of a static member, also referred to as an instance member. This refers to a member that can be accessed through an instance of a class. Instance members can be overriden with the addition of the `Overrides` keyword.

Role of Namespaces

As mentioned in Chapter 1, namespaces are used to organize code both within and among assemblies. Basically, your decisions as a VB .NET developer involve determining to which namespace your classes will belong and whether your assemblies will contribute classes to a particular namespace given that namespaces can cross assembly boundaries. At an organizational level, a company should plan its namespace hierarchy and publish it so that developers can integrate their code into it and so that other developers will be able to easily identify and reuse existing code.

TIP

Typically, the considerations mentioned here are most appropriate for classes you want to publish in DLLs created in class library projects.

For example, the company I work for, Quilogy, might want to group all its reusable code under the `Quilogy` namespace. As a result, individual developers must be aware of the naming structure the company has set up and which child namespaces have been used and which are available. Figure 4.1 shows a sample of a namespace hierarchy that Quilogy might use, including some of the classes that might be developed. Note that in Figure 4.1 the namespaces are derived from the lines of business that Quilogy engages in and that only the `Education` namespace is populated. The `Education` namespace also consists of both classes (`Instructors`) and nested namespaces (`Enrollment` and `Schedule`).

Also keep in mind that namespaces can be nested and that any namespaces or classes defined always exist in the global namespace, which by default is the name of the project. You can change this in the VS .NET IDE by clicking on the project and changing the appropriate project property to a different namespace or to none at all. If you change it to none at all, you would need to place explicit `Namespace` declarations in your code. This flexibility allows you to decouple the name of the DLL from the namespaces it contains and allows any DLL to contribute members (either nested namespaces or classes) to the namespace.

NOTE

You can also override the behavior of the global namespace by using the command-line compiler (vbc.exe) rather than compiling in VS .NET. By specifying the `\rootnamespace` option at the command line, you can dictate that all your classes (types) be placed under the namespace you specify.

For example, the following code snippet shows how the namespace statement is used to create nested namespaces:

```
Namespace Quilogy
    Namespace Education
        Public Class Instructors
        End Class
    End Namespace
End Namespace
```

In this case, the `Instructors` class would be referenced as `Quilogy.Education.Instructors`.

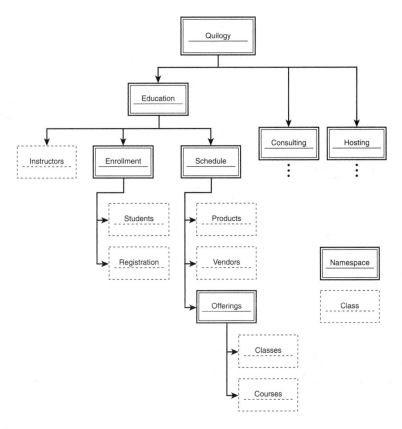

FIGURE 4.1

Sample namespace hierarchy. This chart shows a sample namespace configuration for Quilogy. Note that the namespaces and classes can be nested at the same level.

Because global namespaces are the default, you can also take advantage of this fact to create a naming scheme for your assemblies. By using the global namespace, the highest level namespace that you are exposing in your DLL (in the case of a single-file assembly) will be the name of the DLL. For example, the classes that exist directly under the Quilogy.Education namespace will be placed in the Quilogy.Education.dll because the DLL contains a global namespace equivalent to the name of the DLL. Nested namespaces could then appear within the DLL as well.

In this case, namespaces do have an effect on how assemblies are constructed. In the example in Figure 4.1, the Students and Registration classes would both exist in the same namespace, and so both would exist in an assembly that is created at the boundary of one of the higher-level namespaces (Enrollment, Education, or Quilogy). If followed rigorously, the end result is that if you want to add classes from a new assembly to an existing namespace, you

4

OBJECT-ORIENTED FEATURES

create a new assembly that creates a nested namespace. This technique implies the design rule that you create nested namespaces at assembly boundaries. In other words, you would group classes together in a nested namespace that will be distributed, reused, and secured as a unit.

Finally, remember that namespaces are used to organize code and do not affect the inheritance hierarchy. In other words, a class from one namespace can be used as the base class for a class in a separate namespace. All that is required is that the assembly containing the base class be referenced by the namespace that contains the derived class.

Defining Classes

As mentioned previously, classes are the fundamental programmatic structure you'll use when constructing VB .NET applications. One or more classes are contained in a single source code file and declared using the `Class` keyword. Building on the example from Figure 4.1, the `Offerings` class would be declared as follows:

```
Public Class Offerings
    ' Members to handle course offerings information
End Class
```

Note that VB .NET expands the modifiers you can prefix to the name of the class beyond `Public` and `Private` (the default) and includes `Protected`, `Friend`, and `Protected Friend`. A protected class is one that is nested inside another class and specifies that only derived classes can see it. For example, assume that the `Offerings` class contains a nested `Course` class defined as follows:

```
Public Class Offerings
        Protected Class Course
          Public Function ListCourses() As DataSet
                    ' Query code to get the courses
          End Function
        End Class
End Class
```

By using the keyword `Protected`, a client cannot directly instantiate an object of type `Offerings.Course` to call its `ListCourses` method. The client can instead get access to the `Course` object only through methods of the `Offerings` class itself. In this way, protected access is no different from private access and is analogous to the "Public Not Createable" setting in VB 6.0. However, protected access also allows any classes that inherit from `Offerings` to have full access to the `Course` class as follows:

```
Public Class NewOfferings
    Inherits Offerings

        Public Sub ShowCourse()
```

```
        Dim objCourse As New Course()
          Dim objDs As DataSet
          objDS = objCourse.ListCourses()
          ' Other code to manipulate the courses
    End Sub
End Class
```

Although the `Protected` keyword affects the visibility of nested classes in derived classes, as in VB 6.0, the `Friend` keyword restricts the visibility of a class to code within the project in which it is defined. In the previous example, if the `Offerings` class had been defined with only the `Friend` keyword, it would still have been visible to all calling code within the project but could not have been instantiated by any code outside the project. In addition, any derived classes such as `NewOfferings` also would have to also be marked as `Friend` because not doing so would expand the access to the base class. Finally, a nested class can be marked as `Protected Friend` so that it is visible both in derived classes and code within the same project.

Creating Members

In this section, we'll explore the VB .NET syntax for creating methods, properties, fields, events, and delegates, as well as handling constants.

Creating Methods

As in previous versions of VB, you can create both methods that return a value, using the `Function` statement, and methods that do not, using the `Sub` statement. Both types can accept arguments passed by value (`ByVal`, now the default), by reference (`ByRef`), and an optional array of objects (`ParamArray`) as arguments.

TIP

Parameter arrays have always been an underutilized feature of VB. However, they can be powerful when you want to pass an undefined number of objects into a method. The reason they are underutilized is that the calling code must explicitly pass the parameters in a comma-delimited list rather than simply as an array. In most cases where it makes sense to use a `ParamArray`, the calling code does not know at design-time how many objects it will pass, and so simply defining the arguments using an array of objects typically makes more sense. VB .NET's support for overloaded methods also serves to lessen the need for `ParamArrays` because you can create specific method signatures for each set of arguments.

As in VB 6.0, if the `Optional` keyword is used with any of the arguments, all subsequent arguments must be declared as optional. However, VB .NET requires a default value to be specified in the argument list for any optional parameters. Alternatively, as will be discussed later, the same method can be declared more than once inside a class to create an overloaded method from which the client can choose during development.

To return a value from a class, VB .NET now supports the use of the `Return` statement as well as assigning a value to the function name, shown as follows:

```
Public Function ListCourses(Optional ByVal pVendor As Long = -1) As DataSet
    Dim myDS As DataSet
    ' Code to access the database and populate the dataset
    Return myDS
End Function
```

The method declaration can also include an expanded set of modifiers including `Public`, `Private`, `Friend`, `Protected`, `Protected Friend`, and `Shared`. As you would expect, the first five modifiers in that list serve the same functions as in class modules to restrict access to the method in both derived classes and across projects. The `Shared` keyword, however, is unique to members and is used to implement static members across all instances of a class, as will be discussed shortly.

Creating Properties

One of the syntactical changes in VB .NET is the consolidation of property declarations into the `Property` keyword. Basically the `Property` keyword includes an access modifier, the name of the property, and an optional parameters list in addition to the code to optionally both get and set the value of the property. As in VB 6.0, properties are useful because you can see the value the client is attempting to set the property to and raise exceptions if necessary.

The basics of the `Property` statement can be seen in the following example, where a `LastName` property is implemented for the `Instructor` class:

```
Private mstrLName As String

Property LastName() As String
    Get
        Return mstrLName
    End Get
    Set(ByVal Value As String)
        mstrLName = Value
    End Set
End Property
```

Notice that the code to retrieve the value and to store the value is placed in blocks within the `Property` statement and that the `Value` argument is used to catch the incoming value. As noted in Chapter 3, "VB .NET Language Features," any variables declared within either the `Get` or `Set` blocks are scoped within the block and are accessible only within the block.

The access modifiers for properties include `ReadOnly`, `WriteOnly`, and `Default`. As the names imply, the `ReadOnly` and `WriteOnly` modifiers are used to limit the access to the property. When specified, either the `Get` or `Set` block must be omitted from the `Property` statement as appropriate.

VB .NET also supports parameterized properties by including a parameter list in the declaration of the property. Typically you would use this construct when the property returns an individual array or object instance stored in the class. For example, assume that a class called `Vendors` is used to store a collection of `Vendor` objects defined in the `Vendor` class. To make development simpler, the `Vendors` class is derived from the `System.Collections.CollectionBase` class (as will be discussed later in the chapter) that provides all the low-level handling of collections. To provide access to a particular `Vendor` in the `Vendors` collection, you could create the read-only property shown in Listing 4.1.

LISTING 4.1 Default property. This listing shows how to implement a default property for a class.

```
Public Class Vendors
    Inherits CollectionBase

    ' other properties and methods

    Default ReadOnly Property Item(ByVal index As Integer) As Vendor
        Get
            Return CType(Me.InnerList.Item(index), Vendor)
        End Get
    End Property

    Public Sub Add(ByVal obj As Vendor)
        Me.InnerList.Add(obj)
    End Sub

End Class
```

When the `Vendor` class is instantiated by a client, the client can then add vendors using the public `Add` method and retrieve one by passing an index value to the `Item` property, as shown in the following example:

```
Dim colVendors As New Vendors
Dim objVen As New Vendor
Dim objVen2 As Vendor

colVendors.Add(objVen)
' populate or retrieve the collection
objVen2 = colVendors.Item(4) ' Get 5th item in the collection
```

In the preceding example, you'll also notice that the property is marked as `Default`. Only properties that are parameterized can be marked as default. This allows a client to use the shortcut syntax

```
objVen2 = colVendors(4) ' Get 5th item in the collection
```

rather than accessing the `Item` property directly. Of course, only one property can be marked as the default within a class.

You can also create collection classes by deriving from the `Collection` class in the `Microsoft.VisualBasic` namespace. The difference is that the `Collection` class contains more default behavior such as the inclusion of the `Item` and `Add` methods, whereas `CollectionBase` contains methods that allow you to provide custom behavior as items are added to and removed from the collection.

> **NOTE**
>
> The Services Framework uses parameterized properties in many scenarios, particularly those where an object hierarchy has been implemented (such as the ADO.NET SqlParameterCollection class).

Like methods, properties can be modified with the `Shared`, `Private`, `Overridable`, `Overrides`, and `Overloads` keywords as discussed later. The only point to remember is that if a property is marked as `ReadOnly`, `WriteOnly`, or `Default`, the overriding method in the derived class must also be marked as such.

Creating Fields

Previous versions of VB also had the ability to create fields. Fields are simply variables declared with the `Public` or `Public Dim` keyword at the class level. Variables declared with `Private` or simply `Dim` are not exposed as fields. They are available to any code within the class and can be accessed by clients of the class in the same fashion as properties. The advantage to using fields is that they require very little syntax and are simple. In addition, fields can also be marked with the `ReadOnly` keyword so that any code outside the class constructor cannot change the value. The `ReadOnly` field `Count` in the following code snippet is public so that it is accessible by code both inside and outside the class, but it can be changed only within the constructor (`New`) method of the class:

```
Public Class Instructors
    Public ReadOnly Count As Integer

    Public Sub New()
```

```
        Count = 50 ' Legal
    End Sub

    Public Sub OtherProc()
        Count = 2  ' Generates a compile time error
    End Sub
End Class
```

The primary disadvantage to using fields is that access to them cannot be intercepted by custom code as is the case with properties.

Creating Events and Delegates

The basic event handling syntax has not changed significantly from previous versions of VB, although it has been extended (as you'll see shortly). As in previous versions, events can be declared within a class using the `Event` keyword. An event can be `Public`, `Private`, `Protected`, `Friend`, and `Protected Friend` to the class, can pass arguments either `ByVal` or `ByRef`, and cannot return values. Events can then be raised using the `RaiseEvent` keyword from within the class and passing the required arguments. A partial sample from a class called `RegistrationWatch` is shown in Listing 4.2.

LISTING 4.2 Simple events. This class implements the simple event `NewRegistrations` using the `Event` keyword and fires it using `RaiseEvent`.

```
Public Class RegistrationWatch
    Public Event NewRegistrations(ByVal pStudents As DataSet)

    ' Other methods and properties
    Public Sub Look()
        Dim dsStuds As DataSet
        Dim flNew As Boolean

        ' Method that fires on a timer to look for new registrations
        ' since the last invocation of the method
        ' If one is found then create a DataSet with the new students
        ' and raise the event
        flNew = True
        dsStuds = New DataSet()

        If flNew Then
            RaiseEvent NewRegistrations(dsStuds)
        End If
    End Sub
End Class
```

Notice that the class defines a `NewRegistrations` event as `Public` so that consumers of the class will be able to catch it. The event passes back to the consumer a variable containing an ADO.NET `DataSet` that stores information on the new registrations found. The event is raised in the `Look` method using the `RaiseEvent` statement.

To catch the event, a consumer can declare the `RegistrationWatcher` class using the `WithEvents` keyword (termed *declarative event handling*). Note that, as in VB 6.0, variables declared using `WithEvents` can be either `Public` or `Private`. However, in VB .NET, `WithEvents` can be declared at the module or class level, rather than only in classes and forms as in VB 6.0. The syntax for using `WithEvents` is as follows:

```
Private WithEvents mobjReg As RegistrationWatch
```

To set up the event handler (or event sink), you can then create a procedure that handles the event within the class or module, as shown in the following example:

```
Public Sub RegFound(ByVal pStudents As System.Data.DataSet) _
   Handles mobjReg.NewRegistrations
    MsgBox("New Students Found!")
End Sub
```

Note that VB .NET uses the new `Handles` keyword to indicate precisely which event the procedure handles rather than simply relying on the naming convention used by the event handler as in previous versions. Declarative event handling is certainly the most convenient way to handle events, although as mentioned, it requires the object variable to be scoped correctly and cannot be used to dynamically turn an event handler on or off.

TIP

Although it is true that declarative event handling does not allow you to turn events on and off, if the class raising the event is a custom class, you can implement your own `EnableRaisingEvents` property. The client can then use this property to stop the raising of events. You would then wrap your `RaiseEvent` statements in a check of this property.

When dealing with inheritance, keep in mind that if a class acting as a consumer does not implement the event handlers for a particular object, classes derived from it will not be able to implement them later. In addition, as with other methods, the event handlers can be specified with the `Overridable`, `NotOverridable`, and `MustOverride` keywords.

Events also can be marked as `Shared`, which allows all consumers of a class to receive an event notification when the `RaiseEvent` method is executed in any instance of the class. This might be useful for notifying several consumers when shared data changes, for example, in a service application that periodically queries a database and exposes the data through shared properties.

Dynamic Event Handling

VB .NET expands the ability to use events by implementing *dynamic event handling* in addition to the declarative approach discussed earlier. Dynamic event handling can be very useful when you want to turn event handling on or off (called *hooking* and *unhooking* an event) at a specific time or when the object variable that you want to hook does not reside at the module or class level. To hook and unhook events at run-time, use the AddHandler and RemoveHandler statements.

As an example, consider the RegistrationWatch class shown in Listing 4.3. In this example, we want to create client code in a class that hooks and unhooks the NewRegistrations event based on the setting of the public property. The client class that does this is shown in Listing 4.3.

Listing 4.3 Dynamic events. This class hooks and unhooks events dynamically using the AddHandler and RemoveHandler statements.

```
Public Class Registrations

    Private mRec As Boolean = False
    Private mRegWatch As RegistrationWatch

    Public Property ReceiveNotifications() As Boolean
        Get
            Return mRec
        End Get
        Set (ByVal Value As Boolean)
            mRec = Value
            If mRec = True Then
                ' Add the event handler
                AddHandler mRegWatch.NewRegistrations, _
                    AddressOf Me.NewRegistrations
            Else
                ' Remove the event handler
                RemoveHandler mRegWatch.NewRegistrations, _
                    AddressOf Me.NewRegistrations
            End If
        End Set
    End Property

    Public Sub NewRegistrations(ByVal ds As DataSet)
        ' New Registrations found
        MsgBox("New registrations have been added!")
    End Sub
```

4

Object-Oriented Features

LISTING 4.3   Continued

```
Public Sub New()
    ' Instantiate the class level object
    mRegWatch = New RegistrationWatch()
End Sub

Public Sub TestNotify()
    ' Test method to simulate repeated queries for new registrations
    mRegWatch.Look()
End Sub
End Class
```

In Listing 4.3, the property `ReceiveNotifications` is used to determine whether the class is to receive notifications. The `Set` block of the property then reads the value and calls the `AddHandler` and `RemoveHandler` statements accordingly. Both of the statements accept two parameters:

- A reference to the event to be hooked (in this case, the `NewRegistrations` event of the module level `mRegWatch` variable)
- The address of the method to use as the event handler

Note that the `AddressOf` and `Me` keywords are used to create a pointer to the method and specify a method internal to the class, respectively.

From the client's perspective, the code differs only in that the `ReceiveNotification` property can be set to `True` when notifications are desired (because the `mRec` class level variable defaults to `False`), as shown in the following example:

```
Dim objReg As New Registrations()

objReg.TestNotify() ' No notification
objReg.ReceiveNotifications = True
objReg.TestNotify() ' Notification received
```

Mapping Events to Delegates

As mentioned in Chapter 1, the infrastructure for events is based on the concept of delegates, and therefore, it is not surprising that the event keywords (such as `Event`, `RaiseEvent`, `AddHandler`, and `RemoveHandler`) simply abstract the creation and processing of delegates. However, VB .NET developers can also access delegates directly through the `Delegate` keyword. To understand delegates, let's first explore how delegates are used to implement events in VB .NET.

Remember first and foremost that delegates are simply types that hold references to functions in other objects (type-safe function pointers). There are two basic types of delegates:

single-cast and multi-cast. The former allows a single function pointer to be stored and the latter creates a linked-list of pointers (events are implemented as multi-cast delegates). In addition to the function pointer, the delegate stores the arguments that the function will accept. As a result, from the developer's view, the delegate can be thought of simply as a method signature.

The basic idea behind using a delegate is that a program (called A for this example) creates a delegate that points to one of its own functions and then passes the delegate to some other program (B). At some time in the future, B executes A's function, making sure to push the appropriate arguments on the stack, by running the code at the address provided by the delegate. Of course, this is exactly the model used when dealing with events.

In the example in Listing 4.3, what happens when the `Event` keyword and `RaiseEvent` statements are added to the class is this. Behind the scenes, the VB compiler creates a `Delegate` with the same signature as the event and stores it in a field of the class as follows:

```
Delegate Sub NewRegistrations(ByVal pStudents As DataSet)
```

The compiler also creates add and remove methods for the delegate that take as an argument a reference to a delegate defined (in this case, `NewRegistration`). In addition, the `RaiseEvent` is replaced with a call to the delegate's `Invoke` method, which accepts the single argument as defined in the `Delegate`.

The consumer then uses the `WithEvents` keyword and implements the event handler with the `Handles` statement. At run-time, the delegate is instantiated (it is actually a class derived from `System.Delegate`) and a reference to the event handler is passed to the add method in `RegistrationWatch`. When the delegate is invoked, the function pointer to the event handler is used to call the method. This simple mapping of delegates to events should also explain why it is easy for VB .NET to support the `AddHandler` and `RemoveHandler` statements. They simply call the add and remove methods implemented by the compiler at specified times rather than upon instantiation and deallocation.

To make this a little clearer, examine the code in Listing 4.4 that shows the `RegistrationWatcher` class rewritten with a delegate in place of the event.

LISTING 4.4 Simple delegate. This class uses a delegate in place of an event to perform simple notification.

```
Public Class RegistrationWatch
    Delegate Sub NewRegistrations(ByVal pStudents As DataSet)

    ' Other methods and properties
    Private mfound as NewRegistrations

    Public Sub RegisterClient(ByVal found As NewRegistrations)
```

LISTING 4.4   Continued

```
        mfound = found
    End Sub

    Public Sub Look()
        Dim dsStuds As DataSet
        Dim flNew As Boolean

        ' Method that fires on a timer to look for new registration
        ' If one is found then create a DataSet with the new students
        ' and raise the event
        flNew = True
        dsStuds = New DataSet()

        If flNew Then
            mfound.Invoke(dsStuds) 'invoke the delegate
        End If
    End Sub
End Class
```

The differences between Listing 4.4 and Listing 4.3 can be summarized as follows:

- The `Event` statement has been replaced with `Delegate`.

- The `RaiseEvent` statement has been replaced with `Delegate.Invoke`.

- The `RegisterClient` method is now used to pass in the reference to the delegate stored in a private class variable, whereas the `Look` method simply invokes the delegate at the appropriate time.

Notice also you don't have to explicitly create the add and remove methods, even when specifying the delegate yourself; the VB .NET compiler will add these automatically.

The client code also changes in order to instantiate the delegate as it is being passed to the `Look` method. Note that the address of the event handler is passed as the only argument in the constructor of the delegate, as shown in the following example:

```
Private mobjReg As RegistrationWatch

' in a class or module
mobjReg = New RegistrationWatch()
mobjReg.RegisterClient(New RegistrationWatch.NewRegistrations( _
    AddressOf NewRegistrations))
mobjReg.Look()

Private Sub NewRegistrations(ByVal ds As DataSet)
End Sub
```

Events can also work with delegates as a kind of shortcut for declaring the event signature. For example, rather than declaring an event as

```
Event NewRegistrations(ByVal ds As DataSet)
```

you could make the declarations

```
Delegate Sub NewRegistrations(ByVal ds As DataSet)
Event NewReg as NewRegistrations
```

This allows you to reuse the definition of the delegate inside the event. This can be useful when you have many events that require the same arguments.

Obviously, using delegates in place of events might be construed as overkill because events work quite nicely for scenarios where an event model is required. However, because delegates are function pointers, they also provide other capabilities of which you can take advantage, such as function substitution and asynchronous operation.

Function Substitution with Delegates

The idea of *function substitution* is exactly as it sounds: A section of client code can call one of several functions depending on the delegate it is passed. This promotes the idea of polymorphism because it allows you to write code that is generic as it doesn't know at compile-time which function it is going to call. As an example, consider the Registration class shown in Figure 4.1. Suppose that it contains a RegisterStudent method that implements the business rules necessary to register a student to take a course. As a small part of that process, the cost of the course must be calculated. However, the algorithm for calculating the cost varies depending on how the student was registered and could include a phone call, Web, and registrations received directly from a vendor or partner through a Web service.

To implement this requirement, the Registration class could declare a delegate called CalcCourseCost as follows:

```
Delegate Function CalcCourseCost(ByVal CourseID As String) As Decimal
```

Note that delegates can also return values and therefore be declared as a function. The RegisterStudent method is shown in Listing 4.5.

LISTING 4.5 Skeleton code for the RegisterStudent method. This method uses the delegate passed in as the first parameter to invoke the appropriate calculation function.

```
Public Sub RegisterStudent(ByVal pCalc As CalcCourseCost, _
  ByVal pStud As DataSet)

    ' Implement the business process for registering the student
```

4

OBJECT-ORIENTED
FEATURES

LISTING 4.5 Continued

```
' 1. make sure the student has provided enough info
' 2. make sure the student has not been blacklisted
' 3. possibly suggest another class that is closer based on
' geographic data: raise exception
' 4. make sure the class is not full

' 5. calculate the cost
Dim curCost As Decimal
Dim strCourseID As String

curCost = pCalc(strCourseID)

' 6. persist the registration (database or queue)
' 7. notify the appropriate internal staff of a new registration
' 8. email verification to student
End Sub
```

The method takes both the delegate and the student information packed in a `DataSet` as parameters. After completing the preliminary business rules, the course cost can be calculated simply by invoking the delegate `pCalc` and passing the required `CourseID` argument. Note that this example illustrates that the `Invoke` method of the delegate is actually the default method of a delegate object. The invocation of the calculation function could also be written as `pCalc.Invoke(strCourseID)`.

On the client side, the appropriate delegate must be instantiated. The skeleton code in Listing 4.6 shows code residing in a module or class that first collects the registration method (stored in `RegType`) and uses a `Select Case` statement to instantiate the correct delegate. The delegate is then passed to the `RegisterStudent` method.

LISTING 4.6 Client code using a delegate. This code determines the appropriate delegate at run-time and passes it to the `RegisterStudent` method. Note that the procedures used as the delegates are shown later.

```
Dim objReg As New Registrations()
Dim delCalc As Registrations.CalcCourseCost
Dim RegType As Integer
Dim ds As DataSet

' Determine the registration type
' Create the delegate based on the registration type
Select Case RegType
    Case 1
        delCalc = New Registrations.CalcCourseCost(AddressOf CalcWeb)
```

LISTING 4.6 Continued

```
    Case 2
        delCalc = New Registrations.CalcCourseCost(AddressOf CalcPhone)
    Case 3
        delCalc = New Registrations.CalcCourseCost(AddressOf CalcService)
End Select

' Register the student
objReg.RegisterStudent(delCalc, ds)

' Other code goes here

Public Function CalcWeb(ByVal strCourseID As String) As Decimal
    ' Calculate cost based on web registration
End Function

Public Function CalcPhone(ByVal strCourseID As String) As Decimal
    ' Calculate cost based on phone registration
End Function

Public Function CalcService(ByVal strCourseID As String) As Decimal
    ' Calculate cost based on service registration
End Function
```

> **NOTE**
>
> Experienced VB developers might have noticed that this technique is similar to using the `CallByName` function in VB 6.0. The difference is that `CallByName` could be used only on internal classes or COM objects, whereas delegates can be used with any procedure (in a module or a class) that fits the signature of the delegate.

What About Interfaces?

Developers who have done interface-based programming in VB 6.0 will note that the polymorphism shown in the `CalcCourseCost` example could also be implemented simply by creating separate classes for each calculation method and implementing a common interface (`ICalc`) that exposes a `Calculate` method. Different classes that implement the `ICalc` interface could then be passed to `RegisterStudent` at run-time to call the `Calculate` method. Although this technique would also work, it might be more complicated and less efficient. For example, by using a delegate, you don't have

> to create separate classes because any number of functions (as long as they have the same signature) in the calling code can be used to implement the delegate, and you don't have to pass a full object reference to RegisterStudent, only a delegate. As a rule of thumb, create interfaces when there is a collection of related members that you want to implement across classes and when the particular function will be implemented only once. Use delegates when you have only a single function to implement, the class implementing the delegate doesn't require a reference to the object, or you want to create a delegate for a shared method (all methods defined for the interface are always instance methods).

As mentioned in the "What About Interfaces?" sidebar, using delegates for function substitution can also take the place of using interfaces (discussed later in the chapter). This pattern can be approximated by instantiating a delegate inside a class and then using a private function to invoke the delegate. For example, consider the case in which disparate classes each support the ability to persist their state. In this case, client applications could work with each of these classes polymorphically through the use of a delegate rather than requiring them to implement the same interface or belong to the same inheritance hierarchy. The pattern for such a class is shown in Listing 4.7.

LISTING 4.7 Delegates as interfaces. This class shows how a delegate can be used to expose functionality to client applications polymorphically. It is functionally equivalent to using an interface.

```
Delegate Function Persist() As String

Public Class Registrations
   Public ReadOnly myPersist As Persist

        Public Sub New()
           myPersist = New Persist(AddressOf Me.SaveToDisk)
        End Sub

        Private Function SaveToDisk() As String
           Dim strFile as String

         ' save the contents to disk and return the path name
           Return strFile
        End Function
End Class
```

Note that the delegate is declared external to the class and that the class then instantiates a read-only variable in the constructor, passing it the address of the private SaveToDisk method (which will actually save the results and return the file name). The client application can then call any class that supports the `Persist` delegate by implementing a function that accepts the delegate as parameter, as shown here:

```
Public Function Save(ByVal pPersist As Persist) As String
    Return pPersist.Invoke
End Function
```

The client then invokes the function to save the contents to a file by passing the delegate of the `Registrations` class to the `Save` function, as shown here:

```
Dim objRegister As New Registrations
Dim strPath As String

' ...work with the class
strPath = Save(objRegister.myPersist)
```

In this way, each class can decide internally how to implement the code to save its contents and yet provide a public interface through the `Persist` delegate that client applications can call. Even though this code is slightly more complex from the client application's perspective, it is more flexible because interfaces and inheritance are not required.

Asynchronous Processing with Delegates

A second major use of delegates in .NET is for handling asynchronous processing. One of the benefits of using delegates for asynchronous processing is that they can be used both in conjunction with .NET Remoting (discussed in Chapter 8, "Building Components,") to facilitate communication between processes and machines and with code that resides in the same application domain. This common programming model allows you to write code that is location transparent as well.

Delegates are appropriate for asynchronous calls because they were designed with `BeginInvoke` and `EndInvoke` methods that allow the client to invoke a method asynchronously and then catch its results respectively. You can think of `BeginInvoke` and `EndInvoke` as partitioning the execution of a method from a client's perspective. To specify which procedure to call upon completion of the asynchronous method, you use the `AsyncCallback` object and `IAsyncResult` interface from the `System` namespace. When using delegates with the asynchronous classes and interfaces in the `System` namespace, the CLR provides the underlying services needed to support this programming model including a thread pool and the ability to call objects that reside inside synchronized contexts such as those using COM+ services. (We'll explore more about thread support in the CLR in Chapter 12, "Accessing System Services," as well.) One of the side benefits of this integration is to make it fairly simple to create multi-threaded applications in VB .NET.

4

OBJECT-ORIENTED
FEATURES

> **NOTE**
>
> VB 6.0 developers will recall that because the VB 6.0 runtime was single-threaded, it was very difficult to create any asynchronous code without resorting to using the Win32 API directly (which led to unstable code that was tricky to debug) or tricking the COM library into creating an object in a new single-threaded apartment. Needless to say, neither technique was particularly attractive.

To understand the pattern for asynchronous programming in .NET, consider a method of the `Registration` class that is used to send reminder e-mail notifications to all students who are to attend a class the following week. This `RemindStudent` method might take some time to complete because it must read a list of students from the database, construct an e-mail message for each one, send the e-mail, and update the database appropriately. For the client application's thread to avoid being blocked when the method is called, the method can be called using a delegate (in this case often termed an *asynchronous delegate*).

Because the .NET asynchronous model allows the client to decide whether the called code will run asynchronously, the code for the `RemindStudent` method does not have to be written explicitly to handle asynchronous calls. You can simply declare it and write the code as if it were synchronous as follows:

```
Public Function RemindStudent(ByVal pDaysAhead As Integer, _
     ByRef pErrors() as String) As Boolean
   ' Read from the database and send out the email notification
End Sub
```

Note that the method requires an argument to specify how many days in advance the e-mail should be sent out and returns an array of strings containing any error messages. However, the client code must significantly change. The code in Listing 4.8 is used to call the `RemindStudent` method.

LISTING 4.8 Code used to implement asynchronous programming using delegates.

```
' Async delegate
Delegate Function RemStudentCallback(ByVal pDaysAhead As Integer, _
ByRef pErrors() as String) As Boolean

' Client code inside a class or module

' Declare variables
Dim temp() As String
Dim intDays As Integer = 7
```

Listing 4.8   Continued

```
' Create the Registration class and the delegate
Dim objReg As Registration = New Registration()
Dim StudCb As RemStudentCallback = New RemStudentCallback(AddressOf _
    objReg.RemindStudent)

' Define the AsyncCallback delegate
Dim cb As AsyncCallback = New AsyncCallback(AddressOf RemindResult)

' Can create any object as the state object
Dim state As Object = New Object()

' Asynchronously invoke the RemindStudent method on objReg
StudCb.BeginInvoke(intDays, temp, cb, state)

' Do some other useful work

Public Sub RemindResult(ByVal ar As IAsyncResult)
        Dim strErrors() As String
        Dim StudCb As RemStudentCallback
        Dim flResult As Boolean
        Dim objResult As AsyncResult

        ' Extract the delegate from the AsyncResult
        objResult = CType(ar, AsyncResult)
        StudCb = objResult.AsyncDelegate

        ' Obtain the result
        flResult = StudCb.EndInvoke(strErrors, ar)

        ' Output results
    End Sub
```

To begin, notice that the client code first creates a new instance of the Registration class as normal. However, it then creates a new RemStudentCallback delegate and places in it the address of the RemindStudent method of the newly created object instance (objReg). Once again, the delegate must have the same signature as the RemindStudent method.

Now the code must create an address that can be called back upon completion of the RemindStudent method. To do this, a system delegate class called AsyncCallback is instantiated and passed the address of a procedure called RemindResult. You'll notice that RemindResult must accept one argument: an object that supports the IAsyncResult interface.

After the callback is set up, the `RemindStudent` method is actually invoked using the `BeginInvoke` method of the delegate that was created earlier (`StudCb`). The `BeginInvoke` method accepts the same arguments as the delegate it was instantiated as in addition to the delegate that contains the callback and an object in which you can place additional state information required by the method.

At this point, your code can continue on the current execution path. The delegate will invoke the `RemindStudent` method (on a separate thread if in the same application) and when finished will call the procedure defined in the delegate passed to `BeginInvoke` (in this case, the `RemindResult`). As mentioned previously, this procedure accepts an argument of type `IAsyncResult`. To retrieve the instance of the delegate `RemStudentCallback` from it, you first need to convert it to an object of type `AsyncResult` using the `CType` function. The `AsyncDelegate` property of the resulting `AsyncResult` object contains the reference to the `RemStudentCallback` delegate. The return value and any arguments passed `ByRef` are then captured using the return value and arguments passed to the `EndInvoke` method of the delegate.

Creating Named Constants

There are two ways to expose constants in a class in VB .NET: The first is to use the traditional `Const` keyword at the class level, and the second is to use an enumerated type.

To create a constant, simply declare it and assign it a value as follows:

```
Private Const QUILOGY_CODE As Byte = 1
```

Constants can be defined as any of the simple data types such as `Byte`, `Boolean`, `Char`, `Short`, `Integer`, `Long`, `Single`, `Double`, `Decimal`, `Date`, and `String`. As expected, constants cannot be the targets of assignment statements and must be initialized deterministically. In other words, the code used to initialize the constant must be able to be evaluated at compile-time using a constant expression that contains no variables or functions that return varying results.

TIP

If you would like to create a constant but need to initialize it using a non-deterministic algorithm, you should use a read-only field and initialize it in the class constructor. Read-only fields also have the advantage of being able to support additional types such as custom objects.

Finally, constants in a class are always explicitly shared members, as will be discussed later in the chapter. However, you can also modify them with the `Public`, `Private`, `Protected`, `Friend`, and `Protected Friend` keywords.

The second technique for creating constants in a class is to use an enumeration. As in VB 6.0, enumerations in VB .NET are declared with the Enum keyword and are used to provide a collection of constants that can be used in structures, variables, parameters, or even return values of procedures. The limitations of enumerated types include the following:

- They have a restricted set of data types (Byte, Short, Long, and Integer, which is the default).

- They must be initialized at compile-time under the same restrictions as constants. If you don't explicitly initialize them, they will be initialized starting with 0. VB .NET also supports the syntax where initializing the first constant in the enumeration and leaving the others uninitialized will result in the uninitialized constants being initialized in increments of
1 based on the first constant.

- They are not inheritable.

The typical syntax for declaring an enum is as follows:

```
Public Enum VendorCodes As Byte
    vcQuilogy = 1
    vcMicrosoft = 2
    vcOracle = 3
    vcRational = 4
    vcSybase = 5
End Enum
```

Note that in this case, the Byte data type is used explicitly for the VendorCodes enumerated type rather than defaulting to an Integer. In addition, this syntax implies that all constants within the type are of the same data type unlike a structure.

Using Inheritance

The addition of implementation inheritance is probably one of the most eagerly anticipated new features in VB .NET. To support this feature, the VB .NET syntax has been augmented with keywords that specify how a class and its members can be inherited and used in a derived class.

At the class level, the Inherits keyword is used in the class declaration to create a derived class. After the class is inherited, it automatically has all the functionality exposed in the base class and can additionally create new members and override and overload members in the base class. The class acting as the base class does not need to be declared within the current application or even the same namespace. In fact, any .NET class referenced in an assembly in your project can act as a base class, and at run-time the CLR will be able to access its implementation. This includes classes created in other managed languages such as VC# and managed VC++.

> **NOTE**
>
> The CLR supports only single inheritance, which means that a class can be derived
> from only a single base class. Some languages, such as C++, support multiple inheri-
> tance, in which the members from several classes can be inherited in a derived class.
> However, if you need to bring methods from multiple classes together, you can do so
> through an inheritance tree. Because an inheritance hierarchy can contain multiple
> classes, you can create designs in which, for example, class C derives from class B,
> which derives from class A. In this case, methods implemented by both class A and B
> are available to be overridden by class C or called from clients using class C.

In addition, classes can be specified with the `MustInherit` or `NotInheritable` keywords. By
default, all classes are inheritable within their defined scope as defined by the modifiers discussed in the previous section. However, if you want to create a class that acts as an abstract
base class, you can do so by adding the `MustInherit` keyword. An example of using this technique is shown in Listing 4.9 where a partial abstract base class called `QuilogyDataAccess` is
defined.

LISTING 4.9   Abstract base class. This listing shows an example abstract base class for a
COM+ configured class.

```
Option Explicit On
Option Strict Off

Imports System.Data
Imports System.EnterpriseServices

Namespace Quilogy.Education

    '********************************************************************
    Public Interface IQuilogyQuery
        ' Interface used to query
        Function GetByID(ByVal pID As Long) As DataSet
        Function GetByName(ByVal pName As String) As DataSet
    End Interface

    '********************************************************************
    <Transaction(TransactionOption.Supported), _
      EventTrackingEnabled(True), _
      ConstructionEnabled(Enabled:=True)> _
      Public MustInherit Class QuilogyDataAccess : Inherits ServicedComponent
        Implements IQuilogyQuery
```

LISTING 4.9   Continued

```
    Protected mstrConnect As String

    '**********************************************************************
    Public NotOverridable Overrides Sub Construct(ByVal s As String)
        ' Implements object construction
        mstrConnect = s
    End Sub

    '**********************************************************************
    Overrides Function CanBePooled() As Boolean
        ' Default is that the objects will not be pooled
        Return False
    End Function

    '**********************************************************************
    Public Overridable Function GetByName( _
      ByVal pName As String) As DataSet _
        Implements IQuilogyQuery.GetByName

    End Function

    '**********************************************************************
    Public Overridable Function GetByID(ByVal pId As Long) As DataSet _
        Implements IQuilogyQuery.GetByID

    End Function
    End Class


End Namespace
```

In this example, the abstract base class `QuilogyDataAccess` itself inherits from the `ServicedComponent` Services Framework class to provide access to COM+ transactions (discussed in Chapter 9). The base class also implements the custom interface `IQuilogyQuery` to provide querying capabilities, as will be discussed later in this chapter.

> **NOTE**
>
> The `Inherits` keyword must be placed on a separate line from the `Class` statement. In this example, the lines are separated using a colon rather than a carriage return-line feed. This syntax has the advantage of making the code more readable, although in most instances I would not recommend using the line separator.

4

OBJECT-ORIENTED FEATURES

The obvious advantage to being able to create abstract base classes is that you can create a layer of abstraction that allows other developers to reuse your code and at the same time protect that code from direct instantiation. Keep in mind that you must be careful to include all the functionality required and inherit from the appropriate base class when creating abstract base classes because .NET does not support multiple inheritance. Additional functionality can be provided through interfaces, although by definition they provide only the signatures of methods to implement, not the actual implementation.

When a class is used in an inheritance hierarchy, you can place modifiers on the members that determine how they can be used in the derived class. For example the inheritance behavior of methods can be specified using the Overridable, NotOverridable (the default), MustOverride, Overrides, and Overloads keywords. The first three keywords in the list are used in the original declaration of a method to indicate whether the method can or can't be overridden or whether it must be overridden. Note that if you don't specify otherwise, a method cannot be overridden (a warning is issued; a shadows is assumed) and, when invoked from an instance of a derived class, will execute the implementation in the base class; hence, the genesis of the term *implementation inheritance*.

For example, the method GetByID in Listing 4.1 uses the Overridable keyword to indicate that the method can be overridden in the derived class. If you use the MustOverride keyword, all you can specify is the method declaration, no implementation. This behavior is essentially like implementing an interface on the class in that it ensures that the derived class will create an implementation for the method.

The Overrides keyword is used in the derived class to indicate methods that have been overridden from the base class. In the earlier example, the Construct procedure was overridden in the base class and so you must explicitly note this in the declaration, as shown in the following example:

```
Public NotOverridable Overrides Sub Construct(ByVal s As String)
    ' Implements object construction
    mstrConnect = s
End Sub
```

NOTE

Although it might seem like overkill to require the Overrides keyword—after all, the compiler could simply look to see whether the method name is in the base class and that the signatures match—I like that VB .NET requires it because it forces developers to explicitly note their intention to override a method of the base class rather than simply doing it by accident. At a lower level, the use of the Overridable and NotOverridable keywords allows the JITer to produce more efficient code as well.

Note that overridden methods are just that. When invoked on a derived class, the overridden method in the base class does not run. You can explicitly cause this to happen by using the MyBase object to invoke the overridden method from the derived class.

The Overloads keyword can be used both in a base class and a derived class. In a base class, Overloads is used to create multiple versions of the same method that differ only in their arguments, as you'll see in the following discussion. This allows a client to select which implementation they wish to call at design-time. A typical use for overloaded methods in a base class is to create varying versions of the class constructor, as will be shown later. In VS .NET, overloaded methods are shown by a list of possible signatures in the autocompletion window. In a derived class, Overloads is used to add additional method signatures available to the client. Depending on which one the client chooses, the actual code might execute either in the base class or the derived class.

> **NOTE**
>
> The Overloads keyword is not required when overloading methods within a class but it is required when a derived class overloads a method from the base class. However, if one overloaded method in a class has the Overloads keyword, then they all must.

Finally, the Shadows keyword can be used in a derived class to reuse and redeclare a member from the base class. In other words, even if the base class does not specify that an existing method can be overridden, you can declare a method of the same name in the derived class with the Shadows modifier in order to use the name. In this event, the shadowed method from the base class is not overloaded but becomes unavailable in the derived class and all its descendants. This can be useful when you want to hide all the overloaded members from the base class and expose only one signature for the member to clients of your class.

> **TIP**
>
> If a method specifies neither Shadows nor Overloads then the VB .NET compiler will issue a warning but Shadows will be assumed. However, it is recommended to always explicitly use Shadows when that is your intent.

Using Polymorphism

In addition to the ability to reuse the implementation of a class in derived classes, one of the other primary benefits to using inheritance is polymorphism. Creating an inheritance hierarchy implicitly means that the derived classes have a "is a" relationship with the base class and therefore, they can be treated polymorphically. For example, as discussed previously, if a Velociraptor class is derived from the Theropod class, any client code that is designed to work with the Theropod class will also work with the Velociraptor class since Velociraptor is a Theropod. Consider the following method signature that accepts an argument of type Theropod:

```
Public Sub PrintDinosaur(ByRef oTheropod as Theropod)
```

Because Velociraptor is derived from Theropod, a client application can instantiate a Velociraptor object and pass it to this method as follows:

```
Dim oVec as New Velociraptor
PrintDinosaur(oVec)
```

VB .NET will allow this behavior only if the Option Strict statement is set to Off. If it is on, however, you must first use the CType function to convert the reference oVec to Theropod as follows:

```
PrintDinosaur(CType(oVec, Theropod))
```

Obviously, by writing code that works against your base classes, you'll end up being able to reuse the code to perform work on derived objects as well.

Creating and Using Shared Members

One of the biggest changes in VB .NET that supports true OO programming and that works hand-in-hand with inheritance is the use of shared or static members (sometimes called class members). As the name implies, *shared members* are methods, properties, fields, and events that are shared between all instances of the class and any derived classes for which they are defined. This allows all objects created with the class to access the same data (in the case of properties and fields) and implementation (in the case of methods), and to receive the same fired event (in the case of events).

To mark a member as shared, you simply use the Shared keyword on either Public or Private members. For example, consider the Count field of the Instructors class discussed earlier. Obviously, this kind of data is a good candidate for sharing among all instances of the class because it should be automatically updated for all instances when any one instance adds a new instructor. To implement the shared field, you would simply redefine it at the class level as follows:

```
Public Shared ReadOnly Count As Integer
```

However, by making the field read-only, other methods that are not shared within the class—such as Add—would not be able to increment the Count. Because of this limitation, you could instead create Count as a read-only instance property and store the internal value of the count as a shared private variable as follows:

```
Private Shared mCount As Integer

ReadOnly Property Count() As Integer
    Get
        Return mCount
    End Get
End Property
```

In this way, both the shared constructor and other shared and instance methods have access to mCount.

When using shared members, you must keep in mind that within a shared member you cannot access data that is particular to an instance. In other words, you cannot manipulate variables, properties, or call methods that are not also marked as shared. However, the reverse is not true, so you can safely increment the mCount shared variable from within a virtual method such as Add.

```
Public Function Add() As Integer
    ' Perform the transaction
    mCount += 1
End Function
```

In addition, shared methods and properties cannot be overridden in descendant classes, although they can be overloaded both in the base class and in any derived class. This behavior is the default so that any shared method is the only implementation available for the base class and all its descendants. However, a class can extend the implementation by creating overloaded members that accept different arguments.

> **CAUTION**
>
> If you declare a variable as shared in the base class and declare the same variable in a derived class, regardless of the modifier, the runtime will treat them as two entirely separate entities within their respective scopes. As a result, any code in the derived class that refers to the name will reference the variable defined in the derived class and result in the obfuscation of the shared variable. Similarly, any code in the base class will modify only the shared variable.

To summarize, shared members are useful when all instances of a class will share the same data or when the class has a standard set of methods that will operate identically across all instances of the class and any derived classes.

Using Interface Based Programming

As shown in several examples already in this chapter, as in VB 6.0, VB .NET also supports the concept of interface inheritance. In this section, we'll first review interface-based programming and then discuss the syntax VB .NET uses to create and implement interfaces.

Put simply, an *interface* is a semantically related set of members that define the contract between an object and the client application that uses it. When an object implements an interface, it is essentially agreeing to provide a view of itself that looks like the interface. The interesting thing about using interfaces in your classes is that clients can write code that works against any class that implements the interface rather than custom code for each particular class. This promotes polymorphism and, therefore, code reuse.

NOTE
One of the reasons interface-based programming was not popular in VB 6.0 was because creating interfaces was not intuitive. Because VB 6.0 did not support the explicit creation of interfaces, you had to create a class with methods that had no implementation and compile them into a DLL. The syntax in VB .NET makes creating interfaces an explicit and well-defined activity, which should increase their usage. Actually, VB 6.0 does create an interface automatically for each class in an ActiveX DLL project. However, this interface is hidden and is used behind the scenes by VB.

Although you can first create interfaces for all your classes and therefore take a truly interface-based programming approach, it might not be the most cost-effective use of your time. Typically, interfaces are best leveraged when you want to isolate a set of related methods that will be implemented in different ways by different classes. For example, defining an interface through which to query for data from various classes is a good use of an interface because it can be used in many different classes, and because the implementation in each of those classes is likely to differ. If the implementation were to remain the same, a better technique would be to create a base class and inherit from it so that all the derived classes could reuse the actual code.

In VB .NET, you create an interface with the `Interface` keyword and include the signatures of the members required in the interface. The following snippet shows a small interface that could be implemented by various classes for handling database queries:

```
Public Interface IQuilogyQuery
    Function GetByID(ByVal pid As Long) As DataSet
    Function GetByName(ByVal pname As String) As DataSet
End Interface
```

Note that the method definitions do not contain any "end" statements and thus have no implementation. The interface itself can also be specified with the `Public`, `Private`, `Protected`,
`Friend`, and `Protected Friend` keywords in the same way as classes. This allows interfaces to
be scoped within classes, modules, and applications. And like classes, interfaces are automatically scoped within a namespace, either the global namespace or a specific namespace declared
in your code.

Unlike classes, however, the members defined in the interface cannot be marked with access
modifiers such as `Public` and `Private` or inheritance hints such as `Overridable` or `MustInherit`.
This is because, by definition, all the members of an interface must be implemented by the
class as a part of its contract to any client application that wants to use it. However, one property of the interface can be marked as the `Default` property as long as the property requires a
parameter, as discussed in the section "Creating Properties" in this chapter.

As in VB 6.0, a class can incorporate an interface using the `Implements` keyword. Unlike
implementation inheritance, you can implement more than one interface on a class. This allows
client applications to work with the class in multiple ways depending on which interface they
request.

When an interface is implemented, each of the members of the interface must be created in the
class. The following code shows a class that implements the `IQuilogyQuery` interface:

```
Public Class Offerings
Implements IQuilogyQuery

Public Function GetById(ByVal pid As Long) As DataSet _
   Implements IQuilogyQuery.GetByID
        ' Provide the implementation
     End Function

Public Function GetByName(ByVal pName As String) As DataSet _
   Implements IQuilogyQuery.GetByName
         ' Provide the implementation
     End Function
 End Class
```

Note that the methods that are used to implement the members of the interface are specified
using the `Implements` keyword as well. Although this might seem unnecessary, requiring this
syntax allows your class to implement several interfaces that could include members that have
names that collide. As a result, you can use a name of your choosing for the internal name.

Within a client application, writing code against interfaces rather than specific classes allows
you to write code that is reusable. For example, assume that your client application contains a
procedure that queries a class and uses the resulting data set to populate a grid control on a

4

form. Rather than writing specific procedures for each type that can be used in the application, you could write a single `PopulateGrid` class that takes as a parameter a reference to an object that supports the `IQuilogyQuery` interface. The procedure can then call the `GetByID` method of the underlying class through its interface and retrieve the resulting data set, as shown in the following example:

```
Public Sub PopulateGrid(ByRef oQuery As IQuilogyQuery, ByVal pId As Integer)
    Dim ds As DataSet

    ds = oQuery.GetByID(pid)

    'Populate the grid with the data set
End Sub
```

Before calling the `PopulateGrid` method, the client application can also query the class to make sure that it implements the `IQuilogyQuery` interface by using the `TypeOf` statement. If so, and if `Option Strict` is set to `On`, the `CType` function can be used to cast the object reference to `IQuilogyQuery` during the call.

```
Dim oIns As New Instructors()

If TypeOf oIns Is IQuilogyQuery Then
    PopulateGrid(CType(oIns, IQuilogyQuery), intInsID)
End If
```

Note that if the object does not support the interface and the `TypeOf` check was not done first, the `CType` function will throw an `InvalidCastException`. The exception would also be thrown if `Option Strict` were set to `Off` and the implicit cast failed.

Versioning

As mentioned previously, developers face the decision of whether to use abstract base classes or interfaces or some combination of both in their designs. In addition to the basic decision of whether you need to reuse the implementation of code located in base classes, the issue of versioning is also important.

Because interfaces form a contract between the client and the implementer of the interface, a change to an interface necessarily breaks the contract. As a result, you cannot add or delete members to an interface, change return types from methods, or change the number or data types of arguments without breaking the contract. When the runtime attempts to load a class that implements an interface, it ensures that the interface implements all of the members and that their signatures are correct. If the interface has changed or is not correctly implemented, the runtime will throw a `System.TypeLoadException` at load-time.

Although this might at first seem like a restriction, it is a good thing because the strict enforcement of interface versioning is what allows classes that implement the same interface to be used polymorphically by clients.

Using Constructors and Destructors

As with VB 6.0 classes, the classes in VB .NET support the inclusion of initialization and termination code that runs when a new instance of the class is created and deallocated. However, the names and behavior of these methods differ dramatically.

A constructor in VB .NET is defined as a procedure that has the name New (rather than Initialize as in VB 6.0) and can accept arguments to allow clients to pass data into the instance to assist with initialization. Constructors do not return values and therefore are always declared as a Sub. The constructor can also be overloaded and accept varying arguments to promote polymorphic use of the class.

When the first instance of a class is constructed using the New operator, the run-time will initially attempt to find and execute the shared constructor (defined as Shared Sub New()) on the class. Note that shared constructors are not defined with the Public keyword, cannot accept arguments, and hence cannot be overloaded with another version of the shared constructor. In other words, the following code is illegal because it attempts to overload a shared constructor:

```
Overloads Shared Sub New()
End Sub

Overloads Shared Sub New(ByVal ID As Integer)
End Sub
```

After dealing with the shared constructor, the runtime executes any virtual constructor (a constructor that is not shared), passing in the optional arguments, for the specific instance of the class. After that is completed, the instance is ready for use.

Inherited classes can also have their own shared and instance constructors. In this case, when a new instance of a derived class is created, the runtime first looks for a shared constructor of the base class, and then the shared constructor for the derived class, followed by an instance constructor for the derived class, and finally the instance constructor for the base class. This arrangement makes sense because the shared constructor of the derived class can alter the contents of other shared data and therefore must execute after the shared constructor of the base class.

If the derived class does not contain a shared constructor, the shared constructor of the base class is executed, followed by the instance constructor of the base class, and finally the instance constructor of the derived class.

4

OBJECT-ORIENTED
FEATURES

This discussion implies that constructors cannot be overridden and will always execute regardless of whether a derived class has a constructor as well. As a result, you do not need to use the `MyBase` keyword to explicitly call the `New` method of the base class. However, you can invoke `MyBase.New()` as the first line in a instance constructor if you want to execute the constructor in the base class before that in the derived class.

Parameterized Constructors

The ability to pass data directly into the constructor is referred to as *parameterized construction*. VB .NET allows this by expanding the syntax for the `New` operator. For example, the `Course` class discussed earlier supports construction using the following syntax:

```
Protected Class Course
    Public Sub New(ByVal courseID As Integer)
        ' Initialize with a specific course in mind
    End Sub
    Public Sub New()
        ' Initialize without a course
    End Sub
End Class
```

A client then has the option of creating the class using either constructor by simply providing parameters to the `New` statement in the variable declaration:

```
Dim objCourse As New Course(intCourseID)
```

or separately in a `New` statement:

```
Dim objCourse As Course
objCourse = New Course(intCourseID)
```

Note that as an additional bonus, the IntelliSense feature of VS .NET shows both constructors in a drop-down list as shown in Figure 4.2.

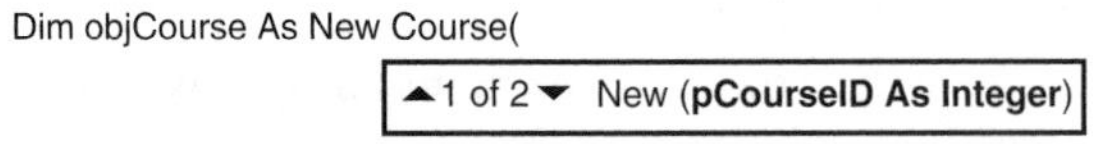

```
Dim objCourse As New Course(
```
```
▲ 1 of 2 ▼  New (pCourseID As Integer)
```

FIGURE 4.2

Calling constructors. This screen shot from VS .NET shows how IntelliSense provides a drop-down list for all constructors of a class.

As with other overloaded methods, overloaded constructors must differ in either the number of arguments or their data types; argument names are not considered. Of course, in this simple example you could also have specified the `courseID` argument as `Optional`, although this would have required you to specify a default value and the IntelliSense feature would not show the varying constructors in a drop-down list. In addition, using overloaded constructors rather than optional arguments frees you from the limitation that each argument following the first optional must also be optional.

> **NOTE**
>
> Although it might seem confusing the `Overloads` keyword is not allowed on over-loaded constructors.

By creating classes with numerous (overloaded) constructors, you also run the risk of duplicating code. You can alleviate duplication in one of two ways. First, you can create private procedures that abstract the non-specific initialization code required and simply invoke that procedure from each constructor. Second, you can place the non-specific initialization code in a shared constructor, although remember that shared constructors can reference only other shared members of the class.

Destructors

Analogous to the `Terminate` method in VB 6.0, each class in VB .NET can implement a `Finalize` method that is called when the object instance is deallocated. The `Finalize` method is a `Sub` procedure that should always be protected and overrides the `Finalize` method of the base class. However, unlike a constructor, the `Finalize` method of the base classes in the hierarchy do not run unless explicitly called with `MyBase.Finalize` in the derived class as follows:

```
Overrides Protected Sub Finalize
    ' Call the base class Finalize
    MyBase.Finalize
End Sub
```

Perhaps the most important difference between `Terminate` and `Finalize`, as mentioned in Chapter 1, is that by default, the `Finalize` method is actually executed by the runtime on a special thread allocated by the Garbage Collector (GC). Subsequent to the object instance no longer being referenced (reachable), the `Finalize` method is executed whenever the runtime feels it is appropriate, such as when a low-resource condition occurs. In other words, you don't necessarily have control of when the `Finalize` method executes. This situation is often referred to as *non-deterministic finalization*. VB .NET still supports the `Nothing` keyword and you are encouraged to set an object instance to `Nothing` when you are finished using it. This information actually helps the GC detect when an object is no longer reachable and allows it to be marked as requiring deallocation.

Using the `Finalize` method for code that frees resources such as file handles and database connections is tempting. However, because of non-deterministic finalization, you'll probably also want to free system resources much sooner than whenever the GC gets around to finalizing your objects.

> **NOTE**
>
> In fact, your classes do not have to implement a `Finalize` method at all. Not doing so actually increases performance for the runtime because the GC does not have to queue up the execution of the `Finalize` method, as mentioned in Chapter 1. However, in some cases you might want to make sure that all resources are cleaned up gracefully, and implementing a `Finalize` method is the only way to ensure that this happens.

The standard technique for allowing objects to clean up their resources in a timely fashion is to implement a `Close` or `Dispose` method in the class. Typically, a `Close` method is used when the object can be "opened" again by calling some other method, whereas `Dispose` is used if the object instance is not to be used after calling `Dispose`. Keep in mind that these methods will not automatically be called and so the documentation for your class must adequately describe its proper use. To provide both explicit and implicit cleanup, you can place your cleanup code in the `Finalize` method and then call `Finalize` from the `Dispose` method as shown in the following code:

```
Public Class Instructors
    Public Sub Dispose
        ' Dispose() calls Finalize so that you can include all
        ' the cleanup code in one place.
        Me.Finalize()
        ' Tell the GC that the object doesn't require any cleanup
        GC.SuppressFinalize(Me)
    End Sub

    Overrides Protected Sub Finalize
        ' Clean up system resources
    End Sub
End Class
```

Note that the `Finalize` method can be called using the `Me` keyword because it is a member of the same object instance. In addition, the Services Framework makes available the `System.GC` class that you can use to interact with the Garbage Collector through its shared methods. In this case, the `SuppressFinalize` method is called to notify the GC that it does not have to `Finalize` this object because it has already been finalized. This saves the GC from having to do extra work when the object becomes unreachable.

One other aspect of the GC that you need to be aware of is that it does not guarantee that objects will be deallocated in any particular order. In other words, the order in which you set them to Nothing is not necessarily the order in which they'll be cleaned up.

This presents an interesting situation when you create one class that references another. For example, assume that the Registration class accepts an argument in its constructor that refers to an instance of the Instructors class defined in the previous code snippet as shown here:

```
Public Class Registration
    Private mIns As Instructors

    Public Sub New(ByRef obj As Instructors)
        mIns = obj
    End Sub

    Protected Overrides Sub Finalize()
        mIns.Dispose()
    End Sub
End Class
```

Obviously, as long as the Registration instance is reachable, the Instructors object will also be reachable because Registration retains a reference to it in the mIns local variable. However, let's assume that both instances become unreachable (are set to Nothing). Because the order of finalization is not guaranteed, the runtime could finalize the Instructors object referred to by the Registration object before the Registration object. In this case, when the finalization occurs on Registration and it attempts to call the Dispose method of Instructors, an exception is thrown. As a result, in designs like these you should either be prepared to catch the resulting exception or not implement a Finalize method in classes like Registration. Optionally, if the Instructors object really does need to be disposed, you can implement a Dispose method in Registration that calls the Dispose method of Instructors.

TIP
When you are dealing with classes that use external resources such as file handles, window handles, database connections, and other resources outside of the runtime, make sure that those resources are released with a finalizer and a Dispose method. However, if your classes simply manipulate other managed classes, either custom or through the Services Framework, you typically do not need to create a finalizer.

In order for other classes to call Dispose methods polymorphically in an early-bound fashion, the Services Framework exposes the IDisposable interface that your classes can implement. By implementing the interface, any client code can query for the interface and call an object's

4

OBJECT-ORIENTED
FEATURES

`Dispose` method without knowing anything else about the object. Windows Forms uses this technique to cleanup controls that are placed on a form. The `Instructors` class implementing `IDisposable` would look like Listing 4.10.

LISTING 4.10 The `Instructors` class implementing the `IDisposable` interface to allow clients to call `Dispose` polymorphically.

```
Public Class Instructors
    Implements IDisposable

    Private mflDisposed As Boolean = False

    Public Sub Dispose Implements IDisposable.Dispose
        ' Dispose() calls Finalize so that you can include
        ' all the cleanup code in one place.
        Me.Finalize()
        ' Tell the GC that the object doesn't require any cleanup
        GC.SuppressFinalize(Me)
        mflDisposed = True
    End Sub

    Overrides Protected Sub Finalize
        ' Clean up system resources
    End Sub

    Public Function GetInstructors() As DataSet
        If mflDisposed Then
            Throw ObjectDisposedException("Instructors")
        End If
    End Function
End Class
```

You'll also notice in Listing 4.10 that the class tracks a private `Boolean` variable to determine when the object was disposed. If any other method is subsequently called, such as `GetInstructors`, the `System.ObjectDisposedException` is thrown indicating to the client that the object is not usable.

Interacting with the GC

As the call to `SuppressFinalize` in the previous section makes clear, you can programmatically interact with the GC through the `System.GC` class through its shared methods.

The first method you can use to affect the GC is `Collect`. Basically, this method forces the GC to collect all unreachable objects and queue them up for finalization. Although it's possible to include this call in your code so that resources are cleaned up at a specific point in time, it is recommended that you design your classes to do explicit cleanup as discussed previously and then leave the actual collection process to the GC. In this way, resources that need to be freed early will be, and those that are less critical won't take up the extra CPU cycles being deallocated unnecessarily.

You can also call the `KeepAlive` method of `System.GC` and pass it a reference to an object you wish to not have garbage collected in the current method. When the runtime sees a call to `KeepAlive`, it assumes that the object is reachable up to the point where the `KeepAlive` method is called (in execution order within the current procedure, not necessarily in line order). In other words, the `KeepAlive` method assures that the object will be kept alive until at least directly after the call to `KeepAlive`. This method is sometimes used when referring to COM objects or other unmanaged objects so that the runtime does not inadvertently lose references to it.

Finally, you can also call the `WaitForPendingFinalizers` method, which suspends the current thread and waits for all `Finalize` methods that have been queued up to run. This is seldom used because this operation could take some time and block the current thread. In fact, `WaitForPendingFinalizers` is not assured ever to return (because the finalization process could trigger another garbage collection, *ad infinitum*) and so should be left safely alone.

Resurrection

As mentioned in Chapter 1, the runtime also allows objects to be re-referenced from within their `Finalize` methods. If this occurs, the object is said to be *resurrected* because it will not be deallocated and is now once again reachable. For example, assume that the `Finalize` method of the `Registration` class includes a line of code that passes a reference to the object using the `Me` keyword to another class or to a public variable within the application. In this case, the original variable used to refer to the `Registration` object would be set to `Nothing`; however, the object itself would still be alive and could be referenced through the new class or variable. The object is then said to be resurrected and can be used normally with the exception that the `Finalize` method will not run a second time. To allow it to run again, you must call the `ReRegisterForFinalize` method of the GC, passing in the `Me` keyword. The code for implementing the `Registration` class with resurrection is as follows:

```
Dim objHolder as Registration

Public Class Registration
    Private mIns As Instructors

    Public Sub New(ByRef obj As Instructors)
        mIns = obj
    End Sub
```

```
Protected Overrides Sub Finalize()
    mIns.Dispose()

    ' Resurrect
    objHolder = Me
    GC.ReRegisterForFinalize(Me)
End Sub
End Class
```

As a final note, keep in mind that as in this case shown here with `mIns`, if the resurrected class contains references to other objects, those references will also be resurrected.

Obviously, the situations in which you'd want to use resurrection are very limited, and as a general rule it should be avoided.

Weak References

The final way in which you can interact with the GC is to utilize *weak references*. Basically, as I discussed in Chapter 1, a weak reference is a reference to an object instance that can be collected by the GC if it deems that resources are scarce. In other words, by creating a weak reference, you are giving permission to the GC to collect the object even though you are still holding a reference to it, albeit a weak one. Of course, weak references imply the existence of strong references. A strong reference is simply one that is created with a standard variable using the `New` operator.

The idea behind weak references is to allow your application to hold references to many easily reconstructable objects without permanently consuming large amounts of memory. Obviously, the higher the cost of re-creating the object, the less likely it will be that you'll choose to use weak references. However, when you use a weak reference, there are a few coding conventions that must be followed.

To create a weak reference, you create an instance of the `System.WeakReference` class and pass it a strong reference to the object you want to hold. For example, the following code snippet creates a strong reference to the `Instructors` class followed by a weak reference:

```
Dim oIns As New Instructors
Dim wrIns As New WeakReference(oIns,False)
```

At this point, the `oIns` variable can go out of scope or otherwise become unreachable and the `Instructors` object will still be alive as long as the GC has not determined that it needs to reclaim memory by deallocating it. In the meantime, the `wrIns` variable can be passed around and perhaps stored in a collection for later use. The second argument to the `WeakReference` constructor shown earlier indicates whether the object should be available until the object is collected (`False`) or until it is actually finalized (`True`).

When the weakly referenced object needs to be used, you'll need to cast it to the correct type; however, you can first check to be sure that the object still exists by checking the `Target` property of the object. If the property is not `Nothing`, you can use the `CType` function to once again create a strong reference to the object.

```
Dim obj As Instructors

If Not wrIns.Target Is Nothing Then
    obj = CType(wrIns.Target, Instructors)
End If
```

Alternatively, you can check the `IsAlive` property to determine whether the object is still available, although doing so is discouraged because there is no guarantee that the object will still be alive even as soon as the very next statement.

At this point, the GC will not collect the object since it is reachable with a strong reference, and you can continue to work with it.

Summary

Because the object-oriented features of the CLR are exposed in VB .NET, developers can now access the extended power inherent in those features. Although this adds nominal complexity to the language and developers must be aware of how to properly use these features, features such as delegates and implementation inheritance can promote both code reuse and polymorphic programming.

In the next chapter, I'll discuss the changes in compilation and deployment that allow you to distribute and secure your code.

4

OBJECT-ORIENTED FEATURES

Packaging, Deployment, and Security

IN THIS CHAPTER

Two of the more difficult and time-consuming aspects of software development on the Windows platform are packaging and deployment. Fortunately, the Common Language Runtime (CLR), through its process of locating and binding assemblies—referred to as *Fusion*—has the ancillary effect of making packaging and deployment much simpler. Fusion alleviates complicated and error-prone registry manipulation, in addition to alleviating the "DLL Hell" that resulted when installing one application caused another not to function. In turn, Fusion simplifies the process of uninstallation as well.

In this chapter, we'll review and drill-down on these concepts first introduced in Chapter 1, "The Microsoft .NET Architecture," before moving on to how VS .NET supports project types for packaging a VB .NET application. Along the way, we'll also discuss several utilities shipped in the .NET SDK, among them a utility that allows server-based resources such as performance counters and Windows services to be installed.

Finally, the chapter ends with a brief discussion of the different ways that code can be secured in .NET, and how this differs from traditional methods. Although a discussion of security might seem incongruent with deployment, the two are actually closely related because the security policies in place affect how an application can be deployed.

> **NOTE**
>
> All code listings and supplemental material for this chapter can be found on the book's Web site at samspublishing.com.

Packaging and Deployment Concepts

This section reviews and provides more detail on the packaging and deployment concepts you need to be familiar with in .NET.

Assemblies Revisited

As you'll recall from Chapter 1, an *assembly* is the smallest unit of deployment and reuse available in .NET. When you compile a project in VB .NET, you are producing an assembly, either an EXE or DLL, that can be reused and deployed. Although the assembly can contain many source code files (.vb), the single resulting PE file contains the *metadata*, analogous to a type library in COM, which fully describes any types (classes) you define within the assembly. Therefore, an application that is self-contained by not relying on external components has no registration requirements and is said to be a "*no-impact application.*" Simply put, this means that the application can be installed on a machine that has the CLR and Services Framework already installed simply by copying it to a local directory.

However, most applications of any complexity rely on external components. If those components are found in managed assemblies, you reference them using the References dialog in VS .NET or the /r switch when using the command-line compiler. Information about these assemblies, including which version to use, is stored in the assembly's *manifest*, packaged in the PE file. Both the metadata and the manifest can be viewed using the ILDasm utility.

> **NOTE**
>
> You can also create assemblies that contain multiple PE files (modules) that were previously compiled. We will discuss this topic further later in the chapter.

Private and Shared Assemblies

When an assembly is referenced in a VB .NET project, the assembly can either be public or private. Private assemblies are created by default in VS .NET and are, as the name implies, private to the application that references them. As a result, they must reside in the same directory as the assembly that references them or in the set of paths searched by the Fusion process. By default, VS .NET copies a private assembly to the application path automatically when it is referenced. This also can be controlled through the Properties window viewed when the referenced assembly is highlighted in the Solution Explorer. In addition to displaying version information about the assembly, the Copy Local option can be used to override the local copy.

> **CAUTION**
>
> Overriding the Copy Local option can cause problems at runtime if the path searched by the Fusion process cannot find the assembly.

The implication for deployment is simply that you need to ensure that private assemblies get deployed to the application directory or a directory that will be searched. Referenced assemblies are also often placed in a subdirectory of the application directory, as noted in Chapter 1. Because the referenced assemblies themselves are self-describing, complete with their own metadata and manifest, the entire application can be copied to a new machine by keeping the relative pathing in order. This is sometimes referred to as *XCOPY deployment* because only the application directory and its subdirectories need to be copied to the new machine. Obviously, this also implies that the application can be uninstalled by only deleting its directory.

The use of private assemblies by default is the reverse of the situation with COM components written in VB 6.0. In that context, components are publicly available and can be referenced by any application on the machine. Defaulting to private assemblies ensures controlled sharing of code by making the sharing process an explicit activity.

5

PACKAGING, DEPLOYMENT, AND SECURITY

> **NOTE**
>
> In addition to providing controlled sharing of code when private assemblies are used, the DLL Hell issue vanishes because two applications cannot point to the same binary at runtime. However, as you'll see in the next section, the CLR also provides a more subtle way to both share assemblies and run multiple versions side-by-side.

Although private assemblies are useful in a variety of applications, often it is advantageous to be able to share assemblies between applications. Typical examples include creating shareable Web Server controls or assemblies that access Component Services to provide the business or data services of a distributed application. In fact, the assemblies of the Services Framework themselves need to be shared on a machine.

Global Assembly Cache

To allow an assembly to be shared, .NET creates a machinewide code cache on each machine that has the CLR installed. As discussed in Chapter 1, this cache is called the *Global Assembly Cache (GAC)*. The interesting aspect of the GAC is that it can contain multiple versions of the same assembly and as such allows applications on the same machine to load different versions. In addition, assemblies placed in the GAC are found more quickly by the CLR and consume less memory because the operating system only loads the code once even if multiple applications reference it. The GAC also provides some additional security because only members of the local Administrators group can add and delete from the GAC.

To place an assembly in the cache, you can use the following methods:

- Using the installer from within the Windows Installer as exposed by VS .NET
- Using the command-line utility GACUtil.exe from the .NET SDK
- Using Windows Explorer to drag and drop the assembly into the cache
- Using the .NET Admin Tool (a Microsoft Management Console snap-in)

Although the first option in the preceding list is preferred for production releases of an application, it will be discussed more thoroughly later in the chapter. The second option often is used during development. For example, the command line:

```
gacutil.exe /i EducationData.dll
```

installs the EducationData assembly into the cache. Analogously, the /u switch can be used to uninstall the assembly. However, simply using the /u switch uninstalls all versions of the assembly. To avoid this, you can use the ver, loc, and PK switches to specify the particular version, culture, and public key of the assembly to uninstall as follows:

```
gacutil.exe /u EducationData.dll, ver=1.0.0.1,loc="en",PK=45e343aae33223ca
```

To graphically manipulate the cache, you can use either the Windows shell extension (`shfusion.dll`) or the .NET Admin Tool. The shell extension is not installed by default, and so should be placed in the .NET Framework directory (*windowsdir*\Microsoft.Net\ Framework*version*) and then registered using Regsvr32.exe. Navigating to the *windowsdir*\ assembly directory then activates the extension and displays the contents of both the Native Image Cache (referred to as Zap) and the GAC, as shown in Figure 5.1.

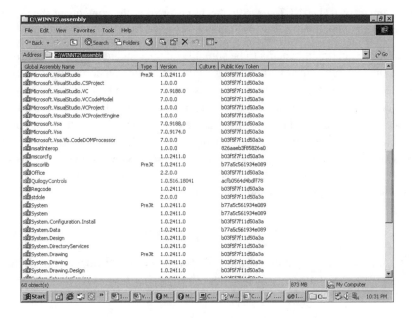

FIGURE 5.1

The Global Assembly Cache as viewed through the shell extension.

By right-clicking on an assembly, its properties can be viewed, or the assembly can be deleted. The .NET Admin Tool is a Microsoft Management Console snap-in (`mscorcfg.msc`) that displays not only the GAC, but also information on configured assemblies, remoting, and security. It also can be found in the .NET Framework directory and executed simply by double-clicking on it.

Strong Names

As you probably noticed in Figure 5.1, the GAC stores a public key token for the assembly. This information is required for the assembly to be stored in the GAC and in part (along with the name, version number, culture information, and digital signature) makes up the identity of the assembly. As mentioned in Chapter 1, together this is referred to as a *strong name*. Creating a strong name for the assembly ensures that it is globally unique by relying on unique key pairs. In particular, a strong name provides the following benefits:

- Name uniqueness   Even if two assemblies with, for example, the same text name and version are created, they will be different in the eyes of the CLR if they are generated with different private keys.

- Version compatibility   Generating a subsequent version of the assembly using the same private key allows the user of the assembly to be sure that it was created by the same publisher as the original version.

- Binary Integrity   The .NET security checks ensure that the contents of the assembly have not been altered since it was compiled.

Although these are important benefits to be sure, they do not include the notion of trust. In other words, an assembly signed with a strong name can ensure version compatibility, but it cannot be used to ensure, for example, that the assembly about to be loaded came from Quilogy. To do so, you also need to sign the assembly using an Authenticode digital signature. Although beyond the scope of this book, this can be done in the .NET SDK using the signcode utility. After an assembly is signed with an Authenticode signature, administrators can create policies that allow it to be downloaded and loaded on users' machines. As discussed later in the chapter, the signature becomes part of the *evidence* used by the CLR's class loader to determine whether the assembly should be loaded.

> **NOTE**
>
> Because creating a strong name for an assembly implies that you want to derive the benefits of using a strong name, assemblies that use them can only reference other strong-named assemblies. Not doing so would allow DLL conflicts to once again crop up.

To sign an assembly with a strong name, you can either use the Assembly Generation tool (Al.exe) that ships with the SDK, or a set of attributes found in the System.Reflection namespace. First, however, you must generate a public-private key pair using the Strong Name tool (Sn.exe) from the SDK. For example, to generate a key pair and save it to the file QuilogyEducation.snk, you would use the following command-line:

```
sn.exe -k QuilogyEducation.snk
```

> **TIP**
>
> Other switches are available with the Strong Name tool to change with which cryptographic service provider (CSP) the key pair is generated. These switches also provide options for extracting the key from a file and using delayed signing.

After the key pair is generated, you can sign the assembly. To sign an assembly at the command-line using the Assembly Generation tool, simply use the \keyfile switch and pass the path to the file that contains the key pair.

More typically, the specification of the key file will be done in VS .NET using attributes. As mentioned in Chapter 1, VS .NET includes an AssemblyInfo.vb file with each project that provides a good place for adding attributes that will become part of the assembly's manifest. The System.Reflection namespace exposes a set of assembly attributes that can be placed here. To illustrate their use, consider the AssemblyInfo.vb file shown in Listing 5.1.

Listing 5.1 AssemblyInfo.vb. This file shows the use of assembly attributes to, among other things, specify a strong name.

```
Imports System.Reflection
Imports System.Runtime.InteropServices

<Assembly: AssemblyTitle("Quilogy Education Data Access")>
<Assembly: AssemblyDescription("Quilogy Data Access")>
<Assembly: AssemblyCompany("Quilogy")>
<Assembly: AssemblyProduct("Education System")>
<Assembly: AssemblyCopyright("Quilogy, Inc. 2001")>
<Assembly: AssemblyTrademark("")>
<Assembly: AssemblyCulture("")>
<Assembly: AssemblyKeyFile("QuilogyEducation.snk")>

<Assembly: AssemblyVersion("1.0.0.*")>
<Assembly: ComVisible(True)>
```

> **Note**
>
> Note that the actual name of the class that defines the attribute is appended with "Attribute". For example, the class that defines the assembly title is actually called AssemblyTitleAttribute, although the short-hand reference that drops the "Attribute" can be used for brevity.

In Listing 5.1, the attributes include typical descriptive information about the assembly, its title, company, product, and copyright. However, the key to creating a strong name is to include the AssemblyKeyFile attribute and passing in its constructor the relative location of the key file.

> **NOTE**
>
> Alternatively, you can use the `AssemblyKeyName` attribute to specify the name of the container that is storing the key pair. A key pair can be stored in the container using switches in the Strong Name tool.

In this example, the `AssemblyVersion` attribute also is used to specify the version information. Note that the asterisks can be used for the third and fourth portions of the version number (build and revision), and they will be autogenerated at compile time.

Although the technique shown here is fine for small organizations or individual development, the key pair used to sign code in a large organization is often closely guarded. In this case, developers typically have access to the public key while the private key remains in the hands of only a few. In terms of generating strongly named assemblies, access to the public key during development is critical because any assemblies referencing the strongly named assembly must contain the token of the public key. To enable development to continue, .NET also supports delayed or partial signing.

As implied by the name, partial signing reserves space at compile time in the PE file for the strong name signature. The signature can then be added later. In the meantime, other assemblies can reference the strongly named assembly. To implement delayed signing, the `AssemblyInfo.vb` file can reference the `AssemblyDelaySign` attribute and pass `True` to the constructor. This implies that the key file referenced in `AssemblyKeyFile` contains only the public key (which can be done using a switch of the Strong Name tool).

After the assembly is partially signed, it must also have its verification turned off. This is because a partially constructed strong name is not valid and will not pass the .NET security checks as discussed previously. To bypass verification, use the Strong Name tool's `-Vr` switch as follows:

```
sn.exe -Vr EducationData.dll
```

At some point later, the assembly is ostensibly passed to the group that has access to the private key where the group signs it with the strong name using the `-R` switch as follows:

```
sn.exe -R EducationData.dll QuilogyEducation.snk
```

where `QuilogyEducation.snk` contains the private key. VS .NET also provides a UI to set the key file and key container, and support delayed signing. By right-clicking on the name of the project in the Solution Explorer and selecting Properties, the property pages dialog is invoked. These settings can be accessed through the Common Properties, Strong Name pane as shown in Figure 5.2.

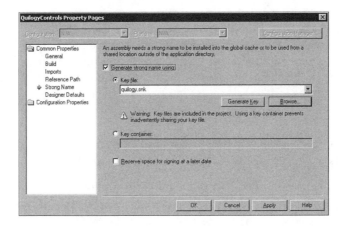

FIGURE 5.2
This properties dialog enables setting or creating a key file to create a strong name in addition to providing support for delayed signing.

In addition to specifying the file that contains the key information, a key file can be generated by clicking the Generate Key button.

Side-by-Side Execution

As discussed in Chapter 1, the CLR's class loader attempts to load a shared assembly using a variety of information, including the version number, GAC, and policy information found in the application, publisher, and machine configuration files.

> **TIP**
>
> The results (and supporting details) of the Fusion process can be seen through a graphical utility in the .NET SDK called the Fusion Bind Log Viewer (`fuslogvw.exe`), which is not installed by default. In addition, you must configure a registry setting for logging to take place. See the online documentation for details.

Keep in mind that the entire reason this careful process is undertaken is to allow side-by-side execution. In other words, for multiple applications to load different versions of the same assembly, the class loader must be careful to load the correct version.

> **TIP**
>
> Remember that simply because the CLR allows side-by-side execution does not mean that all assemblies will function correctly in this mode. For example, consider an

> assembly that caches data in a file during processing. The developer of that assembly must take care not to allow multiple versions of the assembly to try and use the same file. In the same way, an assembly that reads and writes data to the system registry might get confused if more than one version of the assembly modifies the registry entries.

Although the information used by the class loader can be specified by manually editing the configuration files, it is more convenient to use the .NET Admin Tool.

In addition to manipulating the GAC, the .NET Admin Tool allows you to create application- and machinewide configurations for managed applications. In other words, you can bind policies and turn them on and off using this tool rather than edit the files themselves. For example, to configure a managed EXE, you can simply add it to the Applications folder in the .NET Admin Tool by right-clicking on the folder and selecting Add. The application is then scanned for any dependent assemblies, and an application configuration file is created in the application directory. To configure a dependent assembly, simply right-click the child Configured Assemblies icon and select Add. The assembly then can be selected from the cache, from the dependent lists, or entered manually. Once entered, the assembly's binding policy and codebase can be created by right-clicking on the assembly and selecting Properties. Figure 5.3 shows the resulting dialog.

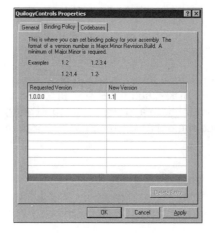

FIGURE 5.3
This properties dialog enables automatic creation of binding redirection information.

In Figure 5.3, the Binding Policy tab is selected to configure the `bindingRedirect` tag. In this example, all requests for version 1.0.0.0 of the QuilogyControls assembly will redirect to any version 1.1 assembly. Note that asterisks are not required in this case. In the associated application configuration file, the following entries are made:

```xml
<?xml version="1.0"?>
<configuration>
  <runtime>
    <assemblyBinding xmlns="urn:schemas-microsoft-com:asm.v1">
      <dependentAssembly>
        <assemblyIdentity name="QuilogyControls"
          publicKeyToken="acfb0564d4bdff78" />
        <publisherPolicy apply="yes" xmlns="" />
        <bindingRedirect oldVersion="1.0.0.0" newVersion="1.1" xmlns="" />
      </dependentAssembly>
    </assemblyBinding>
  </runtime>
</configuration>
```

In an analogous fashion, the `Machine.config` file can be modified by adding configured assemblies to the Configured Assemblies entry under the My Computer icon.

Multifile Assembly Creation

Only single-file assemblies can be created by VB .NET. However, in some instances, you might want to create an assembly that consists of multiple modules compiled separately. The most obvious reason to do so is to be able to include a module written in another language such as VC#. In this way, multiple developers can work on the same project in their language of choice. Although each developer could simply compile his code into an assembly, doing so would have the effect of making some types public that shouldn't be, and might not be desired if you want to enforce versioning of the entire assembly.

> **TIP**
>
> Another good reason to create a multifile assembly is to optimize downloading. For example, when running an application over the Internet, you could put infrequently used types into a module that is only downloaded when needed.

To compile a module, you must first use the command-line compiler for the particular language. Particularly, the `/t` (target) switch must be set to module. For example, the command-line

```
csc.exe /t:module QuilogyTools.cs
```

compiles the VC# module in the `QuilogyTools.cs` file into the PE file `QuilogyTools.netmodule`. Keep in mind that the resulting module contains MSIL instructions and all the metadata. However, it is not an assembly and therefore does not contain a manifest, nor can it be loaded independently by the CLR. This module then can be compiled into a VB .NET component using the VB .NET command-line compiler as follows:

```
vbc.exe EducationData.vb AssemblyInfo.vb /t:library /out:EducationData.dll
        /addmodule:QuilogyTools.netmodule
```

In this case, the VB .NET source code files, `EducationData.vb` and `AssemblyInfo.vb`, are to be compiled into a library (DLL) called `EducationData.dll`. The `/addmodule` switch includes the `QuilogyTools.netmodule` PE file in the build. Keep in mind that the manifest for the assembly is located in the `EducationData.dll` file and that the assembly is still physically represented by two files.

Alternatively, if all the code is already compiled into modules, you can use the Assembly Generation tool (`Al.exe`) to create the assembly as follows:

```
al.exe QuilogyTools.netmodule EducationData.netmodule /target:lib
        /out:EducationData.dll
```

PreJITing Your Code

Until this point, the discussion has assumed that when the CLR loads and executes your assembly, it does so by using JIT compilation, as described in Chapter 1. In fact, although that is the default mode of operation, the .NET SDK also ships with a command-line utility called the Native Image Generator (`Ngen.exe`) that allows you to PreJIT your code to a native image.

Compiling code to a native image at install time or prior to it improves performance by reducing the load time of your application. For example, several of the core assemblies in the Services Framework, such as `System` and `System.Windows.Forms`, have been PreJITed. Having said that, most applications perform well enough with the combination of the PreJITed system assemblies and JIT compiled custom code. In fact, PreJITing is only recommended when your own performance tests indicate that doing so will provide a substantial benefit. This most often occurs with client-side applications, such as Windows Forms executables.

To PreJIT your code, you must run the `Ngen.exe` utility and pass it the location of the assemblies to natively compile. The utility can compile multiple DLLs or one EXE per invocation.

> **NOTE**
>
> If an EXE is specified on the command line, it must be first in the list.

For example, to natively compile the `xmltransfer.exe` executable you could use the command line:

```
Ngen.exe xmltransfer.exe
```

The resulting native image is dependent on the CPU type, the version of the operating system, the identity of the assembly, and the identities of any dependent assemblies. When the native image is generated, it is not placed in the application directory, but rather in a special cache (referred to as the native image cache or the Zap) located under the *windowsdir*\assembly\ NativeImages1_*frameworkversion* directory. During the Fusion process, the CLR also checks this cache for the presence of a native image, and might load it.

The PreJITed native images then can be viewed using the GACUTIL.exe utility with the /l switch, the Windows Explorer shell extension (in the Type column will appear "PreJit"), or the .NET Admin Tool under the Global Assembly Cache node (they'll have a different icon and cache type of "Zap").

Although the CLR will attempt to load a PreJITed image, it might not always be able to do so. For example, if the CLR determines that the MSIL in the assembly has been modified with respect to the native image, the CLR will revert to JIT compiling the MSIL rather than using the "stale" native image. In addition, if any dependent assemblies have been modified, the native image cannot be used. This implies that even if PreJIT is used, the original assembly also must be present on the machine and in the appropriate location for the CLR to find it.

Finally, this version of .NET does not automatically clean up stale native images, nor does it do any automatic creation or deletion. To delete a native image, you can use the context menus in the Windows Explorer or .NET Admin Tool, or the /delete switch of the Ngen utility like so:

```
Ngen.exe /delete xmltransfer.exe
```

Packaging and Deployment Options

Because .NET includes the concepts of self-describing components, private assemblies, and side-by-side execution, packaging and deployment are simplified. In this section, the three most common methods used to package and deploy a managed application are discussed. In addition the section covers the .NET SDK utility that allows server-based resources to be installed.

Deployment Scenarios

There are essentially three different techniques you can use to package and deploy managed code, all of which are supported directly by VS .NET. These include using XCOPY deployment, compressed CAB files, and the Windows Installer. Each is appropriate in particular situations and is discussed in the following sections.

XCOPY Deployment

The simplest way to package and deploy a managed application is to simply not package it at all. As discussed previously in the chapter, if your application uses only private assemblies and assemblies from the Services Framework that ship with .NET, the entire application can be installed on a target machine simply by copying the application directory and its subdirectories. This is referred to as *XCOPY deployment*.

XCOPY deployment is well suited for deploying ASP.NET applications. For example, if the Web project uses only private assemblies, you can easily move it from a development server to test, staging, and ultimately production simply by copying the virtual directory to the new server. In fact, because you can fully control whether the assemblies in your application are shared—and if they are, what versions the application will use through policy—you can run two versions of your ASP.NET application side-by-side on the same Web server. For example, you might want to run separate test and staging versions of your ASP.NET application on the same Web server so that developers can integrate code in the test version, and so it can be certified in the staging environment.

Further, XCOPY deployment also implies that you can deploy only a subset of the files to the target machine if needed. Depending on the runtime host for the application, deploying new versions of DLLs to the application directory does not necessarily require the application to be shut down. As discussed in Chapter 10, "Building Web Forms," the runtime host for ASP.NET behaves in this way, and Web sites can be updated on-the-fly without affecting current users.

VS .NET supports XCOPY deployment for ASP.NET applications with the inclusion of the Copy Project menu option under the Project menu. Much as in Visual Interdev (VID) 6.0, the menu option invokes a dialog used to configure how the copy will take place. Unlike VID 6.0, however, the dialog allows you to optionally copy directly to a file share rather than going through the FrontPage server extensions. In addition, you can copy only those files needed to run the application, only the project files, or the project files and any other files in the directory.

Cabinet Files

To more easily package multiple files and to speed up code downloads from the Internet, your application, or components in it, can be placed into *cabinet files*. Cabinet files are compressed files with a .cab extension, and typically contain individual assemblies that are then pointed to by codebase hints in the application or machine policies. For example, you could deploy a new version of a Windows Form simply by including it in a cabinet file and placing it on the Internet. The user of the application could then change the policy, and the new form would be downloaded the next time the application was executed.

To support the creation of cabinet files, VS .NET includes a project template called Cab Project under the Setup and Deployment Projects folder. You can create a new cabinet file simply by selecting a new project in VS .NET and navigating to the template. Adding files to the cabinet file can be accomplished by right-clicking on the cabinet file in the Solution Explorer and choosing Add.

The cabinet file itself also exposes some properties that can be accessed in the properties window when the cabinet file is highlighted in the Solution Explorer. The Name, FriendlyName, and Version properties are self-explanatory; however, clicking on the WebDependencies property invokes a dialog box that allows you to add the URL, FriendlyName, and Version of other cabinet files. This is useful because the files pointed to in this list are automatically downloaded and installed when the cabinet file is run.

Windows Installer

The most robust way to package and deploy your application is by using the Windows Installer. Although the details of the Windows Installer are beyond the scope of this book, VS .NET includes two project templates in the Setup and Deployment Projects folder to automate the creation of msi files: Setup Project and Web Setup Project.

> **NOTE**
>
> VS.NET also includes a template to create Merge Module projects. These projects allow you to create reusable setup components to share setup code between Windows Installer packages analogous to DLLs that allow the sharing of code between applications. A merge module is packaged as a .msm file, is self-contained, and includes all dependencies for the included files. Merge modules can't be installed alone, but can be added to a Windows Installer by right-clicking on the project and clicking Add, Merge Module.

Typically, the Setup Project template is for use with Windows Forms applications, whereas the Web Setup Project is for use with ASP.NET applications. The primary difference is that the Web Setup Project exposes a special folder type that knows how to automatically configure IIS settings. To illustrate the use of the Web Setup Project, a brief example will be given.

Although XCOPY deployment works well for many Web applications, there are scenarios where you need to perform a more complex and professional installation. For example, when you need to install assemblies in the GAC, manipulate the registry, or ensure that the target system is configured correctly, you should use the Web Setup Project template.

When you create a new project using the template, the project exposes six different views that can be accessed by right-clicking on the project name in the Solution Explorer and selecting View. Basically, views are the components that make up the installation package and can be used to customize it. The views are shown in Table 5.1.

TABLE 5.1 Windows Installer Project Views

View	Description
File System	Specifies how the file system on the target machine will be modified. Includes pointers to special folders including the Web Application and Global Assembly Cache folders.
Registry	Specifies how the registry on the target machine will be modified. Includes pointers to the appropriate keys and allows you to define new keys.
File Types	Specifies new file associations to be installed on the target machine.
User Interface	Specifies the flow of dialog boxes presented to the user during the installation process categorized as Start, Progress, and End. Allows you to add up to 14 additional types of dialogs to display and collect information from the user.
Custom Actions	Specifies the execution of executable and script files during the various phases of the installation (Install, Commit, Rollback, Uninstall).
Launch Conditions	Specifies the requirements that must be met on the target machine. It allows you to search for particular files in the file system, for registry entries, or for a previously installed component and then create a condition on it.

The most important view is the File System view, where you specify the files to be installed on the target machine. This is done by simply right-clicking on the folder in the list and clicking Add. Figure 5.4 shows the File System view with files added for a Quilogy Education Web site.

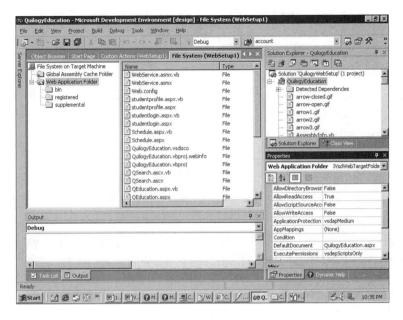

FIGURE 5.4
A Web Setup Project in the File System view. Note that files have been added to the Web Application Folder.

When you add assemblies to the File System view, they are checked for dependencies, and those dependent assemblies are added to the list. You can exclude dependent assemblies by setting their `Exclude` property to `True`.

Additional target directories are predefined and can be accessed by right-clicking on the root node in the view and selecting Add Special Folder. Some of these special folders include Program Files, Windows, Common Files, and System.

One particular aspect to notice in Figure 5.4 is that because the Web Application Folder is highlighted, its properties are shown in the Properties window. Note that this special folder contains properties that allow you to configure the IIS properties. In addition to the properties shown here, you also can configure the name of the virtual directory, logging, and port.

In this case, the ASP.NET application also includes subdirectories (bin, registered, supplemental), which are defined simply by adding Web Folders under the Web Application Folder. Obviously, these folders can contain their own files and their own IIS configurations.

Although space prohibits a discussion of the Registry, User Interface, File Types, and Custom Actions views, the Launch Conditions view is particularly interesting. Figure 5.5 shows this view and its associated properties dialog.

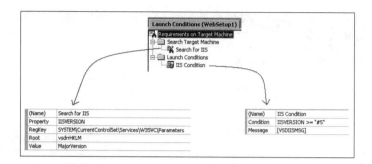

FIGURE 5.5

A portion of the properties windows for both the target search and launch condition used to check for the existence of IIS.

As you'll notice, the `Search for IIS` search target is used to specify a search for a particular registry entry. Additional search types include searching for files and other Windows Installer components. In this case, the properties determine that the `MajorVersion` value of the `Parameters` key is to be returned. The `Property` property is set to `IISVERSION` and is then used in the launch condition.

Launch conditions can be thought of as simple expressions that abort the installation and display a message when they do not evaluate to `True`. In this case, the IIS Condition simply tests the `IISVERSION` property for a value of 5 or greater using the expression `IISVERSION >= "#5"` in the `Condition` property. In addition to checking the IIS version, the Web Setup Project also comes preconfigured with launch conditions that check for a particular file on the file system, a registry entry, a Windows Installer component, and the presence of the .NET Framework. The latter will be particularly useful as managed applications are installed for the first time on target machines whose operating systems do not ship with the CLR.

Installing Server Resources

Managed applications can consist not only of assemblies, registry entries, and ancillary files that must be installed on the target machine, but also associated resources such as performance counters, message queues, services, and event logs. Often, these resources must be created during the installation to ensure that the application functions correctly.

Fortunately, the Services Framework includes an elegant solution to installing these server-based resources in the `System.Configuration.Install` namespace. Simply put, the namespace exposes an `Installer` class that can be derived from within an assembly. This class provides the framework for installing specific components derived from `ComponentInstaller`. Figure 5.6 shows the partial namespace hierarchy for specific classes derived from `ComponentInstaller` and used to install event logs, performance counters, message queues, and services.

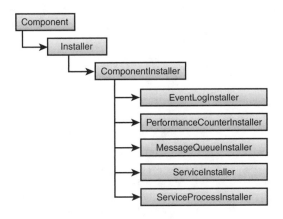

Figure 5.6

The partial hierarchy of the System.Configuration.Install *namespace.*

For example, from within your assembly, you can create a class derived from Installer called myInstaller. Within this class, you can override the Install, Commit, Rollback, and Uninstall methods to include custom code performed when the installer is invoked. However, in the constructor of myInstaller, you also can configure and add one or more objects derived from ComponentInstaller to the Installers collection (such as EventLogInstaller or MessageQueueInstaller). These objects, typically contained in the namespaces they represent, such as System.Messaging, also are installed when myInstaller is invoked. Listing 5.2 presents a simple installer class that installs a message queue.

Listing 5.2 Using an Installer. This class shows how a message queue would be installed.

```
Imports System.ComponentModel
Imports System.Configuration.Install
Imports System.Messaging
Public Class <RunInstaller(True)> myInstaller : Inherits Installer

    Private WithEvents mMSMQInstaller As MessageQueueInstaller

    Public Sub New()
        MyBase.New
        ' Instantiate installers
        mMSMQInstaller = New MessageQueueInstaller()

        With mMSMQInstaller
            .Label = "QuilgoyDocQueue"
            .UninstallAction = UninstallAction.Remove
            .UseJournalQueue = True
```

LISTING 5.2   Continued

```
            .Transactional = True
            .Path = ".\Private$\QuilogyDocs"
        End With

        Installers.Add(mMSMQInstaller)
    End Sub

    ' Catch the events
    Public Sub mMSMQInstaller_AfterInstall(ByVal sender As Object, _
        ByVal e As System.Configuration.Install.InstallEventArgs) _
            Handles mMSMQInstaller.AfterInstall
        Me.Context.LogMessage( _
            "The QuilogyDocQueue was installed successfully.")
    End Sub

    Public Sub mMSMQInstaller_AfterUninstall(ByVal sender As Object, _
        ByVal e As System.Configuration.Install.InstallEventArgs) _
            Handles mMSMQInstaller.AfterUninstall
        Me.Context.LogMessage( _
            "The QuilogyDocQueue was uninstalled successfully.")
    End Sub

    Public Overrides Sub Install(ByVal state As IDictionary)
        MyBase.Install(state)
        ' Add custom actions here
    End Sub

    Public Overrides Sub UnInstall(ByVal state As IDictionary)
        ' Add custom actions here
        MyBase.UnInstall(state)
    End Sub
End Class
```

Notice that in addition to deriving from `Installer`, the `RunInstaller` attribute for the class must be set to `True` or the installer will not be able to be invoked. The constructor of the class is used to create the `MessageQueueInstaller` component and set its properties appropriately.

> **NOTE**
>
> More information about message queues and how they can be used can be found in Chapter 14, "Integrating with the Enterprise."

> **TIP**
>
> You can derive your own classes from `ComponentInstaller` to create installation components for your own assemblies. This can be useful if you create a server-based application and want to encapsulate the installation of all server-based resources.

The installer is then added to the `Installers` collection using the `Add` method. This example also illustrates the handling of the `AfterInstall` and `AfterUninstall` instance events that can be used for logging or for notifying the user as to the result. Other important events include `BeforeInstall`, `BeforeUninstall`, `BeforeRollback`, `AfterRollback`, `Committed`, and `Committing`. You'll notice that the appearance of `Committed` and `Committing` events implies that the installation is transacted. In fact, you also can override the `Commit` and `Rollback` methods to complete the install transaction and restore the preinstallation state of the machine.

Note that the `AfterInstall` and `AfterUninstall` methods use the `Context` property to write a message to the log file and to the console. The `Context` property exposes an instance of the `InstallContext` class that contains information about the current installation. Typical uses of the `InstallContext` object include parsing the parameters passed into the installer into a `StringDictionary` object using the `Parameters` collection and determining whether a given parameter was activated using the `IsParameterTrue` method.

Finally, the `Install` and `Uninstall` methods are overridden so that additional installation and uninstallation code can be added. Note that the methods of the base class must be invoked first using the `MyBase` keyword to process the installers in the `Installers` collection. If your installer doesn't require the addition of custom code, you needn't override these methods.

Running the Installers

There are two techniques you can use to run the installer classes within an assembly. The first is to use the `InstallUtil.exe` command-line utility. If run against an assembly without any switches specified, this utility uses reflection (`System.Reflection` namespace) to search the assembly for any derived `Installer` classes with their `RunInstaller` attribute set to `True`. It then executes the `Install` or `Uninstall` method, depending on the command-line switch used, for each instance of `Installer` it finds. The installation occurs in a transacted manner so that all the installers must succeed. In addition, multiple assemblies can be specified on the command line.

By default, the utility creates `InstallUtil.InstallLog`, *assemblyname*`.InstallLog` (where output from the `LogMessage` method can be found), and *assemblyname*`.InstallState` log files. Optional switches can be used to uninstall (`/u`), suppress console output (`/logToConsole=false`), change the name of the *assemblyname*`.InstallLog` file

(/`logFile=`*filename*), and print the contents of the call stack to the log if an exception occurs (/`showCallStack`). As a result, a typical command-line might look as follows:

```
InstallUtil.exe /logFile=QEd.log /showCallStack
   /logToConsole=false EducationData.dll
```

The second technique you can use to install and uninstall server resources involves the `AssemblyInstaller` class. This class allows you to load an assembly, pass it command-line arguments, and then call the `Install` or `Uninstall` method to invoke the installers contained in the assembly. In this way, it is the programmatic equivalent of the `InstallUtil.exe` utility.

For example, to install the resources in the assembly reference in a variable `strAssembly`, the following code could be used:

```
Dim arCommand() As String = {"LogtoConsole=False"}
Dim oInstall As New AssemblyInstaller(strAssembly, arCommand)
oInstall.Install(Nothing)
```

Note that the constructor of `AssemblyInstaller` can be passed the location of the assembly in addition to an array of strings that specify the command line. These values can alternatively be set with the `Path` and `CommandLine` properties, and are used to build the `InstallContext` passed to the installers found in the assembly. As with `InstallUtil.exe`, only installers with the `RunInstaller` attribute set to `True` will be invoked. To determine ahead of time whether an assembly contains valid installers, you can use the shared `CheckIfInstallable` method, which raises an `Exception` if the specified assembly:

- Does not exist
- Is not a .NET assembly
- Has no public types
- Does not have at least one installer class with the required attributes
- If the installer cannot be instantiated

When configured, the `Install` method is called with an empty object representing the state of the install.

> **NOTE**
>
> Rather than pass a "u" in the command line, the `AssemblyInstaller` class exposes an `Uninstall` method.

Securing Your Code

As mentioned in Chapter 1, the idea of the Internet as the platform for development requires that new security models be developed to deal with code that can be downloaded and run remotely. In the .NET Framework, two mechanisms are provided to allow you to write code that can only be executed appropriately, referred to as *code access security* and *role-based security*.

In this section, a brief overview of the two security models is presented along with the basics of setting and administering security policy. An exhaustive discussion of .NET security will be left to other books.

Code Access Security

Simply put, code access security is the mechanism .NET uses to control access to protected resources such as the file system, the system registry, printing, calling out to unmanaged code, and accessing data through the Internet among others. As a result, the functions of code access security include

- Permissions and sets of permissions predefined by the Services Framework that represent access to various system resources
- The capability for code to request permissions it requires, would be nice to have, or does not require to run
- The capability of the CLR to determine, based on evidence, whether the code has the required permissions
- The capability of users and administrators to set policies to help determine whether the code has permissions
- The capability of developers to define custom permission sets that represent rights needed to execute their code

At the highest level, the CLR defines four policy levels that control security:

- Enterprise
- Machine
- User
- Application domain

As you can imagine, by default, the user and application domain policies are less restrictive than enterprise and machine.

Each policy contains *code groups* and *permission sets*. As the name implies, code groups are logical groupings of code, each of which contains a membership condition and a set of

5

permissions. For convenience of administration, the individual permissions are combined into predefined permission sets such as `FullTrust`, `Execution`, `Internet`, `Nothing`, and so on. Several of the sets can be edited, although typically, administrators create new permission sets for specific scenarios. Table 5.2 lists the default sets of system permissions and their associated class. Each permission is represented in the Services Framework with one or more classes that define the permission and include an attribute used in declarative and imperative security discussed later in the chapter. Many of these classes are found in the `System.Security.Permissions` namespace unless otherwise noted.

TABLE 5.2 Default System .NET Permissions

Permission	Description
Environment Variables	Access to environment variables (`EnvironmentPermission`)
File Dialog	Capability to peruse files on the file system with the dialog (`FileDialog`)
File and Folder	Access to the file system (`FileIO`)
Isolated Storage	Capability to manipulate isolated storage (`IsolatedStoragePermission` and `IsolatedStorageFilePermission`)
Reflection	Capability to view type information from other assemblies (`ReflectionPermission`)
Registry	Capability to manipulate the registry (`RegistryPermission`)
Security	Capability to perform specific security functions such as calling unmanaged code and controlling policy (`SecurityPermission`)
Windowing	Capability to create user interface elements and manipulate the Clipboard (`UIPermission`)
DNS	Capability to use DNS to resolve remote host names (`System.Net.DnsPermission`)
Printing	Capability to print to the default printer, a restricted set of printer options, no printing or unrestricted (`System.Drawing.Printing.PrintingPermission`)
Event Log	Access at four different levels to specific event logs on specific machines (`System.Diagnostics.EventLogPermission`)
Socket Access	Capability to access specific hosts and ports using TCP or UDP (`System.Net.SocketPermission`)
Web Access	Capability to access specific URLs (`System.Net.WebPermission`)
Performance Counter	Access at four different levels to specific performance counters on specific machines (`System.Diagnostics.PerformanceCounterPermission`)

TABLE 5.2   Continued

Permission	Description
Directory Services	Capability to grant, browse or write access to various paths within Active Directory (`System.DirectoryServices.DirectoryServicesPermission`)
Message Queue	Access at five different levels to message queues on specific machines (`System.Messaging.MessageQueuePermission`)
Service Controller	Access at three different levels to services on specific machines (`System.ServiceProcess.ServiceControllerPermission`)

NOTE

In addition to the permissions shown in Table 5.2, other Services Framework classes can expose permissions; for example, the `System.Data.SqlClient` namespace includes a `SqlClientPermission` class and attribute used to make sure that the calling code has an adequate security level.

At load time, the CLR uses *evidence* to determine which code groups at each policy level the assembly belongs to. The evidence includes the Authenticode signer of the code, the URL from where the code was downloaded, the strong name, the zone, and the application directory, in addition to optional custom attributes. After the CLR determines which code groups the code belongs to, it combines the permissions defined for each policy level. Finally, the CLR intersects the permissions from each policy level so that the resulting permission set contains only the permissions that all policy levels have in common.

Next, the set of permissions that has been calculated is compared to attributes defined in the code to determine which permissions are actually granted to the code. For example, code can actually demand permission to access the file system but refuse permission to print. If both permissions appear in the set of permissions calculated for the assembly, the refused permission is removed from the set. Conversely, if permission to access the file system is not granted, an exception is thrown.

Finally, if the code being loaded (assembly or class) demands specific permissions, the CLR also walks the call stack to make sure that all code executed leading up to loading the assembly also has the required permission. If not, the code is not loaded, and an exception is thrown. Although this is expensive, it is required to ensure that code without permissions cannot sneak in the back door by executing code with wider access.

For the code to request permissions, it can use either a declarative or imperative method (which we will discuss next). Although specifically requesting permissions is not required, not doing so means that your code must be ready to handle exceptions, as discussed in the following chapter, that result from insufficient permissions. In addition, requesting specific permissions helps ensure that your code is used only for the purposes it was intended and cannot be used maliciously. Finally, requesting permissions increases the probability that your code will be allowed to run if you request only the permissions it needs.

That having been said, requesting permissions adds complexity to your code and is typically best used when your code is deployed across an intranet or the Internet. For example, if you develop a component that will be shared across your organization, requesting only the specific permissions required by the component can ensure that it runs under the LocalIntranet code group.

Declarative Security

Declarative security uses attributes to place security information in the PE file. These attributes can be placed at the assembly, class, or member level and indicate both the permission and how it will interact with the code. The security attributes are ultimately derived from `CodeAccessSecurityAttribute` found in the `System.Security.Permissions` namespace and are a superset of the permissions shown in Table 5.2. For a complete list of the possible permissions, see the derived class list for the `CodeAccessSecurityAttribute` class in the online help.

The constructor of each attribute accepts one of the nine members of the `SecurityAction` enumeration that indicates how the permission will be used. For example, the declaration of the following method uses the `PrintingPermission` attribute to ensure that the method is executed only if the assembly has the capability to print from a restricted dialog box using the `Demand` member:

```
Imports System.Security.Permissions
Imports System.Drawing.Printing
<PrintingPermission(SecurityAction.Demand, _
  Level:=PrintingPermissionLevel.SafePrinting)> _
Sub PrintResults()
    ' Print results here
End Sub
```

Notice that the `SecurityAction` is specified in the constructor, whereas the `Level` property is set using the `:=` syntax because it does not exist in the constructor. In this case, if the calculated permissions do not include the capability to print, a `SecurityException` is thrown when the code is loaded. It is recommended that your code actually ask for the permissions it needs ahead of time so that in the event the permission is not granted, the exception is caught early rather than frustrating the user by failing later. It follows then that you'll typically want to demand permissions at higher levels such as the class and assembly level.

Demand Versus Assert

Demanding a permission does not mean that the code demanding it will be granted the permission. Demanding the permission is simply a means of telling the CLR at load time that the assembly, class, or method needs the permission to function correctly. If the permission is not in the calculated set or is not granted to all callers in the call stack, an exception is thrown. You can, however, bypass the latter condition by asserting the permission.

To assert a permission, use the `Assert` member of `SecurityAction`. In that case, the permission that is asserted will be added to the set. Obviously, this can lead to security holes but can be useful in situations where your assembly performs some action on a resource that its callers do not know about and would not normally perform. For example, you could create a class that must access a particular registry key for configuration information but does not present this fact to the user. Your code could then assert the permission using the `RegistryPermission` attribute so that its caller would not require the permission.

Obviously, the biggest risk is introduced if, using the previous example, your code allowed the caller to specify the registry key to manipulate, and your code then asserted the permission access it. To be able to assert permissions, your code requires the `SecurityPermission` attribute with the `SecurityPermissionFlag` set to `Assertion`, which is included by default in the `FullTrust`, `LocalIntranet`, and `Everything` permission sets.

The previous example used the `Demand` member of `SecurityAction` to request a permission. Your code can make two other types of security demands: link demands and inheritance demands. Briefly, a *link demand* is made with the `LinkDemand` member of `SecurityAction`, is checked during just-in-time compilation, and checks only the immediate caller instead of performing a stack walk. Although this is good for performance, it can open your code to security attacks. The other type of demand, an *inheritance demand*, is likewise specified with the `InheritanceDemand` member and is placed at the class level to ensure that only code with the specified permission can inherit from the class.

As mentioned earlier, an assembly also can request minimum and optional permissions in addition to refusing permissions. For example, the following declaration requests unrestricted access to the file system as an optional permission:

```
<Assembly: FileIOPermissionAttribute(SecurityAction.RequestOptional, _
    Unrestricted:=True)>
```

If the calculate permission set includes access to the file system, it will be granted to the code. However, because optional permissions imply that the permission might not be granted, your code needs to be able to gracefully handle `SecurityExceptions` thrown using a `Try` block.

5

PACKAGING,
DEPLOYMENT,
AND SECURITY

In addition to requesting specific permissions for the file system, registry, or message queues, you also can request permissions defined in one of the predefined permissions sets that are not modifiable, such as `Nothing`, `Execution`, and `FullTrust`. This is accomplished using the `PermissionSet` attribute and setting its `Name` property like so:

```
<Assembly: PermissionSetAttribute(SecurityAction.RequestMinimum, _
Name:= "FullTrust")>
```

Finally, .NET also supports five additional permissions not shown in Table 5.2 that map to the evidence used to determine membership in code access groups. For example, the following code could be used to ensure that the assembly is only loaded if it is loaded from the Quilogy Web site:

```
<Assembly: UrlIdentityPermissionAttribute(SecurityAction.RequestMinimum, _
          Url:="http://www.quilogy.com/*")>
```

Collectively, these permissions are referred to as identity permissions and also include `PublisherIdentityPermission`, `SiteIdentityPermission`, `StrongNameIdentityPermission`, and `ZoneIdentityPermission`.

Imperative Security

Whereas declarative security is handled through attributes, *imperative security* is handled through a mirrored set of classes derived from `CodeAccessPermission`. The difference is that a permission class is invoked at runtime from within a method and as such can dynamically demand and assert permissions. For example, rather than using the `FileIOPermission` attribute to request read access to a static directory, the `FileIOPermission` class can be instantiated and configured with the appropriate path as follows:

```
Dim oIO As New FileIOPermission(FileIOPermissionAccess.Read, strAppData)
```

where `strAppData` is a file path calculated from user input or read from persistent storage, such as the registry or a database.

Obviously, each permission object must be configured appropriately. To request the permission, the appropriate method must then be called. Permission classes support the methods shown in Table 5.3 derived from the base class `CodeAccessPermission`.

TABLE 5.3   Methods to Request Permissions in Classes Derived from `CodeAccessPermission`

Method	Description
Demand	Determines at runtime whether all callers higher in the stack have been granted the permission. If not, a `SecurityException` is thrown.

TABLE 5.3   Continued

Method	Description
Assert, RevertAssert	Asserts that calling code can access the resource even if it has not been granted the permission. Removed by a call to RevertAssert or RevertAll.
Deny, RevertDeny	Denies callers higher in the stack the capability to access the resources specified by the permission. Effective until the calling code returns to its caller. Removed by a call to RevertDeny or RevertAll.
PermitOnly, RevertPermitOnly	Ensures that only the resources specified by the permission can be accessed even if code higher in the call stack is granted additional permissions. Similar to Deny but more restrictive. Effective until the calling code returns to its caller and can be removed by a call to RevertPermitOnly or RevertAll.
RevertAll	Causes all previous Assert, Deny, or PermitOnly methods to be removed.

As a result, the code can demand the permission by calling the Demand method of the oIO object to initiate a stack walk like so:

```
Try
    oIO.Demand()
Catch e As SecurityException
    ' Catch the error here
End Try
```

Obviously, using imperative security requires more error handling, but also is more flexible because it can be used when the resource your code needs to access is known only at runtime.

Custom Permissions

As with most things in the Services Framework, code access security is extensible, and so you can create your own permissions, permission sets, and code groups. Typically, you would create custom permissions when the permissions exposed by the Services Framework are not granular enough. For example, although the framework includes the SqlClientPermission object to restrict general attributes when connecting to SQL Server, it obviously cannot know anything about a specific schema in the database. As a result, you could create a custom permission that allows access to data from a certain table or specific rows within a table.

To create custom permissions, you create a class that implements the IPermission interface, the easiest way being to derive from CodeAccessPermission. A class derived from

`CodeAccessPermission` must then override the `Copy`, `Intersect`, `IsSubsetOf`, `FromXml`, `ToXml`, and `Union` methods. An example of doing so can be found in the online help. In addition, if you want your permission to support declarative security, you can create a class derived from `CodeAccessSecurityAttribute` as discussed in the online help.

Handling Policies

To configure policies used with code access security, you can use the .NET Admin Tool discussed previously in this chapter. The tool includes a node for each policy level that includes nodes where you can configure the code groups, permission sets, and policy assemblies. Policy assemblies include those assemblies that implement custom permissions and as such are unrestricted on the system.

A system administrator or a user can use the .NET Admin Tool to add custom code groups, for example, to make sure that all code originating from Quilogy is treated as if it were from the local intranet. To do so, simply right-click on the `All_Code` code group at the appropriate policy level and click New. The new code group then can be configured with a membership condition of type URL, as shown in Figure 5.7. A custom permission set also can be created or one of the built-in permission sets can be assigned using the Permission Set table in the dialog.

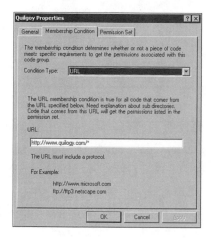

FIGURE 5.7

This dialog shows how a code group is configured. In this case, its membership is restricted to code downloaded from Quilogy.

Role-Based Security

In addition to using code access security, .NET applications also can employ role-based security. As the name implies, the idea behind role-based security is to create security filters based on the role membership of the current user or account. To expose users, accounts, and roles, the Services Framework contains the idea of *identity* and *principal* objects in the System.Security and System.Security.Principal namespaces.

Simply put, in .NET, an identity encapsulates information about the entity being validated and includes the Name (that is, the Windows account) of the entity and the AuthenticationType (that is, NTLM, Kerberos, and so on). The framework supports several identity objects that implement the IIdentity interface, the most basic of which are WindowsIdentity and GenericIdentity. The former encapsulates information about a Windows user, whereas the latter can be used to create an application-specific identity.

NOTE

Other identity objects are used in ASP.NET applications and will be covered in detail in Chapter 10.

Principal objects encapsulate identity and represent the security context of the entity including the roles of which the identity is a member. Principal objects in .NET implement the IPrincipal interface, and not surprisingly include WindowsPrincipal and GenericPrincipal. Primary members of principal objects include the Identity property, which references the identity object and IsInRole method used to determine whether the current identity is in a given role.

Many applications that run within an organization need to restrict access to Windows users based on their group membership. This can be easily accomplished using the WindowsIdentity and WindowsPrincipal objects. For example, to construct a WindowsPrincipal object, you can use the shared GetCurrent method of the WindowsIdentity class to return an identity object representing the current Windows user. The identity object can then be passed to the constructor of a WindowsPrincipal object to build the principal as shown in the following code:

```
Imports System.Security
Imports System.Security.Principal
Dim oPrincipal As WindowsPrincipal
oPrincipal = New WindowsPrincipal(WindowsIdentity.GetCurrent)
```

Building the principal in this way is required because building principal objects is expensive and not undertaken automatically by the CLR unless first instructed to do so. To make sure that the CLR attaches principal objects automatically, you can set a policy using the SetPrincipalPolicy method of the current AppDomain object. The principal can then simply be retrieved using the CurrentPrincipal property of the Thread object as follows:

```
Imports System.Security
Imports System.Threading
Imports System.Security.Principal
AppDomain.CurrentDomain.SetPrincipalPolicy(PrincipalPolicy.WindowsPrincipal)
Dim oPrincipal As WindowsPrincipal
oPrincipal = Thread.CurrentPrincipal
```

After the principal has been retrieved, you can check for group membership specifically using the overloaded `IsInRole` method of the `WindowsPrincipal` object. It supports passing the name of the group to the method as a string, using the role identification number, or the `WindowsBuiltInRole` enumeration.

However, instead of explicitly checking for roles in this way, subsequent declarative and imperative security checks can be performed analogous to the techniques used in code access security.

Although using Windows accounts is fine for intranet applications running on a Windows network, some applications must work with other authentication schemes. For example, many Internet sites store authentication information in a database. For these types of applications, the `GenericIdentity` and `GenericPrincipal` are well suited.

After an application retrieves the username via a logon page or some other means, the application can create a `GenericIdentity` object like so:

```
Dim oIdentity As GenericIdentity
oIdentity = New GenericIdentity(strUser)
```

Note that the constructor of the `GenericIdentity` object also supports an optional second `String` argument to identify the authentication type.

The `GenericPrincipal` object can then be constructed by passing to its constructor a reference to the identity object and an array of roles the user belongs to. The new principal object must then be associated with the `CurrentPrincipal` property of the current thread using the `Thread` class as follows:

```
Dim oPrincipal As GenericPrincipal
Dim arRoles() As String

' arRoles populated from a database
oPrincipal = New GenericPrincipal(oIdentity, arRoles)
Thread.CurrentPrincipal = oPrincipal
```

This is more complex than using Windows accounts because the roles must be explicitly populated and the principal object for the current thread explicitly set. In addition, in applications where the authentication information is stored in a database, the roles must also be read from the database and used to populate the `arRoles` array.

Regardless of which principal is in use, both declarative and imperative security can be used to ensure that your code is executed only by members of specific roles. We will discuss these next.

Declarative Security

To implement declarative security in a role-based environment, .NET supports the `PrincipalPermissionAttribute` class derived from `CodeAccessSecurityAttribute`. As with code-access security, this attribute can be placed at the class and member level and must be passed a member of the `SecurityAction` enumeration and, optionally, the `Name`, `Role`, `Unrestricted`, and `Authenticated` instance properties.

For example, to ensure that the `GetSales` method can only be run by members of the Sales role, the following declarative demand using only the `Role` property can be created:

```
<PrincipalPermission(SecurityAction.Demand, Role:="Sales")> _
Public Sub GetSales()
    ' Get the sales
End Sub
```

To simply make sure that the user is authenticated, the declaration can be made as follows:

```
<PrincipalPermission(SecurityAction.Demand, Authenticated:=True)>
```

> **NOTE**
>
> If declarative demands are made at both the class and member level, the member level takes precedence.

Imperative Security

To perform an imperative demand, use the `PrincipalPermission` class. Although `PrincipalPermission` is not derived from `CodeAccessPermission` because it does not actually protect any resources, it behaves similarly. For example, the overloaded constructor supports the passing of a `PermissionState` constant. Passing in the `Unrestricted` constant is equivalent only to ensuring that the user is authenticated.

The constructor also can accept the identity name and role to check, as in the following code:

```
Dim oPrincipalPerm As New PrincipalPermission(Nothing, "Sales")

Try
    oPrincipalPerm.Demand()
Catch e As SecurityException
    ' Not in the sales role
End Try
```

In this case, the first argument to the constructor is passed `Nothing` to indicate that a particular username is not required, whereas the Sales role is.

Because each instance of `PrincipalPermission` supports only a single role, it is sometimes necessary to combine objects through the `Union` method. In this way, you can allow users from multiple roles to execute the code. For example, the following code creates a demand for both the Sales and Marketing roles:

```
Dim oSalesPerm As New PrincipalPermission(Nothing, "Sales")
Dim oMarketingPerm As New PrincipalPermission(Nothing, "Marketing")

oMarketingPerm.Union(oSalesPerm).Demand()
```

Summary

This chapter focused on the .NET concepts related to deployment and security. In many ways, deployment has been simplified because of the self-describing nature of components created in VB .NET. This, coupled with support for the Windows Installer built into VS .NET, should make packaging and deployment simpler.

The same cannot be said, however, for security. The need for protecting computers that regularly download and run code from the Internet requires .NET to implement a more sophisticated security model. Although these concepts will take some adjustments for VB developers, remember that in many instances, the default policies will be sufficient as long as your code handles exceptions appropriately.

The capability to handle exceptions in an elegant way through the use of structured exception handling also is a new concept to VB developers. This, along with the new debugging and tracing features, will be discussed in the next chapter.

Error Handling and Debugging

IN THIS CHAPTER

In any software development effort, it's important to be able to find and correct errors in your code. This is particularly true of distributed applications that perform mission-critical functions within your organization or are accessed directly by your customers over the Internet. Typically, these errors fall into one of three types:

- Syntax errors
- Runtime errors
- Logic errors

Although syntax errors are addressed at compile time and can be avoided through the use of Option Explicit and Option Strict, both runtime and logic errors often are more subtle and require other techniques to ferret out. VB .NET and VS .NET support several techniques for addressing both runtime and logic errors.

First, this chapter discusses the two techniques you can use in VB .NET for handling exceptions generated at runtime that might arise from unexpected user input or changed conditions within the environment the application is running. Second, the chapter highlights the debugging and tracing features of VS .NET and the Services Framework that make finding logic errors simpler.

NOTE

All code listings and supplemental material for this chapter can be found on the book's Web site at www.samspublishing.com.

Handling Exceptions

VB .NET supports the traditional method of handling exceptions using the On Error statement, referred to as *unstructured exception handling*, in addition to *structured exception handling* using the Try statement. In both cases, the goal is to handle exceptions generated at runtime that in the Common Language Runtime (CLR) are actually objects of type System.Exception or are derived from System.Exception. For example, the predefined CLR exceptions are all of type SystemException, whereas applications typically derive their own exceptions from the ApplicationException class. The primary members of the Exception class are shown in Table 6.1.

TABLE 6.1   Members of the `Exception` Class

Member	Description
HelpLink	Property that specifies a URL that provides help information associated with the exception.
InnerException	Property that specifies a reference to a previous exception in the chain. Useful for wrapping one exception inside another and for propagating the outer exception.
Message	Property that specifies the text string of the error.
Source	Property that specifies the text string containing the name of the application or object that caused the error.
StackTrace	Property that returns a `String` that contains the execution stack captured immediately before the exception is thrown.
TargetSite	Property that returns a `MethodBase` object that contains information about the method from which the exception was thrown.
GetBaseException	Method that traverses the chain of `InnerException` objects and returns a reference to the first one in the chain. If no chain exists, it returns the current exception.
HResult	Property that specifies a 32-bit value that represents a severity code, facility code, and error code. Used in COM interop.

Exception Propagation

It is recommended that most procedures of any complexity, or in which errors are anticipated, contain a way to trap exceptions (either an unstructured handler or a `Try` block). However, in the event that an exception is generated in a method that does not have a mechanism to handle it, VB .NET propagates the exception to the next lower method in the call stack. That method then has the responsibility of handling the exception. This process continues on down the call stack until a handler is found or the application is terminated.

In other words, if method A calls method B, and method B generates a runtime exception without a handler, the handler in method A is called immediately, if it exists, and, in the case of structured exception handling, handles that type of exception. This process continues until every active method has been checked. This functionality implies that not every one of your methods must contain error handlers, only those that are the lowest in the call stack, such as methods invoked from a user interface. However, in many instances, you still will want to handle specific exceptions in individual methods since they can be more easily addressed at that level.

Using Unstructured Exception Handling

The traditional mechanism VB uses to handle runtime exceptions is the error trap. Basically, *error traps* are sections of code within a procedure, denoted by a line label, that are executed when an exception occurs. By default, no error traps are enabled in an application, and any runtime exception produces a dialog that ends the application after it is dismissed.

To set or enable an error trap, use the `On Error Goto` statement followed by a line label. For example, to set an error trap in a method of a class, you would code the following handler:

```
Public Sub ProcessDocs()
On Error Goto MyErr

' other code goes here

Exit Sub
MyErr:
    ' handle the error here
End Sub
```

In this case, any exceptions that occur between the `On Error` statement and the `Exit Sub` immediately will redirect the flow of control to the `MyErr` line label. Note that `Exit Sub` is required if you want to separate the error handling code from the normal flow of execution. Obviously, an analogous `Exit Function` statement can be used in methods that return values.

To disable the currently enabled trap (you can have only one enabled trap per procedure—that is, they cannot be nested), use the `On Error Goto 0` statement. You also can skip all errors that occur in a procedure by using the `On Error Resume Next` statement, although this is recommended only for small procedures in which the possible trappable exceptions are well understood and insignificant. Either of the previous statements might be desirable if you want to use inline error handling (discussed in the next section) within the procedure. In addition, the `On Error Goto -1` statement can be used to clear the current exception in the same way as calling the `Clear` method of the `Err` object.

Speaking of which, inside the error trap, you can use the intrinsic `Err` object to view the `Source`, `Description`, and `Number` of the exception using its properties. The `Err` object simply maps many of the properties of the underlying `Exception` object with the exception of the `LastDllError` property, which is automatically populated with the system error code when an unmanaged DLL function produces an error.

NOTE

The mapping of the `Err` object to the underlying `Exception` object implies that unstructured exception handling in VB .NET is simply layered on top of the structured exception handling mechanism of the CLR.

In addition, the `Err` object can be used to throw an exception using the `Raise` method. This is particularly useful in components that need to handle the exception and then raise a user-defined exception to be handled by the calling application. Keep in mind, however, that the `Raise` method always raises generic exceptions (of type `Exception`) and so is less flexible than the `Throw` statement that can be used to throw an exception of any type derived from `Exception`.

> **NOTE**
>
> Technically, any object that derives from `System.Object` can be thrown as an exception; however, that practice is not recommended because error handlers will be expecting objects that derive from `Exception`.

Along these same lines, it also should be noted that an enabled error trap will trap all types of exceptions, whereas the structured exception handling constructs can be used to filter on a particular type of exception. To do so with unstructured exception handling, you can use the `GetException` method of the `Err` object to retrieve the exception, check its type, and then either handle it or raise it to the caller like so:

```
Dim oException As Exception

oException = Err().GetException()
If TypeOf (oException) Is ArgumentException Then
    ' Handle it
Else
    Throw oException
End If
```

Obviously, in these situations, using structured exception handling makes more sense because it is better able to handle different types of exceptions.

Exiting an Error Trap

When an error trap is activated, you have a choice of five courses of action, which are presented in Table 6.2.

TABLE 6.2   Ways to Exit an Error Trap

Statement	Description
Resume	Forces program execution to continue at the statement that caused the error. For certain kinds of errors that the user can correct, this method is preferred. For instance, an exception occurs when a floppy disk or CD-ROM is not ready for reading. By inserting the proper media, the statement can be re-executed successfully.

TABLE 6.2 Continued

Statement	Description
Resume Next	Forces program execution to continue with the statement following the one that caused the exception. Useful when the statement can be safely bypassed without causing other errors.
Resume *line*	Forces program execution to continue at a specific line label. This often is used to skip an entire section of a procedure and continue with a later section.
Err.Raise	As mentioned previously, invoking the Raise method propagates the exception to the calling method.
(Nothing)	By doing nothing in the error trap, the procedure will simply end after the error handler has finished executing. In many cases, this is the desired action.

When using unstructured exception handling with an On Error statement, remember that the Resume and Resume Next statements execute code only within the procedure in which the error handler actually is found. This means that in the example discussed in the preceding section, if the error handler in method A issues a Resume statement, the statement that is re-executed is actually the call to method B and not the actual statement in method B that initially caused the error. Likewise, if method A issues a Resume Next statement, the statement following the call to method B is executed.

Using Inline Error Handling

In some situations, it might be advantageous to bypass the error trapping mechanism and check for errors after each line of code is executed. In fact, ASP developers are forced to use this technique because VBScript does not support line labeling. This is referred to as *inline error handling* and can be done by first disabling all error traps using the On Error Resume Next statement. Errors then are detected by checking the Number property of the Err object.

Once again, note that if you are using unstructured exception handling, the only way to check for specific exceptions is to check the Number property of the Err object, or cast to the appropriate exception type using GetException as shown earlier.

Keep in mind that if a method that contains an On Error Resume Next statement calls a method with no error handler, and that method produces an unhandled error, the error will be propagated to the calling method. Since the calling method contains an On Error Resume Next statement, the exception will not be handled.

Using Structured Exception Handling

The second type of exception handling that VB .NET supports is structured exception handling through the use of the Try statement. Basically, the Try and End Try statements are used to protect a block of code and can contain filters that allow you to execute code to handle various types of exceptions. In addition, through the use of the `Finally` statement, you can set up a code block that executes regardless of whether an exception is thrown within the block. For example, a typical method, such as the `ReadDataAsXml` method shown in Listing 6.1, might contain a `Try` block.

LISTING 6.1 Using Structured Exception Handling. This method uses structured exception handling to detect different types of exceptions.

```
Imports System.Xml
Imports System.IO
Imports System.Data.SqlClient
Public Sub ReadDataAsXml()
  Dim cn As SqlConnection
  Dim cm As SqlCommand
  Dim ds As New DataSet()

  Try
    ' Open the connection and execute
    cn = New SqlConnection(mstrConnect)
    cm = New SqlCommand(mstrSQL, cn)
    cn.Open()
    cm.CommandType = CommandType.Text
    ds.ReadXml(cm.ExecuteXmlReader, XmlReadMode.Fragment)

    Dim fs As New FileStream(mstrFile, _
      FileMode.OpenOrCreate, FileAccess.Write)

    ds.WriteXml(fs)
    fs.Close()

  Catch eSql As SqlException
    ' Handle SQL Server errors here
  Catch eXml As DirectoryNotFoundException
    ' Handle XML errors here
  Catch e As Exception
    ' Pass all other errors here
    Throw e
  Finally
    ' Cleanup
    cn.Close()
  End Try

End Sub
```

In Listing 6.1, the method first dimensions variables used to communicate with SQL Server. Because these variables are outside the `Try` block, any exceptions thrown from their initialization (for example, if one of them had used a constructor) will not be handled by the `Try` block. Next, the `Try` block protects the initialization and opening of a connection to SQL Server along with the execution of a SQL statement that results in the population of a file with XML.

> **NOTE**
>
> Because `Try` blocks adhere to block scope, the `fs` variable declared in the `Try` block is only visible within the block. This implies that you cannot declare the same variable both inside and outside the `Try` block within the same procedure. Doing so would hide the outer variable, and in any case, causes a compile-time error.

As the code in a `Try` block is executed, several different types of exceptions can be generated. In this case, a `SqlException` might be thrown by the `Open` method of the `SqlConnection` object, or the `ExecuteXmlReader` method of the `SqlCommand` object, whereas a `DirectoryNotFoundException` might be thrown if the filename passed to the `FileStream` object points to an invalid path. Each `Catch` block is designed to handle a certain type of exception. The final block handles a generic `Exception` and can be used much like the `Case Else` statement in a `Select Case` block. In fact, like a `Select Case` statement, the `Catch` blocks are order dependent, and, if the exception matches the filter, the block will be executed and the `Try` block exited.

> **TIP**
>
> Because `Catch` blocks are processed in order, you should put the most specific exceptions first. In other words, put derived exception classes first and base exception classes next on down the hierarchy, followed by the `Exception` class itself.

As mentioned earlier, if you want your application to throw its own exceptions, you can do so by deriving a class from `System.ApplicationException`. This can be useful if you want to add additional state information to the exception that the calling program can use, and is typically used when building middle-tier components that throw exceptions based on business rule violations. In addition, your derived exception class can take advantage of the `InnerException` property discussed in Table 6.1 to encapsulate the original exception. For example, the definition for a class called `QuilogyEdException` would look like the following:

```
Public Class QuilogyEdException : Inherits ApplicationException

  Public Sub New(ByVal message As String)
    MyBase.New(message)
  End Sub

  Public Sub New(ByVal message As String, ByVal innerException As Exception)
    MyBase.New(message, innerException)
  End Sub

  ' other properties here
End Class
```

Note that the class takes advantage of the constructor of `ApplicationException` to accept both the message and a reference to the `InnerException`. Your methods then can use the class in the `Catch` block like so:

```
Catch eXml As DirectoryNotFoundException
  ' Handle XML errors here
  Dim eQuilogy As New QuilogyEdException("XML error occurred", eXml)
  Throw eQuilogy
```

In addition to or instead of filtering by exception type, the `Catch` block supports the `When` clause to evaluate an expression. For example, the `Catch` signature

```
Catch eSql As SqlException When Err().Number = 5
```

can be used to catch only `SqlExceptions` thrown where the error code is 5. This syntax relies on using the intrinsic `Err` object, which does get populated when an exception is thrown. Note, however, that you cannot use both structured and unstructured exception handling in the same procedure. More typically, you would use the `When` clause to check for other conditions that do not necessarily throw exceptions such as returning a result from a DLL function.

As with the `Try` block, the `Catch` block can contain its own variables, and once again you cannot declare a variable in a `Catch` block that has been declared at a higher level within the method.

As you can see in Listing 6.1, the `Finally` block is used to execute any cleanup code necessary for operations in the `Try` or `Catch` blocks. The important point about a `Finally` block is that it executes regardless of whether an exception is thrown and does so even if the `Try` or `Catch` block issues an `Exit Try`, `Exit Sub`, or `Exit Function` statement. In the event that the `Catch` block calls another method, the `Finally` block executes after control is returned to the calling method.

As implied by its name, unstructured exception handling does not use a control structure and as such results in code that is more difficult to write and maintain. In fact, `On Error` statements also don't perform as well and have the obvious limitation of not being able to easily distinguish between different types of exceptions or nest exceptions (Yes, Try blocks can be nested). As a result, structured exception handling is recommended because it provides protected blocks of code using a simple syntax that is consistent with the CLR.

TIP
Structured Exception Handling in the CLR has been optimized for the non-exceptional condition. In other words performance will suffer if you throw lots of exceptions for conditions that are really not errors (for example, to return the status of a method). As a result only throw exceptions when it is necessary to do so.

Changing Exception Handling Settings

Just as you could stipulate when VB 6.0 would enter break mode using the General tab of the Options dialog, VS .NET includes the Exceptions dialog, which can be invoked from the Debug, Exceptions menu.

This dialog, shown in Figure 6.1, shows the hierarchy of exceptions under each of the referenced namespaces in the project. By selecting a namespace or a specific exception, you can set the When the Exception Is Thrown and If the Exception Is Not Handled options at the bottom of the dialog. As the names imply, the former option controls what happens when the specified exception is thrown, and can include automatically opening the debugger, continuing in the normal program flow (for example by executing Catch blocks if present), or simply using the parent setting. Similarly, if the exception is subsequently not handled, the same three options are available.

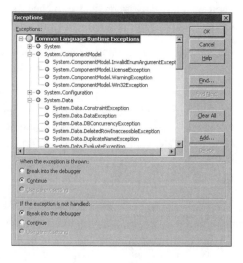

FIGURE 6.1

The VS .NET Exception dialog allows you to determine what happens when certain exceptions are thrown.

As shown in Figure 6.1, the default settings are to continue when an exception is thrown and if not handled launch the debugger. You might want to change the When the Exception Is Thrown setting for specific exceptions early in the development process to ensure that you're aware of the exceptions and take steps to fix them. In addition, note that you can add your own exceptions to this list by clicking the Add button.

Using the VS.NET Debugger

Developers familiar with VB 6.0 should find the debugging tools in the .NET Framework and VS .NET familiar, although definitely enhanced. For example, in addition to the line-by-line debugging and Edit and Continue features available in VB 6.0, the VS .NET debugger includes the following features:

- Cross-language debugging—Using this feature, you can seamlessly step through code in the same project written in different languages. For example, you can step from a VB .NET Web application to private assembly written in VC#.

- Attaching to a running program—Using this feature, you can attach the debugger to an already running application and cause it to enter break mode. You then can step through its code. The attached program does not need to be executed from the VS .NET IDE.

- Remote debugging—Using the running program feature, programs running on remote machines can be attached and debugged just as if they were running locally.

- Debugging multithreaded applications—Unlike in VB 6.0, the VS .NET debugger fully supports debugging multithreaded applications and provides facilities for viewing and manipulating threads.

- Debugging Web applications—Because ASP.NET applications are simply VB .NET applications, they can be debugged just as a forms-based application. Developers familiar with debugging Web applications in Visual Interdev will find this a welcome relief.

This section provides a general overview of the debugging process for detailing how to debug both local and remote projects.

As discussed in Chapter 1, "The Microsoft .NET Architecture," the source code you write in VB .NET is typically compiled first to intermediate language (MSIL) at compile time, and then to native code at runtime using a JITer. To successfully debug an application, the CLR must do the reverse and map native instructions to MSIL, which then are mapped to source code statements.

It turns out that the needed mapping information is stored in a programmer's database (.PDB) file generated by the VB .NET compiler with the /debug switch. The switch is controlled in VS .NET using the Configuration Manager dialog invoked from the Build menu. This dialog shows all the projects in the current solution and allows you to set the active configuration for each, which when set to Debug, instructs the compiler to use the /debug switch. In addition, options such as the Platform (currently only .NET) and Deployment options are supported.

> **TIP**
>
> You also can set the active configuration in the properties window when the solution is selected or through the drop-down list in the standard toolbar.

For ASP.NET applications, where compilation is often done on-the-fly, debugging also is controlled by the debug attribute of the compilation tag in the Web.config and machine.config files. We will discuss this further in Chapter 10, "Building Web Forms."

In both cases, using the debug configuration also creates .PDB files for each of the private assemblies. This is what allows seamless debugging of assemblies written in other languages.

Starting Debugging

When the debug switch is set, you can start the project with the F5 key, the Start option in the Debug menu, or the Start button in the toolbar. Just as in VB 6.0, however, you must first set the startup project by right-clicking on the project in the Solution Explorer window and choosing Set as StartUp Project. Doing so shows the project name in bold. For Web projects, you also must set the startup page in an analogous fashion. You also can run the project without debugging by starting it with Ctrl+F5 or using the Menu option in the Debug menu.

> **NOTE**
>
> Many of the options the debugger uses during a debugging session can be set on the Tools, Options dialog under the Debugging option. Here the display options, as well as features such as Edit and Continue, can be configured.

Starting the application within the IDE allows you to place breakpoints in your code, and when in break mode, use the various debugging windows shown in Table 6.3.

> **TIP**
>
> VB developers should be aware that you now can place breakpoints on Dim statements if the statement creates a new instance of the object.

TABLE 6.3 VS .NET Debugging Windows

Window	Description
Autos	Automatically (hence the name) displays information on the variables in the current statement (the statement about to be executed) and the previous statement. Also displays the return value for functions stepped over (F10). Can use this window to modify variables.
Breakpoints	Displays information on all the breakpoints set in the project. Allows you to conditionally control whether the breakpoints are enabled using an expression or a hit count. Also displays a toolbar that can be used to set and delete breakpoints, as well as find the breakpoint in both the code and Disassembly windows.
Call Stack	Displays the names, parameter types, and parameter values of functions on the call stack.
Disassembly	Displays the assembly code corresponding to the instructions created by the compiler.
Immediate	Used to type in and evaluate expressions when in debug mode. Also referred to as the Command window and available from the View, Other Windows menu.
Locals	Displays all local variables with their value and type in the current scope.
Me	Can be opened from the Me menu option of the Debug, Windows menu when in debug mode. Used to display information about the object referenced as Me in the current scope.
Memory	Opened from the Memory menu option of the Debug, Windows menu. Can be used to view large buffers and other strings that do not display well in the Locals or Watch windows.
Modules	Can be opened from the Modules menu option of the Debug, Windows menu when in debug mode. Shows the DLL or EXEs used by the project.
Output	By default, displays the output from methods of the `System.Diagnostics.Debug` and `System.Diagnostics.Trace` classes. Opened from the View, Other Windows menu.
Quick Watch	Dialog invoked from the Debug menu that allows you to enter and evaluate expressions and watches.
Registers	Can be opened from the Registers menu option of the Debug, Windows menu when in debug mode. Used to display the contents of the registers. Values that have recently changed will be displayed in red.

6

ERROR HANDLING AND DEBUGGING

TABLE 6.3   Continued

Window	Description
Threads	Can be opened from the Threads menu option of the Debug, Windows menu when in debug mode. Used to display information about and manipulate threads in a multithreaded program.
Watch	Used to enter expressions evaluated by the debugger. Unlike in VB 6.0, does not have the capability to break when an expression evaluates to a specific value.

As in VB 6.0, stepping through code is accomplished using the Step Into (F11) and Step Over (F10) options, the former allowing you to do line-by-line debugging, whereas the latter can be used to execute procedures and then continue line-by-line debugging.

Note that if you start the project in the IDE in Release mode, any breakpoints you set will not be honored. Also, if an exception occurs, the Disassembly window will be shown, but not mapped back to source code instructions.

TIP

As a result, you'll typically run in Debug mode within the IDE for development and testing and then set the option to Release before deployment.

NOTE

Although beyond the scope of this book, the .NET SDK also ships with a command-line debugger, CorDbg.exe, that is not installed by default.

As mentioned at the beginning of this section, one of the great features of the VS .NET debugger is that it allows you to seamlessly debug multithreaded applications, a task that wasn't possible in VB 6.0. In addition to the support provided by the Threads window shown in Table 6.3, the Debug Location toolbar (which is not displayed by default but can be accessed by right-clicking on the toolbar area and choosing it) contains a drop-down list of the threads in the currently running application. By simply selecting one, the debugger displays the code the thread is currently executing. By placing breakpoints in this code, you can debug multiple threads simultaneously.

> **NOTE**
>
> Note that when a break-point is encountered within the project, all its threads are suspended.

Attaching to a Running Process

One of the most interesting features of the VS .NET debugger is its capability to attach to and debug a running process. This is evidenced by the fact that if you execute an application outside the VS .NET and it encounters an unhandled exception, a dialog, as shown in Figure 6.2, is presented allowing you to attach to any CLR debugger present on your machine. If no debugger is present, or if you click No, the exception will simply be thrown and the application exited.

> **NOTE**
>
> If the application was not compiled with the debug switch and a debugger is chosen, the debugger will run but will only show the Disassembly window because the required .PDB file used for mapping is not present.

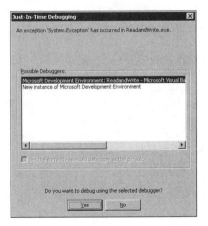

FIGURE 6.2

Attaching to a Debugger. This dialog is invoked when a managed executable encounters an unhandled exception and a debugger is present.

This capability also is present in the Debug menu of VS .NET under the Processes menu option. Using the dialog shown in Figure 6.3, you can attach to any running process by simply selecting it and choosing Attach. You also are prompted for the type of application to debug, which includes CLR, script, and Transact-SQL (T-SQL). When attached, you can use the Debug toolbar or the Break button on the dialog to break execution. When in debug mode, the debugger presents the source code file at its current line of execution and allows you to step through the application.

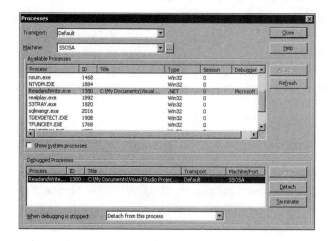

FIGURE 6.3

The Processes dialog controls attaching to running processes on the local machine or remotely.

In addition, notice that the Processes dialog shows the type of application in addition to whether it is currently being debugged. The When Debugging Is Stopped option allows you to terminate or simply detach from the program when you stop the debugger.

Finally, this dialog also enables cross-machine debugging by allowing you to attach to processes running on remote computers. To do so, simply select the Transport and the Machine name. The Transport can be set to Default (local), Native-only TCP/IP (for attaching to native programs without using DCOM), and TCP/IP.

Using Diagnostics

In addition to the debugging features of VS .NET itself, the Services Framework provides support for debugging and tracing through the System.Diagnostics namespace. The final section of this chapter focuses on the Debug and Trace classes and how they can be used to programmatically enhance development.

Using the Debug Class

As in VB 6.0, VB .NET exposes the Debug object to allow you to write debug statements to the Output window during program execution. As you would expect, any debug statements included in your code are only compiled into debug releases. In this way, neither the performance nor code size of your application is affected in the final release. However, VB .NET also supports the DEBUG compilation directive, which can be placed at the top of your source code file to explicitly include or exclude debugging statements in the compiled code. For example, the line

```
#Const DEBUG = True
```

includes debugging statements in an executable even if the configuration is set to Release mode.

> **NOTE**
>
> Alternatively, when using the command-line compiler vbc.exe, you can use the /d switch with the attribute DEBUG set to True as in /d:DEBUG=True.

In .NET, the Debug class, however, is a member of the System.Diagnostics namespace and includes additional functionality. The Debug class exposes a number of shared methods and is accessible globally. For example, rather than simply expose the Print method, the Debug class exposes overloaded Write, WriteIf, WriteLine, and WriteLineIf methods to allow you to output messages based on criteria and optionally including category information. For example, the statement

```
Debug.WriteLineIf(cn.State = ConnectionState.Broken, _
"Connection was broken", "Data Access")
```

only outputs the message if the condition is true. It also prefixes the output with the category Data Access followed by a colon like so:

```
Data Access: Connection was broken
```

The Debug class also contains the IndentSize and IndentLevel properties, which control how many spaces will be used for indentation and at what level the next Write method will indent at. To control indentation on-the-fly, you also can use the Indent and Unindent methods as follows:

```
Debug.IndentSize = 2
Debug.WriteLine("Debugging app")
  ' Do some work
Debug.Indent()
```

```
Debug.WriteLine("Now here")
  ' Do some work
Debug.Unindent()
Debug.WriteLine("Done")
```

Finally, as in VB 6.0, the Debug class supports the Assert method. The Assert method is a tool familiar to C programmers and is used to test for invalid conditions in the application. When the expression passed to this overloaded method evaluates to False, a failure message is output with the format "Fail:" followed by the message passed to the method.

A typical use for Assert is to check for valid parameters—for example, a method that extracts students from an XML file using a Stream—as in the following code:

```
Public Sub ExtractStudents(ByVal pStream As Stream)
    Debug.Assert(pStream.CanRead, "Invalid Stream object in ExtractStudents")
End Sub
```

In the event the CanRead method of the Stream argument returns False, the message

```
Fail: Invalid Stream object in ExtractStudents
```

is output. To enable a dialog to be displayed rather than simply writing the output to the Immediate window (or other listener), you can add the assert element to the application or machine.config file like so:

```
<configuration>
  <system.diagnostics>
     <assert  assertuienabled="true" />
  </system.diagnostics>
</configuration>
```

The assertuienabled attribute controls whether the dialog is displayed in addition to the regular output. To issue a failure message explicitly, you can optionally use the Fail method, although this method will not result in a dialog even if the assertuienabled attribute is set to true.

TIP

Remember that just as with the WriteLine method of the Debug class, the Assert method only executes when debugging is turned on. As a result, make sure that you don't include code essential to the running of your application in the assert. In other words, asserts don't take the place of good validation code; they only help you to check your program's state at debug time.

Using Tracing

The `Trace` class is similar to the `Debug` class, although it is typically used to *instrument* an application for runtime analysis rather than developer testing. In other words, you would use the methods of the `Trace` class to output information that might be helpful to users of the application to pinpoint performance problems or validate input and output of methods in the code. Tracing also is helpful for understanding what is happening in nonvisual processes of an application, such as Web Services. In these cases, tracing can be combined with a custom listener to write out logs that can be subsequently examined by system administrators and other interested parties. As a result, tracing is by default enabled in Release builds of the application, but can be affected using the `TRACE` compilation direction or the command-line `/d:TRACE=True` switch.

> **NOTE**
>
> Two other techniques to provide feedback to users or administrators of a distributed application include using the event log and performance counters. Both topics are discussed in Chapter 13, "Implementing Services."

The `Trace` class supports the same set of members as the `Debug` class and so, for example, can conditionally output messages using `WriteLineIf` and perform assertions using the `Assert` method.

However, tracing also typically is used with switches. Simply put, a switch allows you to control whether output from the `Trace` and `Debug` class is generated. For example, using switches, you can instrument your application to display only trace messages that deal with data access and not the performance of other functions of the application. Whether a switch is enabled can be determined programmatically, although more typically it is done through the configuration file.

To create a switch, you instantiate an object derived from the `Switch` class (either `BooleanSwitch` or `TraceSwitch`) and then configure the switch in the application configuration file. For example, the following declarations in a class create two switches for the class:

```
Private daSwitch As New BooleanSwitch("daSwitch", "Data Access")
Private tsPerfSwitch As New TraceSwitch("tsPerfSwitch", "Performance")
```

The first switch is a `BooleanSwitch` and simply can be set to on or off, which maps to the `Enabled` property of the switch object. The second is a `TraceSwitch` instance, which exposes properties to allow informational messages, warnings, errors, and all messages to be displayed. Note that the constructor populates the `DisplayName` property used to reference the switch and the `Description`.

To configure the switch, an entry is made to the application configuration file as follows:

```
<configuration>
    <system.diagnostics>
        <switches>
            <add name="daSwitch" value=1 />
            <add name="tsPerfSwitch" value=4 />
            <clear/>
        </switches>
    </system.diagnostics>
</configuration>
```

TIP

When authoring classes that are going to be reused by other developers, you also can expose the switches as shared fields within the class. In this way, developers using the class simply can set the Enabled or TraceLevel properties of the field to programmatically enable tracing for the component.

In this case, both switches are enabled because they've been added to the switches element. In this case, the value attribute for the BooleanSwitch is set to 1 to indicate that the switch is enabled, whereas the TraceSwitch value is 4 to indicate that all messages are enabled. The value property maps to the constants in the TraceLevel enumeration as shown in Table 6.4.

TABLE 6.4 TraceLevel Enumeration Constants

Trace Level	Value
Off	0
Error	1
Warning	2
Info	3
Verbose	4

TIP

Of course, if these levels are not sufficient for your application, you can create your own switch class by deriving from Switch and overriding the SwitchSetting method.

Within the application, the switches can be used by testing the `Enabled` property of the `BooleanSwitch` object or the `Level` property of the `TraceSwitch` object. For example, to output tracing information on data access, you could use the following code:

```
If daSwitch.Enabled Then
    Trace.WriteLine(mstrConnect, "Data Acccess")
End If
```

Additionally, the `TraceSwitch` class exposes a `Boolean` property for each level, and so to test for a specific level in a `TraceSwitch`, you could add the following code:

```
If tsPerfSwitch.TraceVerbose = True Then
    Trace.WriteLine("Method " & execMethod & " executed in " & _
    execTime.Tostring & " seconds", "Performance")
End If
```

In this case, the `execMethod` and `execTime` variables represent arguments passed into the procedure.

> **TIP**
>
> Although you could use the `WriteLineIf` method, it is more efficient to perform the test up front because the expression will not have to be evaluated.

Keep in mind that although switches are typically used with tracing, they also can apply to the `Debug` class in the same way.

Obviously, the combination of switches and tracing provide a powerful set of tools to create instrumented applications. The primary advantage of switches is that they can be enabled at runtime without recompiling the application. A typical approach is to create a set of switches for your application that can be turned on and off and break down into the following categories:

- Performance
- User Interface
- Data Access
- Business Logic

In that way, maintenance programmers and system administrators looking to optimize the application are not inundated with messages from all aspects of the system.

> **TIP**
>
> Keep in mind that as with any technology, instrumentation also incurs a cost. Particularly, the cost of executing statements that test switches.

Using Listeners

Up to this point, the discussion has assumed that output from the Debug and Trace classes is sent to the Output window mentioned in Table 6.3. However, tracing especially wouldn't be useful if you couldn't redirect it to the console or a file.

To do so, both the Debug and Trace classes expose a Listeners collection that exposes a set of TraceListener objects through a TraceListenerCollection object. By default, the only object in the collection is an instance of DefaultTraceListener that writes to the Output window. However, it is trivial to add a new listener to the collection to redirect the output. In fact, TraceListener serves as the base class for the EventLogListener and TextWriterTraceListener classes, which write output to the event log and to a file or stream, respectively.

For example, to allow Debug and Trace output to go to the console, you can call the Add method of the collection as follows:

```
Trace.Listeners.Add(New TextWriterTraceListener(Console.Out))
```

Similarly, you can remove the default listener by using the Remove method as follows:

```
Debug.Listeners.Remove("Default")
```

In this case, the listener was removed using the overloaded method that accepts the DisplayName of the listener.

Although in the previous cases, one code example used the Listeners collection of the Trace class and the other the Debug class, in fact both collections refer to the same underlying object. In other words, removing the default listener from the Debug object actually removes it from both Debug and Trace. In the same way, adding a listener adds it to both.

Typically, developers will add a new instance of TextWriterTraceListener and pass in the overloaded constructor a Stream or filename to write to. In this way, you can write all trace and debug output to a log file without having to write your own logging class.

As you might expect, the extensibility of the Services Framework allows you to create your own listener by deriving from TraceListener and overriding its Write and WriteLine methods. This would be especially useful to standardize application tracing throughout an organization.

6

Developing a custom listener also can be a powerful technique because the overloaded `Write` and `WriteLine` methods of the `Debug` and `Trace` classes also support passing objects directly to the listener. In this way, you can write a listener that abstracts the trace processing of an object so that developers using your listener need not be concerned with passing specific data to the listener. To illustrate the basics of this concept, consider the skeleton class shown in Listing 6.2.

LISTING 6.2   Deriving a Listener. This skeleton listing of a derived `TraceListener` class implements a custom `WriteLine` method.

```
Imports System.Data

Public Class DAListener : Inherits TraceListener
    Public Overloads Overrides Sub WriteLine(ByVal message As String)
        ' Write the message to the console
        Console.WriteLine(message)
    End Sub
    Public Overloads Overrides Sub Write(ByVal message As String)
        ' Write the message to the console
        Console.Write(message)
    End Sub

  Public Overloads Overrides Sub WriteLine(ByVal ds As Object)
    ' If its a DataSet then print it to the console
    If TypeOf (ds) Is DataSet Then
      Dim dsStrict As DataSet
      dsStrict = CType(ds, DataSet)
      dsStrict.WriteXml(Console.Out)
    End If
  End Sub
End Class
```

In this case, the class `DAListener` is derived from `TraceListener` and as such must override the `WriteLine` and `Write` methods that accept strings. In addition, it exposes an overloaded `WriteLine` method that accepts an `Object` as a parameter. This object then can be tested for a specific type and handled accordingly. Here, if the object is a `System.Data.DataSet` object, its contents are written to the console as XML.

To use the custom listener, it simply needs to be added to the `Listeners` collection as shown in the following code:

```
Debug.Listeners.Add(New DAListener())

Dim ds As New DataSet()
' Populate DataSet here
Debug.WriteLine(ds)
```

Summary

The error handling and debugging features found in VS .NET and the Services Framework should feel comfortable to existing VB developers because they incorporate many of the features of the VB 6.0 debugger. However, the addition of tracing and a more powerful debugger provide more power and flexibility. This combination makes it much easier to debug your applications and create a robust tracing infrastructure.

This chapter concludes the .NET Concepts section of the book. From here, the book takes you through the application of these concepts manifested in the tiers of a distributed application developed with VB .NET. We'll begin with a discussion of data access using ADO.NET.

Enterprise Techniques

IN THIS PART

Accessing Data with ADO.NET

IN THIS CHAPTER

Far and away the single most important technique for corporate VB developers is *data access*. Most of the applications written in today's corporate environments involve displaying and manipulating operational and line of business data. Historically, Microsoft has provided support for accessing data in a variety of relational and nonrelational data stores by shipping APIs that existing VB, and now ASP, developers have become quite familiar with over the years, including VBSQL, ODBC, DAO, RDO, OLE DB, and ADO. Although this continued evolution meant that VB developers had to learn new techniques along the way, the benefits of learning the models meant a unified relational data access model (ODBC), increased simplicity (DAO), increased performance (RDO), and increased reach to nonrelational sources (ADO).

To that list you can now add the data access classes of the Services Framework. These classes, collectively termed ADO.NET, serve to implement a managed interface to OLE DB and SQL Server, increase performance when using SQL Server, and allow data to be manipulated in a fashion commensurate with distributed application development utilizing the Internet and XML. Even though learning a new data access model might at first be daunting, it will also help you build modern, distributed applications.

In this chapter, I'll discuss the architecture of ADO.NET and how it can be used to build distributed applications. This chapter, and the three chapters that follow, form a progression that illustrates the techniques useful in VB .NET to build distributed applications. The sample code that will be discussed in this and subsequent chapters explicates a somewhat simplified implementation of Quilogy's online education system where students enroll in classes over the Web, and Quilogy employees view and manipulate data through an Intranet site. The enrollment data is stored in a SQL Server 2000 database, so, where appropriate, specific features of SQL Server 2000 will be utilized.

Because data is the foundation for applications such as this one, I'll begin with a discussion of accessing data in the .NET world.

> **NOTE**
>
> All code listings and supplemental material for this chapter can be found on the book's Web site at www.samspublishing.com.

ADO.NET Defined

ADO.NET is comprised of classes found in the System.Data namespace that encapsulates data access for distributed applications. However, rather than simply mapping the existing ADO object model to .NET to provide a managed interface to OLE DB and SQL Server, ADO.NET changes the way data is stored and marshalled within and between applications. The primary reason ADO.NET redefines this architecture is that most applications developed today can benefit from the scalability and flexibility of being able to distribute data across the Internet in a disconnected fashion.

Because the classic ADO model was developed primarily with continuously connected access in mind, creating distributed applications with it is somewhat limiting. A typical example is the need to move data through a `Recordset` object between tiers in a distributed application (defined as an application whose tiers are split across process boundaries). To accomplish this in classic ADO, you have to specifically create a disconnected `Recordset` using a combination of properties including cursor location, cursor type, and lock type. In addition, because the `Recordset` is represented in a proprietary binary format, you have to rely on COM marshalling code built in to OLE DB to allow the `Recordset` to be passed by value (`ByVal`) to another component or client code. This architecture also runs into problems when attempting to pass recordsets through firewalls because these system-level requests are often denied.

On the other hand, if you elected not to use disconnected recordsets, you had to devise your own scheme to represent the data using `Variant` arrays, delimited within a string, or saved as tabular XML using the `Save` method (although the latter option is really viable only when using ADO 2.5 and higher). Obviously, these approaches have their downsides, including problems with performance and maintainability, not to mention interoperability difficulties between platforms.

In addition, the classic ADO model doesn't handle hierarchical data particularly well. Although it is possible to create hierarchical recordsets using the Microsoft data shape provider, it is not simple, therefore is not often used. Typically, `JOIN` clauses are used inside stored procedures or inline SQL to retrieve data from multiple tables. However, this does not allow you to assemble data from multiple data sources and easily determine from where the data comes. As a result, classic ADO provides a flat view of data that is not strongly typed.

To alleviate these problems, ADO.NET is built from the ground up for distributed applications used in today's disconnected scenarios. For example, the central class in ADO.NET is the `DataSet`, which can be thought of as an in-memory XML database that stores related tables, relationships, and constraints. As you'll see, the `DataSet` is the primary mechanism used in VB .NET applications to cache data and pass it between tiers in a distributed application, thereby alleviating the need to rely on proprietary schemes or COM marshalling.

Using XML alleviates several of the burdens of classic ADO. For example, by storing the data as XML, it can easily pass through firewalls without special configuration. In addition, by storing related tables and representing the relationships between those tables, the `DataSet` can store data hierarchically, allowing for the easy manipulation of parent/child relationships. The self-describing nature of XML, combined with the object-oriented nature of VB .NET, also allows for direct programmatic access to the data in a `DataSet` in a strongly typed fashion. In other words, the data need not be accessed using tables, rows, and columns metaphor, but can be accessed in terms of the definition of the data that can be type-checked by the compiler.

Further, this disconnected model, combined with connection pooling schemes, frees resources on the database server more quickly, allowing applications to scale by not holding on to expensive database connections and locks.

In the following section, we'll dig deeper to take a look at how ADO.NET is designed with the goals of disconnected access, scalability, and interoperability in mind.

Relation to OLE DB and ADO

Some readers might get the impression that ADO.NET replaces the existing ADO and OLE DB architecture. However, you should think of ADO.NET as an *enhancement* to this technology for distributed application development that at least in part relies on the underlying OLE DB and ADO architecture. For example, ADO.NET, at this point anyway, does not contain managed code to natively access any data source other than SQL Server. For all other data sources, OLE DB providers are required.

In fact, because ADO.NET was designed for disconnected and distributed applications, it might not be suitable for all types of applications you need to create with VB .NET, especially those that rely on server-side cursors and are continuously connected. As a result, you might want to use classic ADO with VB .NET through the COM Interop layer, which is discussed in detail in Chapter 9, "Accessing Component Services."

> **NOTE**
>
> One of the reasons that ADO.NET does not support the server-side processing model is that attempts to do so with classic ADO proved difficult because database vendors did not support the model in a uniform way. As a result, you won't see this type of support implemented generically in ADO.NET. However, look for server-side cursors and other SQL Server-specific features possibly to be included in subsequent versions of ADO.NET in a `SqlServer` namespace.

System.Data Architecture

You can think of the `System.Data` namespace as consisting of two primary parts:

- The managed providers that allow you to connect to a data source, issue commands against the data source, and read data directly from the data store or into a `DataSet`. The managed providers contain classes analogous to the Connection, Command, and

Parameter objects in classic ADO, as well as adding support for iterating through a result set in a forward-only manner.

- The `DataSet` and its various supporting classes that allow you to manipulate data in a disconnected fashion. As mentioned earlier, the `DataSet` is most like a disconnected `Recordset` although much more powerful and flexible.

Managed Providers

To manipulate data in a data store, you first need to open a connection to it and pass it commands to execute. In ADO.NET, this is accomplished by using a *managed provider* (also referred to as a .NET Data Provider). ADO.NET ships with two managed providers: the *OleDb managed provider* and the *SqlClient managed provider*. The former is contained in the `System.Data.OleDb` namespace, which, like classic ADO, allows you to access any data source for which an OLE DB provider is available. The latter is in `System.Data.SqlClient` and provides native access to SQL Server by writing directly to the tabular data stream (TDS) protocol used by SQL Server. In other words, the OleDb managed provider simply offers a data access model that sits on top of the existing OLE DB infrastructure and requires data source–specific OLE DB providers. Conversely, the SqlClient managed provider takes the place of the existing OLE DB provider for SQL Server (SQLOLEDB) because it writes directly to SQL Server without the assistance of any other software. A diagram of these components and their relation to OLE DB and ADO can be seen in Figure 7.1.

> **NOTE**
>
> Although you might think that the OLE DB Provider for ODBC (MSDASQL) might be transparently supported, it is not. A managed provider for ODBC is now available for download on `msdn.microsoft.com`.

Each of the managed providers includes a set of classes that implement interfaces and derive from classes found in `System.Data`. The common types of classes included in a managed provider are as follows:

- Command   A class that implements `IDbCommand` and includes members used to execute queries against a connection. It can execute queries that do not return results and queries that return an `IDataReader` object for iterating through a result set. Also includes events for responding to schema changes in the underlying data source.
- Connection   A class that implements `IDbConnection` and includes members to connect to a data source, handle transactional behavior and connection pooling, and receive notifications when the state of the connection changes.

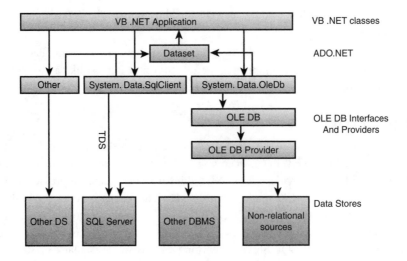

FIGURE 7.1

The data access components used in a VB .NET application. Note that OLE DB is still a part of this data access model.

- DataAdapter   A class derived from `DbDataAdapter` that implements `IDbDataAdapter`. It includes a set of command objects and a connection used to populate a `DataSet` and update the underlying data source. It also maps data source tables and columns to tables and columns in a `DataSet`. Note that only relational providers will inherit directly from `DbDataAdapter`.

- DataReader   A class that implements the `IDataReader` interface, used to read a forward-only stream of records from the data source. Note that this is analogous to a firehose cursor in SQL Server.

- Parameter   A class that implements `IDataParameter`, used to pass parameters to command objects. Parameters are tracked through a `ParameterCollection` object that implements the `IDataParameterCollection` interface.

- Transaction   A class that implements `IDbTransaction`, used to represent a transaction in the data source.

In addition, the managed providers can also include their own classes to represent properties, events, exceptions, command builders for use with a DataAdapter, and errors. The naming convention used is to prefix the name of the base class or interface with the namespace for the managed provider. For example, for the SqlClient managed provider, the classes shown in Table 7.1 are available.

TABLE 7.1   Classes Found in the `System.Data.Sql` Namespace for the SqlClient (SQL Server) Managed Provider

Class	Description
`SqlClientPermission`, `SqlClientPermissionAttribute`	Imperative and declarative security classes used to ensure that a user has sufficient permissions to access SQL Server.
`SqlCommand`	Implements `IDbCommand` and is used to execute Transact-SQL commands such as stored procedures.
`SqlCommandBuilder`	Used to automatically generate commands in a `SqlDataAdapter` used to update a SQL Server database from a `DataSet` object.
`SqlConnection`	Implements `IDbConnection` and represents the connection to the SQL Server database. Includes its own syntax for the connection string.
`SqlDataAdapter`	Derived from `DbDataAdapter` and used to map data from SQL Server to a `DataSet` for select, insert, update, and delete.
`SqlDataReader`	Implements `IDataReader` as a means of returning a forward-only, read-only cursor on a result set.
`SqlException`	Derived from `SystemException` and is thrown whenever SqlClient encounters a warning or errors. Includes at least one instance of `SqlError`.
`SqlError`	Represents an error returned by the `SqlDataAdapter`. Returned through a collection within a `SqlException` object.
`SqlErrorCollection`	Represents a collection of `SqlError` objects returned through a `SqlException`.
`SqlParameter`	Represents a parameter to a `SqlCommand` object.
`SqlParameterCollection`	Represents a collection of `SqlParameter` objects.
`SqlTransaction`	Represents a transaction in SQL Server.

Obviously, by abstracting the basic functionality for managed providers into base classes and interfaces, it is possible for database vendors and corporate developers to write their own managed providers. Although this is possible, it is probably not recommended for the vast majority of developers because the managed providers shipped with .NET handle all the connectivity required for most data sources. However, it might be warranted for companies that have large-scale systems and have developed a proprietary data access interface to their back end.

In one respect, the availability of multiple managed providers represents a decision point for developers using SQL Server (or a back end for which a managed provider is available) as their back-end database. Because the SqlClient managed provider handles TDS natively, it performs better than incurring the extra translation layer when using the OleDb managed provider against SQL Server, as noted in Figure 7.1.

> **NOTE**
>
> In fact, tests indicate that the combination of VB. NET and SqlClient is 10 percent faster than using OLE DB directly in an unmanaged Visual C++ application. Of course, this combination is itself 10 percent faster than VB 6.0 and ADO 2.5.

As a result, most SQL Server developers will likely want to use the SqlClient managed provider. The downside of this choice is that if you change your back-end database, you'll have to change and recompile your code to use the OleDb managed provider. To avoid this, where it is likely that the back-end database might change, you might want to create your own set of generic classes that abstract the instantiation of objects from the managed providers. Obviously, these classes could run the gamut from statically invoking a particular managed provider such as SqlClient to dynamically invoking the correct one based on a property setting. The cost of creating and maintaining this extra layer might be justified if your target database changes.

That being said, for most projects, a better approach is to make sure the data access code is abstracted from the user and business logic in custom classes so that, if necessary, it will be fairly easy to change and yet not incur the overhead of creating and maintaining a separate set of generic data access classes. This is the approach used in this chapter.

Using a Managed Provider

The basics of using a managed provider are analogous to using the `Connection` and `Command` objects in classic ADO. However, a managed provider also includes a DataAdapter used to populate and control `DataSet` objects that have no equivalent in classic ADO.

To illustrate the use of the connection and command objects, Listing 7.1 shows a simple example of connecting to SQL Server using the SqlClient managed provider and executing a simple stored procedure to return the contents of the Courses table using the `SqlCommand` object. The resulting rows are then iterated upon using the `SqlDataReader` class.

LISTING 7.1   Using a Managed Provider. This listing shows the simplest example of executing a stored procedure in SQL Server using the SqlClient managed provider and streaming through the resulting rows.

```
Imports System.Data
Imports System.Data.SqlClient
Dim cnSQL As SqlConnection
Dim cmSQL As SqlCommand
Dim drCourses As SqlDataReader

cnSQL = New SqlConnection( _
    "server=ssosa;trusted_connection=yes;database=enrollment")
cmSQL = New SqlCommand("usp_ListCourses", cnSQL)
cmSQL.CommandType = CommandType.StoredProcedure

Try
  cnSQL.Open()
  drCourses = cmSQL.ExecuteReader()

  Do While drCourses.Read()
    Console.WriteLine(drCourses("Description").ToString())
  Loop
Catch e As SqlException
  Console.WriteLine(e.ToString())
Finally
  cnSQL.Close()
End Try
```

One item to note in Listing 7.1 is that constructor strings are used to pass the connection string, and the command text with a reference to the connection, to the SqlConnection and SqlCommand objects, respectively. Further, you'll notice that the syntax of the connection string passed to SqlConnection is very similar to that used with the SQLOLEDB provider. In addition, the ExecuteReader method is called, which returns a SqlDataReader object used to simply iterate through the rows using the Read method. The SqlDataReader implements a forward-only cursor that allows access to the data through a simple default Item property. For optimum performance, the SqlDataReader provides only the basic constructs for reading data.

NOTE

Although much of the code in this chapter uses the SqlClient managed provider, the code for using the OleDb managed provider is almost exactly analogous.

Using a `SqlDataReader` is the fastest way of getting data from SQL Server and involves no overhead on the client because data is not persisted in memory. The data is simply streamed from the SQL Server to the network buffers on the client machine where SqlClient reads it. However, as with a "firehose" cursor in classic ADO, the database connection will stay open until the `Close` method of the `SqlConnection` is called or until the object goes out of scope. Alternatively, the `ExecuteReader` method accepts a bitwise combination of values from the `CommandBehavior` enumeration. One of these, `CloseConnection`, automatically closes the `SqlConnection` when the `SqlDataReader` is closed.

> **TIP**
>
> In addition, the `CommandBehavior` enumeration can be used to provide the data source with additional information that allows it to optimize performance. For example, the `SingleResult` and `SingleRow` values are used to tell the data source that a single result set, or only a single row will be returned by the query, respectively.
>
> Experienced ADO developers might be wondering whether all the rows can be read from the `SqlDataReader` with a single method call analogous to the `GetRows` method exposed in ADO 2.x. Unfortunately, this functionality does not exist in ADO.NET yet, although all the columns from the current row can be read into an array using the `GetValues` or `GetSqlValues` methods.

Even though it might at first feel strange to access forward-only result sets in this manner, moving the functionality provided by the `SqlDataReader` into the managed provider and away from the `DataSet` (where you might expect to find it because it is analogous to the `Recordset` in most respects) is a good thing because the implementation must clearly be managed by the data source and it allows the `DataSet` to be used strictly as a client-side data cache.

> **TIP**
>
> For more information on creating firehose cursors in classic ADO, see Chapter 14 of my book, *Pure Visual Basic*.

The interesting aspect of `SqlCommand` is that it also implements other methods to execute commands against SQL Server, as shown in Table 7.2.

TABLE 7.2 Execute Methods of `SqlCommand`

Class	Description
ExecuteNonQuery	Executes the command and does not return a result. Useful for executing statements that do not return resultsets, such as stored procedures that modify data.
ExecuteScalar	Executes the command and returns only the first column and first row of the result set as an `Object`. Discards all other data.
ExecuteXMLReader	Executes the command and returns the results as an XML stream. For use with the FOR XML statement in SQL Server 2000.

Several of the methods shown in Table 7.2, such as `ExecuteNonQuery` and `ExecuteScalar`, also exist in the OleDb managed provider and will be discussed in more detail later in the chapter. However, as an example of the customization possible when using managed providers for a particular data source, consider the code in Listing 7.2.

LISTING 7.2 Returning a Stream. This listing shows how a managed provider can implement specific features of the data source—in this case, the capability to return XML as a stream.

```
Imports System.Data
Imports System.Data.SqlClient
Imports System.IO
Imports System.Xml
Dim cnSQL As SqlConnection
Dim cmSQL As SqlCommand
Dim xmlCourses As XmlReader

cnSQL = New SqlConnection( _
  "server=ssosa;trusted_connection=yes;database=enrollment")
cmSQL = New SqlCommand("usp_ListCourses", cnSQL)
cmSQL.CommandType = CommandType.StoredProcedure

Try
  cnSQL.Open()
  xmlCourses = cmSQL.ExecuteXmlReader
  Do While xmlCourses.Read()
    Console.WriteLine(xmlCourses.ReadOuterXml)
  Loop

Catch e As SqlException
```

LISTING 7.2   Continued

```
  Console.WriteLine(e.ToString())
Finally
  cnSQL.Close()
End Try
```

In this example, the same stored procedure is executed as in Listing 7.1. However, rather than execute the procedure using the `ExecuteReader` method, the `ExecuteXmlReader` method is invoked, which is unique to the SqlClient managed provider. In this case, instead of returning a result set that you can iterate using a `SqlDataReader`, an XML stream is returned via an XmlReader object and can be accessed using its Read method (discussed in Chapter 14, "Integrating with the Enterprise"). This is possible because SQL Server 2000 has the capability to generate XML at the server using the `FOR XML` clause. To generate the XML, the usp_ListCourses stored procedure was modified as shown in the following Transact-SQL code example:

```
CREATE PROCEDURE usp_ListCourses
AS
SELECT * FROM Course
ORDER BY CourseNum
FOR XML AUTO
```

Several other techniques for using command objects of the managed providers will be shown later in the chapter.

The other key aspect of using a managed provider is to use the DataAdapter to populate a `DataSet` and control how changes to the `DataSet` are sent to the underlying data store. To do this, the DataAdapter references select, insert, update, and delete command objects that are invoked when the `DataSet` is manipulated. Listing 7.3 creates a new `SqlDataAdapter` and sets the `SelectCommand` and `UpdateCommand` properties.

LISTING 7.3   Using `SqlDataAdapter`. This simple example creates a `SqlDataAdapter` and uses it to specify a stored procedure for updating a `DataSet`.

```
Imports System.Data
Imports System.Data.SqlClient
Dim cnSQL As SqlConnection
Dim daSQL As SqlDataAdapter
Dim parmWork As SqlParameter
Dim dsCourses As New DataSet("Offerings")
Dim intRows as Integer
```

LISTING 7.3   Continued

```
cnSQL = New SqlConnection( _
  "server=ssosa;trusted_connection=yes;database=enrollment")

' Create the adapter and set the SelectCommand through the constructor
daSQL = New SqlDataAdapter("usp_ListCourses", cnSQL)
daSQL.SelectCommand.CommandType = CommandType.StoredProcedure

' Create the update command
daSQL.UpdateCommand = New SqlCommand("usp_UpdateCourse", cnSQL)
daSQL.UpdateCommand.CommandType = CommandType.StoredProcedure

' Set the parameters for the update command
parmWork = daSQL.UpdateCommand.Parameters.Add( _
  New SqlParameter("@Days", SqlDbType.TinyInt))
parmWork.SourceColumn = "Days"
parmWork.SourceVersion = DataRowVersion.Current

parmWork = daSQL.UpdateCommand.Parameters.Add( _
  New SqlParameter("@CourseID", SqlDbType.Int))
parmWork.SourceColumn = "CourseID"
parmWork.SourceVersion = DataRowVersion.Original

parmWork = daSQL.UpdateCommand.Parameters.Add( _
  New SqlParameter("@Cost", SqlDbType.Money))
parmWork.SourceColumn = "CourseWareCost"
parmWork.SourceVersion = DataRowVersion.Current

' Populate the DataSet
intRows = daSQL.Fill(dsCourses, "Courses")

' Make a change to the underlying data
dsCourses.Tables("Courses").Rows(0).Item("Days") = 0

Try
  ' Save the changes
  daSQL.Update(dsCourses,"Courses")
Catch e As Exception
  ' Report the exception
End Try
```

Note that like any Command object in classic ADO, the SqlCommand object referenced in the UpdateCommand property accepts parameters stored in a Parameters collection. The constructor of SqlParameter accepts the name of the parameter and the data type using the SqlDbType enumeration. The SourceColumn and SourceVersion properties are used to instruct the

7

**ACESSING DATA
WITH ADO.NET**

SqlDataAdapter as to which column and which version of the column (Current, Default, Original, Proposed) from the DataRowVersion enumeration should be used from the DataSet to populate the parameter. In this case, the original version of the CourseID is used because it is the primary key, whereas the current versions of Days and CourseWareCost are used because they are updateable.

> **TIP**
>
> Unlike in classic ADO, when using parameters with a SqlCommand or OleDbCommand, the parameters needn't be added to the Parameters collection in the order in which they are defined in the stored procedure. This is because the procedure will be executed using named rather than positional arguments. For example, in Listing 7.3 the @Days parameter is defined prior to the @CourseID, although in the stored procedure the reverse is true. Of course, this means that you must use the exact name of the parameter when adding it to the collection. The upside is that if the parameter is nullable (defined with the NULL keyword in Transact-SQL), you needn't add it to the Parameters collection if it isn't going to be populated.

The SqlDataAdapter can then populate the underlying DataSet using the Fill method, which returns the number of rows added to the underlying DataTable. Note that if the SqlConnection object is not yet open, the Fill method will first open it before executing the query used to retrieve the data before closing it. If the connection is already open, the Fill method uses it and does not close it. This behavior is efficient because holding on to an expensive resource such as database connections is not desirable in distributed applications. Although covered later in the chapter, note that the constructor of the DataSet is used to specify a name for the DataSet, whereas the second parameter to the Fill method specifies the name of the TableMappings collection within the dsCourses DataSet to populate.

A simple change is then made to the Days column of the first row and the Update method of the SqlDataAdapter is then called. The end result is a single call to the usp_UpdateCourse stored procedure with the appropriate parameters.

In both the Fill and Update methods, the second argument is used to specify the DataTable object within the DataSet that is to be populated, about which more is to follow.

As shown in Table 7.1, instead of specifying the insert, update, and delete commands executed by the DataAdapter in code (as shown in Listing 7.3), it is possible to instruct the managed provider to create them on the fly. This can be done with SqlCommandBuilder and OleDbCommandBuilder classes. In fact, by simply instantiating a command builder and passing it the DataAdapter in the constructor, the commands will be built on the fly by the CommandBuilder when they are needed. The code in Listing 7.4 shows how this works using the SqlCommandBuilder class.

Listing 7.4 Using a `CommandBuilder`. This listing shows how to use the `SqlCommandBuilder` to autogenerate commands for data manipulation through the `SqlDataAdapter`.

```
Imports System.Data
Imports System.Data.SqlClient
Dim cnSQL As SqlConnection
Dim daSQL As SqlDataAdapter
Dim cmdSql As New SqlCommandBuilder(daSQL)
Dim cmUpd As SqlCommand
Dim dsCourses As New DataSet("Offerings")

cnSQL = New SqlConnection( _
  "server=ssosa;trusted_connection=yes;database=enrollment")
' Create the adapter and set the SelectCommand through the constructor
daSQL = New SqlDataAdapter("SELECT * FROM fn_ListCourses()", cnSQL)

' Create the command builder
cmdSql = New SqlCommandBuilder(daSQL)

' Populate the DataSet
daSQL.Fill(dsCourses, "Courses")

' Make a change to the underlying data
dsCourses.Tables("Courses").Rows(0).Item("Days") = 0
daSQL.Update(dsCourses,"Courses")

' Get the command that was used to update the database
cmUpd = cmdSql.GetUpdateCommand
Console.WriteLine(cmUpd.CommandText)
```

Notice that rather than creating the `UpdateCommand` explicitly, the `SqlCommandBuilder` is instantiated and passed a reference to daSQL. At this point, no further intervention is required. When the `Update` method of the `SqlDataAdapter` is invoked, the command builder sends a request to SQL Server to discover the column names and data types of the base table used in the `SelectCommand`. In this way, the command builder incurs only the overhead of the extra roundtrip to the server when it is required. It then populates the underlying `SqlDataAdapter` command objects, which are then immediately used to execute the insert, delete, or update (as in this case) using the `sp_executesql` system stored procedure. The commands are then cached for the lifetime of the `SqlDataAdapter`. Note that the code in Listing 7.4 also uses the `GetUpdateCommand` method of the `SqlCommandBuilder` to get a reference to the `SqlCommand` used for the update, and simply prints the `CommandText` that was generated for diagnostic purposes.

Before you plan on relying on the command builders, there are a couple of caveats of which to be aware. First, command builders only work when the statement used for the SelectCommand pulls data from a single base table. In this example, the SelectCommand uses a call to an inline table function in SQL Server 2000 that queries only the Course table and so it is successful. However, if the function were to use a SELECT statement with aggregate functions or a JOIN clause, the command builder would throw a SqlException when trying to generate the commands because either no base table or multiple base tables would be returned. As shown, however, with SQL Server you can use functions and stored procedures that return data from a single table.

TIP

A second type of function supported in SQL Server 2000 is the multi-statement table function. This function returns a result set built on the fly by Transact-SQL inside the function. Although you can use multi-statement table functions in a SelectCommand by simply referencing them in the FROM clause, the SqlCommandBuilder cannot create commands from such a statement because base table information is missing. This is the case even if the function returns data from a single table.

The second point to note is that the SQL syntax that gets built when using a command builder is not necessarily optimal. For example, all the columns returned in the SelectCommand are included inside the WHERE clause for the update and delete commands even if the primary key of the underlying DataTable is set, as shown later in the chapter. This obviously wastes network bandwidth and causes the SQL Server to have to parse the statement and create an optimized query plan before it can be executed. The following is an example of the update CommandText. Note that CourseID is the primary key.

```
UPDATE Course SET CourseNum = @p1 , Description = @p2 , ProductID = @p3 ,
LOBID = @p4 , Days = @p5 , CourseWareCost = @p6
WHERE ( CourseID = @p7 AND CourseNum = @p8 AND Description = @p9 AND
ProductID = @p10 AND LOBID = @p11 AND Days = @p12 AND CourseWareCost = @p13 )
```

In addition, the insert command is built based on only the columns that are set when populating the new row. In other words, if the insert is to succeed, you must ensure that you populate all the columns that are required and that do not have defaults.

The end result is that, for most sophisticated applications, you'll want to populate the data modification commands yourself using more efficient techniques such as stored procedures.

Using Events

Just as the `Connection` and `Command` objects in classic ADO support events, so too do the managed providers. The connection and DataAdapter classes for both OleDb and SqlClient include events that your code can capture. For example, both the `SqlConnection` and the `OleDbConnection` classes support the `InfoMessage` and `StateChanged` events to capture informational messages from the data source and monitor when the connection changes its state, respectively. Meanwhile, `SqlDataAdapter` and `OleDbDataAdapter` support `RowUpdating` and `RowUpdated` events that fire before and after the `UpdateCommand` of the adapter is executed.

To handle one of these events, you can declare the object using the `WithEvents` keyword, a dynamic event handler, or the `Delegate` class explicitly, as discussed in Chapter 4, "Object-Oriented Features." As an example, consider a client that wants to capture messages produced with the `PRINT` statement in Transact-SQL. To do this, an `InfoMessage` event must be handled. Assuming that the `SqlConnection` object is declared as `cnSQL`, a dynamic event handler can be constructed using the `AddHandler` statement as follows:

```
AddHandler cnSQL.InfoMessage, AddressOf SqlConnInfoMessage
```

The private `SqlConnInfoMessage` method must then take as its second argument the type `SqlInfoMessageEventArgs`, which exposes a collection of `SqlError` objects. The code to handle the event, construct a message string, and print it to the console is as follows:

```
Imports System.Data.SqlClient

Private Sub SqlConnInfoMessage(ByVal sender As Object, _
  ByVal e As SqlInfoMessageEventArgs)
Dim i As Integer
Dim strMessage As String

  For i = 0 to e.Errors.Count - 1
    strMessage = "Source: " & e.Errors(i).Source & vbCrlf & _
    "Number: " & e.Errors(i).Number.ToString() & vbCrlf & _
    "State: " & e.Errors(i).State.ToString() & vbCrlf & _
    "Class: " & e.Errors(i).Class.ToString() & vbCrlf & _
    "Server: " & e.Errors(i).Server & vbCrlf & _
    "Message: " & e.Errors(i).Message & vbCrlf & _
    "Procedure: " & e.Errors(i).Procedure & vbCrlf & _
    "LineNumber: " & e.Errors(i).LineNumber.ToString()
    Console.WriteLine(strMessage)
  Next
End Sub
```

Connection Pooling

Developers interested in developing scalable distributed applications for use by hundreds or thousands of concurrent users must concern themselves with using expensive resources such as database connections. As a result, you'll want to make sure that your applications do not hold connections for an extended period of time, and that multiple users can reuse connections no longer in use without having to incur the overhead of rebuilding the connection.

In classic ADO, pooling database connections was handled either through the session pooling mechanism of OLE DB or the connection pooling code implemented by the ODBC Driver manager when using the MSDASQL provider.

TIP

For more information on the differences and specifics of these two methods, see Chapter 14 of my book, *Pure Visual Basic*.

When using the OleDb managed provider, OLE DB session pooling is still available and is handled automatically by OLE DB. However, because the SqlClient managed provider communicates directly with SQL Server using TDS, it must implement its own form of connection pooling, and does so by relying on Windows 2000 Component Services. As discussed in Chapter 9, COM+ in Windows 2000 supports pooled components whereby a predefined number of instantiated object instances are hosted in a pool managed by COM+. If an object instance is available, one is handed out to a client application when it requests a new instance, and subsequently returned to the pool when dereferenced for use by another client. This scheme allows clients to reuse objects that are expensive to create, thereby reducing the resources required on the server. The class that represents a connection to SQL Server, SqlConnection, is a perfect candidate for a pooled component.

To support creating and configuring a connection pool, several additional properties are included in the ConnectionString for the SqlConnection. For example, by simply instantiating and opening a SqlConnection object with the Pooling property set to True (the default), the connection will be added to a new or existing pool. As with OLE DB session pooling, connections are grouped into pools based on the distinct text of the ConnectionString property. Any differences at all in connection strings results in the creation of a new pool.

To illustrate the concept, consider the following code:

```
cnSQL = New SqlConnection( _
   "server=ssosa;uid=dfox;pwd=dlf;database=enrollment;pooling=true")
cnSQL.Open
```

```
cnSQL2 = New SqlConnection( _
   "server=ssosa;trusted_connection=yes;database=enrollment;pooling=true")
cnSQL2.Open

cnSQL3 = New SqlConnection( _
   "server=ssosa;trusted_connection=yes;database=enrollment;pooling=true")
cnSQL3.Open
cnSQL3.Close

cnSQL4 = New SqlConnection( _
   "server=ssosa;trusted_connection=yes;database=enrollment;pooling=true")
cnSQL4.Open
```

In this example, four SqlConnection objects are instantiated and all are left open with the exception of cnSQL3. In this case, because all have the Pooling attribute set to True, two pools are created: one containing cnSQL1 and the other containing cnSQL2 and cnSQL3 (because the ConnectionString for cnSQL1 differs from that of cnSQL2 and cnSQL3). However, when the Close method of cnSQL3 is called, the connection is not torn down but is returned to the pool. As a result, when the Open method of cnSQL4 is called, the connection previously used by cnSQL3 will be pulled from the pool and assigned to cnSQL4, rather than a new connection.

Obviously, this contrived example concerns a single client application, but if you assume that each connection represents a separate user that attempts to create a database connection nearly simultaneously, you begin to see the usefulness of connection pooling. This is especially the case when the methods using the connections are short-lived and acquire and release connections quickly resulting in fewer open connections than users. Unlike OLE DB session pooling, by default, the pooled SqlConnection objects are not destroyed until the process that created them ends or the connection is somehow broken (noticed by the pooler when the connection is actually used). In addition, the pools created are also subdivided based on the transaction context of the calling thread. This allows the client application to use distributed transactions with SqlConnection objects and be sure that all work done by the transaction is committed together.

Finally, the syntax of the ConnectionString has been augmented with additional properties that control the size and behavior of the pool as shown in Table 7.3. Note that because these are included in the ConnectionString, they are set when the pool is first created (because pools are created on the basis of the syntax of the ConnectionString).

TABLE 7.3   SqlClient Connection Pooling Properties

Property	Description
Connect Timeout	Specifies the length of time to wait for a connection to succeed; the default is 15 seconds.

7

ACCESSING DATA WITH ADO.NET

Table 7.3   Continued

Property	Description
Connection Lifetime	Specifies the maximum amount of time in seconds that a connection can live. Default is 0, meaning for the duration of the process. Checked when the connection is returned to the pool.
Connection Reset	Specifies whether the connection is reset when returned to the pool by undoing any session level (SET) statements issued during the user session. Defaults to True but incurs an extra roundtrip when the connection is returned to the pool.
Enlist	Defaults to True and automatically enlists the connection in the current transaction context. Can be turned off to increase performance if your application does not use distributed transactions.
Min Pool Size, Max Pool Size	Default to 0 and 100, respectively, and determine how many connections might live in the pool.
Pooling	Defaults to True. Determines whether pooling is enabled.

Disconnected Data

As previewed in Listings 7.3 and 7.4, the second major partition of the System.Data namespace is the DataSet and its related classes. As previously mentioned, the DataSet is fundamental to ADO.NET because it represents data from one or more underlying data sources in a disconnected fashion. In addition, it includes metadata such as relationships and constraints that provide structure for the data and allows code to navigate through the data. And of course, the DataSet can be both defined with XML using an XSD schema, and stored as XML, so it is a great vehicle for passing data between tiers of a distributed application.

> **Note**
>
> The DataSet class is derived from the System.ComponentModel.
> MarshalByValueComponent class, which allows it to be marshalled by value across
> process boundaries whereby a copy of the serialized object is passed rather than
> a reference to it. In this way, it is analogous to the disconnected Recordset in
> classic ADO.

In addition to scalar properties used to configure the DataSet, the DataSet contains references to the major classes shown in Figure 7.2 and discussed in Table 7.4.

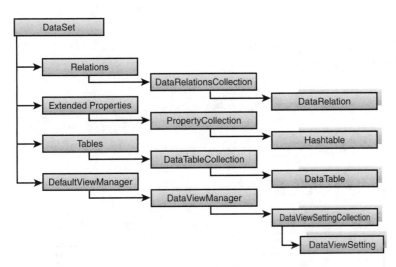

FIGURE 7.2

DataSet *object model. This diagram depicts the primary classes referenced by the* DataSet.

TABLE 7.4   DataSet classes. These are the primary classes referenced by the DataSet.

Class	Description
DataRelationsCollection	Exposed through the Relations property and contains a collection of DataRelation objects that map all the parent/child relationships between DataTable objects in a DataSet.
PropertyCollection	Exposed through the ExtendedProperties property and contains a collection of custom properties based on the Hashtable class.
DataTableCollection	Exposed through the Tables property and contains a collection of DataTable objects contained in the DataSet.
DataViewManager	Exposed through the DefaultViewManager property and used to create custom sort and filter settings (DataViewSetting) for each DataTable in the DataSet. Includes a reference to a DataViewSettingsCollection where settings for each DataTable are stored.

As you'll notice from the table, the DataSet contains references to objects that expose collections containing the data stored in the DataSet. From that perspective, you can also think of the DataSet as simply a container for tables, properties, and relations.

As depicted in Figure 7.2, the DataTableCollection exposes the collection of DataTable objects, which are used to represent the actual data. Figure 7.3 and Table 7.5 expand the DataTable and show its constituent classes.

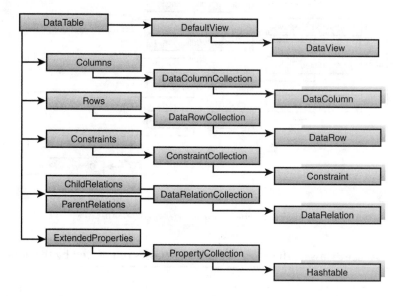

FIGURE 7.3

The relationships between the DataTable *and other* System.Data *classes.*

TABLE 7.5   DataTable Classes

Class	Description
DataView	Exposed through the DefaultView property and contains a reference to a DataView object that contains sort and filter settings for this DataTable object.
DataColumn	In addition to being referenced in Columns collection, also exposed in the PrimaryKey property as an array of objects to enforce the primary key (not shown in Figure 7.3).
DataColumnCollection	Exposed through the Columns property and contains a collection of DataColumn objects that represent each column in the DataTable.

TABLE 7.5   Continued

Class	Description
DataRowCollection	Exposed through the Rows property and contains a collection of DataRow objects in the DataTable.
ConstraintCollection	Exposed through the Constraints property and references a collection of objects derived from Constraint such as ForeignKeyConstraint and UniqueConstraint.
DataRelationCollection	Exposed through the ChildRelations and ParentRelations properties and contains a collection of DataRelation objects contained in the DataSet.
PropertyCollection	Exposed through the ExtendedProperties property and contains a collection of custom properties based on the Hashtable object.

The DataTable is the heart of the DataSet and contains the representation of the actual data. You'll notice that like the DataSet, it contains a series of collection objects that reference the columns, rows, properties, constraints, and relations. From this perspective, the DataTable is analogous to the classic ADO Recordset.

In addition, the DataTable contains a reference to a default DataView object that controls how the data is sorted and filtered. DataView objects can also be created independently to provide multiple views on the same data, for example, when changed rows need to be viewed in one grid control while new rows are viewed in another.

As an example of using the DataSet and its associated collections, consider the code in Listing 7.5. In this example, two SqlDataAdapter objects use stored procedures to fill two DataTable objects within the DataSet dsCourses with data for products and their associated courses.

LISTING 7.5   Manipulating a DataSet. This code example populates a DataSet using a SqlDataAdapter and then exercises the various collections of the DataSet and DataTable.

```
Imports System.Data.SqlClient
Imports System.Data
Dim cnSQL As SqlConnection
Dim daSql As SqlDataAdapter
Dim daSql1 As SqlDataAdapter
Dim drProdCourse As DataRelation
Dim objCon As Constraint
Dim objUn As UniqueConstraint
```

LISTING 7.5   Continued

```
Dim rowProd As DataRow
Dim rowCourse As DataRow
Dim CourseRows() As DataRow
Dim dtProducts As DataTable
Dim dtCourses As DataTable
Dim pk() As DataColumn
Dim dsCourses As New DataSet("Offerings")

cnSQL = New SqlConnection( _
  "server=ssosa;trusted_connection=yes;database=enrollment")

' Create the adapters and set the SelectCommand through the constructor
daSql = New SqlDataAdapter("usp_ListCourses", cnSQL)
daSql.SelectCommand.CommandType = CommandType.StoredProcedure

daSql1 = New SqlDataAdapter("usp_ListProducts", cnSQL)
daSql1.SelectCommand.CommandType = CommandType.StoredProcedure

' Populate the DataSet
daSql.Fill(dsCourses, "Courses")
daSql1.Fill(dsCourses, "Products")

dtProducts = dsCourses.Tables("Products")
dtCourses = dsCourses.Tables("Courses")

' Set the primary keys
ReDim pk(1)
pk(0) = dtProducts.Columns("ProductID")
dtProducts.PrimaryKey = pk
ReDim pk(1)
pk(0) = dtCourses.Columns("CourseID")
dtCourses.PrimaryKey = pk

' Add a relationship
drProdCourse = new DataRelation("ProdCourse", _
                 dtProducts.Columns("ProductID"), _
                 dtCourses.Columns("ProductID"))

drProdCourse.Nested = True
dsCourses.Relations.Add(drProdCourse)

' Look at each row in Products
For Each rowProd in dtProducts.Rows
  CourseRows = rowProd.GetChildRows("ProdCourse")
  Console.WriteLine(rowProd("Name").ToString() & " has " & _
```

LISTING 7.5 Continued

```
                      CourseRows.Length.ToString() & " Courses")

  ' Loop through each correlated row for the Courses
  For Each rowCourse in CourseRows
    Console.WriteLine(vbTab & rowCourse("CourseNum").ToString() _
        & ":" & CStr(rowCourse("Description")))
  Next
  Console.WriteLine()
Next

' Print out the constraints
For Each objCon in dtProducts.Constraints
  If TypeOf objCon Is UniqueConstraint Then
    objUn = CType(objCon,UniqueConstraint)
    Console.WriteLine("UniqueConstraint on " & objUn.Columns(0).ColumnName)
    If objUn.IsPrimaryKey Then
      Console.WriteLine("It is the primary key")
    End If
  End If
Next
```

> **TIP**
>
> Although this example illustrates the use of several DataAdapters being used to pop-
> ulate a single DataSet, multiple result sets can be returned from a single stored pro-
> cedure or SQL batch to the same effect. Doing so will increase performance because
> only a single roundtrip to the server will be incurred. Keep in mind, however, that
> you can associate only a single insert, update, and delete command to a DataAdapter.
> This means that if you plan on updating multiple DataTables within a DataSet using a
> single DataAdapter, you'll need to programmatically switch the insert, update, and
> delete commands before invoking Update or exceptions will certainly result.

The remainder of this section will discuss several features of Listing 7.5 that illustrate the
structure and uses of the DataSet and DataTable classes.

Mapping Data to the DataSet

Note that the second argument of the overloaded Fill method specifies the name of the
DataTableMapping to populate. In this case, because no mapping was created before the Fill
method was invoked, the SqlDataAdapter creates DataTable objects using the provided mapping names, and maps each DataColumn in the DataSet to a column from the underlying

database. However, you can programmatically create a mapping layer before populating the DataSet using the TableMappings collection. This is important for when the schema of the DataSet will not exactly match the names of the columns in the database. For example, instead of simply using the database column names in Listing 7.5, the following code could be inserted before the Fill method is invoked to map some of the columns of the Course table to new values:

```
daSql.TableMappings.Add("Table","Courses")

daSql.TableMappings(0).ColumnMappings.Add("CourseNum","CourseNumber")
daSql.TableMappings(0).ColumnMappings.Add("Description","CourseDesc")
daSql.TableMappings(0).ColumnMappings.Add("ProductID","CourseProdID")
daSql.TableMappings(0).ColumnMappings.Add("LOBID","CourseLineOfBusinessID")
daSql.TableMappings(0).ColumnMappings.Add("Days","CourseDays")
daSql.TableMappings(0).ColumnMappings.Add("CourseWareCost","Cost")


daSQL.Fill(dsCourses)
```

In this example, a DataTableMapping object is added to the collection exposed by the DataAdapter and called "Table." In this case, "Table" has a special connotation because it represents the default table mapping. In other words, when a DataSet is filled, the SqlDataAdapter looks for a table mapping with the name of "Table" and uses it to map the column information in the DataTable. Optionally, another name for the mapping could be used and then passed as the second argument to the Fill method. Because of this default behavior, the second argument to the Fill method is omitted.

After the mapping has been created, columns can be added to it using the ColumnMappings collection by simply passing the name of the database column followed by the name it will have in the resulting DataTable. In this case, all the columns except CourseID are being mapped. If the database column does not exist in the ColumnMappings collection, it will by default automatically be added to the resulting DataTable (although this can be changed by setting the MissingSchemaAction property of the DataAdapter to the Ignore value). After the Fill method is invoked, a DataTable called "Courses" is created and populated with the columns from the ColumnsMapping collection. An example of the resulting XML from the DataSet returned using the WriteXml method of the DataSet follows (note that the Nested property is set to False for this example, as discussed later):

```
<Courses>
  <CourseID>12</CourseID>
  <CourseNumber>SYB </CourseNumber>
  <CourseDesc>FastTrack to Adaptive Server</CourseDesc>
  <CourseProdID>8</CourseProdID>
  <CourseLineOfBusinessID>2</CourseLineOfBusinessID>
  <CourseDays>5</CourseDays>
```

```
  <Cost>300</Cost>
</Courses>
<Courses>
  <CourseID>15</CourseID>
  <CourseNumber>SYBA</CourseNumber>
  <CourseDesc>Administering Adaptive Server</CourseDesc>
  <CourseProdID>8</CourseProdID>
  <CourseLineOfBusinessID>2</CourseLineOfBusinessID>
  <CourseDays>5</CourseDays>
  <Cost>300</Cost>
</Courses>
```

TIP

Optionally, you can programmatically create the DataTable and add new columns and rows to it with the Add method of the Columns collection and the NewRow method, respectively. This might come in handy if you need to add data to the DataSet that does not live in the database, for example, the values of arguments used to query the database.

After the DataSet has been populated, the DataTablesCollection can then be accessed through the Tables property of the DataSet. In Listing 7.5, it is used to assign the tables to object variables for easier access. Note that because the DataAdapters are separate objects, the data they use to populate the tables of the DataSet could come from heterogenous sources. In addition, you can set the PrimaryKey property of the DataTable to an array of DataColumn objects in order to represent a composite key. This also has the effect of automatically creating a UniqueConstraint object and placing it in the ConstraintCollection exposed through the Constraints property.

In situations (like that shown in Listing 7.5) in which you want to populate the schema of the DataSet directly from a database table, you can optionally use the FillSchema method of a DataAdapter to prepopulate the schema. This method accepts the DataSet to populate, the SchemaType and, optionally, arguments such as the table mapping. In addition to the column information, FillSchema will retrieve both the primary key and unique constraints by querying the underlying data source (in SQL Server this entails issuing the SET NO_BROWSETABLE ON statement). For example, the following line of code will prepopulate the schema of the Courses table mapping used in Listing 7.5:

```
daSql.FillSchema(dsCourses, SchemaType.Mapped, "Courses")
```

Note that this method returns the DataTable object that was populated.

7

ACESSING DATA
WITH ADO.NET

> **TIP**
>
> A more convenient way to retrieve the constraint information automatically is to set the `MissingSchemaAction` property of the `DataSet` equal to `MissingSchemaAction.AddWithKey` before invoking the `Fill` method.

Relating Data

To associate the rows in the Courses table with their parent rows in the Products table, you can create a `DataRelation` object as shown in the listing. In this case, the constructor of the `DataRelation` accepts the name of the relation in addition to the parent column and child column within their respective tables. The `DataRelation` is then added to the appropriate `DataRelationCollection` for each table and exposed through the `ChildRelations` and `ParentRelations` properties. For example, in this case the relation is added to the `ChildRelations` collection of `dtProducts` and the `ParentRelations` collection of `dtCourses`.

You'll also notice that the `Nested` property of the `DataRelation` is set to `True`. Setting this property changes the XSD schema produced by the `DataSet` from one that produces a union-like view of the data with one that is hierarchical. For example, changing the `Nested` property from the defaulted value of `False` to `True` changes the resulting XML from the following, where all the Products elements follow all the Courses elements:

```
<Offerings>
  <Courses>
  ...
  </Courses>
  <Courses>
  ...
  </Courses>
  <Products>
  ...
  </Products>
  <Products>
  ...
  </Products>
</Offerings>
```

to this:

```
<Offerings>
  <Products>
    <Courses>
      ...
    </Courses>
```

```
    <Courses>
      ...
    </Courses>
  </Products>
  <Products>
    <Courses>
      ...
    </Courses>
  </Products>
</Offerings>
```

where all the Courses for a particular product are nested within the appropriate Products element. Of course, the underlying XSD also changes to reflect the new hierarchical nature of the `DataSet` and can be queried using the `WriteXmlSchema` method.

> **TIP**
>
> Keep in mind that even though all the database columns are mapped by default to elements in the XML representation of the `DataSet`, you can override this behavior by altering the schema used to produce the XML. One technique for doing so is to change the `ColumnMapping` property of the `DataColumn` object to a value from the `MappingType` enumeration. For example, to change the ProductID column to an attribute, you would use the syntax `dtProducts.Columns("ProductID").ColumnMapping = MappingType.Attribute` in Listing 7.5.

Regardless of which way the XML is nested for display, after the relationship is in place, the code can navigate through the `DataSet`. In this example, each `DataRow` in the `dtProducts` table is iterated using a `For Each` loop. The `GetChildRows` method of the `DataRow` object can then be called to return an array of `DataRow` objects, in this case `CourseRows`, found via the relationships. In turn, the rows in the array are iterated to print out various columns.

Using Constraints

Finally, the code in Listing 7.5 iterates through each `Constraint` object in the `ConstraintCollection` exposed by the `Constraints` property of the `dtProducts DataTable`. Because `Constraint` is the base class, the `TypeOf` statement is used to determine whether the constraint is of type `UniqueConstraint`. If so, the `objCon` variable is cast to the `UniqueConstraint` type using the `CType` function and the first column of the constraint is printed to the console. In this case, the act of creating the relation automatically puts a unique constraint on the ProductID column of the `dtProducts DataTable`. However, unless the primary key is explicitly created, as in this example, the `IsPrimaryKey` property of the `UniqueConstraint` object will be defaulted to `False`.

An excerpt of the sample output for Listing 7.5 is as follows:

```
SQL Server has 3 Courses
        1140:SQL Server 7.0 Intro
        2072:System Administration for SQL Server 2000
        2073:Implementing a Database Design on SQL Server 2000

Visual Basic has 2 Courses
        1013:Mastering Visual Basic
        1016:Enterprise Development with Visual Basic

Visual Interdev has 1 Courses
        1017:Mastering Web Site Development
```

Using Select

The final important concept that you should be familiar with when using the DataTable class
is the ability to select rows with the Select method. This overloaded method returns an array
of DataRow objects corresponding to the criteria provided. For example, in the case of the
Courses DataTable shown in Listing 7.5, you can use the Select method to return only those
rows for a particular product as follows:

```
Dim drRows() As DataRow
Dim strCourseNum as String

drRows = dtCourses.Select("ProductID = 1","CourseNum ASC")

For Each rowProd in drRows
  strCourseNum = rowProd("CourseNum").ToString
Next
```

In addition, the second argument (exposed in an overloaded signature) can include a sort criteria; in this case, sorting by CourseNum in ascending order. Further, a third overloaded method
allows you to select rows based on the values of the DataViewRowState enumeration which
include Added, CurrentRows, Deleted, ModifiedCurrent, ModifiedOriginal, None,
OriginalRows, and Unchanged.

NOTE

Other techniques can also be used to return a subset of data from a DataSet or
DataTable. These include the GetErrors method of the DataTable, which returns an
array of rows that contain errors after a call to Update when the HasErrors property
returns True, and the GetChanges method of the DataSet, which returns a new
DataSet that contains only data that has been modified.

Using Events

Just as the `Recordset` object in classic ADO supports events, both the `DataSet` and `DataTable` classes support a variety of events that you can use to respond to changes in the structure and the data in the application. For example, the `DataSet` supports the `MergeFailed` and `PropertyChanged` events that fire when errors occur as two `DataSet` objects are merged with the `Merge` method and when any property of the `DataSet` changes, respectively. The `DataTable` supports seven events, six of which are logically paired as shown in Table 7.6 along with the arguments passed into the events.

TABLE 7.6 `DataTable` Events

Events	Event Args	Description
ColumnChanging, ColumnChanged	DataColumnChange EventArgs	Fired immediately before and immediately after a column value is modified in the `DataTable`.
RowChanging, RowChanged	DataRowChange EventArgs	Fired immediately before and immediately after a row has been successfully edited in a `DataTable`.
RowDeleting, RowDeleted	DataRowChange EventArgs	Fired immediately before and immediately after a row has been successfully deleted in a `DataTable`.
Disposed	EventArgs MarshalByValueComponent	Inherited from and fires when the object is disposed.

These events can be used to add functionality to your applications such as creating a client-side audit trail by capturing the `RowChanged` event and inspecting the `DataRowAction` enumeration exposed through the `Action` property of the `DataRowChangeEventArgs`. For each row marked as `Delete`, `Add`, `Change`, and `Commit`, your application could log the fact to a file. For example, the `RowChanged` event of the `dtCourses` table created in Listing 7.5 can be handled by using the following `AddHandler` statement:

```
AddHandler dtCourses.RowChanged, AddressOf CoursesRowChanged
```

The `CoursesRowChanged` method is then implemented to handle the event, extract the `Action` and the primary key of the row from the event arguments, and log them to a log file using a private `LogToFile` method, as follows:

```
Private Sub CoursesRowChanged(ByVal sender As Object, _
  ByVal e As DataRowChangeEventArgs)

Dim strAction As String

  Select Case e.Action
    Case DataRowAction.Add
      strAction = "Action=Add"
    Case DataRowAction.Change
      strAction = "Action=Change"
    Case DataRowAction.Commit
      strAction = "Action=Commit"
    Case DataRowAction.Delete
      strAction = "Action=Delete"
    Case Else ' Do Nothing
      Return
  End select

  LogToFile(strAction & ", CourseID = " & e.Row.Item("CourseID").ToString() & _
    " at " & DateTime.Now.ToShortTimeString()
    & " " & DateTime.Now.ToShortDateString())
End Sub
```

Although the preceding discussion highlights the constituent pieces and mechanics of a DataSet and using the managed providers, it does not place them in the context of an actual application. The remainder of the chapter will be devoted to using ADO.NET in a distributed application.

Application Scenario: The Quilogy Education System

With the fundamentals of accessing data through managed providers and returning data through a DataSet out of the way, we can now begin to focus on putting the ADO.NET components in their proper context. The code developed in the remainder of this chapter includes an application architecture and data access techniques used in developing an online Quilogy Education system. The code for this application can be found on the companion Web site at www.samspublishing.com.

One of the key features of the sample application is the ability for students to access information about Quilogy Education offerings through a public Web site. Several features of the site include the ability to query for course schedules, enroll in a class, and log on to the site with a password in order to view transcripts. Obviously, each of these three actions involves either collecting data from the user services tier of the application and sending it to the business and data services for processing, or querying the database for data and passing it back to the user services for presentation. Both of these scenarios lend themselves very well to using the DataSet because of its structured and disconnected nature.

However, the application must also be able to query the server directly to validate logins, save enrollments, and perform other data access tasks. For these tasks, it will be more efficient for the managed provider to execute statements directly rather than using a DataSet. In addition, because the data store used in this application is SQL Server 2000, the SqlClient managed provider will be used because it communicates natively with SQL Server using TDS, thereby increasing performance. As a result, the application will be architected as shown in Figure 7.4.

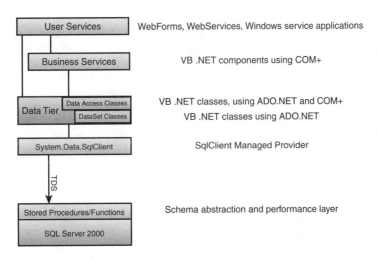

FIGURE 7.4
The architecture of the application used for the Quilogy Education Web site.

To handle both types of data access, two sets of classes will be created within the data services tier, as shown in Figure 7.4:

- A set of DataSet classes used to encapsulate the data passed between tiers of the application will be developed.

- A set of data access classes will be developed through which the other components of the system will request and receive data, possibly by returning instances of the DataSet classes.

The data access classes in particular will use the SqlClient managed provider to access SQL Server.

You'll also notice from Figure 7.4 that when making requests of SQL Server, the application will use stored procedures and functions rather than inline SQL. Doing so has the advantage of providing an interface that abstracts the database schema from developers and their code so that the data is both simpler for developers to use and insulates code from schema changes (as long as the signatures of stored procedures and functions remain the same). It also increases performance because stored procedures don't require the additional resolution and query plan creation incurred when using inline SQL.

There are two main advantages to this architecture:

- It abstracts the data access code from the business and user services tiers. In this way, changes to the location and structure of the data do not have rippling effects on either the business rules or user interface.
- By creating custom DataSet classes to embody the data being passed between tiers, we can provide strongly typed access to it that makes coding more efficient and less error prone.

In the next few sections, we'll take a look at defining the data structure of the Quilogy Education application. We'll begin by creating the custom DataSet classes used in the application and will then implement the data access classes.

Defining the Data Structure

ADO.NET is designed to facilitate the passing of data between tiers of a distributed application easily using the DataSet. As a result, the sample Quilogy Education application takes advantage of the DataSet to collect information from users and pass it to business and data access components in the middle and data tiers.

To support the passing of data, the data tier is responsible for defining the structure of the data passed back and forth. To do this, the application will use multiple classes derived from DataSet, the most important of which are shown in Table 7.7.

TABLE 7.7   Application DataSets—the DataSet Classes Used in the Quilogy Education Application

Class	Description
TranscriptData	Defines the data returned for a student when she views her transcript.
ScheduleData	Defines the data returned when querying for a list of available classes given a variety of criteria.
EnrollmentData	Defines the data captured when enrolling a student in a class.
StudentData	Defines the demographic data for one or more students.

The remainder of this section will discuss the varying techniques used to create the custom `DataSet` classes shown in Table 7.7.

Creating a `DataSet`

ADO.NET supports three basic techniques for creating the structure of data sets including automatic creation, programmatic creation, and using the XML Schema.

Automatic Schema Creation

The first option, automatic creation, was used in Listing 7.5 when populating the `DataSet` that contained the Courses and Products `DataTable` objects by simply invoking the `Fill` method of the `SqlDataAdapter` and passing in the name of a `DataTableMapping` that does not exist. In that case, the column names and data types extracted from the database are used as the names of the `DataColumn` objects; by default, each `DataColumn` is mapped to an element in the XML schema of the `DataSet`. In addition, the XSD schema creates a unioned rather than hierarchical representation of the data when there are multiple `DataTable` objects. For example, Listing 7.6 shows the XSD schema that was automatically created for the `DataSet` in Listing 7.5 containing the Courses and Products `DataTable` objects.

> **NOTE**
>
> A discussion of the elements that make up the structure of XSD schemas is beyond the scope of this book. For more information see www.w3c.org/XML/Schema/.

LISTING 7.6   XSD Schema. The schema produced for the `DataSet` created in Listing 7.5 using automatic population.

```
<xsd:schema id="Offerings" targetNamespace="" xmlns=""
xmlns:xsd="http://www.w3.org/2001/XMLSchema"
xmlns:msdata="urn:schemas-microsoft-com:xml-msdata">
  <xsd:element name="Offerings" msdata:IsDataSet="true">
    <xsd:complexType>
      <xsd:choice maxOccurs="unbounded">
        <xsd:element name="Courses">
          <xsd:complexType>
            <xsd:sequence>
              <xsd:element name="CourseID" type="xsd:int" minOccurs="0" />
              <xsd:element name="CourseNum" type="xsd:string" minOccurs="0" />
              <xsd:element name="Description" type="xsd:string" minOccurs="0"
              <xsd:element name="ProductID" type="xsd:int" minOccurs="0" />
              <xsd:element name="LOBID" type="xsd:int" minOccurs="0" />
              <xsd:element name="Days" type="xsd:unsignedByte" minOccurs="0" /
              <xsd:element name="CourseWareCost" type="xsd:decimal"
```

7

ACCESSING DATA
WITH ADO.NET

LISTING 7.6   Continued

```
              minOccurs=" />
          </xsd:sequence>
        </xsd:complexType>
      </xsd:element>
      <xsd:element name="Products">
        <xsd:complexType>
          <xsd:sequence>
            <xsd:element name="ProductID" type="xsd:int" minOccurs="0" />
            <xsd:element name="Name" type="xsd:string" minOccurs="0" />
            <xsd:element name="VendorID" type="xsd:int" minOccurs="0" />
          </xsd:sequence>
        </xsd:complexType>
      </xsd:element>
    </xsd:choice>
  </xsd:complexType>
</xsd:element>
</xsd:schema>
```

You'll notice that the schema contains the root element Offerings, which consists of repeating Courses elements followed by repeating Products elements. You'll also notice that the elements are not related to each other. In addition, the schema does not indicate which elements are required, maps each column to an element, and uses the database column names.

If this approach were used in an application architected as shown in Figure 7.4, the data access classes would be responsible for building the DataSet objects on the fly, and returning them through methods exposed by the data access classes. The methods would return the type DataSet rather than a strongly typed class inherited from DataSet because the DataSet is created in a just-in-time fashion. This technique has the benefit of simplicity because the creation of custom DataSet classes is not required, but is limiting in other respects.

Although automatic creation is certainly the simplest way to build the DataSet, it is obviously limited in several ways including:

- The names of the DataColumn objects are controlled by the underlying data store rather than the application

- The structure of the XML produced is flat rather than hierarchical and does not contain constraint information

- The DataSet produced is not strongly typed

The first limitation means that the data store and DataSet are tightly coupled so that changes to database column names and table structures will have rippling effects as the data is used in applications within bound controls and code written to manipulate the data in the presentation services. The second limitation severely restricts the use of the XML produced to applications that manipulate the data as a `DataSet` rather than an XML document. This is the case because vital metadata about the relationships between elements is not automatically shown. Finally, by using late-bound access to the `DataSet`, your code is less readable. This increases development time along with the possibility of run-time rather than compile-time errors.

As a result, in all but the simplest applications, you'll want to decouple the structure of the `DataSet` from the data store used to populate it and include all the relevant metadata using a typed `DataSet`. Doing so also decreases the amount of code you'll need to write in the data access classes. To create a typed `DataSet`, you'll need to rely on other techniques discussed later in this section.

DataSet Population from XML Documents

Although this discussion has thus far focused on creating `DataSet` objects from a persistent data store such as SQL Server, you can also create and populate a `DataSet` from standalone XML documents as well. This would be advantageous when you want to load XML documents and save them directly to a relational database.

To create the structure of a `DataSet` from an XML document, the `DataSet` class supports the `InferXmlSchema` method as the analog to automatic schema creation using the `Fill` method. For example, consider the following simple XML document:

```
<Course ID="22321">
  <Class>
    <City>Kansas City</City>
    <Date>1/1/2001</Date>
    <Students>12</Students>
    <Instructor>
      <FName>Mike</FName>
      <LName>Willoughby</LName>
    </Instructor>
  </Class>
</Course>
```

This document can be passed to the `InferXmlSchema` method to automatically create the schema as follows using a process referred to as *inference* (note that the data, however, is not loaded):

```
Dim dsCourseData As New DataSet
dsCourseData.InferXmlSchema("CourseData.xml", Nothing)
```

The method has a variety of overloaded signatures that allow you to pass the XML using a `Stream`, `XmlReader`, or `TextReader` (discussed in Chapters 12 and 14). Note that the second argument is set to `Nothing`, but can be populated with an array of strings containing namespace URIs that are to be ignored when creating the schema. In this way, you can selectively create a schema from only certain elements in the document. The resulting schema is shown in Listing 7.7. Refer to the .NET Framework online documentation for the rules regarding how the schema is inferred.

LISTING 7.7   Inferred XSD Schema. This listing shows the XSD schema resulting from calling the `InferXmlSchema` method of the `DataSet` class.

```
<xsd:schema id="NewDataSet" targetNamespace="" xmlns=""
  xmlns:xsd="http://www.w3.org/2001/XMLSchema"
  xmlns:msdata="urn:schemas-microsoft-com:xml-msdata">
  <xsd:element name="Course">
    <xsd:complexType>
      <xsd:sequence>
        <xsd:element name="Class" minOccurs="0" maxOccurs="unbounded">
          <xsd:complexType>
            <xsd:sequence>
              <xsd:element name="City" type="xsd:string" minOccurs="0"
                msdata:Ordinal="0" />
              <xsd:element name="Date" type="xsd:string" minOccurs="0"
                msdata:Ordinal="1" />
              <xsd:element name="Students" type="xsd:string" minOccurs="0"
                msdata:Ordinal="2" />
              <xsd:element name="Instructor" minOccurs="0"
                maxOccurs="unbounded">
                <xsd:complexType>
                  <xsd:sequence>
                    <xsd:element name="FName" type="xsd:string"
                      minOccurs="0" msdata:Ordinal="0" />
                    <xsd:element name="LName" type="xsd:string"
                      minOccurs="0" msdata:Ordinal="1" />
                  </xsd:sequence>
                  <xsd:attribute name="Class_Id" type="xsd:int"
                    use="prohibited" />
                </xsd:complexType>
              </xsd:element>
            </xsd:sequence>
            <xsd:attribute name="Class_Id" msdata:AutoIncrement="true"
              type="xsd:int" msdata:AllowDBNull="false" use="prohibited" />
            <xsd:attribute name="Course_Id" type="xsd:int" use="prohibited" />
          </xsd:complexType>
        </xsd:element>
      </xsd:sequence>
      <xsd:attribute name="Course_Id" msdata:AutoIncrement="true"
        type="xsd:int" msdata:AllowDBNull="false" use="prohibited" />
      <xsd:attribute name="ID" type="xsd:string" />
    </xsd:complexType>
```

Listing 7.7   Continued

```
    </xsd:element>
    <xsd:element name="NewDataSet" msdata:IsDataSet="true">
      <xsd:complexType>
        <xsd:choice maxOccurs="unbounded">
          <xsd:element ref="Course" />
        </xsd:choice>
      </xsd:complexType>
      <xsd:unique name="Class_Constraint1" msdata:ConstraintName="Constraint1"
        msdata:PrimaryKey="true">
        <xsd:selector xpath=".//Class" />
        <xsd:field xpath="@Class_Id" />
      </xsd:unique>
      <xsd:unique name="Constraint1" msdata:PrimaryKey="true">
        <xsd:selector xpath=".//Course" />
        <xsd:field xpath="@Course_Id" />
      </xsd:unique>
      <xsd:keyref name="Course_Class" refer="Constraint1" msdata:IsNested="true">
        <xsd:selector xpath=".//Class" />
        <xsd:field xpath="@Course_Id" />
      </xsd:keyref>
      <xsd:keyref name="Class_Instructor" refer="Class_Constraint1"
        msdata:IsNested="true">
        <xsd:selector xpath=".//Instructor" />
        <xsd:field xpath="@Class_Id" />
      </xsd:keyref>
    </xsd:element>
</xsd:schema>
```

Inferring schemas in this fashion is most useful in a design environment in which you need to reverse-engineer existing XML documents to create DataAdapters that populate them. You'll also want to edit the resulting schema to include appropriate data types, required elements and attributes, and additional constraint information because the data types are all defaulted to string, the elements and attributes are not required, and only the constraints required to associ-ate the nested elements are automatically created as evidenced by Listing 7.7.

To populate the DataSet from an XML document, you can use the ReadXml method analogous to the Fill method as follows:

```
dsCourseData.ReadXml("CourseData.xml")
```

In this case, the file is passed using relative pathing as the only argument, although the method actually supports eight different signatures and also can accept data from an XmlReader, Stream, or TextReader. Note that calling ReadXml and leaving off the optional second argu-ment both infers the schema and loads the data. The second argument can be set to one of the

XmlReadMode enumerations: `Auto`, `DiffGram`, `IgnoreSchema`, `InferSchema`, `ReadSchema`, or `Fragment`. As you might expect, `Auto` is the default and in this case both infers the schema and loads the data. The ignore, infer, and read schema options can be used to bypass the schema if one exists in the document, infer the schema only, or read only the schema from the document, respectively. The `Fragment` option allows the `DataSet` to read an XML document with an inline XDR (XML Data Reduced) schema, such as those produced by SQL Server 2000 when using the `FOR XML` statement.

> **NOTE**
>
> The XDR schema specification was Microsoft's initial attempt, proposed to the W3C, at creating an XML grammar for specifying the structure of an XML document. The W3C considered several competing specifications and eventually landed on XSD as the recommended specification.

The `DiffGram` option will be discussed in more detail later in the chapter.

Programmatic Creation

The second technique for creating a `DataSet` is to use the programmatic interfaces exposed by the `DataSet`. Often this technique is used in conjunction with creating a *typed* `DataSet`. As mentioned in the first part of this section, the application architecture in this case calls for the creation of custom `DataSet` classes to represent the information shown in Table 7.7.

To create a typed `DataSet`, you can simply create a custom class and inherit from the `DataSet` class. In this way, all the members—in addition to your own members—of the `DataSet` class are available to consumers of the typed `DataSet`. You can then add custom code to programmatically create `DataTable` objects, relations, and constraints as required.

For example, the simple `TranscriptData` class from Table 7.7 inherits from `DataSet`. In its constructor is a call to a private method that is responsible for building and customizing the `DataTable` object, as shown in Listing 7.8.

LISTING 7.8   A Simple Typed `DataSet`. In this example, a typed `DataSet`, `TranscriptData`, is created by inheriting from `DataSet`. It includes code to create the structure of the `DataSet` when a new instance is created.

```
Option Strict On
Option Explicit On

Imports System
Imports System.Data
Imports System.Runtime.Serialization
```

LISTING 7.8 Continued

```
Namespace Quilogy.Education

  <Serializable()> _
  Public Class TranscriptData : Inherits DataSet

    Private studentClass As DataTable

    Public Event ValidationWarning(ByVal pMessage As String)

    Public Const STUDENT_ID As String = "StudentID"
    Public Const ENROLL_ID As String = "EnrollID"
    Public Const CLASS_DATE As String = "Date"
    Public Const CITY As String = "City"
    Public Const INSTRUCTOR As String = "Instructor"
    Public Const INS_EMAIL As String = "InstructorEmail"
    Public Const VENDOR_NAME As String = "VendorName"
    Public Const COURSE_NUM As String = "CourseNum"
    Public Const COURSE_DESC As String = "CourseDesc"
    Public Const DAYS As String = "Days"
    Public Const ORGANIZATION As String = "StudentOrganization"


    Public Sub New()
      '  Initialize a TranscriptData instance by building the table
      MyBase.New()
      InitClass()
    End Sub

    Public Sub New(ByVal info As SerializationInfo, _
      ByVal context As StreamingContext)
      '  Initialize a TranscriptData instance
      MyBase.New()
      InitClass()
      Me.GetSerializationData(info, context)
    End Sub

    Private Sub InitClass()
      ' Create the tables in the dataset
      BuildTables()
      ' Initialize the class
      Me.DataSetName = "QuilogyTranscript"
      Me.Namespace = "www.quilogy.com/education/transcript"
      Me.Prefix = "qedts"
      Me.CaseSensitive = False

      ' Capture the ColumnChangingEvent
```

LISTING 7.8 Continued

```
      AddHandler studentClass.ColumnChanging, _
        AddressOf Me.TranscriptColChanging
    End Sub

    Private Sub TranscriptColChanging(ByVal sender As Object, _
      ByVal e As DataColumnChangeEventArgs)
      Dim strOrig As String
      ' Do simple data validation
      Select Case e.Column.ColumnName
        Case COURSE_DESC
          ' Truncate long descriptions
          If Len(e.ProposedValue) > 255 Then
            strOrig = CType(e.ProposedValue, String)
            e.ProposedValue = Left(CType(e.ProposedValue, String), 255)
            RaiseEvent ValidationWarning("The " & COURSE_DESC & " '" & _
              strOrig & "' was truncated to '" & _
              CType(e.ProposedValue, String) & "'")
          End If
      End Select
    End Sub

    Public ReadOnly Property ClassTable() As DataTable
      Get
        Return studentClass
      End Get
    End Property

    Private Sub BuildTables()
      Dim pk() As DataColumn

      ' Create the transcript table
      studentClass = New DataTable("Class")

      With studentClass.Columns
        .Add(STUDENT_ID, GetType(System.Int32))
        .Add(ENROLL_ID, GetType(System.Int32))
        .Add(CLASS_DATE, GetType(System.DateTime))
        .Add(CITY, GetType(System.String))
        .Add(INSTRUCTOR, GetType(System.String))
        .Add(INS_EMAIL, GetType(System.String))
        .Add(VENDOR_NAME, GetType(System.String))
        .Add(COURSE_NUM, GetType(System.String))
        .Add(COURSE_DESC, GetType(System.String))
        .Add(DAYS, GetType(System.Byte))
        .Add(ORGANIZATION, GetType(System.String))
      End With
```

Listing 7.8   Continued

```
        ' Set the column attributes
        With studentClass
            .Columns(STUDENT_ID).ColumnMapping = MappingType.Attribute
            .Columns(ENROLL_ID).ColumnMapping = MappingType.Hidden
            .Columns(CLASS_DATE).AllowDBNull = False
            .Columns(CLASS_DATE).Caption = "Class Date"
            .Columns(CITY).AllowDBNull = False
            .Columns(COURSE_NUM).AllowDBNull = False
            .Columns(DAYS).DefaultValue = 0
            .Columns(VENDOR_NAME).Caption = "Vendor Name"
            .Columns(COURSE_NUM).Caption = "Course Number"
            .Columns(COURSE_DESC).Caption = "Description"
            .Columns(ORGANIZATION).Caption = "Your Organization"
        End With

        ' Set the primary key
        ReDim pk(1)
        pk(0) = studentClass.Columns(ENROLL_ID)
        studentClass.PrimaryKey = pk

        ' Add the table to the collection
        Me.Tables.Add(studentClass)

    End Sub
  End Class
End Namespace
```

Perhaps the first aspect of Listing 7.8 you'll notice is that the `TranscriptData` class is defined within a `Namespace` statement. In this case, the class will exist in the `Quilogy.Education` namespace discussed in Chapter 4, Figure 4.1.

Second, notice that all the work is done in the constructor of the class. Here, the base class constructor is called prior to a private method, `InitClass`, which in turn calls `BuildTables` to create a `DataTable` object and populates it with `DataColumn` objects. In addition, the `InitClass` method initializes the `DataSet` by setting the name and namespace properties.

> **Note**
>
> The `TranscriptData` class also contains an overloaded constructor that accepts `SerializationInfo` and `StreamingContext` objects as parameters and calls `GetSerializationData`. This "private" constructor is called by the runtime when the `DataSet` is serialized so that it can be transported across `AppDomains`. In addition, the

> class signature must include the System.SerializableAttribute to indicate to the runtime that the DataSet can be serialized. Obviously, the addition of these constructs is required only in a derived DataSet; objects declared simply as DataSet can be deserialized automatically. For more information on serialization see Chapter 8.

Because this is a simple DataSet, within BuildTables only a single DataTable, mdtClass, is created and exposed with the read-only property ClassData. After the columns are added, they are customized using the properties of the DataColumn object. For example, the CLASS_DATE, CITY, and COURSE_NUM columns are set to not allow nulls, whereas the mapping of STUDENT_ID and ENROLL_ID are changed from element to attribute and hidden, respectively. Finally, the primary key of the DataSet is created using the ENROLL_ID column before the DataTable is added to the DataTableCollection of the DataSet. Notice that the names of the columns are created as constants so that they can be easily changed if necessary without affecting code that uses this class.

Because TranscriptData is a custom class like any other in VB .NET, it can also include its own members. In this case, not only is the ClassTable property added to expose the mdtClass DataTable, but a Public event, ValidationWarning, has been defined as well. This event is raised in the Private TranscriptColChanging procedure that handles the ColumnChanging event for mdtClass discussed in Table 7.6. You'll notice that in this event handler, the DataColumnChangeEventArgs class exposes a ProposedValue that you can inspect and change to do simple data validation along with a reference to the actual DataColumn being changed. In this case, if the COURSE_NUM column has been changed to a string with a length greater than 255 characters, it is truncated and a ValidationWarning event is fired with the particulars.

TIP

> Note that if an exception is raised in the ColumnChanging event handler, the ProposedValue will not be reflected in the DataColumn and so it can be used for more sophisticated validation as well.

Using the class in Listing 7.8, a consumer of the TranscriptData class can be assured that the structure of the DataSet is immutable and can simply populate it as follows:

```
Imports Quilogy.Education
Imports System.Data.SqlClient
Dim dsTs As New TranscriptData
Dim parmWork As SqlParameter
```

```
Dim daSql As SqlDataAdapter
Dim parmSql As SqlParameter

daSql = New SqlDataAdapter("usp_GetTranscript", cnSQL)

daSql.SelectCommand.CommandType = CommandType.StoredProcedure
parmSql = daSQL.SelectCommand.Parameters.Add( _
  New SqlParameter("@StudentID", SqlDbType.Int))
parmSql.Value = intStudentID

daSql.Fill(dsTs,dsTs.ClassTable.TableName)
```

7

In this particular case, the name of the `DataTable` is passed as the second argument to the `Fill` method because no explicit table mapping was created. As a result, the `usp_GetTranscript` stored procedure should produce columns with the same names as the `DataColumn` objects added to the table in Listing 7.8. If this is not the case, the default behavior mandates that the additional columns will also be added to the `DataSet`. As stated previously, to ensure that only columns in the table mapping are populated, you can set the `MissingSchemaAction` property to `Ignore`. Optionally, if the stored procedure does not produce the requisite columns, a table mapping can be created by the developer writing the code in the previous example.

The resulting XSD and XML data returned by the `WriteXml` method of the `DataSet` for a particular student can be seen in Listing 7.9.

LISTING 7.9   Completed Schema and Data for a Transcript. This listing shows the XSD schema produced in Listing 7.7 along with data returned from a stored procedure.

```
<qedts:QuilogyTranscript xmlns:qedts="www.quilogy.com/education/transcript">
  <xsd:schema id="QuilogyTranscript"
  targetNamespace="www.quilogy.com/education/transcript"
  xmlns="www.quilogy.com/education/transcript"
  xmlns:xsd="http://www.w3.org/2001/XMLSchema"
  xmlns:msdata="urn:schemas-microsoft-com:xml-msdata"
  attributeFormDefault="qualified" elementFormDefault="qualified">
    <xsd:element name="QuilogyTranscript" msdata:IsDataSet="true"
      msdata:Prefix="qedts">
      <xsd:complexType>
        <xsd:choice maxOccurs="unbounded">
          <xsd:element name="Class">
            <xsd:complexType>
              <xsd:sequence>
                <xsd:element name="Date" msdata:Caption="Class Date"
                  type="xsd:dateTime" msdata:Ordinal="2" />
                <xsd:element name="City" type="xsd:string"
                  msdata:Ordinal="3" />
```

LISTING 7.9 Continued

```xml
            <xsd:element name="Instructor" type="xsd:string"
              minOccurs="0" msdata:Ordinal="4" />
            <xsd:element name="InstructorEmail" type="xsd:string"
              minOccurs="0" msdata:Ordinal="5" />
            <xsd:element name="VendorName" msdata:Caption="Vendor Name"
              type="xsd:string" minOccurs="0" msdata:Ordinal="6" />
            <xsd:element name="CourseNum" msdata:Caption="Course Number"
              type="xsd:string" msdata:Ordinal="7" />
            <xsd:element name="CourseDesc" msdata:Caption="Description"
              type="xsd:string" minOccurs="0" msdata:Ordinal="8" />
            <xsd:element name="Days" type="xsd:unsignedByte" default="0"
              minOccurs="0" msdata:Ordinal="9" />
            <xsd:element name="StudentOrganization"
              msdata:Caption="Your Organization" type="xsd:string"
              minOccurs="0" msdata:Ordinal="10" />
          </xsd:sequence>
          <xsd:attribute name="StudentID" form="unqualified"
            type="xsd:int"/>
          <xsd:attribute name="EnrollID" type="xsd:int"
            msdata:AllowDBNull="false" use="prohibited" />
        </xsd:complexType>
      </xsd:element>
    </xsd:choice>
  </xsd:complexType>
  <xsd:unique name="Constraint1" msdata:PrimaryKey="true">
    <xsd:selector xpath=".//Class" />
    <xsd:field xpath="@EnrollID" />
  </xsd:unique>
</xsd:element>
</xsd:schema>
<Class StudentID="3" xmlns="www.quilogy.com/education/transcript">
  <Date>2001-08-24T00:00:00.0000000-05:00</Date>
  <City>Indianapolis</City>
  <Instructor>Michael Smith</Instructor>
  <InstructorEmail>msmith@quilogy.com</InstructorEmail>
  <VendorName>Microsoft</VendorName>
  <CourseNum>2072</CourseNum>
  <CourseDesc>System Administration for SQL Server 2000</CourseDesc>
  <Days>0</Days>
  <StudentOrganization>Quilogy</StudentOrganization>
</Class>
<Class StudentID="3" xmlns="www.quilogy.com/education/transcript">
  <Date>2001-08-23T00:00:00.0000000-05:00</Date>
  <City>Kansas City</City>
```

LISTING 7.9 Continued

```
    <Instructor>Michael Smith</Instructor>
    <InstructorEmail>msmith@quilogy.com</InstructorEmail>
    <VendorName>Microsoft</VendorName>
    <CourseNum>1016</CourseNum>
    <CourseDesc>Enterprise Development with Visual Basic</CourseDesc>
    <Days>5</Days>
    <StudentOrganization>Quilogy</StudentOrganization>
  </Class>
</qedts:QuilogyTranscript>
```

Although this approach provides a strongly typed `DataSet` with a predefined structure, you'll notice that it does not provide strongly typed access to the actual columns within the `DataSet`. As a result, you're vulnerable to run-time errors if typos are introduced when accessing columns. For example, to retrieve the CourseNum from the second row of the `DataSet` shown in Listing 7.9, the following code could be used:

```
strCourse = dsTs.ClassTable.Rows(1).Item("CourseNum"))
```

Obviously, if the literal string shown in this line were mistyped, the compiler would not be able to catch the error and an exception would be thrown at runtime. Finally, IntelliSense will not be activated to show a drop-down list of the available columns when typing statements such as these. However, with the addition of the public constants for the columns names, typing this line of code is a little easier:

```
strCourse = dsTs.ClassTable.Rows(1).Item(TranscriptData.COURSE_NUM))
```

In either case, and more importantly, if the code was modifying the CourseNum field, the data would not be type-checked at compile-time and in fact would be coerced into the type defined for the column in the `DataSet`, another potential source of errors. As a result, this approach can be considered as a midway technique between using an untyped `DataSet`, as discussed in the first part of this section, and using a fully typed `DataSet` discussed later in the chapter.

The advantage to this approach is that although the class, `TranscriptData`, and its `DataTable` are well-defined, the columns can be changed rather easily by modifying the code in the private `BuildTables` method and simply adding constants. If the structure of the `DataSet` changes, it will definitely affect code that uses it; however, the public interface of the `TranscriptData` class will not change. This increases flexibility while still providing a typed class.

Creating from a Schema

The final technique for creating a `DataSet` is to load it directly from a predefined XML Schema (XSD). The schema itself can be one that already exists in a file or graphically designed using the XML Designer included in VS.NET. This tool allows you to create the schema and save it as an XSD file in your project.

7

ACCESSING DATA WITH ADO.NET

By right-clicking on the project in the VS.NET project explorer and selecting "Add Class," the resulting dialog allows you to select XML Schema. Within the designer, you can right-click to add elements, attributes, types, and groups. You can also add relationships between elements to create a hierarchical schema. In addition, you can view the XML produced for the schema or copy and paste an existing schema in the XML pane available via the buttons along the bottom of the designer. For example, the simple ScheduleData schema was created using the designer, as shown in Figure 7.5. It contains two high-level elements, Criteria and Offering, which each contain a series of elements and attributes that define the information needed to display a course schedule.

FIGURE 7.5

XML Designer. This figure shows the designer surface where elements are created and associated with other elements graphically.

To make things even easier tables can be dragged and dropped onto the XML Schema designer surface from the Server Explorer window. Doing so is a great way to jump start the graphical creation of a DataSet.

After the schema has been successfully created with the XML Designer or received from another source, it can be read into a DataSet at runtime to create the underlying DataSet collections using the ReadXmlSchema method of the DataSet class. This method has several overloaded signatures to accept input from a TextReader, Stream, XmlReader, or simply a file on the file system. For example, a derived DataSet such as ScheduleData could use the ReadXmlSchema method in its constructor to create the DataSet structure, rather than manipulating the collections programmatically, as follows:

```
Public Class ScheduleData : Inherits DataSet

  Public Sub New()
    '   Initialize a ScheduleData instance by building the table
    MyBase.New

    ' Create the tables in the dataset
    Me.ReadXmlSchema("scheduleSchema.xsd")
  End Sub
End Class
```

The advantage to this approach is that if changes are required to the schema, they can be made in a file rather than having to modify code and recompile the class. The disadvantage, of course, is the extra file system access required. Therefore, for online applications, this technique is not recommended, although for applications such as a Windows service it can be used to increase maintainability and flexibility.

> **TIP**
>
> As discussed earlier, the ReadXml method is used to read the XML document into the DataSet. For example, if a Windows service is written to process XML documents, it might first create an instance of the DataSet and populate the schema by calling ReadXmlSchema. Each document is then loaded using the ReadXml method with the appropriate XmlReadMode value set.

Finally, just as you can read a schema and populate a DataSet from an XML file or stream, you can also write both the schema and data using the WriteXmlSchema and WriteXml methods of the DataSet class. For example, to write both the schema and data to a file, call the WriteXml method as follows:

```
Dim dsTs As TranscriptData

dsTs.WriteXml("transcripts.xml", XmlWriteMode.WriteSchema)
```

The optional second argument to the WriteXml method affects how the data is written to the file by using the XmlWriteMode enumeration and can also be set to IgnoreSchema to write only the data and DiffGram.

> **TIP**
>
> When using the DiffGram enumeration of XmlWriteMode, the XML document produced is called an *updategram* and contains elements that show the before and after states of the data. This updategram can be used to create an XML representation of the data set that includes changes to pass to another method for update. In addition, the XML grammar used is the same as that supported by SQL Server 2000 so that the updategram can be passed directly to SQL Server 2000 to update tables in a database. Note that the ReadXml method also supports the XmlReadMode enumeration DiffGram so that an updategram can be loaded into a DataSet.

Both the WriteXml and WriteXmlSchema methods support overloaded versions that can write to a Stream, TextWriter, XmlWriter, or file.

Strongly Typed `DataSets`

As discussed in the previous section and shown in Listing 7.8, creating a typed `DataSet` by inheriting from the `DataSet` class allows you to extend the `DataSet` while encapsulating the structure and functionality. However, the `TranscriptData` class is only a partially typed `DataSet` because you can reference the class itself and its `DataTable` through strongly typed variables, but not the rows or columns. Doing so would increase the readability and ease of working with the `DataSet`.

Creating a Strongly Typed `DataSet`

To create a strongly typed `DataSet`, you could simply manually extend the `TranscriptData` class to include subclasses for the `DataRow` and `DataColumn` objects exposed by the `DataSet`. However, the VS .NET and the .NET Framework do this for you by including a `DataSet` creation tool in the XML Designer and the XML Schemas/DataTypes support utility (XSD.exe) in the .NET Framework SDK.

The process of creating a strongly typed `DataSet` in the XML Designer is trivial. After defining your XML schema graphically as described in the previous section, you can then select the Generate `DataSet` option from the context menu. Behind the scenes, the XML representing the XSD is altered and a .vb file is created that includes a class definition with the same name as the schema. You can view the source code file by clicking the Show All Files toolbar button in the Solution Explorer. The new `DataSet` then can be declared and instantiated by client code.

Optionally, you can choose to use the command-line XSD utility to create the strongly typed `DataSet`.

> **NOTE**
>
> The XSD utility can also be used to create a strongly typed DataSet from an XDR schema, infer XSD schemas from XML documents, convert XDR schemas into XSD schemas, and generate schemas from types in an assembly.

To illustrate the use of XSD.exe, consider the XSD schema shown in Listing 7.10. This schema was created to correspond to the data that is captured when registering one or more students for a class at Quilogy.

LISTING 7.10   XSD Schema for Enrollment Data. This schema includes the data captured for an enrollment in a Quilogy class.

```
<qedr:QuilogyEnrollment xmlns:qedr="www.quilogy.com/education/registration">
  <xsd:schema id="QuilogyEnrollment"
    targetNamespace="www.quilogy.com/education/registration"
```

LISTING 7.10   Continued

```xml
        xmlns="www.quilogy.com/education/registration"
        xmlns:xsd="http://www.w3.org/2001/XMLSchema"
        attributeFormDefault="qualified"
        elementFormDefault="qualified">
            <xsd:element name="Enrollment">
              <xsd:complexType>
                <xsd:sequence>
                  <xsd:element name="Cost" type="xsd:decimal" minOccurs="0" />
                  <xsd:element name="Student" minOccurs="0"
                    maxOccurs="unbounded">
                    <xsd:complexType>
                      <xsd:sequence>
                        <xsd:element name="FName" type="xsd:string"
                          minOccurs="0" />
                        <xsd:element name="LName" type="xsd:string" />
                        <xsd:element name="Organization" type="xsd:string"
                          minOccurs="0" />
                        <xsd:element name="Comments" type="xsd:string"
                          minOccurs="0" />
                        <xsd:element name="ContactInfo" minOccurs="0"
                          maxOccurs="unbounded">
                          <xsd:complexType>
                            <xsd:sequence>
                              <xsd:element name="Address" type="xsd:string"
                                minOccurs="0" />
                              <xsd:element name="City" type="xsd:string"
                                minOccurs="0" />
                              <xsd:element name="State" type="xsd:string"
                                minOccurs="0" />
                              <xsd:element name="ZipCode" type="xsd:string"
                                minOccurs="0" />
                              <xsd:element name="Phone" type="xsd:string"
                                minOccurs="0" />
                              <xsd:element name="Email" type="xsd:string"
                                minOccurs="0" />
                            </xsd:sequence>
                          </xsd:complexType>
                        </xsd:element>
                      </xsd:sequence>
                      <xsd:attribute name="StudentID" form="unqualified"
                        type="xsd:int" />
                      <xsd:attribute name="Existing" form="unqualified"
                        type="xsd:string" />
                    </xsd:complexType>
                  </xsd:element>
```

7

ACCESSING DATA
WITH ADO.NET

LISTING 7.10   Continued

```
        </xsd:sequence>
        <xsd:attribute name="ClassID" form="unqualified" type="xsd:int"
          use="required" />
        <xsd:attribute name="WebEnroll" form="unqualified" type=
        ➡"xsd:string"
          use="required" />
        <xsd:attribute name="PaymentType" form="unqualified" type=
        ➡"xsd:string"
          use="required" />
      </xsd:complexType>
    </xsd:element>
  </xsd:choice>
</qedr:QuilogyEnrollment>
```

Note that this schema includes both student and class data that reflect the person taking the course and the class he signed up for. To create a strongly typed class from this schema, the XSD.exe utility can be run at the command line as follows:

```
xsd /l:vb /d QuilogyEnrollment.xsd
```

where the /l command specifies the language in which to create the DataSet and /d indicates that you want to create a class derived from DataSet. Alternatively, the utility can create a simple class (by specifying the /c option instead of the /d option) that does not derive from DataSet and that uses the System.Xml.Serialization namespace to serialize the class to the XML schema.

> **NOTE**
>
> The full code for the generated QuilogyEnrollment class can be found on the companion web site at www.samspublishing.com.

The resulting .vb file contains a single high-level class—in this case, called QuilogyEnrollment—derived from the DataSet class with the structure (as viewed in the Class Explorer window in VS .NET) shown in Figure 7.6. To get an understanding of the how the tool creates the DataSet, the classes and their descriptions are listed in Table 7.8.

FIGURE 7.6

Strongly typed DataSet. *This figure shows the Class Explorer view in VS .NET for the* EnrollmentData *class generated by the XSD.*

TABLE 7.8   Strongly Typed DataSet

Class	Description
QuilogyEnrollment	Highest level class derived from DataSet. Includes a private InitClass method that creates the table structure and relationships. Exposes DataTable objects as properties.
StudentDataTable	Child class of QuilogyEnrollment derived from DataTable and implements IEnumerable. Exposes each DataColumn as a property and declares each of the public events. Contains an InitClass private method used to create the columns. Includes AddStudentRow, NewStudentRow, and RemoveStudentRow methods.
StudentRow	Child class of QuilogyEnrollment derived from DataRow. Exposes each column as a strongly typed property. Includes methods to handle database null values and return all related ContactInfoRow objects.
StudentRowChangeEvent	Child class of EnrollmentData derived from EventArgs. Used to pass data for the events associated with StudentDataTable.
ContactInfoDataTable	Analogous to StudentDataTable.
ContactInfoRow	Analogous to StudentDataRow.
ContactInfoRowChangeEvent	Analogous to StudentDataRowChangeEvent.
EnrollmentDataTable	Analogous to StudentDataTable.

TABLE 7.8 Continued

Class	Description
EnrollmentRow	Analogous to StudentDataRow.
EnrollmentRowChangeEvent	Analogous to StudentDataRowChangeEvent.

As you can see from Table 7.8, the QuilogyEnrollment class uses a series of child classes to implement each of the DataTable and DataRow objects. In this case, three tables are created: one that represents the high-level Enrollment element (EnrollmentDataTable), one that represents each Student element within an Enrollment element (StudentDataTable), and a third to represent the ContactInfo element (ContactInfoDataTable) within the Student element.

As discussed earlier, DataTable objects are related within a DataSet using a DataRelation. In this case, the parent/child relationships of EnrollmentDataTable to StudentDataTable and StudentDataTable to ContactInfoDataTable are handled by two private DataRelation objects created in the InitClass method of QuilogyEnrollment, as illustrated in the following code:

```
' Class level declarations
Private relationEnrollment_Student As DataRelation
Private relationStudent_ContactInfo As DataRelation

' In InitClass of EnrollmentData
Me.relationStudent_ContactInfo = New DataRelation("Student_ContactInfo", _
  New DataColumn() {Me.tableStudent.Student_IdColumn}, _
  New DataColumn() {Me.tableContactInfo.Student_IdColumn}, false)
Me.relationStudent_ContactInfo.Nested = true
Me.Relations.Add(Me.relationStudent_ContactInfo)
Me.relationEnrollment_Student = New DataRelation("Enrollment_Student", _
  New DataColumn() {Me.tableEnrollment.Enrollment_IdColumn}, _
  New DataColumn() {Me.tableStudent.Enrollment_IdColumn}, false)
Me.relationEnrollment_Student.Nested = true
Me.Relations.Add(Me.relationEnrollment_Student)
```

As you'll notice, the relationships are created based on the Enrollment_IdColumn and Student_IdColumn columns, added to the appropriate DataTables. These columns act as the primary and foreign keys that implement the relationships. To make sure that these columns do not appear in the XML document and to adhere to the schema, both of these columns are created with a MappingType of Hidden. In addition, the primary key columns, Enrollment_Id in EnrollmentDataTable and Student_Id in StudentDataTable, are set to be auto-incrementing. In this way, each row will be assigned a unique primary key. The following code shows the creation of the Student_Id column in the StudentDataTable's InitClass method:

```
Me.columnStudent_Id = New DataColumn("Student_Id", GetType(System.Int32), "", _
  System.Data.MappingType.Hidden)
Me.columnStudent_Id.AutoIncrement = true
Me.columnStudent_Id.AllowDBNull = false
Me.columnStudent_Id.Unique = true
Me.Columns.Add(Me.columnStudent_Id)
Me.PrimaryKey = New DataColumn() {Me.columnStudent_Id}
```

In addition to the properties shown, you can also set the initial value (defaulted to 0) and increment (defaulted to 1) for the column using the `AutoIncrementSeed` and `AutoIncrementStep` properties, respectively. Note that this unique key is found only within the client-side data cache (`DataSet`) and is not propagated back to the database. In other words, it is simply used as a tool for relating `DataTable` objects within the `DataSet`.

Using a Strongly Typed `DataSet`

After the `DataSet` has been created, a client can access it with distinct types exposed by the class. This allows for compile-time checking of the code and the assistance of IntelliSense. For example, using the `QuilogyEnrollment` class produced earlier, the code in Listing 7.11 can be used to add a new enrollment to the `DataSet`.

LISTING 7.11   Using the `DataSet`. This example shows how to use a strongly typed `DataSet`.

```
Dim dsEnrollment As New QuilogyEnrollment()
Dim drEnroll As QuilogyEnrollment.EnrollmentRow
Dim drStudent As QuilogyEnrollment.StudentRow
Dim drContactInfo As QuilogyEnrollment.ContactInfoRow
Dim drStudents() As QuilogyEnrollment.StudentRow
Dim strName As String

' Add a new enrollment
drEnroll = dsEnrollment.Enrollment.AddEnrollmentRow(1745, "Y", "CC", 1234)

' Add a student
dsEnrollment.Student.AddStudentRow(0, "N", "Sammy", "Sosa", "Chicago Cubs", _
  "There better be coffee", drEnroll)

' Add the contact information for the student
drContactInfo = dsEnrollment.ContactInfo.NewContactInfoRow
drContactInfo.Address = "3345 North Shore Drive"
drContactInfo.City = "Chicago"
drContactInfo.State = "IL"
drContactInfo.ZipCode = "43211"
drContactInfo.Phone = "3145551212"
drContactInfo.Email = "ssosa@cubs.com"
```

LISTING 7.11   Continued

```
drContactInfo.StudentRow = drStudent

dsEnrollment.ContactInfo.AddContactInfoRow(drContactInfo)

' Retrieve the students for the enrollment
drStudents = drEnroll.GetStudentRows
strName = drStudents(0).FName & " " & drStudents(0).LName

' Query the user
If MsgBox("Add enrollment for " & strName & " to class " & _
  drEnroll.ClassID & "?", MsgBoxStyle.YesNo Or MsgBoxStyle.Question, _
  "ClassID") = MsgBoxResult.Yes Then
  dsEnrollment.AcceptChanges()
Else
  dsEnrollment.RejectChanges()
End If
```

> **NOTE**
>
> Keep in mind that if you add a namespace declaration to the DataSet class, such as Quilogy.Education, the namespace will be appended to the root namespace for the project. In that case, you would need to prefix the project name to the Imports statement. When creating assemblies that contain only classes that have explicit namespace declarations, you might want to set the root namespace to an empty string by right-clicking on the project and selecting Properties. The resulting dialog box allows you to set or clear the root namespace.

You'll notice that in Listing 7.11, two distinct techniques for populating the DataTable objects are provided using overloaded methods such as AddStudentRow. First, a version of the method is created for each class that accepts arguments that map to the various columns. Internally, this method uses the ItemArray property to set all the columns in a DataRow by passing an array of Object types in a single statement. It can also be used to retrieve the contents of a DataRow into an array of objects. The second technique, as shown when adding the contact information, uses the other method signature—in this case, AddContactInfoRow—which accepts the ContactInfoRow as the parameter. In this case, the row is prepopulated using the strongly typed properties of the derived DataRow class. Note that the ContactInfoRow class exposes a StudentRow property that is used to call the SetParentRow method of the DataRow using a DataRelation object.

Listing 7.11 also exercises the methods used to return an array of child rows using the private `DataRelation` objects discussed earlier. In this case, the `GetStudentRows` method returns an array of `StudentRow` objects associated with the `EnrollmentRow`. Internally, this method calls the `GetChildRows` method of the `DataSet` and passes it the relation through which to get the rows.

Finally, the client code uses a message box to query the user and invokes the `AcceptChanges` or `RejectChanges` method of the `DataSet` as a result. As in a database, these methods serve to provide a certain level of transactional behavior at the `DataRow`, `DataTable`, and `DataSet` level. This is accomplished by manipulating the `RowState` property of the `DataRow` objects in the various `DataTables`. For example, `AcceptChanges` "commits" all the rows within the `DataSet` by changing the `RowState` property of any rows that are `New` or `Modified` to the `Unchanged` value of the `DataRowState` enumeration while removing any rows that have been `Deleted`. Conversely, `RejectChanges` changes the `RowState` of all `Modified` and `Deleted` rows to `Unchanged`.

> **NOTE**
>
> DataRow also supports the `BeginEdit` and `EndEdit` methods that put the row in edit mode and take it out again. These are used to suspend events and allow multiple changes to be made to the row without validation occurring. Both methods are called implicitly; first when a column value is changed, and then when `AcceptChanges` or `RejectChanges` is called.

After the registration is added to the `DataSet`, as shown in Listing 7.11, the XML produced by calling the `WriteXml` method is shown as follows:

```xml
<QuilogyEnrollment xmlns="www.quilogy.com/education/registration">
  <Enrollment ClassID="1745" WebEnroll="Y" PaymentType="CC">
    <Cost>1234</Cost>
    <Student StudentID="0" Existing="N">
      <FName>Sammy</FName>
      <LName>Sosa</LName>
      <Organization>Chicago Cubs</Organization>
      <Comments>There better be coffee</Comments>
        <ContactInfo>
          <Address>3345 North Shore Drive</Address>
          <City>Chicago</City>
          <State>IL</State>
          <ZipCode>43211</ZipCode>
          <Phone>3145551212</Phone>
        <Email>ssosa@cubs.com</Email>
```

```
        </ContactInfo>
      </Student>
    </Enrollment>
</QuilogyEnrollment>
```

Having seen the different techniques for creating data sets, you might be wondering which of them to use. Obviously that question can only be answered by your particular project. However, several considerations include the size of the project, its expected lifetime, and the skill level of the development staff. Generally, the larger the project (meaning the wider reach it has within the organization) and the longer it is expected to function, the more you would move toward a strongly typed approach. By doing so, you can more easily justify the increased maintenance costs and will likely expose the classes to developers with a wider range of skills. However, for the majority of projects, a weakly typed `DataSet` approach, like that shown in Listing 7.8, is warranted because it provides the primary benefits of typed `DataSets` and still allows for flexibility. As a result, in the remainder of this chapter, we'll use `DataSet` classes based on that approach.

XML Integration

As should be evident from this chapter, the `DataSet` provides a relational view of data using an XML data store. Although this chapter has spent some time reviewing the relationships between the structure of the `DataSet`, the XML schema, and the XML produced, you can use a `DataSet` quite apart from any reference to XSD and XML in both weakly and strongly typed implementations. In fact, for developers not familiar with XML, this provides a great layer of abstraction.

On the other hand, many developers have worked with XML documents programmatically using the various versions of the Microsoft XML Parser (MSXML) via the Document Object Model (DOM). As will be discussed in Chapter 14, "Integrating with the Enterprise," those developers can still use the DOM through the `System.Xml` classes, the most important of which is `XmlDocument`. However, until now those same developers had to write their own translation layer when attempting, for example, to read an XML document and save the contents to a relational database. Fortunately, the Services Framework integrates the programming models provided by the relational view of data using `DataTable` and `DataRow` objects in ADO.NET and the node-based hierarchical view using the DOM. This intermediary is the `XmlDataDocument` class, which resides in the `System.Xml` namespace.

Using `XmlDataDocument`

At the most basic level, the `XmlDataDocument` provides an XML view of a `DataSet` in a separate object so that it can be manipulated using the DOM. However, the `XmlDataDocument` can also be loaded with data independently, resulting in the creation of a `DataSet` and relational schema when the `DataSet` property of the object is accessed. Keep in mind that the

XmlDataDocument and DataSet are separate objects at run-time and are kept in sync using events. As a result, creating an XmlDataDocument based on a large DataSet will incur extra overhead.

> **NOTE**
>
> You can think of the XmlDataDocument as a more robust way of loading XML into a DataSet. Rather than use the ReadXmlSchema, ReadXml, WriteXmlSchema, and WriteXml methods, you could instantiate and load an XmlDataDocument object and subsequently view it as a DataSet using the DataSet property.

To use an XmlDataDocument, you can optionally pass an instance of a DataSet to the constructor. By doing so, the XmlDataDocument is populated and can then be traversed using the DOM. Because XmlDataDocument is derived from XmlDocument, all the classes and methods familiar to users of the DOM are available. For example, the following code instantiates a new XmlDataDocument with the dsEnrollment DataSet populated in Listing 7.11. It then navigates through the XML using the methods of the DOM:

```
Imports System.Xml
Dim xmlData As New XmlDataDocument(dsEnrollment)
Dim elRroot, elEnroll, elStudent As XmlElement
Dim intClassID As Integer
Dim strLastName As String
Dim curCost As Double

elRroot = xmlData.DocumentElement

For Each elEnroll In elRroot.GetElementsByTagName("Enrollment")
  intClassID = CInt(elEnroll.Attributes("ClassID").Value)
  curCost = CDbl(elEnroll.FirstChild.FirstChild.Value)

  For Each elStudent In elEnroll.GetElementsByTagName("Student")
    strLastName = elStudent.GetElementsByTagName("LName").Item(0)
    ➥.FirstChild.Value
  Next
Next
```

You can also go the other direction by loading the XmlDataDocument using the Load or LoadXml methods. The data can then be manipulated using the DataSet property. The following code example is the reverse of the previous one:

```
Imports System.Xml
Imports System.Data
    Dim xmlData As New XmlDataDocument()
    Dim drRow, drStudent As DataRow
    Dim strLastName As String
    Dim intClassID As Integer
    Dim curCost As Double

    xmlData.DataSet.ReadXmlSchema("QuilogyEnrollment.xsd")
    xmlData.Load("regdata.xml")

    For Each drRow In xmlData.DataSet.Tables("Enrollment").Rows
      intClassID = CInt(drRow.Item("ClassID"))
      curCost = CDbl(drRow.Item("Cost"))

      For Each drStudent In drRow.GetChildRows( _
        xmlData.DataSet.Tables("Enrollment").ChildRelations(0))
        strLastName = drStudent.Item("LName").ToString
      Next
    Next
```

Note that in this case, the schema and the XML are loaded from files.

After the initial mapping of the DataSet to the XmlDataDocument is complete, if new nodes are added to the XmlDataDocument that do not correspond to defined columns in a DataTable within the DataSet, the nodes will be added to the XmlDataDocument but not synchronized to the DataSet.

Although using the XmlDataDocument as an alternative view of a DataSet might at first seem unnecessary, it can be used to provide functionality not supported by the DataSet. As an example, consider an application that needs to automatically create multiple Web pages for an online catalog from data in a relational database each night. One technique for doing so is to fill a DataSet, view it through an XmlDataDocument, and then use the System.Xml.Xsl.XslTransform class to output the data in HTML format using an XSL stylesheet.

The code in Listing 7.12 shows an example of a method used to transform a DataSet into HTML or XML using an XmlDataDocument and save the resulting document to a file on the file system.

LISTING 7.12 Using the `XmlDataDocument`. This listing shows how you can use the `XmlDataDocument` to programmatically transform a `DataSet` into an HTML document.

```
Imports System.Xml
Imports System.Data
Imports System.Xml.Xsl
Imports System.Xml.XPath

Public Sub TransformDS(ByRef dsData As DataSet, ByVal xslFile As String, _
  ByVal destFile As String)

  Dim xmlData As XmlDataDocument
  Dim xslTrans As New XslTransform()
  Dim xmlWriter As XmlTextWriter

  Try
    ' Load the stylesheet and transform
    xslTrans.Load(xslFile)
  Catch e As Exception
    Console.WriteLine("Could not load file " & xslFile & " : " & e.Message)
    Return
  End Try

  Try
    ' Create an XmlTextWriter to write to the file
    xmlWriter = New XmlTextWriter(destFile, Nothing)

    ' Populate the XmlDataDocument and do the transform
    xmlData = New XmlDataDocument(dsData)
    xslTrans.Transform(xmlData.DocumentElement, Nothing, xmlWriter)
  Catch e As Exception
    Console.WriteLine("Could not write to " & destFile & " : " & e.Message)
  Finally
    xmlWriter.Close()
  End Try

End Sub
```

In this example, notice that the `XslTransform` object, `xslTrans`, first loads the stylesheet passed in as an argument using the `Load` method. After opening the destination file using an `XmlTextWriter` object, the `XmlDataDocument` object is populated by passing the `DataSet` as an argument to the constructor. The root node of the `XmlDataDocument`, in this case `xmlData.DocumentElement`, is then passed to the `Transform` method along with the `XmlWriter` used to output the results of the transformation. The `Transform` method navigates through an XML document using a cursor model, applying the style sheet rules found in the XSL document. The second parameter to `Transform`, here set to `Nothing`, can be used to specify a list of parameters that are fed into the XSL stylesheet to allow for dynamic execution.

To use the method in Listing 7.12, the client application would simply create the `DataSet` and pass it to the method as follows:

```
Dim cnSQL As SqlConnection
Dim daSQL As SqlDataAdapter
Dim dsCourses As New DataSet("Offerings")

cnSQL = New SqlConnection( _
   "server=ssosa;trusted_connection=yes;database=enrollment")

' Create the adapter and set the SelectCommand through the constructor
daSQL = New SqlDataAdapter("usp_ListCourses", cnSQL)
daSQL.SelectCommand.CommandType = CommandType.StoredProcedure

' Populate the DataSet
daSQL.Fill(dsCourses,"Courses")

' Transform and Save
TransformDS(dsCourses, "CourseList.xsl","Courses.htm")
```

Handling Data Access

In addition to custom `DataSet` classes, the data services tier shown in Figure 7.4 consists of data access classes. These classes are responsible for communicating with the back-end database by abstracting the calls to the managed provider. They are called from both the presentation and business services tiers.

When communicating with the SQL Server database, the data access classes will use stored procedures exclusively. In addition to the performance and abstraction benefits already mentioned, by allowing stored procedures to be the gatekeepers of the data, security can be enhanced, and some business logic or data validation can be introduced at the data source. Specifically, a SQL Server administrator can grant access to a stored procedure without granting direct access to the tables and views the stored procedure references. In this way, all access to the database objects must be performed through approved and maintained stored procedures.

TIP
Although there has been some debate as to the appropriate amount and type of code to place in stored procedures, their importance in SQL Server will only increase

> as Microsoft works to embed the CLR into a future release code named "Yukon." This will enable you to write stored procedures in VB .NET, or any .NET language, the ease and productivity of which will likely lead to their increased usage.

Once again, the primary benefit to using stored procedures, rather than inline SQL, is that the code running on a middle-tier server need not generate SQL or have an understanding of the database schema.

In the Quilogy Education sample application, there exist data access classes for each of the major namespaces shown in Figure 4.1. In the remainder of this chapter, we'll focus on the `Students` class responsible for manipulating student data within the database. The primary methods of this class are shown in Table 7.9.

TABLE 7.9 Students Data Access Class

Method	Description
GetTranscript	Returns the `TranscriptData` class for a particular student.
Login	Validates a student login and returns the student's demographic information in a `StudentData` class.
ChangePass	Allows a student to change his password.
Save	Both inserts and updates student data through a `StudentData` class.
CheckIfExists	Determines whether a student exists in the database, given the student's e-mail address and last name.
ClassesTaken	Returns the number of classes taken by a particular student.

Obviously other methods could be added to this list—for instance, for querying a list of students based on some criteria—but those shown here represent the core functionality required for the online application.

To get a feel for the structure of a data access class, the code for the class and the `GetTranscript` method is shown in Listing 7.13.

LISTING 7.13 Students Data Access Class. This class encapsulates the data access code for student data.

```
Option Explicit On
Option Strict On

Imports System.Data
Imports System.Data.SqlClient
```

LISTING 7.13 Continued

```
Imports Quilogy.Education
Imports System.EnterpriseServices
Imports System.Runtime.InteropServices

Namespace Quilogy.Education.Enrollment

    Public Class Students
        ' Students Data Access Class

        Private cnSQL As SqlConnection
        Private strConnect As String

        '**********************************************************************
        Public Sub New(ByVal connect As String)
            strConnect = connect
            cnSQL = New SqlConnection(strConnect)
        End Sub

        '**************************************************
        Public Function GetTranscript(ByVal studentID As Integer) _
          As TranscriptData
            ' Fill a dataset with transcript data based on the student ID

            Dim dsTs As New TranscriptData()
            Dim daSql As SqlDataAdapter
            Dim parmSql As SqlParameter

            ' Check the incoming parameters
            If studentID <= 0 Then
                Throw New ArgumentOutOfRangeException( _
                  "StudentID cannot be less than or equal to 0")
                Return Nothing
            End If

            ' Setup the data adapter
            daSql = New SqlDataAdapter("usp_GetTranscript", cnSQL)

            ' Call the stored procedure
            daSql.SelectCommand.CommandType = CommandType.StoredProcedure
            parmSql = daSql.SelectCommand.Parameters.Add( _
              New SqlParameter("@StudentID", SqlDbType.Int))
            parmSql.Value = studentID

            daSql.MissingSchemaAction = MissingSchemaAction.Ignore
            daSql.Fill(dsTs, dsTs.ClassTable.TableName)
```

LISTING 7.13 Continued

```
            Return dsTs

        End Function
    End Class
End Namespace
```

Note that the class exists in the `Quilogy.Education.Enrollment` namespace and must import not only the ADO.NET namespaces such as `System.Data` and `System.Data.SqlClient`, but also the `Quilogy.Education` namespace because the `TranscriptData` class exists there.

You'll also notice that the constructor of this class accepts an argument used as the `ConnectionString` of the `SqlConnection` object stored at the class level and then instantiates the `SqlConnection` object.

> **NOTE**
>
> Although there are several ways to pass the connection string to a class (for example, by referencing a separate class created explicitly for configuration settings), this approach is flexible in situations where the `Students` class might be used in a variety of scenarios. As you'll see in Chapter 9, if the class is to use COM+ services, it can take advantage of object construction through an overridden method where the connection string is configured in the COM+ application.

The actual `GetTranscript` method first checks the incoming parameter and might throw the `ArgumentOutOfRangeException` if it is invalid. The method then uses the familiar `SqlDataAdapter` to execute the stored procedure, as discussed previously in this chapter. Note once again that the stored procedure was specifically created to map to the columns of the `DataTable` within `TranscriptData`. If the stored procedure cannot be created to match the `DataSet`, a `TableMapping` must be created before the `Fill` method is called. To ensure that the `DataTable` contains only the columns specified in the `TranscriptData` class, the `MissingSchemaAction` property is set to `Ignore` so that any additional columns returned from the stored procedure are not added to the `DataSet`.

A client using the `Students` class would contain code like the following:

```
Imports Quilogy.Education.Enrollment
Imports Quilogy.Education
Dim objStudents As New Students(strConnect)
Dim dsTranscript As TranscriptData
Dim intStudentID As Integer
```

```
Try
  dsTranscript = objStudents.GetTranscript(intStudentID)
Catch e As ArgumentOutOfRangeException
  ' Possibly prompt the user again or try to repopulate intStudentID
  Return
Catch e As SqlException   ' Must be a database error
  ' Display an error to the user
  Return
End Try
```

Both of the `Quilogy.Education` namespaces must be imported because the `Students` class is found in one and the `TranscriptData` class in another. Note also that the `Try` block contains two `Catch` statements, the first to catch the `ArgumentOutOfRangeException` that might occur because of invalid parameters, and the second to catch any database errors.

Modifying Data

One of the most important responsibilities of the data access classes is to modify data in the underlying database. In the `Students` class, the `Save` method is exposed to handle both the insertion of a new student and the update of demographic information. The entire method is shown in Listing 7.14.

Listing 7.14   The `Save` Method. This method calls a stored procedure to insert or update a student in the database.

```
Public Function Save(ByVal student As StudentData) As Integer
  ' Handles both inserts and updates through the proc
  ' and returns the new StudentID

  Dim cmSql As SqlCommand
  Dim parmSql As SqlParameter

  ' Check the incoming parameter
  If student Is Nothing Then
    Throw New ArgumentNullException("No data found!")
    Return 0
  End If

  cmSql = New SqlCommand("usp_SaveStudent", cnSQL)

  ' Create the parms and extract the data
  With cmSql
    .CommandType = CommandType.StoredProcedure
    .Parameters.Add(New SqlParameter("@StudentID", SqlDbType.Int))
    .Parameters("@StudentID").Value = _
       student.StudentTable.Rows(0).Item(StudentData.STUDENT_ID)
```

LISTING 7.14   Continued

```
    .Parameters.Add(New SqlParameter("@FName", SqlDbType.VarChar))
    .Parameters("@FName").Value = _
      student.StudentTable.Rows(0).Item(StudentData.FIRST_NAME)
    .Parameters.Add(New SqlParameter("@LName", SqlDbType.VarChar))
    .Parameters("@LName").Value = _
      student.StudentTable.Rows(0).Item(StudentData.LAST_NAME)
    .Parameters.Add(New SqlParameter("@Company", SqlDbType.VarChar))
    .Parameters("@Company").Value = _
      student.StudentTable.Rows(0).Item(StudentData.ORGANIZATION)
    .Parameters.Add(New SqlParameter("@Email", SqlDbType.VarChar))
    .Parameters("@Email").Value = _
      student.StudentTable.Rows(0).Item(StudentData.EMAIL)
    .Parameters.Add(New SqlParameter("@Address", SqlDbType.VarChar))
    .Parameters("@Address").Value = _
      student.StudentTable.Rows(0).Item(StudentData.ADDRESS)
    .Parameters.Add(New SqlParameter("@City", SqlDbType.VarChar))
    .Parameters("@City").Value = _
      student.StudentTable.Rows(0).Item(StudentData.CITY)
    .Parameters.Add(New SqlParameter("@State", SqlDbType.VarChar))
    .Parameters("@State").Value = _
      student.StudentTable.Rows(0).Item(StudentData.STATE)
    .Parameters.Add(New SqlParameter("@ZipCode", SqlDbType.VarChar))
    .Parameters("@ZipCode").Value = _
      student.StudentTable.Rows(0).Item(StudentData.ZIP_CODE)
    .Parameters.Add(New SqlParameter("@Phone", SqlDbType.VarChar))
    .Parameters("@Phone").Value = _
      student.StudentTable.Rows(0).Item(StudentData.PHONE)
End With

' Set up the return value
parmSql = New SqlParameter("RETURN", SqlDbType.Int)
parmSql.Direction = ParameterDirection.ReturnValue
cmSql.Parameters.Add(parmSql)

' Call the proc
cnSQL.Open()
cmSql.ExecuteNonQuery()
cnSQL.Close()

' Return the new or old student id
Return CType(parmSql.Value, Integer)

End Function
```

In Listing 7.14, notice that because no `DataSet` is being returned from the method, the `SqlCommand` object is used to execute a stored procedure to perform the insert or update. After instantiating the `SqlCommand`, the parameters are added to the `Parameters` collection. Note that the `SqlParameter` class supports several overloaded constructors, one of which allows you to specify all the important properties. In this case, however, the method simply provides the name of the parameter and the data type. The `Direction` property is defaulted to `ParameterDirection.Input` and so only the `Value` property must be additionally set. This is accomplished by accessing the data in the `StudentData` class passed in as a parameter to the method. It is assumed that only one student exists in the `StudentData` `DataSet`, although modifying the code to handle several students using a loop is straightforward.

The final parameter added after the `With` block corresponds to the return value of the stored procedure. SQL Server stored procedures can return a 32-bit integer value indicating status or other application-specific information. In this case, the `usp_SaveStudent` procedure returns the new or existing StudentID assigned to the student. Within SQL Server, this value is generated by adding the `IDENTITY` property to the StudentID column in the table. Unlike in classic ADO, however, the parameter specifying the return value does not have to be the first added to the `Parameters` collection and need not have a specific name.

The `SqlConnection` is then opened and the procedure executed using the `ExecuteNonQuery` method of the `SqlCommand` object. This method specifies that the command will not return a result set resulting in more efficient execution. The new or existing StudentID is then returned by accessing the `Value` property of the `Parameter` and converting it to an `Integer`.

Batch Updating

One of the interesting aspects of this technique is that the determination of whether to perform an `INSERT` or `DELETE` statement in the database ultimately rests with the stored procedure rather than the `Save` method. This simplifies the calling convention for client applications and requires one less stored procedure per table.

An alternative approach to the one shown here is to instantiate a `SqlDataAdapter` in the `Save` method and populate the `InsertCommand` and `UpdateCommand` properties to point to stored procedures, and then calling the `Update` method as was done in Listing 7.3. Although this would handle multiple rows without adding a loop, it would entail writing a few more lines of code to configure the commands, and you'd have to be certain that the `RowState` properties of the individual rows were set correctly as they determine which command is executed for each row.

This technique can also be used with `IDENTITY` values that are created on the server by adding a parameter to represent the return value (as was done in Listing 7.14) to the `SqlCommand` that populates the `InsertCommand` property of the `SqlDataAdapter`.

The `SourceColumn` property of the parameter can then be set to the column in the `DataSet`. When the `InsertCommand` is executed, the `IDENTITY` value will then be returned from the stored procedure and be reflected in the `DataSet`.

Although space prohibits a more complete discussion, the approach described in the previous paragraphs is more suited to true batch scenarios in which an application might insert, update, or delete multiple rows in the `DataSet` and then want to synchronize them with the database. In these scenarios, the code responsible for updating the data store will use the `GetChanges` method of the `DataSet` to create a copy of the `DataSet` that contains either all the changed rows, or those filtered by the `DataRowState` enumeration. It should then check the `HasErrors` property of each `DataTable` to determine whether there are validation errors on any of the rows. If so, the `HasErrors` property of each `DataRow` can be inspected to find those rows that have errors, although a quicker way to return rows that contain errors is to call the `GetErrors` method of the `DataTable`, which returns an array of `DataRow` objects. For each of these rows the `RowError` property will contain a string specifying the error.

After the errors have been corrected, the copy created with `GetChanges` can be sent to a method in the data services tier. At this point, the method can execute the `Update` method of a DataAdapter to perform the inserts, updates, and deletes. If the update completes successfully, the `AcceptChanges` method can be called to reset the row states to unmodified. Conversely, `RejectChanges` can be called if errors occur. The data services tier might then return the `DataSet` to the presentation tier where it can be merged with the existing data using the `Merge` method.

TIP

If you write your own custom validation code in the presentation services tier, you can use the `SetColumnError`, `GetColumnError`, and `ClearErrors` methods of the `DataRow` to manipulate the error information.

System Assigned Keys

As pointed out earlier, this particular application relies on SQL Server `IDENTITY` values to generate system assigned keys to identify students, enrollments, courses, products, and other entities. These columns are in turn defined as the primary keys on their respective tables. However, in distributed applications, relying on keys generated from a single database might not be advisable in all scenarios.

One technique for bypassing `IDENTITY` values, and yet retaining system assigned keys, is to use Globally Unique Identifiers (GUIDs) for the keys.

> **NOTE**
>
> GUIDs are difficult to read, increase the size of the data being passed around, and increase the table size in SQL Server. However, your users shouldn't be seeing system-assigned keys and their impact on performance is negligible. Although I'm not advocating the exclusive use of GUIDs, they make sense for some applications, particularly those that use data from distributed database servers, use replication, or are architected in such a way that returning the newly assigned key from the database server is difficult.

These 16-byte unique values (calculated using an algorithm based on the MAC address of the network card and other information) work particularly well with SQL Server because versions 7.0 and higher support the `uniqueidentifier` data type. VB .NET supports GUIDs by allowing the `DataSet` to automatically create these values in the same way as a database populates default constraints on columns. In addition, the Services Framework includes a `Guid` structure in the `System` namespace that can be used to generate new guids on demand.

The Quilogy Education application can be modified to support GUIDs in the following way:

1. The primary key of the tables (for example Student) must be replaced by a uniqueidentifier. Listing 7.15 shows what the new table would look like.

LISTING 7.15   Student Table. This version of the Student table uses a `UniqueIdentifier` as the data type for the StudentID.

```
CREATE TABLE [Student] (
    [StudentID] [uniqueidentifier] NOT NULL
      CONSTRAINT [DF_StudentID] DEFAULT (NewID()),
    [FName] [varchar] (50)  NULL ,
    [LName] [varchar] (50) NOT NULL ,
    [Company] [varchar] (50) NULL ,
    [ZipCode] [char] (10) NULL ,
    [City] [varchar] (50) NULL ,
    [State] [varchar] (50) NULL ,
    [Email] [varchar] (100) NULL ,
    [Address] [varchar] (1000) NULL ,
    [Pwd] [varchar] (10) NULL ,
    [Phone] [varchar] (12) NULL ,
    CONSTRAINT [PK_Student1] PRIMARY KEY  CLUSTERED
    (
        [StudentID]
    )  ON [PRIMARY]
)
```

Note that a default constraint is added to the StudentID column that invokes the `NewID` function. This Transact-SQL function generates a new GUID and will place it in the column if not provided in the `INSERT` statement.

2. The `StudentData` class can be modified to change the data type of the StudentID column from `Integer` to `System.Guid`. In the `BuildTables` method, the code that adds the columns would be changed as follows where mdtStudent references the private `DataTable` object:

```
With mdtStudent.Columns
  .Add(STUDENT_ID, GetType(System.Guid))
  ' Add the other columns
End With
```

3. The `DefaultValue` property of the `DataColumn` can be set to the `NewGuid` method of the `System.Guid` structure to generate a GUID when a new row is added to the `DataTable`.

```
With mdtStudent.Columns
  .Columns(STUDENT_GUID).DefaultValue = System.Guid.NewGuid
  ' Set the other properties
End With
```

The benefit of using this approach is that methods of the `Students` class, such as `Save`, do not have to return the StudentID information to the code that calls it. By generating the GUID directly in the `DataSet`, the client already has access to it.

Returning Other Types of Data

In addition to being able to pass input parameters to and catch return values from stored procedures, ADO.NET supports output parameters. For example, the `CheckIfExists` method of the `Students` class is used to determine whether a student already exists in the database, given the student's e-mail address and last name. If so, the method returns the StudentID. Rather than have the stored procedure that implements this functionality return a resultset, it returns the StudentID as an output parameter. From SQL Server's perspective, this is more efficient than creating a result set. The Transact-SQL code for the stored procedure usp_StudentExists can be seen as follows:

```
CREATE PROC usp_StudentExists
@Email varchar(100) ,
@LName varchar(50),
@StudentID int OUTPUT
AS

SELECT @StudentID = StudentID
FROM Student
WHERE Email = @Email AND LName = @LName
```

7

ACCESSING DATA
WITH ADO.NET

Even though this method could also have been implemented using a return value, output parameters are useful when you have more than one value to return (what would typically be referred to as returning a single row, multi-column result set) or need to return a single value of a data type other than Integer.

The CheckIfExists method is shown in Listing 7.16.

LISTING 7.16   Using Output Parameters. This method uses an output parameter to return the StudentID.

```
Public Function CheckIfExists(ByVal email As String, _
  ByVal lastName As String) As Integer

  Dim cmSql As SqlCommand
  Dim parmSql As SqlParameter

  ' Check the incoming parameter
  If email.Length = 0 Or lastName.Length = 0 Then
    Throw New ArgumentNullException("Must supply email address and last name")
    Return 0
  End If

   cmSql = New SqlCommand("usp_StudentExists", cnSQL)

  ' Create the parms and extract the data
  With cmSql
    .CommandType = CommandType.StoredProcedure
    .Parameters.Add(New SqlParameter("@LName", SqlDbType.VarChar))
    .Parameters("@LName").Value = lastName
    .Parameters.Add(New SqlParameter("@Email", SqlDbType.VarChar))
    .Parameters("@Email").Value = email
    .Parameters.Add(New SqlParameter("@StudentID", SqlDbType.Int))
    .Parameters("@StudentID").Direction = ParameterDirection.Output
  End With

  ' Call the proc
  cnSQL.Open()
  cmSql.ExecuteNonQuery()
  cnSQL.Close()
  ' Check if Null before Return
  If cmSql.Parameters("@StudentID").Value Is DBNull.Value Then
    Return 0
  Else
    Return CType(cmSql.Parameters("@StudentID").Value, Integer)
  End If

End Function
```

One other interesting note found in Listing 7.16 is that the value returned by the output parameter might be NULL if the student did not exist. Null values can be checked for by comparing them to DBNull.Value, a singleton class in the System namespace. Note that comparing a NULL value returned from the database to Nothing will always return False and therefore lead to errors.

Related to the use of output parameters is the support for the ExecuteScalar method found in both the OleDbCommand and SqlCommand classes. This method returns only the first row and first column of a result set, and is useful in situations in which an existing stored procedure must be used. This technique does not save any resources on the server side, but is more efficient than using the ExecuteReader method and then manipulating the resulting SqlDataReader.

As an example of using this method, the ClassesTaken method of the Students class calls the stored procedure usp_GetClasses that performs an aggregate query using the COUNT() function, as follows:

```
CREATE PROC usp_GetClasses
@StudentID int
AS

SELECT COUNT(*)
FROM Enrollment
WHERE StudentID = @StudentID
```

This value is then returned using the ExecuteScalar method as shown in Listing 7.17.

LISTING 7.17 Returning a Scalar Value. This procedure returns the first column from the first row of the result set using ExecuteScalar.

```
Public Function ClassesTaken(ByVal studentID As Integer) As Integer
  ' Get the number of classes taken by this student

  Dim cmSql As SqlCommand
  Dim parmSql As SqlParameter

  ' Check the incoming parameter
  If studentID <= 0 Then
    Throw New ArgumentOutOfRangeException("StudentID must be greater than 0")
    Return 0
  End If

  cmSql = New SqlCommand("usp_GetClasses", cnSQL)

  ' Create the parms and extract the data
```

LISTING 7.17   Continued

```
With cmSql
  .CommandType = CommandType.StoredProcedure
  .Parameters.Add(New SqlParameter("@StudentID", SqlDbType.Int))
  .Parameters("@StudentID").Value = studentID
End With

' Call the proc
cnSQL.Open()
ClassesTaken = CType(cmSql.ExecuteScalar, Integer)
cnSQL.Close()

End Function
```

Summary

In many ways, ADO.NET has changed the programming model for developers by focusing on a more message-based and disconnected architecture. However, as you can see from this chapter, many of the concepts learned in classic ADO can be translated without difficulty. Hopefully, this new model will make accessing data both simpler and more efficient.

Now that the data access tier has been developed, you can move on to the next chapter where the discussion will focus on the creation of business components that take advantage of Component Services and interoperate with COM components.

Building Components

IN THIS CHAPTER

Chapter 7, "Accessing Data with ADO.NET," laid the groundwork for building distributed applications by describing techniques used to access data from relational and nonrelational data sources using the `System.Data` namespace. It also presented a design pattern (refer to Figure 7.4) using derived `DataSet` and data access classes to comprise the data services tier of a multitiered distributed application.

This chapter builds on that foundation to describe how the classes in both the business and data services tiers can be built as components to include functionality, such as

- Interaction with VS .NET to promote reusability and Rapid Application Development (RAD)
- Invocation across AppDomains and servers using .NET Remoting
- Calling unmanaged code

Together with Chapter 9, "Accessing Component Services," these two chapters provide techniques for building and using middle-tier components in .NET. As in Chapter 7, much of the information in this discussion takes place in the context of the Quilogy education sample application.

> **NOTE**
>
> All code listings and supplemental material for this chapter can be found on the book's Web site at www.samspublishing.com.

Designing Components

To begin, there are several design issues surrounding building middle-tier components that must be addressed. These issues include a justification for the architecture shown in Figure 7.4, and how .NET handles marshalling data across tiers, as well as how it handles exceptions.

> **NOTE**
>
> In this discussion, the term "application" means the entire solution, not simply a single CPU process running on a single machine or server. An application could be comprised of many processes spread across servers.

Some existing VB 6.0 and ASP developers might be wondering why we're approaching a distributed application in a tiered fashion as shown in Figure 7.4 in the first place. After all, the data access techniques shown in Chapter 7 could just as easily be employed in code written directly within .ASPX pages.

Although that is true, and many existing ASP applications were developed using just such a two-tiered Web architecture, those applications are more difficult to maintain and, more importantly, to enhance as time goes by. The reason is because the code that implements the user interface (presentation), business logic, and data access is tightly coupled, making it difficult to change one without changing (perhaps inadvertently) the other two. The object-oriented nature of VB.NET makes it natural to place code that implements each type of service (presentation, business logic, and data access) in classes that communicate through well-defined interfaces. This not only protects the structure and location of the data from changes, as stated in Chapter 7, but also the algorithms that implement business processes as well as user interface elements.

The second major reason we're employing this architecture is that it can promote scalability. Just as with classic COM, splitting services into separate components allows them to be physically located on distinct servers. This allows the processing to be amortized across multiple servers, albeit at the cost of increased network traffic. In addition, if the components are created in a stateless fashion, each tier can be "scaled-out" by creating an array or farm of servers at each tier. Products such as Microsoft Application Center 2000 can be used to fully implement this architecture.

A side benefit of all this is that some of the components are likely candidates for reusability across applications because they are loosely coupled and perform well-defined functions.

That being said, developing a multitiered distributed application requires more discipline and a larger learning curve for VB and ASP developers used to creating two-tiered applications. As a result, a subset of Web applications (those that are small in scope in terms of the development team, user population, or usable lifetime) are certainly candidates for a two-tiered approach. However, for most line of business and enterprise applications, the architecture discussed in this chapter is recommended.

Building Classes Versus Components

To begin to get a handle on how you should design components in VB .NET, it is helpful to distinguish between classes and components.

So far, this book has shown many examples of creating classes. *Classes* are the programmatic structure by which you encapsulate behavior and that are built using the object-oriented features of the CLR, including inheritance, polymorphism, and encapsulation.

However, when a class is compiled into an assembly, in many cases, you want an instance of that class (now referred to as a *type*) to be able to be shared between applications at runtime and reused, much like an ActiveX control is in classic COM. A *component* then is the definition of a shareable class. Building components from your classes allows you to satisfy these requirements as discussed in the next two sections.

Marshalling Objects

To use objects in distributed applications, you often need to be able to pass them between tiers that might reside in multiple AppDomains spread across servers. Objects that are able to be shared across AppDomains either by passing a proxy to the object or a copy of the object itself are, in .NET parlance, termed *remotable*. These remotable classes and their descendants, because they are shareable in this respect, are usually referred to as components.

> **NOTE**
>
> Marshalling refers to the process an execution environment such as the Common Language Runtime (CLR) uses to construct a method call to a remote object, including packaging parameters on the originating end of the call and unpackaging them on the receiving end. An in-depth discussion of .NET Remoting can be found later in the chapter.

Unfortunately, a class derived only (and implicitly) from `System.Object` can only be used within the AppDomain in which it is created. In other words, objects instantiated from a class derived only from `System.Object` cannot interoperate with objects living in other AppDomains in the same process, across processes, or across machines. In addition, the lifetime of objects instantiated from these classes is controlled automatically by the CLR's garbage collector as discussed in Chapter 4, "Object-Oriented Features."

You can derive from three primary classes to create remotable components. Their names and primary uses can be seen in Table 8.1 and Figure 8.1.

TABLE 8.1   Component Classes

Class	Description
`System.ComponentModel.Component`	Derived from `System.MarshalByRefObject` and used as the base class for components that must be passed by reference because they have distributed identity (that is, an instance lives where it was created) and that use deterministic finalization. A class derived from `Component` never leaves its AppDomain and should be used by classes that hold on to resources such as file handles and database connections or that encapsulate reusable functionality.

TABLE 8.1 Continued

Class	Description
System.ComponentModel.MarshalByValueComponent	Derived from Object and used as the base class for components that must be passed by value because they encapsulate state information (that is, a copy of data as in a DataSet) and that use deterministic finalization. A class derived from MarshalByValueComponent can be serialized and remoted across AppDomains.
System.EnterpriseServices.ServicedComponent	Derived from ContextBoundObject and ultimately from MarshalByRefObject and used as the base class for components that access Component Services, such as transactions and object pooling. A object derived from ServicedComponent can be hosted in a Component Services process or in the AppDomain of the client that created it. Note that classes derived from ServicedComponent are referred to as *serviced components*.

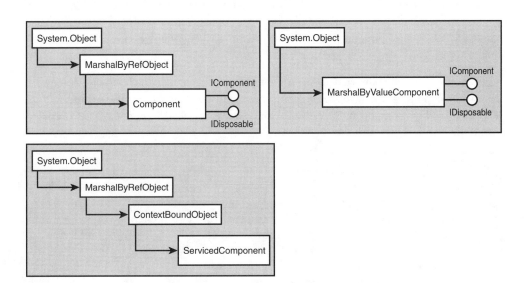

FIGURE 8.1
The inheritance hierarchy for the three primary types of components you can create.

In Figure 8.1, two of the component classes, Component and ServicedComponent, are ultimately derived from MarshalByRefObject, and so are able to be remoted only by passing a proxy to the object created from the type across AppDomains. This works well for components that simply perform business logic or data access and that might reside on a separate server. For example, the business and data access classes used in the sample application might reside on a separate server hosted by Windows 2000 Component Services. As a result, you do not need to (and would not want to) pass the objects themselves between tiers. On the other hand, objects created from the `DataSet` classes will be passed back and forth between the data and presentation tiers, possibly across machine boundaries through input parameters and return values. For them to be remoted by value (much like a disconnected `Recordset` in classic ADO), they are derived from `MarshalByValueComponent`.

Finally, classes derived from `Component` must exist in the AppDomain in which they were created, but might be referenced by clients across AppDomain boundaries by reference. Typically, reusable classes (like controls) whose instances will exist in a single AppDomain are derived from `Component`.

Technically, and as shown in Figure 8.1, the difference between components and classes is that components, as in the case of the `Component` and `MarshalByValueComponent` classes, implement the `IDisposable` and `IComponent` interfaces. As mentioned in Chapter 4, `IDisposable` is an interface that allows classes to implement deterministic finalization through an explicit `Dispose` method rather than relying solely on the garbage collection algorithms of the CLR. `IComponent` simply extends this interface by adding a `Disposed` event and support for interacting with a component's site. In this way, classes that implement the `IComponent` interface can be dragged and dropped onto the VS .NET Web Forms designer surface to support rapid application development.

For our purposes, I lump classes derived from `ServicedComponent`, which are not technically components, into this group because the nomenclature is the same and it makes sense to think of classes hosted by Component Services as components. Serviced components are discussed in detail in Chapter 9.

NOTE

A *site*, as the name implies, refers to the placement of a component into a container. For example, the Web Forms designer is a container that implements the `System.ComponentModel.IContainer` interface. When a component is placed in the container, a site is created and can be referenced using the `Component` property of the `ISite` interface. For the types of development typically done in business applications, you won't have to worry about creating containers and dealing with sites.

What About Controls?

Conspicuously absent from this discussion is any mention of UI controls. The Services Framework supports two classes from which controls are derived: `System.Web.UI.Control` (discussed in Chapter 10, "Building Web Forms") for ASP.NET controls and `System.Windows.Forms.Control` (beyond the scope of this book) for Windows Forms controls. The latter is derived from `Component` and also implements several interfaces that allow it to interact with forms, whereas the former derives directly from `System.Object` and implements the `IComponent` and `IDisposable` interfaces, as well as interfaces to support data binding and child controls. You can think of controls as simply subsets of components.

In summary, components are classes that are remotable, might implement deterministic finalization, and can be reused.

NOTE

It is possible to create nonremotable "components" in the strict sense by creating a class that implements `IComponent`.

Understanding how to build components and how the CLR passes objects instantiated from components between tiers allows us to derive components for the Quilogy sample application from the appropriate classes:

- The business and data access components rely on Component Services and do not need to be passed by value, so they will be derived from `ServicedComponent` as discussed in Chapter 9.

- The `DataSet` objects will be passed by value and hence are derived from `DataSet`, which is derived from `MarshalByValueComponent`.

- Utility classes, such as the logging class shown later in the chapter, will be derived from `Component` because they do not need to be passed between tiers and are reusable between projects.

Passing Data

What does this discussion imply for how our components pass and return data?

First, as in previous versions of VB, you should avoid passing arguments by reference across process or machine boundaries. Doing so requires that the object live in the process in which it was created and incurs the overhead of cross process or machine calls each time the data is accessed. Luckily, VB .NET now defaults to passing parameters `ByVal` rather than `ByRef`.

Second, it means that any objects passed as parameters to an object that resides in a separate AppDomain should be one of three types:

- A simple type such as `Integer` or `String` that can be passed by value
- An object that derives from `MarshalByValueComponent` so that it will be serialized by the CLR
- An object that is marked with the `Serializable` attribute or implements the `ISerializable` interface so that it will be serialized by the CLR

Returning data from methods defined as functions should adhere to these same rules.

Handling Exceptions

In addition to returning data, your components also might throw exceptions. As a result, you'll want to adhere to a standard technique used to check for possible errors and handle exceptions gracefully. This is especially important for components that use distributed transactions because they might need to inform Component Services that the transaction should abort.

For example, as mentioned in Chapter 6, "Error Handling and Debugging," you should check for valid values in arguments passed into a method and raise an `ArgumentException` (or one of its descendants) if the argument does not pass muster. In addition, you should create standard error logging methods in your class, or better yet, abstract them into a class that could be compiled as a module and included in other assemblies, to log errors to a text file or a Windows event log. In this way, the code in a method would use a `Try` block to catch the exception, record it using a standard logging class, and then pass the exception back to the caller using the `Throw` statement.

> **NOTE**
>
> Techniques for persisting errors to text logs and events logs will be shown in Chapter 13, "Implementing Services." In addition, you could use the tracing functionality described in Chapter 6.

Finally, keep in mind that the CLR has been optimized for nonexceptional cases. In other words, exceptions introduce performance overhead, so your methods should only throw exceptions when an actual error occurs and not as the normal course of events.

Serializing Classes

As pointed out in Table 8.1, a class derived from `MarshalByValueComponent` can be serialized by the CLR as it is passed between AppDomains. Serialization is simply the process of converting the state of an object into a representation of bytes that can be transmitted. When the bytes are received on the other end, they are automatically deserialized back into an object.

> **NOTE**
>
> The type of serialization described in this section should not be confused with serializing an object to XML using the `XmlSerializer` class. That technique also can be used when you want to pass the state of an object across AppDomain boundaries, as will be discussed in Chapter 14, "Integrating with the Enterprise."

However, to allow the runtime to perform the serialization, you must mark the class with the `System.Serializable` attribute. In fact, adding the `Serializable` attribute is all you need to enable the runtime to serialize and deserialize objects created from your class. This can be useful if you prefer not to include deterministic finalization in your classes, don't need the RAD services provided by `IComponent`, or need to derive your class from a base class other than `MarshalByValueComponent` (because VB .NET does not support multiple inheritance).

> **NOTE**
>
> Although beyond the scope of this book, your classes optionally can implement the `ISerializable` interface. Doing so allows you to provide custom code that is called when the object is serialized and deserialized to tailor the way in which data is serialized.

In addition, adding serialization support gives you the option of adding methods to your classes that serialize and deserialize an object on demand. This can be useful when you need to persist an object to disk and on a later run of the application re-create it with the previous state. For example, consider the `ImportTask` class shown in Listing 8.1. This simple class represents one that might be created to perform a task that imports a series of files into a database using its `ProcessFiles` method.

LISTING 8.1 Custom Serialization. This class includes the `Serializable` attribute and methods to serialize and deserialize instances on demand.

```
Imports System.IO
Imports System.Runtime.Serialization.Formatters.Binary
 <Serializable()> Public Class ImportTask

  Private mintDocs As Integer
  Private mstrFile As String
  Private marErrors() As Exception
```

8

BUILDING COMPONENTS

LISTING 8.1 Continued

```vb
Public Property DocsProcessed() As Integer
  Get
    Return mintDocs
  End Get
  Set(ByVal Value As Integer)
    mintDocs = Value
  End Set
End Property

Public Property LastFile() As String
  Get
    Return mstrFile
  End Get
  Set(ByVal Value As String)
    mstrFile = Value
  End Set
End Property

Public Sub New(ByVal create As Boolean)
  If create Then
    ' Create some internal state
    ReDim marErrors(1)
    marErrors(0) = New Exception("Sample Error 1")
    marErrors(1) = New Exception("Sample Error 2")
  End If
End Sub

Public Function ProcessFiles() As Exception()
  ' This method would perform the algorithm and may
  ' return after a certain amount of time, or an error,
  ' or after a certain number of files were processed

  ' Return the errors thus far
  Return marErrors
End Function

Public Sub SaveState()
  ' Save the current state of the current object
  Dim fsSave As FileStream
  Dim bf As New BinaryFormatter()

  fsSave = New FileStream("ImportState.dat", FileMode.Create, _
    FileAccess.Write, FileShare.None)
```

LISTING 8.1 Continued

```
    bf.Serialize(fsSave, Me)
    fsSave.Close()
End Sub

Public Shared Function LoadState() As ImportTask
    ' Load the state of an object
    Dim fsSave As FileStream
    Dim bf As New BinaryFormatter()
    Dim objTask As ImportTask

    If Not File.Exists("ImportState.dat") Then
        Throw New Exception("No state previously saved.")
    End If

    fsSave = New FileStream("ImportState.dat", FileMode.Open, FileAccess.Read)

    ' Deserialize
    objTask = CType(bf.Deserialize(fsSave), ImportTask)
    fsSave.Close()

    Return objTask
End Function

End Class
```

Notice that the class itself is marked as serializable using the Serializable attribute from the System namespace. Although typically only used at the class level, this attribute also can be placed on individual fields and properties to allow them to be serialized. Conversely, the System namespace also contains a NonSerialized attribute that you can use to exclude members from being serialized.

The ImportTask class contains a virtual or instance method called SaveState that saves the state of the object instance to a file. The state includes the private variables tracked by the class. These not only include simple types such as an Integer but also more complex types such as the array of Exception objects. The object's state is saved by using the BinaryFormatter class of the System.Runtime.Serialization.Formatters.Binary namespace, which translates the object into a compact binary format that is fast to parse. This class is used internally by the runtime when objects are serialized for transport between AppDomains.

8

**BUILDING
COMPONENTS**

> **NOTE**
>
> The runtime also contains a `SoapFormatter` to translate objects into a format that can be transmitted as SOAP. You can find more information on SOAP in Chapter 11, "Building Web Services."

The `Serialize` method of the `BinaryFormatter` class accepts a `FileStream` that represents the file (discussed in Chapter 12, "Accessing System Services") and the object to serialize, in this case the current instance represented by `Me`.

The object is deserialized using the shared `LoadState` method and the `Deserialize` method of the `BinaryFormatter` class. This method can be called without a current instance and returns a valid instance of `ImportTask` (if the file used to save the state exists, of course).

A client might use the class as in the following code:

```
Dim objTask As New ImportTask(True)
Dim arErrors() As Exception

' Start the process of importing
arErrors = objTask.ProcessFiles()

' Need to shut down or perform other work so save the state
objTask.SaveState()
objTask = Nothing
arErrors = Nothing

' Later we want to rehydrate the object and start again
objTask = ImportTask.LoadState()
arErrors = objTask.ProcessFiles()
```

Of course, the client application would likely only save the state between invocations of the application.

Building Reusable Components

One of the benefits of component-based programming is the capability to reuse components in different projects to promote a Rapid Application Development (RAD) approach. VB always has supported this paradigm by making a toolbox available from which developers could pick and choose components to add to their projects. It is no surprise that VS .NET contains the same paradigm and that classes you create can be transformed into components to be added to the toolbox for reuse in your projects.

To create a reusable component in VB .NET, you perform several steps, including deriving the class from `Component` or `MarshalByValueComponent`, or simply implementing the `IComponent` interface, using designer attributes to allow your component to be configured from the property dialog in VS .NET, and adding the component to the toolbox. This section will show how a `QuilogyLog` component can be created and reused across projects. The code for the component can be seen in Listing 8.2.

TIP

The process described in this section is analogous to creating a classic COM component, registering it on a machine, and using the Project References dialog in VB 6.0 to add a reference to the component.

LISTING 8.2 Reusable `QuilogyLog` Class. This listing shows the reusable class that can be added to the toolbox in VS .NET. Note the designer attributes placed at the property level.

```
Option Strict On

Imports System.IO
Imports System.ComponentModel

Namespace Quilogy.Utils

  <DefaultProperty("Source")> _
  Public Class QuilogyLog : Inherits Component

    ' Logging class
    Private mstrSource As String
    Private mstrFile As String
    Private mflFileOnly As Boolean

    Public Sub New()
      ' Default the value
      Me.LogFile = "AppLog.txt"
      Me.FileOnly = False
    End Sub

    Public Sub New(ByVal source As String, ByVal fileName As String, _
      ByVal fileOnly As Boolean)
      Me.Source = source
      Me.LogFile = fileName
      Me.FileOnly = fileOnly
    End Sub
```

8

BUILDING
COMPONENTS

LISTING 8.2   Continued

```vbnet
<Browsable(True), _
Category("Logging Options"), _
Description("Path of the file used to log to.")> _
Public Property LogFile() As String
  Get
    Return mstrFile
  End Get
  Set(ByVal Value As String)
    mstrFile = Value
  End Set
End Property

<Browsable(True), _
Category("Logging Options"), _
Description("Log source to use in the Application log")> _
Public Property Source() As String
  Get
    Return mstrSource
  End Get
  Set(ByVal Value As String)
    mstrSource = Value
  End Set
End Property

<Browsable(True), _
Category("Logging Options"), _
Description("Log to the text file only?")> _
Public Property FileOnly() As Boolean
  Get
    Return mflFileOnly
  End Get
  Set(ByVal Value As Boolean)
    mflFileOnly = Value
  End Set
End Property

Public Sub LogText(ByVal message As String, _
  ByVal isError As Boolean)
  ' Write to both the text file and the Quilogy log
  Dim objLog As New EventLog("Application")
  Dim strType As String

  objLog.Source = mstrSource
```

LISTING 8.2   Continued

```
If Len(message) = 0 Then
  Throw New ArgumentException("No message passed.")
  Return
End If

Try
  ' Create or open the log file
  If Len(mstrFile) = 0 Then
    Throw New Exception("Must set the LogFile property first")
    Return
  End If

  Dim objFs As FileStream = New FileStream(mstrFile, _
    FileMode.OpenOrCreate, FileAccess.Write)
  Dim objSw As StreamWriter = New StreamWriter(objFs)
  objSw.BaseStream.Seek(0, SeekOrigin.End) ' point to the end

  ' Write the log entry
  objSw.Write("Log Entry : ")
  objSw.Write("{0} {1}", DateTime.Now.ToShortTimeString(), _
    DateTime.Now.ToShortDateString())

  If isError Then
    strType = "Error"
  Else
    strType = "Information"
  End If

  objSw.WriteLine(":" & strType & "[" & message & "]")
  objSw.Flush()  ' Update underlying file
  objSw.Close()

Catch e As Exception
  Throw New Exception("Could not create or open " & _
    mstrFile & ": " & e.Message)

Finally
  If Not mflFileOnly Then
    Try
      ' Make sure the source is registered, it should be
      If (Not EventLog.SourceExists(objLog.Source)) Then
        EventLog.CreateEventSource(objLog.Source, "Application")
      End If
```

LISTING 8.2   Continued

```
            ' Write the message to the log
            If isError Then
              objLog.WriteEntry(message, EventLogEntryType.Error)
            Else
              objLog.WriteEntry(message, EventLogEntryType.Information)
            End If
          Catch e As Exception
            ' Not so important so skip it
            Throw New Exception("Error logging to Application log: " & _
              e.Message)
          Finally
            objLog.Dispose()
          End Try
        End If
      End Try

    End Sub

  End Class

End Namespace
```

First, for the QuilogyLog component to be available to be added to the toolbox, it must derive from Component or implement IComponent. This is the case because components must implement deterministic finalization (IDisposable) and be able to be placed in a designer (IComponent) within VS .NET. In this example, the QuilogyLog class will derive from Component and contain three properties:

- LogFile to specify the path to the file used to log application events

- Source used to specify the source name for the event log

- FileOnly to indicate whether to log only to the text log

The class also will contain one method, LogText, that logs the given message to the file and optionally to the event log.

Second, notice in Listing 8.2 that the class uses a set of designer attributes in the System.ComponentModel namespace to specify how the component's properties will appear in the Properties window in VS .NET. For example, the LogFile property statement includes references to three attributes:

- Browsable to make sure that the property shows up in the properties window

- Category to group properties by functionality

- Description to display in the help pane of the Properties window

In addition, at the class level, the `DefaultProperty` attribute is used to specify that the `Source` property is the default and should be the one that has focus when the developer views the properties.

Also notice that this class contains an overloaded constructor, and that the version that does not accept arguments defaults the `LogFile` and `FileOnly` properties. This is done so that when the designer creates an instance of the component, the default values will be set. As an alternative to this approach, you could use the `DefaultValue` attribute for each property as well.

After the assembly containing the component has been compiled, you can add it to the toolbox by right-clicking on the General tab and selecting Customize Toolbox. Figure 8.2 shows the resulting dialog. By selecting the .NET Framework Components tab and using the Browse button, you can point to the DLL that contains the component. In Figure 8.2, notice that the `QuilogyLog` component has been selected and that it is contained in the `Quilogy.Utils` namespace.

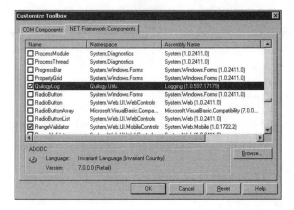

FIGURE 8.2
You can use this dialog to add components to the toolbox.

TIP

You can place multiple components in a single assembly simply by placing more than one class in the assembly, although each of them must derive from `Component` or implement `IComponent`.

After the component is selected, it is placed in the toolbox and can be dragged and dropped on a designer surface. The designer then writes the appropriate code into the target component (Web Form, Windows Form, or other component), as shown in Figure 8.3. Notice that the properties are shown and categorized in the Properties window, and that the `QuilogyLog` component has a graphical representation in the designer.

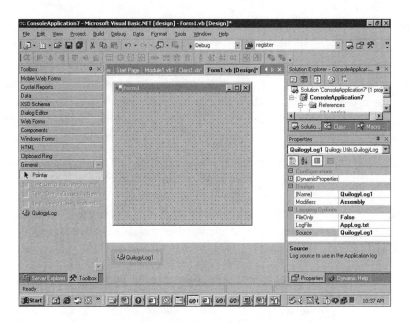

FIGURE 8.3
The VS .NET IDE after the QuilogyLog *components have been added to the Web Form designer surface. Note the properties window in the lower right-hand corner.*

The code generated by the designer is included in the InitializeComponent method as follows:

```
Protected WithEvents QuilogyLog1 As Quilogy.Utils.QuilogyLog

Private Sub InitializeComponent()
    Me.QuilogyLog1 = New Quilogy.Utils.QuilogyLog()
    Me.QuilogyLog1.FileOnly = False
    Me.QuilogyLog1.LogFile = "AppLog.txt"
    Me.QuilogyLog1.Source = Nothing
End Sub
```

Compiling and Versioning

Deriving your classes from Component allows them to be reused by adding them to the toolbox. However, keep in mind that the CLR supports side-by-side execution for components and that, as a result, a component dragged from the toolbox, or for that matter referenced using the Add References dialog, might be a private assembly and copied to the application directory of the client application.

As mentioned in Chapter 5, "Packaging, Deployment, and Security," for the same version of a component to be used by all applications on the same machine, it must be a shared assembly and compiled with a strong name and placed in the Global Assembly Cache (GAC). As you compile your components, make sure that you change only the Quick Fix Engineering (QFE) number for components that must remain compatible and keep the major and minor versions the same.

Using .NET Remoting

With the concepts covered thus far, you should be able to create components that encapsulate business logic and data access, enable objects to be serialized, and promote reuse through reusable components. However, because most corporate developers are interested in creating distributed applications where the presentation, business, and data services might exist on multiple physical machines, we now need to explore how these components can be invoked across processes and machines using .NET Remoting.

At its core, .NET Remoting includes the runtime components and Services Framework classes included in the `System.Runtime.Remoting` namespace that allows managed classes (types) to communicate across AppDomain boundaries. These classes are built on the substrate provided by the `System.Net` classes that will be discussed in Chapter 13, "Implementing Services." Specifically, as mentioned at the beginning of this chapter, types either can be referenced outside their AppDomain if they derive from `MarshalByRefObject` or copied between AppDomains if they are serializable. These types are said to be remotable because .NET Remoting can either create a proxy on the client through which it references an object on the server or serialize the object for transport.

> **NOTE**
>
> Under the covers, this version of .NET Remoting uses either SOAP 1.1 or a binary encoding to marshal objects and HTTP or TCP to make remote calls. However, both the serialization formatter (that is, SOAP, binary) and the communication channel (that is, HTTP, TCP) are "pluggable" and can be replaced as the Internet evolves. Because SOAP and HTTP are used natively, you can think of every remotable object as a Web Service.

Although .NET Remoting is a big subject and serves as the basis for Web Services as discussed in Chapter 11, in the context of components (CLR Object Remoting), it can be used in distributed applications in the following primary ways:

- To provide location transparency when instantiating business and data access components. Just as in DCOM, .NET Remoting, through the use of configuration files, allows the client to be unconcerned with where the object actually resides. In many of these cases, the VB. NET object will be hosted by Component Services on the remote server, although a standalone managed application also can act as a host.
- To provide a mechanism for clients to connect to a single instance of an object across the network. For example, by hosting a VB. NET object in a Windows Service, many clients

can connect to the service and use its services. In addition, because delegates are supported by .NET Remoting, the clients can register for notification as events occur within the service.

The remainder of this section focuses on how .NET Remoting works and specifically how components in the Quilogy education application can be called remotely.

Hosting Components

For a remotable type to be available to be called from a client, it needs to be made available by a hosting (server) application. In other words, the host application must register the fact that it can host certain types and indicate how the objects will be created and destroyed. Specifically, the hosting application must provide the assembly name in which the type is contained, the type name of the remotable object, a URI that the client can use to locate the object, and the activation mode of the type.

Before examining these attributes, it should be noted that the hosting application can specify this information using either a programmatic approach or a configuration file. By programmatically configuring the type for remoting, the hosting application can make runtime decisions about the parameters mentioned in the previous paragraph to, for example, change the activation mode or use a different type at runtime. On the other hand, by placing the remoting information for the type in a configuration file, it is abstracted from the code and can thus be changed without having to recompile or alter the code—for example, when moving from a test to a production environment.

Host Registration

As mentioned previously, the hosting application must provide the assembly and type name to be remoted. This implies that the type must be available on the server, and, in fact, when the server registers the remotable type, the runtime creates an instance of the type and creates an object reference (technically an ObjRef) for it. The runtime packages the ObjRef together with its metadata and the configuration information in an internal remoting table. At this point, the type is ready to be referenced from a client. When the hosting application ends, all its entries are removed from the remoting table making the types unavailable.

In addition to registering the type for remoting, the server also must listen for connections from clients by registering one or more *channels*. In .NET Remoting, this channel is either an HTTP, TCP, or pluggable channel that represents an endpoint that the server uses to service clients. Once again, the channel information can be specified programmatically or through a configuration file. Behind-the-scenes messages are passed between clients and servers by first encoding the message using SOAP or a binary encoding and then transporting it over one of the channels.

When the server registers the channel, it starts listening for calls on that channel using a thread from the runtime's thread pool. When one is encountered, the message is unpacked, and the runtime examines the remoting table to see whether the target type exists in the table. If so, the configuration information is used to activate the object and/or forward the call to the object. Because channels and remotable types do not require a one-to-one correspondence, the server can listen for calls to any of its remotable objects on any of its channels. For example, the server can listen for calls on a TCP channel for clients on the local LAN and simultaneously on an HTTP channel for clients on the Internet. In addition, each client connection on a channel is handled by its own thread, thereby increasing concurrency.

When the server registers the remote object, it can choose between two different activation modes, *single call* and *singleton.* A type activated using single call ensures that a new instance of the type is created for each call. This stateless approach is analogous to the way in which components running Component Services behave when using JIT activation, and should be used when you want to ensure that each client has its own instance of the object and state is not saved between calls. Conversely, all clients that call a singleton type always interact with the same instance of the type. Using singletons is great for sharing information between clients but leads to possible conflicts between threads making calls on the single instance. As a result, you'll need to employ techniques for synchronizing access to the object using techniques such as the Monitor class of the System.Threading namespace discussed in Chapter 12. To illustrate these concepts, consider the simple code shown in Listing 8.3 that implements a server application hosting a singleton object called QuilogyStats.

LISTING 8.3 Hosting a Remotable Object. This console application hosts the QuilogyStats object using the server activation model.

```
Option Strict On
Option Explicit On

Imports System
Imports System.Web.Services
Imports System.Threading
Imports System.Runtime.Remoting
Imports System.Runtime.Remoting.Channels.Tcp
Imports System.Runtime.Remoting.Channels.Http
Imports System.Runtime.Remoting.Channels
Imports RemotingServer

Module Module1

  Sub Main()
    ' Register the Channel
    Dim chan As New TcpChannel(8085)
    ChannelServices.RegisterChannel(chan)
```

8

BUILDING
COMPONENTS

LISTING 8.3 Continued

```
' Register the remotable type
RemotingConfiguration.RegisterWellKnownServiceType( _
    GetType(QuilogyStats), _
    "RemotingHost.QuilogyStats", WellKnownObjectMode.Singleton)

' Wait for client connections
System.Console.WriteLine("Waiting for connections...")
System.Console.ReadLine()

End Sub

End Module
```

In this example, a console application is being used to host a remotable type called QuilogyStats. To do so the application first creates and registers a TCP channel on port 8085 using the ChannelServices class. To instruct the runtime to choose an inactive channel (HTTP or TCP), simply pass the appropriate constructor a zero.

> **NOTE**
>
> Although a server can listen on multiple channels, only one process on the machine can be listening on the same port at any one time.

The application then registers the remote object using the shared RegisterWellKnownServiceType method of the RemotingConfiguration class. This methods takes three parameters that include the type that will be remotable, the URI that the client will use to identify the type, and the activation mode. In this case, we're using WellKnownObjectMode.Singelton, so all clients will be calling the same instance of QuilogyStats. At this point, the server simply waits for connections using Console.ReadLine.

The QuilogyStats class implemented in an assembly called RemotingServer is shown in Listing 8.4.

LISTING 8.4 Remotable Class. This class implements a remotable class called QuilogyStats that is derived from MarshalByRefObject.

```
Option Strict On

Imports System.Threading
Imports System.Security.Principal
Imports System.Runtime.Remoting.Lifetime
```

LISTING 8.4 Continued

```vb
Public Class QuilogyStats : Inherits MarshalByRefObject
  Implements IQuilogyStats

  Private mRegistrations As Integer
  Private mRevenue As Double
  Private mLastUpdate As Date

  Public ReadOnly Property LastUpdate() As Date _
    Implements IQuilogyStats.LastUpdate
    Get
      Return mLastUpdate
    End Get
  End Property

  Public Sub New(ByVal s As String)
    Console.WriteLine(s)
  End Sub

  Public Sub New()
    ' Dummy data
    mRegistrations = 74
    mRevenue = 83560
    mLastUpdate = Now()
  End Sub

  Public Function RegistrationsToday() As Integer _
    Implements IQuilogyStats.RegistrationsToday

    Monitor.Enter(Me)
    ' Manipulate mRegistrations
    Return mRegistrations
    Monitor.Exit(Me)
  End Function

  Public Function RevenueToday() As Double _
    Implements IQuilogyStats.RevenueToday

    Monitor.Enter(Me)
    ' Manipulate mRevenue
    Return mRevenue
    Monitor.Exit(Me)
  End Function

End Class
```

8

**BUILDING
COMPONENTS**

In Listing 8.4, note that `QuilogyStats` derives from `MarshalByRefObject` to make it remotable, and that its methods are implemented from the interface `IQuilogyStats`. As discussed in the next section, implementing interfaces for remotable types is a good practice because it allows the representation of the object to be referenced by clients separate from the implementation.

The `QuilogyStats` class simply exposes two methods and a property that are used to return information about the daily registration process. When used as a singleton, this class would ostensibly contain code that refreshes its instance variables periodically or allows the client to do so to provide updated information. Note also that because each client connection is handled on a separate thread, the possibility exists that two clients could be running code in one of the methods simultaneously. As discussed in Chapter 12, using the `Enter` and `Exit` methods of the `Monitor` class synchronizes access to the body of the method.

> **NOTE**
>
> As implied by the earlier discussion, if a method of the `QuilogyStats` class takes as a parameter another type or if the method returns a type, that type must either be marked as `Serializable` or inherit from `MarshalByRefObject`.

Alternatively, the server application could have specified this information in a configuration file and used the `Configure` method of the `RemotingConfiguration` class to load it. For example, the same information could have been specified in the application configuration file, in this case `remoting.exe.config`, as shown in Listing 8.5.

LISTING 8.5 Server Configuration File. This file can be loaded by the hosting application to configure remoting.

```
<configuration>
  <system.runtime.remoting>
    <application>

      <service>
        <wellknown mode="Singleton"
          type="RemotingServer.QuilogyStats,RemotingServer"
          objectUri="RemotingHost.QuilogyStats" />
      </service>

      <channels>
        <channel type="System.Runtime.Remoting.Channels.Tcp.TcpChannel,
          System.Runtime.Remoting" port="8085" />
```

LISTING 8.5   Continued

```
        </channels>

    </application>
  </system.runtime.remoting>
</configuration>
```

The `Main` procedure of the server could then have been altered as follows:

```
Sub Main()
    ' Register the remotable types
    RemotingConfiguration.Configure("remoting.exe.config")

    ' Wait for client connections
    System.Console.WriteLine("Waiting for connections...")
    System.Console.ReadLine()
End Sub
```

Keep in mind that you also can mix and match these approaches by, for example, adding the channel information to a configuration file and still calling `RegisterWellKnownServiceType` in your code. In addition, you can also call the shared `Configure` method of the `RemotingConfiguration` class multiple times with various service and channel definitions defined in each file. This can be useful by allowing you to separate remoting configuration information that might change based on the deployment scenario from other types of configuration information.

> **NOTE**
>
> Remoting configuration information can also be added to the application configuration files using the .NET Admin Tool. A Remoting Services node is exposed under the Applications node when a new application is added to the list.

Obviously, this example shows how you would configure a type to be remotable in a managed executable you wrote just for that purpose. However, you also can host remotable objects in Windows Service applications, Windows Forms applications, and ASP.NET applications. In the first two cases, you must create the channel and remoting table entry either programmatically or through a configuration file loaded using the `Configure` method as shown previously. In the latter case, you simply need to add a `system.runtime.remoting` element to the Web.config file for the ASP.NET application, and ASP.NET reads the information and configures the remoting table automatically.

8

**BUILDING
COMPONENTS**

> **NOTE**
>
> More information on Web.config and ASP.NET can be found in Chapter 10, "Building Web Forms."

Other Hosts

In addition to creating your own host application for remote objects, other executable processes can be used.

Serviced components already hosted in Component Services (that is those that run in a Server application under the control of DLLHost.exe), can be called in one of two ways. First, because they are exposed by Component Services, they are accessible through DCOM. In other words, you can treat them as if they were unmanaged COM+ components and reference the type library generated by Regsvcs.exe in your application, as discussed in the next chapter. The registry on the client machine then can be updated manually, or with DCOMCnfg.exe to point to the server computer.

Alternatively, in Windows 2000, you can use IIS to act as the listener for the component, whether serviced or not, by creating an ASP.NET application and placing a reference to the component in the Web.config file. The Web application then listens for HTTP connections to the component and routes them, in the case of serviced components, to Component Services. In this case, the communication from the client to IIS is handled through SOAP.

> **TIP**
>
> When using IIS as the remote host, do not specify any channel information in the Web.config file because IIS will use HTTP and select its own port. Although not required of other remote hosts, when using IIS, the objectURI attribute must be set to a string that ends in ".soap" or ".rem".

In Windows .NET Server, the integration of Component Services and SOAP is much tighter, so the Component Services snap-in provides a check box that enables a component to be called via SOAP. This applies to both managed and unmanaged components.

> **TIP**
>
> To get an idea of how SOAP uses XML to describe the metadata of a component, you can modify the code in Listing 8.3 to add an HTTP channel on which to listen. Then

go to MSIE and enter the URL of the remote object appended with `?wsdl`—for example, `http://ssosa:9000/remotinghost.quilogystats?wsdl`. The XML generated is the Web Services Description Language (WSDL) that SOAP clients use to formulate method calls.

Activating Components

From the client's perspective, the remotable object can be activated using either server or client activation. Server activation is simpler and is used when the remote object doesn't store state between calls (`SingleCall`) or when multiple clients are accessing the same instance of an object (`Singleton`). Up until this point, the discussion on hosting components focused on setting up components for server activation. Client-activated objects gain more control over the remote object by being able to pass parameters into the constructor and controlling the lifetime of the object through a leasing model. In addition, the state of the remote object remains between calls. As on the server, the client can explicitly use either of these methods programmatically or through configuration files.

Using Server Activation

To activate a remote object using server activation, the client can use either the `New` operator if a configuration file is in place or the shared `GetObject` method of the `System.Activator` class. In the latter approach, the client must register a client channel used for communication from the server, and then pass the type and URL used to access the remote object as configured on the server. For example, a client application that wants to get a reference to the singleton `QuilogyStats` component shown in Listing 8.3 would do the following:

```
Dim chan As New TcpChannel(8086)
Dim obj As RemotingServer.IQuilogyStats

ChannelServices.RegisterChannel(chan)

obj = CType(Activator.GetObject(GetType(RemotingServer.IQuilogyStats), _
    "tcp://ssosa:8085/RemotingHost.QuilogyStats"),RemotingServer.IQuilogyStats)

intReg = obj.RegistrationsToday
```

Although the name of the method used in this case is familiar, don't confuse it with the intrinsic `GetObject` method used in previous versions of VB that was used to communicate with COM servers already running. In VB .NET, `GetObject` might return a reference to a newly created instance of the object (`SingleCall`), or an existing instance (`Singleton`), depending on how the remote object is configured at the server.

Note that the client needs to set a reference to the assembly that contains the `Remoting Server.IQuilogyStats` interface because the client must read the metadata to make the call. In this case, the remote object has implemented the `IQuilogyStats` interface, which was compiled in a separate assembly and then made available on the client machine. This technique is useful when multiple developers need to program against the remote object while it is still under development. Using interface-based programming in these instances is recommended because the alternatives for providing metadata are simply to copy the assembly containing the remote object to the client or to use the command-line `Soapsuds.exe` utility.

Soapsuds can be used to build an assembly from the WSDL generated by a remote object when listening on an HTTP channel. In addition, it can generate source code for a proxy class derived from `System.Runtime.Remoting.Services.RemotingClientProxy` that can be used by the client to communicate with the remote object via SOAP. The big benefit of Soapsuds is that it relieves the burden of distributing the assembly to clients by allowing them to easily create their own metadata. However, Soapsuds does not work with a component exposed through TCP channels only because, in this case, messages are transported via a binary encoding and not SOAP.

> **NOTE**
>
> Interestingly, just as a proxy for managed components can be created with `Soapsuds.exe`, an unmanaged component using COM Interop (covered in Chapter 9) can be called via SOAP by creating an entry for it in the configuration file or programmatically using `RegisterWellKnownServiceType`. This technique allows SOAP access to existing COM and COM+ components using IIS as the listener.

Obviously, to provide location transparency, the URL can be read from isolated storage (discussed in Chapter 12), the registry, the application configuration file, or an application-specific settings file.

As an alternative to the programmatic approach, the client also can use a configuration file so that some of the configuration information can be abstracted from the source code. Unfortunately, this approach only works with components when the assembly exists on the client machine. In other words, if you simply compile the interfaces for the remote object into an assembly and reference them on the client, the `New` operator cannot be used to instantiate the class because the actual type is not in the assembly. However, this approach is useful when the component can be instantiated on the client or the server. For example, by copying the assembly containing the component to the local machine, a configuration file can be created as shown in Listing 8.6.

LISTING 8.6 Client Configuration File. This listing shows a configuration file that can be loaded by the client to abstract the remoting information.

```
<configuration>
  <system.runtime.remoting>
    <application>

      <client>
        <wellknown type="RemotingServer.QuilogyStats, RemotingServer"
          url="tcp://ssosa:8085/RemotingHost.QuilogyStats" />
      </client>

      <channels>
        <channel type="System.Runtime.Remoting.Channels.Tcp.TcpChannel,
          System.Runtime.Remoting" port="8086" />
      </channels>

    </application>
  </system.runtime.remoting>
</configuration>
```

Note that this file contains a `client` element rather than a `service` element, and defines the client channel, in this case a TCP channel on port 8086 to use.

Now, rather than use `GetObject`, the client can simply load the configuration file and use the `New` operator as follows:

```
Dim obj As RemotingServer.QuilogyStats

RemotingConfiguration.Configure("remotingclient.exe.config")

' Remote object
obj = New RemotingServer.QuilogyStats
intReg = obj.RegistrationsToday
```

Using Client Activation

In both of the preceding instances, the client used server activation to activate the remote object. However, the client can gain more control over the remote object by using client activation. Client activation can be used in scenarios where the client needs to make repeated calls to the same instance of the object on the server.

Before a client can activate an object, the server must register the remote object as able to be client activated. This is done by calling the `RegisterActivatedServiceType` method of the `RemotingConfiguration` class and simply passing in the type like so:

```
RemotingConfiguration.RegisterActivatedServiceType( _
  GetType(RemotingServer.QuilogyStats))
```

The equivalent entry also can be made to the server configuration file by adding an "activated" element that specifies this information as follows:

```
<service>
    <activated type="RemotingServer.QuilogyStats, RemotingServer" />
</service>
```

At this point, when the server begins listening for messages, it does not create an instance of the object but waits for the client to make a request before activating one using any parameters passed to the constructor. You can create a server that registers both an activated and well-known type for use by different types of clients. Obviously, when using client activation, each client receives its own instance of the object, which stays alive on the server until the client releases it or its lease expires.

For a client to activate the object and pass it arguments to satisfy the constructor, the CreateInstance method of the Activator class is used. This method has several overloaded signatures, but in one of its basic forms, it accepts the type of the object to activate along with arrays that represent the arguments to pass to the constructor and the attributes used to activate the object. For example, the code in Listing 8.7 would be executed by the client to return an instance of the remote object created on the server.

LISTING 8.7   Client Activated Object. This code shows how a client would activate an object and pass it a constructor using the client activation model.

```
Dim chan As New TcpChannel(8086)
Dim obj As RemotingServer.QuilogyStats
Dim arConstructor(0) As Object
Dim arActivation(0) As Object
Dim objUrl As New UrlAttribute("tcp://ssosa:8085")

ChannelServices.RegisterChannel(chan)

' Set up the constructor and activation attributes
arConstructor(0) = "logfile.txt"
arActivation(0) = objUrl

' Activate the object on the server, passing a string in the constructor
obj = CType(Activator.CreateInstance(_
  GetType(RemotingServer.QuilogyStats), _
  arConstructor, arActivation), RemotingServer.QuilogyStats)

intReg = obj.RegistrationsToday
```

Notice that, in this case, the QuilogyStats class has been augmented with a constructor that accepts the name of a log file used to log statistics about the registration process. Because the constructor only accepts one argument, the `Object` array is dimensioned with one element. Likewise, the only activation attribute that needs to be set is the URL, so the array is dimensioned to one element, and a `UrlAttribute` object (from the `System.Runtime.Remoting.Activation` namespace) is placed in the array. Note that because the remote object doesn't already exist, you don't need to set up an endpoint. Simply specifying the machine name and port is sufficient.

> **TIP**
>
> In the case of client activated objects, the class must be accessible on the client so that the appropriate constructor can be found. This means that you cannot use the interface-based approach to activate a remote object using only its interface. If you do, a `MissingMethodException` exception is thrown with the message "Constructor not found."

If a client configuration file is used, then an `activated` element can be placed in the `client` element that simply refers to the type and assembly that will use client activation. The client then can load the configuration file using the `Configure` method and instantiate the object as normal using the constructor.

Managing Object Lifetime

As mentioned previously, client-activated objects also support lifetime management. It does this based on the concept of leases, support for which can be found in the `System.Runtime.Remoting.Lifetime` namespace. This technique is used so that the garbage collector on the server can eventually collect all the remotable objects, and also used as an alternative to reference counting as employed by COM. The idea is that the runtime includes a lease manager for each AppDomain that occasionally polls all client-activated remote objects (by default every 10 seconds) to determine whether their leases have expired. If so, the runtime might make a call to a client sponsor object to notify it of the fact. The sponsor then has the option of renewing the lease or letting it expire. If it expires, the remote object is destroyed, and any subsequent calls to it result in exceptions.

To get a reference to the lease, you simply need to create a variable of type `ILease` and call the shared `GetLifetimeServices` method of the `RemotingServices` class passing in the client-activated object. The `ILease` interface supports properties that return the time until the lease expires (`CurrentLeaseTime`), whether the lease has expired (`CurrentState`), the initial lease time (`InitialLeaseTime`), the amount of time to add to the lease when a call is made on the remote object (`RenewOnCallTime`), and the time the server waits for a sponsor to respond (`SponsorShipTimeout`). In addition, a client can renew a lease using the `Renew` method.

NOTE

The members of the `ILease` and `ISponsor` interfaces rely on the `TimeSpan` structure to identify a period of time. This structure is discussed more thoroughly in Chapter 13.

For example, the code in Listing 8.7 could be augmented to get a reference to the lease for `QuilogyStats` and renew the lease for a period of one day:

```
Dim objLease As ILease

objLease = RemotingServices.GetLifetimeService(obj)
objLease.Renew(New TimeSpan(24, 0, 0))
```

However, this is not required because by default, remote objects include an `InitialLeaseTime` of five minutes and a `RenewOnCall` time of two minutes. Therefore, each call to a method of the object after being dormant for five minutes renews it for two minutes. In most scenarios, this is sufficient because the reference to the remote component might not last more than two minutes.

However, in scenarios where one Windows Service application used a client-activated object in another service, you might need to manage the lease by creating a sponsor object on the client. Basically, a sponsor can be created from any class that implements the `ISponsor` interface and derives from `MarshalByRefObject`. The sponsor object acts as a callback from the server used to notify the client application when the lease expires. For example, to register a sponsor with the server, you might use the following code:

```
Dim objSpons As New QuilogyStatsSponsor()

objLease = RemotingServices.GetLifetimeService(obj)
objLease.Register(objSpons)
```

Note that the `ILease` interface contains a `Register` method (along with a complementary `Unregister` method) that allows you to pass the sponsor object to the server. The server then calls back on the `Renewal` method of the interface when the lease expires. The `QuilogyStatsSponsor` class is defined as follows:

```
Public Class QuilogyStatsSponsor : Inherits MarshalByRefObject
  Implements ISponsor

  Public Function Renewal(ByVal objLease As ILease) As TimeSpan _
    Implements ISponsor.Renewal
    ' Keep it alive
    Return New TimeSpan(0, 2, 0)
  End Function
End Class
```

In this case, when the Renewal method is called, the lease is renewed for an additional two minutes.

If you don't want to deal with leases or want to customize how the lease is created at the server, your remote object can override the InitializeLifetimeService method of MarshalByRefObject. For example, to ensure that no lease is created for the QuilogyStats component, the method can be overridden and the InitialLeaseTime property set to zero:

```
Public Overrides Function InitializeLifetimeService() As Object
    Dim objLease As ILease

    objLease = MyBase.InitializeLifetimeService
    If objLease.CurrentState = LeaseState.Initial Then
        objLease.InitialLeaseTime = TimeSpan.Zero
    End If
End Function
```

When the client attempts to retrieve the lease using GetLifetimeService, Nothing is returned. Obviously, other properties of the lease also could be set here. Note that only when the state of the lease is set to the value Initial of the LeaseState enumeration can the properties be manipulated.

Using Advanced Remoting

The previous description is a cursory explanation of .NET Remoting. It does not address several advanced features that developers of distributed applications are definitely interested in. Among these are security and asynchronous operation using delegates, which we will discuss next.

Securing Remoting

As discussed in Chapter 5, VB .NET code can be protected using various security techniques, such as code access and role-based security. .NET Remoting does not add another layer of security but simply uses the underlying models and techniques already exposed. For example, when communicating with a remote object, the actual communication is carried out by classes in the System.Net namespace discussed in Chapter 13. These classes expose methods and properties used to set the credentials used for authentication.

To illustrate, assume that a remote object is hosted by IIS over an HTTP channel. Because the IIS server can use anonymous, basic, digest, or Windows Integrated authentication, sending credentials from a client to a remote object using these authentication schemes involves creating credentials on the client that the runtime will pass to the server. In this case, assume that the server is using basic authentication. You can use the static GetChannelSinkProperties method of the `ChannelServices` class to specify a username and password that will be used to authenticate when the remote object is called as follows:

```
Dim objD As IDictionary

objD = Channelservices.GetChannelSinkProperties(obj)
objD("UserName") = "dfox1"
objD("Password") = "sfdfs"
```

Note that `obj` is the reference to the remotely activated object.

In addition to Web security, you can use the role-based security of .NET to check for the appropriate role either declaratively or imperatively, as discussed in Chapter 5. .NET Remoting automatically sends the required identity information to the server.

Using Asynchronous Remoting

You shouldn't be surprised to learn that .NET Remoting also automatically supports asynchronous calls from the client. It does so using the same asynchronous pattern using delegates as shown in Chapter 4.

For example, to call the `RegistrationsToday` method of the remote `QuilogyStats` object asynchronously, the client must first create a delegate with the same signature as the method to be called—in this case, a function that returns an `Integer`:

```
Public Delegate Function RegToday() As Integer
```

In addition, the client needs to set up a handler that is called when the asynchronous call completes:

```
Public Sub Done(ByVal ar As IAsyncResult)
    ' Notify the client that the processing is complete
End Sub
```

To call the method after the client activates the remote object, it can then instantiate an `AsyncCallback` object and pass it the address of the handler. In addition, the delegate is instantiated and passed the address of the method on the remote object to call. By using the `BeginInvoke` method of the delegate and passing in the `AsyncCallback` object, the runtime calls the remote object and waits for notification on another thread, as shown in Listing 8.8.

Listing 8.8 Asynchronous Remoting. This listing shows how a client application can use the asynchronous pattern with a remote object.

```
Dim cbRegToday As AsyncCallback
Dim delRegToday As RegToday
Dim ar As IAsyncResult
```

LISTING 8.8 Continued

```
Dim obj As RemotingServer.IQuilogyStats
Dim chan As New HttpChannel()

' Register the channel to receive the callback and activate the object
ChannelServices.RegisterChannel(chan)
obj = CType(Activator.GetObject(GetType(RemotingServer.IQuilogyStats), _
  "http://ssosa:9000/RemotingHost.QuilogyStats"),RemotingServer.IQuilogyStats)

' Setup the callback and invoke the method asynchronously
cbRegToday = New AsyncCallback(AddressOf Done)
delRegToday = New RegToday(AddressOf obj.RegistrationsToday)
delRegToday.BeginInvoke(cbRegToday, Nothing)
```

As a result, the Done method is called on a separate thread when the RegistrationsToday method completes.

Calling Unmanaged DLLs

Despite the breadth of functionality available in the Services Framework, on occasion you'll need to make calls to the Win32 API or a custom or third-party unmanaged DLL. Fortunately, the CLR makes this process simple using the Platform Invoke (PInvoke) service. To make life even easier for VB developers, PInvoke has been exposed through the intrinsic Declare statement in VB.NET. However, as with previous versions of VB, you need to be aware of several considerations before calling into unmanaged DLLs.

The basic syntax for calling a DLL function using the Declare statement remains relatively unchanged. For example, to call the GetSystemDirectory Win32 API function, you can use the following Public or Private Declare statement in a module or a class:

```
Declare Auto Function GSD Lib "Kernel32" _
  Alias "GetSystemDirectory" _
 (ByVal s As StringBuilder, ByVal len As Integer) As Integer
```

The DLL that contains the function (referred to as the *entry point*) is specified by the Lib statement, and the function can be referred to with a different name using the Alias statement. However, those familiar with the Declare statement should immediately see two other differences. The first is the Auto keyword. This keyword controls how PInvoke finds the actual name of the function to call and how it marshals strings. Using Auto instructs PInvoke at runtime to look for either an ANSI version of the function or a Unicode version depending on the operating system the code is running on. Typically, Win32 exports an ANSI version of the function for use on Windows 95 and 98 appended with an "A" and the Unicode version used on Windows NT and 2000 appended with a "W."

8

BUILDING
COMPONENTS

> **NOTE**
>
> Yes, there is an easier way to get the system directory by using the shared `SystemDirectory` property of the `Environment` class. The use of `GetSystemDirectory` here is only for illustration.

In place of the `Auto` keyword, you can also explicitly use `Ansi` (the default) or `Unicode` to call the appropriate version of the function. By doing so, you disable the capability of PInvoke to build the name, and the exact spelling of the function name, `GetSystemDirectoryW` or `GetSystemDirectoryA` in this case, must be specified in the `Declare` statement. Not surprisingly, an attribute called `DLLImport` can be used to override this setting by changing its `ExactSpelling` field to `False` as follows:

```
Imports System.Text
Imports System.Runtime.InteropServices
<DLLImport("Kernel32", ExactSpelling:=False)> _
Declare Ansi Function GSD Lib "Kernel32" _
  Alias "GetSystemDirectoryA" _
 (ByVal s As StringBuilder, ByVal len As Integer) As Integer
```

> **NOTE**
>
> As implied by the previous code example, `DLLImport` also allows you to specify the name of the DLL in its constructor, which is equivalent to the `Lib` statement in the declare. In addition, `DLLImport` contains `EntryPoint` and `CharSet` fields that map to the `Function` or `Alias` and character set portions of the declare. Three other attributes, `CallingConvention`, `PreserveSig`, and `SetLastError`, are defaulted for VB .NET developers, so you shouldn't need to change them.

In this case, because `Ansi` is specified, PInvoke uses the explicit name of the function specified, `GetSystemDirectoryA`. Because ANSI is being used, PInvoke will make the call, marshalling the strings as ANSI (1 byte per character) and then converting them back to Unicode upon return.

The other significant change from previous versions of VB is that because an `Integer` data type in VB .NET maps to the `System.Int32` data type, you no longer need to use the `Long` data type when calling Win32. In addition, as is common, the `GetSystemDirectory` function accepts a string buffer and the length of the buffer. Rather than use the `String` data type, you should pass an instance of `StringBuilder` to the function because the `String` data type is immutable in the CLR. The `StringBuilder` allows the new string to be copied back into the managed code, simulating a call by reference. You pass the `StringBuilder` by value (`ByVal`). For example, to call the function you would do the following:

```
Dim sbReturn As StringBuilder

sbReturn = New StringBuilder(256)
intRet = GetSystemDirectory(sbReturn, sbReturn.Capacity)
```

A table of other common Win32 data types and their appropriate VB .NET equivalents can be found in the online documentation.

Wrapping Unmanaged DLLs

As with previous versions of VB, it is good coding practice to abstract the `Declare` and associated constants, structures, and the actual calls to external DLLs in wrappers. In this way, the code that calls the DLL is isolated and can be modified without affecting other code. Although this was typically done with standard modules in previous versions of VB, in VB .NET this is more appropriate for a class.

When you create a VB .NET class that abstracts unmanaged DLLs, you basically have two options. First, you can place each function in a separate class and expose properties to set up the call before invoking it. Second, and preferably, you can group related functions into a shared class and expose roughly one shared method or property for each unmanaged function. In this way, you can create a private assembly that is easily shared with other developers.

To illustrate the latter technique, consider the `Win32Info` class shown in Listing 8.9. This class is a member of the `Quilogy.Utils` namespace and is used to provide information and interact with the operating system.

LISTING 8.9 Wrapping Unmanaged DLLs. This class is a wrapper for several Win32 API functions that return system information and send messages.

```
Option Explicit On
Option Strict On

Imports System
Imports System.Runtime.InteropServices

Namespace Quilogy.Utils

    Public Class Win32Info
```

LISTING 8.9   Continued

```
' Recognized processor types
Public Enum ProcessorType
    INTEL_386 = 1
    INTEL_486 = 2
    INTEL_PENTIUM = 3
    MIPS_R4000 = 4
    ALPHA_21064 = 5
    ALPHA_21066 = 6
    ALPHA_21164 = 7
    PPC_601 = 8
    PPC_603 = 9
    PPC_603PLUS = 10
    PPC_604 = 11
    PPC_604PLUS = 12
    PPC_620 = 13
    INTEL_UNKNOWN = 14
    MIPS_UNKNOWN = 15
    ALPHA_UNKNOWN = 16
    PPC_UNKNOWN = 17
    UNKNOWN = 99
End Enum

' Local storage
Private Shared mbProcs As Byte = 0
Private Shared mType As ProcessorType = ProcessorType.UNKNOWN

Public Shared ReadOnly Property Processors() As Byte
    ' Return the number of processors
    Get
        If mbProcs = 0 Then
            mbProcs = GetProcessors()
        End If

        Return mbProcs
    End Get
End Property

Public Shared ReadOnly Property Processor() As ProcessorType
    ' Return the processor type
    Get
        If mType = 0 Then
            mType = GetProcType()
        End If
        Return mType
```

LISTING 8.9   Continued

```
            End Get
        End Property

        Public Shared Sub SendMessage(ByVal message As String, _
          ByVal recip As String, _
         Optional ByVal from As String = Nothing)
            ' Send a message
            NetSend(message, recip, from)
        End Sub

    End Class
End Namespace
```

In this case, the class exposes `Processors` and `Processor` properties that return the number of processors in the machine on which the code is running, and the type of processors used through the `ProcessorType` enumeration. In addition, the class exposes one method, `SendMessage`, which uses the Messenger service to send a message to a particular client or set of clients.

This class does not actually contain any of the `Declare` statements for the underlying Win32 APIs called. Those are abstracted to a module shown in Listing 8.10.

LISTING 8.10   Calling Win32. This module contains the actual calls to the unmanaged DLLs in addition to the constants, structures, and other supporting declarations.

```
Option Strict On

Imports System.Runtime.InteropServices
Imports System.Text

Module APIs
    '***************************************************
  <StructLayout(LayoutKind.Sequential)> _
  Public Structure SYSTEM_INFO
    Public dwOemId As Integer
    Public dwPageSize As Integer
    Public lpMinimumApplicationAddress As Integer
    Public lpMaximumApplicationAddress As Integer
    Public dwActiveProcessorMask As Integer
    Public dwNumberOfProcessors As Integer
    Public dwProcessorType As Integer
    Public dwAllocationGranularity As Integer
    Public wProcessorLevel As Short
```

8

BUILDING COMPONENTS

LISTING 8.10 Continued

```
    Public wProcessorRevision As Short
End Structure

'**************************************************
Private Const PROCESSOR_ARCHITECTURE_ALPHA As Integer = 2
Private Const PROCESSOR_ARCHITECTURE_INTEL As Integer = 0
Private Const PROCESSOR_ARCHITECTURE_MIPS As Integer = 1
Private Const PROCESSOR_ARCHITECTURE_PPC As Integer = 3
Private Const PROCESSOR_ARCHITECTURE_UNKNOWN _
  As Integer = 65535

Private Const FORMAT_MESSAGE_FROM_SYSTEM As Integer = 4096
Private Const NERR_Success As Integer = 0
Private Const MAX_LENGTH As Integer = 256

'**************************************************
Private Declare Auto Function Win32NetMessageSend Lib "netapi32.dll" _
  Alias "NetMessageBufferSend" _
  (ByVal lpstrServer As String, ByVal lpstrMsgName As String, _
  ByVal lpstrFromn As String, ByVal lpbyteBuf As String, _
  ByVal dwLen As Integer) As Integer

Private Declare Auto Sub Win32GetSystemInfo Lib "Kernel32" _
  Alias "GetSystemInfo" (ByRef s As SYSTEM_INFO)

Private Declare Auto Function Win32GetLastError _
  Lib "kernel32" () As Integer

Private Declare Auto Function Win32FormatMessage Lib "kernel32" _
  Alias "FormatMessage" _
  (ByVal dwFlags As Integer, ByVal lpSource As Integer, _
  ByVal dwMessageId As Integer, ByVal dwLanguageId As Integer, _
  ByVal lpBuffer As StringBuilder, ByVal nSize As Integer, _
  ByVal Arguments As Integer) As Integer

'**************************************************
Public Function GetProcessors() As Byte
  ' Call the Win32 API function and get the number of processors
  Dim s As New SYSTEM_INFO()

  Try
    Win32GetSystemInfo(s)
    Return CType(s.dwNumberOfProcessors, Byte)
  Catch e As Exception
```

LISTING 8.10   Continued

```
    Return 0
  End Try

End Function

'***************************************************
Public Function GetProcType() As _
  Quilogy.Utils.Win32Info.ProcessorType
  ' Call the Win32 API function and get the processor type
  Dim s As New SYSTEM_INFO()

  Try
    Win32GetSystemInfo(s)
  Catch e As Exception
    Return Quilogy.Utils.Win32Info.ProcessorType.UNKNOWN
  End Try

  Select Case s.dwOemId
    Case PROCESSOR_ARCHITECTURE_INTEL
      Select Case s.wProcessorLevel
        Case 3
          Return Quilogy.Utils.Win32Info.ProcessorType.INTEL_386
        Case 4
          Return Quilogy.Utils.Win32Info.ProcessorType.INTEL_486
        Case 5
          Return Quilogy.Utils.Win32Info.ProcessorType.INTEL_PENTIUM
        Case Else
          Return Quilogy.Utils.Win32Info.ProcessorType.INTEL_UNKNOWN
      End Select
    Case PROCESSOR_ARCHITECTURE_MIPS
      Select Case s.wProcessorLevel
        Case 4
          Return Quilogy.Utils.Win32Info.ProcessorType.MIPS_R4000
        Case Else
          Return Quilogy.Utils.Win32Info.ProcessorType.MIPS_UNKNOWN
      End Select
    Case PROCESSOR_ARCHITECTURE_ALPHA
      Select Case s.wProcessorLevel
        Case 21064
          Return Quilogy.Utils.Win32Info.ProcessorType.ALPHA_21064
        Case 21066
          Return Quilogy.Utils.Win32Info.ProcessorType.ALPHA_21066
        Case 21164
          Return Quilogy.Utils.Win32Info.ProcessorType.ALPHA_21164
```

8

**BUILDING
COMPONENTS**

LISTING 8.10   Continued

```
            Case Else
              Return Quilogy.Utils.Win32Info.ProcessorType.ALPHA_UNKNOWN
          End Select
      Case PROCESSOR_ARCHITECTURE_PPC
        Select Case s.wProcessorLevel
          Case 1
            Return Quilogy.Utils.Win32Info.ProcessorType.PPC_601
          Case 3
            Return Quilogy.Utils.Win32Info.ProcessorType.PPC_603
          Case 4
            Return Quilogy.Utils.Win32Info.ProcessorType.PPC_604
          Case 6
            Return Quilogy.Utils.Win32Info.ProcessorType.PPC_603PLUS
          Case 9
            Return Quilogy.Utils.Win32Info.ProcessorType.PPC_604PLUS
          Case 20
            Return Quilogy.Utils.Win32Info.ProcessorType.PPC_620
          Case Else
            Return Quilogy.Utils.Win32Info.ProcessorType.PPC_UNKNOWN
        End Select
      Case Else
        Return Quilogy.Utils.Win32Info.ProcessorType.UNKNOWN
    End Select
End Function


Public Sub NetSend(ByVal message As String, ByVal recip As String, _
  ByVal from As String)
  ' Send a message
  Dim intRet As Integer
  Dim intLen As Integer
  Dim sbReturn As StringBuilder


  intLen = Encoding.Unicode.GetByteCount(message)
  ' Send the message from the local server
  intRet = Win32NetMessageSend("", recip, from, message, intLen)

  If intRet <> NERR_Success Then
    sbReturn = New StringBuilder(MAX_LENGTH)

    ' Get the message
    intRet = Win32FormatMessage( _
      FORMAT_MESSAGE_FROM_SYSTEM, 0, intRet, 0, _
      sbReturn, sbReturn.Capacity, 0)
```

LISTING 8.10 Continued

```
      If intRet > 0 Then
        Throw New Exception("Message was not sent:" & sbReturn.ToString)
      Else
        Throw New Exception("Message was not sent: Unknown error")
      End If
    End If
  End Sub

  Private Function GetErrorMsg() As String
    Dim intRet As Integer
    Dim sbReturn As New StringBuilder(MAX_LENGTH)

    ' Get the last error and message
    intRet = Win32GetLastError()
    If intRet = 0 Then
      Return Nothing
    Else
      intRet = Win32FormatMessage( _
        FORMAT_MESSAGE_FROM_SYSTEM, 0, intRet, 0, _
        sbReturn, sbReturn.Capacity, 0)
      Return sbReturn.ToString
    End If

  End Function

End Module
```

In Listing 8.10, the public GetProcessor and GetProcType methods both call the
GetSystemInfo Win32 API function aliased as Win32GetSystemInfo.

> **TIP**
>
> The "Win32" is prefixed to the function so that it is easier to differentiate between
> functions in .NET and external functions.

This function has a simple Declare statement but returns a structure called SYSTEM_INFO
passed by reference. The structure is declared as Public and maps the members as Integer
and Short values. In addition, the StructLayout attribute is used with a LayoutKind of
Sequential to make sure that the runtime does not reorder the members of the structure

(which it occasionally does for efficiency). For more control, you can explicitly set the offsets in the structure using the `Explicit LayoutKind` with the `FieldOffset` attribute as follows:

```
<StructLayout(LayoutKind.Explicit)> _
  Public Structure Rect
    <FieldOffset(0)> Public left As Integer
    <FieldOffset(4)> Public top As Integer
    <FieldOffset(8)> Public right As Integer
    <FieldOffset(12)> Public bottom As Integer
  End Structure
```

After the function returns the structure, it is a simple matter to read the appropriate field and return the correct result.

The other key point in Listing 8.10 is the public `NetSend` method. This method is called by the class method in Listing 8.9 and is responsible for making the call to Win32 and raising any exceptions. Notice that the underlying `NetMessageBufferSend` function is called as a Unicode function, so the byte length passed as the final argument should be double the character length. One way to determine the number of bytes in a `String` is to use the `GetByteCount` method of the `Encoding` class.

After the `Win32NetMessageSend` function is called, the return value is inspected. In this case, if the value is not equal to the constant `NERR_Success`, then an error occurred. Typically, error strings can be retrieved using the `FormatMessage` function. Once again, this function fills a string buffer with the retrieved message when passed the error code. In this case, the method throws an exception that includes the text of the message.

TIP
Although not used in any of the other methods, the `GetErrorMsg` method can be used with API functions that set the error code for the current thread but do not return it. This method calls the `GetLastError` function to retrieve the error code followed by `FormatMessage` to get the error string. Functions such as `GetCurrentDirectory` that use a positive return value to indicate success and 0 to indicate failure, then require that `GetLastError` be called to discover the actual error code.

Because the class and its methods are shared (calls to Win32 APIs should rarely require any instance storage), a client can use this class by simply importing the assembly and calling a method. In the following code, the `SendMessage` method is called to send a network message to a specific machine in the event of a fatal error in the application:

```
Imports Quilogy.Utils
Win32Info.SendMessage("Fatal Error Occurred on web server", _
  strAdminPC, "Quilogy Education Application")
```

Using Callbacks

In addition to passing simple data types and structures, you also can use Win32 callbacks. As you might expect, this is done using delegates, which were described in Chapter 4.

For example, assume that you wanted to call the EnumWindows Win32 function to return a list of all the Window handles on the current system. This function takes as a parameter the address of a callback function. To specify the callback function, simply create a delegate with the appropriate signature as follows:

```
Imports System.Runtime.InteropServices
Declare Auto Function Win32EnumWindows Lib "User32" _
  Alias "EnumWindows" (ByVal cb As EnumCallBack, _
  ByVal appspecific As Integer) As Integer


Delegate Function EnumCallBack(ByVal hwnd As Integer, _
ByVal lParam As Integer) As Boolean
```

Once again, the delegate is passed ByVal because it encapsulates the address of a method. The client code then simply needs to instantiate the delegate, pass it the address of the callback method, and pass the delegate to the function as follows:

```
Dim dCB As New EnumCallBack(AddressOf WinCB)
Dim intRet As Integer

intRet = Win32EnumWindows(dCB, 0)

  ' Other code here
Public Function WinCB(ByVal hwnd As Integer, _
  ByVal lParam As Integer) As Boolean
  ' Use the Window handle
  Return True
End Function
```

Note that the WinCB method of the module or class will be called repeatedly as long as the method returns True. Unlike the delegates described in Chapter 4, however, in this case, the work of the Win32 function occurs on the same thread as the caller. In other words, the call to EnumWindows will block until all the Windows are enumerated.

Summary

This chapter looked at the various aspects of the Services Framework and VB .NET that you can use to create components. This included the techniques used to serialize objects, reuse components, and use components across the network with .NET Remoting.

Although this chapter laid the groundwork for working with components, many of the middle-tier services that VB developers have come to expect, including just-in-time activation and transactional support, will be covered in the next chapter.

Accessing Component Services

IN THIS CHAPTER

Chapter 8, "Building Components" laid the groundwork for building components in VB .NET by describing how components are created, reused, and able to be remoted across AppDomain boundaries. This chapter builds on that foundation to describe how the classes in both the business and data services tiers can be integrated with Component Services (also referred to as COM+ in this discussion) to take advantage of services, such as transactions and object pooling in addition to looking at how .NET components can interoperate with classic COM components.

Once again many of examples in this chapter come from the Quilogy education sample application, specifically, with the components used to handle the process of registering a student in a Quilogy class.

> **NOTE**
>
> All code listings and supplemental material for this chapter can be found on the book's Web site at www.samspublishing.com.

As noted in the previous chapter, the Services Framework supports accessing Component Services by deriving classes from the ServicedComponent class in the System.EnterpriseServices namespace. Although serviced components can run on NT 4.0 and hence in Microsoft Transaction Server (MTS), the most development will be done on Windows 2000 and Windows .NET Server, so this discussion focuses on using COM+ services.

Both the business and data access classes in the Quilogy sample application use COM+ primarily for distributed transactions. However, this section shows not only how these features can be used but also how managed components can use other services such as object pooling, shared properties, COM+ events, and queued components.

Is COM+ Necessary?

It is certainly true that many applications do not require Component Services. For these applications, the architecture described in this part of the book still is recommended without the reliance on Component Services. However, in many enterprise scale applications, the need to use transactions across disparate data sources, queued components, and object pooling makes Component Services an attractive host for business and data access components. That being said, because Component Services is built on the classic COM infrastructure, the integration between managed code and Component Services requires that the runtime identify the managed component as a COM component. As a result, you'll notice that the integration between the two technologies is not always seamless. Look for this to improve greatly in coming releases.

Before we explore serviced components, a short review of COM+ and a discussion of the differences between it and MTS are in order.

Migrating from MTS to COM+

Since its release in 1997, Microsoft Transaction Server (MTS) has been heavily employed by developers of distributed applications built on Windows NT 4.0. In short, MTS allows a developer to create components that contain data access and business logic and run them on a middle-tier server (hence the term component-oriented middleware). In addition, these components can create distributed transactions to modify data in different data sources while maintaining transactional consistency. For developers, this architecture produces several benefits, including

- The components can run in a dedicated server process (thereby taking the load off the client and providing process isolation).
- You can centralize business logic so that it can be easily updated.
- You can allow both thin and fat client applications access to the components.
- You can allow components to update multiple data sources consistently within a single transaction.

MTS was updated as a part of Windows 2000 under the name COM+ or Component Services. Although you can think of COM+ as MTS version 3.0, albeit with plenty of subtle and some not so subtle changes, for the sake of this discussion, I'll assume that you are familiar with these basics of MTS.

NOTE

Fore more information on MTS and its architecture see Chapter 16 of my book *Pure Visual Basic*.

9

Administrative Changes

COM+ is administered through the Component Services snap-in instead of the MTS Explorer. Each "package" in MTS is now called an "application" and, as in MTS, serves the function of security and isolation when configured as a "Server application" in the Activation tab of the properties dialog. When running as a Server application, components in the application run in a separate process, which is now hosted by instances of DLLHOST.EXE rather than MTX.EXE. Hosting components in this way allows them to actually execute on a middle-tier server. Both unmanaged components and managed components can be hosted by DLLHOST.EXE. As in MTS, components within an application alternatively can be loaded into the process of their creator when the application is configured as a "Library application," which is the default.

In COM+, components are either "configured" or "nonconfigured." Simply put, a configured component is a classic COM component or a managed component derived from ServicedComponent that has been registered with the Component Services snap-in and that can use one or more of the COM+ services. A nonconfigured component does not have access to the COM+ services and will not be hosted by Component Services.

As you'll see, configuration information can be provided through attributes in VB .NET and supports manual, first-use, and programmatic registration with Component Services. Configuring a component allows the system software that underlies COM+ and provides unmanaged APIs to register and create component instances (the COM+ Library) to store additional information about the component in the COM+ Catalog. The COM+ Catalog is a private binary database of information separate from the registry that is managed by the Component Services snap-in. The COM+ Catalog then is used by the COM+ Library to determine which services the component will use and how the component will be instantiated. This arrangement is analogous to MTS where you think of a component registered with MTS as "configured," although behind the scenes the two methods differ. The configuration attributes also can be accessed directly using the Component Services snap-in.

You also can programmatically administer the COM+ Catalog using the classic COM component COMAdminCatalog and its associated collections. In this release, the Services Framework does not contain classes to handle this; you must rely on the interoperation services described later in this chapter.

Architectural Changes

It's not surprising to learn that COM+ takes the best features of MTS and builds them into the classic COM infrastructure to provide tighter integration and to simplify life for both the operating system and the developer. After all, MTS was developed and shipped as a part of the NT Option Pack after NT 4.0 had been released and as a result had to fool the COM Library to work its magic. Four of these changes include the method of interception, automatic deactivation, the addition of object pooling and construction, and use of the registry.

Interception

Both MTS and COM+ use a technique called *interception* to provide a layer of abstraction between the client and the component, which provides the opportunity to add a variety of runtime services. In other words, when a base client (the client that first requests an instance of a component running in COM+) asks for an instance of a component, MTS and COM+ intercept the call, create the instance, and hand a pointer to the object back to the client. Although the general technique remains the same, the details differ.

In MTS, the interception is performed by a separate *context wrapper* object that stores all the MTS-related information for the object and through which all calls to and from the object must pass. In COM+, however, all component instances are automatically created inside a COM+ *context* that contains all the COM+-related information. This difference underlies the fact that MTS was added on top of COM, while COM+ is integrated into the operating system.

> **NOTE**
>
> You'll notice that in the Services Framework `ServicedComponent` derives from `ContextBoundObject`, which provides access to the COM+ context information.

You can think of contexts as subdivisions within a process where one or more objects live.

Fortunately, the programming model exposed by the `System.EnterpriseServices` namespace is similar to the MTS object model VB 6.0 developers used and parallels the COM+ Services Type Library. For example, the `ContextUtil` class (shown in Table 9.1) includes a number of shared members used to provide the component with information about the context just as the `ObjectContext` provided information about the context wrapper in MTS. In fact, `ContextUtil` exposes a combination of the members provided by the `IObjectContext` and `IContextState` interfaces in COM+.

TABLE 9.1 `ContextUtil` Class.

Member	Description
ActivityID	Property that returns a GUID representing the activity containing the component. Useful for debugging.
ApplicationID	Property that returns a GUID representing the application containing the component. Useful for debugging.
ApplicationInstanceID	Property that returns a GUID representing the current application instance containing the component. Useful for debugging.
ContextID	Property that returns a GUID for the current context. Useful for debugging.
DeactivateOnReturn	Boolean property that controls whether the component is deactivated when it returns from the current method (also called the "doneness bit").
IsInTransaction	Boolean property that returns whether the component is participating in a distributed transaction.
IsSecurityEnabled	Boolean property that returns whether role-based security is turned on.
MyTransactionVote	Specifies whether the current context will vote to commit or abort the transaction using the `TransactionVote` enumeration (also called the "context consistency bit").

TABLE 9.1 Continued

Member	Description
PartitionID	Property that returns a GUID representing the current partition. Useful for debugging in Windows .NET Server, which supports partitioned applications.
Transaction	Property that returns an object representing the current transaction if there is one.
TransactionID	Property that returns a GUID representing the current transaction if there is one. Useful for debugging.
DisableCommit	Method that sets both the context consistency and doneness bits to False (that is, the component will vote to roll back the transaction when completed but the component will not be deactivated).
EnableCommit	Method that sets the context consistency bit to True and the doneness bit to False (that is, the component will vote to commit the transaction when completed, but the component will not be deactivated).
GetNamedProperty	Method that returns a named property of the current context. Useful for returning the intrinsic ASP objects when the component is called from ASP.
IsCallerInRole	Boolean method that returns whether the caller is in the specified role.
SetAbort	Method that sets the context consistency bit to False and the doneness bit to True (that is, the component will cause the transaction to abort and will be deactivated when the method returns).
SetComplete	Method that sets both the context consistency and doneness bits to True (that is, the component will vote to commit the transaction when completed and will be deactivated when the method returns).

The difference between the MTS and COM+ architecture can be seen in Figure 9.1. The key difference to notice in Figure 9.1 is that calls into and out of a COM+ object automatically pass through context-aware proxies where COM+ can make decisions about transaction enlistment and other runtime services. In MTS, the context wrapper does not necessarily get notified, and developers must ensure that it receives information about the calls using the CreateInstance and SafeRef methods.

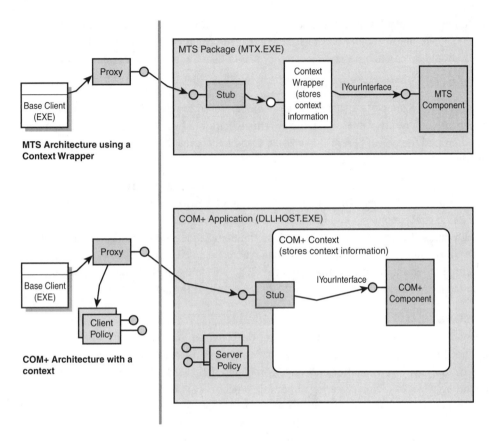

FIGURE 9.1

The difference between the context wrapper object used in MTS and the context used in COM+.

For example, consider a method called `Transfer` in a managed banking component that calls `Deposit` and `Withdraw` methods. If the component being called resides in MTS, you'll have to write the following code in VB 6.0 to ensure that the `Bank.Services` component runs in the same activity (a logical thread of execution set up for a single base client) and is enlisted in the MTS transaction of its caller:

```
Dim objBank as Bank.Services

Set objBank = GetObjectContext.CreateInstance("Bank.Services")

objBank.Deposit(strAccount, dblAmount)
objBank.Withdraw(strAccount, dblAmount)
```

If the component resides in COM+, however, you can simply instantiate it using the New operator, and COM+ automatically consults the context information to determine whether the component should be created in the same activity and enlisted in the transaction as shown below.

```
Set objBank = New Bank.Services
```

In addition, MTS supports a shared SafeRef method used to pass an object reference out of a component via a return value or parameter. This is required because an MTS proxy must be created around the object before it is passed. Components residing in COM+ are not required to do this.

Obviously, both MTS and COM+ are implemented as unmanaged code and make use of the unmanaged APIs designed before managed code and CLR were developed. As a result, the role of the ServicedComponent class is to act as a broker between the unmanaged COM+ world and the managed world. For example, code in the ServicedComponent class handles activation of a serviced component by calling the CoCreateInstance API in the COM+ Library and retrieving configuration information from the COM+ Catalog. In addition, it creates the proxy on the managed side that interacts with the COM+ context through the ContextUtil class.

Deactivation

A second architectural change is the timing of deactivation. As you're probably aware, MTS introduced the concept of Just-In-Time activation (JITA). JITA allows MTS and Component Services to destroy objects after they have completed their work and rebuild them on demand without the client knowing or caring about this process. This technique is primarily used to ensure transactional consistency and results in the design of stateless components. For JITA to take place in MTS, you had to explicitly call the SetAbort or SetComplete methods of the ObjectContext object within each method of your component.

In COM+, however, JITA has been decoupled from transactions, which has several effects. You can enable JITA on a component without using a transaction by setting a property within the Activation tab in the component's property dialog. You can use the Component Services snap-in or an attribute in VB .NET to configure each method of a component to trigger a deactivation of the object (setting the doneness bit to True) when the method completes, as shown in Figure 9.2. Of course, if the component is deactivated it loses all of its state information. This is available when either JITA is enabled or a transaction mode other than Not Supported or Disabled is selected.

Automatic deactivation allows components that do not explicitly contain calls to SetAbort and SetComplete—such as third-party components for which you do not have the source code or components that do not participate in transactions—to use JITA. For transactional components, this feature also automatically calls SetComplete if the method returns normally and SetAbort if the method throws an exception.

FIGURE 9.2
Configuring a method in the Component Services snap-in to use JITA without programmatic interaction.

Object Pooling and Construction

In addition, COM+ now supports object pooling as well as JITA, as foreshadowed by the
`CanBePooled` method of the `IObjectControl` interface available in MTS. Components created
in VB 6.0 cannot take advantage of object pooling because it requires the components to support the Thread Neutral Apartment (TNA) architecture rather than the simpler Single Threaded
Apartment (STA). VB .NET is no longer bound by this restriction and can create pooled
objects simply through the use of attributes and overridden methods.

COM+ supports a new interface called `IObjectConstruct`. This interface solves the common
problem of how to pass simple information into a component on activation, the primary example being a database connection string. In MTS, developers chose between passing an ADO
connection string from the client application to each method of the component, hard-coding
the string within the components, or reading it from the system registry or a file with each
method call. Each of these options obviously has its downside that involves trade-offs between
maintainability and performance.

COM+ solves this problem with `IObjectConstruct` by allowing components to implement this
interface. Doing so enables COM+ to call the implementation of the `Construct` method of
`IObjectConstruct` each time an instance of the component is created. This is analogous to the
constructor of a VB .NET class or the command-line parameters available to executable files.
However, COM+ only calls the interface if object construction is enabled on the Activation tab
of the component's property sheet or if the appropriate attribute is set.

Registry Settings

The registry entries associated with configured components in COM+ are different from those required for registered components in MTS. When a component was registered with MTS, its `HKEY_LOCAL_MACHINE\SOFTWARE\Classes\CLSID` key was modified by MTS to look like this:

```
{CLSID for component}
InProcServer32=""
LocalServer32="c:\winnt\system32\mtx.exe /p:{package GUID}"
```

In this case, the `InProcServer32` key was blanked out, and the `LocalServer32` key was created. It contained the new activation string that pointed to the host executable. This explicit call to the host executable MTX.exe was required because NT 4.0 knew nothing about MTS and its services. This arrangement also required that the MTS Explorer and the MTS VB 6.0 Add-In made available an option to ensure that these registry entries remain correct in the event that you recompile the component on the server or register it using Regsvr32.EXE.

With unmanaged components, the registry entries are identical for configured and nonconfigured components in COM+. However, because the CLR controls the execution of managed components, the CLSID key in the registry is modified to point to `mscoree.dll` and includes information about the assembly, class, version, and threading model. As with unmanaged components, the COM+ Catalog contains the additional settings for configured components.

> **Note**
>
> You might be wondering how a managed component obtained a CLSID in the first place, because, after all, GUIDs are not a part of the .NET infrastructure. When a serviced component is registered with COM+, the registration utility, Regsvcs.exe, can dynamically create, or read from attributes specified in the code, the required GUIDs, including CLSIDs and interface identifiers (IIDs), and place them in the registry. In addition, the utility creates a type library that can be used by unmanaged clients to make calls to the component.

Implementing COM+ Services

To access COM+ services, the component must first be derived from `ServicedComponent`, as mentioned previously. However, that's just the start. The class also can contain attributes and override methods of its base class to use the services provided by COM+. In addition to showing how serviced components can access transasctions, JITA, and object construction, this section briefly covers how more advanced COM+ services such as shared properties, events, and queued components can be used.

In the sample application, much of this configuration work is abstracted into a base class called QuilogyDataAccessBase, shown in Listing 9.1. As you'll see, it incorporates transactional behavior, object construction, and debugging into a class that developers can derive from to create a Quilogy data access component.

LISTING 9.1 QuilogyDataAccessBase Base Class. This class is used to derive all the data access classes in the Quilogy sample application.

```
Option Explicit On
Option Strict On

Imports System.Runtime.InteropServices
Imports System.EnterpriseServices
Imports System.Diagnostics
Imports System.Data.SqlClient

Namespace Quilogy.Education

  <ClassInterface(ClassInterfaceType.AutoDual), _
    Transaction(TransactionOption.Supported), _
    EventTrackingEnabled(True), _
    ConstructionEnabled(Enabled:=True, _
        Default:="server=ssosa;database=enrollment;trusted_connection=yes")> _
    Public MustInherit Class QuilogyDataAccessBase
    Inherits ServicedComponent

    Protected connect As String
    Protected cnSql As SqlConnection
    Public Debug As Boolean = False

    '******************************************************************
    Public ReadOnly Property ConstructString() As String
      Get
        Return connect
      End Get
    End Property

    '******************************************************************
    Protected NotOverridable Overrides Sub Construct(ByVal s As String)
      ' Implements object construction
      connect = s
      cnSql = New SqlConnection(connect)
    End Sub

    '******************************************************************
```

LISTING 9.1   Continued

```vb
Protected Overrides Function CanBePooled() As Boolean
  ' Default is that the objects will not be pooled
  Return False
End Function


'*********************************************************************
Protected Overrides Sub Activate()
  If Debug Then
    WriteTrace("Activate")
  End If
End Sub


'*********************************************************************
Protected Overrides Sub Deactivate()
  If Debug Then
    WriteTrace("Deactivate")
  End If
End Sub


'*********************************************************************
Public Sub WriteTrace(ByVal eventMessage As String)
  ' Writes the event to the Application log
  Dim objLog As EventLog

  Try
    objLog = New EventLog("Application")
    objLog.Source = Me.GetType.ToString

    If (Not EventLog.SourceExists(objLog.Source)) Then
      EventLog.CreateEventSource(objLog.Source, _
        "Application")
    End If

    ' Write the message to the log
    objLog.WriteEntry(DebugTrace(eventMessage), _
      EventLogEntryType.Information)
    objLog.Dispose()

  Catch e As Exception
    ' Not important so skip it
  Finally
    ' Make sure the transaction if any can commit
    If ContextUtil.IsInTransaction Then
      ContextUtil.EnableCommit()
    End If
```

LISTING 9.1   Continued

```
      End Try
    End Sub

    '*******************************************************************
    Protected Function DebugTrace(ByVal eventMessage As String) As String
      ' Used to write events to the application event log
      Dim strTrace As String

      strTrace = "Class: " & Me.GetType.ToString & vbCrLf
      strTrace &= "Event: " & eventMessage & vbCrLf
      strTrace &= "Construct String: " & connect & vbCrLf
      strTrace &= "Activity:" & ContextUtil.ActivityId.ToString & vbCrLf
      strTrace &= "Context:" & ContextUtil.ContextId.ToString & vbCrLf
      strTrace &= "Transaction?" & _
        ContextUtil.IsInTransaction.ToString & vbCrLf
      strTrace &= "Security?" & _
        ContextUtil.IsSecurityEnabled.ToString & vbCrLf
      If ContextUtil.IsInTransaction Then
        strTrace &= "TransactionId:" & _
          ContextUtil.TransactionId.ToString & vbCrLf
        strTrace &= "Direct Caller:" & _
          SecurityCallContext.CurrentCall.DirectCaller.AccountName & vbCrLf
        strTrace &= "Original Caller:" & _
          SecurityCallContext.CurrentCall.OriginalCaller.AccountName
      End If

      Return strTrace
    End Function
  End Class
End Namespace
```

Notice in Listing 9.1 that the `QuilogyDataAccessBase` class is a member of the
`Quilogy.Education` namespace and is marked as `MustInherit` because it is a base class and is
derived from `ServicedComponent`.

NOTE

The class is marked with the `EventTrackingEnabled` property set to `True`. This property ensures that statistics will show up in the Component Services snap-in for the
component when the View, Status View option is chosen when the Components
folder is highlighted. Keep in mind that statistics are only viewable, however, in applications configured as Server applications.

There are also a couple of design considerations you should be aware of when creating serviced components that are not immediately obvious in Listing 9.1. First, your class should not contain a parameterized constructor. This is the case since the COM+ Library has no mechanism to pass the arguments around. Second, shared or private methods will not be able to be called in a serviced component.

Automatic Transactions

The primary service provided by COM+ is certainly distributed transactions. By abstracting the concept of the transaction from the physical data stores involved and using the Microsoft Distributed Transaction Coordinator (MSDTC) service, COM+ allows components written in different languages and using different data stores (Oracle, SQL Server, Microsoft Message Queue or MSMQ, DB2, among others) to enlist in the same transaction. In addition, it allows for the creation of components that are loosely coupled because each component can do its work and not have to worry about the larger transaction in which it is running. The component simply votes on the outcome as it leaves a method. These types of transactions are referred to as *automatic transactions* because the actual initiation and commit/rollback is handled automatically by the MSDTC service. This is contrasted with *manual transactions* that can be defined in stored procedures or using ADO.NET methods like the BeginTransaction method of the SqlConnection class.

Activities Make It Easy

At a higher level, all the work, including transactions, done by COM+ on behalf of a base client is contained within activities. Basically, an *activity* is a logical thread of execution for a base client that is created each time a client creates an object that resides in COM+. All subsequent objects created by the *root* (defined as the first object created in the activity) and its children also reside in the same activity.

Using the concept of activities, COM+ ensures that only one object in the activity is executing concurrently on behalf of the base client and that all objects in the activity are isolated from objects in other activities. This makes the programming model for COM+ simple for developers who don't have to worry about issues such as synchronization and the physical threads that are running the components. Activities are also the containers for distributed transactions. In other words, transactions do not cross activities.

In COM+, a *transaction* is a logical unit of work that executes within a single activity. Each component that you create can be marked with an attribute or in the Component Services snap-in that indicates to what level objects created from the component participate in transactions. By marking a component as Requires a New Transaction or Requires a Transaction, COM+ enlists with the MSDTC to ensure that the work performed by its objects can be coordinated with work performed by other objects created in the activity. Although the details of the algorithm used are beyond the scope of this book, the MSDTC service uses a two-phase commit protocol to ensure that all the data sources affected by the activity either commit or roll back their changes together.

In the Quilogy sample application, the `RegisterStudent` method of the `Registrations` business class calls the `Students` and `Classes` data access classes. This entire process needs to be scoped in a single transaction so that the entire registration process succeeds or fails as a logical unit of work.

To declaratively set the transactional behavior of the `QuilogyDataAccessBase` class, the `Transaction` attribute (`TransactionAttribute` class) is set at the class level. Note that the attribute's constructor accepts a value from the `TransactionOption` enumerated type, which supports the five COM+ values (`Disabled`, `NotSupported`, `Required`, `RequiresNew`, `Supported`). If the component is set to `Supports`, as is the case here, COM+ enlists the MSDTC only if the object is created in an activity for which a transaction is already present.

TIP

Using `Supports` is particularly handy in cases where the component might sometimes be instantiated by clients who do not want to use transactions. For example, the methods of the `Students` data access class discussed in the previous chapter that simply return data will not typically be invoked within a transaction. By not doing so, system resources are conserved because there is a cost to creating a distributed transaction.

Obviously, using `Disabled` or `NotSupported` never enlists the MSDTC. Generally, components that run in COM+ use `Requires` or `Supports`. However, `RequiresNew` can be useful when the component is used for logging or audit trails and thus should be isolated from commits or rollbacks happening within other transactions within the activity.

TIP

Remember that a derived class can override any attribute settings of the base class. For example, even though the base class `QuilogyDataAccessBase` has a transaction option of `Supported`, a derived class can override this by specifying a transaction option of `RequiresNew` or some other value. Further, a derived class could add additional properties such as `JustInTimeActivation` not set by the base class.

The actual work of voting for the outcome of the transaction can be handled in several ways. First, as mentioned previously, the method can use automatic deactivation to vote for the transaction to commit or roll back based on whether the method returns normally or throws an exception. For example, the `ChangePass` method of the `Students` class derived from `QuilogyDataAccessBase` might use the following technique to automatically call `SetComplete` or `SetAbort` when its database work is complete:

```
<Autocomplete(True)> Public Function ChangePass(ByVal email As String, _
  ByVal oldPwd As String, ByVal newPwd As String) As Boolean
  ' execute a proc
End Function
```

> **TIP**
>
> As you might expect, if a serviced component participating in a transaction throws an unhandled exception, the `SetAbort` method will be called automatically.

Second, the `EnableCommit` and `DisableCommit` methods can be called. These methods simply register the transaction vote but do not deactivate the component. They come in handy when subsequent calls to the component instance can affect the outcome. For example, the public `WriteTrace` method of the `QuilogyDataAccessBase` class makes a call to `EnableCommit` in its `Finally` block to ensure that the transaction, if any, will be able to commit regardless of the outcome of the method. Finally, a method can explicitly call the `SetAbort` or `SetComplete` methods to vote on the transaction and deactivate the component following the call to the method.

To illustrate the use of transactions in a VB .NET class, consider the code in Listing 9.2, which implements the `Registrations` class of the Quilogy education application. This class requires enlistment in a new transaction and contains a `RegisterStudent` method that uses the `ContextUtil` class to affect the outcome of the transaction.

LISTING 9.2   Transactional VB .NET. This listing shows the `RegisterStudent` method and how it uses the `ContextUtil` class to work within a distributed transaction.

```
Option Explicit On
Option Strict On

Imports System.Runtime.InteropServices
Imports System
Imports System.Data
Imports System.EnterpriseServices
Imports System.Diagnostics
Imports System.Data.SqlClient
```

LISTING 9.2   Continued

```
Imports Quilogy.Education.Schedule

Namespace Quilogy.Education.Enrollment

  <Transaction(TransactionOption.Required)> _
  Public Class Registration : Inherits QuilogyDataAccessBase

  Public Function RegisterStudent( _
    ByVal enroll As EnrollmentData) As Integer

    Dim arStud(), arContact() As DataRow
    Dim drStud, drEnroll As DataRow
    Dim intStudentID, intClassID, intEnrollID As Integer
    Dim strEmail, strLastName As String
    Dim objStudents As Students
    Dim dsStudents As StudentData
    Dim decCost As Decimal
    Dim objClasses As New Classes

    ' Implement the business process for registering the student

    If enroll Is Nothing Then
      ContextUtil.SetAbort()
      Throw New ArgumentNullException("No enrollment data found")
    End If

    ' Validate Student
    drEnroll = enroll.EnrollmentTable.Rows(0)
    intClassID = Convert.ToInt32(drEnroll(EnrollmentData.CLASS_ID))
    If intClassID = 0 Then
      ContextUtil.SetAbort()
      Throw New ArgumentOutOfRangeException("Must provide a classID")
    End If

    ' Make sure the class is not full
    If objClasses.IsFull(intClassID) Then
      ContextUtil.SetAbort()
      Throw New Exception("Class is already full")
    End If

    ' Get the student info
    Try
      arStud = drEnroll.GetChildRows("Enrollment_Student")
      drStud = arStud(0)
      intStudentID = Convert.ToInt32(drStud(EnrollmentData.STUDENT_ID))
```

9

ACCESSING
COMPONENT
SERVICES

LISTING 9.2   Continued

```
        If intStudentID = 0 Then
          ' Check if student exists
          arContact = drStud.GetChildRows("Student_ContactInfo")
          strEmail = arContact(0).Item(EnrollmentData.EMAIL).ToString
          strLastName = arContact(0).Item(EnrollmentData.LAST_NAME).ToString

          objStudents = New Students
          intStudentID = objStudents.CheckIfExists(strEmail, strLastName)

          If intStudentID = 0 Then
            ' Student did not exist
            ' Build the new student data structure
            dsStudents = New StudentData()
            drStud = dsStudents.StudentTable.NewRow()
            With drStud
              .Item(StudentData.FIRST_NAME) = _
                arContact(0).Item(EnrollmentData.FIRST_NAME)
              .Item(StudentData.LAST_NAME) = strLastName
              .Item(StudentData.ORGANIZATION) = _
                arContact(0).Item(EnrollmentData.ORGANIZATION)
              .Item(StudentData.EMAIL) = strEmail
              .Item(StudentData.ADDRESS) = _
                arContact(0).Item(EnrollmentData.ADDRESS)
              .Item(StudentData.CITY) = arContact(0).Item(EnrollmentData.CITY)
              .Item(StudentData.STATE) = _
                arContact(0).Item(EnrollmentData.STATE)
              .Item(StudentData.ZIP_CODE) = _
                arContact(0).Item(EnrollmentData.ZIP_CODE)
              .Item(StudentData.PHONE) = _
                arContact(0).Item(EnrollmentData.PHONE)
            End With
            ' Save the student
            intStudentID = objStudents.Save(dsStudents)
          End If

          ' Set the student id in the enrollment data
          drStud(EnrollmentData.STUDENT_ID) = intStudentID
        End If

    Catch e As Exception
      ContextUtil.SetAbort()
      Dim newE As New Exception( _
        "Student could not be validated or saved. ", e)
      Throw (newE)
    End Try
```

LISTING 9.2   Continued

```
    Try
      ' Calculate the cost
      decCost = Convert.ToDecimal(objClasses.CalcCost(intClassID, _
        RegistrationType.Web))
      drEnroll(EnrollmentData.COST) = decCost
      ' Persist the registration
      intEnrollID = objClasses.AddEnrollment(enroll)
      Return intEnrollID

    Catch e As Exception
      ContextUtil.SetAbort()
      Dim newE As New Exception( _
        "Could not calculate the cost.", e)
      Throw (newE)
    End Try

    ContextUtil.SetComplete()
    Return intEnrollID

  End Function
  End Class
End Namespace
```

> **NOTE**
>
> The code shown in Listing 9.2 requires that the DataSet and data access classes
> created in Chapter 7 be referenced, hence the inclusion of the
> `Quilogy.Education.Schedule` namespace.

In Listing 9.2 notice that the class is derived from `QuilogyDataAccessBase` and overrides the transaction option by setting it to `Required`. If everything succeeds the `RegisterStudent` method calls the `SetComplete` method of the `ContextUtil` class and returns the new enrollment ID (`intEnrollID`).

Object Activation and Construction

As mentioned previously, JITA has been decoupled from transactions in COM+. As a result, a VB .NET class that does not support transactions can use JITA by decorating the class with the `JustInTimeActivation` attribute and passing `True` or `False` in the constructor. If transactions are used, JITA support is enabled automatically and cannot be disabled.

At the method level you can then set automatic deactivation in two ways: by setting the `DeactivateOnReturn` property to `True` within a method or by marking the method with the `AutoComplete` attribute and passing its constructor an expression of `True`.

CAUTION

Unless the method is implemented using a custom interface (or the class is decorated with the `ClassInterface` attributes discussed later in the chapter) in VB .NET, it will not show up in the Component Services snap-in. As a result, you will not be able to configure it for automatic deactivation unless you use one of the techniques discussed in the previous paragraph.

When building a COM+ component in VB 6.0, developers had to implement the `IObjectControl` and `IObjectConstruct` interfaces to be notified when an object instance was activated and deactivated and to catch the construction string passed to the component, respectively. In the Services Framework, however, the `ServicedComponent` class implements these interfaces for you and exposes methods that can be overridden to take their place.

To be notified of activation and deactivation events, you can simply override the `Activate` and `Deactivate` events of the base class. Notice that in Listing 9.1 the `QuilogyDataAccessBase` class does this and makes a call to the `WriteTrace` method if the `Debug` field is set to `True`. In addition, the `CanBePooled` method is exposed and in this case returns `False` because the default behavior of the component will not be pooled.

The `Activate` method is fired when any instance of the class is returned to a client. This is true for both new instances and instances taken from a pool. The `Deactivate` event occurs when a component that supports JITA is released by the client or when a pooled object returns to the pool.

NOTE

Alert readers might be wondering about the integration of JITA and garbage collection in the CLR. Basically, when a method call returns from a serviced component marked for deactivation, the finalizer of the object is run immediately and it is deallocated by the runtime. However, the proxy and the COM+ context remain as you would expect so that subsequent method calls can be intercepted and a new managed object created. If no further calls are made, the proxy object is eventually garbage collected. To clean up the proxy object and the COM+ context the `SerivcedComponent` class contains the `DisposeObject` method that can be called by the client. While this is the most efficient technique it adds an extra burden on the client developer.

The DebugTrace method exercises the ContextUtil class to build a string that can be written to an event log. It also uses the SecurityCallContext class to discover information about the caller of the component, as discussed later in the chapter.

A second feature of COM+ that affects activation is object construction. As with IObjectControl, the IObjectConstruct interface is exposed through the Construct method of the ServicedComponent class. This method is passed the string configured in the Activation tab, as shown in Figure 9.3, when an instance of the component is created.

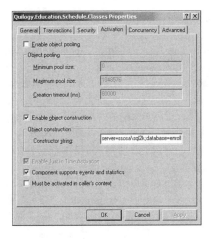

Figure 9.3

The Activation tab of the component properties dialog in Component Services used to configure object construction.

As you can see in Listing 9.1 the Construct method of QuilogyDataAccessBase places the construction string passed into the method in a Protected variable called connect and instantiates the SqlConnection object that its various methods will use. In addition, the class contains a single read-only property, ConstructString, that returns connect. The Construct method is marked as NotOverridable because a derived class shouldn't be able to change the behavior. Other uses for object construction might be to pass the name of an MSMQ queue to write to or the name of an Exchange server to query.

If a derived class does not want to use object construction, it can override the ConstructionEnabled attribute that decorates the QuilogyDataAccessBase class and instead read the connection string from some other source or pass it to each method. The Default parameter can be specified in the attribute to set the default connection string. This obviously assists during development but should be changed in the Component Services snap-in in a production environment.

Object Pooling

The capability to create pooled objects is a feature that VB developers have salivated over since they first became aware of the CanBePooled method of the IObjectControl interface in MTS 2.0. Previous versions of VB did not support this feature, which actually was not implemented until COM+, because VB could not create objects that could be accessed by more than a single thread.

> **NOTE**
>
> Although this limitation has been overcome by the fact that VB .NET components run within the CLR, object pooling is only useful in certain application scenarios, particularly when the cost of initializing the component is high. For example, if your component reads and parses large amounts of data as it is being initialized, or acquires access to a particularly expensive resource, you might consider pooling that object to bypass the cost of the construction. However, typical data access components do not have this requirement because they only acquire database connections that are themselves pooled by ADO.NET and so are not particularly good candidates for pooling.

To implement object pooling, you simply need to add the ObjectPooling attribute to the class declaration and provide the arguments for the constructor. One of the overloaded constructors accepts arguments that set the Enabled, MinPoolSize, and MaxPoolSize properties. The Enabled property controls whether pooling will be done as new component instances are requested, whereas the other two control how many instances are in the pool at a given time. For example, if the Registrations class were to be pooled with an initial size of 5 objects and a maximum size of 15, the class signature would be defined as follows:

```
<ObjectPooling(True, 5, 15)> Public Class Registrations
    Inherits ServicedComponent

End Class
```

Keep in mind that the minimum number of objects will be created and added to the pool when the application in which the component resides is first started. As a result, you'll probably want to keep the MinPoolSize fairly small or administratively start the application before clients start requesting objects. In addition, you can configure the CreationTimeout property using the Component Services snap-in to specify how long COM+ waits for instantiation of an object before throwing an exception. The default is 60 seconds.

The `Activate` and `Deactivate` methods also can be used with object pooling to be notified as clients reference and release objects. These methods might be used to clean up any class level variables used by the class. However, because the CLR uses garbage collection, the `Deactivate` method might not run until the object is collected. To get around this, you can use the shared `DisposeObject` method of `ServicedComponent` to immediately instruct the CLR to place the instance back into the pool. This method accepts a reference to the serviced component of which to dispose.

The `CanBePooled` method also is called when the component is returned to the pool. A component that uses external resources should make sure that those resources are still available and return `False` if the instance of the component is no longer viable.

Shared Properties

Although powerful, object pooling is not the best solution for storing global or session state between invocations of a component. This is the case because, by default, shared data is not protected against concurrent access by multiple clients, and you're never guaranteed to get the same component back again on subsequent calls. To support shared global state, the `System.EnterpriseServices` namespace includes support for the Shared Property Manager (SPM) familiar to MTS and COM+ developers.

Simply put, the SPM provides a mechanism for multiple instances of different components within the same COM+ application (read process) to share transient state. *Transient state* is data that is held in memory only and does not survive a restart of the application. Uses for transient state might include counters or the generation of unique numbers.

> **NOTE**
>
> The SPM protects against concurrent access using locking so that two components cannot update the same property at the same time.

The SPM is modeled as a set of groups shared by the process, each of which can include one or more properties. Within the Services Framework, support for the SPM is included in the `SharedPropertyGroupManager`, `SharedPropertyGroup`, and `SharedProperty` classes.

Although the Quilogy sample application does not use the SPM, Listing 9.3 presents a method showing its use for creating unique receipt numbers.

LISTING 9.3   Using the SPM. This listing implements a method that increments a receipt counter held as a property by the SPM.

```vb
Imports System.EnterpriseServices
<AutoComplete(True)> Public Function GetReceipt() As Integer
  Dim objManager As New SharedPropertyGroupManager()
  Dim objReceipt As SharedPropertyGroup
  Dim objOrder As SharedProperty
  Dim fExists As Boolean

  Try
    'Create the property group if not already created
    objReceipt = objManager.CreatePropertyGroup("Receipts", _
     PropertyLockMode.SetGet, PropertyReleaseMode.Standard, fExists)
    'Create the property if not already created
    objOrder = objReceipt.CreateProperty("Order", fExists)
    'Increment the property or initialize it
    If fExists Then
      objOrder.Value = Convert.ToInt32(objOrder.Value) + 1
    Else
      objOrder.Value = 10000
    End If

  Catch e As Exception
    Dim eX As New Exception("Receipt was not generated.", e)
    Throw eX
  End Try

  Return Convert.ToInt32(objOrder.Value)

End Function
```

In Listing 9.3, the method first creates or obtains a reference to the Receipts group using the CreatePropertyGroupManager method of the SharedPropertyGroupManager class.

The second and third arguments of this method are used to set the PropertyLockMode and PropertyReleaseMode, respectively. In this case, the SetGet constant is selected so that the property is locked only while it is being accessed and not for the remainder of the method, set using the Method value of the enumeration. The PropertyReleaseMode affects the lifetime of the property group. The Process constant specifies that the group should remain alive while the process (COM+ application) is running. The Standard value allows the group to be destroyed after all clients have released their references.

> **TIP**
>
> As mentioned previously, if configured as a Server Application, the components will run in a separate process hosted by DLLHOST.EXE. In this case, if you mark any components as Must Be Activated in Caller's Context from the Activation tab of the component's properties (Figure 9.3), that component will not be able to see the property groups. As a result, all components that must share properties should have the same activation attributes set. This option also can be set with an attribute called `MustRunInClientContext`.

The final argument is passed by reference and returns a `Boolean` that indicates whether the group already existed. In either case, the `Order` property is created or simply referenced using the `CreateProperty` method of the `SharedPropertyGroup`. If the property already existed (returned through the `CreatePropertyMethod` in the same way), it is incremented; if not, the property is initialized to 10000. The new value is then returned from the method.

COM+ Events

One of the most interesting services in COM+ is Loosely Coupled Events (LCE), or COM+ Events. To understand its significance, consider the following scenario.

Suppose that each time a new class offering was added to the Quilogy database, several business processes had to be invoked, including notifying the instructor of the assignment in addition to regenerating a static Web report for the public Web site. Suppose also that these business processes are implemented in components. In the MTS world, the data access component used to add the class would need to reference the business components and call their appropriate methods directly in the code. As a result, the three components are now tightly coupled, meaning that a change to either of the business components might affect the data access component and vice versa. In addition, this design is not flexible; adding additional business processes or adding logic to run the process only in certain circumstances requires modifying the data access component.

A better metaphor for this scenario is the use of an event model consisting of *publishers* and *subscribers*. It would be better if the data access component (publisher) could simply fire an event that could be independently subscribed to by both of the business components (subscribers). That way, the components could be modified without affecting each other and new subscriber components developed without the knowledge of the publisher. This is precisely what COM+ Events is designed to do.

At its core, LCE uses one of the most powerful concepts in computer science, abstraction, to define an architecture where the publisher of an event is separated from subscribers to the event by placing an *event class* between them. The event class is simply a component that exposes interfaces termed *event interfaces* that contain one or more methods that the publisher component uses to initiate an event. Subscriber components written in VB .NET then implement the event interface using the Implements keyword to perform their specific logic. Administrators or the subscriber components themselves can register a subscription with the COM+ Catalog to identify to which event classes the component wants to subscribe. If the subscription is created through the administrative interface, it is said to be *persistent* and as the name implies, can survive a system restart. Components that create their own subscriptions programmatically are termed *transient* and only receive event notifications when the component is running.

> **NOTE**
>
> The subscriptions discussed here are persistent. The Services Framework does not directly support the capability to create transient subscriptions. In order to do so you would need to reference the ComAdmin type library and use COM Interop as discussed later in the chapter.

LCE Internals

LCE works through an operating system service called the COM+ Events Service. This service manufactures the event class and makes it available for publishers to instantiate as they would any normal COM+ component. The difference lies in the fact that the event service then intercepts calls from publishers on event interfaces and matches those calls with the subscriber components that have registered subscriptions. The service subsequently creates a new instance of each persistent subscriber component and calls the implemented method. For transient subscriptions, the Events Service uses a callback interface that the subscriber stores in the COM+ Catalog to invoke the implemented method. The publication of event classes and subscriptions are managed by the COM+ Catalog made available to administrators through the Component Services snap-in.

Including this layer of abstraction as a part of the COM+ infrastructure creates two primary benefits. First, components can be created that are not dependent on each other (loosely coupled), which simplifies development and creates a flexible system whereby subscribers can be developed later. Second, the layer of abstraction provides an opportunity to extend the architecture to add features such as filtering at either end of the system. As a result, publishers can determine not only which subscribers should receive events but in what order, and allow subscribers to respond to only those events in which they are interested based on the data passed as arguments.

The Services Framework provides support for LCE by exposing an attribute used to decorate event classes. For example, the following code implements an event class called `OfferingsEvents`:

```vb
Imports System.EnterpriseServices
Public Interface IOfferingEvents
  Sub NewClass(ByVal classID As Integer, ByVal location As Integer)
  Sub ClassCancelled(ByVal classID As Integer, ByVal location As Integer)
End Interface

<EventClassAttribute()> _
Public Class OfferingsEvents : Inherits ServicedComponent
  Implements IOfferingEvents

  Public Sub NewClass(ByVal classID As Integer, _
    ByVal location As Integer) Implements IOfferingEvents.NewClass
    ' do something
  End Sub

  Public Sub ClassCancelled(ByVal classID As Integer, _
    ByVal location As Integer) Implements IOfferingEvents.ClassCancelled
    ' do something
  End Sub
End Class
```

The event class implements a public interface, `IOfferingEvents`, that contains two methods, `NewClass` and `ClassCancelled`, that will be fired when a class is scheduled or removed, respectively. The interesting aspect of this class is that the methods do not contain any implementation. This is the case because the event class will be instantiated by a publisher and then intercepted by the COM+ Events Service and used to invoke any components that have subscribed to this event class. In other words, the implementation is not necessary because the subscribers provide it.

9

> **NOTE**
>
> You might be wondering, why not simply have a way to register `IOfferingEvents` directly with Component Services rather than resorting to this apparently kludgy design? The primary reason is that by registering event classes rather than interfaces, LCE can work with languages that don't support creating interfaces directly. One primary example is VB 6.0.

A subscriber component can then be created by implementing the IOfferingsEvents interface and providing an implementation for the methods. For example, assume that the Instructors component will be used to send an e-mail message to the instructor each time a class is added or removed. The relevant parts of the Instructors class are as follows:

```
Public Class Instructors : Inherits ServicedComponent
    Implements IOfferingEvents

    Public Sub NewClass(ByVal classID As Integer, _
      ByVal location As Integer) Implements IOfferingEvents.NewClass
        ' Query the database to get the instructor ID and email address along
        ' with relevant course information such as date and course number
        ' Send the email message
    End Sub

    Public Sub ClassCancelled(ByVal classID As Integer, _
      ByVal location As Integer) Implements IOfferingEvents.ClassCancelled
        ' Query the database to get the instructor ID and email address along
        ' with relevant course information such as date and course number
        ' Send the email message
    End Sub
End Class
```

Because the Services Framework does not support the creation of subscriptions through attributes, the subscription must be created by right-clicking on the Subscriptions folder and clicking New Subscription after the subscriber component has been configured in Component Services. The resulting wizard prompts you first for the interface or selected method within the interface to which you want to subscribe.

> **TIP**
>
> Even though the subscriber class, Instructors in this case, must implement all methods of IOfferingEvents, you can choose to only subscribe to a certain method using this dialog. In this way, a subscriber could be notified of new classes but not cancelled classes. Obviously, if you do so, the implementation of the unsubscribed method need not contain any code.

The wizard then presents a list of all the event classes that implement the interface you chose so that you can hook up the subscription to an event class. After providing a name and enabling the subscription, the resulting subscription can be seen in Figure 9.4.

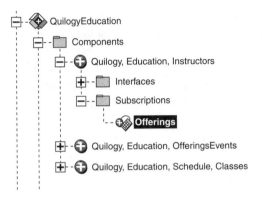

FIGURE 9.4

The Component Services snap-in with a subscription to the OfferingsEvents *EventClass.*

As you would expect, if the event class is marked as at least supporting transactions, any subscriber components can be enlisted in the transaction of the publisher. In this example, the event class probably would not be marked as supporting transactions because failure to send an e-mail message to an instructor should not roll back the entire transaction.

Finally, to actually fire the event a class, Classes in this case, can instantiate the event class and invoke the method that subsequently will notify the subscribers as follows:

```
Public Function Save(ByVal classData As ClassData) As Integer
  Dim intClassID, intLocation As Integer
  Dim objOffEvent As OfferingsEvents

  ' Save the class here

  ' Fire the event
  objOffEvent = New OfferingsEvents()
  objOffEvent.NewClass(intClassID, intLocation)
End Function
```

Similarly, the Remove method of the Classes class could invoke the ClassCancelled event of OfferingsEvents. Keep in mind that when a publisher calls a method on an event class, the invocation is synchronous from the perspective of the publisher. In other words, the call to NewClass will block until all subscribers have completed their work, even if they are not participating in the publisher's transaction. As a result, you would not want to perform a long-running operation in a subscriber component unless that component was queued, as discussed in the next section. Finally, the FireInParallel property of the EventClass attribute can be set to True, or the event class can be marked in the component's property dialog to Fire in Parallel. This has the effect of causing subscriber components to be invoked on multiple threads, thereby possibly decreasing the blocking time on multiprocessor systems.

9

ACCESSING COMPONENT SERVICES

As mentioned previously, adding this layer of abstraction also allows for filtering at either the publisher or subscriber end. One way to filter at the subscriber end is to create a parameter filter. By right-clicking on the subscription in the Component Services snap-in and clicking on the Options tab, you are presented with a Filter Criteria text box. Here you can specify a `Boolean` expression used for the filter. For example, to filter only on a specific location, the filter for the Offerings subscription shown in Figure 8.7 might be set as `location = 1`, where `location` is the name of one of the arguments to the method. If the criteria evaluates to `False`, the subscriber component is not created.

> **NOTE**
>
> Filtering on the publisher side and invoking events across servers are advanced topics beyond the scope of this book. Consult the COM+ documentation at `msdn.microsoft.com` for more information.

Queued Components

A second new service added to COM+, Queued Components, provides developers with a simple way to invoke components asynchronously. As you're probably aware and as will be discussed in Chapter 13, MSMQ allows you to create applications that are asynchronous by providing a queuing infrastructure that you can incorporate into your VB .NET applications through the `System.Messaging` namespace.

Unfortunately, using MSMQ requires you to write code explicitly for use with MSMQ. COM+, however, provides a layer of abstraction on top of MSMQ so that you can administratively configure components to receive their invocations in a queued fashion through MSMQ rather than synchronously, as is typically the case. This capability allows you to create applications that do not have to be aware of component lifetimes and can be more scalable because the actual processing of the method calls can be deferred. For example, consider the situation where the Quilogy Web site receives a large number of enrollment requests due to an e-mail newsletter about a new VB .NET course. Because the process of enrolling in a class might require several steps that involve database and e-mail access, it might be advantageous to collect and validate the enrollment information and simply queue the database and other work for later processing. As the traffic subsides, these queued enrollment requests are processed by a queued component. In this way, the user is served more quickly, but the enrollment request is still processed.

Behind the scenes, a COM+ application marked as Queued in the Queuing tab of the application's property dialog is associated with a series of MSMQ queues automatically by COM+. In addition, each interface within the component that is expected to receive asynchronous calls must be marked as such in the component's property dialog. Then, as calls to the components in the application are made, a message recorder on the client machine builds a message and sends it to the queue on the server when the reference to the component is released. The application can then be configured to listen for messages in its queue using a setting on the Queuing tab when the application is started. When the application starts, messages from its queue are dequeued and "played back" through the component in the order they were received. Of course, only a Server Application running in a dedicated process can be queued and listen for messages.

TIP

You can control when messages are processed by starting and shutting down the COM+ application at predefined intervals. For example, if you wanted to process registrations only at a certain time of day, you could create a service application that wakes up at that time and uses the ComAdmin library to start the application and shut it down after the queue was drained.

Queuing Support

The Services Framework supports queued components by providing attributes to configure an assembly and its interfaces for queuing. For example, the assembly that contains the `Registrations` class can be configured as a queued application using assembly level attributes in the AssemblyInfo.vb file as follows:

```
<Assembly: ApplicationActivation(ActivationOption.Server)>
<Assembly: ApplicationQueuing(Enabled:=True, QueueListenerEnabled:=True)>
```

In this case, the COM+ application is configured as a server application, and both queuing and listening are enabled using the `ApplicationActivation` and `ApplicationQueuing` attributes, respectively. In addition, interfaces within the component can be marked as enabled for queuing using the `InterfaceQueued` attribute as follows:

```
<InterfaceQueuing(True)> Public Interface IQuilogyRegistrations
    Sub RegisterStudent(ByVal student As StudentData)
End Interface

Public Class Registrations : Inherits ServicedComponent
    Implements IQuilogyRegistrations

    Public Sub RegisterStudent(ByVal student As StudentData) _
      Implements IQuilogyRegistrations.RegisterStudent
    ' do the work here
    End Sub
End Class
```

9

ACCESSING
COMPONENT
SERVICES

This implies that classes that want to use queuing should expose their functionality as an interface. In addition, interfaces exposed for queuing cannot contain methods that return values (functions) or arguments passed ByRef because the actual execution of the method is divorced from its invocation. In fact, if you attempt to use return values or pass arguments by reference in a class with the InterfaceQueued attribute, an exception is thrown when the component is registered with COM+. Consequently, in components that use queuing, a good design rule is to segregate the methods that will be called asynchronously into their own interface.

As with COM+ events, queued components can participate in transactions to ensure that the MSMQ message is delivered to the queue only if the entire transaction commits. In other words, in a queued scenario, the transaction boundary from the client side is at the delivery of the message, not the playback into the component when it is activated. However, the playback of the message into the component is also transacted in the sense that if the component uses a transaction and calls other components that do as well, the entire playback of the method call will be transacted. If the transaction is rolled back, the message remains in the queue to be played back again. Although this could go on *ad infinitum* behind the scenes, queued components contain six queues representing the retry level of the message. After the message has failed in the sixth queue, it is moved to the "dead queue" where it stays.

The Services Framework also supports an attribute, ExceptionClass, for setting up a reference to a queuing exception class. This attribute is used at the class level and specifies which component to call should a message finally reach the dead queue. The exception class needs to implement the same interface as the queued component but likely handles the data differently—for example, by logging the error to a database for possible human intervention later.

Even though a component is configured to be called in a queued fashion, it does not have to be. A client determines whether the methods are called asynchronously by the way in which the object is instantiated. If the object is created simply using the New operator, the call takes place synchronously as normal. However, if the call uses the COM CoGetObject API with a *moniker*, the call will be made as a queued call.

NOTE

A moniker is simply a COM object that knows how to call other objects. Windows 2000 supports the "queue" moniker that is used to instantiate queued components. A good overview of monikers can be found in *Understanding ActiveX and OLE* by David Chappell.

To use the queue moniker client code can invoke the shared `BindToMoniker` method the `Marshal` class found in the `System.Runtime.InteropServices` namespace. The `Marshal` class contains a host of shared functions that are useful for dealing with unmanaged code such as handling unmanaged memory allocation and communicating with COM components.

To instantiate the `Registrations` class as queued and call its `RegisterStudent` method, the following client code would suffice:

```
Imports System.Runtime.InteropServices
Dim oReg As IQuilogyRegistrations
Dim ds As StudentData

Try
  oReg = CType(Marshal.BindToMoniker( _
    "queue:/new:Quilogy.Education.Registrations"), IQuilogyRegistrations)
  oReg.RegisterStudent(ds)
Catch e As Exception
  '      Catch errors
Finally
  Marshal.ReleaseComObject(oReg)
End Try
```

> **NOTE**
>
> You can include many parameters in the moniker to specify everything from the computer to which the message should be sent to the priority level and encryption to use. For more information on the specifics and advanced topics, such as receiving notification from queued components, see *Understanding COM+* by David S. Platt (Microsoft Press, ISBN 0-73560666-8).

Note that the string passed to the `BindToMoniker` method includes the queue moniker along with the reference to the fully qualified class name. If the component is not marked as queued or cannot be located a `COMException` will be thrown. Since the `oReg` object is being called as a COM object the `ReleaseComObject` method is called in the `Finally` block.

As you can imagine, the combination of COM+ Events and queued components can be powerful in scenarios where a component fired through a published event also is queued. For example, the component that sends out instructor notification e-mail messages also can be marked as queued so that the process of sending internal e-mail can be offloaded to nonpeak hours. In this case, you get the benefits of abstraction at both the implementation and execution perspectives.

COM+ Security

Although there are several ways to secure code written in VB .NET unique to the CLR (as discussed in Chapter 5), the Services Framework also allows serviced components to interoperate with COM+ security. This might be required in situations where the component is running in an application with unmanaged components or when COM+ security is all that is required for the particular solution. The important point to note is that you must make a design decision as to the security model you will use since CLR role-based security does not interoperate with COM+ security.

As you might be aware, COM+ security is based only on the concepts of identity and roles. Simply put, each COM+ application can contain one or more roles that are populated with Windows 2000 groups or accounts. A role can then be activated for particular components, interfaces, or methods within the application.

For COM+ to check for security, the Enforce Security Checks option must be selected in the application's property dialog in the Component Services snap-in. Although beyond the scope of this book, the particular settings for whether security is checked at the process level only or for both the process and component level, how the calls are authenticated, and the impersonation level of the caller also can be configured at the application level. The Services Framework supports these options through the `ApplicationAccessControl` attribute. For example, the AssemblyInfo.vb file might contain the following attribute declaration that turns on security and enforces checks at both the application and component level.

```
<Assembly: ApplicationAccessControl(True, _
  AccessChecksLevel:=AccessChecksLevelOption.ApplicationComponent)>
```

To support the creation and assignment of roles the `SecurityRole` attribute can be used at either the assembly, class, or interface level. If used at the assembly level it adds roles to the application like so.

```
<Assembly: SecurityRole("Sales", True)>
<Assembly: SecurityRole("Marketing", False)>
```

In this case two roles will be added to the application if they don't already exist. The second argument sets the `SetEveryoneAccess` property to `True` and determines if the built-in `Everyone` account is added to the role. This can be useful for minimal security roles that typically read but do not update data.

In addition, each component also can be configured to enforce security checks and enable roles through its property dialog or attributes. To make sure security is turned on you can use the `ComponentAccessControl` attribute at the class level and pass it True in the constructor. To make sure a role has been added to the application and to enable it for the component, you once again use the `SecurityRole` attribute at the class level and pass in the role to be enabled.

The preceding discussion assumes that at development time you know which roles will be applied at the application and component levels. However, this is not always the case. As a result, you are not required to use the `ApplicationAccessControl` or `ComponentAccessControl` attributes since these settings can be made administratively in the Component Services snap-in.

As discussed in the next section, roles also can be enabled at the interface or method level using the `SecurityRole` and `SecureMethod` attributes. However, any role enabled at the component level will supersede settings at the interface level. The same is true for roles at the method level if enabled at the interface level. In any case, typically, you'll want to group a related set of methods in a class and apply roles to the entire collection of methods rather than individual methods, thereby making administration simpler.

Interface and Method Level Security

While the simplest and easiest way to administer COM+ security is to group related methods in a class and use the `SecurityRole` attribute, you also can apply security at the individual interface and method levels for finer grained control. This might be required when a class implements several interfaces, each of which requires different security settings or when methods within the class need to be protected.

In order to use either interface or method level security you must create explicit interfaces for your serviced components to implement. This allows the interface and its methods to be configured with attributes in the COM+ catalog and makes it visible when registered in the Component Services snap-in.

> **NOTE**
>
> If your serviced component will be called exclusively from unmanaged clients you can alternatively use the `ClassInterface` attribute with the `ClassInterfaceType` enumeration set to `AutoDual` at the class level. This will create a COM interface that will show up in the Component Services snap-in and which you can then configure manually.

In addition, you must apply the `SecureMethod` attribute to the class or assembly if the serviced component will be called from managed clients. This ensures that COM+ security will be activated.

With these conditions met you can use the following steps to enable interface or method level security respectively.

- To use interface level security, apply the SecurityRole attribute to the interface, passing in the name of the role you wish to enable for the interface.

- To use method level security, apply the SecurityRole or SecureMethod attribute to the methods within the interface or class you wish to protect. Obviously, you would use SecureMethod when you do not know ahead of time for which roles the method should be enabled.

To illustrate method level security consider the altered Registrations class shown below decorated with attributes.

```
Public Interface IQuilogyRegistrations
  Sub RegisterStudent(ByVal student As StudentData)
  Function GetRegistrations() As DataSet
End Interface

<ComponentAccessControl(True), _
SecureMethod()> _
Public Class Registrations : Inherits ServicedComponent
  Implements IQuilogyRegistrations

  <SecurityRole("Sales")> _
  Public Sub RegisterStudent(ByVal student As StudentData) _
    Implements IQuilogyRegistrations.RegisterStudent
    ' do the work here
  End Sub

  <SecurityRole("Sales"), _
   SecurityRole("Marketing")> _
  Public Function GetRegistrations() As DataSet _
    Implements IQuilogyRegistrations.GetRegistrations
    ' do the work here
  End Sub
End Class
```

First, notice that the class implements the IQuilogyRegistrations interface, which is required in order for method level security to work. If you don't implement an interface, a ServicedComponentException will be thrown. The Registrations class is then decorated with the ComponentAccessControl and SecureMethod attributes. The former turns on security checks at the component level while the latter makes sure that interface or method level security can be used from managed clients. The SecurityRole attribute is then applied to both methods in the class and passed the appropriate roles. In this way only members of the Sales role can call the RegisterStudent method while both Sales and Marketing role members can call the GetRegistrations method.

Using Security Context

Once COM+ security is enabled, as can be checked using the `IsSecurityEnabled` method of the `ContextUtil` class, the Services Framework supports COM+ security by providing the `SecurityCallContext` class. This class provides both shared and instance methods used to discover information primarily about the chain of callers that led up to the call. Listing 9.1 showed how to access members of this class to build the string used to write to the event log. Its methods can be seen in Table 9.2.

TABLE 9.2   `SecurityCallContext` Members

Member	Description
CurrentCall	Shared property that returns the current `SecurityCallContext` object.
Callers	Instance property that returns a `SecurityCallers` collection of `SecurityIdentity` object. Includes all the callers in the call chain.
DirectCaller	Instance property that returns a `SecurityIdentity` object for the direct caller of the current method.
IsSecurityEnabled	Instance property that returns a `Boolean` indicating whether security checks are enforced. Same as the method of the same name in `ContextUtil`.
MinAuthenticationLevel	Read-only property that returns an `Integer` specifying the minimum authentication level.
NumCallers	Instance property that returns the number of callers in the call chain.
OriginalCaller	Instance property that returns a `SecurityIdentity` object for the original caller in the call chain.
IsCallerInRole	Instance method that returns a `Boolean` indicating whether the `DirectCaller` is a member of the given role. Same as the method of the same name in `ContextUtil`.
IsUserInRole	Instance method that returns a `Boolean` indicating whether the given user (`String`) is a member of the given role (`String`).

One of the interesting aspects of this class is the `Callers` property. This property returns a collection of `SecurityIdentity` objects in the `SecurityCallers` class. You can use this class to enumerate all the callers in the call chain. This can be useful for debugging a call to a method. For example, your component could implement the following loop to add the callers to a delimited string:

```
Dim objCaller As SecurityIdentity
Dim strCallers As String

strCallers = "Callers=" & SecurityCallContext.CurrentCall.NumCallers.ToString

For Each objCaller In SecurityCallContext.CurrentCall.Callers
   strCallers &= strCallers & objCaller.AccountName & vbCrlf
Next
```

Registering Serviced Components

As mentioned previously, a serviced component can be configured in the COM+ Catalog using either first-use or manual registration with Component Services. The former technique registers the component the first time it is instantiated by a managed client based on attributes specified in the AssemblyInfo.vb file, whereas the latter requires a utility, Regsvcs.exe, to be run to install the component with Component Services.

In both scenarios, because Component Services is based on COM+, registry entries that identify the component will be created. In addition, in either case, the assembly containing the serviced component must be compiled with a strong name using the project property dialog or the AssemblyKeyFile attribute as discussed in Chapter 5.

First-Use Registration

Dynamic, or first-use registration occurs, as the name implies, when the serviced component is first instantiated by a client. Because first-use registration involves additional overhead, including reading the attribute information, creating or finding the COM+ application, and placing component information in the COM+ Catalog, this technique typically should be used in development and testing scenarios only. In addition, the client code that is instantiating the component must be running under an account that has administrative privileges. That is, an account that is in the local Administrators group or is a member of a group in the Administrators group.

To specify the information required to install the component, you can use a series of attributes at both the assembly and component level. The following code from an AssemblyInfo.vb file highlights those used at the assembly level:

```
<Assembly: ApplicationName("Quilogy Education")>
<Assembly: Description("Quilogy business and data access components")>
<Assembly: ApplicationID("A39EB4BA-B559-4420-84B7-F2E9A37D102B")>
<Assembly: ApplicationActivation(ActivationOption.Server)>
```

In this example, the COM+ application name and GUID are specified using the ApplicationName and ApplicationID attributes. First-use registration uses these attributes to determine with which application to register the components in the assembly. Precedence is given to the `ApplicationID` if it is provided. The `ApplicationActivation` attribute specifies where the application will be hosted, as seen earlier.

At the component level, registration is more complex. First, if the assembly contains an `AssemblyVersion` attribute like

```
<Assembly: AssemblyVersion("1.0.*")>
```

then by default a new version is generated, and therefore the new component is added to the application each time it is referenced. This can lead to multiple versions of the same component showing up in the Component Services snap-in. In some cases this might actually be a good thing because it allows managed clients to use the appropriate version at runtime. To avoid this, you can use an invariant version number like

```
<Assembly: AssemblyVersion("1.0.0.1")>
```

so that the assembly is generated with the same version information and therefore the component is replaced rather than added to the application. A second technique is to specify a `Guid` from the `System.Runtime.InteropServices` namespace for each class as follows:

```
<Guid("0D8C6A7C-527A-3075-81D8-B7E63E15F91E")> _
Public Class Classes :  Inherits Quilogy.Education.QuilogyDataAccessBase

End Class
```

In this case, the GUID takes precedence during the registration process and replaces a component with the same GUID. Other attributes have been shown through the course of this chapter, including `Transaction`, `ConstructionEnabled`, `EventClass`, `ExceptionClass`, and `JustInTimeActivation`. Attributes you can set at the class level also include those shown in Table 9.3.

TABLE 9.3   Additional Component-Level Attributes

Attribute	Description
Description	Sets the description that shows up in the Component Services property dialog.
EventTrackingEnabled	Enables or disables statistics and events for the component that show up in the Component Services snap-in.
MustRunInClientContext	Forces the component to be created in the caller's context.
Synchronization	Sets the `SynchronizationOption` for the component. This is defaulted to `Required` if JITA is enabled. If automatic transactions are enabled, it is set to the matching value.

Obviously, in a first-use scenario, it is critical to set all the attributes your component requires to run correctly because the component runs with these settings at least during its first execution. Additionally, dynamic registration only works when the serviced component is instantiated from a managed client.

As the name implies, after first-use registration is complete, the component is registered with Component Services and subsequent calls do not reinvoke the process.

Manual Registration

Components also can be registered manually from an assembly using the (Regsvcs.exe) .NET Services Installation Tool. This utility is passed the name of an assembly and can create the COM+ application, or use an existing one, and builds a type library for use with unmanaged clients.

The utility includes a number of command-line switches where you can specify the COM+ application (/appname), specify whether to create a new application (/c), or find an existing one (/fc); reconfigure an existing application or not (/reconfig or /noreconfig); specify the name of the type library (/tlb) or use an existing type library (/extlb); or uninstall the components in the assembly (/u).

Manual registration more often will be used in production environments to bypass the cost of first-use registration. It also must be used with components accessed by unmanaged clients because the instantiation of the component from an unmanaged client obviously will not invoke first-use registration since the registry has not been configured. In addition, the configuration of specific security settings and roles probably will require manual registration.

CAUTION

Anytime a serviced component is instantiated, the CLR looks at the `ApplicationName` or `ApplicationID` and the `AssemblyVersion` or `Guid` attributes to determine which COM+ application and component to instantiate. If these do not match with an existing application and component, a new component—perhaps in a new application—might be created. In other words, just because a component has been manually registered does not mean that new versions automatically will use the same COM+ application and configured component.

Interoperating

Although the Services Framework certainly covers a lot of ground and provides access to the bulk of system services required by most applications, at times, you'll need to call an existing unmanaged COM component from managed code. This might include both custom components that are already deployed in production or that you do not want to port to VB .NET and third-party components such as the ActiveX Data Objects Multidimensional (ADOMD) for use with Analysis Services in SQL Server 2000 that have no equivalent in VB .NET. In these cases, .NET provides a simple way to interoperate with existing COM components.

Conversely, although probably less frequently, you might want to expose a VB .NET class to development tools that produce unmanaged code. For example, the Quilogy `Classes` class might need to be accessed from a form-based application created in VB 6.0. Once again, the CLR provides a fairly seamless way to make these calls.

Taken together, the COM to .NET and the .NET to COM scenarios fall under the category of COM Interop. This section takes a look at both scenarios and discusses both the implementation the CLR uses and its application. Much of the managed code used to handle interoperation is found in the `System.Runtime.InteropServices` namespace.

Accessing COM Components from .NET

As mentioned in Chapter 1, "The Microsoft .NET Architecture," although the concepts that COM is built on, such as object reuse and interface-based programming, live on in .NET, the implementation details differ greatly. For example, COM uses reference counting, whereas .NET uses garbage collection; COM uses its own set of data types whereas .NET uses the Common Type System; COM uses type libraries, whereas .NET uses metadata; and so on. As a result, for you to be able to access classic COM components from VB .NET, the CLR needs to provide a translation between these execution environments.

The CLR accomplishes this through the use of a *runtime callable wrapper (RCW)*, as shown in Figure 9.5.

As shown in Figure 9.5, the RCW is an object that acts as a proxy to an unmanaged COM object and translates all calls to the COM object from managed code. The CLR creates one RCW for each COM object that caches all references to the object from managed code. In this way, the RCW can manage the lifetime of the COM object by dereferencing it at the appropriate time. As a result, all calls to the COM object pass through the RCW, which also is responsible for marshalling data between the two. Because COM types differ from managed types, the RCW provides the conversion. For example, the managed `System.String` type is marshalled to `BSTR` as used in VB 6.0. Finally, COM objects also implement a variety of interfaces, not the least of which are `IUnknown` and `IDispatch`. Without getting into the details, the RCW consumes these interfaces and therefore hides them from a managed client. However, it retains all other custom interfaces implemented by the component and adds them to the metadata. When it does so, it exposes all members of all implemented interfaces as a part of the managed class. In this way, a client does not have to, but certainly can, cast to the appropriate interfaces before making a call to one of its methods.

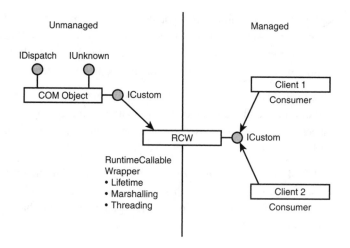

Unmanaged

Managed

IDispatch   IUnknown

COM Object — ICustom

RCW — ICustom

Client 1

Consumer

RuntimeCallable
Wrapper
• Lifetime
• Marshalling
• Threading

Client 2

Consumer

FIGURE 9.5

The CLR uses the RCW to translate all calls to a COM object from managed code.

> **NOTE**
>
> This arrangement will seem natural to VB 6.0 developers because they always have had the option of simply defining methods and properties at the class level and not dealing with interfaces. However, COM always uses interfaces, even with VB 6.0. The VB 6.0 compiler hid this fact from developers by performing some under the covers work to create a hidden interface that implemented the methods of the class. This became the default interface for the component.

The RCW also is responsible for managing when the COM object's reference count is decremented. The default behavior is to simply wait until the RCW is garbage collected and at that time the COM object's `Release` method is called. Of course, once the reference count reaches 0, the COM object deallocates itself. However, you also can control when `Release` is called by explicitly calling the `ReleaseComObject` method of the `Marshal` class as discussed previously. In both cases the RCW remains until it is garbage collected. Typically, you'll use this method when the COM object holds some resource that you wish to release as soon as possible. Once `ReleaseComObject` has been called, however, calling it again will throw a `NullReferenceException`.

Calling a COM Component

For example, consider a COM component built with VB 6.0 used to send enrollment verification and reminder e-mail messages to students. This component uses the `CDONTS` library to send messages using the SMTP service in Windows 2000. Rather than rewrite the component in VB .NET, Quilogy might choose to simply call it from the `RegisterStudent` method of the `Registrations` class. Listing 9.4 shows the simplified code for the `QuilogyEd.Email` class in VB 6.0.

LISTING 9.4   VB 6 Component. This code implements the `Email` component used to send e-mail from `CDONTS` and will be called from a managed client.

```
Option Explicit

Public Function SendReminder(ByVal ClassID As Long, _
  ByRef Students As Integer, ByVal Connect As String) As Boolean

  ' Sends email reminders to all students in the class
  SendReminder = True
End Function


Public Function SendEnrollVerify(ByVal EnrollID As Long, _
  ByVal Connect As String) As Boolean

' Looks up the student and class info and sends an email to that affect
    Dim objMsg
    Dim strFrom As String
    Dim strTo As String
    Dim strSubject As String
    Dim strBody As String

  ' Defaults
  strFrom = "education@quilogy.com"
  strSubject = "Enrollment Verification"

  ' Access the database and populate the message properties
  strTo = "dfox@quilogy.com"
  strBody = "You have been successfully enrolled in course 2072: "
  strBody = strBody & "Administering SQL Server 2000 in Kansas City"

  On Error GoTo VerifyErr

  ' Build the message
  Set objMsg = New CDONTS.NewMail

  objMsg.From = strFrom
  objMsg.To = strTo
  objMsg.Subject = strSubject
  objMsg.Body = strBody
  objMsg.Importance = CdoImportance.CdoNormal
```

9

Listing 9.4   Continued

```
    ' Send the message
    objMsg.Send
    SendEnrollVerify = True

  Exit Function
  VerifyErr:
    SendEnrollVerify = False
    Err.Raise vbObjectError + 1000, _
      "Verification email not sent: " & Err.Description

End Function
```

This class exposes two methods, SendReminder and SendEnrollVerify, that accept arguments such as the ClassID and EnrollID along with the ADO connection string to use. In addition, the SendReminder method uses a ByRef argument to return the number of students to which the reminder message was sent. Obviously, these methods also would access the database to build the appropriate message based on the primary key values passed to them. The SendEnrollVerify method instantiates a NewMail object and uses it to send the message.

To use this component, you first must import it as a managed type in VB .NET. Although this can be done with the Type Library Importer (tlbimp.exe) or programmatically through the System.Runtime.InteropServices.TypeLibConverter class, the simplest approach is to use the Add Reference dialog in VS .NET. After right-clicking on References and invoking the dialog, you can use the COM tab to select any registered component in the same way you use the References dialog in VB 6.0. If the component is not already registered, you can use the Browse button to find the component or its associated .tlb or .olb file containing the type library.

> **Note**
>
> In order to facilitate the use and interoperability of common COM objects, publishers of COM components can produce what is referred to as the primary interop assembly (PIA). This is a strongly named metadata assembly that is placed in the GAC and through which all clients will gain access to the COM component. You can think of PIAs as the "authorized" way to gain access to these components. Microsoft ships several PIAs including one for ADO that are installed with VS .NET. Behind the scenes the CLSID key in the registry for the COM component can be updated with an Assembly value that points to the PIA. In this way when you select a registered COM component from the Add References dialog, VS .NET will attempt to load the PIA if it exists and if not, prompt you to create the metadata assembly. Note that you can create your own PIAs for COM components in your organization using this technique as well.

When you select the COM component, a process is run to read the type library and create a corresponding managed type complete with metadata, in this case called Interop.QuilogyEd_2_0.dll. The metadata assembly (also called a wrapper object) is placed in the bin directory of your application and automatically referenced in your project. The metadata assembly contains a managed class that looks like the COM class complete with a namespace. For example, the `QuilogyEd.Email` component is translated into an `Email` class that exists in the `QuilogyEd` namespace. This allows you to add an `Imports` statement in your source file and simply reference the class as `Email`. The metadata also contains the translations from COM types to managed types. For example, the arguments for the `SendReminder` method used the `Long`, `Integer`, and `String` (BSTR) data types in VB 6.0. These are translated to `Integer`, `Short`, and `System.String` in the managed class, as shown in Figure 9.6. The complete mapping of COM data types to managed types can be found in the online documentation. Note also that you needn't reference any component referenced by the COM object, in this case `CDONTS`, because the instantiation of the `CDONTS` object is handled by the COM Library in the standard fashion.

```
' Email verification to student
Try
    objEmail = New Email()
    objEmail.SendEnrollVerify(intEnrollID, objclasses.ConstructString)
    objEmail.SendReminder |
Catc SendReminder (pClassID As Integer, ByRef pStudents As Short, pConnect As String) As Boolean
    ' Not critical so don't rollback transaction
    objLog.LogText("Email not sent: " & e.Message, True)
End Try
```

FIGURE 9.6

The VS .NET IDE as a developer accesses the Email *component. The data types shown in the Intellisense pop-up have been converted from their VB 6.0 equivalents.*

By examining the MSIL of the metadata assembly using ILDasm, you can see that an interface called _Email was created that contains the two methods and subsequently implemented by a class called `Email`. This is the case because the VB 6.0 compiler always creates a COM interface prefixed with an underscore for the class and marks it as the default interface, which, of course, shows up in the type library generated for the component. As mentioned previously, if this component had implemented additional interfaces (other than those consumed by the RCW), they would have shown up in the metadata, and their methods would have been added to the `Email` class.

9

ACCESSING
COMPONENT
SERVICES

TIP

At distribution time the metadata assembly either needs to be placed in your application directory (if it is private) or in the GAC (if it has a strong name and you wish to

> share it). The COM component that is referenced simply needs to be registered on the machine using Regsvr32.exe or the DllRegisterServer API.

The interesting aspect of treating COM components as managed types is that you can use them as such. For example, it is possible to extend the Email class from the COM object to add functionality to it like so:

```
Imports QuilogyEd
Public Class EmailEx : Inherits Email
...
End Class
```

In this way, not only can you use existing code but you can also leverage it to add functionality.

In addition to inheriting from a COM object, you can take advantage of containment to expose the functionality of the COM object to managed clients. The basic technique is to reference the COM object and then declare it as a private object inside your own VB .NET wrapper class. In the constructor of the VB .NET class you then instantiate the COM object. The VB .NET class can then provide methods that are used to call underlying methods in the COM object. The advantage to this approach is that you can customize the interface presented to the client and at the same time extend the functionality by using techniques such as parameterized construction and shared methods not available in COM.

TIP

Although for the vast majority of cases, the default way in which the RCW represents a COM component will suffice, you can provide a custom RCW by building a special managed class that implements the ICustomMarshaler interface. By doing so, you could hide an older interface exposed by a COM component and translate it into a new interface for use by managed clients. However, this is beyond the scope of this book; consult the documentation for implementing these techniques.

Using the default RCW is especially fitting for components written in previous versions of VB because they always include type libraries that are registered and use automation-compliant data types. However, if you currently are building a component in VB 6.0 that will be used in VB .NET, keep in mind that interop performs better if you use simple data types, such as Boolean, Integer, and Double rather than arrays, dates, and strings. And as always, design your components to minimize the number of calls it takes to complete an operation.

In addition, making calls between managed code and COM objects requires that the CLR take into account the differing threading models. Basically, because most COM objects (especially those written in VB 6.0) use single-threaded apartments (STA), whereas managed code does not use the concept of apartments, the runtime must marshal all calls through a proxy if their threading models differ. This adds overhead and can degrade performance. To avoid the overhead, you can set the `ApartmentState` property of the current thread to STA before making the first call to the unmanaged component. For example, the code that calls the `SendEnrollVerify` method would be modified as follows:

```
Imports System.Threading
Imports QuilogyEd
Thread.CurrentThread.ApartmentState = ApartmentState.STA
objEmail = New Email()
objEmail.SendEnrollVerify(intEnrollID, objClasses.ConstructString)
```

> **NOTE**
>
> Details about the `Thread` class can be found in Chapter 11, "Accessing System Services."

While this technique reduces the overhead when calling a COM object, you can only set the `ApartmentState` property once and therefore subsequent calls to `ApartmentState` are ignored.

Accessing .NET Components from Unmanaged Code

On the other side of the coin, classes you create in VB .NET can be exposed to COM clients such as previous versions of VB and ASP script. Although this probably fits a minority of the interoperability scenarios, it might be useful when you want to gain the productivity advantages of VB .NET or leverage the Services Framework to build components but still use previous versions of VB or VID for the user interface.

As you might guess from the previous section, the CLR abstracts COM clients from managed code through the use of a wrapper. In this case, it is called a *COM callable wrapper (CCW)* and is depicted in Figure 9.7.

Notice, in Figure 9.7, that the CCW has analogous responsibilities to the RCW and that one CCW is created for each instance of a managed class that must be called from COM. In addition, the CCW is responsible for exposing the managed class and its interfaces to COM, marshalling data, and handling object lifetimes. For example, the CCW synthesizes the `IUnknown`, `IDispatch`, `IConnectionPoint`, and other COM interfaces that an unmanaged client might call in the course of using the component. In this way, developers of managed components do not have to concern themselves with the COM infrastructure. However, before a managed class can be called from COM, several issues must be considered.

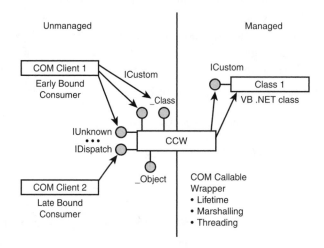

FIGURE 9.7

COM Callable Wrapper. This diagram depicts the role of the CCW in abstracting the managed implementation of a class from a COM client.

First, for a managed class to be creatable by a COM client, the class must adhere to certain rules. Among these are that the class must be Public, must not be an abstract class (MustInherit), must expose some public members (other than shared members and constant fields), and must have no constructor or one that does not accept arguments because COM does not support parameterized constructors. If the class is Public but only has a parameterized constructor or is a base class, it still can be referenced, although you need to wrap the construction of objects created from the class in a "creatable" class. In addition, shared members and constants are not supported.

Second, the inheritance hierarchy of a managed class is supported, although it appears flattened to the COM client. For example, if a managed class contains a child class to handle exceptions, the child class appears as a peer to the parent class to a COM client. No notion of parent-child relationship is supported in COM, and additional dot-notation to access the child class is not required. This same rule applies to interfaces contained within a class as well.

Third, derived classes expose all the members defined within the class and any of its base classes. In other words, just as with the RCW, the resulting COM class contains all the members that can be accessed through it and its base classes, as you would expect. Further, all the methods implemented in an interface by the VB .NET class also will be exposed as members of the COM class. As a result, casting for interfaces using the TypeOf statement in VB 6.0 is not required, and VBScript clients (read ASP) will be able to call all of the interface methods implemented by the VB .NET class. However, the COM class does expose the interfaces so that it is possible to use the object polymorphically.

> **TIP**
>
> VB .NET classes that raise exceptions trigger error handlers in VB 6.0 and ASP code. In both cases, the intrinsic Err object is populated.

Fourth, the managed class must take as arguments and return data types that are able to be automatically translated to COM types or that also have been registered. For example, if you pass the derived DataSet StudentData into the Save method of the Students class, it appears in a type library as an "Unsupported variant type." At runtime, if you attempt to call the method, you likely will get the error dialog shown in Figure 9.8 because the type is not supported. To avoid this problem, restrict yourself to using simple data types when you're designing methods that must be used from COM. For example, instead of using StudentData, you might define the parameter simply as String and then serialize the data to XML before passing it to the method.

> **NOTE**
>
> Other strategies to accomplish this include providing one implementation of the method for COM clients and marking the other as ComVisible equals False or providing a custom marshaller using the ICustomMarshaler class to translate the managed type to a COM type on-the-fly.

FIGURE 9.8

This dialog might appear at runtime in a VB 6.0 application if you attempt to use data types in a managed class that cannot be translated to COM types.

Finally, attributes can be used to customize the way in which the managed class is exposed to COM clients, the most important of which is ComVisible. By default, all public types and their public members are visible to COM. However, you can use the ComVisible attribute at the assembly, interface, class, structure, delegate, enumeration, field, method, and property levels to hide individual members. The obvious case is to place the attribute on some method that should not be called from COM because of the type it supports. For example, the following simple `Utilities` class exposes a `ReverseString` method while hiding the `GetID` function because it uses a data type not supported in COM. It also exposes a child class called `Security`, which is accessed as a peer to `Utilities`:

```
Imports System.Runtime.InteropServices
Imports System.Security.Principal

<ClassInterface(ComInterfaceType.InterfaceIsIDispatch)> _
Public Class Utilities

    Public Function ReverseString() As String
      ' Implementation here
    End Function

    <ClassInterface(ComInterfaceType.InterfaceIsIDispatch)> _
    Public Class Security

        Public Function GetUserName() As String
          ' Implementation here
        End Function

        <ComVisible(False)> _
        Public Function GetID() As IPrincipal
          ' Implementation here
        End Function

    End Class
End Class
```

Conversely, the `ComVisible` attribute can be used to explicitly include types by setting it to False at the assembly level, and then explicitly applying it to a method you wish to expose to COM.

Registration

For the classes in a managed assembly to be instantiated at runtime, they must be registered as COM components in the registry. This is accomplished with the use of the Assembly Registration Tool command-line utility (RegAsm.exe). If no parameters are specified, the tool simply registers the classes in the registry under the HKEY_CLASS_ROOT hive and generates the appropriate class identifier (CLSID) and programmatic identifier (ProgID) keys.

TIP

You can use the /regfile option of the RegAsm utility to generate a .reg file without actually registering the types. This allows you to view the changes that are about to be made to registry before actually making them. In addition, the .reg file can be distributed and used to update other computers as well.

NOTE

If the managed class was registered with Component Services using the RegSvcs utility or using first-use registration, the registration and type library generation will have already occurred.

Any COM-creatable class (as defined previously) also can include registration and unregistration methods that are called during the registration and unregistration processes. These are defined by decorating a method with the `ComRegisterFunction` and `ComUnregisterFunction` attributes, respectively. During registration and unregistration, the appropriate method is called and passed the registry key to be updated and the fully qualified name of the class being registered. You can use these methods to customize the registration process, although for the vast majority of components, this will be unnecessary.

After the component is registered, its `InProcServer32` value in the `CLSID` key is set to mscoree.dll because the CLR actually will be executing the managed code. Mscoree.dll exports the appropriate function (`DllGetClassObject`) to allow the COM Library to reference an object called a *class factory* used to create an instance of the component just as it would an unmanaged component. In addition, the assembly version, culture, and public key information is added to the registry so that the appropriate version is loaded by the class loader. The component also is registered in a special category for .NET components so that development tools (such as OleView shipped with Visual Studio 6.0) can categorize them. The `ProgID` is defaulted to *namespace.class* but can be overridden with the `ProgId` attribute set at the class level. Figure 9.9 shows the Registry tab in the OleView tool for the `Utilities` class.

NOTE

The path to the assembly is not provided in the registry, so the rules about how assemblies are located and loaded still apply, even if the caller is a COM client. If the assembly is private, it must reside in the same directory as the calling application. A shared assembly exists in the GAC and will be discovered by the CLR's class loader at runtime. As a result, managed classes used by multiple unmanaged clients on the same machine should be installed in the GAC.

```
CLSID =
 ¦--{69A0415E-A6E3-31A8-8548-FAA7ABE3436D} = NETCOM.Utilities
 ¦    ¦--Implemented Categories
 ¦    ¦     ¦--{62C8FE65-4EBB-45e7-B440-6E39B2CDBF29}
 ¦    ¦--InprocServer32 [<no name>] = mscoree.dll
 ¦    ¦--InprocServer32 [ThreadingModel] = Both
 ¦    ¦--InprocServer32 [Class] = NETCOM.Utilities
 ¦    ¦--InprocServer32 [Assembly] = NETCOM, Version=1.1.8948.8, Culture=neutral, PublicKeyToken=null
 ¦    ¦--InprocServer32 [RuntimeVersion] = v1.0.2615
 ¦    ¦--ProgId = NETCOM.Utilities
NETCOM.Utilities = NETCOM.Utilities
 ¦--CLSID = {69A0415E-A6E3-31A8-8548-FAA7ABE3436D}
```

FIGURE 9.9

The typical way in which the registry is configured for a managed class that will be called from a COM client.

At this point, the managed class can be instantiated using late binding, for example, by an ASP client. This works because the CCW automatically supports COM automation through the IDispatch interface for all managed components.

A COM Primer

For those who are unaware, late binding in COM is used when a VB client declares a variable as Object or Variant or when the object is accessed from VBScript in an ASP page. In these cases, the compiler cannot tell ahead of time which CLSID and IID will be requested, so the determination must be made at runtime. At runtime, VB uses a *dispatch interface* (IDispatch) and calls its GetIDsOfNames method, passing it the name of the method. It then uses the returned id (called a dispid) to call the Invoke method to execute the method and return the result.

Essentially, this means that two calls to the object must be made each time a method or property is accessed, thereby decreasing performance. For objects that reside in a separate process from the client, or perhaps even on a separate server, this greatly affects the responsiveness of the call. On the up side, when using late binding, you don't have to worry about breaking compatibility with COM clients when you change the interface of your class. For more information on how COM works see Chapter 23 of *Pure Visual Basic*.

Type Libraries

To use early binding and help the CLR marshal data at runtime, it is recommended that you create and register a type library for the managed class. A type library can be created manually using the Type Library Exporter command-line utility (TlbExp.exe) or programmatically with the `TypeLibConverter` class. However, it is simpler to use the `/tlb` switch of RegAsm to automatically create and register the type library.

> **TIP**
>
> If you specify an `AssemblyDescription` attribute, it will be used as the name of the type library.

As you might be aware, development tools like VB 6.0 often load type libraries to view the signatures of the members of a component to make programming against the components simpler and to provide type checking. The information in the type library also can be used by the compiler to ensure early binding by adding memory offsets (through a v-table) or method identifiers called dispatch ids (`dispids`) into the executable code so that at runtime the application can call the appropriate methods more efficiently.

By default, when the type library for a managed class is generated using any of the previous methods, the default interface for the class is set to `_Object`. This interface exposes the members of `System.Object` but does not contain custom members added to the class. As a result, although the type library can be referenced from the VB 6.0 IDE using the Project, References menu, the custom members will not be visible, and the compiler will result to late binding at runtime.

To create an explicit interface for the managed class, you must specify the `ClassInterface` attribute as shown in the previous code example. By setting it to a `ClassInterfaceType` of `AutoDual`, the type library will contain an interface with the same name as the class prefixed with an underscore. The default setting is `AutoDispatch`, although it also can be set to `None`. The resulting interface is marked as the default and contains all the members of the class and any base classes, including `System.Object`. Development tools like VB 6.0 can then use the Object Browser and IntelliSense to view the method signatures and assist in writing type-safe code. Once again, this arrangement should be familiar to VB 6.0 developers because VB 6.0 uses this strategy to create its own type libraries. Figure 9.10 shows the result of the type library registered and referenced from VB 6.0.

You'll also notice in Figure 9.10 that the members inherited from the `System.Object` class are also then exposed in the type library. In the same way, you can control how interfaces are exposed in the type library by decorating the `Interface` statement with the `ComInterfaceType`

9

ACCESSING
COMPONENT
SERVICES

attribute and setting it to `InterfaceIsDispatch`, `InterfaceIsDual`, `InterfaceIsIUnknown`, or `InterfaceIsNone`.

FIGURE 9.10

The Object Browser in VB 6.0 can be used to view the methods and properties of a managed class for which a type library is created.

Although beyond the scope of this book, you also can customize the way in which individual elements of the type library are created using a series of attributes, including `Guid`, `DispId`, `MarshalAs`, and `StructLayout`, to name a few. Consult the documentation for using these advanced options.

> **NOTE**
>
> Each time a type library is generated for a given assembly, it is created in exactly the same manner. In other words, the creation of the type library is deterministic. However, if you recompile the assembly and regenerate the type library, new GUIDs will be created, thereby breaking compatibility. To get around this, you'll need to specify invariant `Guid` attributes for the class, interfaces, and the type library. The type library GUID is set by decorating the assembly with a `Guid` attribute in the AssemblyInfo.vb file, which VS .NET does for you. In addition, because the CLR does not require the immutability of interfaces, it's up to you to make sure that you don't break existing COM clients by changing interface definitions.

Activation

With the type library registered, a COM client can use early binding to efficiently access the component. Of course, because the CLR can move objects around in memory, the COM client doesn't actually receive a memory address as it would when accessing a COM component via a v-table. The CCW simply generates a stub that is then used to call the actual method.

The activation process for a managed component called from a COM client occurs as you would expect:

1. The VB client executes the `New` or `CreateObject` statement.

2. Behind the scenes, the unmanaged code calls the `CoCreateInstance` function in the COM Library with the `CLSID` of the component, as typically happens.

3. The COM Library then uses the `CLSID` to look up the `InProcServer32` key in the registry.

4. Because `InProcServer32` points to mscoree.dll, the DLL is loaded, and `DllGetClassObject` is called to return the object used to instantiate the class (a class factory).

5. `DllGetClassObject`, in turn, reads the *Class* value in the registry to determine which class to load.

6. The CLR's class loader then determines whether an instance of the class is already loaded. If so, the cached class factory is returned from `DllGetClassObject`.

7. If the class is not loaded, the *Assembly* value is read from the registry, and the assembly is located using the standard rules.

8. After the assembly is located, it is loaded, and an instance of the class factory is returned from `DllGetClassObject`.

9. The COM Library then calls the `CreateInstance` method of the class factory to create the object.

10. The VB client is returned a reference to the object.

Summary

This chapter focused on the aspects of the Services Framework and VB .NET that you can use to create components that use Component Services. The components built for the Quilogy education application included data access and business components that take advantage of Component Services as described in this chapter. Along the way, this chapter also covered how COM components and VB .NET components can interoperate.

With the data access and business services built, it is now time to build the presentation tier using ASP.NET.

Building Web Forms

IN THIS CHAPTER

This chapter and Chapter 11, "Building Web Services," deal with developing the user services tier in a distributed application with VB .NET. Because the .NET platform was optimized for development using Web technologies, these chapters discuss using ASP.NET to create more traditional Web applications in addition to Web Services. Information on creating Windows Forms applications is beyond the scope of this book and can be found in the online help.

As just mentioned, ASP.NET actually encompasses two programming models: Web Forms and Web Services. This chapter focuses on the general architecture and features of ASP.NET that apply to both Web Forms and Web Services, and takes a more detailed look at Web Forms. Chapter 11 deals specifically with Web Services. Because this is a large topic, the discussion will be circumscribed to topics relevant to building a public Web site where Quilogy students can view course schedules, log in, and view their transcripts. However, before delving into the details, we need to put ASP.NET in perspective.

> **NOTE**
>
> All code listings and supplemental material for this chapter can be found on the book's Web site at www.samspublishing.com.

Understanding ASP.NET

At its core, ASP.NET is more than simply an evolution of the Active Server Pages (ASP) technology with which most readers are familiar. Rather, it actually encompasses an entirely new architecture that includes two programming models (Web Forms and Web Services) and a host of services based on the .NET Framework. Coupled with VS .NET, the result is a unified Web development platform that allows you to build user services using an object-oriented and event-driven paradigm.

In addition, because the platform is based on .NET, it also derives all of .NET's benefits discussed throughout this book, including language interoperability; CLR services such as strong typing, type-safety, early binding, and inheritance; JIT compilation; and access to both low-level and enterprise system services using the Services Framework. The result is a Web development environment that is natural and easily accessible to VB developers.

However, ASP.NET is much more than the programming models mentioned previously. In fact, ASP.NET consists of a series of managed classes contained in the System.Web namespace, which I'll collectively refer to as the ASP.NET runtime, that provide the following services, as will be discussed later in the chapter:

- XML-based configuration files   Each Web site can contain a configuration file that controls settings such as authentication and state management, and can be customized for the particular application.

- State management   As with ASP, ASP.NET provides session and application state management services that can be extended across servers for use in Web farm scenarios.

- Caching engine   ASP.NET offers a sophisticated caching engine that allows you to increase performance and scalability. The engine can cache either full or partial page output in addition to expensive objects.

- Tracing   ASP.NET provides tracing functionality that allows you to view performance data and insert custom diagnostic messages in your code.

- Security   ASP.NET provides authentication providers, authorization semantics, and impersonation that together make for a flexible and extensible security architecture.

- Runtime extensibility   Although not used by corporate developers as often as the other items in this list, the fact that ASP.NET is built on the Common Language Runtime (CLR) means that its runtime is extensible. For example, you can create your own managed classes to process certain types of resources and can include your own modules, much like the intrinsic `Session` module. This allows developers to add functionality that is not provided out of the box and to eliminate the "black box" feel of classic ASP. In addition, this is a great place for ISV's to add value by providing their own functionality that is reused across pages and applications. In short, this extensibility allows VB .NET developers to create advanced functionality, previously the purview of C++ developers.

ASP.NET Architecture

Before discussing these features, a brief overview of ASP.NET from the ground up is warranted.

At the lowest level, an ASP.NET application is comprised of a collection of files found in a virtual directory and its subdirectories on an IIS Web server. Like other VB .NET applications, an ASP.NET application is compiled and runs within an AppDomain that is, in this case, hosted by an executable called aspnet_wp.exe spawned by the inetinfo.exe (IIS) process. As a result, all the application's ASP.NET pages are compiled into an assembly placed in the `bin` directory under the virtual directory. The ASP.NET runtime is the software that sits between the request from the client and actual page processing. To illustrate how this works, consider Figure 10.1.

When a client makes a request for files associated with ASP.NET (with extensions such as .aspx, .ascx, and .asmx), IIS processes the request with the registered ISAPI extension (aspnet_isapi.dll). The ISAPI extension is responsible for invoking aspnet_wp.exe, which then loads and interacts with the CLR to create the AppDomain, if necessary, and load the required

10

assemblies. The ASP.NET runtime then processes the request based on its configuration information to perform any preprocessing required. After the preprocessing is concluded, the ASP.NET classes within the assembly are instantiated, and methods called that emit the HTML ultimately are sent back to the requesting client.

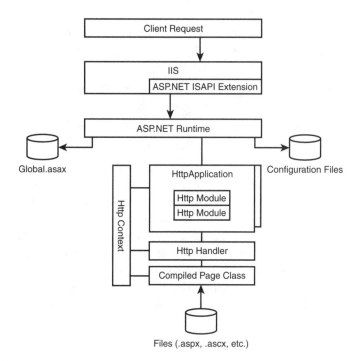

FIGURE 10.1

ASP.NET includes an extensible runtime architecture.

Improving Fault Tolerance

In addition to allowing for compiled code, the reliance on AppDomains makes for a lightweight isolation boundary between Web applications. In other words, multiple ASP.NET applications running in different AppDomains within the same process can be independently stopped, and cannot inadvertently access memory within another AppDomain, thereby taking down the aspnet_wp process. Further, if errors such as access violations, memory leaks, or deadlocks do occur, the next incoming request causes a new AppDomain to be launched to process the request. Finally, application DLLs are never locked, so new versions of dependent assemblies can be deployed without shutting down the application or Web server. When the DLL is detected, a new AppDomain (for the same application) is launched to handle new requests, whereas any existing AppDomains finish processing requests before being terminated.

One of the tasks of the ASP.NET runtime is to apply configuration information as shown in Figure 10.1. This information is loaded and parsed from XML configuration files at both the machine and individual directory levels. Although the content of the files and how they are processed will be discussed in more detail later in the chapter, each ASP.NET directory can contain a Web.config file. Simply put, this file contains settings that allow the runtime to make decisions about how the request is to be processed. Examples include which authorization and impersonation scheme to use, which class (HTTP Handler) will handle the request, and whether the request should be processed by an HTTP Module.

Each ASP.NET application optionally can contain a Global.asax file that, like the Global.asa file found in ASP, is used to handle events raised by the application. However, in ASP.NET, the Global.asax file is dynamically parsed and compiled into a class derived from the HttpApplication class found in the System.Web namespace. If no Global.asax file exists, then a generic HttpApplication class is created. The ASP.NET runtime maintains a pool of objects created from the HttpApplication class and uses them to actually service requests. When a request is made for a resource, the ASP.NET runtime assigns one of the objects to fulfill the request and, when completed, returns the instance to the pool.

The six events supported by default in the Global.asax file include Start and End for the Session and Application objects and the BeginRequest and EndRequest events for the Application object. You can use these events to do preprocessing on a request as in the following code:

```
Sub Application_BeginRequest(ByVal sender As Object, ByVal e As EventArgs)
' Fires at the beginning of each request

  If InStr(Me.Request.Url.ToString, "Main", CompareMethod.Text) > 0 Then
    Dim o As New QAConfig()
    Me.Context.Items.Add("QAConfig", o)
  End If

End Sub
```

In this example, the Application_BeginRequest event is used to determine whether the user has requested a particular page. If so, a custom class called QAConfig is instantiated and the instance placed in the HttpContext object that is carried throughout the request, as shown in Figure 10.1.

TIP

As implied in the previous code example, the HttpContext object exposes an Items property that can contain a key-value collection that implements the IDictionary interface. This can be convenient for storing information that must persist

> throughout the request. However, the collection is reinitialized with each request and cannot be used to store session or application state.

NOTE

There are actually 11 other per-request events that can be handled as well, ranging from authentication to errors. For more information, see the online help.

When changes to the Global.asax file are detected, ASP.NET finishes all pending application requests before firing the Application_End event. When the next request is received, the Application_Start event is fired, and the Global.asax file is reparsed and recompiled. This has the effect of rebooting the application and destroying any state information and user sessions.

TIP

You optionally can compile a class derived from HttpApplication in your own assembly and place it in the bin directory within the Web site. However, the Global.asax file still needs to refer to the class.

As shown in Figure 10.1, in addition to the HttpApplication instances, ASP.NET supports a series of modules (*called HTTP Modules*) that can participate in the application. This is where ASP.NET implements the familiar Session state object, as well as new features, such as authentication and output caching. However, by deriving a class from HttpModule and registering it with Web.config, you can add your own modules that support custom filtering, authentication, and state services, among others.

Finally, particular file types are subsequently processed by *HTTP Handlers*. These managed classes derive from HttpHandler and are used to perform custom processing of certain resources. For example, the PageHandlerFactory class in the System.Web.UI namespace handles all requests for .aspx pages. Again, the specification of the handler must be present in the configuration information so that the runtime can make the proper association. The implementation of both custom HTTP Modules and HTTP Handlers is beyond the scope of this book.

NOTE

Developers familiar with the Internet Server Application Programming Interface (ISAPI) will note that HTTP Modules are roughly equivalent to ISAPI filters, whereas HTTP Handlers equate to ISAPI extensions.

Note that the HTTP Context is flowed through the entire lifetime of the request. This `HttpContext` object encapsulates all the HTTP-specific information about the request, including references to the familiar `Server`, `Request`, and `Response` objects, in addition to the `Session`, `Application`, and other objects the runtime uses to implement the features discussed previously (such as tracing and caching). The managed class representing the resource requested by the client has access to the context and is processed by the handler.

Programming Models

As mentioned previously, ASP.NET supports two programming models: Web Forms and Web Services.

Web Forms

The idea behind Web Forms is to provide a form-based development paradigm for Web applications. To that end, the architecture relies on a page processing HTTP Handler that makes calls to managed classes ultimately derived from `System.Web.UI.Control`. In fact, the classes that represent your Web pages are compiled along with static HTML defined for the Web Form into the application assembly. Typically, the page classes you create are derived from the `System.Web.UI.Page` class, which is derived from `Control`.

As mentioned, the assembly is loaded by the runtime and emits HTML that is streamed to the browser. Along the way, the `Page` class can include references to other assemblies that contain classes derived from `Control` (ASP.NET server controls) that add HTML to the stream of data sent to the browser, in addition to assemblies that implement business and data services.

> **NOTE**
>
> VB 6.0 developers who developed IIS applications (WebClasses) will no doubt find the previous description familiar. However, the major difference is that the WebClass architecture was not built for scalability, and it was difficult to meld the UI with the application logic. You can think of Web Forms as an evolution of WebClasses, although the latter is much simpler and more flexible. For more information on WebClasses, see Chapter 17 of my book *Pure Visual Basic*.

This programming model is advantageous for several reasons:

- Separation of UI from application logic   The capability to separate the user interface elements (HTML) from the logic that manipulates them is beneficial both from a readability and maintenance perspective. In previous versions of ASP, HTML, client-side logic, and server-side code were commingled on the same page, making it difficult to maintain and leading to "spaghetti code." Although not required in ASP.NET, the default behavior in VS.NET is to include the HTML in a separate file (.aspx) from the class file

(.vb) that contains the logic. This arrangement often is referred to as "code behind forms," or simply CBF.

- WYSIWYG editing   The separation of UI from logic allows development tools such as VS.NET to provide WYSIWYG editing capabilities. The commingled nature of classic ASP code does not lend itself to strong WYSIWYG editing. In addition, Web Forms ships with more than 40 controls that can be graphically manipulated in an editor.

- Event-based programming   The combination of code behind forms and WSYWIG editing allows for an event-based programming model. By simply double-clicking on a control, a server-executed event handler can be created within the Page class. The Web Form architecture allows events generated within the browser to be posted and handled on the server.

- Compiled code   Obviously, because the assembly encapsulates both the UI and the code, they are not interpreted but rather compiled together, thereby increasing performance.

- Browser independence   Because UI elements can be abstracted into controls implemented as managed classes, they dynamically can alter the HTML they render based on browser type. This allows Web applications to potentially run under a single code base with minimal branching based on browser type.

- Extensibility   The reliance on an object-oriented runtime and programming model allows Web Forms to be extensible through the inclusion of third-party controls and the development of custom server and user controls.

Web Services

Although covered in detail in Chapter 11, Web Services allow other Web-enabled applications to access server functionality remotely. This "headless UI" approach relies on industry standards, such as HTTP, XML, and SOAP, to allow applications to communicate.

As you'll see, the scalability and performance improvements of ASP.NET, and the inclusion of Web Services, portends of a world where distributed applications are stitched together using a variety of private and publicly available Web Services.

Differences from ASP

From a developer's perspective, by far the biggest difference between classic ASP and ASP.NET is the inclusion of CBF. As most readers are probably aware, in the ASP environment, both server- and client-side script are commingled on the ASP page. As the page is processed by the ASP engine, the server-side code is interpreted and the resulting HTML added back into the response stream sent to the browser that initiated the request. As a result, the performance of ASP applications is not optimum, and the readability and maintainability of ASP applications suffer.

NOTE

Many ASP developers use server-side includes to separate some of the server-side script from the UI. This is a good practice and should be encouraged, although the code in the include is still interpreted.

However, under ASP.NET, this model is reversed, and the entire page actually is an executable class that produces HTML. This allows the HTML to be separate from the code at design time and compiled together for runtime execution.

The inclusion of CBF allows for the separation of UI and logic and makes possible an event-based programming model. Developers coming exclusively from an ASP background likely will find writing code in response to events executing on the server a more abstract task than simply building pages by mixing blocks of server script with HTML. However, this abstraction is part of what allows ASP.NET to provide the features listed in the previous section.

Although ASP.NET is different in many respects, one of its design goals was to be fully backwards compatible with ASP. As you'll see, this goal was not fully realized, but ASP developers will find most of the concepts and syntax familiar. For example, it is possible, though not recommended, to develop .aspx pages that look like classic ASP pages.

One of the points of incompatibility between ASP and ASP.NET is that ASP.NET does not support VBScript on the server, so the code within the page must be written in one of the supported languages such as VB .NET, VC#, or JScript. All the code within a page also must be written in the same language. Although VB .NET has a similar syntax to VBScript, it is more structured. This implies that language changes, such as those discussed in Chapter 3, "VB .NET Language Features," must be made. To illustrate some of the differences, consider the simple ASP page shown in Listing 10.1 used to retrieve orders from the Northwind database that ships with SQL Server.

LISTING 10.1 Simple ASP. This simple ASP page uses ADO to retrieve orders, display them in a table, and provide navigation.

```
<%@ Language=VBScript %>
<HTML>
<BODY>
<font face="verdana">
<h2>
<img src="win2000.gif"><br>
Northwind Most Recent Orders</h2>

<%
```

10

LISTING 10.1   Continued

```
Set cn = Server.CreateObject("ADODB.Connection")
cn.Provider = "SQLOLEDB"
cn.Open "server=ssosa;database=northwind;uid=sa"

Set rs = Server.CreateObject("ADODB.Recordset")

' Line up the cache size with the PageSize
rs.CacheSize = 10
rs.CursorLocation = 2 'adUseClient
rs.Open "Select * From Orders",cn,3,1 'Static and Readonly

'Check for empty resultset
If rs.EOF And rs.BOF Then
    Response.Write("No more orders")
    Response.End
End If

rs.PageSize = 10

' Determine how many pages are in this recordset
intPageCount= rs.PageCount

' Now see where the user requested we go
If Len(Request.Form("txtPage")) > 0 Then
    intPage = Request.Form("txtPage")
Else
    Select Case Request.Form("Action")
        Case "<<"
            intPage = 1
        Case "<"
            intPage = Request ("intPage") -1
            If intPage < 1 Then intPage = 1
        Case ">"
            intPage = Request ("intPage") + 1
            If intPage > intPageCount Then
                intPage = intPageCount
            End If
        Case ">>"
            intPage = intPageCount
        Case Else
            intPage = 1
    End Select
End If

rs.AbsolutePage = intPage
```

LISTING 10.1   Continued

```
%>

<table>
<tr>
    <td><strong>Record</strong></td>
    <td><strong>Order ID</strong></td>
    <td><strong>Order Date</strong></td>
    <td><strong>Customer ID</strong></td>
    <td><strong>Ship Name</strong></td>
</tr>

<%

For intRecord = 1 To rs.PageSize %>
<tr>
    <td><% =rs.AbsolutePosition %></td>
    <td><a href="orderdetail.asp?id=<% =rs.Collect("OrderID") %>">
        <% =rs.Collect("OrderID") %></a></td>
    <td><% =rs.Collect("OrderDate") %></td>
    <td><% =rs.Collect("CustomerID") %></td>
    <td><% =rs.Collect("ShipName") %></td>
</tr>
    <%
    rs.MoveNext
    If rs.EOF Then Exit For
Next

%>
</table>
<%
rs.Close
Set rs = Nothing
cn.Close
Set cn = Nothing
%>

<form name="MovePage" action="paging.asp" method="post">
<input type="hidden" name="intpage" value="<% =intpage %>">
<input type="submit" name="action" value="&lt;&lt;">
<input type="submit" name="action" value="&lt;">
<input type="submit" name="action" value="&gt;">
<input type="submit" name="action" value="&gt;&gt;"><br>

Go to page:<input type="text" name="txtPage" size=4>
<input type="submit" name="go" value="Go"><br>
```

LISTING 10.1 Continued

```
Page: <% =intpage & " of " & intPageCount %>
</form>

</BODY>
</HTML>
```

This page retrieves and places 10 orders within an HTML table. Buttons on the form then allow the user to scroll through the rows and pick the page he wants to view.

Listing 10.2 shows the minimum changes that need to be made to run this same page in ASP.NET. Notice that several of the lines are in boldface type to indicate where code changes have been made.

LISTING 10.2 Simple ASP.NET. This page contains the minimum changes to allow the ASP page in Listing 10.1 to run in ASP.NET.

```
<%@ Page aspCompat="True" Language="vb" CodeBehind="Paging.aspx.vb"
  AutoEventWireup="false" Inherits="QuilogyEducation.Paging"
  enableViewState="False"%>
<HTML>
<BODY>
<font face="verdana">
<h2>
<img src="http://ssosa/win2000.gif"><br>
Northwind Most Recent Orders</h2>

<%
Dim cn
Dim rs
Dim intPageCount As Integer
Dim intPage As Integer
Dim intRecord As Integer

cn = Server.CreateObject("ADODB.Connection")
cn.Provider = "SQLOLEDB"
cn.Open("server=ssosa;database=northwind;uid=sa")

rs = Server.CreateObject("ADODB.Recordset")

' Line up the cache size with the PageSize
rs.CacheSize = 10
rs.CursorLocation = 2 'adUseClient
rs.Open("Select * from Orders",cn,3,1) 'Static and Readonly
```

LISTING 10.2 Continued

```
'Check for empty resultset
If rs.EOF And rs.BOF Then
    Response.Write("No more orders")
    Response.End
End If


rs.PageSize = 10


' Determine how many pages are in this recordset
intPageCount= rs.PageCount


' Now see where the user requested we go
If Len(Request.Form("txtPage")) > 0 Then
    intPage = Request.Form("txtPage")
Else
    Select Case Request.Form("Action")
        Case "<<"
            intPage = 1
        Case "<"
            intPage = CType(Request("intPage"),Integer) -1
            If intPage < 1 Then intPage = 1
        Case ">"
            intPage = CType(Request("intPage"),Integer) + 1
            If intPage > intPageCount Then
                intPage = intPageCount
            End If
        Case ">>"
            intPage = intPageCount
        Case Else
            intPage = 1
    End Select
End If


rs.AbsolutePage = intPage
%>


<table>
<tr>
    <td><strong>Record</strong></td>
    <td><strong>Order ID</strong></td>
    <td><strong>Order Date</strong></td>
    <td><strong>Customer ID</strong></td>
    <td><strong>Ship Name</strong></td>
</tr>
```

LISTING 10.2 Continued

```
<%
For intRecord = 1 To rs.PageSize %>
<tr>
    <td><% =rs.AbsolutePosition %></td>
    <td><a href="orderdetail.asp?id=<% =rs.Collect("OrderID") %>">
        <% =rs.Collect("OrderID") %></a></td>
    <td><% =rs.Collect("OrderDate") %></td>
    <td><% =rs.Collect("CustomerID") %></td>
    <td><% =rs.Collect("ShipName") %></td>
</tr>
    <%
    rs.MoveNext
    If rs.EOF Then Exit For
Next

%>
</table>
<%
rs.Close
rs = Nothing
cn.Close
cn = Nothing
%>

<form name="MovePage" action="paging.aspx" method="post">
<input type="hidden" name="intpage" value="<% =intPage %>">
<input type="submit" name="action" value="&lt;&lt;">
<input type="submit" name="action" value="&lt;">
<input type="submit" name="action" value="&gt;">
<input type="submit" name="action" value="&gt;&gt;"><br>

Go to page:<input type="text" name="txtPage" size=4>
<input type="submit" name="go" value="Go"><br>

Page: <% =intPage & " of " & intPageCount %>
</form>

</BODY>
</HTML>
```

To begin, notice that the Page directive at the top of the page now includes several new options, in addition to the Language. In this case, the aspCompat option is set to True to indicate that the page uses components (ADO in this case) that need to be executed in a Single Threaded Apartment (STA). This is required because .aspx pages are by default accessible by multiple threads, which could corrupt the component.

> **TIP**
>
> The `aspCompat` setting must be on when accessing COM+ 1.0 components as well. In addition, because ASP.NET uses a new security model, you'll need to run the COM+ components under their own identity and make sure that the account used is configured using DCOMCNFG.exe.

Second, the `Page` directive includes the `CodeBehind` option that specifies the .vb file that contains the `Page` class. When creating .aspx pages in VS .NET, this is set up automatically, although it is unused in this case. `AutoEventWireUp` and `enableViewState` also are set to `False` to indicate that the page's event handlers are not automatically created and that the state of the page will not be saved between requests, respectively.

> **NOTE**
>
> Although Web Forms promote the separation of UI and application logic, you can create .aspx pages that contain all the server-side logic normally found in the code behind file in `SCRIPT` blocks decorated with the `runat=server` attribute. Many of the sample Web Forms shown on sites such as www.gotdotnet.com use this approach. In these cases, there is no need for a code behind file (in fact the `Page` directive is not necessary) nor the explicit declaration of a `Page` class.
>
> In addition, when the file is updated, the page is dynamically compiled and cached, which does not update the assembly in the `bin` directory. The same holds true for .aspx files that use code behind, although the associated .vb file will not be compiled. As a result, if you change the code in a .vb file, an explicit build is required for the changes to be reflected when the page is executed.

> **TIP**
>
> When working outside VS .NET, use the `SRC` attribute rather than the `CodeBehind` attribute to point to the file that contains the code.

The move from VBScript to VB .NET also entails the following code changes:

- Because VB .NET requires variable declaration, the variables are declared. Note that `cn` and `rs` are defaulted to `System.Object` (`Variant` is no longer supported) and use late binding to the ADO `Connection` and `Recordset` objects.

- As the objects are created and destroyed, the Set statements are removed because Set and Let are no longer required.

- The arguments to the Open methods of the Connection and Recordset now must be contained in parentheses.

- The intPage Request variable is now cast explicitly to an Integer using the CType function in two places. This is required because VB .NET automatically casts it to a String and then concatenates a "1" to it, rather than produce an Integer. In general, you should always cast to the explicit data type in VB .NET.

Now, when the page is compiled, it runs as expected.

In addition to the changes that must be made to the example in Listing 10.1, ASP.NET also does not support mixing HTML and server-side code within a procedure. For example, the block

```
<% Sub Hello %>
    <b>Hello</b>
<% End Procedure %>
```

does not compile in VB .NET because the compiler assumes that the intent was to terminate the procedure block when it encounters the <b>.

Although performing a lightweight translation such as this allows the page to work, it does not take advantage of the features of ASP.NET. Particularly, using classic ADO rather than ADO.NET hurts performance because the aspCompat option must be specified, performing all the logic inline with the HTML doesn't take advantage of CBF and IntelliSense in VS .NET, and not using ASP.NET server controls, such as the DataGrid, means that additional looping and paging code must be written.

Although all existing ASP pages will and should be modified to run under ASP.NET to take advantage of the performance and scalability increases alone, developers with ASP skills should find their skills still applicable in a .NET world.

NOTE

Because of the architecture improvements, ASP.NET applications typically run two to three times faster than equivalent ASP or JSP (Java Server Pages) applications. This was demonstrated by developing five versions of a sample application called Nile 2.0 using competing architectures. You can download the source code from the MSDN Code Center at http://msdn.microsoft.com/code.

That being said, there is additional good news for ASP developers. The ASP.NET engine only processes pages specific to it and can therefore coexist on the same Web server with ASP. In other words, you can continue to run ASP applications without modification alongside ASP.NET apps and even place ASP pages in the same virtual directory as ASP.NET pages. In the latter case, each page will be processed by the appropriate server extension.

> **NOTE**
>
> Although you can place ASP pages in an ASP.NET application, they will not be able to share Session and Application state. However, Global.asa and Global.asax files can coexist in the same virtual directory.

Can't We All Just Get Along?

In addition to adding ASP pages to sites created with VS .NET, Microsoft has created an easy way of connecting VS .NET to existing VID Webs. To do so, assume you have an existing VID Web application called "myVI6web." To convert this site to a VS .NET compatible Web, VS .NET has a hidden gem called New Project in Existing Folder. To use it, follow these steps:

1. Open up VS .NET.
2. Select File, New, Project. VS .NET displays the New Project dialog box.
3. Select Visual Basic Projects, New Project In Existing Folder.
4. Enter **myVI6web** for a project name. (The project name always will be your existing VID project Web.)
5. Click OK. VS .NET prompts you with the Create a New Project in an Existing Folder dialog.
6. Enter the URL address to the existing VID project.
7. Click OK. Because VS .NET is designed by default to use UNC paths, VS .NET warns you that the Web server is not accessible. You must tell VS .NET to use FrontPage Server extensions.
8. Click OK. VS .NET now converts the VID Web to a VS .NET compatible Web. This is done by VS .NET adding two configuration files called myVI6web.vbproj and myVI6web.vbproj.webinfo to the virtual directory. These files allow VS .NET to discover information about the project. Because these files are text files (in fact, they are XML files), you can still connect to the Web site using VID or any FrontPage-compliant tool.

10

**BUILDING
WEB FORMS**

> After the project has been loaded in VS .NET, you can start editing files. However, when you first view the project through the solution explorer, none of the files will be visible.
>
> To show the files, select Project, Show All Files. Although these files are editable, they are not really a part of the VS .NET project. By default, only files that are part of the VS .NET project are compiled into an assembly when the project is built. To include any existing ASP.NET files, right-click on the existing file and select Include In Project.
>
> After you select the option to include any existing ASP.NET files, or folders, into the project, VS .NET offers you the option of creating a code behind class file. Do not choose this option if you want to continue to use the page with ASP. As you become more proficient with VS .NET and begin converting your code to ASP.NET, you can move to the code-behind model.

Example Application

With the introduction to ASP.NET out of the way, we can begin discussing Web Forms and specific ASP.NET features that bear on the development of the Quilogy education Web site. This site is comprised of the ASP.NET pages listed in Table 10.1.

TABLE 10.1   Pages in the Quilogy Example Web Site

Page	Description
QEducation.aspx	Home page that displays menus and class search control
QSearch.ascx	User control that displays class search options
Schedule.aspx	Page that displays class schedules dynamically queried from the database
StudentLogin.aspx	Page that collects login information from students
StudentProfile.aspx	Page that displays the student's demographic data
Register.aspx	Page that allows a student to register for a class
Transcript.aspx	Page that displays a student's transcript

In addition, this site contains HTML menu pages and client-side JavaScript used to implement the various menus processed using server-side includes and <script> tags. The complete Web application can be downloaded from the book's companion Web site at www.samspublishing.com.

> **NOTE**
>
> Keep in mind that these non-ASP.NET resources are processed directly by IIS and not through the ASP.NET runtime.

Obviously, the application uses the ADO.NET classes and components discussed in Chapter 7, "Accessing Data with ADO.NET"; Chapter 8, "Building Components"; and Chapter 9, "Accessing Component Services," to provide the business and data services. The pages shown in Table 10.1 provide the user services.

Web Forms Architecture

To understand how the ASP.NET pages listed in Table 10.1 are processed, it is important to understand the architecture of a Web Form. This architecture can be broken down into the page processing flow and the event model.

Page Processing Flow

As mentioned previously, ASP.NET pages contain both UI and logic in separate files. The code file contains a class derived from the Page class, whereas the .aspx file contains a Page directive that points to the code file. When compiled and executed by the ASP.NET runtime, the page acts like other components and goes through a series of stages during its life cycle. However, like any resource requested from a Web server, the component is stateless and is re-created with each round-trip to the server.

Table 10.2 shows the stages the page goes through and where you'll typically interact with them.

TABLE 10.2 Page Processing States

Stage	Description
Initialize	Used to initialize variables used throughout the request and exposed through the Init event of the Page class. Can be handled, but controls will not be populated at this point.
Load View State	Loads any previously saved state of controls on the page and populates the object model. Typically handled by the Page class automatically.
Load	All the controls are populated and the object model updated. The Page class exposes the Load event where developers add code to populate controls (perhaps with a database query).

TABLE 10.2   Continued

Stage	Description
Data Binding	Any controls that are going to be bound to a data source are processed. The Page class exposes the DataBinding event, although it is not typically handled.
Event Handling	Fires any server-side event handlers in response to actions the user initiated. The majority of a developer's code is processed in this stage.
Prerender	The output is about to be created. The Page class exposes a PreRender event to give the developer one last chance to update controls.
Save State	The state of the controls on the page (termed the *view state*) is persisted to a string that is round-tripped to the client in a hidden Form field.
Render	Output is generated to be sent to the client. Typically handled automatically.
Cleanup and Dispose	The page has finished rendering and cleanup can begin. The Page class exposes the Unload and Disposed events where developers will close files, release database connections, and so on.

Notice that most of the interaction with the page from the developer's perspective occurs in the Load event and the event handlers for the individual controls. Many of the other stages are handled automatically by the Page class (actually ultimately derived from the Control class).

The key point to notice in Table 10.2 is that the Web Forms architecture creates the appearance of a static form-based development environment by saving the ViewState of ASP.NET server controls on the page. Each page contains a FORM tag with the attribute runat set to the literal string "server." When this attribute is encountered, a form tag is written to the HTML stream that posts the form back to itself, a technique many ASP developers implemented manually. In addition, however, a hidden INPUT tag named __VIEWSTATE is added to the form and contains a compressed binary string that represents the state of the properties in the controls on the form. This technique is useful because it alleviates developers from having to manually save the state of their controls, and does so in a browser-independent and efficient manner. The state information then is placed back into the controls during the Load View State phase shown in Table 10.2. This allows the controls to be programmatically manipulated without worrying about repopulating them.

> **TIP**
>
> The view state of individual controls and the form as a whole can be controlled by setting the `EnableViewState` property in code, or as an attribute in the `Page` directive. By default it is set to `True`, but setting it to `False` can improve performance by decreasing the amount of data round-tripped.

When the form is posted back to the server, the runtime also is smart enough to know whether this is a postback or an initial load and exposes that fact through the `IsPostBack` property of the page. The result is that you can isolate code in the `Load` event that need only execute the first time the page is displayed.

Page Processing Example

To illustrate the page structure and handling basic events, consider the QEducation.aspx page shown in Listings 10.3 and 10.4.

LISTING 10.3   QEducation.aspx. This listing shows an abbreviated version of the UI for the Quilogy education home page.

```
<%@ Register TagPrefix="QEd" TagName="QSearch" Src="QSearch.ascx"%>
<%@ Page Language="vb" AutoEventWireup="true" Codebehind="QEducation.aspx.vb"
    Inherits="QuilogyEducation.QEducation" EnableSessionState="True"
    clientTarget="DownLevel"%>

<HTML>
  <HEAD>
    <TITLE>Quilogy - Services: Education</TITLE>
    <!DOCTYPE HTML PUBLIC="-//W3C//DTD HTML 4.0 Transitional//EN">
    <LINK href="supplemental/site.css" type=text/css rel=stylesheet>
  </HEAD>
  <BODY language=javascript leftMargin=0 topMargin=0
    marginheight="0" marginwidth="0">
    <FORM id="QEducation" method=post runat=server>
    <!-- #include file="navbar.htm" -->
    <TABLE cellSpacing=0 cellPadding=0 width="100%" border=0>
        <TR>
            <TD class="caption">
            <div id="studentdata" runat="server"></div>
            </TD>
        </TR>
        <TR>
            <TD align=left bgColor=#f3f0de>
            <TABLE cellSpacing=0 cellPadding=0 width=740 border=0>
```

LISTING 10.3   Continued

```
                <TR>
                    <TD valign=center align=left width=211>
                    <IMG SRC="supplemental/services-maineducation.gif"
                      width=211 height=45 border=0>
                    </TD>
                    <TD width=529>
                    <IMG height=6 src="supplemental/trans.gif"
                      width=300 border=0>
                    <BR>
                    <TABLE cellSpacing=0 cellPadding=2 border=0>
                      <QEd:QSearch id="QSearch" runat="server"></QEd:QSearch>
                    </TABLE>
                    </TD>
                </TR>
            </TABLE>
            </TD>
        </TR>
        <TR>
            <TD bgColor=#dbd3bf>
    <IMG height=1 src="supplemental/trans.gif" width=1 border=0>
            </TD>
        </TR>
        <TR>
            <TD bgColor=#ece8cd><!-- #include file="edmenu.htm" --></TD>
        </TR>
    </TABLE>
<!-- #include file="bottombar.htm" -->
    <asp:LinkButton id=lnkSignOut runat="server"
      cssclass="caption">Click here to Sign Out</asp:LinkButton>
    </FORM>
</BODY>
</HTML>
```

LISTING 10.4   QEducation.aspx.vb. This listing shows the code behind file for the Quilogy education home page.

```
Option Strict Off

Imports System.Web.UI.HtmlControls
Imports System.Security.Principal
Imports System.Web.Security
Imports System.Text
Imports System.Web.Caching
```

LISTING 10.4   Continued

```
Public Class QEducation
    Inherits System.Web.UI.Page
    Protected WithEvents lnkSignOut As System.Web.UI.WebControls.LinkButton
    Protected WithEvents studentdata As _
      System.Web.UI.HtmlControls.HtmlGenericControl

    Protected Sub Page_Init(ByVal Sender As System.Object, _
      ByVal e As System.EventArgs) Handles MyBase.Init
        'CODEGEN: This method call is required by the Web Form Designer
        'Do not modify it using the code editor.
        InitializeComponent()
    End Sub

    Private Sub Page_Load(ByVal sender As System.Object, _
      ByVal e As System.EventArgs) Handles MyBase.Load
        ' If the user is authenticated then set the welcome message

        If Context.User.Identity.IsAuthenticated Then
            studentdata().InnerText = "Welcome " & Me.Session("StudentName")
            lnkSignOut.Visible = True
        Else
            studentdata().InnerText = "Welcome to Quilogy Education! "
            studentdata().InnerText &= "Please select an option"
            lnkSignOut.Visible = False
        End If

    End Sub

    Private Sub lnkSignOut_Click(ByVal sender As System.Object, _
      ByVal e As System.EventArgs) Handles lnkSignOut.Click
        ' Sign out
        FormsAuthentication.SignOut()
        Session.Clear()
        Response.Redirect("\QuilogyEducation\QEducation.aspx")
    End Sub
End Class
```

The items to note in these listings include the fact that in Listing 10.3, the .aspx page contains a FORM tag with the runat=server attribute set, and that it includes a Register directive that references the QSearch.ascx file, which is a Web Forms user control. This control contains the drop-down lists required to search the class schedule. In addition, the studentdata DIV tag includes the runat=server attribute, enabling it to be "seen" when the page is processed on the server. In addition, an ASP.NET LinkButton control is placed at the bottom of the page to enable a logged-in user to sign out.

10

BUILDING
WEB FORMS

NOTE

The event handlers in ASP.NET include the familiar arguments to represent the initiator of the event (Sender) and any event-specific information (typically EventArgs).

TIP

When working in the HTML or Design view in VS.NET for a page, you can set the targetSchema property in the Properties window to MSIE 5.0, MSIE 3.02/Navigator 3.0, or Navigator 4.0. Doing so exposes the tags supported by those browsers to IntelliSense. This can be helpful when reviewing and coding HTML meant for a particular browser level. Warnings appear in the Task List menu when elements are found that do not correspond to the schema. The targetSchema also can be set directly with the vs_targetSchema metatag in the <head> section of the page.

In Listing 10.4, the Load event is handled and is used to populate the studentdata control by setting its InnerText property. Although controls will be discussed in more detail later, it should be noted that the DIV tag was declared as HtmlGenericControl and so supports the typical Document Object Model (DOM) methods and properties including InnerText. The Load event also checks the IsAuthenticated property of the User object to customize the welcome message if the user is authenticated.

NOTE

In addition to the code shown here, in many instances, the Load event consists of an If Then statement that checks the IsPostBack property of the Page class to determine whether the page is being loaded for the first time. This is especially true if the page queries a database. The proper use of IsPostBack is important because it can reduce the amount of code run when the page is being processed, thereby increasing performance.

The result of the page can be seen in Figure 10.2.

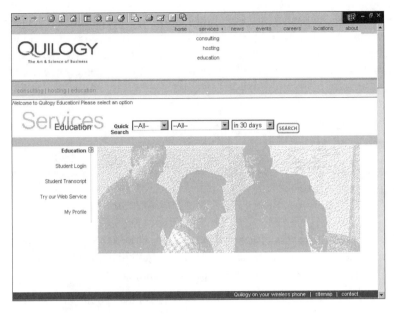

FIGURE 10.2
The Quilogy education home page with the user control allowing users to search the class schedule.

Event Model

The implementation of ViewState makes a server-based event model possible. In fact, by relying on this model, you can work with the Web Form in virtually the same way as you can a form in VB 6.0.

> **NOTE**
>
> As you might expect, server events can only be processed when using ASP.NET server controls. This includes both Web server controls and all HTML server controls except HtmlGenericControl.

However, because most events originate on the client, the page must be posted back to the server for processing. Obviously, this can cause overhead, so most server controls support a limited set of server events, usually restricted to click and changed. Not surprisingly, events that cause a form post are referred to as *postback events*. However, for some events, such as the TextChanged event of the server TextBox control, the event is captured on the client and is not actually processed until the next postback. The obvious advantage is that this minimizes round-trips.

Along the same lines, changed events, such as the `SelectedIndexChanged` event of the `DropDownList` control, might need to be processed immediately—for example, in the case where the selection triggers the population of another `DropDownList`. In these cases, you can set the `AutoPostBack` property of the control to `True`, and its changed event will be posted immediately.

> **NOTE**
>
> Some controls contain specialized changed events, such as the `SelectionChanged` event of the `WebCalendar` Web server control. These will be posted immediately when `AutoPostBack` is set to `True`.

During the Event Handling phase of page processing shown in Table 10.2, the form's changed events are processed first, followed by any click events, both in no particular order. As a result, you should not write code that is dependent on events firing in a specific order.

As you might expect, client events have priority over server events. In other words, you certainly can create both client and server event handlers for the same control. This allows you to take advantage of DHTML events, such as `onmouseover`, when using a browser that supports HTML 4.0. However, if you create an event handler for the same event on both the client and the server, the server event is ignored.

Finally, Web server controls can contain child controls that themselves raise events. In these cases, rather than having each child control raise a separate event that you must handle, the events are "bubbled" to the container, and a generic `ItemCommand` event is raised. This includes arguments that allow you to programmatically determine which child control raised the event.

To illustrate these concepts, review the code in Listings 10.5 and 10.6. In this example, a Web Form with two Web server `DropDownList` controls and a `Hyperlink` control are used to display information about dinosaurs.

LISTING 10.5   Simple Event Example. This listing shows the .aspx file for a simple page that displays information about dinosaurs.

```
<%@ Page Language="vb" AutoEventWireup="false" Codebehind="WebForm1.aspx.vb"
Inherits="QuilogyEducation.WebForm1"%>

<HTML>
  <HEAD>
<meta content="Microsoft Visual Studio.NET 7.0" name=GENERATOR>
<meta content="Visual Basic 7.0" name=CODE_LANGUAGE>
<meta content=JavaScript name=vs_defaultClientScript>
```

LISTING 10.5   Continued

```
<meta content="Internet Explorer 5.0" name=vs_targetSchema>
  </HEAD>
<body MS_POSITIONING="GridLayout">
<form id=WebForm1 method=post runat="server">

<asp:dropdownlist id=lstGenus runat="server" autopostback="True">
</asp:dropdownlist>
<asp:dropdownlist id=lstSpecies runat="server">
</asp:dropdownlist>
<asp:HyperLink id=HyperLink1 runat="server">HyperLink
</asp:HyperLink>
</form>

<script language="javascript"  event="onchange" for="lstSpecies">
    window.alert(lstSpecies.value);
</script>

 </body>
</HTML>
```

LISTING 10.6   Simple Event Code. This listing shows the code behind file for a page that displays dinosaur information using events.

```
Public Class WebForm1 : Inherits System.Web.UI.Page
    Protected WithEvents lstGenus As System.Web.UI.WebControls.DropDownList
    Protected WithEvents lstSpecies As System.Web.UI.WebControls.DropDownList
    Protected WithEvents HyperLink1 As System.Web.UI.WebControls.HyperLink

    Private Sub Page_Load(ByVal sender As System.Object, _
      ByVal e As System.EventArgs) Handles MyBase.Load
        'Put user code to initialize the page here
        If Not Me.IsPostBack Then
            lstGenus.Items.Add("Pick One")
            lstGenus.Items.Add("Tyrannosaurus")
            lstGenus.Items.Add("Triceratops")

            lstSpecies.Visible = False
            HyperLink1.Target = "_blank"
            HyperLink1.Visible = False
        Else
            lstSpecies.Visible = True
            HyperLink1.Visible = True
        End If
    End Sub
```

LISTING 10.6   Continued

```
Private Sub lstGenus_SelectedIndexChanged(ByVal sender As System.Object, _
    ByVal e As System.EventArgs) Handles lstGenus.SelectedIndexChanged

    lstSpecies.Items.Clear()

    Select Case lstGenus.SelectedIndex
        Case 1
            lstSpecies.Items.Add("T. rex")
            lstSpecies.Items.Add("T. lancensis")
            HyperLink1.Text = "Go T.Rex"
            HyperLink1.NavigateUrl = _
    "http://www.enchantedlearning.com/subjects/dinosaurs/dinos/Trex.shtml"
        Case 2
            lstSpecies.Items.Add("Triceratops horridus")
            lstSpecies.Items.Add("Triceratops ingus")
            HyperLink1.Text = "Go Triceratops"
            HyperLink1.NavigateUrl = _
    "http://www.enchantedlearning.com/subjects/dinosaurs/dinos/Triceratops.shtml"
        Case Else
            HyperLink1.Visible = False
            lstSpecies.Visible = False
    End Select

End Sub

End Class
```

Notice in Listing 10.5 that the autopostback attribute of the lstGenus DropDownList control is set to True. In Listing 10.6, the Load event uses the Add method of the Items collection to load three options into the DropDownList and makes the second drop-down and the hyperlink invisible.

To respond to the onchange event generated at the client, an event handler for the SelectedIndexChanged event of lstSpecies is used in Listing 10.6. This handler clears lstSpecies and repopulates it with selections appropriate for the genus selected. In addition, it changes the properties of the Hyperlink server control to display a hyperlink to the appropriate dinosaur. Because AutoPostBack is set to True, the form is posted to the server immediately when a new item is selected.

Finally, note that a client-side script block was created to handle the onchange event of the cboSpecies control. Because this is a client-side script, the event is captured only on the client and the alert method executed. Keep in mind that if the event were associated with the lstGenus control, only the client event would execute.

Although the server-side code is straightforward, the way it is rendered within the browser is more complicated, as shown in Listing 10.7.

LISTING 10.7 Client Rendered Events. This listing shows the page constructed in Listings 10.5 and 10.6 as it is rendered in MSIE 6.0.

```
<HTML>
  <HEAD>
<meta content="Microsoft Visual Studio.NET 7.0" name=GENERATOR>
<meta content="Visual Basic 7.0" name=CODE_LANGUAGE>
<meta content=JavaScript name=vs_defaultClientScript>
<meta content="Internet Explorer 5.0" name=vs_targetSchema>
  </HEAD>
<body MS_POSITIONING="GridLayout">
<form name="WebForm1" method="post" action="webform1.aspx" id="WebForm1">
<input type="hidden" name="__VIEWSTATE"
value="dDw2NDg1MzUyMDA7dDw7bDxpPDE+Oz47bDx0PDtsPGk8MT47aTwzPjtpPDU+Oz47bDx0PQ8
03A8bDxpPDA+O2k8MT47aTwyPjs+O2w8cDxQaWNrIE9uZTtQaWNrIE9uZT47cDxUeXJhbm5vc2F1nV
zO1R5cmFubm9zYXVydXM+O3A8VHJpY2VyYXRvcHM7VHJpY2VyYXRvcHM+Oz4+O2w8TwxPjs+PjsPj
t0PHQ8cDxwPGw8VmlzaWJsZTs+O2w8bzx0Pjs+Pjs+O3Q8TwyPjtAPFQuIHJleDtULiBsYW5jZWza
XM7PjtAPFQuIHJleDtULiBsYW5jZW5zaXM7Pj47Pjs7PjtuPHA8cDxsPFRleHQ7VGFyZ2V0V0O1Zpcli
bGU7TmF2aWdhdGVVcmw7PjtsPEdvIFQuUmV4O019ibGFuaztvPHA2h0dHA6Ly93d3cuZW5jaGFuGGV
kbGVhcm5pbmcuY29tL3N1YmplY3RzL2Rpbm9zYXVycy9kaW5vcy9UcmV4LnNodG1sOz4+Oz47Oz4Pj
47Pj47Pg==" />


<select name="lstGenus" id="lstGenus"
  onchange="javascript:__doPostBack('lstGenus','')">
  <option value="Pick One">Pick One</option>
    <option selected="selected" value="Tyrannosaurus">Tyrannosaurus</option>
    <option value="Triceratops">Triceratops</option>
</select>

<select name="lstSpecies" id="lstSpecies">
  <option value="T. rex">T. rex</option>
    <option value="T. lancensis">T. lancensis</option>
</select>

<a id="HyperLink1"
  href="http://www.enchantedlearning.com/subjects/dinosaurs/dinos/Trex.shtml"
  target="_blank">Go T.Rex</a>

<input type="hidden" name="__EVENTTARGET" value="" />
<input type="hidden" name="__EVENTARGUMENT" value="" />
<script language="javascript">
<!--
```

LISTING 10.7   Continued

```
    function __doPostBack(eventTarget, eventArgument) {
        var theform = document.WebForm1
        theform.__EVENTTARGET.value = eventTarget
        theform.__EVENTARGUMENT.value = eventArgument
        theform.submit()
    }
// -->
</script>
</form>

<script language="javascript"  event="onchange" for="lstSpecies">
    window.alert(lstSpecies.value);
</script>

 </body>
</HTML>
```

First, as expected, each DropDownList is rendered as a SELECT tag and the Hyperlink as an anchor (<a>). Second, the hidden INPUT tag __VIEWSTATE is used to encode the values of the properties of the controls. Third, the onchange event handler of the lstGenus control is set to execute the __doPostBack JavaScript function. As you can see, this function, generated by the ASP.NET runtime, accepts arguments that map to the event arguments on the server and then populates hidden INPUT tags with the values before invoking the submit method of the form. When the form is submitted, the ViewState and event arguments are unpacked, the object model for the controls is populated on the server, and the appropriate event is executed on the server.

ASP.NET Features

Now that you understand how Web Forms are architected, we'll shift the discussion to the primary features of ASP.NET used in the Quilogy example application, including configuration, security, state management, caching, and tracing.

Configuration Files

Many of the features discussed in this section are specified in the configuration files discussed previously. To recap, the ASP.NET runtime loads and parses XML configuration files to determine how resources are processed and general constraints on the application.

The processing of configuration files is actually hierarchical. First, the runtime looks for a file called Machine.config in the .NET Framework directory (*windowsdir*\Microsoft.Net\ Framework*version*\config\). This file contains configuration information for more than

ASP.NET, but a significant portion of it is devoted to the `system.web` tag that provides the default settings for ASP.NET. Among these are tags that set the default options for the ASP.NET runtime, compilation, tracing, page directives, authentication, authorization, impersonation, session state, modules, and browser compatibility, among others, as denoted in the online documentation. For example, the `httpHandlers` child element determines which resources are processed by which ASP.NET runtime classes, a portion of which follows:

```
<httpHandlers>
  <add verb="*" path="trace.axd"
     type="System.Web.Handlers.TraceHandler,System.Web" />
  <add verb="*" path="*.aspx"
     type="System.Web.UI.PageHandlerFactory,System.Web" />
  <add verb="*" path="*.asmx"
      type="System.Web.Services.Protocols.WebServiceHandlerFactory,
      System.Web.Services" validate="false"/>
</httpHandlers>
```

Note that .aspx pages are handled by the `PageHandlerFactory` class.

Second, the runtime looks for a Web.config file in the root directory of the application for the requested resource and overlays these settings on Machine.config. These settings apply to files in the root directory and any child directories. Likewise, if Web.config files exist in any child directories, the settings will be read, and a unique set of configuration information applied to each URL. In this way, configuration information applies hierarchically with the nearest Web.config file taking precedence. Alternatively, you can encapsulate certain elements in a location element that references the child directory to which the settings apply. In this way, you needn't manage multiple Web.config files for these settings.

There are several advantages to this system, including the fact that configuration files are human readable and can be changed at any time, and all subsequent requests automatically will pick up the new settings without requiring a restart of the Web application. In addition, the configuration files are extensible so that you can add your own application level settings and read them programmatically within a page.

One obvious use for extending the configuration system is to store database connection strings.

TIP

Reading database connection strings from a configuration file is analogous to using construction strings when building components that run in Component Services. The former technique is preferred when the connection string must be particular to the Web application, whereas the latter is used when the component might be called from a variety of user services.

10

BUILDING
WEB FORMS

To extend the configuration system, you must first define the element or section that will contain your settings. This is done by adding an element to the configSections element. For example, the Machine.config file, by default, defines a section called appSettings that is suitable for storing your own application information. This section is defined in Machine.config as follows:

```
<configSections>
    <section name="appSettings"
        type="System.Configuration.NameValueFileSectionHandler, System" />
</configSections>
```

Note that the type attribute of the section element defines which class handles (processes) the information stored in the tag. In this case, the appSettings tag consists of name-value pairs processed by the NameValueFileSectionHandler class. Other built-in handlers in the System.Configuration namespace include DictionarySectionHandler, NameValueSectionHandler, and SingleTagSelectionHandler. Each of these defines how the tag is to be structured and parsed at runtime.

> **NOTE**
>
> Although beyond the scope of this book, you can create your own handler by creating a class that implements the IConfigurationSectionHandler interface.

Next, in the Web.config file, you can add an appSettings section with a custom value as follows:

```
<appSettings>
  <add key="SQLConnect" value="data source=ssosa;
  initial catalog=enrollment;user id=sa;pooling=true" />
</appSettings>
```

In this case, the section handler specifies that key and value attributes are used to define the information. You then can read the settings programmatically using the ConfigurationSettings class of the System.Configuration namespace. For example, the studentlogin.aspx page calls the Login method of the Quilogy.Education.Enrollment.Students class to validate the login. The connection string is passed in the constructor of the class as follows:

```
Imports Quilogy.Education.Enrollment
Imports System.Configuration
Protected Sub cmdLogin_Click(ByVal sender As System.Object, _
  ByVal e As System.EventArgs) _
    Handles cmdLogin.Click
    Dim oStud As New Students(ConfigurationSettings.AppSettings( _
      "SQLConnect").ToString)
End Sub
```

The `AppSettings` shared property of the `ConfigurationSettings` class is used to explicitly retrieve name-value pairs from the `appSettings` tag. To more generically retrieve configuration information, you can use the `GetConfig` method of either the `ConfigurationSettings` class or the `HttpContext` class as exposed through the `Context` property of the `Page` class like so:

```
Dim o As System.Object
o = Context.GetConfig("appSettings")
Dim oStud As New Students(o("SQLConnect").ToString)
```

Note that because configuration files are encoded as XML, they are case-sensitive. In the previous example, passing the value of "AppSettings," rather than "appSettings," would result in an unhandled exception.

Security

One of the services provided by ASP.NET and specified in the configuration files is security. To be more precise, ASP.NET includes settings to handle impersonation, authentication, and authorization. Of course, because an ASP.NET application is hosted by IIS, the security configuration of the IIS server acts as a gatekeeper to ASP.NET security, and hence is relevant to this discussion.

To begin, keep in mind that a virtual directory in IIS 5.0 can be secured in several ways that are each checked when a request is made for a resource on the server, the settings for which are stored in the IIS metabase. First, IP address restrictions can be placed on the directory to allow or disallow certain IP addresses, subnets, or domains. If the IP address passes this test, the user might be authenticated using either anonymous (unauthenticated), basic (clear text), digest (using a Windows 2000 Domain Controller), or Windows Integrated authentication (NTLM or Kerberos). Regardless of which option is set, the end result is that IIS passes an access token for the authenticated account to the ASP.NET application. Because IIS works with only Windows accounts, the token either represents the anonymous user (typically `IUSR_server`) or the user account logged in to the client workstation. In addition, at the directory level, permissions can be set to allow read, write, and execute.

After the IIS requirements are met, the ASP.NET security settings are invoked. Keep in mind, however, that only resources processed by the ASP.NET server extension (aspnet_isapi.dll) use ASP.NET security.

At the most basic level, you can set the trust level of the managed code running within an ASP.NET site by placing a `<trust>` element in the `<system.web>` element in the Web.config file and setting its level attribute. By default, the trust level is set to Full, whereby ASP.NET does not restrict the security policy of code running within the site. The level attribute can alternatively be set to High, Low, or None to apply predefined security policies configured in the Machine.config file. In this way you ensure right from the start that code running within an ASP.NET Web site cannot gain access to resources on the machine.

Impersonation

Perhaps the simplest security scheme you can implement with ASP.NET, and the one that requires the least code, is to use impersonation. *Impersonation* allows the ASP.NET code to run under either the identity of the access token passed from IIS, or a specific user account specified in the configuration settings. Impersonation is configured by adding the `identity` element to the Web.config file and setting the `impersonate` attribute to `true`. Optionally, `name` and `password` attributes can be included to specify that the application run under a specific user account. For example, to run the ASP.NET application using the access token passed from IIS, you would add the following line to the Web.config file:

```
<identity impersonate="true" />
```

If a name and password are provided, they will be used in preference over the IIS token. By default, impersonation is set to `false`, which means that ASP.NET code will run under the SYSTEM account used by the ASP.NET runtime process (aspnet_wp.exe).

It is also possible to change the account under which aspnet_wp.exe executes by changing the `processModel` element in the `system.Web` section of Machine.config as follows:

```
<system.web>
  <processModel enable="true" username="domain\user" password="pwd"/>
</system.web>
```

The `username` attribute also can be set to `"SYSTEM"` (the default) or `"MACHINE"`, which causes the ASP.NET runtime process to run under a special account called ASPNET created when ASP.NET is installed on the server. In both cases, the password must be set to `"AutoGenerate"`.

> **NOTE**
>
> For security reasons, it is recommended that you change the account under which the runtime executes to limit the permissions given. However, that account must have read/write access to the ASP.NET temporary files under the *windowsdir*\Microsoft.Net\Framework directory, read/write access to the system temporary directory for compilers to use, and read access to both the application directories and the Services Framework system assemblies in *windowsdir*\Microsoft.Net\Framework. Because of security restrictions, if you do use a different account, you cannot explicitly specify the account to impersonate within the `identity` element.

If impersonation is set to `true`, then you must ensure that the access token passed to ASP.NET has the appropriate NTFS permissions because they will be checked.

> **NOTE**
>
> In addition, because Windows 2000 supports delegation, you can use impersonation to pass the credentials of the client all the way to a back-end resource, such as Component Services or SQL Server.

Typically, impersonation is used in conjunction with basic, digest, or Windows Integrated authentication in IIS and Windows authentication in ASP.NET, as discussed in the following section. This configuration is well suited to intranet scenarios because the users must have Windows accounts, and those accounts will use NTFS permissions, SQL Server, and Component Services roles to access the appropriate resources. In addition, Windows Integrated authentication only works on MSIE and does not work with proxy servers. Conversely, for Internet scenarios, this would not be a good choice because users will not typically have Windows accounts.

Authentication

ASP.NET supports four forms of authentication: Windows, Passport, Forms, and None. The type of authentication is configured using the authentication element in the Web.config file using the mode attribute, and is implemented by classes in the `System.Web.Security` namespace called providers. These providers are implemented as HTTP Modules (derived from `IHttpModule`) and are specified in the Machine.config file in the `httpmodules` element. For example, when using forms authentication, the `FormsAuthenticationModule` provider is used.

Windows Authentication

By default, Windows authentication is configured in the Machine.config file like so:

```
<authentication mode="Windows" />
```

The job of the `WindowsAuthenticationModule` is to construct a `WindowsIdentity` object (found in the `System.Security.Principal` namespace) based on the access token sent to ASP.NET from IIS. The `identity` object then attaches a `WindowsPrincipal` object to the `HttpContext` exposed through its `User` property. As is true of other context members, such as `Session` and `Application`, the `User` property also is exposed directly by the `Page` object.

When the authentication occurs, the `Authenticate` event of the `WindowsAuthenticationModule` class fires and can be handled in the Global.asax file by creating a method called `WindowsAuthentication_OnAuthenticate`. Although not typically used, in this way, you can attach a custom object that implements the `IPrincipal` interface to the context. This basic architecture is the same for each of the authentication providers discussed in this chapter.

> **NOTE**
>
> As you would expect, Windows authentication works only when IIS authentication is set to an authentication scheme other than anonymous. When set to anonymous, the `Name` and `AuthenticationType` properties of the `WindowsIdentity` object are set to `Nothing`, and the `IsAuthenticated` property is set to `False`.

Remember that a `WindowsPrincipal` object is primarily used to determine which roles a user is a member of using the `IsInRole` method, and to expose the `WindowsIdentity` object through its `Identity` property. In this way, you can programmatically check for role membership using .NET Framework roles as discussed in Chapter 5, "Packaging, Deployment, and Security." To access the `WindowsIdentity` object, for example, to print the name and authentication type of the authenticated user, you could add the following lines to the `Load` event of the `Page` (assuming that `txtUser` is a Web server control):

```
txtUser.Text = Context.User.Identity.Name
txtAuth.Text = Context.User.Identity.AuthenticationType
```

> **TIP**
>
> Because `User` is also a member of the `Page` object, you could replace `Context` with the keyword `Me` or simply omit it altogether. `Context` is used here as a reminder that the `HttpContext` information is flowed through the request.

Behind the scenes, the `User` property, and its `Identity` property, return objects that support the `IPrincipal` and `IIdentity` interfaces, respectively. These interfaces support only a subset of the members of the underlying `WindowsPrincipal` and `WindowsIdentity` objects. As a result, to call all the methods of the `WindowsPrincipal` and `WindowsIdentity` objects, you'll need to cast the objects to these classes like so:

```
Imports System.Security.Principal
Dim oPrincipal As WindowsPrincipal
Dim oIdentity As WindowsIdentity

oPrincipal = Context.User
oIdentity = Context.User.Identity
```

Doing so allows you to call the overloaded `IsInRole` method of the `WindowsPrincipal` object to check for role membership in Windows groups as well. For example, to determine whether the current user is a member of the `Administrators` local group on the IIS machine, you would use the `WindowsBuiltInRole` enumeration with the `Administrator` constant as follows:

```
Imports System.Security.Principal
If oPrincipal.IsInRole(WindowsBuiltInRole.Administrator) Then
    cmdAdminFunctions.Visible = True
End If
```

Similarly, you can use the `WindowsIdentity` methods, such as `Impersonate`, to programmatically impersonate another account or properties, such as `IsAnonymous`, to determine whether anonymous authentication is being used.

Windows authentication often is used with impersonation to provide seamless access to resources for intranet users. However, it also can be used effectively without impersonation so that the UI can check for role or group membership to simply customize the user interface. In either case, when Windows authentication is enabled, ASP.NET automatically uses file authorization implemented by the `FileAuthorizationModule` to perform ACL checks on requested resources using the user's credentials.

Passport Authentication

Although impersonation and Windows authentication are appropriate for intranet sites, they clearly are not useful in Internet sites that require authentication and personalization because it is not feasible to issue Windows accounts to an unlimited number of potential users. As one alternative, these sites can take advantage of Passport authentication.

Simply put, Passport (`www.passport.com`) is a federated authentication and profile service created by Microsoft, and is the first of the .NET My Services publicly available (formerly Hailstorm) described in Chapter 1, "The Microsoft .NET Architecture." This service is responsible for authenticating users based on an e-mail address and password. In other words, when a user attempts to access a page on your server protected by Passport, he is redirected to a Passport server where his credentials are checked.

NOTE

Windows XP also supports a Passport-aware client authentication exchange protocol that can be used rather than redirecting to the Passport site.

If the user is authenticated, he is redirected back to the original page requested along with an encrypted ticket. This ticket then is used to authenticate subsequent requests and can include an expiration time and be reused on other sites that support Passport.

> **TIP**
>
> Passport stores several cookies on the client browser (for example to store profile information), so cookies must be enabled for Passport authentication to work correctly. If cookies are disabled, the user will be redirected to the Passport login page each time he requests a protected resource.

To use Passport, you must first set up a Preproduction (PREP) passport and register your PREP site ID (which can be done at `www.passport.com/business`). This test environment allows you to test your implementation before going live by agreeing to the license agreement and obtaining a Production Site ID. The site IDs are keys encrypted using the Triple DES encryption scheme that Passport uses to encrypt and decrypt the query strings passed between the sites. Passport also requires that you download and install the Microsoft Passport SDK, which also can be downloaded from its site.

> **NOTE**
>
> Although Microsoft currently is waiving any fees for this service, in the future it will charge a "nominal annual license fee to service operators" according to the Passport Web site.

By setting the mode attribute of the authentication element to "Passport" in the Web.config file, the `PassportAuthenticationModule` is used. This module provides a wrapper around the Passport SDK and is responsible for detecting the absence of the passport ticket and redirecting to the login form on the Passport server. It also decrypts the returned ticket and constructs a `PassportIdentity` object (that implements the `IIdentity` interface) that is exposed through the `User` property of the `HttpContext`. As with Windows authentication, a Global.asax event called `PassportAuthentication_OnAuthenticate` can be created to customize the authentication process.

The `PassportIdentity` object can be used to interact with the Passport service using the primary members shown in Table 10.3.

TABLE 10.3 Important `PassportIdentity` Members

Class	Description
Decrypt	Shared method that decrypts data using the key for the current site.
Encrypt	Shared method that encrypts data using the key for the current site.

TABLE 10.3 Continued

Class	Description
Signout	Shared method that signs the current user out of his session.
HasSavedPassword	Instance property that returns whether the user has chosen to save his password on the Passport login page.
HasTicket	Instance property that returns whether there is a Passport ticket as a cookie on the query string.
AuthURL2	Instance method that returns a string containing the Login server URL for the user. Can be used to generate a link for a user who has not signed in, or whose ticket has expired.
IsAuthenticated	Instance property that returns whether the user has been authenticated by Passport.
Item	Instance property that returns the default collection of profile information.
Name	Instance property that returns the name of the Passport user.
TicketAge	Instance property that returns the time, in seconds, since the last ticket was issued or refreshed.
TimeSinceSignIn	Instance property that returns the time, in seconds, since the user logged in to Passport.
GetProfileObject	Instance method that returns the Passport profile information passed as an argument.
LoginUser	Instance method that logs in the user by redirecting to the Passport site or using a Passport-aware client authentication exchange.

For example, to query for an authenticated user's profile information, you can determine whether the user is logged in using IsAuthenticated and then use the Item property (or the GetProfileObject) property to populate a form in the Load event of a page that shows the user's profile information as follows:

```
Dim oIdentity As PassportIdentity

oIdentity = Context.User.Identity

If oIdentity.IsAuthenticated Then
    txtZip.Text = oIdentity.Item("PostalCode")
    txtBDay.Text = oIdentity.Item("BirthDate")
    txtGender.Text = oIdentity.Item("Gender")
    txtNickname.Text = oIdentity.Item("Nickname")
End If
```

10

Note that as in Windows authentication, the `Identity` property of the `User` object exposed through the `Context` object can be cast to the appropriate identity object, in this case `PassportIdentity`. In addition, profile information can be extended to include custom attributes, in addition to core attributes like those shown in the preceding code.

Although using Passport creates an external dependency for your sites, the obvious advantage is that it offloads the storage and security of passwords and profile information. However, to provide privacy, the architecture of Passport ensures that participating sites are only allowed to see a user's e-mail address if he has indicated that it can be shared. If so, the `PreferredEmail` attribute of the user's profile contains a value that can be queried using the `Item` collection, as shown previously. As a result, you cannot use the e-mail address of the user as the primary key of a private database that tracks additional information (such as orders or course registrations).

You can, however, use the `MemberIDLow` and `MemberIDHigh` attributes of the Passport profile, which contain two 32-bit values that together make up the 64-bit Passport unique identifier (PUID) for the Passport user. The PUID is factored into two attributes because many scripting languages cannot handle 64-bit values. These properties can be concatenated as a string using their hex equivalents to form a unique identifier that can be stored in a database. The `GetPUID` method shown in Listing 10.8 can be added to the `Page` class to return the unique string derived from these attributes.

LISTING 10.8 Deriving a Passport Unique Identifier. This method derives the PUID from the attributes of the Passport profile.

```
Imports System.Web.Security
Imports System.Text
Private Function GetPUID() As String
    Dim oIdentity As PassportIdentity
    Dim PPID As String
    Dim intHigh As Integer
    Dim intLow As Integer
    Dim strHex As String

    Try
        ' Get the passport identity
        oIdentity = Context.User.Identity

        ' get values, convert to hex and pad
        If oIdentity.IsAuthenticated Then
            intHigh = oIdentity.Item("MemberIdHigh")
            intLow = oIdentity.Item("MemberIdLow")
            strHex = Hex(intHigh)
            PPID = strHex.PadLeft(8, "0")
```

LISTING 10.8   Continued

```
            strHex = Hex(intLow)
            PPID = PPID & strHex.PadLeft(8, "0")
        End If
    Catch e As Exception
        ' Skip the error and return Nothing
    End Try

    Return PPID

End Function
```

The resulting unique string then can be stored in your database and used as a primary key. If your site requires an e-mail address so that you can send confirmations and other information to the user, you can additionally request that information on a Web Form and store it separately in your database linked to the PUID. For users who have a `PreferredEmail` address registered with Passport, you can synchronize the two using the profile.

Forms Authentication

The final authentication technique exposed by ASP.NET, and the one used in the Quilogy education example, is Forms Authentication.

Forms Authentication is appropriate when your application needs to collect the user's credentials through an HTML form and authenticate the user with a custom scheme. In the Quilogy example application, the user is required to enter his e-mail address and password, which is validated against a private Quilogy database. The Forms Authentication module implemented through the `FormsAuthenticationModule` class. This class provides the services to automatically issue a client-side redirect for unauthenticated requests to the appropriate login page, and track authenticated users through the use of cookies. For this reason, Forms Authentication is also sometimes referred to as "cookie authentication."

> **NOTE**
>
> The next version of ASP.NET is said to include a query string version of Forms Authentication that will not require cookies.

To enable Forms Authentication, simply set the mode attribute of the authentication element in Web.config to "Forms." In addition, the child forms element can contain name, loginurl, protection, timeout, and path attributes that control the name of the cookie used for authentication, the login page to redirect to, the level of encryption to use, the timeout period for the

10

cookie, and the path on the browser where cookies are to be stored. For example, for the Quilogy site, the authentication element is configured as follows:

```
<authentication mode="Forms">
    <forms loginUrl="studentlogin.aspx" />
</authentication>
```

Note that, by default (as configured in the Machine.config file), the name attribute is set to ".ASPXAUTH" and the protection attribute is set to "All" to indicate that both data validation and encryption are done on the cookie using Triple DES encryption. Alternative values include None, Encryption (only), and Validation. The timeout value, by default, is set to 30 minutes, and, like ASP.NET sessions, is a sliding value updated with each request. The default path is simply "/".

Before authentication can take place, however, the Web site must be configured to allow or deny access to certain resources. This is accomplished through the authorization element in Web.config, which instructs ASP.NET to use URL authorization implemented by the URLAuthorizationModule class.

By default, all users are allowed to access ASP.NET resources, although specific users and roles can be granted and denied access by adding allow and deny child elements as shown in the following code:

```
<authorization>
<allow users="*" />
    <!-- Allow all users -->
    <!-- <allow users="[comma separated list of users]"
        roles="[comma separated list of roles]"/>
        <deny users="[comma separated list of users]"
        roles="[comma separated list of roles]"/> -->
</authorization>
```

In the Quilogy example, all users (including unauthenticated users) should have access to a core set of services, including the home page, to be able to query for class schedules. However, only authenticated users can view their transcript and register for a class. To restrict only a subset of pages, you can place them in a subdirectory and include a Web.config file in the directory that denies access. In this case, the restricted subdirectory contains the Register.aspx and Transcript.aspx pages in addition to the Web.config file shown here:

```
<?xml version="1.0" encoding="utf-8" ?>
<configuration>
    <system.web>
        <authorization>
            <deny users="?" /><!-- Deny anonymous -->
        </authorization>
    </system.web>
</configuration>
```

Because the processing of configuration information is hierarchical, the Web.config file need only contain settings that differ from the parent directory. Now, if a user clicks the Student Transcript link from the home page, he is automatically redirected to studentlogin.aspx as defined in the authentication tag.

After the login page has been redirected to, it can present a form to collect the user's credentials, as does the studentlogin.aspx page shown in Listings 10.9 and 10.10.

LISTING 10.9   The studentlogin.aspx page. This page (simplified) shows the Web Form used to collect credentials.

```
<%@ Page Language="vb" AutoEventWireup="false"
  Codebehind="studentlogin.aspx.vb" Inherits="QuilogyEducation.studentlogin"
  EnableSessionState="True"%>

<HTML>
  <HEAD>
<meta content="Microsoft Visual Studio.NET 7.0" name=GENERATOR>
<LINK href="supplemental/site.css" type=text/css rel=stylesheet>
  </HEAD>
<body MS_POSITIONING="GridLayout">
<!-- #include file="navbar.htm" -->
<TABLE cellSpacing=0 cellPadding=0 width="100%" border=0>
  <TR>
    <TD align=left bgColor=#f3f0de>
      <TABLE cellSpacing=0 cellPadding=0 width=740 border=0>
        <TR>
          <TD vAlign=center align=left width=211><IMG height=45
              src="supplemental/services-maineducation.gif"
              width=211 border=0 ></TD>
        <TD width=529>
          <form id=studentlogin method=post
          runat="server">
          <TABLE cellSpacing=0 align=center bgColor=#f3f0d>
            <tr>
              <td class=body-copy>
                <div id=txtMessage runat="server">Enter
                your Email address and password to login</DIV></TD></TR>
            <tr>
              <TD class=body-copy><B
                >Email Address: </B></TD>
              <TD><ASP:TEXTBOX id=txtEmail runat="server"></ASP:TextBox>
              </TD></TR>
            <TR>
              <TD class=body-copy><B
                >Password: </B></TD>
```

LISTING 10.9   Continued

```
                <TD><ASP:TEXTBOX id=txtPass runat="server" TextMode="Password">
                    </ASP:TextBox></TD></TR>
            <TR>
                <TD class=caption>Forgot your password?
                  Click <A href="Forgot.aspx" >here</A></TD>
                <TD><ASP:BUTTON id=cmdLogin runat="server" text="Submit">
                    </ASP:Button></TD></TR></TABLE></FORM></TD></TR>
      <!-- #include file="bottombar.htm" --></TABLE></TD></TR></TABLE>
</body>
</HTML>
```

LISTING 10.10   The studentlogin.aspx.vb file. This file contains the code used to log in a student using Forms Authentication.

```
Imports System.Drawing
Imports System.Web.UI.WebControls
Imports System.Web.UI.HtmlControls
Imports Quilogy.Education
Imports Quilogy.Education.Enrollment
Imports System.Configuration
Imports System.Web.Security

Public Class studentlogin
    Inherits System.Web.UI.Page
    Protected WithEvents txtPass As System.Web.UI.WebControls.TextBox
    Protected WithEvents txtEmail As System.Web.UI.WebControls.TextBox
    Protected WithEvents txtMessage As _
      System.Web.UI.HtmlControls.HtmlGenericControl
    Protected WithEvents cmdLogin As System.Web.UI.WebControls.Button

    Private Sub InitializeComponent()
    End Sub

    Protected Sub Page_Init(ByVal Sender As System.Object, _
      ByVal e As System.EventArgs) Handles MyBase.Init
        'CODEGEN: This method call is required by the Web Form Designer
        'Do not modify it using the code editor.
        InitializeComponent()
    End Sub

    Protected Sub cmdLogin_Click(ByVal sender As System.Object, _
      ByVal e As System.EventArgs) _
      Handles cmdLogin.Click
        Dim dsStud As StudentData
```

LISTING 10.10   Continued

```
        Dim oStud As New Students( _
          ConfigurationSettings.AppSettings("SQLConnect").ToString)
        Dim dr As DataRow

        Try
            dsStud = oStud.Login(txtEmail().Text, txtPass().Text)
            If dsStud.StudentTable.Rows.Count > 0 Then
                ' Success, so set the session level variables accordingly
                dr = dsStud.StudentTable.Rows(0)
                Session("StudentData") = dsStud
                Session("StudentID") = dr(dsStud.STUDENT_ID)
                Session("StudentName") = dr(dsStud.FIRST_NAME).ToString & _
                  " " & dr(dsStud.LAST_NAME).ToString

                ' Manually authenticate
                FormsAuthentication.SetAuthCookie(txtEmail.Text, False)

                ' Authenticated so send them to requested URL
                If InStr(FormsAuthentication.GetRedirectUrl( _
                        txtEmail.Text, False),"default.aspx") > 0 Then
                    Response().Redirect("\QuilogyEducation\QEducation.aspx")
                Else
                    FormsAuthentication.RedirectFromLoginPage(txtEmail.Text, _
                     False)
                End If

            Else
                txtPass().Text = ""
                txtMessage().InnerText = "Login unsuccessful"
            End If
        Catch Ex As Exception
            txtPass().Text = ""
            txtMessage().InnerText = "Login unsuccessful: " & Ex.Message
        End Try

    End Sub

End Class
```

Notice that the page simply presents two Web server `TextBox` controls to collect the e-mail address and password and a `Button` to implement the login button. When the login button is clicked, the form is posted and the `cmdLogin_Click` procedure is executed.

Because the method used to validate a student's e-mail address and password against the database is implemented by a method of the `Students` class, a `Student` object is created and passed the connection string stored in the configuration file. The `Login` method then is called, which, if validated, returns a `StudentData DataSet` object. The `DataSet` is populated with the student's profile information. By checking the number of rows returned, the procedure can determine whether the student exists. If so, the `StudentID` and name are extracted from the `DataSet` and placed into `Session` level variables that are used in other pages within the application.

The interaction with the forms authentication module occurs when the procedure uses the `SetAuthCookie` method of the `FormsAuthentication` class to instruct the module to construct an authentication ticket (represented by the `FormsAuthenticationTicket` class) and send it to the browser on the next response.

TIP

The second argument to `SetAuthCookie` is set to `False`, indicating that the cookie should be retained in the browser's memory and not persisted to disk. A common technique is to add a check box to the login page to prompt the user to have the site "remember me." If so, you can set the argument to `True`, and on subsequent visits to the site, retrieve the username (in this case the e-mail address) from the `Context. User.Identity.Name` property in the `Session_Start` event of the Global.asax file. Alternatively, you can cast the `Identity` object to `FormsIdentity` and retrieve the information from its `Ticket` property. In addition, you might want to place your own cookies on the client with additional information using the `Response.Cookies` collection.

Calling this method is only necessary if the login page was navigated to directly, and not automatically, as a result of a redirect by the `FormsAuthenticationModule`. In other words, the cookie is created automatically if the `FormsAuthenticationModule` redirects the user to the login page, so calling `SetAuthCookie` is not required. However, in this case, because the login page is an unprotected resource, the user can navigate to it freely, and the authentication module will not know that it is to construct the cookie unless it is specified programmatically.

NOTE

Another use for `SetAuthCookie` occurs in the studentprofile.aspx page where new users can fill in their profile information and save it to the database. The process creates a default password and then authenticates the user using the `SetAuthCookie` method. In this way, new users are not required to re-login after they complete the profile.

The `FormsAuthentication` class is a helper class that contains a collection of shared methods as shown in Table 10.4.

TABLE 10.4   FormsAuthentication Helper Class Methods

Method	Description
Authenticate	Attempts to validate the given name and password against credentials stored in the configuration file.
Decrypt	Given an encrypted ticket from the GetAuthCookie method, it returns an unencrypted FormsAuthenticationTicket object.
Encrypt	Given a FormsAuthenticationTicket, it produces an encrypted string suitable for use in the cookie.
GetAuthCookie	Returns the encrypted HttpCookie object.
GetRedirectUrl	Returns the URL the user was originally navigating to before being redirected to the login page.
HashPasswordForStoringInConfigFile	Given the password and a string identifying the hash type, returns a hash password you can store in a configuration file.
Initialize	Reads the configuration information and gets cookie values and encryption keys.
RedirectFromLoginPage	Redirects the user to the originally requested page.
RenewTicketIfOld	Renews the ticket if more than half-way to its expiration.
SetAuthCookie	Given a username, it creates a ticket sent to the browser in the next response. Also can specify whether the cookie is to be persistent.
SignOut	Removes the authentication ticket.

The procedure then invokes the `GetRedirectFromUrl` method to determine whether the user navigated to the login page directly, or was redirected there by the authentication process. If the former is the case, the method returns "default.aspx," and the user is manually redirected to the home page using `Response.Redirect`. If the user originally requested another page (such as the transcript), the `RedirectFromLoginPage` method performs the redirection.

10

At this point, the cookie is sent to the browser and the user is authenticated. As you would expect, the `HttpContext` object is populated with a `FormsIdentity` object (which implements `IIdentity`) exposed through the `Identity` property of the `User` object. The `FormsIdentity` object only extends the interface by adding a `Ticket` property, which returns the `FormsAuthenticationTicket` object associated with the request. The `Name` and `AuthenticationType` properties are, not surprisingly, set to the name passed into `SetAuthCookie` (e-mail address in this case) and "Forms," respectively. As with the other forms of authentication, a `FormsAuthentication_OnAuthenticate` method can be added to the Global.asax file to customize the authentication process.

> **NOTE**
>
> As you might have gathered, in this case, the user's password is captured in an HTML form and is transmitted as clear text to the Web server. In some applications that expose sensitive data, this might be a security concern. One way around this is to protect the login page using HTTPS. Note that the authentication ticket itself is encrypted by default, so subsequent requests are secure.

Although for most scenarios you'll want to store the association of usernames to passwords in a database accessed through the data services tier, Forms Authentication also supports authentication against credentials stored in the configuration file. By placing a `credentials` element inside the `forms` element, you can embed user elements that include `name` and `password` attributes. The `credentials` element also must include a `passwordFormat` attribute that indicates how the passwords are stored. For example, the following `forms` element contains the credentials for three users with their passwords stored as a SHA1 hash digest:

```
<forms loginUrl="studentlogin.aspx" >
  <credentials passwordformat="SHA1" >
    <user name="Willie" password="GASDFSA9823598ASDBAD"/>
    <user name="Mickey" password="ZASDFADSFASD23483142"/>
    <user name="Duke" password="HASDFADSFASD23483367"/>
  </credentials>
</forms>
```

To authenticate against these credentials, the `Authenticate` method of the `FormsAuthenticationClass` can be passed the name and password.

> **TIP**
>
> To create hashed passwords for storing in configuration files, you can write your own utility using the `HashPasswordForStoringInConfigFile` method of the `FormsAuthentication` class.

State Management

Perhaps one of the most significant changes in ASP.NET from ASP is the way that state can be managed. The stateless nature of HTTP makes this an important topic, so the more services the ASP.NET infrastructure provides in this area, the more seamless the programming model becomes.

This section explores how state information can be saved using the State Bag, `Session` state, and `Application` state.

State Bag

As already mentioned, ASP.NET tracks a certain amount of state information automatically through the view state of Web Forms. Particularly, the properties of the `Page` object itself, and the server controls, are represented in the hidden `__VIEWSTATE` control on the page in the browser, and the `ViewState` property of the `Page` object.

Although this is great for controls, when an ASP.NET page is loaded or posted back to the server, the page is reconstructed and re-executed from scratch. In other words, if your `Page` class contains class-level variables or custom properties, these are not saved in the `ViewState`. To add custom information to the `ViewState`, you can programmatically manipulate the underlying `StateBag` object.

The `StateBag` class is found in the `System.Web.UI` namespace and simply exposes a collection of `StateItem` objects by implementing the `ICollection`, `IDictionary`, and `IEnumerable` interfaces. You can add items to the `StateBag` of a page by simply calling the `Add` method and providing the key and the value as arguments. For example, the Schedule.aspx page is used in the Quilogy example site to display the requested class schedule based on the user's selections. The page populates a Web server `DataGrid` to display the results.

To allow the user to sort the list by course, date, and so on, the page posts a server event that reloads the grid and sorts the data. Although working with the `DataGrid` will be covered in more detail later in the chapter, the page also implements a toggle on the sort. The first time the user clicks a column, it will be sorted in ascending order; if clicked a second time, it will be sorted in descending order. To implement this feature, the page must remember what column was previously sorted and in what order.

To add this information to the `ViewState`, the method that populates the grid contains the following code:

```
' Add to the state bag if not already present
If Me.ViewState("SortField") Is Nothing Then
    Me.ViewState.Add("SortField", pSort)
    Me.ViewState.Add("SortDesc", True) ' default to true so first time is ASC
End If
```

```
' Toggle the sort if we're clicking on the same column
If pSort <> "" And pSort = Me.ViewState("SortField").ToString Then
    flDesc = Not Me.ViewState("SortDesc")
    If flDesc Then
        pSort = pSort & " DESC"
    Else
        pSort = pSort & " ASC"
    End If
End If

' Set the field and order in the StateBag
Me.ViewState("SortDesc") = flDesc
Me.ViewState("SortField") = pSort
```

Note that the code first checks to determine whether a "SortField" key exists in the StateBag exposed through the ViewState property of the Page class. If not, the keys are created and populated with the column that is to be sorted and the default sort order (ascending in this case). The new column to sort on is then compared with the information in the StateBag, and, if equal, the sort order is toggled. Finally, the new column and sort order are placed back in the StateBag.

Using the StateBag in this way has several advantages over Session state. Particularly, there is less overhead involved because the values are not persisted anywhere and simply travel with the form. In addition, the StateBag promotes information hiding because only this particular Web Form needs to see these values. In classic ASP, you would have had to create your own state bag-like implementation using hidden form fields, or you would have had to use the Session object.

Session State

The stateless nature of HTTP makes the inclusion of a mechanism to save state between user requests a must. Unfortunately, the implementation of the Session object in classic ASP has two main weaknesses. First, the 120-bit SessionID used to identify the session is always stored as a cookie on the browser. Therefore, if, for example, the security policy of a user's employer disallows cookies, the Session object can not be populated.

Second, the data associated with the session and accessed through the SessionID is stored on the Web server that processed the initial request and started the session. As a result, the session data can not be shared in a Web farm scenario where multiple Web servers are processing requests from multiple clients. Although programmatic techniques and system software such as the Windows 2000 clustering services and Application Center 2000 can be configured to force a client to access the same Web server for each request, the overhead and possible imbalance that this situation creates reduces scalability.

> **TIP**
>
> As with classic ASP, tracking session state requires overhead, so if a particular page will not be accessing the `Session` object, you should set the `EnableSessionState` attribute of the `Page` directive to `False`. You also can turn off session state for the entire site by setting the mode attribute of the `sessionState` element to `Off` in Web.config.

Fortunately, the ASP.NET session implementation addresses both of these weaknesses.

As mentioned previously in this chapter, the `Session` object itself is implemented through the `SessionStateModule` class derived from the `IHttpModule` interface. By default, it is included as a part of the HTTP request and configured in the `httpModules` element of the Machine.config file like so:

```
<httpModules>
    <add name="Session"
       type="System.Web.SessionState.SessionStateModule,System.Web" />
</httpModules>
```

This class is responsible for creating `SessionID`s and managing the session state using an instance of the `HttpSessionState` class. The object is then attached to the `HttpContext` object and exposed through the `Session` property. As in other situations, classes such as `Page` also expose the `Session` property that points to the `HttpSessionState` object.

> **NOTE**
>
> As in classic ASP, the Global.asax file includes `Session_OnStart` and `Session_OnEnd` methods to intercept the `Start` and `End` events of the `SessionStateModule`.

The interesting aspect of this architecture is that by abstracting the management of session state into a separate module, it can be expanded to include more capabilities. The attributes that specify which capabilities the `SessionStateModule` should use are defined in the Web.config file under the `sessionState` element.

By default, sessions in ASP.NET are configured in the same way as classic ASP; that is, an in-memory cookie is sent to the browser that contains the `SessionID`, the session data itself is stored in the memory of the server that initiated the session, and the session timeout is set to 20 minutes. As a result, the Web.config file will look like the following:

```
<sessionState mode="InProc" cookieless="false" timeout="20" />
```

Note that the mode attribute is set to InProc to indicate that the session state is stored in memory by ASP.NET.

Cookieless Sessions

To change these settings, you simply need to alter the Web.config file. By setting the cookieless attribute to True, ASP.NET no longer sends a cookie, but creates a new server variable called HTTP_ASPFILTERSESSIONID and populates it with the SessionID. The SessionID is then inserted into the query string. For example, after a session is established, a call to one of the ASP.NET pages in the Quilogy sample site would look like the following:

```
http://ssosa/QuilogyEducation/(12mfju55vgblubjlwsi4dgjq)/qeducation.aspx
```

The SessionStateModule then extracts the SessionID from the query string and associates the user request with the appropriate session. In this way, cookies are not required, nor are hidden form fields, so that pages without forms can still participate in the session.

> **NOTE**
>
> Using a cookieless session has no impact on where the session data is stored, only on how it is accessed.

SQL Server Storage

To address the storage of session data, the mode attribute of the sessionState element in Web.config can be set to "SqlServer." When this is set, the SessionStateModule attempts to store session data on the SQL Server pointed at by the sqlConnectionString attribute. This attribute should contain the data source and security credentials necessary to log on to the server. The Web.config file for the Quilogy sample application looks like the following:

```
<sessionState mode="SQLServer"
    sqlConnectionString="data source=ssosa;
    trusted_connection=yes;pooling=true" cookieless="false"
    timeout="20" />
```

> **NOTE**
>
> Depending on how SQL Server is configured, both Windows and SQL Server authentication are supported. Placing the parameter "trusted_connection=yes" in the connection string instructs ASP.NET to connect to SQL Server using Windows authentication. Note, however, that if impersonation is enabled, the access token passed from IIS to ASP.NET is used to attempt to log in to SQL Server. If IIS is configured for anonymous access, this will be the IUSR_server account, and it would need

permissions in SQL Server. If impersonation is not enabled, the account of the ASP.NET runtime process (aspnet_wp.exe) is used, (which by default is SYSTEM and has system administrator rights in SQL Server). It is recommended that you enable both forms of authentication on SQL Server and create a specific SQL Server account to use for the SessionStateModule with the appropriate permissions. Session state also can take advantage of connection pooling, a setting that is recommended.

To configure the SQL Server with the appropriate objects, you also need to run the install script found in the *windowsdir*\Microsoft.Net\Framework*version*\config directory. By executing this script, an ASPState database and the appropriate stored procedures are created on the SQL Server.

The script also creates a scheduled job to be executed by the SQL Server Agent service that runs by default every minute. This job deletes all the expired sessions from the database. Obviously, this job can be modified to run less frequently to reduce database conflicts.

CAUTION

Because you cannot specify the name of the database to use within SQL Server for storing state (it must be called ASPState), Application Service Providers (ASPs) would need to install separate instances of SQL Server for each client if they want to provide full isolation between client Web sites.

When configured, the application code should run identically. However, keep in mind that the SessionStateModule serializes all the data in the session's collections at the end of each Web request using the .NET serialization services discussed in Chapter 8. This serialized data is then saved to the database. On each new request, the data is read from the database and deserialized into the appropriate objects. This implies that all objects saved in the Session object's collections must be able to be serialized and deserialized. Also, it is apparent that storing many or large objects in session state increases the amount of database traffic.

TIP

To see the additional traffic generated by storing session data on SQL Server, use the SQL Profiler utility to record the traffic.

Obviously, storing session state in the database is a trade-off of scalability and reliability over performance in the following ways:

- Session data decoupled from the Web server can be easily shared across servers in a Web farm, thereby increasing scalability.

- Session data stored on a separate machine is not lost when the application crashes or is restarted.

- Session data stored separately from ASP.NET worker processes can be accessed by multiple processors concurrently, thereby eliminating cross-processor lock contention.

- Session data stored separately from the Web server does not impact the memory requirements of the Web server as does in-process storage.

If none of the previous considerations are relevant to your application, use the in-process setting because it performs better.

State Server

In addition to storing session data in a SQL Server, ASP.NET also provides for storing data in a separate in-memory cache controlled by a Windows service. The service is called the ASP.NET State service (aspnet_state.exe), and can be run either on the same machine as the Web server, or on a separate machine. To use the service, the `mode` attribute of the `sessionState` element in Web.config is set to `"StateServer"`, and the `stateConnectionString` attribute must include the server and port used to connect to the service like so:

```
<sessionState mode="StateServer" stateConnectionString="tcpip=ssosa:42424"
    cookieless="false" timeout="20" />
```

In this case, the state service is running on a machine called "ssosa" at the port 42424, which is the default. The port can be configured at the server by modifying the `Port` value in the `aspnet_state` registry key under the `HKLM\SYSTEM\CurrentControlSet\Services`.

Obviously, using the state service has the same advantage of process isolation and sharability across a Web farm. However, if the state service is stopped, all session data is lost. In other words, the state service does not persistently store the data as does SQL Server; it simply holds it in memory.

Application State

It should be noted that as in classic ASP, application level state is supported in ASP.NET. It is implemented by the creation of an `HttpApplicationState` object the first time a resource is requested for the virtual directory. This object then is attached to the `HttpContext`, and made available throughout the Web request through the `Application` property. As a result, even custom HTTP Modules can manipulate the application state.

However, unlike the SessionStateModule, the application state is not shared between servers. Each Web server creates its own HttpApplicationState object. This implies that application state is best used as a read-only cache of data and not to store data that the users might change. For example, a good use of application state is to cache DataSet objects that contain infrequently updated data such as state and country lists. Each server within a Web farm can then read the data on demand (or in the Application_OnStart event) and populate its own cache.

In addition, because data in the HttpApplicationState object can be accessed concurrently by more than one thread, it supports the familiar Lock and Unlock methods to synchronize access. For example, the following code locks the states variable while it is being populated:

```
Context.Application.Lock()
    Dim ds As DataSet
    ' Populate DataSet…
    Context.Application("StateList") = ds
Context.Application.UnLock()
```

Both the HttpApplicationState and SessionStateModule classes support the declaration of static objects in the Global.asax file. In other words, you can declare an object with the object tag inside the Global.asax file like so:

```
<OBJECT RUNAT=SERVER SCOPE=APPLICATION ID="Utils" PROGID="Quilogy.Utils" />
```

In this case, the Quilogy.Utils class can be referenced using the StaticObjects collection of the HttpApplicationState object.

Caching

One of the tried-and-true techniques used in a variety of scenarios to improve performance is to cache frequently used items in memory. ASP.NET builds on the caching behavior of browsers, proxy servers, and Web servers to provide two types of caching behavior that you can take advantage of in your applications: caching page output and a caching engine.

Page Output Caching

The first type of caching that you can use involves caching page output. This can be useful in scenarios where the page output is built through an expensive database query or other server-side code. You can implement this type of caching using either the OutputCache page directive, or programmatically modifying the HttpCachePolicy object through the Cache property of the HttpResponse (Response) object.

To use the page directive, simply add the directive at the top of the page along with attributes that minimally specify the duration and the location where caching takes place:

```
<@ OutputCache Duration="60" Location="Server" >
```

In this example, the page can only be cached by the server and will be cached for 60 seconds. Behind the scenes, the ASP.NET uses the `InitOutputCache` method of the `Page` object to set the caching options and in this case translates them to the following calls:

```
Response.Cache.SetExpires(DateTime.Now.AddSeconds(60))
Response.Cache.SetCacheability(HttpCacheability.Server)
```

The `HttpCacheability` enumeration also supports `NoCache`, `Private`, and `Public` constants to indicate that no caching will occur, that caching can only occur on the client (browser), and that caching can occur on clients and proxy servers. Each of these sets the Cache-Control HTTP header to the appropriate value.

TIP

You also can call the `SetSlidingExpiration` method and pass it `True` to renew the Cache-Control HTTP header with each response. This is equivalent to setting the Enable Content Expiration option for the page in the Internet Services Manager.

The caching options also allow you to cache multiple versions of the same page by using the `VaryByHeader` and `VaryByParam` attributes. For example, the `VaryByHeader` attribute can be set to allow a version of the page to be cached for each type of browser using the `UserAgent` value like so:

```
<@ OutputCache Duration="60" Location="Server" VaryByHeader="UserAgent" >
```

In turn, this translates to

```
Imports System.Web
Dim o As HttpCacheVaryByHeaders
o = Me.Response.Cache.VaryByHeaders
o.UserAgent = True
```

Similarly, `VaryByParam` can be used to store multiple versions of the same page based on the query string or form POST parameters. For example, if a page is called with `Vendor`, `Location`, and `Advance` parameters in the query string, multiple versions of the page can be cached using the directive:

```
<@ OutputCache Duration="60" Location="Server"
  VaryByParam="Vendor;Location;Advance" >
```

Note that an asterisk can be used to denote all parameters as well.

> **TIP**
>
> You also can include a `VaryByCustom` attribute that allows you to specify that multiple versions of the page are cached based on custom attributes of the browser that you define in the Global.asax file by overriding the `GetVaryByCustomString` method. For more information, see the online help.

In addition to caching full page output, you also can cache partial page output. This is accomplished by creating a Web Forms user control (discussed later in the chapter) and placing the `OutputCache` directive at the top of the control. In this way, for example, the portion of the page that performs intensive database queries can be cached while the remainder of the page can be reprocessed with each request.

In addition to using the `VaryByParam` attribute (which is required) on a user control, you also can use the `VaryByControl` attribute. This attribute specifies a semicolon-delimited list of custom properties that, if unique, results in the output for the control to be cached.

Caching Engine

The second way that you can cache information is to use, for lack of a better term, the caching engine. This cache, implemented by the `Cache` object in the `System.Web.Caching` namespace, can be accessed through the `Cache` property of the `HttpContext` object. The `Cache` class is implemented as a typical dictionary-type object that includes `Add`, `Insert`, `Remove`, `Count`, and `Item` properties that you can use to manipulate the items in the cache.

The cache is application-wide, so any items you add to it are available to any client using the application. As a result, you need to make sure that items are uniquely identified if you're going to use them to store user-specific information.

> **CAUTION**
>
> ASP.NET uses the cache to store some of its own information with the key prefixed with "System." Do not tamper with these items.

Although at the surface it appears that the cache is simply a service analogous to the `HttpApplicationState` object, the interesting aspect of the cache is that it includes the capability to age-out its items, invoke a callback method when an item is removed, and create dependencies between items. For example, consider the following code:

```
Imports System.Web.Caching
Dim strData As String
Dim onRemove = New CacheItemRemovedCallback(AddressOf MyDataGone)

Context.Cache.Add("MyData", strData, _
    New CacheDependency(Server.MapPath("\\myServer\myData.xml")), _
    Cache.NoAbsoluteExpiration, TimeSpan.FromSeconds(30), _
    CacheItemPriority.High, CacheItemPriorityDecay.Never, onRemove)
```

In this example, the `Add` method of the `Cache` object is used to add a string identified with the "MyData" key to the cache. Typically, you'll use the `Insert` method because the `Add` method is not overloaded and therefore requires all the arguments.

In this case, a dependency is created on MyData to an external XML file called myData.xml. This means that the item will be removed from the cache if the file moves or is deleted. The MyData item does not expire at a certain date as indicated by the `NoAbsoluteExpiration` property of the `Cache` class but does expire in 30 seconds. Its `CacheItemPriority` is set to `High` to indicate that it is least likely to be purged as a result of the system freeing memory by deleting items from the cache. The values in this enumeration form a sliding scale including `NotRemoveable`, `High`, `AboveNormal`, `Normal` (Default), `BelowNormal`, and `Low`. As items remain in the cache, their priorities can change depending on how frequently they are accessed. The `CacheItemPriorityDecay` defines how fast the decay occurs and can be set to `Never`, `Slow`, `Medium` (Default), and `Fast`. In this case, the priority does not change. The last argument specifies an optional delegate of type `CacheItemRemoved` that will be invoked when the item is removed from the cache. The signature of the method `MyDataGone` used to catch the invocation is as follows:

```
Imports System.Web.Caching
Public Sub MyDataGone(ByVal key As String, ByVal value As Object, _
    ByVal r As CacheItemRemovedReason)
    ' Repopulate the cached item
End Sub
```

The `CacheItemRemovedReason` enumeration passed as an argument to the method indicates why the item was removed and can return `DependencyChanged`, `Expired`, `Removed`, or `Underused`.

TIP

In both the `Add` and `Insert` methods of the `Cache` class, the *slidingExpiration* parameter (the fifth parameter in the `Add` method shown in the previous code example) optionally can be set to `TimeSpan.Zero` or `Cache.NoSlidingExpiration`. In both cases, the cached item then expires in accordance with the *absolutateExpiration* parameter.

One interesting use of the cache can be to simulate a timer on the Web Form to ensure that a user responds within a certain time period. For example, in the Quilogy education site, an authenticated user can query for a class schedule and click a link to sign up for the class. The Register.aspx page is then invoked, which calculates the cost of the class and presents the user with a confirmation page with the class information and cost. Behind the scenes, the page places the cost in the cache with a key that is the student ID from the database. This occurs in the page's Load event, as shown in Listing 10.11.

LISTING 10.11   Caching the Price. The Load event of the Register.aspx page determines the class price and places it in the cache.

```
Imports Quilogy.Education.Enrollment
Imports Quilogy.Education
Imports Quilogy.Education.Schedule
Imports System.Configuration
Imports System.Web.Caching
Private Sub Page_Load(ByVal sender As System.Object, _
  ByVal e As System.EventArgs) Handles MyBase.Load
    ' Load the controls

   If Not Me.IsPostBack Then
       If Request("ClassID") Is Nothing Then
           txtWho.InnerText = "No class was picked. Search again"
           txtWho.Style.Item("Color") = "Red"
           Return
       End If

       ' Now display the class
       txtWhen.InnerText = Request("When").ToString
       txtCourse.InnerText = Request("Course").ToString
       txtWho.InnerText = Session("StudentName").ToString

       ' Calculate the cost for display
       Dim oClasses As New Classes( _
         ConfigurationSettings.AppSettings("SQLConnect"))
       Dim decCost As Decimal
       decCost = oClasses.CalcCost(Request("ClassID"), RegistrationType.Web)
       txtCost.InnerText = FormatCurrency(decCost, 0, TriState.False, _
         TriState.False, TriState.False)

       ' Add the quote to the cache
       Cache.Insert(Session("StudentID"), decCost, Nothing, _
         Cache.NoAbsoluteExpiration, TimeSpan.FromSeconds(20))
    End If

End Sub
```

Notice that the cost of the class is calculated based on the particular `ClassID` and the registration type. In this case, registering on the Web triggers a discount. The cost actually is placed in the cache using one of the overloaded `Insert` methods with a timeout period set to 20 seconds. Figure 10.3 shows the registration page.

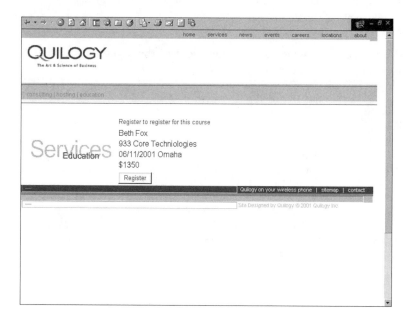

FIGURE 10.3

The Student Confirmation page presents the user with the information regarding her registration and allows her to click Register to actually register.

When the user clicks the Register button, the Web Form is posted to the server, and the `cmdSubmit_Click` event procedure is invoked, as shown in Listing 10.12.

LISTING 10.12   Checking the Cache. This procedure is invoked when the user clicks the Register button. It checks the cache and displays an expired message if the item no longer exists.

```
Imports Quilogy.Education.Enrollment
Imports Quilogy.Education
Imports Quilogy.Education.Schedule
Imports System.Configuration
Imports System.Web.Caching
Private Sub cmdSubmit_Click(ByVal sender As System.Object, _
```

Listing 10.12   Continued

```vb
ByVal e As System.EventArgs) Handles cmdSubmit.Click
    Dim oReg As Registration
    Dim dsEnroll As New EnrollmentData()
    Dim dr As DataRow
    Dim drStud As DataRow
    Dim intEnrollID As Integer

    ' First make sure the course quote has not expired
    If Cache(Session("StudentID")) Is Nothing Then
        txtMessage.InnerText = "Sorry. The price quote has expired. " & _
            "Please reselect your class and register within 20 seconds."
        cmdSubmit.Visible = False
        Return
    End If

    ' Would redirect here to process payment type
    ' and then insert the enrollment

    Try
        oReg = New Registration( _
          ConfigurationSettings.AppSettings("SQLConnect"))
        ' Build the enrollment DataSet
        dr = dsEnroll.EnrollmentTable.NewRow
        dr(dsEnroll.CLASS_ID) = Request("ClassID")
        dr(dsEnroll.WEB_ENROLL) = "Y"
        dr(dsEnroll.PAYMENT_TYPE) = "CC"
        dsEnroll.EnrollmentTable.Rows.Add(dr)
        drStud = dsEnroll.Tables("Student").NewRow
        drStud(EnrollmentData.STUDENT_ID) = Session("StudentID")
        ' Placeholder since it cannot be null
        drStud(EnrollmentData.LAST_NAME) = "Dummy"
        dsEnroll.Tables("Student").Rows.Add(drStud)
        drStud.SetParentRow(dr)

        ' Register the Student
        intEnrollID = oReg.RegisterStudent(dsEnroll)
        If intEnrollID > 0 Then
            txtMessage.InnerText = "Registration Successful. Thanks"
            cmdSubmit.Visible = False
        End If

    Catch Ex As Exception
        txtMessage.InnerText = "An error occurred: " & Ex.Message
        txtMessage.Style.Item("Color") = "Red"
```

LISTING 10.12   Continued

```
    End Try

End Sub
```

This procedure first checks the cache to determine whether the student's item is there and, if not, whether the item was removed. In this case, a message is displayed indicating that the price quote has expired and the Register button is made invisible. If the quote has not expired, the procedure builds an `EnrollmentData` `DataSet` and uses the `Registration` class to add the enrollment by calling the `RegisterStudent` method.

Tracing

To assist in debugging and creating a performance profile of your applications, ASP.NET includes an intrinsic `TraceContext` object found in the `System.Web` namespace that stores information about each request. This object is attached to the `HttpContext` object and exposed through the `Trace` property. As a result, it also is available through the `Trace` property of the `Page` object.

Simply put, the `TraceContext` object collects information on each method executed as the page is processed along with timings, a control tree that shows each server control processed and how many bytes it rendered, the cookies collection, the HTTP headers collection, and the server variables. A full description of each of the sections and the information presented can be found in the online help. All this information can be displayed either at the bottom of a page or on its own page by requesting the Trace Viewer page for the application like so:

```
http://ssosa/QuilogyEducation/Trace.axd
```

> **NOTE**
>
> The Trace.axd file is handled by a special `httpHandler` configured in the Machine.config file.

The simplest way to show trace information for a specific page is to add the `Trace` attribute to the `Page` directive and set it to "True". All the trace information will then be streamed to the browser after the page has been processed.

> **TIP**
>
> This is the equivalent of setting the `IsEnabled` property of the `TraceContext` object to `True`.

To configure tracing at the application level, you can include the `trace` element in the Web.config file like so:

```
<trace enabled="true" requestLimit="40" pageOutput="false"
    traceMode="SortByTime" localOnly="true" />
```

This configuration indicates that tracing is enabled and `pageOutput` is set to `False`, so trace information will be accessible through the .axd file even if the `Page` directive is not modified. In addition, up to 40 requests will be cached and the Trace Viewer will only be accessible on the host Web server. The `traceMode` attribute specifies how custom trace information is displayed in the page.

Custom trace information can be written to the page using the `Write` and `Warn` methods of the `TraceContext` object. Both of these methods are overloaded and support an argument that can contain a user-defined category to more easily categorize messages. The only difference between the methods is that `Warn` writes the text in red. Typically, you'll use tracing in the same way that ASP developers use `Response.Write`—that is, to check for the existence of particular values to debug their code. For example, in Listing 10.12, a trace message might be written to ensure that the cost made it into the cache like so:

```
Context.Trace.Write("Cache", "Cache=" & Cache(Session("StudentID")))
```

This information then appears in the Trace Information section of trace output as shown in Figure 10.4.

> **TIP**
>
> Along these same lines, keep in mind that you can debug a Web application in VB.NET in the same way that you debug a forms application by using breakpoints, watches, and so on. However, when you deploy the application, be sure to turn off debugging by setting the `debug` attribute of the `compilation` element of the Web.config file to `False`.

10

BUILDING WEB FORMS

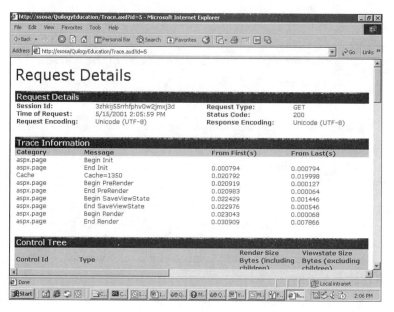

FIGURE 10.4

Application-level trace output—note that the Trace.Write *output appears after the initialization event.*

ASP.NET Server Controls

Perhaps the aspect of ASP.NET that provides the most benefit to developers is the inclusion of server controls. Obviously, the use of controls should be familiar to VB developers who have long benefited from the rapid application development and reuse that comes with taking advantage of functionality encapsulated into controls. ASP.NET server controls rely on the event model and processing architecture discussed previously in the chapter to bring this same paradigm to Web development.

In fact, the architecture of server controls is so integral to ASP.NET that the Page class discussed in this chapter is ultimately derived from the base class System.Web.UI.Control. In this way, you can think of an ASP.NET page as simply another server control with additional functionality. As a result, the hierarchy of server controls can be broken down as shown in Figure 10.5.

As shown in Figure 10.5, five classes derive directly from Control. The TemplateControl class is an abstract base class from which both the Page and UserControl classes are derived. As will be discussed in this section, most of the interesting classes are descendants of the HtmlControl class, that map directly to HTML elements, and descendants of WebControl, which typically provide a richer interface (such as events) and do not necessarily map to HTML controls.

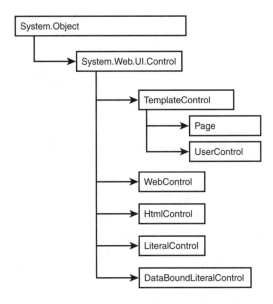

FIGURE 10.5

The ASP.NET server control hierarchy—note that the Page *class is actually a descendant of the* Control *class.*

> **NOTE**
>
> The LiteralControl class is used by ASP.NET during page processing to represent all HTML elements that do not have the runat=server attribute set. The DataBoundLiteralControl class represents those same elements, but allows the Text property of the element to be persisted in the view state. This is useful, as will be discussed later, when the <%# .. %> syntax is used to bind a value to an HTML element.

HTML Server Controls

As mentioned previously, any HTML element can be converted to an HTML server control either by placing the runat=server and ID attributes in the control, or by dragging the control onto the form from the toolbox. The advantage to doing so is that the view state of the control will get saved so that you can work with the control programmatically using dot notation within the code behind file. Typically, HTML server controls should be used when you're modifying existing HTML to run under ASP.NET, or when the control needs to interact with both client and server scripts.

> **TIP**
>
> Keep in mind that there is additional cost in converting HTML elements to server controls, and so it should be done only when working with the control on the server is required.

Sixteen HTML server controls that ship with ASP.NET map directly to HTML elements. These are shown in Figure 10.6. All these controls derive from `HtmlControl`, shown previously in Figure 10.5, and exist in the `System.Web.UI.HtmlControls` namespace. As you can see, the primary division for HTML server controls is between those derived from the abstract base classes `HtmlInputControl` and those derived from `HtmlContainerControl`. As implied by the names, `HtmlInputControl` is used as the base class for controls defined with the <input> tag in HTML, whereas `HtmlContainerControl` defines the members for controls that must have a closing tag such as <form>, <table>, and <tr>.

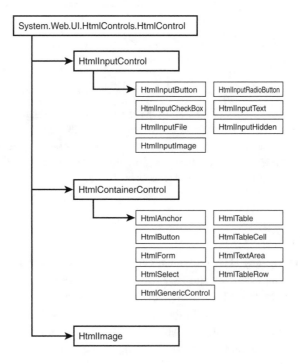

FIGURE 10.6

The inheritance hierarchy for HTML server controls. Note that all but one derive from `HtmlInputControl` *and* `HtmlContainerControl`.

Obviously, each of the controls exposes particular properties that you would expect for the type of control it is. For example, the HTML server control defined in the .aspx page as

```
<a href="http://www.quilogy.com " id="lnkQ">Go to Quilogy!</a>
```

is translated into an instance of the HtmlAnchor class that supports the Href property and the ServerClick event that allow for the interception of the click and the modification of the destination URL.

If the element does not map to any of the existing HTML server controls—for example the DIV element—the control is created using the HtmlGenericControl class. This class supports a generic set of properties and methods, the most important of which are InnerText, InnerHTML, and Style. Several of the pages in the Quilogy example application use a DIV tag called txtMessage in this way to display error and status information to the user.

Because not all the attributes of HTML elements (even those that map to HTML server controls) are exposed through the controls, each control inherits the Attributes collection from HtmlControl that exposes all the attributes set for the control in name-value pairs. For example, the HtmlInputText control does not expose the autocomplete attribute of the INPUT tag because it is a Microsoft extension to HTML. To set the property for a control named txtCity running in MSIE, the following line can be executed:

```
txtCity.Attributes("autocompete") = "yes"
```

If you want to revert an HTML server control to an HTML element, simply remove the runat=server attribute and be sure to delete the declaration of the control in the .vb file along with any references to it in the code. You must keep the ID attribute if the control is referred to by client-side script.

Extending HTML Server Controls

Because HTML server controls are implemented as managed classes, they can be extended through inheritance. For example, assume that you want to place a TEXTAREA control on the Register.aspx page to capture any user comments during the registration process. If you want to extend the HtmlTextArea control to include custom members or default certain properties, you can create an inherited control such as HtmlComments as follows:

```
Protected Class HtmlComments : Inherits HtmlTextArea
    Public Sub New()
        MyBase.New()

        ' Set the defaults
        MyBase.Rows = 10
        MyBase.Cols = 50
        MyBase.Value = "Enter your comments here"
    End Sub
```

```
    ' Add additional members or override members here
End Class
```

In this case, the control actually resides within the `Page` class and so is protected; it also can be compiled in its own assembly and reused in different applications.

However, for extended controls such as `HtmlComment` to be instantiated on the page, they must be created programmatically. Dynamic creation in this way often is useful when you don't know ahead of time how many controls must be displayed on a page.

NOTE

Some server controls such as `Repeater`, `DataList`, and `RadioButtonList` automatically render additional elements when the control is processed depending on how many rows are bound to it from a `DataSet`.

Programmatic creation is accomplished by creating an instance of the control and placing it in a container control. ASP.NET provides the Web server `Panel` and `PlaceHolder` controls to act as a container if no other container is appropriate. The `Panel` control can be added to the .aspx page and positioned appropriately. Both the `Panel` and the `HtmlComments` control in this case then are declared at the class level as follows:

```
Imports System.Web.UI.HtmlControls
Imports System.Web.UI.WebControls
Protected WithEvents InfoPanel As Panel
Protected WithEvents txtComments As HtmlComments
```

Within the `Load` event, you can then instantiate the `HtmlComments` control and add it to the `Controls` collection of the `Panel` control as follows:

```
txtComments = New HtmlComments()
InfoPanel.Controls.Add(txtComments)
```

The new `TEXTAREA` control with the defaulted properties then is displayed on the page. Controls added programmatically are automatically incorporated into the view state of the page, and will retain their properties when the form is posted to the server.

NOTE

A typical use for dynamic creation is to instantiate a `LiteralControl` object passing the element to be created in its constructor. The `LiteralControl` can be used to represent a static HTML element such as a horizontal rule (HR) or line break (BR). An alternative technique would be to issue a `Response.Write` from within the server code.

Web Server Controls

The second type of ASP.NET server control that you can use are Web server controls. These controls are found in the System.Web.UI.WebControls namespace, and are derived from the WebControl class or directly from System.Web.UI.Control, as shown in Figure 10.7.

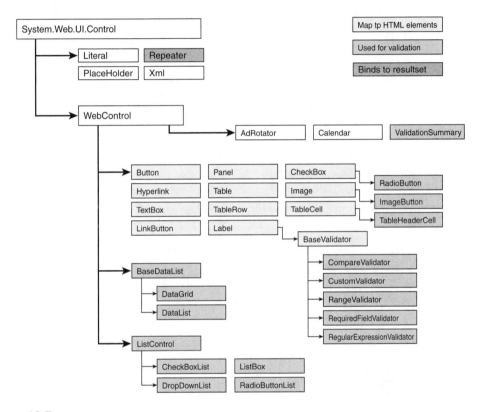

FIGURE 10.7

Web server control hierarchy.

The Literal, PlaceHolder, Repeater, and Xml controls are derived directly from Control. This is because these controls don't represent specific HTML elements, but rather contain or produce output from other controls.

Figure 10.7 also shows that certain Web server controls such as Button, Checkbox, Hyperlink, and so on, map directly to HTML elements, whereas others derived from BaseValidator are used to validate input. Still others have the capability to be bound to a DataSet or DataRepeater to display multiple rows of data. The AdRotator and Calendar controls are separate because they support other functionality using multiple elements.

Because space prohibits a discussion of each of the types of controls, this section focuses on the validation controls, data binding, using mobile controls, and building a Web server control used in the Quilogy sample application.

Using Validators

One of the most common requirements in a Web application is to validate user input. Unfortunately, in the past, this has been complicated because developers had to deal with where to perform the validation (client or server) in addition to possibly writing validation code in multiple languages (JavaScript or VBScript) depending on the targeted browsers. Fortunately, the Web server controls derived from `BaseValidator`, as shown in Figure 10.7, make this process almost effortless, and handle both browser issues and client versus server validation. In many respects, the validation controls are the quintessential example of the power of Web server controls.

As noted in Figure 10.7, six validation controls (not counting the base class `BaseValidator`) handle everything from making sure that a control is populated to handling custom validation code running on the server. To illustrate the use of these controls, the two pages in the Quilogy education example that require user input, the StudentLogin.aspx and StudentProfile.aspx pages, will be used.

The Student Profile page both collects data for a user who wants to register with the site, and displays the profile of a registered user for editing. The page requires that the last name and e-mail address are filled in and validates the format of the e-mail address, ZIP Code, and phone number (if provided). Listings 10.13 and 10.14 shows the .aspx page and the code behind file. Note that the validation controls are in bold.

LISTING 10.13 The StudentProfile.aspx page with Validation Controls. This page shows the use of the `RequiredValidator` and `RegularExpressionValidator` controls.

```
<%@ Page Language="vb" AutoEventWireup="false"
  Codebehind="studentprofile.aspx.vb"
  Inherits="QuilogyEducation.studentprofile" EnableSessionState="True" %>

<HTML>
  <HEAD>
    <TITLE>Student Profile
    </TITLE>
    <meta name="GENERATOR" content="Microsoft Visual Studio.NET 7.0">
    <meta name="CODE_LANGUAGE" content="Visual Basic 7.0">
    <meta name=vs_defaultClientScript content="JScript">
    <meta name=vs_targetSchema content="Internet Explorer 5.0">
    <LINK href="supplemental/site.css" type=text/css rel=stylesheet>
  </HEAD>
```

LISTING 10.13   Continued

```html
<body MS_POSITIONING="GridLayout">
  <!-- #include file="navbar.htm" -->
    <TABLE cellSpacing=0 cellPadding=0 width="100%" border=0>
      <TR>
        <TD align=left bgColor=#f3f0de>
          <TABLE cellSpacing=0 cellPadding=0 border=0>
            <TR>
              <TD valign=center align=left width=211>
                <IMG SRC="supplemental/services-maineducation.gif"
                width=211 height=45 border=0>
              </TD>
              <TD width=529 class="body-copy">
                <div class="body-copy" id="txtMessage" runat="server">
                  <strong>Enter your information and click Save</strong>
                </div>
                <asp:ValidationSummary id=ValidationSummary
                runat="server" ShowMessageBox=True CssClass="body-copy"
                DisplayMode= BulletList HeaderText="Errors occurred.">
                </asp:ValidationSummary>
                <!-- Place content here -->
                <form id="studentprofile" method=post runat="server">
                  <table>
                    <tr class="body-copy">
                      <td><strong>First Name</strong></td>
                      <td>
                      <asp:TextBox ID="txtFName" Runat="server"
                      Text="<%# mdrStud(mdsStud.FIRST_NAME).ToString %>">
                      </asp:TextBox></td>
                      <td><strong>Last Name</strong>
                        <asp:RequiredFieldValidator id=LNameValidator
                        ControlToValidate="txtLName" Display=Dynamic
                        CssClass="body-copy" runat="server"
                        ErrorMessage="Last Name is required" Text="*" >
                        </asp:RequiredFieldValidator>
                      </td>
                      <td>
                        <asp:TextBox ID="txtLName" Runat="server"
                        Text="<%# mdrStud(mdsStud.LAST_NAME).ToString %>">
                        </asp:TextBox></td>
                    </tr>
                    <tr class="body-copy">
                      <td><strong>Organization</strong></td>
                      <td>
                        <asp:TextBox ID="txtOrg" Runat="server"
                        Text=
```

LISTING 10.13   Continued

```
                                "<%# mdrStud(mdsStud.ORGANIZATION).ToString %>">
                                </asp:TextBox></td>
                            <td><strong>Email</strong>
                                <asp:RequiredFieldValidator id="EmailValidator"
                                ControlToValidate="txtEmail" Display=Dynamic
                                CssClass="body-copy" runat="server"
                                ErrorMessage="Email address is required"
                                Text="*">
                                </asp:RequiredFieldValidator>
                                <asp:RegularExpressionValidator
                                id="EmailAtValidator" runat="server"
                                ErrorMessage="Email Address must contain @"
                                ValidationExpression="(.)+(@)+(.)+"
                                Display=Static Text="*" CssClass="body-copy"
                                ControlToValidate="txtEmail">
                                </asp:RegularExpressionValidator>
                            </td>
                            <td>
                                <asp:TextBox ID="txtEmail" Runat="server"
                                Text="<%# mdrStud(mdsStud.EMAIL).ToString %>" >
                                </asp:TextBox></td>
                        </tr>
                        <tr class="body-copy">
                            <td><strong>Address</strong></td>
                            <td colspan=3>
                                <asp:TextBox ID="txtAddress" Runat="server"
                                Text="<%# mdrStud(mdsStud.ADDRESS).ToString %>"
                                width=407px height="26px" >
                                </asp:TextBox></td>
                        </tr>
                        <tr class="body-copy">
                            <td><strong>City</strong></td>
                            <td>
                                <asp:TextBox ID="txtCity" Runat="server"
                                Text="<%# mdrStud(mdsStud.CITY).ToString %>" >
                                </asp:TextBox></td>
                            <td>
                                <strong>State</strong></td>
                            <td>
                                <asp:TextBox ID="txtState" Runat="server"
                                Text="<%# mdrStud(mdsStud.STATE).ToString %>"
                                width=41px height="26px" >
                                </asp:TextBox>    
                                <strong>Zip </strong>
```

LISTING 10.13   Continued

```
                          <asp:RegularExpressionValidator id=ZipValidator
                          runat="server"
                          ErrorMessage="Zip Code not formatted correctly"
                          ValidationExpression="[0-9]{5}-[0-9]{4}|[0-9]{5}"
                          Display=Static Text="*" CssClass="body-copy"
                          ControlToValidate="txtZip">
                          </asp:RegularExpressionValidator>
                          <asp:TextBox ID="txtZip" Runat="server"
                          Text="<%# mdrStud(mdsStud.ZIP_CODE).ToString %>"
                          width=70px height="24px" >
                          </asp:TextBox></td>
                    </tr>
                    <tr class="body-copy">
                    <td><strong>Phone</strong>
                      <asp:RegularExpressionValidator
                      id="PhoneValidator" runat="server"
                      ErrorMessage="Phone must be (xxx) xxx-xxxx"
                      ValidationExpression="[(|][0-9][0-9][0-9][)] " & _
                      "[0-9][0-9][0-9]-[0-9][0-9][0-9][0-9]"
                      Display=Static Text="*" CssClass="body-copy"
                      ControlToValidate="txtPhone">
                      </asp:RegularExpressionValidator>        </td>
                    <td>
                      <asp:TextBox ID="txtPhone" Runat="server"
                      Text="<%# mdrStud(mdsStud.PHONE).ToString %>" >
                      </asp:TextBox></td>
                    <td>
                      <asp:Button ID="cmdSave" Text="Save" Runat="server"
                      accesskey=s height="24px" width="78px">
                      </asp:Button>
                    </td>
                  </tr>
                </table>
              </form>
            </TD>
          </TR>
        </TABLE>
      </TD>
    </TR>
  </TABLE>
  <!-- #include file="bottombar.htm" -->

  </body>
</HTML>
```

LISTING 10.14   The Code-Behind File for the StudentProfile.aspx Page. Note that the IsValid property returns True if the validation controls succeed.

```
Option Strict Off

Imports System.Drawing
Imports System.Web.UI.WebControls
Imports System.Web.UI.HtmlControls
Imports Quilogy.Education
Imports Quilogy.Education.Enrollment
Imports System.Data
Imports System.Configuration
Imports System.Web.Security


Public Class studentprofile
    Inherits System.Web.UI.Page
    Protected WithEvents txtLName As System.Web.UI.WebControls.TextBox
    Protected WithEvents txtPhone As System.Web.UI.WebControls.TextBox
    Protected WithEvents txtFName As System.Web.UI.WebControls.TextBox
    Protected WithEvents txtCity As System.Web.UI.WebControls.TextBox
    Protected WithEvents txtEmail As System.Web.UI.WebControls.TextBox
    Protected WithEvents cmdSave As System.Web.UI.WebControls.Button
    Protected WithEvents txtZip As System.Web.UI.WebControls.TextBox
    Protected WithEvents txtState As System.Web.UI.WebControls.TextBox
    Protected WithEvents txtOrg As System.Web.UI.WebControls.TextBox
    Protected WithEvents txtAddress As System.Web.UI.WebControls.TextBox
    Protected WithEvents txtMessage As _
      System.Web.UI.HtmlControls.HtmlGenericControl

    Protected mdsStud As StudentData
    Protected WithEvents LNameValidator As _
      System.Web.UI.WebControls.RequiredFieldValidator
    Protected WithEvents ValidationSummary As _
      System.Web.UI.WebControls.ValidationSummary
    Protected WithEvents EmailValidator As _
      System.Web.UI.WebControls.RequiredFieldValidator
    Protected WithEvents ZipValidator As _
      System.Web.UI.WebControls.RegularExpressionValidator
    Protected mdrStud As DataRow

    Protected Sub Page_Init(ByVal Sender As System.Object, _
      ByVal e As System.EventArgs) Handles MyBase.Init
        'CODEGEN: This method call is required by the Web Form Designer
        'Do not modify it using the code editor.
        InitializeComponent()
    End Sub
```

LISTING 10.14   Continued

```vb
Private Sub Page_Load(ByVal sender As System.Object, _
  ByVal e As System.EventArgs) Handles MyBase.Load

    If Not Me.IsPostBack Then
        If Context.User.Identity.IsAuthenticated Then
            ' Go get the studentData
            Dim oStud As New Students( _
              ConfigurationSettings.AppSettings("SQLConnect").ToString)
            mdsStud = oStud.GetStudent(Session("StudentID"))
            mdrStud = mdsStud.StudentTable.Rows(0)
            txtMessage().InnerText = "Profile for " & _
              Session("StudentName")
        Else
            ' Create an empty StudentData DataSet with a single row
            mdsStud = New StudentData()
            mdrStud = mdsStud.StudentTable.NewRow
            txtMessage().InnerText = _
            "To become a registered user enter your info and click Save."
        End If

        ' Bind all of the controls on the page
        Me.DataBind()
    End If

End Sub

Protected Sub cmdSave_Click(ByVal sender As System.Object, _
  ByVal e As System.EventArgs) Handles cmdSave.Click
    Dim intStudentID As Integer
    Dim oStud As Students
    Dim dsStud As StudentData
    Dim dr As DataRow

    ' First see if the form is valid
    If Not Me.IsValid Then
        Return
    End If

    ' Place the data into the DataSet
    dsStud = FillDs()

    Try
        ' Create the student object
        Dim strConnect As String
```

LISTING 10.14   Continued

```vb
            strConnect = _
              ConfigurationSettings.AppSettings("SQLConnect").ToString
            oStud = New Students(strConnect)

            ' Save the student data
            intStudentID = oStud.Save(dsStud)

            If intStudentID > 0 Then
                txtMessage().InnerText = "Profile Successfully Saved."
                txtMessage().Style.Item("Color") = "Green"

                ' If they're a new student then setup
                ' their session and authentication
                If Session("StudentID") Is Nothing Then
                    txtMessage().InnerText &= _
                      " Your password has been set to your email address."
                    Session("StudentID") = intStudentID
                    ' Set the authentication cookie
                    FormsAuthentication.SetAuthCookie(txtEmail.Text, False)
                End If

                dr = dsStud.StudentTable.Rows(0)
                Session("StudentName") = dr(StudentData.FIRST_NAME).ToString _
                  & " " & dr(StudentData.LAST_NAME).ToString
                cmdSave.Visible = False
                Return
            End If

        Catch Ex As Exception
            txtMessage().InnerText = "An error occurred: " & Ex.Message
            txtMessage().Style.Item("Color") = "Red"
        End Try

    End Sub

    Private Function FillDs() As StudentData
        Dim dr As DataRow
        Dim dsStud As New StudentData()

        Try
            dr = dsStud.StudentTable.NewRow

            If Not Session("StudentID") Is Nothing Then
                dr(StudentData.STUDENT_ID) = Session("StudentID")
            End If
```

LISTING 10.14   Continued

```
            dr(StudentData.FIRST_NAME) = txtFName.Text
            dr(StudentData.LAST_NAME) = txtLName.Text
            dr(StudentData.ORGANIZATION) = txtOrg.Text
            dr(StudentData.ADDRESS) = txtAddress.Text
            dr(StudentData.CITY) = txtCity.Text
            dr(StudentData.STATE) = txtState.Text
            dr(StudentData.EMAIL) = txtEmail.Text
            dr(StudentData.PHONE) = txtPhone.Text
            dr(StudentData.ZIP_CODE) = txtZip.Text

            ' Add the row to the DataSet if building it
            dsStud.StudentTable.Rows.Add(dr)
            ' Note that this will validate data entry as well
            Return dsStud

        Catch e As Exception
            txtMessage().InnerText = "An error occurred: " & e.Message
            txtMessage().Style.Item("Color") = "Red"
        End Try

    End Function

End Class
```

In Listing 10.13, a ValidationSummary control is near the top of the page. This control allows you to display all the error messages reported from any other validation controls on the form in a single place. In this way, the messages can be centralized so that users don't have to scan the page searching for error messages. Note that the DisplayMode property is set to BulletList to indicate that the errors display in a list of bulleted items directly beneath the HeaderText. The ShowMessageBox property takes effect when the validation is done on the client, and displays a message box with all the errors, in addition to printing them to the validation summary control.

NOTE

Error messages print out in red by default. This can be changed by setting the properties of the control (such as ForeColor) or using a Cascading Style Sheet (CSS). In this case, the CSSClass property is set to "body-copy", which sets the font according to the style sheet linked in the LINK tag at the top of the page.

10

**BUILDING
WEB FORMS**

By default, the validation controls perform the validation on the client if the browser supports DHTML. This is the case because client-side validation reduces server round-trips and makes the application more responsive. To force validation to occur on the server for individual controls, you can set the EnableClientScript property of the control to False, whereas for the entire page, you can set the ClientTarget attribute of the Page directive to "downlevel."

NOTE

Along those same lines, validation can be disabled on the server by setting the Enabled property of the validation control to False. If validation must be disabled from client-side script, you can set the Page_ValidationActive global variable to False. This variable is included on pages that use client validation through a Javascript file (WebUIValidation.js) included with the page.

The actual validation takes place when one of the other validation controls is placed on the .aspx page. For example, the RequiredFieldValidator control is placed in the same cell as the label for the last name column. Notice that the ControlToValidate field references the control that is required, and the Display property is set to Dynamic. Basically, on browsers that support DHTML, this controls whether space on the page is reserved for the error message (by using the Visible attribute of the SPAN tag used to display the error message). Reserving space can ensure that the displaying of the error message does not adversely affect the page layout. In addition, both the ErrorMessage and Text properties are set. Typically, you'd only set the ErrorMessage property, although in this case, because the page includes a ValidationSummary control, the Text property specifies the message that will be displayed at the location of the validation control, whereas the ErrorMessage is displayed in the ValidationSummary control. In this way, you can provide a visual cue to the user as to which fields were in error and still group all the error messages in one place. For example, Figure 10.8 shows the student profile page that results when the user does not enter any information.

TIP

One of the advantages to using a RequiredFieldValidator with client-side validation is that if the user deletes the contents of a required control, the error message displays immediately when the control loses focus, rather than when the form is about to be submitted as is typically the case. However, if a ValidationSummary control is used, only the Text property is made visible. The ErrorMessage associated with the summary control will not be visible until the form is submitted.

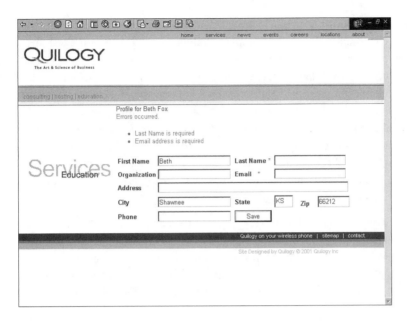

FIGURE 10.8

The StudentProfile.aspx page when errors are detected by the validation controls.

The third type of validation control found in Listing 10.13 is the `RegularExpressionValidator`. Here it is used to ensure that the e-mail address contains an "@" and that the ZIP Code and phone number are formatted correctly. Note that the `ValidationExpression` property is populated with a regular expression. In the case of the `EmailAtValidator` control, the expression ensures that at least one character (.)+ precedes the "@" symbol (@) followed by at least one more character (.)+. Other regular expressions can be seen for the ZIP Code and phone number.

In the case where a single control is the target of two validation controls, there is a precedence to how they are fired. In this case, the `RequiredFieldValidator` is fired first, followed by the `RegularExpressionValidator`.

TIP

It might seem strange that no validation control checks whether the text entered into a control is of a certain length. However, you can easily implement this functionality (as is done in the password field in the StudentLogin.aspx page) by using a `RegularExpressionValidator` with a `ValidationExpression` of something like "(.){5,10}". Translated, this means that the control can contain at least 5, and no more than 10, of any character.

Processing Validation

When using client-side validation, after all the validated controls pass the test, the form is posted back to the server, and normal processing can occur. However, if the validation controls actually perform their validation on the server, the validation occurs before the server event that initiated the postback occurs. Rather than taking any special action (other than error reporting), if errors are encountered, the validation controls simply set the `IsValid` property of the individual controls and the `Page` object to `False`. As a result, code on the server must check for this value before proceeding. Notice that the `cmdSave_Click` method of the `Page` class shown in Listing 10.14 checks the `IsValid` property of the `Page` before attempting to save the profile to the database. Not checking this property results in errors reported to the client, but normal processing to otherwise continue.

Like other server controls, validation controls can be manipulated in the code behind file. For example, you could programmatically change the `ValidationExpression` property based on data read from a database. Although this is possible, keep in mind that because validation controls are actually processed before your custom code is run, you'll need to invoke the `Validate` method of the validation control manually to revalidate with the new property values.

Customizing Validation

Although not used in the Quilogy education site, you certainly have the option of customizing the validation process. This is accomplished on the server by adding a `CustomValidator` control to the page and setting its `ControlToValidate` property to the appropriate control. Then, within the page class, you can create a method to handle the `ServerValidate` event of the control with a signature as follows (where `CustomValidator` is the name of the `CustomValidator` control):

```
Protected Function CustomValidator_ServerValidationFunction( _
  ByVal source As System.Object, _
   ByVal value As System.String) As Boolean
```

This method then performs the validation by referring to the value argument that contains the value of the control being validated. Returning `True` from this function means that the validation was successful. This technique can be used, for example, to dynamically validate the control against values read from a database.

An analogous technique can be used to do custom validation on the client by populating the `ClientValidationFunction` property with the name of a client-side function like so:

```
<asp:CustomValidator id="CustomValidator1" runat=server
   ControlToValidate="txtEmail"
   ErrorMessage="Email address must contain an @"
   ClientValidationFunction="validateEmail(obj, val)" >
</asp:CustomValidator>
```

Just as with server validation, the `obj` and `val` arguments represent the `CustomValidator` and value of the control to be validated.

You work with the other validation controls, `CompareValidator` and `RangeValidator`, to compare a control's value with a literal or another control, to check data types, and to check against a minimum and maximum value in an analogous fashion.

Using Data Binding

Of course, one of the most powerful uses of server controls is to display data retrieved from a database. To that end, ASP.NET supports data binding to either a single value, or to an entire resultset through specific Web server controls, such as `Repeater`, `DropDownList`, `DataList`, and `DataSet`.

Simple Data Binding

In fact, you can bind any property or field exposed by the `Page` class to any attribute in an ASP.NET page simply by using a data binding expression. For example, consider the code in Listing 10.13. Web Server `TextBox` controls are used to display the profile information for a student. This information is queried from the database using the `GetStudent` method of the `Students` data access class. The resulting row is placed in a page-level variable called `mdrStud`, which is then bound to the individual `Text` properties of the control using the syntax that follows:

```
<asp:TextBox ID="txtFName" Runat="server"
  Text="<%# mdrStud(mdsStud.FIRST_NAME).ToString %>" >
</asp:TextBox><
```

The data binding expression itself is contained in the `<%# %>` tags, and in this case, extracts the first name column using the exposed constant `FIRST_NAME`.

In addition, for the bound expression to be evaluated and placed in the appropriate property, the `DataBind` method of the control or the page as a whole must be invoked. In this example, Listing 10.14 contains the line

```
Me.DataBind
```

in the `Load` event of the page.

TIP

Although data binding displays the appropriate values in the page and the view state tracks these values through multiple round-trips to the server, the underlying property or variable does not get updated. In other words, the `mdrStud` DataRow is not updated to reflect a value typed in by the user because the majority of Web applications are used for read-only data. As a result, the StudentProfile class contains the FillDs method to extract the values from the controls and place them into the DataRow when the user attempts to save his changes.

Binding to a Resultset

In addition to binding to individual values, some Web server controls support binding to either a DataReader or a DataSet to display the entire resultset. Figure 10.7 highlights the controls that do so. This is typically the simplest way to display an entire resultset.

To illustrate how this works, the Schedule.aspx page includes a DataGrid Web server control called dgSchedule, the relevant portions of which are shown in Listings 10.15 and 10.16.

LISTING 10.15   Using a DataGrid. This excerpt from the Schedule.aspx page illustrates using a DataGrid with explicitly defined columns.

```
<ASP:DataGrid id="dgSchedule" runat="server" CssClass="body-copy"
  Width="920px" ShowFooter="True"
  CellPadding=3 BackColor=#f3f0de
  BackImageUrl="/QuilogyEducation/supplemental/education-main.jpg">
  <Columns>
    <asp:TemplateColumn ItemStyle-CssClass="caption">
      <ItemTemplate >
        <a href="/QuilogyEducation/registered/Register.aspx?ClassID=
          <%# Container.DataItem("ClassID") %>
          &Course=<%# Trim(Container.DataItem("CourseNum")) & " " & _
          Container.DataItem("Description") %>&When=<%# Container.DataItem( _
            "ClassDate") & " " & Container.DataItem("City") %>">Sign me up</a>
      </ItemTemplate>
    </asp:TemplateColumn>
    <asp:BoundColumn DataField="ClassDate" HeaderText="Date"
    HeaderStyle-Font-Bold=True SortExpression="ClassDate" />
    <asp:BoundColumn DataField="City" HeaderText="Location"
    HeaderStyle-Font-Bold=True SortExpression="City" />
    <asp:TemplateColumn HeaderText="Course" HeaderStyle-Font-Bold=True
    SortExpression="CourseNum">
      <ItemTemplate>
        <a href="ClassDetail.aspx?ClassID=<%# Container.DataItem("ClassID")%>">
          <%# Container.DataItem("Vendor") & " " & _
          Trim(Container.DataItem("CourseNum")) & ": " & _
          Container.DataItem("Description") & " (" & _
          Container.DataItem("Days") & " days)"  %></a>
      </ItemTemplate>
    </asp:TemplateColumn>
```

LISTING 10.15   Continued

```
    <asp:BoundColumn DataField="Product" HeaderText="Product"
     HeaderStyle-Font-Bold=True SortExpression="Product" />
    <asp:BoundColumn DataField="StartTime" HeaderText="Start Time"
     HeaderStyle-Font-Bold=True SortExpression="StartTime" />
    </Columns>
</ASP:DataGrid>
```

LISTING 10.16   Binding to a `DataGrid`. This listing shows how you can bind a `DataSet` to a `DataGrid` control.

```
Option Strict Off

Imports Quilogy.Education
Imports Quilogy.Education.Schedule
Imports System.Configuration
Imports System.Web.UI.WebControls
Imports System.web.UI

Public Class Schedule : Inherits System.Web.UI.Page
    Protected WithEvents dgSchedule As System.Web.UI.WebControls.DataGrid
    Protected WithEvents txtMessage As _
      System.Web.UI.HtmlControls.HtmlGenericControl

#Region " Web Form Designer Generated Code "

    'This call is required by the Web Form Designer.
    <System.Diagnostics.DebuggerStepThrough()> _
    Private Sub InitializeComponent()
    End Sub

    Protected Sub Page_Init(ByVal Sender As System.Object, _
      ByVal e As System.EventArgs) Handles MyBase.Init
        'CODEGEN: This method call is required by the Web Form Designer
        'Do not modify it using the code editor.
        InitializeComponent()

        ' Allow paging and sorting
        dgSchedule.AllowPaging = True
        dgSchedule.PagerStyle.Mode = Web.UI.WebControls.PagerMode.NumericPages
        dgSchedule.PagerStyle.PageButtonCount = 5
        dgSchedule.PageSize = 10
        dgSchedule.AutoGenerateColumns = False
        dgSchedule.AllowSorting = True
    End Sub
```

10

LISTING 10.16   Continued

```
#End Region

    Private Sub Page_Load(ByVal sender As System.Object, _
      ByVal e As System.EventArgs) Handles MyBase.Load
    'Put user code to initialize the page here
    If Not Me.IsPostBack Then
      GetSchedule("")
    End If

    End Sub

  Private Sub GetSchedule(ByVal pSort As String)
    Dim oClasses As Classes
    Dim dsSched As ScheduleData
    Dim flDesc As Boolean = False

    If Not Request("Vendor") Is Nothing Then
      ' Try and get the schedule
      Try
        oClasses = New Classes( _
          ConfigurationSettings.AppSettings("SQLConnect"))
        dsSched = oClasses.GetSchedule(Request("Location"), _
          Request("Vendor"), Request("Advance"))
        dgSchedule.DataSource = dsSched.OfferingsTable.DefaultView

        ' Add to the state bag if not already present
        If Me.ViewState("SortField") Is Nothing Then
          Me.ViewState.Add("SortField", pSort)
          Me.ViewState.Add("SortDesc", True) ' default to true
        End If

        ' Toggle the sort if we're clicking on the same column
        If pSort <> "" And pSort = Me.ViewState("SortField").ToString Then
          flDesc = Not Me.ViewState("SortDesc")

          If flDesc Then
            pSort = pSort & " DESC"
          Else
            pSort = pSort & " ASC"
          End If
        End If

        ' Set the field and order in the StateBag
        Me.ViewState("SortDesc") = flDesc
        Me.ViewState("SortField") = pSort
```

LISTING 10.16   Continued

```
        ' Sort the table
        dsSched.OfferingsTable.DefaultView.Sort = pSort
        dgSchedule.DataBind()

    Catch Ex As Exception
      txtMessage().Style.Item("Color") = "Red"
      txtMessage.InnerText = "An error occurred: " & Ex.Message
    End Try

  End If
End Sub

Private Sub dgSchedule_SortCommand(ByVal source As Object, _
  ByVal e As System.Web.UI.WebControls.DataGridSortCommandEventArgs) _
  Handles dgSchedule.SortCommand
  ' Sort by the sort expression of the bound column
  GetSchedule(e.SortExpression)
End Sub

Private Sub dgSchedule_PageIndexChanged(ByVal source As Object, _
  ByVal e As System.Web.UI.WebControls.DataGridPageChangedEventArgs) _
  Handles dgSchedule.PageIndexChanged
  ' Make sure the page index gets changed to the new page
  dgSchedule.CurrentPageIndex = e.NewPageIndex
  GetSchedule("")
End Sub

End Class
```

In Listing 10.16, the GetSchedule method is called from the Load event of the page and is responsible for retrieving the schedule based on a query string that includes the vendor, location, and the number of days in advance of the class. The GetSchedule method retrieves a ScheduleData DataSet (discussed in Chapter 7, "Accessing Data with ADO.NET") from the GetSchedule method of the Classes data access class. The DataSource property of the dgSchedule DataGrid then is set to the DefaultView property of the OfferingsTable DataTable, and is sorted according to a possible sort expression passed into the method. The DataBind method of the DataGrid then is executed and automatically binds each row of the view to the grid.

The DataGrid itself is defined in the .aspx page shown in Listing 10.15. The AutoGenerateColumns property in the GetSchedule method is set to False so that the bindings can be explicitly specified. This comes in handy when you have columns that you want to hide, or columns that will be based on an expression calculated from several columns as is the case here.

10

The `DataGrid` in this case contains two different types of columns denoted by the `BoundColumn` and `TemplateColumn` elements.

TIP

The `DataGrid` also supports `ButtonColumn`, `EditCommandColumn`, and `HyperlinkColumn` elements to display the data in varying ways.

Using the `BoundColumn` element is simple and allows you to specify the `DataField`, `HeaderText`, `HeaderStyle`, and `SortExpresison` attributes among others. For example, the `City` column is defined to simply display the "City" column from the `DataSet` with a bolded header of "Location." If the `AllowSorting` property of the grid is set to `True`, and the `SortExpression` of the column is set as in this case, a hyperlink on the column header is generated and performs a postback to raise the `SortCommand` event of the `DataGrid`. As you can see in Listing 10.16, this event then requires the schedule with the appropriate sort column.

NOTE

The tracking of the state of the previous sort was discussed earlier in the "State Bag" section and will not be reproduced here.

In addition, by turning on paging using the `AllowPaging` property and setting the various paging properties in the `Page_Init` event, the `DataGrid` will display a subset of the rows (10 at a time in this case) and include navigation links. Clicking the links will fire the `PageIndexChanged` event of the `DataGrid` where the new page will be available in the `NewPageIndex` property of the `DataGridPagechangedEventArgs` object.

The other type of column shown here is the `TemplateColumn`. Other Web server controls, such as the `Repeater` (used in the Transcript.aspx page) and the `DataList` also expose template columns to provide maximum flexibility when displaying the column. In the `DataGrid`, the `TemplateColumn` element itself supports four subelements that include `ItemTemplate`, `EditItemTemplate`, `HeaderTemplate`, and `FooterTemplate`. As you might have guessed, the contents of the `ItemTemplate` element are used to display the column when the grid is not in edit mode, whereas the `EditItemTemplate` can be used to render a `DropDownList`, `TextBox`, or some other editable control. In this way, it is simple to provide in-place editing of the grid. As the names imply, the `HeaderTemplate` and `FooterTemplate` elements simply render HTML in the column header and footer sections of the resulting HTML table.

In Listing 10.15, the template column called "Course" is actually a concatenation of several columns from the DataSet. The columns are accessed using a data binding expression that references the Container object. This object represents the current DataGridItem (representing the row) in the DataGrid control, and is used to bind the appropriate column in the DataRow. Basically, this is what goes on behind the scenes when using a BoundColumn.

> **NOTE**
>
> You also can use the shared Eval method of the DataBinder class to perform binding. This method uses reflection to evaluate the expression dynamically and can be used to output a string for display. For example the code:
>
> ```
> <%# DataBinder.Eval(Container.DataItem, "Cost", "{0:c}") %>
> ```
>
> can be used to format the cost as a locale-specific currency string. However, using Eval is also more costly because reflection is used to dynamically retrieve the type information.

The other template column shown in Listing 10.15 is more complicated because it generates a hyperlink to navigate to the protected Register.aspx page. Figure 10.9 shows the resulting course schedule.

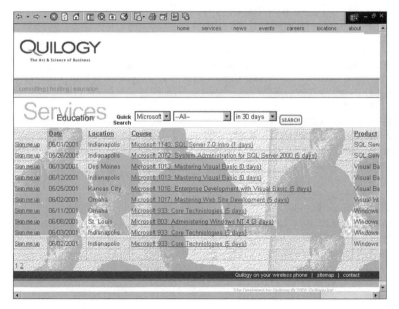

FIGURE 10.9

This page is implemented using a DataGrid control and custom template columns.

10

BUILDING
WEB FORMS

Although the `DataGrid`, `DataList`, or `Repeater` controls expose similar basic functionality, when determining which to use, your decision should be based on the flexibility of the control and the features it provides versus the cost of implementation in terms of development effort and performance. For example, the `DataList` supports additional template types, such as `AlternatingColumn`, can produce a multicolumn layout, and be rendered with `SPAN` tags rather than an HTML `TABLE`. The grid allows paging and automatic sorting, which the `DataList` does not.

In addition to binding to controls like the `DataGrid` and `DataList`, the controls derived from `ListControl` also support data binding to a resultset. This comes in handy when you need to populate a `DropDownList` control with items from the database, as is done in the QSearch.ascx user control. The control contains drop-downs with the vendors and locations, in addition to the number of days in advance that the user can select from to query the class schedule defined as follows:

```
<asp:DropDownlist class=body-copy id=cboVendor runat="server">
</asp:DropDownlist></TD>
<asp:DropDownlist class=body-copy id=cboLocation runat="server">
</asp:DropDownlist>
<asp:DropDownlist class=body-copy id=cboThru runat="server">
</asp:DropDownlist>
```

Although user controls will be covered in more detail later in the chapter, for now, Listing 10.17 shows the relevant code from the control.

LISTING 10.17   Populating Bound List Controls. This excerpt from the QSearch.ascx control populates vendor and location drop-downs using a `DataReader` and a single stored procedure.

```
Option Strict Off
Imports System.Web.UI.WebControls
Imports System.Data.SqlClient
Imports System.Data
Imports System.Configuration
Private Sub LoadControls()

    ' Load the drop downs
    cboThru.Items.Add(New ListItem("in 30 days", "30"))
    cboThru.Items.Add(New ListItem("in 60 days", "60"))
    cboThru.Items.Add(New ListItem("in 90 days", "90"))
    cboThru.Items.Add(New ListItem("in 120 days", "120"))
    cboThru.Items.Add(New ListItem("--All--", "0"))
```

LISTING 10.17   Continued

```
Dim dr As SqlDataReader
Dim cn As New SqlConnection( _
  ConfigurationSettings.AppSettings("SQLConnect"))
Dim cm As New SqlCommand("usp_GetSearch", cn)

Try
  ' Open the connection and execute the DataReader
  cn.Open()
  cm.CommandType = CommandType.StoredProcedure
  dr = cm.ExecuteReader()

 ' Use Databinding
 With cboVendor
   .DataSource = dr
   .DataTextField = "Name"
   .DataValueField = "VendorID"
   .DataBind()
 End With

  ' Get the next resultset
  dr.NextResult()

 With cboLocation
   .DataSource = dr
   .DataTextField = "City"
   .DataValueField = "LocID"
   .DataBind()
 End With

Catch E As Exception
 txtMessage.InnerText = "The controls could not be populated:" & E.Message
 txtMessage.Style("Color") = "Red"
Finally
  ' Cleanup
  If Not dr Is Nothing Then dr.Close()

  ' Now add the items to get all the values
  cboLocation.Items.Add(New ListItem("--All--", 0))
  cboVendor.Items.Add(New ListItem("--All--", 0))
End Try
End Sub
```

The LoadControls method is called when the page loads and first manually populates the cboThru control with options for 30, 60, 90 days, and so on, in the future.

> **NOTE**
>
> These values also can be placed inline in the .aspx or .ascx page using the ListItem element.

Next, a SqlConnection object is instantiated along with a SqlDataReader and SqlCommand. The usp_GetSearch stored procedure simply contains SELECT statements that retrieve the rows from the Vendor and Product tables in the database. The procedure is then executed using the ExecuteReader method of the SqlCommand. The data binding is accomplished by simply setting the DataSource property of the cboVendor and cboLocation controls to the SqlDataReader and setting the DataTextField and DataValueField properties to the field to display and the field to return when selected, respectively. As before, the DataBind method then is called to perform the binding.

The interesting aspect of this example, however, is that because both resultsets are generated from the same stored procedure, the NextResult method of the SqlDataReader is invoked to return the next resultset. The result is that both controls are populated with a single round-trip to the database server, and the overhead of creating a DataSet is avoided on the Web server. This makes for a highly efficient query.

> **NOTE**
>
> This example does not strictly follow the architecture of performing all data access from separate data access classes. But in this case, the usp_GetSearch stored procedure is likely to be particular to this application, and therefore would not justify the creation of a sharable class to encapsulate it. Remember that a cost is associated with strictly following any architecture, and you should make determinations of when it really is cost effective.

Using Mobile Controls

As you might imagine, because server controls are fully rendered on the server and customize their output depending on the browser type, they are perfect candidates to target content for a wide spectrum of devices. To that end, Microsoft also released the .NET Mobile SDK in conjunction with the .NET Framework to support a multitude of devices including the Pocket PC, Wireless Application Protocol (WAP) capable phones using Wireless Markup Language (WML), such as the Sprint PCS TouchPoint phones, and so-called "smart phones," such as the phones recently developed under the code name "Stinger." The idea behind the SDK is to enable write-once, run-anywhere functionality for Web applications on these smaller devices.

Not surprisingly, when installed, the functionality of the Mobile SDK is exposed through the `System.Web.Mobile` and `System.Web.UI` namespaces and contains various server controls such as `Form`, `ObjectList`, `TextView`, `Label`, `TextBox`, `Command`, `Calendar`, and validation controls that can be used to create the equivalent elements on the supported devices. In addition, a project template is available in VS .NET to create a .aspx file targeted for the Mobile SDK.

Basically, the server controls that ship with the Mobile SDK are used in the same way as the server controls previously discussed, including support for data binding. The primary difference, however, is that each page is derived from the `System.Web.UI.MobileControls.MobilePage` class, and each .aspx page can contain multiple `Form` controls. Each `Form` control maps to a screen visible on the device, and forms are navigated to using the `ActiveForm` property of the `MobilePage` class. As a result, all the screens in your mobile application can be contained in the same `MobilePage` class.

> **NOTE**
>
> The `MobilePage` class only renders the `ActiveForm`, so you don't suffer a performance hit by including many `Form` controls in a single page. You can create multiple pages if you want to present a different URL to the user, or if you want to segment your code.

To give you a feel for what an application developed with the Mobile SDK would look like, consider the QEducationMobile.aspx page shown in Listings 10.18 and 10.19. The portions of the page shown here implement the UI for querying and displaying the Quilogy course schedule. Not shown are the pages that allow a user to register her mobile device with the site and query her transcript information.

LISTING 10.18 QEducationMobile.aspx. This page includes five `Form` controls used to query and display e-mail messages.

```
<%@ Page Language="vb" AutoEventWireup="false"
Codebehind="QEducationMobile.aspx.vb"
Inherits="QuilogyEducation.QEducationMobile" %>
<%@ Register TagPrefix="mobile" Namespace="System.Web.UI.MobileControls"
Assembly="System.Web.Mobile" %>

<meta content="Microsoft Visual Studio.NET 7.0" name=GENERATOR>
<meta content="Visual Basic 7.0" name=CODE_LANGUAGE>
<meta content="Mobile Web Page" name=vs_targetSchema>

<body xmlns:mobile="Mobile Web Form Controls">
```

LISTING 10.18   Continued

```
<mobile:form id=frmVendor runat="server">
  <mobile:Label id=Label1 runat="server">Choose a Vendor</mobile:Label>
  <mobile:SelectionList id=cboVendor runat="server"></mobile:SelectionList>
  <mobile:Command id=cmdNext runat="server">Next</mobile:Command>
</mobile:form>

<mobile:form id=frmMain runat="server">
  <mobile:Label id=lblWelcome
  runat="server">Welcome to Quilogy</mobile:Label>
  <mobile:List id=lstSelections runat="server">
    <Item Value="1" Text="View Schedule"></Item>
  </mobile:List>
</mobile:form>

<mobile:form id=frmCity runat="server">
  <mobile:Label id=Label2 runat="server">Choose a City</mobile:Label>
  <mobile:SelectionList id=cboLocation runat="server">
  </mobile:SelectionList>
  <mobile:Command id=cmdGo runat="server">Get Schedule</mobile:Command>
</mobile:form>

<mobile:form id=frmSchedule runat="server">
  <mobile:Label id=lblQuery runat="server">Label</mobile:Label>
  <mobile:ObjectList id=olClasses runat="server">
  </mobile:ObjectList>
  <mobile:Call id=Register runat="server" PhoneNumber="1-800-676-939"
  AlternateURL="http://www.quilogy.com">Register Now</mobile:Call>
</mobile:form>

<mobile:form id=frmError runat="server">
  <mobile:Label id=lblError runat="server">Label</mobile:Label>
  <mobile:Command id=cmdHome runat="server">Home</mobile:Command>
</mobile:form>

</body>
```

LISTING 10.19   Mobile Forms. This code behind file implements the UI for viewing course schedules.

```
Option Strict On

Imports System.Drawing
Imports System.Web.Mobile
Imports System.Web.UI.MobileControls
```

LISTING 10.19 Continued

```vb
Imports System.Web.UI.WebControls
Imports System.Web.UI.HtmlControls
Imports System.Data.SqlClient
Imports System.Configuration
Imports Quilogy.Education
Imports Quilogy.Education.Schedule
Imports Quilogy.Education.Enrollment

Public Class QEducationMobile
    Inherits System.Web.UI.MobileControls.MobilePage
    Protected WithEvents Label1 As System.Web.UI.MobileControls.Label
    Protected WithEvents frmVendor As System.Web.UI.MobileControls.Form
    Protected WithEvents frmCity As System.Web.UI.MobileControls.Form
    Protected WithEvents Label2 As System.Web.UI.MobileControls.Label
    Protected WithEvents cboLocation As _
        System.Web.UI.MobileControls.SelectionList
    Protected WithEvents cmdNext As System.Web.UI.MobileControls.Command
    Protected WithEvents frmSchedule As System.Web.UI.MobileControls.Form
    Protected WithEvents lblQuery As System.Web.UI.MobileControls.Label
    Protected WithEvents cmdGo As System.Web.UI.MobileControls.Command
    Protected WithEvents olClasses As System.Web.UI.MobileControls.ObjectList
    Protected WithEvents frmError As System.Web.UI.MobileControls.Form
    Protected WithEvents lblError As System.Web.UI.MobileControls.Label
    Protected WithEvents Register As System.Web.UI.MobileControls.Call
    Protected WithEvents frmMain As System.Web.UI.MobileControls.Form
    Protected WithEvents lstSelections As System.Web.UI.MobileControls.List
    Protected WithEvents lblWelcome As System.Web.UI.MobileControls.Label
    Protected WithEvents cmdHome As System.Web.UI.MobileControls.Command
    Protected WithEvents cboVendor As System.Web.UI.MobileControls.SelectionList

#Region " Web Forms Designer Generated Code "

    'CODEGEN: This procedure is required by the Web Form Designer
    'Do not modify it using the code editor.
    Private Sub InitializeComponent()

    End Sub

    Private Sub Page_Init(ByVal Sender As System.Object, _
        ByVal e As System.EventArgs) Handles MyBase.Init
        'CODEGEN: This method call is required by the Web Form Designer
        'Do not modify it using the code editor.
        InitializeComponent()

        olClasses.AutoGenerateFields = False
```

10

BUILDING WEB FORMS

LISTING 10.19   Continued

```
    Dim oField(6) As ObjectListField

    oField(0) = New ObjectListField()
    oField(0).DataField = "Description"
    oField(0).Title = "Class"
    olClasses.Fields.Add(oField(0))

    oField(1) = New ObjectListField()
    oField(1).DataField = "ClassDate"
    oField(1).Title = "Date"
    olClasses.Fields.Add(oField(1))

    oField(2) = New ObjectListField()
    oField(2).DataField = "CourseNum"
    oField(2).Title = "Course"
    olClasses.Fields.Add(oField(2))

    oField(3) = New ObjectListField()
    oField(3).DataField = "Days"
    oField(3).Title = "Days"
    olClasses.Fields.Add(oField(3))

    oField(4) = New ObjectListField()
    oField(4).DataField = "StartTime"
    oField(4).Title = "Time"
    olClasses.Fields.Add(oField(4))

    oField(5) = New ObjectListField()
    oField(5).DataField = "Product"
    oField(5).Title = "Product"
    olClasses.Fields.Add(oField(5))

  End Sub

#End Region

  Private Sub Page_Load(ByVal sender As System.Object, _
    ByVal e As System.EventArgs) Handles MyBase.Load
    'Put user code to initialize the page here
    If Not Me.IsPostBack Then
      LoadControls()
      Me.ActiveForm = frmMain
    End If
  End Sub
```

LISTING 10.19   Continued

```
Private Sub LoadControls()

  ' Load the drop downs

  ' Loads the other drop downs from the database
  Dim dr As SqlDataReader
  Dim cn As New SqlConnection( _
    ConfigurationSettings.AppSettings("SQLConnect"))
  Dim cm As New SqlCommand("usp_GetSearch", cn)

  Try
    ' Open the connection and execute the DataReader
    cn.Open()
    cm.CommandType = CommandType.StoredProcedure
    dr = cm.ExecuteReader(CommandBehavior.CloseConnection)

    ' Use Databinding
    With cboVendor
      .DataSource = dr
      .DataTextField = "Name"
      .DataValueField = "VendorID"
      .DataBind()
    End With

    ' Get the next resultset
    dr.NextResult()

    With cboLocation
      .DataSource = dr
      .DataTextField = "City"
      .DataValueField = "LocID"
      .DataBind()
    End With

  Catch E As Exception
    ' Go to an error form to show the exception
    Me.ActiveForm = frmError
    lblError.Text = "An error occurred: " & E.Message

  End Try

End Sub

Private Sub cmdNext_Click(ByVal sender As Object, _
  ByVal e As System.EventArgs) Handles cmdNext.Click
```

LISTING 10.19   Continued

```
  Me.ActiveForm = frmCity
End Sub

Private Sub cmdGo_Click(ByVal sender As Object, _
  ByVal e As System.EventArgs) Handles cmdGo.Click
  GetSchedule()
  Me.ActiveForm = frmSchedule
End Sub

Private Sub GetSchedule()
  Dim oClasses As Classes
  Dim dsSched As ScheduleData
  Dim flDesc As Boolean = False
  Dim intVendor As Integer
  Dim intLocation As Integer

  ' Set the message text
  lblQuery.Text = cboVendor.Selection.Text & ":" & _
    cboLocation.Selection.Text & " 30 days out"

  ' Get the values from the drop downs
  intVendor = CType(cboVendor.Selection.Value(), Integer)
  intLocation = CType(cboLocation.Selection.Value(), Integer)

  ' Try and get the schedule
  Try
    oClasses = New Classes(ConfigurationSettings.AppSettings("SQLConnect"))
    dsSched = oClasses.GetSchedule(intLocation, intVendor)

    dsSched.OfferingsTable.Columns.Add(New DataColumn("myID", _
      GetType(String), "CourseNum + ' ' + ClassDate"))
    olClasses.DataSource = dsSched.OfferingsTable.DefaultView

    Dim oField As New ObjectListField()
    oField.DataField = "myID"
    oField.Title = "ID"
    olClasses.Fields.Add(oField)
    oField.Visible = False

    olClasses.LabelField = "myID"
    olClasses.DataBind()

  Catch Ex As Exception
    Me.ActiveForm = frmError
    lblError.Text = "An error occurred: " & Ex.Message
```

LISTING 10.19 Continued

```
    End Try

  End Sub


  Private Sub lstSelections_ItemCommand(ByVal source As Object, _
    ByVal e As System.Web.UI.MobileControls.ListCommandEventArgs) _
    Handles lstSelections.ItemCommand
    ' Navigate to the appropriate form
    Select Case e.ListItem.Value()
      Case "1"
        Me.ActiveForm = frmVendor
    End Select
  End Sub

  Private Sub cmdHome_Click(ByVal sender As System.Object, _
    ByVal e As System.EventArgs) Handles cmdHome.Click
    Me.ActiveForm = frmMain
  End Sub

End Class
```

In Listing 10.18, the page contains five Form controls that display a menu pain (frmMain), a drop-down to select the vendor (frmVendor), a drop-down to select the city (frmCity), the results of the query (frmSchedule), and an error page (frmError). The code behind in Listing 10.19 looks similar to other pages with the exception that the controls used are different, and the ActiveForm property is set at various points (as in the Load event) to navigate to the appropriate form. One interesting point to note in Listing 10.19 is that the LoadControls method looks similar to the code shown in Listing 10.17, and can take advantage of data binding just as in a standard Web form. However, in this case, the cboVendor and cboLocation controls are found on separate mobile forms and are instances of System.Web.UI.MobileControls.SelectionList.

TIP

If your application needs to support both desktop and mobile devices, it becomes even more imperative that you separate your data access from the UI. In this way, you'll be able to reuse much of the code and only reimplement the barest navigation as in this example. For example, the bulk of the code in LoadControls methods in Listing 10.17 and 10.19 could be abstracted into a method accessible to both the Web form and Mobile form.

10

BUILDING
WEB FORMS

Another interesting aspect of Listing 10.19 is that the course schedule information is displayed in an `ObjectList` control called `olClasses`. The `olClasses` control is initialized in the `Page_Init` method where its `AutoGenerateFields` property is set to `False`, and fields of type `ObjectListField` are explicitly created and added to the `Fields` collection. In each case, the `DataField` property maps to a `DataColumn` in a `DataTable` that will be bound to the `ObjectList`. Within the `GetSchedule` method, the `Classes` data access class is used to retrieve a `ScheduleData DataSet` object using the `GetSchedule` method. This `DataSet` then is bound to `olClasses` using the `DataSource` property.

In addition, a new `DataColumn` called `myID` is created that combines the course number with the class date. A corresponding `ObjectListField` then is added to the collection of fields and made invisible. This is necessary because the `ObjectList` can only display a single column in list mode, and enough information to identify the class offering must be shown. To show the new `myID` field in list mode, the `LabelField` property of `olClasses` is set to `myID`.

The powerful aspect of the `ObjectList` is that it also acts as a selection list and allows the user to drill-down on the item as shown in Figure 10.10.

FIGURE 10.10

The UP.Simulator can be used to test your mobile forms. Note the graphical display in the VS .NET editor as well.

TIP

Figure 10.10 was generated using the UP.Simulator from Openwave Systems, Inc. You can download the simulator at `http://developer.openwave.com`.

In this case, when the user selects the clas offering, the `ObjectList` displays in detail mode and shows all the fields whose `Visible` property is not set to `False`. Note that no extra code had to be written to use this functionality.

Obviously, this discussion only scratches the surface of the power of Mobile controls. However, to further illustrate the point, notice that the `frmSchedule` form contains a control called `Register` of the type `System.Web.UI.MobileControls.Call`. This control exposes a `PhoneNumber` property used to represent, in this case, the class registration number for Quilogy. Depending on which device is detected, this control can render by simply displaying the phone number on HTML devices like the PocketPC or actually dialing the number on a Web-enabled phone.

Creating Web Server Controls

It should come as no surprise that you also can author your own Web server controls in the same way you can author your own components to reuse, as discussed in Chapter 8. Although control authoring is a large topic, in the limited space here, I'll show a simple example of creating a Web server control to display detail information about a class. For more information, see the "Developing ASP.NET Server Controls" topic in the online help.

In Listing 10.16, the `TemplateColumn` called "Course" creates a hyperlink to the ClassDetail.aspx page passing the `ClassID` in the query string. The entirety of the .aspx file for this page can be seen in the following code:

```
<%@ Register TagPrefix="QuilogyControls" Namespace="QuilogyWebControls"
   Assembly="QuilogyWebControls" %>
<%@ Page Language="vb" AutoEventWireup="false"
   Codebehind="ClassDetail.aspx.vb"
   Inherits="QuilogyEducation.ClassDetail"%>

<HTML>
  <HEAD>
    <LINK href="supplemental/site.css" type=text/css rel=stylesheet>
  </HEAD>
  <body MS_POSITIONING="GridLayout" bgcolor="#ECE8CD">
    <!-- #include file="navbar.htm" -->
    <form id="ClassDetail" method="post" runat="server" class="body-copy">
      <QuilogyControls:ClassData id="ClassData1" runat=server>
```

```
      </QuilogyControls:ClassData>
    </form>
  <!-- #include file="bottombar.htm" -->
  </body>
</HTML>
```

The interesting aspect of this page is that the detail information is rendered by the `ClassData` Web server control. Note that the `Register` directive at the top of the page includes `TagPrefix`, `Namespace`, and `Assembly` attributes that specify how and from where the control will be referenced.

The control itself then is defined in a separate assembly created in VS.NET using the Web Control Library template. When the template is chosen, a component is created that includes a class that inherits from `System.Web.UI.WebControls.WebControl`. It is the developer's job to then implement the appropriate methods to create the server control.

Listing 10.20 shows the code for the simple `ClassData` control.

Listing 10.20 Simple Web Server Control. This listing shows the code for the control used to display class details.

```
Imports System.ComponentModel
Imports System.Web.UI
Imports System.Data.SqlClient
Imports System.Data
Imports System.Configuration

<DefaultProperty("ClassID"),
  ToolboxData("<{0}:ClassData1 runat=server></{0}:ClassData1>")> _
Public Class ClassData : Inherits System.Web.UI.WebControls.WebControl

    Protected WithEvents txtMessage As _
      System.Web.UI.HtmlControls.HtmlGenericControl
    Private strCourse As String
    Private strCost As String
    Private strLocation As String
    Private strDays As String
    Private strTime As String
    Private strSyllabus As String
    Private strProduct As String
    Private strVendor As String
    Private strCourseNum As String
    Private strClassDate As String

    Private Sub Control_Load(ByVal sender As System.Object, _
      ByVal e As System.EventArgs) Handles MyBase.Load
```

LISTING **10.20**   Continued

```
txtMessage = New HtmlControls.HtmlGenericControl("<div>")

If Me.ClassID = 0 Then
  txtMessage.InnerText = "The ClassID was not set properly"
Else
  ' Query the database here for the class stuff
  Dim cn As New SqlConnection( _
    ConfigurationSettings.AppSettings("SQLConnect"))
  Dim cm As New SqlCommand("usp_GetClass", cn)
  Dim dr As SqlDataReader

  Try
    ' Execute the procedure and get the class values
    cm.CommandType = CommandType.StoredProcedure
    cm.Parameters.Add(New SqlParameter("@ClassID", SqlDbType.Int))
    cm.Parameters(0).Value = Me.ClassID

    cn.Open()
    dr = cm.ExecuteReader
    If dr.IsClosed Then
      txtMessage.InnerText = "No class found"
      Return
    Else
      dr.Read()
    End If

    strCourse = dr("Description").ToString
    strCourseNum = dr("CourseNum").ToString
    strLocation = dr("City").ToString
    strDays = dr("Days").ToString
    strTime = dr("StartTime").ToString
    strSyllabus = dr("Syllabus").ToString
    strClassDate = dr("ClassDate").ToString
    strProduct = dr("Product").ToString
    strVendor = dr("Vendor").ToString
    strCost = dr("Cost").ToString

    txtMessage.InnerText = _
      "Here are the class details for the class you selected"
  Catch Ex As Exception
    txtMessage.InnerText = "An error occurred: " & Ex.Message

  Finally
    If Not dr Is Nothing Then dr.Close()
    cn.Close()
```

LISTING 10.20   Continued

```
          End Try

      End If

  End Sub

  Protected Overrides Sub Render(ByVal output As _
    System.Web.UI.HtmlTextWriter)
      Dim strImg As String

      ' Set the image to include
      Select Case strVendor
        Case "Microsoft"
          strImg = "http://www.quilogy.com/logo/ms-mctec.gif"
        Case "Oracle"
          strImg = "http://www.quilogy.com/images/banners/oracle.gif"
        Case "Sybase"
          strImg = "http://www.quilogy.com/logo/sybase-partner.gif"
      End Select
      output.Write("<img src='" & strImg & "' />")

      ' Set the message
      output.WriteFullBeginTag("div")
      output.Write(txtMessage.InnerHtml)
      output.WriteEndTag("div")
      output.Write("<hr>")

      ' Build the description
      output.Write("<b>Course:</b> " & strCourseNum & " " & strCourse & _
        "<br>")
      output.Write("<b>Where?:</b> " & strLocation & _
        "  <a href='http://www.quilogy.com/loc-page.asp?location=" & _
        strLocation & "'>Need directions?</a><br>")
      output.Write("<b>When?:</b> " & strTime & " on " & _
        strClassDate & "<br>")
      output.Write("<b>How Long?:</b> " & strDays & " days <br>")
      output.Write("<b>Product:</b> " & strProduct & "<br>")
      output.Write("<b>Retail Price:</b> " & strCost & "<br>")
      output.Write("<b>Vendor:</b> " & strVendor & "<br>")
      output.Write("<hr>")
      output.Write("<a href='" & strSyllabus & "'>Course Description</a>")
  End Sub

  <Bindable(True)> _
  Public Property ClassID() As Integer
```

LISTING 10.20   Continued

```
Get
  Return Me.ViewState("ClassID")
End Get
Set(ByVal Value As Integer)
  ' Save in the view state
  Me.ViewState("ClassID") = Value
End Set
End Property
```

```
End Class
```

In Listing 10.20, the control only implements the `Load` and `Render` methods and includes a single property called `ClassID`. The code in the `Load` method should be familiar because it simply uses the value of the `ClassID` property to execute the `usp_GetClass` stored procedure and extract the values using a `SqlDataReader` into class-level `String` variables. In addition, it creates a `DIV` tag using a new instance of an `HtmlGenericControl` called `txtMessage` that it uses to report errors and show status information.

The bulk of the work takes place in the `Render` method. Keep in mind that controls go through the same life cycle as discussed in Table 10.1, so during the render phase, the `Render` method is called. The single argument, `Output`, passes in an `HtmlTextWriter` whose method you call to build the HTML that the server control renders to the browser. In this case, we're simply writing a series of tags to display a logo for the appropriate vendor, followed by the message, and finally the details of the class. The `HtmlTextWriter` class is derived from `TextWriter` and contains many methods that simplify the creation of HTML including the `WriteFullBeginTag` and `WriteEndTag` methods shown in this example.

The `ClassID` property is also interesting because it persists the value of the property to the state bag using the `ViewState` property. By doing so, the page that hosts the control can perform a postback and retain the value of the `ClassID` property it placed in the instance of the control. For example, the ClassDetail.aspx page contains the following code:

```
Private Sub Page_Load(ByVal sender As System.Object, _
  ByVal e As System.EventArgs) Handles MyBase.Load
    'Put user code to initialize the page here
    If Not Me.IsPostBack Then
      ClassData1.ClassID = Request("ClassID")
    End If
End Sub
```

In this case, the `ClassID` property is populated when the page is initially loaded, and thereafter it will be retained in the view state. When the user clicks on the course description in the Schedule.aspx page, the resulting details page is shown in Figure 10.11.

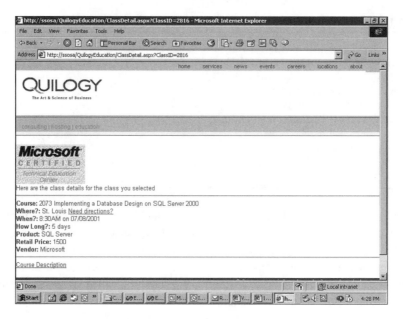

FIGURE 10.11
The ClassData *control displaying the class details.*

TIP

In addition to the simple rendering shown here, the Render method is where you can check for the browser type and customize the output accordingly. Note that the control exposes a Page property that gives you access to the Request object from which you can extract the UserAgent to determine the browser type.

Creating Composite Controls

Finally, although this control rendered all its HTML itself, you can optionally create a *composite control*. Composite controls are conceptually similar to user controls discussed in the next section and, as the name implies, are created by combining existing controls. A composite control can be created by simply instantiating other server controls in a fashion similar to the txtMessage control in Listing 10.20, and then overriding the CreateChildControls method like so:

```
Protected Overrides Sub CreateChildControls()
    Controls.Add(txtMessage)
End Sub
```

Here, a `txtMessage` control is added to the `Controls` collection exposed by the control where you also can position and format the controls appropriately. With composite controls, you don't need to override the `Render` method because each control renders itself, although doing so improves performance.

> **NOTE**
>
> One of the weaknesses of creating your own server controls is that there is no designer to automatically perform the layout for you.

As with other Web server controls, custom controls can raise events and perform their own postback processing by using delegates and implementing the `IPostBackDataHandler` interface. In addition, custom controls can process templates and child elements, generate client-side script, and perform data binding in the same manner as the `DataGrid` control discussed previously. For details on these advanced topics see the online help.

As you would expect, a Web server control can be compiled and added to the toolbox if the control uses a strong name and is installed in the Global Assembly Cache. The `ToolboxData` attribute is used to indicate the tag used when the control is added to a Web Form.

Because additional development effort is involved with creating server controls, only develop your own when the control can be reused across the company or in multiple applications, and when you want to protect the internals of the control.

Web Forms User Controls

Although you can develop your own server controls by deriving from `WebControl` as shown in Listing 10.20, for most applications, a simpler technique to encapsulate UI functionality, and that also promotes reusability, is to create a user control.

A *user control* is simply a page with a .ascx extension that can be referenced from a host page. The user control then behaves like any other page and can contain controls, respond to events, and so forth. The advantage to a user control is simply that you get the benefits of the Web Forms designer and the ease of development while sacrificing reusability across applications.

In the Quilogy sample, the drop-down lists that allow a user to select the vendor, city, and time frame are implemented as a user control called QSeach.ascx. The control is used in both the Schedule.aspx and QEducation.aspx pages. The UI for the control is created as you would expect, whereas Listing 10.21 shows an excerpt of the code behind.

Listing 10.21   Search User Control. This listing shows the code behind for the QSearch.ascx user control to query the class schedule.

```vb
Option Strict Off

Imports System.Web.UI.WebControls
Imports System.Data.SqlClient
Imports System.Data
Imports System.Configuration


Public Class QSearch : Inherits System.Web.UI.UserControl
    Protected WithEvents cboVendor As System.Web.UI.WebControls.DropDownList
    Protected WithEvents cboLocation As System.Web.UI.WebControls.DropDownList
    Protected WithEvents cboThru As System.Web.UI.WebControls.DropDownList
    Protected WithEvents txtMessage As _
      System.Web.UI.HtmlControls.HtmlGenericControl
    Protected WithEvents imgSearch As _
      System.Web.UI.HtmlControls.HtmlInputImage

    Private Sub imgSearch_ServerClick(ByVal sender As System.Object, _
      ByVal e As System.Web.UI.ImageClickEventArgs) _
      Handles imgSearch.ServerClick
        ' Now search for the classes and display them in a grid
        If cboVendor.SelectedItem.Value = 0 And _
          cboLocation.SelectedItem.Value = 0 Then
            txtMessage.InnerText = "Please Select a City OR Vendor"
            txtMessage.Style.Item("Color") = "Red"
            Return
        Else
            Response.Redirect("/QuilogyEducation/Schedule.aspx?Vendor=" & _
              cboVendor.SelectedItem.Value & "&Location=" & _
              cboLocation.SelectedItem.Value & "&Advance=" & _
              cboThru.SelectedItem.Value)
        End If
    End Sub

    Private Sub QSearch_Load(ByVal sender As Object, ByVal e As _
System.EventArgs) _
      Handles MyBase.Load

        If Not Me.IsPostBack Then
          LoadControls()

          ' Make sure the boxes are reset if needed
          If Not Request("Vendor") Is Nothing Then
            cboVendor.Items.FindByValue( _
              Request("Vendor").ToString).Selected = True
```

LISTING 10.21 Continued

```
            cboLocation.Items.FindByValue( _
              Request("Location").ToString).Selected = True
            cboThru.Items.FindByValue( _
              Request("Advance").ToString).Selected = True
        Else
            cboLocation.Items.FindByValue("0").Selected = True
            cboVendor.Items.FindByValue("0").Selected = True
        End If
    End If

    End Sub

End Class
```

Note that the LoadControls method shown in Listing 10.17 also is a member of the QSearch class in Listing 10.21.

The processing of the control follows the same life cycle shown in Table 10.1, although the control class itself derives from the System.Web.UI.UserControl class rather than the Page class. In this case, the Load event calls the LoadControls method if the form in which this control is sitting has not been posted. In addition, it reselects the appropriate values (if a query string is available) or simply the first value in the drop-down by using the FindByValue method and Selected property of the DropDownList controls.

Referencing the user control on a page is similar to referencing a Web server control through the use of the Register directive. The tag that will be used in addition to the location of the .ascx file can be specified by setting the TagPrefix, TagName, and Src attributes as follows:

```
<%@ Register TagPrefix="QEd" TagName="QSearch" Src="QSearch.ascx"%>
```

The control can then be included in the page like so:

```
<QEd:QSearch id="QSearch" runat="server"></QEd:QSearch>
```

As mentioned previously, user controls are great candidates to use output caching (referred to as *fragment caching*) to increase performance by caching only partial pages.

> **NOTE**
>
> Another interesting use for user controls is to provide user interface widgets when developing portal sites. For example, when developing an intranet portal, you could develop individual user controls to display news items, notifications, links, and weather and then load them into a single container page.

10

BUILDING WEB FORMS

Note that like other pages, user controls can post events; however, you should handle the events in the code for the user control and not in the hosting page. In Listing 10.21, the `imgSearch_ServerClick` method handles the `ServerClick` event of the `HtmlInputImage` control that the user clicks on to make his selection.

Summary

This chapter focused on detailing the architecture and implementation of ASP.NET as it relates to building distributed applications. ASP.NET offers a wealth of features, such as state management, caching, and tracing, to create scalable and reliable applications, while allowing the infrastructure to be extensible.

Further, the Web Forms programming model implements an event-driven and object-oriented paradigm for Web development. This, coupled with the rapid application development (RAD) inherent in using server controls and the separation of UI and application logic, makes Web Forms a great programming model for distributed applications.

Although Web Forms enables you to develop a graphical UI for your user services tier, Web Services enables the creation of a programmatic UI. It is to the programmatic side that we now turn our attention.

Building Web Services

IN THIS CHAPTER

The four previous chapters in this section discussed accessing data, building components, and providing a user interface to a Web application. Taken as a whole, those chapters provide a basis for building multitiered distributed applications in VB .NET that are analogous to the Windows DNA applications built using the previous generation of Visual Studio. However, the .NET Framework also adds a new dimension to distributed application development by providing support for Web Services (also referred to as XML Web Services).

In many respects, this chapter is the most important in this book because it discusses a key innovation in VB .NET that makes it possible to develop applications where the Internet is the platform. In other words, the architecture of the Common Language Runtime (CLR) and the major components of the Services Framework were developed primarily to make building and consuming Web Services both simple and integral to the product. As a result, VB .NET developers need to have a thorough understanding of the uses for Web Services and how they can be developed and deployed in VB .NET. This final chapter of the section begins with a discussion of the architecture and technology involved, and then shows how a sample Web Service is built and consumed using the Quilogy education application.

> **NOTE**
>
> All code listings and supplemental material for this chapter can be found on the book's Web site at www.samspublishing.com.

Web Service Architecture

At its most basic level, a Web Service is simply a programmable application component accessible via standard Web protocols. In other words, you can think of a Web Service as an endpoint on the Internet or on an intranet that exposes functionality without a user interface. This functionality is exposed through standard protocols that allow developers to find and incorporate Web Services through a new breed of development tools, VS .NET being among the first. As such, a Web Service is not directly accessible to an end user, but must be called from inside a Web- or form-based application.

A Web Service is conceptually similar to a middle-tier component that exposes its methods as a "black box." However, Web Services don't rely on proprietary component architectures—instead, they use Internet standards that make them platform and language independent. These Web Services then become the building blocks for application development as developers incorporate them into their applications to provide essential features—a truly programmable Web.

Because a Web Service is a programmable application component, it comes as no surprise that, from the developer's perspective, the functionality of the Web Services is exposed as one or more methods that accept arguments and might return both scalar values (`True`, `False`, `Integer`, `String`, and so on) or complex data (such as an XML document). In this way, creating a Web Service is analogous to creating any component in VB .NET.

In addition, because Web Services rely on standard Web protocols, they are obviously well-suited for the Web world, where clients make a series of short-lived connections to Web sites, rather than hold a persistent connection between requests. As such, Web Services are typically comprised of a set of well-defined and granular services analogous to the components you would build for a transactional COM+ environment. However, because Web Services in .NET are a component of ASP.NET, they also can take advantage of features of ASP.NET, such as session and application state.

The standard protocols that comprise the infrastructure—HTTP, XML, and Simple Object Access Protocol (SOAP)—provide a remote procedure call (RPC)-like communication model that is message-based. Further, the ubiquity of HTTP and the wide adoption of XML and SOAP in the industry make the availability of Web Services to any device and platform a reality. In this way, Web Services eliminate many of the battles of the late 1990s over object technologies by providing an industry standard way of exposing functionality and consuming it.

Component Warriors

Of course, the most heated battle in the object wars is between DCOM and CORBA's Internet Inter-ORB Protocol (IIOP). Both protocols provide a means for remotely activating components and using their services and are in heavy use in the industry. However, the cost of implementing these technologies is high, they don't communicate without the inclusion of special bridging software, and they don't work well over the Internet. For example, using IIOP typically means buying ORB licenses, and DCOM requires both clients and servers to be configured with system software while it is unlikely that DCOM or IIOP packets will be able to penetrate a well-configured firewall. The combination of HTTP and XML eliminates these barriers.

In the long run, the low bar for entry and reliance on industry standards will free developers from having to use any specific language or toolset to create software that interoperates. For example, in the past, developers on the Windows platform would build COM components and COM clients that could interoperate with each other using DCOM. However, this interoperation rarely, if ever, went beyond the developer's organization because of the limitations of DCOM and the absence of COM on any but the Windows platform. One of the key aspects of a Web Service is that it abstracts the implementation of the application logic from the means used to communicate with it so that consumers of Web Services need only know where the service is located and the signatures of its methods. In this way, you can think of a Web Service as simply another interface, albeit a programmatic one, to components you build with VB .NET.

Of course, in the short term, using a development tool that abstracts much of the heavy lifting required to build Web Services, such as VS .NET, allows developers to remain highly productive and build Web Services within their language of choice. As mentioned in Chapter 1, "The Microsoft .NET Architecture," the real strength and promise of .NET is not that the CLR will be ported to other platforms, such as Linux (although that might well happen); rather, it is that software built using .NET that will be able to interoperate with software written for other platforms in an industry-standard way.

With VS .NET, Microsoft is hoping that as developers begin to adopt the Web Service model, it will become the fundamental way in which devices (not just PCs but also phones, PDAs, and a host of other Internet-enabled hardware) communicate. In addition, it will become as routine for applications to expose and consume Web Services as it is today for applications to reuse components. A Web laden with interoperable Web Services is the vision of a truly programmable Web where the Internet is the platform.

In the remainder of this section, we'll discuss some common scenarios where Web Services can be employed and drill down on the technology involved before walking through the implementation of a Web Service.

Uses for Web Services

Although as mentioned in the previous section, the long-term vision for Web Services is that almost every application either expose or consume Web Services as a matter of course. In the short term, Web Services will be deployed strategically using .NET and other tools. The two most common scenarios will be for widely reusable functionality and application integration.

> **NOTE**
>
> Of course, Microsoft also sees Web Services as the core technology for a set of services termed *Foundation Services* in its .NET vision that fall under the .NET My Services initiative. As discussed in Chapter 1, .NET My Services will allow collaboration between applications by integrating various pieces of information about consumers and making it available via highly secure Web Services.

In the first scenario, developers built Web Services to expose services that can be reused in a variety of applications and across organizations. For example, a news organization could publish a Web Service that contains methods to pull today's headlines and the text of each article. A developer of a portal site could then incorporate this Web Service into his Web site by subscribing to the service or being charged a per-use fee. Another example might be an express shipping company that provides a free Web Service with methods to calculate the shipping costs given the parameters of a package, and schedule a pickup. An order-fulfillment system could then programmatically calculate shipping costs and schedule pickups without human intervention. These types of Web Services provide value by allowing developers to quickly weave together applications that use a variety of Web Services. The benefit to the organization is that developers needn't spend their time reinventing the wheel defining and writing interfaces to these services.

But How Do I Make Money?

The question that inevitably arises in any discussion of Web Services is the revenue model that could be employed to actually make money from them. Although it is anticipated that initially interorganization Web Services will be deployed as value-added services that simply provide an alternative way to receive information, as Web Services become ubiquitous, they will need to stand on their own. Because Web Services can support the same authentication techniques as Web sites, models that might be used include subscriptions and pay-per-use. The latter option is especially interesting because Web Services easily can be made to track the number of method calls from, or bytes returned to, a particular client. By charging a few cents per invocation or byte, Web Services could be billed in the same way telephone calls are today.

Within an organization, Web Services can be employed to deal with application integration issues. Initially, this likely will be their primary use for corporate VB .NET developers. For example, consider the familiar scenario where an organization has purchased or built a variety of line-of-business systems. Although these systems perform their appropriate functions, their functionality and data are isolated from each other. Using Web Services, the organization's developers could tie these systems together by building a Web Service layer for each application and integrating the results into a portal. In this way, the investment in the line-of-business applications is not wasted, and users can benefit from the insights gained through correlating data from a variety of sources. Of course, this idea also can be extended to interorganization processes to implement purchasing and supply chain solutions, as well.

On a smaller scale, a Web Service might be implemented to synchronize data between a commercial application deployed to the laptops of a sales force, and a central repository at corporate headquarters. These types of services provide value by preserving investment in current systems while making the data available for sharing to a wider audience.

The example Web Service implemented in this chapter falls into the former category as a service that Quilogy might implement to publish course schedules and provide services to organizations and their students who take Quilogy courses.

Web Service Technology

Web Services are based on several key technologies, among them HTTP, XML, and SOAP. This section explores the foundation of Web Services and where in the Services Framework they are implemented.

As mentioned previously, the widespread adoption of HTTP (and thus TCP/IP) provides the transport layer for Web Services requests and responses. The great aspect of this is that Web Services can be hosted by any Web server (such as IIS in the case of VB .NET Web Services) and an increasing number of server applications that support HTTP. The end result is that requests for Web Services can be made from any Web-enabled device, and those requests easily pass through firewalls. However, because Web Services are hosted in IIS, they also can be secured, as discussed later in the chapter, using standard Web authentication techniques such as those accessible from ASP.NET as discussed in Chapter 10, "Building Web Forms."

Although HTTP provides the underlying transport, the key technology that makes Web Services possible is clearly XML. As discussed in Chapter 7, "Accessing Data with ADO.NET," XML is useful because it allows data to be self-describing. In addition, XML is highly portable because parsers exist for all languages and operating systems, and these parsers can handle data encoded using the Universal Character Set (UCS). However, XML is not only a means to exchange data; just as HTML provides a standardized language to display data for human eyes, XML provides the basis for the development of grammars (standardized XML languages) that allow software to interoperate. These standardized languages include the XML grammar to describe the common messaging format (SOAP), the grammar to describe Web Services called Web Services Description Language (WSDL), and the mechanism used to discover Web Services (DISCO and UDDI).

To provide a mental map for developers new to Web Services and these XML-based technologies, Figure 11.1 draws a comparison between technologies used to develop distributed applications in a Windows DNA environment and those used with Web Services.

Before moving on to how the Services Framework supports Web Services, we need to place these technologies into perspective by peeking under the covers.

A Brief Overview of SOAP

Simple Object Access Protocol (SOAP) is an XML grammar designed to leverage XML and HTTP to provide access to services in a platform-neutral way. Using this combination embodied in SOAP (and some platform-specific translation as embodied in the Services Framework), client applications can transparently call CORBA/IIOP components running on a Sun Solaris box as easily as they can call COM+ components on Windows 2000. By incorporating SOAP, a development tool like VS .NET has access to a much broader set of services than those provided by its native platform. Although space prohibits a complete discussion of the grammar itself (see Don Box's overview on MSDN at `http://msdn.microsoft.com/msdnmag/issues/0300/soap/soap.asp` and the SOAP specification at `http://www.w3c.org`.), a quick look at the basic XML message structure is warranted.

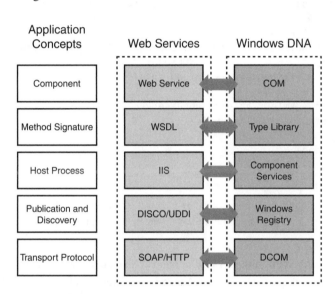

FIGURE 11.1

This diagram provides a mapping of application concepts to both Web Services and Windows DNA.

NOTE

The Services Framework incorporates support for SOAP 1.1, the specification for which can be found at `http://www.w3.org/TR/2000/NOTE-SOAP-20000508/`.

Of course the interesting aspect of SOAP, and its real power, is that it defines an RPC-style calling mechanism for HTTP using XML. For example, consider a Web Service developed by a financial institution that exposes a method allowing a customer to query his account balance given the account number and PIN number. Using SOAP, the client application creates an XML payload that serializes the method call and its parameters and sends it to the Web server using an HTTP POST. The complete HTTP message with its headers would look something like this:

```
POST /WebServices.asp HTTP/1.1
Host: mybankserver.com
User-Agent: MSDNWS
Content-Type: text/xml; charset utf-8
Content-Length: 206
SOAPAction: mybanksserver.com/WebServices/QueryBalance

<?xml version="1.0" encoding="utf-8"?>
<soap:Envelope xmlns:xsi=http://www.w3.org/2001/XMLSchema-instance
  xmlns:xsd="http://www.w3.org/2001/XMLSchema"
  xmlns:soap="http://schemas.xmlsoap.org/soap/envelope">
  <soap:Body>
      <QueryBalance xmlns="http://mybankserver.com/WebServices">
          <Account>66555443</Account>
          <PIN>7654</PIN>
      </QueryBalance>
  </soap:Body>
</soap:Envelope>
```

Note that the HTTP Content-Type is text/xml, and that SOAP mandates the inclusion of the SOAPAction HTTP header field to indicate the intent of the request and to allow firewalls to filter SOAP requests.

The XML payload embodied in the request contains mandatory Envelope and Body elements. Within the Body, the method name QueryBalance is itself represented as an element whose child elements correspond to the arguments passed to the method. SOAP also allows for an optional Header element within the Envelope that specifies processing instructions for the server. If the Header includes the attribute mustUnderstand set to a value of "1," the server cannot ignore the header. Headers can be useful when exchanging SOAP messages using products such as BizTalk Server 2000. SOAP also allows more complex data types to be represented in the request.

NOTE

Actually, SOAP defines two ways that a Web Service method, referred to as an *operation*, can be encoded in a request or response. The example here assumes that the Document style (discussed in Section 5 of the SOAP specification) is being employed where an XSD schema is used to describe both the request and response. The SOAP request generated from the client must then adhere to this schema. Alternatively, an RPC style (defined in Section 7) can be employed where the parameters to the method are mapped directly to elements of the same name.

When the request has been processed by the Web Service, it returns a SOAP response message packaged in an HTTP response that contains an XML payload indicating the return values from the method as follows:

```
HTTP/1.1 200 OK
Content-Length: 245
Content-Type: text/xml charset=utf-8

<?xml version="1.0" encoding="utf-8"?>
<SOAP:Envelope xmlns:xsi=http://www.w3.org/2000/10/XMLSchema-instance
    xmlns:xsd="http://www.w3.org/2000/10/XMLSchema"
    xmlns:soap="http://schemas.xmlsoap.org/soap/envelope">
  <soap:Body>
    <QueryBalanceResponse xmlns="http://mybankserver.com/WebServices">
       <QueryBalanceResult>7641</QueryBalanceResult>
    </QueryBalanceResponse>
  </soap:Body>
</soap:Envelope>
```

Notice that the same `Content-Type` is used along with the familiar `Envelope` and `Body` elements. The return values are then packaged in a `QueryBalanceResponse` element whose children represent each output parameter—in this case, the balance of the account.

SOAP also includes a standard error-passing mechanism using a `Fault` element that includes attributes such as `faultcode`, `faultstring`, and `detail`. A client application then can easily determine when errors occurred in the Web Service and alert the user or log the error appropriately.

Although this example shows some of the basics of SOAP, two questions remain: How do clients discover Web Services, and when they do, how do they determine which methods a particular Web Service supports? One answer to the latter question is the use of the Web Services Description Language (WSDL).

Web Services Description Language

WSDL (http://msdn.microsoft.com/xml/general/wsdl.asp) is an XML grammar that can be used to describe the capabilities of a Web Service. A client can use WSDL as the template to build SOAP messages to correctly call the service. In this way, you can think of a WSDL document as the contract between the client and server analogous to the interface definition of a COM+ component as exposed through a type library. Although space prohibits anything more than a cursory examination of WSDL, consider the WSDL contract generated for the simple banking Web Service discussed previously and shown in Listing 11.1.

LISTING 11.1 The WSDL Contract. This XML document defines the contract that a consumer uses to call a simple banking Web Service.

```xml
<?xml version="1.0" ?>
<definitions xmlns:s=http://www.w3.org/2000/10/XMLSchema
  xmlns:http="http://schemas.xmlsoap.org/wsdl/http/"
  xmlns:mime="http://schemas.xmlsoap.org/wsdl/mime/"
  xmlns:urt=http://microsoft.com/urt/wsdl/text/
  xmlns:soap="http://schemas.xmlsoap.org/wsdl/soap/"
  xmlns:soapenc="http://schemas.xmlsoap.org/soap/encoding/"
  xmlns:s0="http://mybanksserver.com/WebServices"
    targetNamespace="http://mybanksserver.com/WebServices"
  xmlns="http://schemas.xmlsoap.org/wsdl/">
<types>
    <s:schema attributeFormDefault="qualified"
      elementFormDefault="qualified"
    targetNamespace=" http://mybanksserver.com/WebServices">
        <s:element name="QueryBalance">
            <s:complexType>
                <s:sequence>
                  <s:element name="Account" nullable="true"
                    type="s:string" />
                  <s:element name="PIN" type="s:int" />
                </s:sequence>
            </s:complexType>
        </s:element>
        <s:element name="QueryBalanceResponse">
          <s:complexType>
              <s:sequence>
                <s:element name="QueryBalanceResult" type="s:decimal" />
              </s:sequence>
          </s:complexType>
      </s:element>
        <s:element name="decimal" type="s:decimal" />
    </s:schema>
</types>
<message name="QueryBalanceSoapIn">
  <part name="parameters" element="s0:QueryBalance" />
</message>
<message name="QueryBalanceSoapOut">
    <part name="parameters" element="s0:QueryBalanceResponse" />
</message>
<portType name="BankingSoapPortType">
  <operation name="QueryBalance">
      <input message="s0:QueryBalanceSoapIn" />
      <output message="s0:QueryBalanceSoapOut" />
```

LISTING 11.1 Continued

```
      </operation>
    </portType>
    <binding name="BankingSoapBinding" type="s0:BankingSoapPortType">
      <soap:binding transport="http://schemas.xmlsoap.org/soap/http"
        style="document" />
      <operation name="QueryBalance">
          <soap:operation
            soapAction="http://mybanksserver.com/WebServices/QueryBalance"
            style="document" />
            <input>
                <soap:body use="literal" />
            </input>
            <output>
                <soap:body use="literal" />
            </output>
      </operation>
    </binding>
    <service name="Banking">
      <port name="BankingSoap" binding="s0:BankingSoapBinding">
          <soap:address location="http://mybankserver.com/WebServices" />
      </port>
    </service>
</definitions>
```

The WSDL contract is comprised of a series of abstractions that define the Web Service. A convenient way to read the document is from the bottom up. For example, note that the service element near the bottom of Listing 11.1 identifies the Web Service ("Banking") and specifies the available ports. A port identifies an endpoint through which a client can communicate with the service. In this case, the only endpoint is BankingSoap, which specifies the network address and encapsulates the definition of the SOAP messages to be passed using a binding.

NOTE

Web Services created with VB .NET are not limited to communicating strictly through a SOAP port. They also can include HTTP GET and POST ports. This makes it possible for developers to incorporate Web Services as long as they can call a simple URL. This permits even development tools that don't yet support SOAP to take advantage of Web Services.

The binding (BankingSoapBinding) in turn specifies the operations (methods) available, their style (document or RPC), and how they are identified through the SOAPAction header. The binding then points to the port type (`BankingSoapPortType`), which includes each operation and its associated input and output messages. The messages (`QueryBalanceSoapIn` and `QueryBalanceSoapOut`) define the structure of the XML messages passed to (`QueryBalance`) and received from (`QueryBalanceResponse`) the service by pointing to elements defined in the `types` element. Because the document style of encoding is to be used, this element consists of type definitions that use the XML Schemas (XSD) specification to define the structure of the types. As you can see, the `QueryBalance` element includes child elements to pass the account and pin parameters, whereas the `QueryBalanceResponse` element includes the return value of the method as decimal.

By retrieving and parsing the WSDL contract, a client application can create XML payloads to be sent to the server that conform to the calling conventions expected by the Web Service. Conversely, when the result is returned, the client can interpret the results based on the WSDL contract.

However, you might be wondering how prospective consumers of a Web Service know that a WSDL contract exists and how to find it. This is accomplished through the process of Web Service discovery and the use of Universal Discovery, Description and Integration (UDDI).

Web Service Discovery

Web Service Discovery is a process that VS .NET uses to enumerate the WSDL contracts on a Web Server or within any virtual directory on a Web Server. A Web Service can be exposed by placing an XML file with the extension vsdisco in the virtual directory. This document can include a reference to the WSDL contract in addition to references to other disco files. For example, the following vsdisco file could be placed in the virtual directory for the banking Web Service:

```xml
<?xml version="1.0" ?>
<disco:discovery xmlns:disco="http://schemas.xmlsoap.org/disco"
    xmlns:scl="http://schemas.xmlsoap.org/disco/scl">
    <scl:contractRef ref="http://mybankserver.com/webservices/banking.wsdl"/>
    <disco:discoveryRef ref="moreservices/default.vsdisco" />
</disco:discovery>
```

In this example, the WSDL contract is specified in the file banking.wsdl, and the disco file points to a relative path (`moreservices`) that contains another disco file to enumerate other services. To allow consumers to find the disco file without knowing its name, you can place a `link` tag in the `HEAD` tag of the default page for the virtual directory like so:

```html
<HEAD>
    <link type="text/xml" rel="alternate" href="banking.vsdisco"/>
</HEAD>
```

In the same way, a disco file could be placed in the root directory of the Web Server and enumerate all the available WSDL contracts on the server. In this way, by simply pointing to the Web Server, a developer can get access to all its Web Services.

To alleviate the burden of setting up what amounts to a directory on the Web Server, discovery also can be enabled dynamically. By placing a `dynamicDiscovery` element in the disco file, all the Web Services in the virtual directory and any child directories will be exposed. In addition, you can include `exclude` elements to disable searching of specific directories. For example, the following disco file alternatively could be used:

```
<?xml version="1.0" encoding="utf-8" ?>
<dynamicDiscovery xmlns="urn:schemas-dynamicdiscovery:disco.2000-03-17">
    <exclude path="_vti_cnf" />
    <exclude path="_vti_pvt" />
    <exclude path="_vti_log" />
    <exclude path="_vti_script" />
    <exclude path="_vti_txt" />
    <exclude path="Web References" />
</dynamicDiscovery>
```

By default, when you create a new Web Service in VS .NET, dynamic discovery is enabled in this way by adding a similar vsdisco file to the virtual directory. In the same manner, as previously mentioned, this file can be linked to the default page for the virtual directory, or placed in the root of the Web Server to allow dynamic discovery on the entire site.

NOTE

As discussed later in the chapter, the discovery process occurs when a developer uses the Add Web Reference option from the Project menu, or by right-clicking on References in the VS .NET Solution Explorer.

UDDI

Although Web Service Discovery allows developers to find Web Services in a particular virtual directory or within a particular Web server, it does not address finding Web Services across servers or across companies. Keep in mind that for developers, the vision of a programmable Web means that within VS .NET, you should be able to click on Project, Add Web Reference and find the WSDL contract for Web Services published across the world. This is the aim of Universal Description, Discovery, and Integration (UDDI).

UDDI is an industry initiative (www.uddi.org) with more than 220 participating companies that aims to integrate business services over the Internet by promoting a common protocol to publish and connect to Web Services using directories. A Web Service directory or registry is where businesses can publish their Web Services that are searchable. Although in the beta stage now, you can publish information about your company and Web Services at uddi.microsoft.com. The UDDI specification calls for four types of information to be published in the registry including business information, service information, binding information, and specifications for services.

The Add Web References dialog includes an automatic link to the UDDI directory, as discussed later in the chapter. In addition, developers can download the UDDI SDK from the same site. Features of the SDK include .NET classes that allow you to programmatically search the registry and host a lightweight registry of your own for internal use.

The promise of a global directory coupled with WSDL means that development tools and custom code can be written to automatically find and use Web Services without human interaction. For example, UDDI could be used to automatically locate an equivalent public Web Service by comparing the XSD schemas of operations in WSDL documents (referred to as a Technology Model or tModel in UDDI parlance) if the preferred Web Service was not responding.

Web Services in the Services Framework

When a developer has a basic understanding of XML, the jump to SOAP and WSDL is not daunting. However, these industry standards are still somewhat in flux and will change as time passes. Luckily for VB .NET developers, this plumbing has been subsumed into the Services Framework to abstract developers from the details. From the VB .NET perspective, developing a Web Service is analogous to developing a Web site using ASP.NET and can be built using VB .NET syntax.

This abstraction has the immediate benefit of making Web Service development simpler so that the bar for entry is easily reachable. In addition, with subsequent releases to VS .NET, the latest Web standards will be rolled into the Services Framework, shielding developers from the task of updating their code to meet new W3C standards.

NOTE

For developers who continue to use VB 6.0, the SOAP Toolkit for Visual Basic is available. Simply put, the toolkit is a COM and IIS language binding for SOAP and provides the underlying code necessary to expose a COM object as a Web service on IIS and consume a Web Service using a COM-compliant development tool such as Visual Basic. The core pieces of the toolkit include the Remote Object Proxy Engine (ROPE), the WSDL Wizard, and both ASP and ISAPI listeners for IIS. In addition, the UDDI SDK from Microsoft also supports a Visual Studio 6.0 library to allow searching UDDI registries.

Not surprisingly then, high-level support for Web Services in the Services Framework is included in the System.Web.Services namespace, as shown in Table 11.1.

TABLE 11.1 Classes in the System.Web.Services Namespace

Class	Description
WebMethodAttribute	Attribute placed on a method of class to allow it to be included in the WSDL contract.
WebService	Optional base class for a Web Service that includes access to ASP.NET functionality.
WebServiceAttribute	Attribute placed at the class level to add optional information, such as a Name, Description, and Namespace.
WebServiceBindingAttribute	Attribute placed at the class level to define additional SOAP bindings for the Web Service. Includes properties for the binding Name, Location, and Namespace.

With the context set, the remainder of this chapter focuses on implementing and consuming a Web Service with VB .NET.

Web Service Implementation

To create a Web Service hosted in its own site, you simply need to create a new project in VS .NET and select the Web Service template from the new project dialog. VS .NET then creates a virtual directory on the IIS server of your choice and a working directory on your local machine under the Visual Studio Projects folder in My Documents. In addition, you can add a Web Service to an existing Web application by right-clicking on the project in the Solution Explorer and choosing Add Web Service. As mentioned in Chapter 10, the way with which you work with the files in the project is analogous to using Visual Interdev (VID) in VS 6.0.

Like a Web application created with ASP.NET, a separate Web Services project will contain Global.asax and Web.config files, which allows you to write code that handles Application and Session events, as well as configuring authentication and session state modes as discussed in Chapter 10. In other words, a Web Service in VS .NET has access to all the underlying functionality of ASP.NET while providing a new way of communicating with code on the server.

The Web Service itself is exposed by the creation of a .asmx file. This file is the endpoint for the Web Service through which its methods will be called as defined in the port element of the WSDL document. This architecture implies that multiple Web Services can be exposed through a single virtual directory by including more than one .asmx file. The HTTP handler for the .asmx file does most of the work and encapsulates the code required to listen for requests, parse them, invoke the proper method, and send results.

The methods of the Web Service must be placed into a class that can be either created inline in the .asmx file, or referenced in a separate file. The default behavior is for VS .NET to create a code-behind file with a .vb extension that has the same name as the .asmx file. This file then is referenced in the WebService directive. In other words, a file called WebService.asmx would contain the following text:

```
<%@ WebService Language="vb"
  Codebehind="WebService.asmx.vb"
  Class="QuilogyEducation.EducationService" %>
```

Note that the CodeBehind attribute is used to specify the name of the file containing the QuilogyEducation.EducationService class. In addition, there is no runat=server tag because all Web Service code runs on the server.

TIP

Although you can place the code inline in the .asmx file, it is not recommended because the VS .NET code editor will not be able to use IntelliSense and keyword coloring because the file does not have a .vb extension. In addition, the inclusion of the .vb file allows the Web Service class to be compiled into a DLL prior to invocation. Classes within the .asmx file must be compiled on-the-fly.

When you right-click on the .asmx file and select View Code, the .vb file is loaded into the editor based on the value of the CodeBehind attribute.

Creating a Web Service Class

The class that implements the Web Service is, in many respects, the same as any other custom class with the following exceptions:

- For the class to have access to ASP.NET intrinsics, such as Application and Session state, the class must be derived from WebService, as shown in Table 11.1.

- For a method to be exposed through the Web Service, it must include the WebMethod attribute.

As a result, the recommended approach for creating Web Services is to create separate Web Services classes that act as wrappers to the business and data access classes discussed in Chapter 7 and shown in Figure 7.4. Under this model, the Web Services classes are a part of the user services layer in a distributed application. On reflection, it is apparent that this is appropriate because Web Services are fundamentally just a programmatic, HTTP-based interface to business logic and, as such, should be logically separate.

For example, consider a simple Web Service that Quilogy might provide to its customers. The actual functionality of the Web Service is the same as that provided by the Web application, namely the capability to query course schedules and review transcripts. An appropriate strategy is to simply add a .asmx file to the Web application that exposes the functionality already present in the business and data access classes. Listing 11.2 shows the .asmx file that exposes the `Login`, `GetTranscript`, and `GetSchedule` methods.

LISTING 11.2 Quilogy Education Web Service. This listing shows a simple Web Service that exposes three methods that wrap methods of the data access classes.

```vb
Option Strict On

Imports System.Web.Services
Imports System.Web.Services.Protocols
Imports Quilogy.Education
Imports Quilogy.Education.Enrollment
Imports Quilogy.Education.Schedule
Imports System.Xml.Serialization
Imports System.Xml
Imports System.Configuration


<WebService(Namespace:="www.quilogy.com/edservice", _
 Description:="Quilogy's Education Web Service", _
 Name:="QuilogyEducation")> _
Public Class EducationService : Inherits WebService

  '****************************************************************
  <WebMethod(Description:="Retrieves a student's transcript", _
    EnableSession:=True)> _
  Public Function GetTranscript() As TranscriptData
    Dim dsTrans As TranscriptData
    Dim objStud As New Students()

    ' Check the incoming argument
    If Session("StudentID") Is Nothing Then
      Throw New ArgumentNullException( _
        "You must login before calling the GetTranscript method")
      Return Nothing
    End If

    ' Call the data access component
    dsTrans = objStud.GetTranscript( _
      Convert.ToInt32(Session("StudentID")))
    Return dsTrans

  End Function

  '****************************************************************
  <WebMethod(Description:="Allows a student to login", EnableSession:=True)> _
```

Listing 11.2   Continued

```vb
Public Function Login(ByVal EmailAddress As String, _
  ByVal Password As String) As Boolean
  Dim objStud As Students
  Dim dsStud As StudentData
  Dim drStud As DataRow

  ' Check the incoming arguments
  If EmailAddress Is Nothing Or Password Is Nothing Then
    Throw New ArgumentNullException( _
      "You must supply an email address and password")
    Return False
  End If

  ' Call the data access component
  objStud = New Students()
  dsStud = objStud.Login(EmailAddress, Password)

  If Not dsStud Is Nothing Then
    ' Extract the student ID
    drStud = dsStud.StudentTable.Rows(0)
    Session("StudentID") = drStud(StudentData.STUDENT_ID)
    Return True
  Else
    Throw New Exception( _
      "Student is not registered or credentials were incorrect")
    Return False
  End If

End Function

'*****************************************************************
<WebMethod( _
  Description:="Retrieves a course schedule")> _
Public Function GetSchedule(ByVal Location As String, _
  ByVal Vendor As String, ByVal DaysOut As Byte) As ScheduleData
  Dim objClasses As New Classes( _
    ConfigurationSettings.AppSettings("SQLConnect"))
  Dim intLocID As Integer
  Dim intVendorID As Integer
  Dim dsSched As ScheduleData

  ' Translate the arguments
  Select Case Location
    Case "St. Louis", "STL"
      intLocID = 4
```

LISTING 11.2 Continued

```
    Case "Kansas City", "KC"
      intLocID = 1
    Case "Des Moines", "DSM"
      intLocID = 2
    Case "Omaha", "OMA"
      intLocID = 3
    Case "Nashville", "NSH"
      intLocID = 5
    Case Else
      intLocID = 0 'All cities
  End Select
  Select Case Vendor
    Case "Microsoft", "MSFT"
      intVendorID = 1
    Case "Oracle"
      intVendorID = 4
    Case "Sybase", "SYB"
      intVendorID = 2
    Case Else
      intVendorID = 0
  End Select

  ' Call the data access component
  dsSched = objClasses.GetSchedule(intLocID, intVendorID, DaysOut)
  Return dsSched
End Function

End Class
```

The first thing to note about the EducationService class is that it derives from WebService. As mentioned in Table 11.1, this is optional because the real work of interacting with the class as a Web Service is done by the HTTP handler. WebService simply contains instance properties that expose the ASP.NET Application, Server, Session, and User objects in the HttpContext.

> **TIP**
>
> As was true of the Web Forms application in Chapter 10, this Web Service will by default allow the password to be sent in clear text to the Web server when the Login method is called. To avoid this, an alternative architecture would be to place the Login method in a separate .asmx file placed in virtual directory on the same site protected by SSL. In this way the password is protected while the other methods can be called without the overhead of SSL.

Second, the class contains the optional `WebService` attribute that includes properties, such as `Namespace`, `Description`, and `Name`. These properties allow you to set the namespace used in the `SoapAction` attribute in the WSDL contract. For example, by setting the `Namespace` to `www.quilogy.com/edservice`, the `SoapAction` for the `GetTranscript` method becomes `www.quilogy.com/edservice/GetTranscript`. If unset, the default namespace is `www.tempuri.org`. In an analogous way, the `Name` property is used to set the name of the `Service` element in the WSDL contract. By default, it is set to the name of the Web Service class; in this case, it has been overridden with `QuilogyEducation`. Finally, the `Description` property is used by the HTTP handler to display a human readable description when the .asmx file is requested by a browser without a query string. The description is stored in the documentation element of the service element in the WSDL contract. For example, when the WebService.asmx file is browsed, the HTML service help page appears, as shown in Figure 11.2.

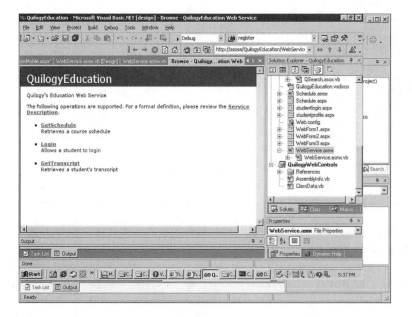

FIGURE 11.2
The Service Help Page is manufactured by ASP.NET when a .asmx file is called from a browser without a query string.

The page in Figure 11.2 typically is used for testing the Web Service and, to a lesser extent, as an information vehicle for prospective clients. By default, the service help page also contains links to the WSDL and to each method. The method links are particularly helpful because they show the calling and return XML syntax for each method, allowing a developer of a client application to understand exactly how to call the Web Service. For example, the HTTP SOAP request and response messages for the `GetSchedule` method can be seen in Listing 11.3.

LISTING 11.3 SOAP Messages. This listing shows the HTTP SOAP messages used with the `GetSchedule` method of the Quilogy Education Web Service.

Request

```
POST /Quilogyeducation/webservice.asmx HTTP/1.1
Host: ssosa
Content-Type: text/xml; charset=utf-8
Content-Length: length
SOAPAction: "www.quilogy.com/edservice/GetSchedule"

<?xml version="1.0" encoding="utf-8"?>
<soap:Envelope xmlns:xsi="http://www.w3.org/2001/XMLSchema-instance"
  xmlns:xsd="http://www.w3.org/2001/XMLSchema"
  xmlns:soap="http://schemas.xmlsoap.org/soap/envelope/">
  <soap:Body>
    <GetSchedule xmlns="www.quilogy.com/edservice">
      <Location>string</Location>
      <Vendor>string</Vendor>
      <DaysOut>unsignedByte</DaysOut>
    </GetSchedule>
  </soap:Body>
</soap:Envelope>
```

Response

```
HTTP/1.1 200 OK
Content-Type: text/xml; charset=utf-8
Content-Length: length

<?xml version="1.0" encoding="utf-8"?>
<soap:Envelope xmlns:xsi="http://www.w3.org/2001/XMLSchema-instance"
  xmlns:xsd="http://www.w3.org/2001/XMLSchema"
  xmlns:soap="http://schemas.xmlsoap.org/soap/envelope/">
  <soap:Body>
    <GetScheduleResponse xmlns="www.quilogy.com/edservice">
      <GetScheduleResult>dataset</GetScheduleResult>
    </GetScheduleResponse>
  </soap:Body>
</soap:Envelope>
```

Note that the bolded items in Listing 11.3 are placeholders that would contain actual data. This page also can be modified to provide custom information about the Web Service—for example, your company's logo—by customizing the DefaultWsdlHelpGenerator.aspx page found in the *windowsdir*\Microsoft.NET Framework*version*\CONFIG directory.

Using GET and POST

As mentioned previously, another interesting aspect of a Web Service created with ASP.NET is that it not only provides a SOAP port in the WSDL contract but also HTTP-GET and HTTP POST ports. In this way, a Web Service can be called by clients that don't yet support SOAP. This can be seen clearly by examining the WSDL contract provided by the service help page. The relevant sections supporting HTTP-GET are produced in Listing 11.4.

LISTING 11.4   Support for HTTP-GET in WSDL. This excerpt from the WSDL contract for the Quilogy Education Web Service shows how HTTP GET is supported by ASP.NET.

```
<message name="GetTranscriptHttpGetIn" />
<message name="GetTranscriptHttpGetOut">
  <part name="Body" element="s0:TranscriptData" />
</message>
<message name="LoginHttpGetIn">
  <part name="EmailAddress" type="s:string" />
  <part name="Password" type="s:string" />
</message>
<message name="LoginHttpGetOut">
  <part name="Body" element="s0:boolean" />
</message>
<message name="GetScheduleHttpGetIn">
  <part name="Location" type="s:string" />
  <part name="Vendor" type="s:string" />
  <part name="DaysOut" type="s:string" />
</message>
<message name="GetScheduleHttpGetOut">
  <part name="Body" element="s0:ScheduleData" />
</message>
<portType name="QuilogyEducationHttpGet">
  <operation name="GetTranscript">
    <documentation>Retrieves a student's transcript</documentation>
    <input message="s0:GetTranscriptHttpGetIn" />
    <output message="s0:GetTranscriptHttpGetOut" />
  </operation>
  <operation name="Login">
    <documentation>Allows a student to login</documentation>
    <input message="s0:LoginHttpGetIn" />
    <output message="s0:LoginHttpGetOut" />
  </operation>
  <operation name="GetSchedule">
    <documentation>Retrieves a course schedule</documentation>
    <input message="s0:GetScheduleHttpGetIn" />
    <output message="s0:GetScheduleHttpGetOut" />
  </operation>
```

LISTING 11.4 Continued

```
</portType>
<binding name="QuilogyEducationHttpGet" type="s0:QuilogyEducationHttpGet">
  <http:binding verb="GET" />
  <operation name="GetTranscript">
    <http:operation location="/GetTranscript" />
    <input>
      <http:urlEncoded />
    </input>
    <output>
      <mime:mimeXml part="Body" />
    </output>
  </operation>
  <operation name="Login">
    <http:operation location="/Login" />
    <input>
      <http:urlEncoded />
    </input>
    <output>
      <mime:mimeXml part="Body" />
    </output>
  </operation>
  <operation name="GetSchedule">
    <http:operation location="/GetSchedule" />
    <input>
      <http:urlEncoded />
    </input>
    <output>
      <mime:mimeXml part="Body" />
    </output>
  </operation>
</binding>
<service name="QuilogyEducation">
  <port name="QuilogyEducationHttpGet" binding="s0:QuilogyEducationHttpGet">
    <http:address location="http://ssosa/QuilogyEducation/WebService.asmx" />
  </port>
  <documentation>Quilogy's Education Web Service</documentation>
</service>
```

Once again, reading from the bottom up, the port `QuilogyEducationHttpGet` is defined in the `port` element of the `service` element. The port points to the `binding` element, which defines the three operations (methods) of the Web Service. In turn, each operation is defined and includes input and output messages. Note that each message is defined as a series of part elements. The input messages for a `GET` request define each query string parameter as a part element, whereas the output message simply defines a single element that will be returned. In this way, the request can be made using HTTP-GET, but the result is an XML document.

Although supporting HTTP-GET and POST extends the reach of Web Services, it does so at a price. For example, all three protocols support the same basic set of scalar data types, such as strings and integers, as shown in Table 11.2. However, only SOAP allows classes and structures serialized as XML to be passed to a method. In addition, a method called via SOAP can use the ByRef keyword to pass classes that are copied in and out of the method to support passing objects by reference. On the flip side, SOAP requires a larger payload and more complex parsing, and so entails more overhead than HTTP-GET and POST.

TABLE 11.2 Scalar VB .NET Data Types Supported by Web Services

VB .NET Data Type	XML Schema Data Type
Boolean	boolean
Double	double
Enum	enum
Integer	int
Long	long
Short	short
String	string
Byte	unsignedbyte

The WSDL in Listing 11.4 allows a client to create the following URL to call the Login method of the Web Service:

```
http://server/QuilogyEducation/WebService.asmx/
  Login?EmailAddress=dfox@quilogy.com&Password=dlfrr55
```

and receive the following response:

```
HTTP/1.1 200 OK
Content-Type: text/xml; charset=utf-8
Content-Length: 83

<?xml version="1.0"?>
<boolean xmlns="www.quilogy.com/edservice">True</boolean>
```

For a method to be included in the WSDL contract, it must be marked with the WebMethod attribute. Methods so marked are referred to as *web methods*. The WebMethod attribute includes the instance properties shown in Table 11.3.

TABLE 11.3 Properties of the `WebMethod` Attribute

Class	Description
BufferResponse	Boolean. When set to `True` (the default), the response for the web method is buffered. This is analogous to setting `Repsonse.Buffer` to `True` in classic ASP. Set this property to `False` when the web method returns a large amount of data.
CacheDuration	Integer. Gets or sets the number of seconds a response from the web method is placed in the cache. If the web method is called again within the duration, the same response is returned. Defaults to 0 and should only be set when the web method returns large amounts of static data to conserve resources.
Description	String. Sets the description displayed in the service help page shown in Figure 11.2 and placed in the documentation element of the WSDL contract for the operation.
EnableSession	Boolean. When set to `True`, the `Session` object is available to be used. The default is `False` and so it must be used when web methods use session state.
MessageName	String. Used to provide an alias for the method or property name of the web method. Used with overloaded (polymorphic) methods in a Web Service class.
TransactionOption	TransactionOption. Set to a constant in the enumeration to indicate the transaction support of the web method. Used to allow the web method to be the root of a distributed transaction when set to `TransactionOption.RequiresNew` or `TransactionOption.Required`.

In Listing 11.2, each `WebMethod` attribute includes the `Description` property. Developers with a background in ASP will note that both the `Login` and `GetTranscript` methods refer to the `Session` object to store and retrieve the student's unique identifier from the database. In this way, Web Service classes are unlike serviced components because they can store state information. This is useful, particularly for authentication, as is done in this case, so that the client application needn't worry about database identifiers. As a result, both methods set the `EnableSession` property of the `WebMethod` attribute to `True`.

NOTE

In this example, the Quilogy Education Web Service uses its own authentication scheme by storing e-mail addresses and passwords in a SQL Server 2000 database.

> However, Web Services created in ASP.NET can alternatively use the same authentication options as in a Web application, namely Windows, Forms, and Passport, by setting the appropriate options in the Web.config file. When authenticating in this way, the ASP.NET User object is available and contains the user's identity. Obviously, Web Services created for use within an organization most likely will use Windows authentication, whereas public Web Services will use Forms, Passport, or a custom scheme.

Although not used in Listing 11.2, it should be noted that the `TransactionOption` and `MessageName` properties are particularly useful. In the case of the former, you can use the property to allow the web method to participate in a distributed transaction as the root object. In this way, a web method could call multiple methods exposed by serviced components and coordinate their work. The `MessageName` property is useful if your Web Service class contains overloaded methods, and you want to expose each method in the WSDL contract. Overloaded methods cannot be used because WSDL does not allow two operations to have the same name.

Web Service Design Issues

Although getting a Web Service up and running is straightforward, there are several issues to consider, including passing objects and error handling.

Perhaps the biggest consideration when designing the interface for a Web Service is that if your Web Service is to be called using `HTTP-GET` or `POST`, the web methods cannot accept objects as arguments.

On the flip side, as you might have noticed from Listing 11.2, both the `GetTranscript` and `GetSchedule` web methods return the derived `DataSet` classes, `TranscriptData` and `ScheduleData`, respectively. In both cases, the `DataSets` are populated by the data access classes discussed in Chapter 7 and returned through the web method. Because these classes are derived from `DataSet`, which is derived from `MarshalByValueComponent`, ASP.NET can represent the object with an XSD schema and serialize it to XML for inclusion in the response message sent back to the client. This implies that any object you want to return from a web method needs to derive from `MarshalByValueComponent`, implement the `ISerializable` interface, or use the `Serializable` attribute discussed in Chapter 8, "Building Components."

NOTE

In this case, the WSDL actually contains a reference to the XSD schemas of the `TranscriptData` and `ScheduleData` types by including the import element. For example, to get the XSD schema for the `TranscriptData` type, the location attribute points to the .asmx file with the query string `schema=QuilogyTranscript`.

In addition, the protocols used to call the web method also affect how error handling is done. If the method contains a `Try Catch` block that throws an exception, or if the methods called in the web method throw an exception, these automatically are translated into a `SoapException` and returned to the client as SOAP client fault code. For example, the `Login` method in Listing 11.2 throws an `ArgumentNullException` if the `EmailAddress` or `Password` is not passed to the method. When the method is called using SOAP, this exception is intercepted by ASP.NET and returned to the client according to the SOAP specification.

> **TIP**
>
> In addition, you can customize the information returned to the client by building a `SoapException` object yourself and then throwing the exception. This is done by creating an `XmlNode` and appending to it child nodes. This node then is passed to the constructor of `SoapException`, which then populates the `Detail` property of `SoapException` object. An example of this can be found in the online help in the documentation for the `SoapException` class. Using this technique, you can provide additional information to a client about the causes of the error.

However, throwing exceptions from web methods called by `HTTP-GET` or `POST` does not work so gracefully. In fact, an exception thrown when using either of these protocols results in an HTTP 500 error with the client unable to read the error string. As a result, for methods that simply perform an operation such as updating a database, you'll want to return status codes indicating success or failure, and perhaps include a separate method that returns the text of the last error that the client can subsequently call. This technique is analogous to that used by the Win32 API for calls to functions within its DLLs. For example, the code in Listing 11.5 shows how the `Login` method might be modified to support this technique.

LISTING 11.5   Error Handling with `HTTP-GET` and `POST`. This listing shows changes to the `Login` method and the inclusion of the `GetLastError` method to enable `GET` and `POST` clients to see error information.

```
<WebMethod(Description:="Allows a student to login", EnableSession:=True)> _
Public Function Login2(ByVal EmailAddress As String, _
  ByVal Password As String) As Boolean
    Dim objStud As Students
    Dim dsStud As StudentData
    Dim drStud As DataRow

    ' Check the incoming arguments
    If EmailAddress Is Nothing Or Password Is Nothing Then
        Session("strLastError") = _
```

LISTING 11.5   Continued

```
            "You must supply an email address and password"
        Return False
    End If


    ' Call the data access component
    objStud = New Students()
    Try
        dsStud = objStud.Login(EmailAddress, Password)
    Catch e As Exception
        Session("strLastError") = e.Message
    End Try


    If Not dsStud Is Nothing Then
        ' Extract the student ID
        drStud = dsStud.StudentTable.Rows(0)
        Session("intStudentID") = drStud(StudentData.STUDENT_ID)
        Return True
    Else
        Session("strLastError") = _
          "Student is not registered or credentials were incorrect"
        Return False
    End If
End Function

<WebMethod(Description:="Returns the last error", EnableSession:=True)> _
Public Function GetLastError() As String
    Return Session("strLastError")
End Function
```

In this case, all exceptions are caught and the Session variable strLastError is set to the
error string that can be subsequently returned through the GetLastError method.

Customizing SOAP

In addition to information you can add to the WSDL contract using the WebService and
WebMethod attributes, you also can modify the WSDL using attributes found in the various
namespaces in the Services Framework.

Setting the Encoding Style

As noted previously, ASP.NET Web Services support both the Document and RPC encodings
in the SOAP specification. By default, ASP.NET uses the Document style and, therefore,

includes XSD schema information in the WSDL document that describes the SOAP request and response messages. To explicitly set which encoding to use, you can apply the `SoapRpcService` or `SoapDocumentService` attributes found in the `System.Web.Services.Protocols` namespace to the Web Service class.

When using `SoapDocumentService`, you also can specify how parameters are encoded by setting the `ParameterStyle` and `Use` properties. The `ParameterStyle` property can be set to one of the constants in the `SoapParameterStyle` enumeration. The default is `Wrapped` so that parameters are wrapped within a single element beneath the `Body` element but also can be set to `Bare`. The `Use` property determines whether the parameters are encoded using the encoding specified in section 5 of the SOAP specification (`SoapBindingUse.Encoded`) or in a predefined XSD schema (`SoapBindingUse.Literal`).

The encoding also can be set at the method level by applying the `SoapRpcMethod` or `SoapDocumentMethod` attributes to the particular methods. In this way, you can override the class level setting for individual methods.

> **TIP**
>
> If you apply the `SoapRpcMethod` attribute to a Web method, it cannot return objects, such as the `DataSet`, because no XSD schema will be generated. Doing so causes an exception to be thrown.

Both the `SoapRpcMethod` and `SoapDocumentMethod` attributes support properties including `Action`, `Binding`, `OneWay`, `RequestElementName`, `RequestNamespace`, `ResponseElementName`, and `ResponseNamespace`. As expected, each of these (with the exception of `OneWay`) changes the way the WSDL is produced for the Web Service. For example, the `Action` property can be used to override the default `SoapAction` associated with the method, whereas the `RequestElementName` is used to override the request element name, which by default is set to the method name appended with "Request."

Two of the more interesting properties of these attributes are `Binding` and `OneWay`. The `Binding` attribute can be used to specify which binding in the WSDL contract a method belongs to. Simply put, bindings allow operations to be grouped together. By supporting multiple SOAP bindings, the Web Service can support more than one set of operations, similar to supporting multiple interfaces.

The second interesting property is `OneWay`. By setting this property to `True`, the Web Service is instructed to immediately return an HTTP 202 status code, indicating that the request has been received and processing started. The client then can go about its business and will not receive an acknowledgement that the web method completed. This can be useful in scenarios where the web method kicks off a long-running process that is better handled asynchronously. In these cases, a good design technique is to provide a method that the client can use to check on the status of the task at a later time. This can be accomplished by issuing the client a ticket of some type that it can pass back to the Web Service that acts as an identifier for the long-running process. Of course, this also implies that a method marked as `OneWay` must be `Sub` procedure and not a `Function`.

Setting Bindings

Bindings themselves are specified using the `WebServiceBinding` attribute shown earlier in Table 11.1. By default, all web methods are included in the default SOAP binding defined with the name of the Web Service appended with "Soap." By including one or more `WebServiceBinding` attributes to the class declaration, the Web Service can support multiple "interfaces." Note, however, that although a Web Service can include multiple SOAP bindings, a method can belong to only one of them. Obviously, by not specifying the `Binding` property, the web method belongs to the default binding. For example, if the `GetTranscript` method was placed in a separate binding, the class and method definitions would be altered as follows:

```
<WebService(Namespace:="www.quilogy.com/edservice", _
 Description:="Quilogy's Education Web Service", _
 Name:="QuilogyEducation"), _
 WebServiceBinding(Name:="TranscriptBinding")> _
Public Class EducationService : Inherits WebService

    <WebMethod(Description:="Retrieves a student's transcript", _
      EnableSession:=True), _
        SoapDocumentMethod(Binding:="TranscriptBinding")> _
    Public Function GetTranscript() As TranscriptData
    End Function

End Class
```

Changing Parameter Elements

In addition to customizing the encoding style, you can specify the names of the elements in the SOAP Body using the `XmlElement` attribute found in the `System.Xml.Serialization` namespace. For example, in the `GetSchedule` method declaration in Listing 11.2, you can add the `XmlElement` attribute to the parameters as follows.

```
Public Function GetSchedule( _
   <XmlElement("city")> ByVal Location As String, _
   <XmlElement("provider")> ByVal Vendor As String, _
   <XmlElement("advance")> ByVal DaysOut As Byte) As ScheduleData
```

In this case, the elements expected in the SOAP message will be changed to the constructor of the XmlElement attribute, rather than using the name of the parameter.

Extending Web Services

The examples of customizing the SOAP messages discussed in this chapter provide great flexibility when implementing a Web Service. Additionally, the Services Framework supports the capability to extend the Web Service infrastructure using the SoapExtension and SoapExtensionAttribute classes in the System.Web.Services.Protocols. In a nutshell, you can create a class derived from SoapExtension that contains an overridden ProcessMessage method. This method is called at various stages when processing a SOAP message, as defined in the SoapMessageStage enumeration. Obviously, you can choose which stages to process, such as BeforeDeserialize to catch incoming SOAP messages, and then manipulate the contents of the message represented as a SoapMessage object.

In addition, you need to create a derived SoapExtensionAttribute class used to apply your SOAP extension to a Web method. For example, your class could expose a property that specifies the name of the log file to use to log SOAP messages.

Uses for extensions include logging, compression, encryption, and custom security. See the example in the online help for more information.

Consuming a Web Service

When the Web Service is exposed on an IIS Server, it can be called in several different ways. As discussed previously, the simplest technique is for clients to issue an HTTP-GET or POST against the URL and catch the resulting XML. For a .NET client, this can be accomplished easily using the System.Net classes as discussed in Chapter 12, "Accessing System Services." VB 6.0 clients can use functions from the WinInet DLLs or the Inet ActiveX control that ships with VB 6.0.

> **TIP**
>
> Keep in mind that even if a content provider does not explicitly expose its content as a Web Service, you still can interact with the content in a programmatic manner using VB .NET. For example, as we will discuss in Chapter 12, you can use the `System.Net` classes to programmatically download and parse the contents of an HTML page. You can subsequently display the contents in another form to users or invoke hyperlinks programmatically. Of course, this sort of interaction is more complex than using Web Services because the structured nature of XML neatly discloses the message structure needed to interact with the service.

For a .NET client, however, support is built in to VS .NET to allow both discovery and referencing of Web Services to take place. For example, assume that ACME Corp, a client of Quilogy, wants to incorporate the Quilogy Education Web Service into its intranet site to allow its employees to view transcripts and query for course schedules from within its site. If the site is built with VB .NET, they can do this by clicking on Add Web Reference from the context menu associated with the project in the Solution Explorer window. The resulting dialog contains an address bar that allows the developer to enter the URL of the Quilogy Web Service. By entering the address of the .asmx file or the .asmx file appended with the query string ?WSDL, the service will be located and the right Available References window populated, as shown in Figure 11.3.

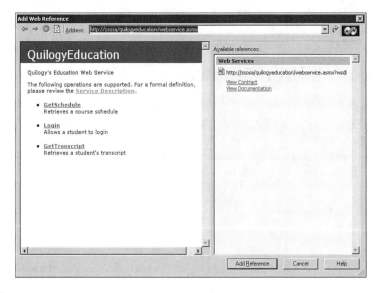

FIGURE 11.3

A client-side developer can set a reference to a Web Service from within VS .NET.

If the developer does not know the URL of the Web Service or wants to search for other Web Services, he can click on the Microsoft UDDI link in the window on the left. The UDDI registry then is navigated to allow the developer to search for various Web Services using the HTML interface. A company that registers its Web Services with UDDI will make them available to the entire installed base of VS .NET. For example, Quilogy could publish a free Web Service in UDDI that allows clients to query the list of free Microsoft seminars Quilogy provides. By clicking on UDDI in the Web References dialog and navigating to Quilogy, the service can be found, as shown in Figure 11.4.

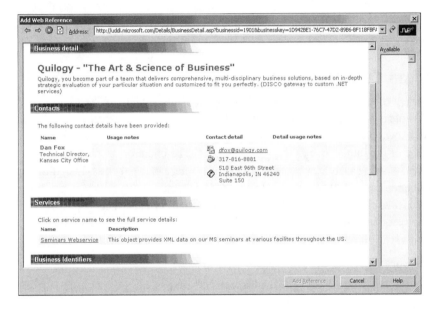

FIGURE 11.4
What a Web Service registered with UDDI would look like when found.

In either case, the developer can then click on the Add Reference button to add a Web reference to his project. Note that Web references can be added to any type of VS .NET project, including Windows Services, Windows Forms, and even other Web Service projects.

The result is a Web References folder in the Solution Explorer, as shown in Figure 11.5, that contains a reference to the Web Service. By default, the reference is named according to the Web Server contacted (in this example, the SSOSA server hosts the Web Service), although it can be changed by right-clicking on the reference and selecting Rename. You might want to rename it if the Web Service can be accessed dynamically from other servers.

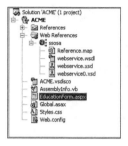

FIGURE 11.5
The Web Reference folder—note that the WSDL contract and XSD files for two DataSet *classes were downloaded from the Web Service.*

Using the Client Proxy

When the Web reference is added, VS .NET downloads the WSDL contract into the Web References folder and reverse engineers it to build a client proxy class that can be used from within the Web application. The class will have the same name as the Web Service and exist in a namespace of the same name as the Web reference. The client proxy class allows the developer to work with the Web Service as if it were any other managed class. In addition, if the Web Service returns any DataSet objects, the XSD schema for the DataSets are downloaded, and typed DataSets (covered in Chapter 7) are generated for each. This is possible because the WSDL contract contains an import element with a location attribute that references a URL, allowing VS .NET to retrieve the schema of the DataSet using the query string:

```
http://server/WebService.asmx?schema=DataSetName
```

In this way, developers also can programmatically work with the XML returned as if it were simply a managed class.

> **NOTE**
>
> Obviously, developers using Web Services sometimes will need to update the reference if the publisher of the service changes it. By right-clicking on the Web reference and selecting Update Web Reference, the WSDL again will be downloaded and the client proxy class regenerated. In addition, the Properties window for the WSDL contract and any XSD files downloaded contain a property that shows the Custom Tool used to generate the client proxy and typed DataSet classes. By right-clicking on the file and selecting Run Custom Tool, the class representing the Web Service or DataSet is regenerated.

The code for the client proxy class does not appear in the Solution Explorer (except for in the Class view). However, you can view the class (and modify it if you're careful) by selecting Show All Files from the toolbar in the Solution Explorer or looking in the project folder (in this case in the Web application directory under the Inetpub/wwwroot directory).

The client proxy class itself is derived from System.Web.Services.Protocols. SoapHttpClientProtocol, which contains methods that enable finer-grained control of communication with the Web Service, as shown in Table 11.4.

TABLE 11.4 Useful Instance Methods of SoapHttpClientProtocol

Method	Description
CookieContainer	Gets the collection of cookies sent to the Web Service.
Credentials	Gets or sets the username and/or password and authentication type used with the Web Service.
Proxy	Gets or sets proxy information for making Web Service requests through a firewall.
RequestEncoding	Gets or sets the encoding method used, such as ASCII, Unicode, UTF7, or UTF8.
Timeout	Sets the length of time in seconds a synchronous call to a Web Service will wait.
Url	Gets or sets the URL of the Web Service.

For example, the Url property can be set programmatically to allow the Web Service to be accessed from a server other than that specified in the WSDL contract. In addition, user credentials can be passed to the service using the Credentials property, and proxy server information used to penetrate a firewall can be set using the Proxy property. The use of Credentials and Proxy are covered in more detail in Chapter 13, "Implementing Services."

> **NOTE**
>
> If you have many Web Services to create proxies for, or need to automate the creation of the client proxy, you can use the Web Services Description Language Utility (wsdl.exe) command-line utility. This exe accepts parameters, such as the language, to create the proxy in, the URL of the WSDL contract, the protocol (HTTP-GET, HTTP-POST, SOAP) to create the proxy for, and the namespace to use.

In addition to the base class methods, of course, the client proxy class includes methods that map to the operations exposed by the Web Service. And so a client-side developer of the

ACME site can call the methods by simply instantiating the proxy class. For example, assume that a developer at ACME Corp. created a Web Form that collected the employee's e-mail address and password and then used the information to call the `Login` method of the Web Service. If the login is successful, the `GetTranscript` method is called, and results are bound to a `DataGrid`. Listing 11.6 shows the event handler for the button that kicks off this process.

LISTING 11.6   Calling a Web Service. Using the client proxy makes calling a Web Service as simple as using any other managed class.

```
Imports System.Drawing
Imports System.Web.UI.WebControls
Imports System.Web.UI.HtmlControls

Public Class EducationForm
    Inherits System.Web.UI.Page
    Protected WithEvents txtPWD As System.Web.UI.HtmlControls.HtmlInputText
    Protected WithEvents txtMessage As _
      System.Web.UI.HtmlControls.HtmlGenericControl
    Protected WithEvents Button1 As System.Web.UI.HtmlControls.HtmlInputButton
    Protected WithEvents DataGrid1 As System.Web.UI.WebControls.DataGrid

    Protected Sub Button1_ServerClick(ByVal sender As System.Object, _
      ByVal e As System.EventArgs) Handles Button1.ServerClick
        Dim strUser As String
        Dim strPWD As String
        Dim flSuccess As Boolean
        Dim objQuilogy As New ssosa.QuilogyEducation()
        Dim dsTranscript As ssosa.QuilogyTranscript

        ' Collect the user input
        strUser = Session("strEmail").ToString
        strPWD = txtPWD().Value

        ' Login
        Try
            flSuccess = objQuilogy.Login(strUser, strPWD)
        Catch Ex As Exception
            txtMessage().InnerText = Ex.Message
        End Try

        If flSuccess Then
            dsTranscript = objQuilogy.GetTranscript()
        End If

        ' Bind the transcript to a grid control
```

LISTING 11.6   Continued

```
        DataGrid1().DataSource = dsTranscript
        DataGrid1().DataMember = "Class"

    End Sub

End Class
```

Note that the `Login` and `GetTranscript` methods are called as they would be with any other class, and that a `Try Catch` block can be used to handle any SOAP client fault codes returned from the Web Service.

In addition to the synchronous versions of the methods exposed by the Web Service, the client proxy class also exposes begin and end methods for each method (for example, `BeginGetTranscript`, `EndGetTranscript`). These methods can be used to call the Web Service asynchronously using the same pattern discussed in Chapter 4, "Object-Oriented Features," for asynchronous delegates, and Chapter 12 for asynchronous reads and writes. Although not particularly useful when calling Web Services from Web applications, asynchronous calls can be important for Web Form and Web Service applications.

You also might notice that the code in the proxy class takes advantage of the `SoapDocumentMethod` attribute to customize the SOAP sent to the server. It also can use the `SoapDocumentService`, `SoapRpcMethod`, and `SoapRpcService` attributes, as well.

Summary

This chapter discussed the ins and outs of creating and consuming Web Services with VB .NET. As you are aware by now, although Web Services are in many ways similar to component-based programming used in previous versions of VB, they also make possible a new paradigm of programmatic interaction using the Web as the platform.

This chapter also concludes Part II of the book devoted to showing how VB .NET can be used to build distributed applications. Part III of the book, beginning with the next chapter, deals with using the Services Framework to integrate your applications into the enterprise.

Integration

IN THIS PART

Accessing System Services

IN THIS CHAPTER

To build effective applications on any platform, you must take full advantage of the services the platform provides. This is especially true of services that interface with the file system, memory, or the operating system kernel because they are typically costly to implement on your own if indeed they are available at all. This chapter covers several of the basic system services provided in .NET including I/O, multithreading, process monitoring, and encryption.

> **NOTE**
>
> All code listings and supplemental material for this chapter can be found on the book's Web site at www.samspublishing.com.

Understanding I/O Concepts

For most existing VB developers, the way in which the Services Framework handles I/O likely will require some getting used to, although developers familiar with the Scripting.FileSystem object used in VB 6.0 should see some similarities.

> **NOTE**
>
> The Microsoft.VisualBasic namespace contains the FileSystem class that includes analogs to many of the statements and functions historically used by VB developers, such as FileOpen, Input, LineInput, FreeFile, PrintLine, and so on. Although these methods certainly can be used, I would employ them more for translating existing VB 6.0 code than for new development. For new development, try using the Services Framework classes to make your code more understandable to other .NET developers and to take advantage of features such as asynchronous file access.

Basically, the Services Framework encapsulates I/O in the System.IO namespace, and does so by abstracting the concept of a stream used to read and write data, from the "backing store" or medium used to store the data. Because of this abstraction, you can think of the System.IO namespace as consisting of three logical components, as shown in Figure 12.1.

At the core, the System.IO namespace contains the Stream class. Stream is a base class (marked as MustInherit) that provides a way to read and write bytes to a backing store. As a result, it includes methods to perform these operations both synchronously (Read, Write) and asynchronously (BeginRead, BeginWrite, EndRead, EndWrite), in addition to methods that manipulate the current position in the Stream, such as Seek. Stream also exposes a variety of properties to indicate the capabilities of the Stream, such as CanRead, CanSeek, and CanWrite. Because Stream is a base class, the Services Framework includes two classes that inherit from it to support specific backing stores. The `FileStream` class supports stream operations against physical files, whereas the `MemoryStream` class supports stream access to physical memory. In addition, other namespaces, such as `System.Net.Sockets`, implement classes that derive from `Stream`, such as `NetworkStream`, to provide the underlying stream of data for network access. The `BufferedStream` class does not actually implement a backing store, but can be used with other `Stream` classes to provide buffered access to data to, for example, decrease the overhead of continual file system accesses.

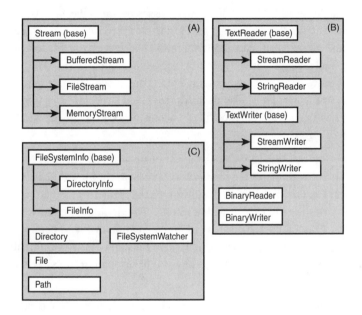

12

ACCESSING SYSTEM SERVICES

FIGURE 12.1

The major classes of the `System.IO` *namespace broken down into components, including streams (A), readers and writers (B), and file system classes (C).*

TIP

Just as the Services Framework implements classes derived from `Stream`, you can create your own derived stream classes from `Stream` or even one of its descendants such as `FileStream`. Why would you want to do this? Because a `Stream` class can encapsulate access to any backing store, you could derive a `Stream` class to write to a proprietary file format in a particular location, thereby freeing the user of the class from having to learn both the file format and the particulars of where the data is stored. As a bonus, if you derive from `Stream`, you only need to override the synchronous `Read` and `Write` methods, and the base class implementation of the asynchronous methods will work automatically.

The second component of System.IO includes the reader and writer classes. As the names imply, these classes are used to read and write bytes from a Stream in a particular way. Although you simply can use the Read and Write methods of the Stream classes directly, doing so means that you would have to read and write data as a Byte array using offsets. To read data from a text file, you would have to call the Read method of the FileStream class for a particular range of data and then convert the data to strings, definitely something you'd rather have the Services Framework take care of.

There are two basic divisions in the reader/writer classes between the TextReader and TextWriter classes and the BinaryReader and BinaryWriter classes. TextReader and TextWriter are base classes that read and write individual text characters to a stream while their analogs read and write primitive types in binary. In turn, the TextReader and TextWriter serve as the base classes for the StreamReader and StringReader, and StreamWriter and StringWriter classes, respectively. The StreamReader and StreamWriter classes read and write text to a Stream in a particular encoding, whereas the StringReader and StringWriter simply read and write from strings.

The final component of System.IO includes the various classes that deal specifically with the file system and interact with the FileStream class. As shown in Figure 12.1, these include the DirectoryInfo and FileInfo classes derived from FileSystemInfo and are used to manipulate files and directories in conjunction with a FileStream. In addition, the NotInheritable (sealed) Directory, File, and Path classes aid in the creation of file system objects in addition to providing methods to copy, delete, open, and move files and directories. Finally, the FileSystemWatcher and associated classes allow you to respond to file system events to take action as files and directories are manipulated.

Because the bulk of the I/O in most applications, other than database I/O, is performed through the file system, the remainder of this section focuses on accessing the file system.

Reading and Writing Files

The most basic use of System.IO is to read and write files. In this section, we'll take a look at a host of topics related to file I/O including reading and writing both text and binary files, navigating the file system, integrating asynchronous I/O, responding to file system events, and dealing with isolated storage.

Using Text Files

The first step in reading and writing files consists of creating a FileStream class and pointing it at the appropriate file while specifying how to open it within the constructor. You can identify the file either through the name (using a relative or absolute path) or the operating system's file handle. The handle can be obtained using the Handle property and can thus be passed between methods easily. Typical arguments to the constructor include one of the FileMode enumerations that specify how the file is to be opened (Append, Create, CreateNew, Open, OpenOrCreate, Truncate) and one of the FileAccess enumerations that determines whether the file is opened for Read, ReadWrite, or Write.

> **TIP**
>
> A common example is to use the OpenOrCreate enumeration to open the file if it exists and create it if it doesn't. Using this enumeration moves the position of the file pointer from the beginning of the stream, so you can then determine whether to append or truncate the file based on its contents.

A member of the FileShare enumeration (None, Read, ReadWrite, Write) might optionally be specified to indicate whether two processes can simultaneously read from the same file. This can be useful in cases where one application is reading a file while the other appends data to it.

The second step in reading from or writing to a file is to associate the FileStream with an instance of a reader or writer class. Which one you choose, for example StreamWriter or BinaryWriter, depends on the specifics of your application. In the case of a writer, you can then call the Write or WriteLine methods to place data in the stream backed by the file. The encoding used to read the file is autodetected by the first call to the Read method when using the StreamReader class, whereas the Encoding can be specified in the constructor of the StreamWriter class. The default is UTF-8 unicode.

> **TIP**
>
> You optionally can perform the first two steps described using the File class and its shared methods OpenText, CreateText, or AppendText. This is preferable if you also want to inspect or set the attributes of the file or perform an additional operation on it such as moving it.

The writer classes support the Flush and Close methods to write any buffered data to the current Stream and close the current stream (referenced through the BaseStream property), respectively. Invoking Flush might be useful in situations where you want to be sure that a certain amount of data is written to the stream in case of subsequent errors. For example, when writing to a log file, you might want to call Flush after each of a configurable number of entries to ensure that data is written to the file incrementally. Alternatively, the AutoFlush property can be used to tell the writer to flush its contents after every call to Write, although doing so might impede performance.

> **TIP**
>
> The `Flush` method of writer classes, such as `StreamWriter`, often is confused with the `Flush` method of a `Stream` class, such as `FileStream`. The former flushes all buffers for the current writer and writes the data to the `BaseStream`, whereas the latter updates the stream with the current state of its own buffer. The upshot of these two methods, as they relate to file access, is that calling `Flush` for the `FileStream` can only write data to the file that has been released from the `StreamWriter`'s buffer, whereas `StreamWriter.Flush` releases the data *and* writes it to the stream immediately.
>
> This is because `StreamWriter` does a small amount of buffering (4096 bytes by default) on its own. As a result, to ensure that data is written to the file immediately, call the `Flush` method of the `StreamWriter`. You can set the buffer size for the `StreamWriter` using an argument to the constructor.

After the writing is completed, call the `Close` method of the `FileStream`. To illustrate these concepts, review the code in Listing 12.1.

LISTING 12.1   Writing Data Using `StreamWriter`. This method writes data to a text file from a `SqlDataReader` using the `StreamWriter` class.

```
Option Strict On

Imports System.Data.SqlClient
Imports System.IO
Public Sub WriteToFile(ByVal FileName As String, ByVal Delimiter As Object, _
  ByRef Reader As SqlDataReader)

  Dim objSr As StreamReader
  Dim fsSave As FileStream
  Dim srWriter As StreamWriter
  Dim i As Integer
  Dim intFields As Integer
  Dim intRowCount As Integer

  If Reader.IsClosed Then
    Throw New Exception("SqlDataReader is closed " & _
      FileName & " not created.")
    Return
  End If
```

LISTING 12.1   Continued

```
Try
  ' Overwrite file if exists
  fsSave = New FileStream(FileName, FileMode.Create, _
    FileAccess.Write, FileShare.None)
  ' Associate the stream writer with the file
  srWriter = New StreamWriter(fsSave) ' UTF-8 and a 4096 byte buffer
Catch e As IOException
  Throw New Exception("I/O error. Cannot access the file " & _
    FileName & " :" & e.Message)
End Try

' Write the header
srWriter.WriteLine(FileName & " created on " & _
  DateTime.Now.ToShortDateString)

intFields = Reader.FieldCount - 1

' First write the column names
For i = 0 To intFields
  srWriter.Write(Reader.GetName(i))
  If i <> intFields Then
    srWriter.Write(Delimiter)
  End If
Next i
srWriter.Write(vbCrLf)   'Write the CRLF at the EOL

' Now write the data
Do While Reader.Read
  ' Flush every 100 rows
  intRowCount = intRowCount + 1
  If intRowCount Mod 100 = 0 Then
    srWriter.Flush()
  End If

  For i = 0 To intFields
    If Reader.IsDBNull(i) Then
      srWriter.Write("NULL")
    Else
      srWriter.Write(Reader.GetValue(i).ToString)
    End If
    If i <> intFields Then
      srWriter.Write(Delimiter)
    End If
  Next i
```

LISTING 12.1   Continued

```
    srWriter.Write(vbCrLf) ' Write the CRLF at the EOL
Loop

'   Close the StreamWriter and the File
srWriter.Close() ' Calls Flush
fsSave.Close()

End Sub
```

In this example, a method called WriteToFile is implemented to write the contents of a SqlDataReader to a delimited text file. The filename, delimiter, and SqlDataReader are passed into the method, and the method checks to be sure that the SqlDataReader is open and ready for reading.

In this case, the FileStream, fsSave, is instantiated using the FileMode of Create so that any existing file is overwritten or a new file is created. In addition, the FileShare parameter is set to None so that other processes cannot read or write to the file. If for some reason the file cannot be overwritten or created, an IOException is thrown, which is passed back to the caller. After the StreamWriter is associated with the FileStream, a header line is written using WriteLine before the SqlDataReader is accessed to write out the column names followed by the actual data in a Do Loop. If the data returned from the database is null, the literal string "NULL" is output to the file. To ensure that the file is written to after every 100 records, a row counter is incremented and the Flush method of the StreamWriter is called if the Mod operator returns 0.

After all the records have been written, the StreamWriter and the FileStream are closed, which flushes all the data from the current buffer and closes the file. To call this method, client code like the following could be used to write out the contents of the Students table to a tab-delimited file:

```
Dim cnSQL As SqlConnection
Dim cmSQL As SqlCommand
Dim sdrCourses As SqlDataReader

cnSQL = New SqlConnection( _
  "server=ssosa;trusted_connection=yes;database=enrollment")
cmSQL = New SqlCommand("usp_GetStudents", cnSQL)
cmSQL.CommandType = CommandType.StoredProcedure

cnSQL.Open()
sdrCourses = cmSQL.ExecuteReader()

WriteToFile("students.txt", vbTab, sdrCourses)
cnSQL.Close()
```

Reading a text file using the `StreamReader` class is basically the converse of using `StreamWriter`. Listing 12.2 shows a method that uses the `StreamReader` to return the last student ID from the file created in Listing 12.1.

LISTING 12.2   Using a `StreamReader`. This method uses a `StreamReader` to read the contents of the file produced in Listing 12.1 and return the last StudentID.

```
Option Strict On

Imports System.IO
Public Function LastStudent(ByVal FileName As String, _
    ByVal Delimiter As Object) As Integer

    Dim fsRead As FileStream
    Dim srReader As StreamReader
    Dim intPos As Long
    Dim strStudent As String
    Dim strLine As String

    Try
      ' Read the file if it exists
      fsRead = New FileStream(FileName, FileMode.Open, _
        FileAccess.Read, FileShare.Read)
      ' Associate the stream writer with the file
      srReader = New StreamReader(fsRead) ' UTF-8 and 4096 byte buffer
    Catch e As IOException
      Throw New Exception("I/O error. Cannot access the file " & _
        FileName & " :" & e.Message)
    End Try

    ' Go near the end of the file
    intPos = srReader.BaseStream.Seek(-500, SeekOrigin.End)

    ' Loop to find the last record
    Do While True
      strStudent = strLine
      strLine = srReader.ReadLine
      If strLine Is Nothing Then
        ' End of file
        Exit Do
      End If
    Loop
```

LISTING 12.2   Continued

```
' Load the student into an array and return the first element (0)
Return CInt(strStudent.Split(CChar(Delimiter))(0))

End Function
```

In this example, the file is accessed using the `Open` member of the `FileMode` enumeration and is opened in a shared mode for reading. If the file does not exist, an `IOException` is thrown. After the file is open and associated with the `StreamReader`, the `Seek` method is used to quickly position the stream near the end of the file. In this case, an offset of -500 bytes from the end of the stream is used as specified by the `SeekOrigin` enumeration. When positioned near the end of the stream, the `Do Loop` is used to read each remaining line (delimited by a CRLF) using the `ReadLine` method. If the method returns `Nothing`, then the end-of-file has been reached. The last string read from the file now contains the student record of interest. By using the `Split` method of the `String` class, the string is parsed into an array of strings demarcated by the delimiter. Because student ID will be the first element of the array, the ordinal 0 can be used to return it.

Using Binary Files

Reading and writing binary files is analogous to handling text files with the exception that you use the `BinaryReader` and `BinaryWriter` classes and work directly with arrays of `Byte`. To provide an example of using these classes, Listing 12.3 implements `GetPhoto` and `PutPhoto` methods to retrieve and insert images of instructors using SQL Server.

The `GetPhoto` method accepts the ID of the instructor along with an optional file path indicating where the image should be saved. If successful, the method returns the fully qualified path name. The `PutPhoto` method accepts the path to a valid file and the ID of the instructor to associate it to.

> **NOTE**
>
> The `Optional` parameter in the `GetPhoto` method also could have been implemented using an overloaded method. However, in cases where it is trivial to check for the existence of the argument, you save yourself some coding by taking advantage of VB .NET's optional syntax. If the method contains multiple optional parameters or significantly affects the method's algorithm, then using an overloaded method is recommended.

LISTING 12.3 Reading and Writing Binary Data. These methods use the `BinaryReader` and `BinaryWriter` classes to read and write image files to SQL Server.

```
Option Strict On

Imports System.Data.SqlClient
Imports System.IO
  Public Function GetPhoto(ByVal InsID As Integer, _
    Optional ByVal FilePath As String = Nothing) As String

    Dim byteBuffer() As Byte
    Dim cmSQL As SqlCommand
    Dim sdrIns As SqlDataReader
    Dim fsSave As FileStream
    Dim brWriter As BinaryWriter
    Dim strFile As String

    ' Make sure directory exists
    If Not Directory.Exists(FilePath) And Not FilePath Is Nothing Then
      Throw New Exception("The path " & FilePath & " does not exist.")
    End If

    Try
      ' Execute proc
      cmSQL = New SqlCommand("usp_GetPhoto", mcnSQL)
      cmSQL.Parameters.Add(New SqlParameter("@InsID", SqlDbType.Int))
      cmSQL.Parameters("@InsID").Value = InsID
      cmSQL.CommandType = CommandType.StoredProcedure
      mcnSQL.Open()
      sdrIns = cmSQL.ExecuteReader()
    Catch e As Exception
      If mcnSQL.State = ConnectionState.Open Then mcnSQL.Close()
      Throw New Exception("Database Error: " & e.Message)
    End Try

    ' Save file and return file name
    Do While sdrIns.Read
      byteBuffer = CType(sdrIns.Item("Photo"), Byte())
    Loop

    If byteBuffer Is Nothing Then
      mcnSQL.Close()
      Throw New Exception("No photo exists for " & InsID)
    End If
```

LISTING 12.3 Continued

```
  If FilePath Is Nothing Then
    strFile = Directory.GetCurrentDirectory & _
      Path.DirectorySeparatorChar & "Ins" & InsID & ".jpg"
  Else
    strFile = FilePath & Path.DirectorySeparatorChar & "Ins" & InsID & ".jpg"
  End If

  ' Write to a binary stream
  Try
    fsSave = New FileStream(strFile, FileMode.Create, _
      FileAccess.Write, FileShare.None)

    ' Associate the stream writer with the file
    brWriter = New BinaryWriter(fsSave)
    brWriter.Write(byteBuffer)
    ' Optional ... fsSave.Write(byteBuffer,0,byteBuffer.Length)
    brWriter.Close()
    fsSave.Close()
  Catch e As IOException
    mcnSQL.Close()
    Throw New Exception("Error writing file " & strFile & ": " & e.Message)
  End Try

  mcnSQL.Close()
  Return strFile

End Function


Public Function PutPhoto(ByVal InsID As Integer, _
  ByVal FilePath As String) As Boolean

  Dim byteBuffer() As Byte
  Dim cmSQL As SqlCommand
  Dim fsSave As FileStream
  Dim brReader As BinaryReader

  ' Write to a binary stream
  Try
    fsSave = New FileStream(FilePath, FileMode.Open, _
      FileAccess.Read, FileShare.None)
    ' Associate the stream writer with the file
    brReader = New BinaryReader(fsSave)
    ReDim byteBuffer(CInt(fsSave.Length))
    brReader.Read(byteBuffer,  0, CInt(fsSave.Length))
```

LISTING 12.3   Continued

```
    brReader.Close()
    fsSave.Close()
Catch e As IOException
    Throw New Exception("Error reading file " & FilePath & ": " & e.Message)
End Try

Try
    ' Execute proc
    cmSQL = New SqlCommand("usp_SavePhoto", mcnSQL)
    cmSQL.Parameters.Add(New SqlParameter("@InsID", SqlDbType.Int))
    cmSQL.Parameters("@InsID").Value = InsID
    cmSQL.Parameters.Add(New SqlParameter("@likeness", SqlDbType.Image))
    cmSQL.Parameters("@likeness").Value = byteBuffer
    cmSQL.CommandType = CommandType.StoredProcedure
    mcnSQL.Open()
    cmSQL.ExecuteNonQuery()
Catch e As SqlException
    Throw e
Finally
    mcnSQL.Close()
End Try

Return True

End Function
```

The GetPhoto method in Listing 12.3 uses a SqlCommand and SqlDataReader to execute a stored procedure, which returns the Photo column from SQL Server. Because this column is defined as Image in SQL Server, it can be read into an array of bytes simply by assigning its Value property to byteBuffer, defined as a dynamic Byte array. After the buffer has been populated, the FileStream is used to open the receiving file, and the BinaryWriter is instantiated and associated with the FileStream. The overloaded Write method of the BinaryWriter is then used to pass the byteBuffer to the underlying stream. Note that the Write method can also specify an offset in the buffer to begin writing and a count of how many bytes to write.

NOTE

Because the FileStream class also supports a Write method, you optionally can write directly to the stream without going through the BinaryWriter. However, the Write method of the FileStream is not overloaded.

The PutPhoto method does the reverse by reading the binary file passed into the method. It does this by opening the file for Read and then using the BinaryReader to Read all its contents into a Byte array defined as byteBuffer. Note that byteBuffer must be sized appropriately, in this case using the Length property of the FileStream class. The reader is then closed, and the byteBuffer passed as the Value of a parameter to the appropriate SqlCommand object. The SqlCommand executes the usp_SavePhoto stored procedure using ExecuteNonQuery as discussed in Chapter 7, "Accessing Data with ADO.NET."

Navigating Directory Entries

Navigating and accessing individual directories and files are accomplished using the classes marked with (C) in Figure 12.1. The interesting point to note is that the File and Directory classes are used statically to manipulate objects in the file system, whereas the DirectoryInfo and FileInfo classes represent individual file system entries. In other words, the methods of File and Directory can be used to perform operations on files and directories, whereas classes derived from FileSystemInfo represent specific instances of files and directories. In addition, the File and Directory classes accept String arguments and return arrays of strings when queried for data, whereas the FileSystemInfo classes accept and return other instances of a FileSystemInfo class.

> **NOTE**
>
> The Path class also is used statically to return platform-independent delimiters and other information about the file system. You'll notice its use in the GetPhoto method in Listing 12.3.

To illustrate working with these classes, Listing 12.4 implements an ArchiveFiles method. This method accepts a path and optional criteria to use to select files from a directory and move them to an archive directory created on-the-fly while changing the archive bit of file.

LISTING 12.4   Navigating the File System. This listing illustrates the use of the DirectoryInfo, FileInfo, File, and Directory classes.

```
Option Strict On

Imports System.IO
    Public Function ArchiveFiles(ByVal FilePath As String, _
        Optional ByVal Criteria As String = Nothing) As Object

        Dim objFile As FileInfo
        Dim objDir As DirectoryInfo
        Dim objArchive As DirectoryInfo
```

LISTING 12.4   Continued

```
Dim arErrors() As Exception
Dim i As Integer
Dim objExcep As Exception

i = 1

' Make sure directory exists
If Not Directory.Exists(FilePath) Then
  Throw New Exception("Directory " & FilePath & " does not exist")
  Return Nothing
Else
  objDir = New DirectoryInfo(FilePath)
End If

' Create the archive directory
objArchive = Directory.CreateDirectory(FilePath & _
  Path.DirectorySeparatorChar & "Archive")

' Get all the files in the directory
If Criteria Is Nothing Then
  Criteria = "*.*"
End If

For Each objFile In objDir.GetFiles(Criteria)
  Try
    ' Move the file and delete
    objFile.MoveTo(objArchive.FullName & _
      Path.DirectorySeparatorChar & objFile.Name)

    ' Set the archive bit
    File.SetAttributes(objArchive.FullName & _
      Path.DirectorySeparatorChar & objFile.Name, FileAttributes.Archive)
  Catch e As Exception
    ReDim Preserve arErrors(i)
    objExcep = New Exception("Error processing " & _
      objFile.Name & ": " & e.Message)
    arErrors(i - 1) = objExcep
    i = i + 1
  End Try
Next

Return arErrors

End Function
```

In this example, the Directory class is first used to determine whether the path exists and to throw an exception if not. If the directory does exist, a DirectoryInfo object is instantiated to refer to the directory. An archive directory then is created using the CreateDirectory method of the Directory class. In the event that the archive directory already exists, no exception is raised.

Although the GetFiles method of the DirectoryInfo object is overloaded to omit search criteria, in this case, the ArchiveFiles method simply determines whether the criteria was set and, if not, defaults it to find all the files. The GetFiles method then returns an array of FileInfo objects conforming to the criteria. The FileInfo objects are then iterated using the For Each loop and moved to the archive directory using the MoveTo method. After the move, the archive attribute is set using the File class.

Finally, if the file cannot be archived, the exception is intercepted and added to an array. This array is returned to the caller for later inspection. As a result, the client code used to call this method might look like the following:

```
Dim Excep as Exception
Dim objErrors as Object

objErrors = ArchiveFiles("D:\Project\Data", "*.xml")

If Not objErrors Is Nothing Then
  For Each Excep in CType(objErrors, Exception())
    WriteToLog(Excep.Message)
  Next
End If
```

Using Asynchronous File I/O

As mentioned previously, one of the great features of how I/O is handled in the Services Framework is that it provides an easily accessible implementation for asynchronous processing. The model is based on the asynchronous delegate model first discussed in Chapter 4, "Object-Oriented Features," by splitting the Read and Write methods of the Stream classes into BeginRead, EndRead, and BeginWrite, EndWrite pairs of methods that are invoked on either end of an asynchronous file I/O operation. Sitting in the middle of these operations is an instance of the AsyncCallback delegate.

To illustrate implementing an asynchronous write, the GetPhoto method from Listing 12.3 has been rewritten as GetPhotoAsync in Listing 12.5. This method writes the photo asynchronously using a worker thread allowing the main thread of the application to continue with more important work.

LISTING 12.5   Asynchronous File I/O. The `GetPhotoAsync` method performs an asynchronous write of the instructor photo. Note that only the actual file I/O is asynchronous.

```
Option Strict On

Imports System.Data.SqlClient
Imports System.IO
Public Sub GetPhotoAsync(ByVal InsID As Integer, _
    Optional ByVal FilePath As String = Nothing)

    Dim byteBuffer() As Byte
    Dim cmSQL As SqlCommand
    Dim sdrIns As SqlDataReader
    Dim fsSave As FileStream
    Dim strFile As String
    Dim cbWritePhoto As New AsyncCallback( _
      AddressOf WritePhotoCallback)

    ' Make sure directory exists
    If Not Directory.Exists(FilePath) And Not FilePath Is Nothing Then
      Throw New Exception("The path " & FilePath & " does not exist.")
      Return
    End If

    Try
      ' Execute proc
      cmSQL = New SqlCommand("usp_GetPhoto", mcnSQL)
      cmSQL.Parameters.Add(New SqlParameter("@InsID", SqlDbType.Int))
      cmSQL.Parameters("@InsID").Value = InsID
      cmSQL.CommandType = CommandType.StoredProcedure
      mcnSQL.Open()
      sdrIns = cmSQL.ExecuteReader()
    Catch e As Exception
      Throw New Exception("Database Error: " & e.Message)
      If mcnSQL.State = ConnectionState.Open Then mcnSQL.Close()
      Return
    End Try

    ' Save file and return file name
    Do While sdrIns.Read
      byteBuffer = CType(sdrIns.Item("Photo"), Byte())
    Loop

    If byteBuffer Is Nothing Then
      Throw New Exception("No photo exists for " & InsID)
      mcnSQL.Close()
      Return
```

LISTING 12.5   Continued

```
    End If

    If FilePath Is Nothing Then
      strFile = Directory.GetCurrentDirectory & _
        Path.DirectorySeparatorChar & "Ins" & InsID & ".jpg"
    Else
      strFile = FilePath & Path.DirectorySeparatorChar & _
        "Ins" & InsID & ".jpg"
    End If

    ' Write to a binary stream
    Try
      fsSave = New FileStream(strFile, FileMode.Create, _
        FileAccess.Write, FileShare.None)

      ' Write asynchronously
      fsSave.BeginWrite(byteBuffer, 0, byteBuffer.Length, _
        cbWritePhoto, fsSave)

    Catch e As IOException
      Throw New Exception("Error writing file " & strFile & ": " & e.Message)
      mcnSQL.Close()
      Return
    End Try

    mcnSQL.Close()
    Return

  End Sub

  Public Sub WritePhotoCallback(ByVal ar As IAsyncResult)
    Dim fsStream As FileStream

    ' Used to get the current thread ID
    '   Dim ThreadID As Integer = Thread.CurrentThread.GetHashCode()
    '   Console.WriteLine(ar.CompletedSynchronously)

    ' Get the FileStream
    fsStream = CType(ar.AsyncState(), FileStream)

    ' Finish the writing and close the stream
    fsStream.EndWrite(ar)
    fsStream.Close()

  End Sub
```

In Listing 12.5, much of the method is identical to `GetPhoto` with a few minor exceptions. First, an instance of `AsyncCallback`, called `cbWriteImage`, is created by passing the address of the `WritePhotoCallback` method to the constructor using the `AddressOf` operator. This designates the method that will be called when the write operation on the `FileStream` completes.

Second, in the `Try` block at the end of the method, the `BinaryWriter` is not used in favor of calling the `BeginWrite` method of the `FileStream` object directly. Note that this method requires that you pass the offset into the buffer to start writing from, the number of bytes to write, the callback delegate, and an object that can be used to track the state. In this case, we're passing the `FileStream` so that it can be closed in the `WritePhotoCallback` method. When the `BeginWrite` method is invoked, the actual write operation usually continues on a new worker thread, which, when completed, calls the `WritePhotoCallback` method using the delegate `cbWritePhoto`.

12

**ACCESSING
SYSTEM SERVICES**

NOTE

The word "usually" is used in the preceding paragraph because if the amount of I/O is small, the work might actually be performed synchronously on the caller's thread. `BeginWrite` makes this determination as the write is performed and before the callback method is executed. The `IAsyncResult` object passed to the callback method contains a `CompletedSynchronously` property that can be inspected to see whether indeed that was the case. In addition, the commented code in Listing 12.5 shows how you can determine which thread executed the I/O by using the `CurrentThread` property of the `Thread` class from the `System.Threading` namespace.

The `WritePhotoCallback` also is shown in Listing 12.5. This method first contains code that pulls the `FileStream` out of the `AsyncState` property of the result object (defined as `IAsyncResult`), and then uses it to finish the operation by calling `EndWrite` and `Close` on the stream.

Obviously, to take advantage of asynchronous I/O, the calling code would need to call the `GetPhotoAsync` method in a situation where, after the call was made, it could continue on to other useful work. For example, if the caller wanted to save all the instructor images to files, a tight loop, like the following, could be executed where `intNumInstructors` is set to the number of instructors employed by Quilogy:

```
For i = 1 to intNumInstructors
  GetPhotoAsync(i)
Next
```

Note that in this case, only the actual writing of the image to the file system is performed on a worker thread, whereas the database access carried out with each call to `GetPhotoAsync` occurs on the caller's thread. The other point to keep in mind is that the caller's application must remain alive until all the worker threads complete, or some of the files might not get written.

Responding to File System Events

One of the most interesting and useful features of the System.IO namespace is the inclusion of the FileSystemWatcher class. This class can be used to monitor a particular directory and its subdirectories for a configurable set of changes to the files or directories contained therein. As changes occur, events are raised from an instance of the FileSystemWatcher class that can be handled by the client code. This capability might be useful, for example, in a Windows service application that needs to monitor an FTP drop-off site as discussed in Chapter 13, "Implementing Services."

> **NOTE**
>
> To use the FileSystemWatcher class, your code must be monitoring a fixed disk on an operating system that supports file system events, such as Windows NT 4.0, Windows 2000, or Windows XP using the NTFS file system. In addition, the class will not raise events for CDs or DVDs. You can, however, monitor directories on a remote machine using a UNC path provided that any permissions restrictions are satisfied.

The basic steps required to use FileSystemWatcher are to instantiate the object, configure its properties to determine which directories to monitor and which events to raise, and add event handlers to handle the events raised at runtime.

The overloaded constructor of the FileSystemWatcher class allows you to specify the Path and Filter properties to indicate which directory to monitor, as well as the types of files to raise events for (such as "*.xml"). By default, all files will be included. In addition, IncludeSubDirectories property can be set to True if you want to monitor all the subdirectories of the Path, although the default is False.

Because different actions can be taken on a directory entry, it is usually a good idea to filter these using the NotifyFilter property. This property is set to one or more values using a bitwise OR from the NotifyFilters enumeration (Attributes, CreationTime, DirectoryName, FileName, LastAccess, LastWrite, Security, Size). For example, by setting the NotifyFilter property to NotifyFilters.FileName BitOr NotifyFilters.LastAccess, events are raised each time a file is accessed.

Which filters are set have a direct effect on which events are raised. There are five events for which you can add handlers, as shown in Table 12.1.

TABLE 12.1 FileSystemWatcher Events

Event	Description
Created	Raised whenever a directory or file is created if the NotifyFilter contains the appropriate value (FileName or DirectoryName).
Deleted	Raised whenever a directory or file is deleted if the NotifyFilter contains the appropriate value (FileName or DirectoryName).
Renamed	Raised whenever a directory or file is renamed if the NotifyFilter contains the appropriate value (FileName or DirectoryName).
Changed	Raised whenever a directory or file is changed if the NotifyFilter contains the appropriate value (FileName or DirectoryName). More than one Changed event can be fired per entry based on the values in the NotifyFilter property.
Error	Raised when the internal buffer is overrun with events.

To illustrate the use of the FileSystemWatcher class, Listing 12.6 shows a custom class called NotifyNewFiles.

LISTING 12.6 Encapsulating FileSystemWatcher. This listing shows the NotifyNewFiles class, which abstracts the FileSystemWatcher to look for only Created events on files in a particular directory.

```
Option Strict On

Imports System.IO
Public Class NotifyNewFiles

  Public Event Created(ByVal FileName As String)
  Public Event Overrun(ByVal Message As String)

  ' Allows events to be raised
  Public Property Enabled() As Boolean
    Get
      Return mEnabled
    End Get
    Set(ByVal Value As Boolean)
      mEnabled = Value
      mWatcher.EnableRaisingEvents = mEnabled
    End Set
  End Property
```

12

**ACCESSING
SYSTEM SERVICES**

LISTING 12.6   Continued

```
' Determines the path to monitor
Public Property Path() As String
  Get
    Return mPath
  End Get
  Set(ByVal Value As String)
    mPath = Value
    mWatcher.Filter = mPath
  End Set
End Property

' File filter to search on
Public Property Criteria() As String
  Get
    Return mCriteria
  End Get
  Set(ByVal Value As String)
    If Value.Length = 0 Then
      mCriteria = "*.*"
    End If
    mCriteria = Value
    mWatcher.Filter = mCriteria
  End Set
End Property

Private mWatcher As FileSystemWatcher
Private mPath As String
Private mCriteria As String = "*.*"
Private mEnabled As Boolean = False

Public Sub New()
  mWatcher = New FileSystemWatcher()
  InitWatcher()
End Sub

Public Sub New(ByVal FilePath As String)
  mPath = FilePath
  mWatcher = New FileSystemWatcher()
  InitWatcher()
End Sub

Public Sub New(ByVal FilePath As String, ByVal Criteria As String)
  mPath = FilePath
  Me.Criteria = Criteria
```

LISTING 12.6   Continued

```
  mWatcher = New FileSystemWatcher()
  InitWatcher()
End Sub

Private Sub InitWatcher()
  ' Initialize the watcher class
  With mWatcher
    .Filter = mCriteria
    .Path = mPath
    .NotifyFilter = NotifyFilters.FileName
    .IncludeSubdirectories = False
  End With

  ' Add event handlers
  AddHandler mWatcher.Created, _
    New FileSystemEventHandler(AddressOf Me.MyWatcher)
  AddHandler mWatcher.Error, _
    New ErrorEventHandler(AddressOf Me.MyWatcherErr)
End Sub

Private Sub MyWatcher(ByVal sender As System.Object, _
  ByVal e As FileSystemEventArgs)
  RaiseEvent Created(e.FullPath)
End Sub

Private Sub MyWatcherErr(ByVal sender As System.Object, _
  ByVal e As ErrorEventArgs)

  Dim strMessage As String

  strMessage = "The internal buffer was overrun, too many files "
  strMessage &= "to handle, some will be missed."
  RaiseEvent Overrun(strMessage)
End Sub

End Class
```

The NotifyNewFiles class abstracts and simplifies the use of the FileSystemWatcher and raises its own Created event when a file is created in a directory specified in its Path property. Both the path and the filter (exposed as the Criteria property) can alternatively be set in one of the overloaded constructors. Note that if the Path property is set to a directory that does not exist, an ArgumentException is thrown by the FileSystemWatcher class itself.

The configuration of the private class level mWatcher variable, which references the instance of the FileSystemWatcher class, takes place in the InitWatcher private method called by the constructors. In this class, mWatcher only looks for file changes because the NotifyFilter property is set to NotifyFilters.FileName, and only in the directory set in the Path property because IncludeSubdirectories is set to False. The method also sets up the handlers for the Create and Error events and hooks them to the private MyWatcher and MyWatcherErr methods. These methods in turn raise the Create and Error events back to the user of the class. The FileSystemEventArgs object passed into the Created event handler supports several properties, the most important of which is FullPath, which returns the entire path for the file on which the event occurred.

A client using the NotifyNewFiles class simply needs to instantiate it and set the directory to look for, as follows:

```
Dim objNew As NotifyNewFiles
objNew = New NotifyNewFiles("c:\My Documents")
objNew.Enabled = True

AddHandler objNew.Created, AddressOf NewFile
```

The exposed Enabled property maps to the EnableRaisingEvents method of the FileSystemWatcher object. The method used to handle the Created event is then specified as follows, assuming that a ProcessFile method is available to process the file passed into the event:

```
Private Sub NewFile(ByVal FilePath As String)
   ProcessFile(FilePath)
End Sub
```

Issues to Consider

When writing code that responds to file system events, two issues might cause unexpected problems. The first is a timing issue that often occurs with large files, and the second occurs when monitoring a heavily accessed directory.

First, because writing a file to the file system is actually a multistep process that involves writing the entry in the file table and then writing the content to the file, the FileSystemWatcher begins processing events before the content is completely written. In fact, the Created event actually is fired when the entry is written to the file table. As a result, on all but the smallest files, you cannot immediately begin processing the file when the Created event is fired, as shown in the previous code example. Instead, use a small utility method, such as the following, that waits until the file can be opened exclusively before attempting to process it:

```
Private Sub WaitForExclusiveAccess(ByVal fullPath As String)
    While (True)
      Try
```

```
        Dim f As Stream
        f = File.Open(fullPath, FileMode.Append, _
          FileAccess.Write, FileShare.None)
        f.Close()
        Exit Sub
      Catch e As Exception
        Thread.Sleep(100)
      End Try
    End While
  End Sub
```

The code for the `NewFile` method would then be changed as follows:

```
Private Sub NewFile(ByVal FilePath As String)
  WaitForExclusiveAccess(FilePath)
  ProcessFile(FilePath)
End Sub
```

The second possible problem occurs when you attempt to monitor a directory on which many file events occur in a short period of time. This is a problem because internally the `FileSystemWatcher` records operating system notification of file system changes in an 8KB (8192 bytes) buffer which is then translated to Win32 API calls so that notifications can be made. Obviously, many changes have the capability to overrun the buffer so that some events will be missed.

In the `NotifyNewFiles` class in Listing 12.6, the `Error` event, which is fired if the buffer is exhausted, is handled to enable the client to know whether events might possibly be missed. To control the size of the buffer, the `InternalBufferSize` property of the `FileSystemWatcher` class can be used.

> **NOTE**
>
> An `InternalBufferSize` of 4096 bytes can track changes on approximately 80 files because each event takes 16 bytes plus the amount needed to store the name in Unicode (2 bytes per character). For best performance, size the buffer in increments according to the default page size of the operating system, which in Windows 2000 is 4KB.

Using Isolated Storage

The final concept that fits under the umbrella of file I/O and that developers should be familiar with is using *isolated storage*. Basically, isolated storage consists of a set of classes that abstract the location of user and assembly-specific files from the code reading from and writing to those files. In addition, access to those files is restricted to the user of the code that created them.

Although isolated storage has obvious uses for storing user preference information in a traditional Windows application over using the registry, distributed applications also can take advantage of it—for example, when you're writing a Windows service application that accepts connections from multiple clients. In this instance, the service could impersonate the user and use isolated storage to store and retrieve distinct configuration information.

Conceptually, isolated storage exposes *stores* of information in which directories and files are created and retrieved. Each store is represented by an instance of the `IsolatedStorageFile` class in the `System.IO.IsolatedStorage` namespace. `IsolatedStorageFile` itself is derived from the `IsolatedStorage` class. Within the stores, files are manipulated using the `IsolatedStorageFileStream` class derived from `FileStream`.

> **NOTE**
>
> Administrators can use a security policy on a machine to restrict the size of stores (referred to as *quotas*) and the way in which those stores can be used (none; isolated by user and assembly; isolated by user, assembly, and domain; unrestricted;, administrator). Ultimately, the runtime uses an `IsolatedStorageFilePermission` object to grant access to isolated storage based on the trust level of the code, the security policy, and whether the code requests permissions using the `IsolatedStorageFilePermissionAttribute`.

Two different kinds of stores can be accessed: one that is unique to the user and assembly that created it, and one that is based on the user, assembly, and domain. Basically, the difference is that the former allows stores to be accessed by an assembly and user, regardless of which application the assembly is used in, whereas the latter only allows access if the user, assembly, and specific application (domain) were used to create the store. These two different kinds of stores are created and accessed using two different methods of the `IsolatedStorageFile` class, `GetUserStoreForAssembly` and `GetUserStoreForDomain`.

After the store has been accessed, it can be manipulated using methods of the `IsolatedStorageFile` class, such as `CreateDirectory`, `DeleteFile`, `GetFileNames`, and `GetDirectoryNames` to name a few. Listing 12.7 uses isolated storage to save and retrieve an array of ZIP Codes for a specific user.

LISTING 12.7   Using `IsolatedStorage`. These methods save and retrieve an array to a file in isolated storage.

```
Option Strict

Imports System.IO.IsolatedStorage
```

LISTING 12.7 Continued

```
Public Sub SavePrefs(ByVal ar As ArrayList, ByVal FileName As String)

    Dim isfStore As IsolatedStorageFile
    Dim ifsFile As IsolatedStorageFileStream
    Dim swWriter As StreamWriter
    Dim i As Integer

    ' Get the isolated storage and open the file
    Try
      isfStore = IsolatedStorageFile.GetUserStoreForDomain
      isfStore.CreateDirectory("Prefs")
      ifsFile = New IsolatedStorageFileStream("Prefs/" & FileName, _
        FileMode.Create, isfStore)

      swWriter = New StreamWriter(ifsFile)
    Catch e As Exception
      ifsFile.Close()
      Throw New Exception("Could not access isolated storage: " _
        & e.Message)
    End Try

    ' Write to the file
    Try
      For i = 0 To ar.Count - 1
        swWriter.WriteLine(ar(i).ToString)
      Next
    Catch e As Exception
      Throw New Exception("Could not write to " & FileName & _
        ": " & e.Message)
    Finally
      swWriter.Close()
      ifsFile.Close()
    End Try

End Sub


Public Function LoadPrefs(ByVal FileName As String) As ArrayList

    Dim isfStore As IsolatedStorageFile
    Dim ifsFile As IsolatedStorageFileStream
    Dim srReader As StreamReader
    Dim i As Integer
    Dim arArray As New ArrayList()
    Dim strArray As String
```

LISTING 12.7 Continued

```
' Get the isolated storage and open the file
Try
  isfStore = IsolatedStorageFile.GetUserStoreForDomain

  isfStore.CreateDirectory("Prefs")
  ifsFile = New IsolatedStorageFileStream("Prefs/" & _
    FileName, FileMode.Open, FileAccess.Read, isfStore)

  srReader = New StreamReader(ifsFile)
Catch e As Exception
  ifsFile.Close()
  Throw New Exception("Could not access isolated storage: " & e.Message)
End Try

Try
  ' Write to the file
  strArray = srReader.ReadLine
  Do While Not strArray Is Nothing
    arArray.Capacity = i + 1
    arArray.Add(strArray)
    i = i + 1
    strArray = srReader.ReadLine
  Loop
Catch e As Exception
  Throw New Exception("Could not read from " & _
    FileName & ": " & e.Message)
Finally
  srReader.Close()
  ifsFile.Close()
End Try

Return arArray

End Function
```

Although the code is self-explanatory, note that in the SavePrefs method, the file is saved to a directory called "Prefs" within the isolated storage using the CreateDirectory method. Because IsolatedFileStream is derived from FileStream, it can be used in conjunction with StreamWriter and StreamReader objects to write and read the file. To use these methods, code such as the following can be used:

```
Dim zips As New ArrayList()
Dim i As Integer
```

```
zips.Add("66212")
zips.Add("66218")
zips.Add("52747")

SavePrefs(zips, "zips.dat")
zips.Clear()
zips = LoadPrefs("zips.dat")

For i = 0 To zips.Count - 1
  Console.WriteLine(zips(i).tostring)
Next
```

12

Creating Multithreaded Applications

One of the most eagerly anticipated features available in VB .NET is the capability to natively create and manage threads. Although it was possible to create a multithreaded VB 6.0 application using the Win32 `CreateThread` API, or by fooling the COM library into creating a component in a separate thread, these techniques were both difficult to debug and maintain.

> **NOTE**
>
> See Chapter 13 of *Pure Visual Basic* for a description of how to use the COM method to create a multithreaded form-based application in VB 6.0.

The main reason for these difficulties, of course, was that VB 6.0 wasn't built to handle multi-threaded applications, which resulted in access violations and memory corruption. In stark contrast, the Common Language Runtime (CLR) was designed for a multithreaded environment, and indeed the Services Framework incorporates them implicitly in the basic architecture of delegates, as you've seen in both Chapter 4 and this chapter. However, the Services Framework also supports explicit use of threading APIs using the `System.Threading` namespace.

For readers unfamiliar with threads, simply put, they allow your application to spawn multiple units of execution independently scheduled and prioritized by preemptive multitasking operating systems such as Windows 2000. Based on the thread priority and the particular scheduling algorithm, the OS schedules each thread to run for a certain amount of time called a *time slice*. When the time slice elapses, the thread is suspended and placed back into a queue while another thread is then allocated a time slice. When the thread is suspended, its state (or context) is saved so that it can continue its work where it left off. The CLR supports threading by starting each `AppDomain` with a main thread and allowing it to create multiple worker threads, each with its own exception handlers and context data.

The obvious advantage to using more than one thread in an application is that your application can appear to be performing several activities simultaneously as the various threads are swapped in and out of the CPU. In fact, on machines with multiple processors, the threads from a single AppDomain can be scheduled across any available processor, allowing work to actually be done concurrently. In distributed applications, this can increase scalability because more clients can share the CPU resources available on a server, and desktop applications, such as spreadsheets and word processors, frequently take advantage of threads to perform background operations, such as recalculation and printing. However, how does this concept apply to distributed applications you'll write with VB .NET?

For starters, keep in mind that you're already using a multithreaded architecture that you get for free if you're building distributed applications like those described in this book. This is the case because application services such as IIS, Component Services, and SQL Server, all are multithreaded. For example, as clients request Web pages, their requests are carried out by worker threads controlled by IIS and the ASP.NET runtime. One of these threads might execute an ASP.NET page that calls a component hosted in Component Services. The component could be configured to run as a Server Application, so it is executed on a thread allocated from a thread pool for the application. The component, in turn, might use a database connection pulled from a pool of worker threads allocated by the SQL Server engine. As a result, as multiple users request pages that instantiate components and access the database, their activities are not serialized and, therefore, constrained by single-threaded execution.

Because most of the code you write in distributed applications executes within the middle tier, there are a limited number of scenarios for which you'll likely need to create threads explicitly. Some of these scenarios include lengthy operations, such as file I/O and database maintenance tasks, servicing multiple clients in a Windows service application, and listening for messages from a Microsoft Message Queue. As a result, this section covers the basics to prepare you for using threads, although for further information and additional samples, consult the documentation.

> **CAUTION**
>
> Because threads are expensive for the operating system to track and schedule, do not go wild creating a new thread for everything your application does. Because memory must be allocated for each thread, too many threads can and will decrease the overall performance of the system. In addition, threads introduce considerations that VB developers have not had to deal with before, such as synchronizing access to shared resources. As a result, only add support for multiple threads after careful consideration.

The rest of this section discusses using both individual threads and multiple threads through the use of a thread pool.

Using Threads

The primary class used to create and manipulate threads is, not surprisingly, the Thread class. It contains methods that allow you to Start, Resume, Abort, Suspend, and Join (wait for) a thread, in addition to querying and setting the thread's state using members such as Sleep, IsAlive, IsBackground, Priority, ApartmentState, and ThreadState.

> **NOTE**
>
> Most members of Thread are virtual members and can only be accessed from a particular instance of the Thread class. To manipulate a particular thread, you either need to create a new instance of the Thread class or get a reference to the current Thread using the shared CurrentThread property. The primary exception to this is the Sleep method, which suspends the current thread for a specific number of milliseconds.

To start a new thread, you must specify an entry point for the thread to begin its execution. The requirement is that the method, either a method on an object or within a module, include no arguments and for obvious reasons should be defined as a Sub procedure. It is also possible to execute a method within the same object on a separate thread.

For example, consider the following code. In this example, the GetPhotos method of the Instructors class is to be executed on a separate thread. This method (not shown) queries the database for all the instructor images and saves each one to a file on the file system. Unlike the asynchronous I/O example shown in Listing 12.5, both the database access and the file access are performed on a separate thread.

```
Option Strict

Imports System.Threading
Dim tPhoto As Thread
Dim tsStart As ThreadStart
Dim objIns As New Instructors

tsStart = New ThreadStart(AddressOf objIns.GetPhotos)
tPhoto = New Thread(tsStart)

tPhoto.Priority = ThreadPriority.BelowNormal
tPhoto.Name = "SavingPhotos"

tPhoto.Start()
```

```
' Wait for the started thread to become alive
While (tPhoto.ThreadState = ThreadState.Unstarted)
  Thread.Sleep(100)
End While

' Perform other work here

If tPhoto.IsAlive Then
  MsgBox("Still processing images...")
  MsgBox("Waiting to finish processing images...")
  tPhoto.Join
End If

MsgBox("Done processing images.")
```

In this example, starting a thread actually involves instantiating a `ThreadStart` delegate with the address of the entry point using the `AddressOf` operator. The delegate is then passed to the constructor of the `Thread` class. Before the thread actually is started, the `Priority` is set to `BelowNormal` so that the main thread continues to service requests more promptly. Four other priorities can be set using the `ThreadPriority` enumeration (`AboveNormal`, `Highest`, `Lowest`, and `Normal`) even though the Win32 API supports more than 30 priority levels.

NOTE

As mentioned, the priorities exposed by the `ThreadPriority` enumeration map to a small subset of the 32 levels of priority available in the Win32 API. In fact, they map from lowest priority (`Lowest`) at a 6 to highest (`Highest`) at 10. You would typically want to lower the priority to ensure that the thread did not use too many CPU cycles, thereby interfering with other threads.

The code then sets the `Name` property of the thread. Although at first glance this seems strange because a thread or its name should never appear in the user interface, the name does appear in the debugger and also can be useful for logging purposes. The `Start` method is then used to actually begin execution.

TIP

Sometimes it comes in handy to get a numeric identifier for the thread for logging and reporting purposes. One technique for doing so is to call the `GetHashCode` method on the `CurrentThread` property or an instance of the `Thread` class. This returns a number that you can log to your application or event log.

After starting the thread, the code goes into a loop to wait until the thread has started by repeatedly checking the ThreadState property for a value other than Unstarted, which is the initial state of the thread. Nine other states ranging from Running to Stopped are exposed by the ThreadState enumeration. Calling the shared Sleep method of Thread class tells the thread running the statement to sleep for a specified number of milliseconds, in this case, the main thread and not the one represented by tPhoto. Finally, after performing some other work, the main thread checks to see whether tPhoto still is executing by checking the IsAlive property. If so, messages to that effect are relayed to the user before calling the Join method. This method synchronizes the two threads by blocking (suspending execution of the current thread) until the thread on which the method was called has stopped.

> **TIP**
>
> Unrelated to the Priority property previously mentioned, the CLR makes a distinction between threads that run in the foreground and those that run in the background. If a thread is marked as a background thread, the CLR does not wait for it to finish in the event that the AppDomain is shut down. As discussed in the previous section, the threads created by the runtime when using asynchronous file I/O are background threads, so you'd want to make sure that the main thread of your code did not finish before the I/O was complete. Conversely, by default threads created as shown previously are marked as foreground and consequently their IsBackground property is set to False.

Although not shown in the previous example, during execution, the thread can be suspended using the Suspend method and then subsequently resumed with Resume. In addition, the thread can be deallocated using the Abort method, which raises a ThreadAbortExcpetion inside the thread. However, ThreadAbortException is not catchable, and the runtime simply executes all the pending Finally blocks before killing the thread. It is recommended that you call Join on the thread after Abort to ensure that the thread has stopped executing.

Synchronizing Access to Resources

Typically you'll want to run processes on separate threads that do not require access to shared resources. The recommended way to do this is as follows:

1. Encapsulate the process that is to be run in a class that exposes an entry point used to start the process—that is, Public Sub Start() and instance variables to handle the state.

2. Create a separate instance of the class.

3. Set any instance variables required by the process.

4. Invoke the entry point on a separate thread.

5. Do not reference the instance variables of the class.

By following this approach, all the instance variables will be "private" to the thread and can be used without fear of synchronization problems.

However, that might not always be possible in the case of database connections or file handles, for example. To ensure that threads wait for each other when accessing these resources, you can use the Monitor class and its associated Enter, Exit, TryEnter, Wait, Pulse, and PulseAll methods.

For example, assume that the Instructors class used in the previous code example includes a class level SqlConnection object shared by all methods and used to connect to the database. This is an example of a resource shared by all methods in the class.

> **NOTE**
>
> Although using connection pooling, as discussed in Chapter 7, would provide a more scalable solution, this example serves our current purpose and allows all database access to go through a single database connection. This approach might be warranted for applications that require a constant database connection, but probably not for distributed applications.

In this case, assume that after the call to GetPhotos, the client continues on and subsequently calls a method that attempts to use the connection object. Because the connection might be in use by GetPhotos, the method might throw an exception if the SqlConnection is busy processing other results.

To avoid this situation, the GetPhotos method can use shared methods of the Monitor class to create a *critical section* inside its code. Simply put, a critical section is a block of code enclosed by calls to the Enter and Exit methods of the Monitor class through which access must be synchronized based on the object passed to the Enter method. In other words, if the GetPhotos method wants exclusively to use the SqlConnection for a block of statements, it must create a critical section by passing the SqlConnection to the Enter method of Monitor at the beginning of the section, and invoke Exit when it is finished. The object passed can be any object derived from System.Object.

If the object currently is being used by another thread, the Enter method blocks until the object is released. Alternatively, you can call the TryEnter method, which will not block, and simply returns a Boolean value indicating whether the object is in use. Once safely in the critical section, the GetPhotos method can use the SqlConnection to execute a stored procedure and write out the results. After closing the resulting `SqlDataReader`, the `Pulse` method of the `Monitor` class is called to inform the next thread in the wait queue that the object is free. This moves the thread to the ready queue so that it is ready for processing. The `PulseAll` method informs all waiting threads that the object is about to be freed. Finally, a call to `Exit` is made, which releases the monitor and ends the critical section. Listing 12.8 shows the skeleton code for `GetPhotos` with the monitoring code.

LISTING 12.8 Synchronizing Resources. This example shows how the `GetPhotos` method would use the `Monitor` class to ensure that two threads do not attempt to use the `SqlConnection` object simultaneously.

```
Public Sub GetPhotos()

  Dim cmSQL As SqlCommand
  Dim sdrIns As SqlDataReader

  Try
    ' Execute proc
    cmSQL = New SqlCommand("usp_GetPhotos", mcnSQL)
    cmSQL.CommandType = CommandType.StoredProcedure

    ' Enter critical section
    Monitor.Enter(mcnSQL)
'    Alternate code
'    Do While Not Monitor.TryEnter(mcnSQL)
'      Thread.CurrentThread.Sleep(100)
'    Loop
    sdrIns = cmSQL.ExecuteReader()
  Catch e As Exception
    ' Other error hanlding
    Monitor.Exit(mcnSQL)
  End Try

  Do While sdrIns.Read
    ' Read the data and write it to a binary stream
  Loop

  sdrIns.Close
  Monitor.Pulse(mcnSQL)
  Monitor.Exit(mcnSQL)
  ' Exited critical section

  Return
End Sub
```

Obviously, critical sections should be created only when absolutely necessary because the effect of blocking threads slows overall throughput.

A simpler technique that can be used to synchronize instance variables shared between threads is to use the `Interlocked` class. This class contains shared `Increment` and `Decrement` methods that combine the operations of changing the variable and checking the result into a single atomic operation. This is needed because a thread could change the value of a variable and then have its time slice expire before being able to check the result. In the intervening time before the thread was again run, the variable could have been changed by another thread.

For example, the following code increments the `mPhotosProcessed` instance level variable of the `Instructors` class:

```
Interlocked.Increment(mPhotosProcessed)
```

The `Interlocked` class also supports `Exchange` and `CompareExchange` to set a variable to a specified value, and to do so only if the variable is equal to a specified value, respectively.

VB .NET also supports the `SyncLock` and `End SyncLock` statements intrinsically that perform the same function as using the `Monitor` class. In other words, you can block a critical section with the `SyncLock` block, and it calls the `Enter` and `Exit` methods automatically. The `SyncLock` statement accepts an expression that must evaluate to a reference type, such as a class, module, interface, array, or delegate, because it is passed to the `Enter` method behind the scenes. For example, the code in Listing 12.8 could alternatively use the `SyncLock` statements as follows:

```vbnet
Public Sub GetPhotos()

  Dim cmSQL As SqlCommand
  Dim sdrIns As SqlDataReader

  Try
    ' Execute proc
    cmSQL = New SqlCommand("usp_GetPhotos", mcnSQL)
    cmSQL.CommandType = CommandType.StoredProcedure

    ' Enter critical section
    SyncLock mcnSQL
      sdrIns = cmSQL.ExecuteReader()

      Do While sdrIns.Read
       ' Read the data and write it to a binary stream
      Loop
      sdrIns.Close
    End SyncLock
    ' Exited critical section
  Catch e As SqlException
```

```
  ' Other error hanlding
  End Try

  Return
End Sub
```

One nice aspect of SyncLock is that it implicitly uses structured exception handling and calls the Exit method of the Monitor class even if an exception is generated. As a result, you cannot use the SyncLock statement in methods that use unstructured exception handling because the two cannot be mixed.

Using Thread Local Storage

Although ideally your threads will use instance variables that are in effect private to the thread, there might be times when your thread must access an instance of an object shared by other threads. If so, your thread might need to store and retrieve its own truly private data. This might be the case, for example, when a thread in a thread pool monitors an MSMQ Server queue and needs to store data pulled from the queue to be used for later processing.

As it turns out, each thread in a Windows operating system contains its own thread local storage (TLS) used to track state information. Luckily, the Services Framework provides access to TLS through an attribute and members of the Thread class.

Using the ThreadStatic Attribute

The simplest way to access TLS is to apply the ThreadStatic attribute to a shared field in your class. This attribute is found in the System namespace and ensures that each thread gets its own copy of the field. To illustrate this attribute, consider the following class definition:

```
Public Class Instructors
  <ThreadStatic()> Shared PhotosProcessed As Integer

  Public Sub ProcessPhotos(ByVal arIns As ArrayList)
    ' Do the work and update the counter
    PhotosProcessed = 5
  End Sub

End Class
```

In this case, if the client code uses the same instance of Instructors in multiple threads to call the ProcessPhotos method, each thread gets its own copy of the PhotosProcessed field and can track how many photos are processed on that thread. This makes accessing TLS straightforward.

Using Data Slots

For finer grained control of TLS, the Thread class exposes a set of methods to create and manipulate memory areas in the TLS called *data slots*.

As to the particulars, the Thread class exposes the shared AllocateNamedDataSlot method that creates a new data slot with a given name on all threads in the AppDomain. This slot subsequently can be populated and read using the SetData and GetData methods. For example, assume that a class called WorkerClass performs some processing activity and we want to create a certain number of threads to perform the work. The following code creates a data slot called "ID" for all threads, and then spins up the appropriate number of threads on the StartWork method of the objWorker instance:

```
Dim dssSlot As LocalDataStoreSlot
Dim tNew As Thread
Dim objWorker As WorkerClass

dssSlot = Thread.AllocateNamedDataSlot("ID")

For i = 0 to intMaxThreads
  tNew = New Thread(New ThreadStart(AddressOf objWorker.StartWork)
  tNew.Start
Next
```

Notice that because all the new threads will share the instance variables associated with objWorker, the StartWorker method, and any methods called by Start, would need to use synchronization to prevent concurrent access to these variables. However, if the threads each require their own data to be shared between methods, they can place a copy in the "ID" slot in TLS like so:

```
Public Sub Start()
  Dim dssIDSlot As LocalDataStoreSlot
  Dim myID As Integer

  '  Do other work

  dssIDSlot = Thread.GetNamedDataSlot("ID")
  Thread.SetData(dssIDSlot, myID)
  Call NextProcess()
End Sub

Private Sub NextProcess()
  Dim myID As Integer
  Dim dssIDSlot As LocalDataStoreSlot

  dssIDSlot = Thread.GetNamedDataSlot("ID")
  myID = Thread.GetData(dssIDSlot)

  '  Do other work
End Sub
```

When the `NextProcess` method is called, the data can once again be read from the slot, using `GetData` as shown.

Once again, it should be pointed out that the design pattern discussed in the previous section is the one that should be employed where possible. Only when your designs are more complicated and require concurrent access to the same object from multiple threads would you consider using TLS.

Using Thread Pools

Although you can create and manage your own threads using the `Thread` class, the `System.Threading` namespace also provides a simple way to use threads from a pool allocated by the CLR. This is possible because the CLR automatically creates and manages one thread pool per process that it uses to handle asynchronous operations, such as file I/O and events, as you've seen earlier. Within the pool, one thread is assigned `Highest` priority and is used to monitor the status of the other threads on the queue. Using the `ThreadPool` class, your code can tap into this pool to make more efficient use of this architecture already employed by the runtime. In essence, the `ThreadPool` class allows you to post *work items*—that is, methods to execute—to the pool that subsequently are serviced by worker threads.

As mentioned earlier, using threads should be reserved only for applications that require it and only after careful analysis. For example, a good use of the thread pool might be in a Windows service application that listens for new messages entering one or more message queues. Although as you'll see in Chapter 14, "Integrating with the Enterprise," the `System.Messaging` namespace supports asynchronous operations, creating a thread pool allows you to control specifics, such as how many threads are processing messages and how long the threads live.

To give you an example of using the `ThreadPool` class, the simplified classes in Listing 12.9 will be used to monitor an MSMQ queue.

LISTING 12.9   The `QueueListener` Class. This class uses the `ThreadPool` class to monitor an MSMQ queue.

```
Option Strict On

Imports System.Threading
Imports System.Messaging

Public Class QueueListener
  ' Used to listen for MSMQ messages

  Private mstrMachine As String
  Private mstrQueue As String
  Private mWorkItems As Integer = 7
```

LISTING 12.9   Continued

```vbnet
Private mFinished As Boolean = False
Private mEvs() As ManualResetEvent

Public Class EventState
  ' Used to store the event and any other state data required by the listener
  Public ResetEvent As ManualResetEvent
  Public ThreadName As String

  Public Sub New(ByVal myEvent As ManualResetEvent)
    MyBase.New()
    ResetEvent = myEvent
  End Sub

  Public Sub New(ByVal myEvent As ManualResetEvent, _
  ByVal Name As String)
    MyBase.New()
    ResetEvent = myEvent
    ThreadName = Name
  End Sub
End Class

Public Property WorkItems() As Integer
  Get
    Return mWorkItems
  End Get
  Set(ByVal Value As Integer)
    If Value > 15 Then
      mWorkItems = 15
    Else
      mWorkItems = Value
    End If
  End Set
End Property

Public Sub New(ByVal Machine As String, ByVal Queue As String)
  ' Constructor accepts the necessary queue information
  mstrMachine = Machine
  mstrQueue = Queue
End Sub

Public Sub Listen(ByVal state As Object)
  ' Method that each thread uses to listen for messages

  Dim evsState As EventState
```

LISTING 12.9 Continued

```vb
evsState = CType(state, EventState)

' Create a MessageQueue object
Dim objMQ As System.Messaging.MessageQueue = _
  New System.Messaging.MessageQueue()
' Create a Message object
Dim objMsg As System.Messaging.Message
' Event from the state
Dim evs As ManualResetEvent

' Cast the state into the event
evs = evsState.ResetEvent

' Set the priority and name
Thread.CurrentThread.Priority = ThreadPriority.BelowNormal
Try
  If Not evsState.ThreadName Is Nothing Then
    Thread.CurrentThread.Name = evsState.ThreadName
  End If
Catch e As Exception
  ' Thread name can only be set once
  ' Don't set it and get out
End Try

Try
  ' Set the path property on the MessageQueue, assume private in this case
  objMQ.Path = mstrMachine & "\private$\" & mstrQueue
  ' Repeat until Interrupt received
  While True
    Try
      ' Sleep in order to catch the interrupt if it has been thrown
      Thread.CurrentThread.Sleep(20)

      ' Set the Message object to the result from the receive function
      ' Will block for 1 second if a message is not received
      objMsg = objMQ.Receive(New TimeSpan(0, 0, 0, 1))

      ' Message found so signal the event to say we're working
      evs.Reset()
      ' Processing the message
      ProcessMsg(objMsg)
      ' Done processing

    Catch e As ThreadInterruptedException
      ' Catch the ThreadInterrupt from the main thread and exit
```

LISTING 12.9 Continued

```
            Exit While
        Catch excp As MessageQueueException
          ' Catch any exceptions thrown in receive
          ' Probable timeout
        Finally
          ' Done with this iteration of the loop so set the event
          evs.Set()
        End Try

        ' If finished then exit thread
        If mFinished Then
          Exit While
        End If

      End While

    Catch e As ThreadInterruptedException
      ' Catch the ThreadInterrupt from the main thread and exit
    End Try

End Sub

Private Sub ProcessMsg(ByVal Msg As Message)
  ' Here is where we would process the message
End Sub

Public Sub Monitor()
  Dim intItem As Integer
  Dim objState As EventState

  ReDim mEvs(mWorkItems)
  mFinished = False

  For intItem = 0 To mWorkItems - 1
    Console.WriteLine("Queue to Thread Pool {0}", intItem)
    mEvs(intItem) = New ManualResetEvent(False)
    objState = New EventState(mEvs(intItem), "Worker " & intItem)
    ThreadPool.QueueUserWorkItem( _
      New WaitCallback(AddressOf Me.Listen), objState)
  Next

End Sub

Public Sub Finish(Optional ByVal Timeout As Integer = 0)
  ' Make sure everyone gets through the last iteration
```

LISTING 12.9 Continued

```
  mFinished = True
  ' Block until all have been set
  Try
    If Timeout = 0 Then
      ' Waiting until all threads signal that they are done.
      WaitHandle.WaitAll(mEvs)
    Else
      WaitHandle.WaitAll(mEvs, Timeout, True)
    End If
  Catch e As Exception
    ' All handles may not have been created
  End Try

  End Sub

End Class
```

Listing 12.9 contains two classes: `EventState`, which is a protected child class, and
`QueueListener`. As you'll see, `EventState` contains a field called `ResetEvent` of the type
`ManualResetEvent` that will be used to ensure that any worker thread can finish its work without interruption by signaling what state it is in using the `ResetEvent` field. The class also contains a `ThreadName` field used to set the name of the thread associated with the class for
debugging purposes.

> **TIP**
>
> Figure 12.2 shows VS .NET in debug mode when running this multithreaded listener
> application. Note that the drop-down window displays each thread with its associ-
> ated name. By selecting the thread, the code window shifts to the point at which
> that thread currently is executing. Note that a thread can have its name set only
> once, and so in a situation where work items might end up using the same thread,
> the code must trap for an exception when setting the `Name` property.

The `QueueListener` class actually polls the MSMQ queue on multiple threads and contains a
constructor that accepts the machine name and queue name to monitor. The public `Listen`
method receives messages from the queue, whereas the public `Monitor` method initiates the
process and creates the thread pool. The private `ProcessMsg` method is a stub used to process a
message when it is received. Finally, the public `Finish` method can be called with an optional
timeout argument to allow the threads used by the `QueueListener` class to complete their work
within a specified time period.

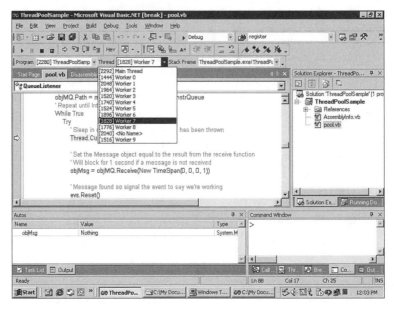

FIGURE 12.2

The debugger with the threads drop-down exposed. Clicking on a thread shows the point at which the thread is paused.

To begin, notice that the `Listen` method accepts a state object as a parameter. This object contains an instance of `EventState` that is used by `Listen` to signal when the method is in the midst of processing a message and when it is done. Doing so ensures that the `Finish` method blocks until all the threads finish their current processing. After setting the `ThreadPriority` and `Name` and retrieving the `EventState`, the method simply contains a `While` loop inside a `Try` block. This loop repeatedly calls the `Receive` method of the `MessageQueue` class that returns the first available message within a specified timeout period. In this case, a `TimeSpan` object (discussed in Chapter 13) is used to instruct the `Receive` method to block for one second before returning if there is no message. In the event that no message is received, a `MessageQueueException` is thrown. Note that if a message is received, the method continues and calls the `Reset` method of the `ResetEvent` field in the `EventState` object. In either case, the `Finally` block calls the `Set` method of the `ResetEvent` field to signal that the thread is finished processing for this iteration of the loop.

As mentioned previously, the `ResetEvent` field of `EventState` contains an instance of `ManualResetEvent`, an event object whose signaled and nonsignaled states can be changed manually using the `Reset` and `Set` methods. When the `Reset` method is called, the state is changed to nonsignaled to indicate that the thread is busy. When the state is set to signaled with the `Set` event, the thread is finished doing its useful work and can be safely destroyed.

The interesting work is actually performed by the `Monitor` method. In this method, a class level array of `ManualResetEvent` objects is created of the same size as the number of work items that will be serviced by the pool.

> **NOTE**
>
> Work items are not the same as threads in this context. Work items are serviced by threads, but the runtime decides when threads get created to handle your work items. For example, if the workload is initially light, the runtime might not spin up worker threads to handle your work items right away. In this example, to make sure that the runtime has available threads for other purposes, such as firing events, the `WorkItems` property is capped at 15.

The number of work items can be set by the `WorkItems` property of the `QueueListener` class, although it is defaulted to seven. A `For` loop is then used to create each of the `ManualResetEvent` objects and associate them with a new instance of `EventState`. The resulting object, `objState`, then is passed as the second argument to the shared `QueueUserWorkItem` method of the `ThreadPool` class. As implied by the name, this method queues a work item to the thread pool managed by the runtime to be serviced by the next available worker thread. The first argument specifies the method to call back into when the work item begins execution, in this case `Listen`.

By passing the `EventState` as the second argument, the `Listen` method can retrieve the object and use any state information stored inside as discussed previously. In this case, the state consists of the name of the thread to use in debugging and a `ManualResetEvent` object used to synchronize the thread. After the loop has completed, the specified number of work items will have been queued for execution by the thread pool. At this point, the threads will continually check the specified queue for new messages.

When the client finally calls the `Finish` method to complete execution, the method first sets the private `mFinished` variable to `True`. This variable is checked on each iteration of the loop in the `Listen` method, and if set to `True`, exits the loop, freeing the thread to return to the pool. The `Finish` method then uses the shared `WaitAll` method of the `WaitHandle` class to block until all the `ManualReset` event objects in the `mEvs` array have been set to a signaled state (`True`). The optional second argument used if the timeout value is passed to the method, specifies the time period to wait for this to occur before unblocking the current thread. Using this approach ensures that the `Finish` method blocks until each worker thread has completed its current iteration of the loop in the `Listen` method. Note that the threads actually are returned to the pool and not destroyed. As a result, another call to `Monitor` reuses the existing threads and does not incur the overhead of re-creating them.

For the client using the `QueueListener` class, the implementation is straightforward, as shown in the following code:

```
Dim objQ As New QueueListener("ssosa", "tester")

objQ.WorkItems = 10
objQ.Monitor()

' Do other work here

objQ.Finish()
```

After instantiating a new object and passing it the machine name and queue to listen for, the number of work items is set and the `Monitor` method called. At some point later, the client can call the `Finish` method with the optional timeout to clean up the worker threads.

Although this example was created to illustrate how to use the `ThreadPool` class, it obviously is not the only way to create a pool of threads to perform actions such as monitoring a message queue. For example, the `QueueListener` class could be easily modified to create and track an array of `Thread` objects from within the class to implement the thread pool. The `Finish` method could then have executed a loop after setting the `mFinished` flag looking at the `IsAlive` property to determine when the thread pool was drained, rather than using a `ManualResetEvent` object. In addition, the technique shown in the previous section for using TLS could have been used to pass state information to the threads. In many respects, this architecture would allow you more control over the threads because you have explicit control over when they are created and destroyed.

Manipulating Windows Processes

Just as you might want to write code to manage threads within your own process, it also is often necessary to manipulate other processes on the machine or across the network. Once again, the Services Framework provides classes in the `System.Diagnostics` namespace that you can use to monitor and manage these external processes.

The primary class that enables this functionality is `Process`. It contains methods and properties that allow you to enumerate the processes on a local or remote machine through shared methods, such as `GetCurrentProcess`, `GetProcessByID`, `GetProcesses`, and `GetProcessesByName`, in addition to identifying all the relevant information regarding a process, such as its `Id`, `MainModule`, `MainWindowTitle`, `WorkingSet`, and `Threads` among others. Finally, `Process` allows you to interact with processes by using the `Start`, `Kill`, `WaitForExit`, and `WaitForInput` methods.

Although you certainly can obtain a host of information about a particular process using the `Process` class, in most business applications, developers are more worried about being notified when a specific process starts or stops because the code you're writing might have dependencies on other executables. In VB 6.0, this scenario caused VB developers no end of headaches as they searched in vain for asynchronous ways to poll for a process and often resorted to the less than optimal `DoEvents` statement. Now, however, by combining the `Process` class with the `Thread` class, it is relatively simple to create a flexible solution to this common problem.

To solve this problem, the example for this section consists of a custom class called `ProcessNotify` that illustrates the use of the `Process` class, and can be used to notify a caller when a process starts or completes.

> **TIP**
>
> This class encapsulates notifications for processes only. If your code is dependent on a Windows service, a better approach would be to use the `ServiceController` class discussed in Chapter 13.

Listing 12.10 presents the code for the `ProcessNotify` class.

LISTING 12.10   The `ProcessNotify` Class. This class uses the `System.Diagnostics.Process` class to notify clients when a process starts and stops.

```vb
Option Strict On

Imports System.Diagnostics
Imports System.Threading

Public Class ProcessNotify
  ' Notifies the caller when a specific process ends

  ' Events raised to the client
  Event ProcessComplete(ByVal ProcName As String)
  Event ProcessStarted(ByVal ProcName As String)

  ' Private data
  Private mstrMachine As String
  Private mProcess As Process
  Private marProcess() As Process
  Private mStart As String
  Private mtWait As Thread
  Private mCancelled As Boolean = False

  ' Pass through properties
  Public ReadOnly Property HasExited() As Boolean
    Get
      If mProcess Is Nothing Then
```

LISTING 12.10 Continued

```
          Return True
      Else
          Return mProcess.HasExited
      End If
   End Get
End Property

Public ReadOnly Property ProcessID() As Integer
   Get
      If mProcess Is Nothing Then
         Return 0
      Else
         Return mProcess.Id
      End If
   End Get
End Property

Public Sub New(ByVal Machine As String)
   mstrMachine = Machine
End Sub

Public Sub New()
   mstrMachine = "."
End Sub

Public Overloads Sub GetProcess(ByVal Name As String)
   ' Get the process by name, note that it returns an array
   marProcess = Process.GetProcessesByName(Name, mstrMachine)
   If marProcess.Length > 1 Then
      Throw New Exception(Name & " returns more than one process.")
      Return
   End If
   If marProcess.Length = 0 Then
      Throw New ArgumentException(Name & " was not found.")
      Return
   End If
   ' Set the process
   mProcess = marProcess(0)
End Sub

Public Overloads Sub GetProcess(ByVal ProcessID As Integer)
   ' Get the process by ID
   mProcess = Process.GetProcessById(ProcessID, mstrMachine)
   If mProcess Is Nothing Then
      Throw New ArgumentException(ProcessID & " process id not found.")
```

LISTING 12.10   Continued

```
      Return
    End If
End Sub

Public Function GetProcesses() As String()
  ' Translate to a string array

  Dim arProcess() As Process
  Dim objProc As Process
  Dim arNames() As String

  arProcess = Process.GetProcesses(mstrMachine)
  ReDim arNames(arProcess.Length)

  For Each objProc In arProcess
    arNames(0) = objProc.ProcessName
  Next
  Return (arNames)
End Function

Public Sub WaitForStart(ByVal IsAsync As Boolean, _
  ByVal Name As String)
  ' Block until the process starts or raise an event

  mStart = Name

  If IsAsync Then
    ' May need to reregister if already called once
    If mCancelled Then
      GC.ReRegisterForFinalize(Me)
      mCancelled = False
    End If

    ' Start another thread to wait
    mtWait = New Thread(New ThreadStart(AddressOf PollForProcess))
    mtWait.Priority = ThreadPriority.Lowest
    mtWait.Name = "Wait for started"
    mtWait.Start()
  Else
    ' Tight loop
    WaitForProc(mStart)
  End If

End Sub
```

LISTING 12.10   Continued

```
Private Function WaitForProc(ByVal Name As String) As Boolean
  ' Tight loop to wait for the process
  While True
    Try
      GetProcess(mStart)
    Catch e As Exception
      ' Do nothing since the process has not started
      Thread.Sleep(500)
    End Try

    If Not mProcess Is Nothing Then
      Exit While
    End If
  End While

  Return True
End Function

Private Sub PollForProcess()
  ' Block the current thread and raise the event when started
  WaitForProc(mStart)
  RaiseEvent ProcessStarted(mStart)
  CancelWait()
End Sub

Public Sub WaitForCompletion(ByVal IsAsync As Boolean, _
  Optional ByVal Timeout As Integer = 0)
  If mProcess Is Nothing Then
    Throw New Exception("No process set.")
    Return
  End If

  ' If asynchronous then setup the event handler
  If IsAsync = True Then
    AddHandler mProcess.Exited, AddressOf Me.ProcComplete
    mProcess.EnableRaisingEvents = True
  Else
    ' Otherwise block the current thread
    If Timeout = 0 Then
      mProcess.WaitForExit()
    Else
      mProcess.WaitForExit(Timeout)
    End If
    ' Destroy internal state
    mProcess.Dispose()
```

LISTING 12.10   Continued

```
      mProcess = Nothing
    End If
  End Sub

  Public Sub CancelWait()
    ' Kill the background thread is waiting
    Try
      mtWait.Abort()
    Catch e As Exception
      ' Do nothing, occurs when there is no background thread
    End Try

    ' Don't finalize if this has already been called
    mCancelled = True
    GC.SuppressFinalize(Me)
  End Sub

  Private Sub ProcComplete(ByVal sender As Object, _
    ByVal e As EventArgs)
    ' Raise the event to notify we're complete
    RaiseEvent ProcessComplete(mProcess.ProcessName)
    mProcess.EnableRaisingEvents = False

    ' Destroy internal state
    RemoveHandler mProcess.Exited, AddressOf ProcComplete
    mProcess.Dispose()
    mProcess = Nothing
  End Sub

  Protected Overrides Sub Finalize()
    MyBase.Finalize()
    ' Make sure the background thread is cleaned up
    CancelWait()
  End Sub
End Class
```

The constructor of `ProcessNotify` class is overloaded to accept a machine name. Note that the literal string "." represents the machine on which the code is running and is used to populate the private `mstrMachine` variable.

This class contains several public methods used to retrieve process information and obtain a reference to the process that will be monitored. The method `GetProcesses` returns an array of strings that simply contain the names of all the processes by calling the shared `GetProcesses` method of the `Process` class. Note that an array of `Process` objects is returned, and that this method simply strips out the ProcessName property. The particular process that will be monitored is set using either of the overloaded GetProcess methods where the user can pass in the name, or the operating system ID of the process.

Because the name is not necessarily unique, the method checks for this condition and raises an exception (although a more robust implementation could return an array of possibilities from which the client could choose). If the process is found, the mProcess variable is populated with the Process object. After mProcess is populated, the two read-only properties, HasExited and ProcessID, can be called to transparently invoke the underlying properties of the mProcess object to obtain information that might be useful to the client.

The interesting aspect of the class is the implementation of the wait methods, WaitForCompletion and WaitForStart. WaitForCompletion accepts a flag indicating whether the wait should be asynchronous and, if not, what the timeout period should be until the method returns. In the event that the client wants an asynchronous notification, an event handler for the Exited event of the Process class is created that points to the private ProcComplete method, and the EnableRaisingEvents property is set to True. When the process does exit, the private ProcComplete method then raises the public ProcessCompleted event, passing back the name of the process that ended before cleaning up the event handler and resetting the EnableRaisingEvents property. The mProcess variable is disposed and deallocated because the process it represents is no longer viable.

If the asynchronous argument is set to False, the WaitForExit method of the Process is called with or without a timeout value to block the current thread until the process exits. Once again, the mProcess variable is cleaned up when the process exits.

Although the Process class supports the Exited event and the WaitForExit method to handle the case when the client needs to synchronize with the ending of a process, it has no analog for waiting for a process to start. The WaitForStart method of the ProcessNotify class implements a mechanism to handle this scenario.

Like the WaitForCompletion method, this method accepts an argument to indicate whether the wait operation should block the current thread or simply raise an event at the appropriate time. It also accepts the name of the process to look for (obviously the Id could not be used here because it is not assigned by the operating system until the process starts). If the asynchronous flag is set to False, the private WaitForProc method is called and executes a tight loop repeatedly calling the GetProcess method. If the process is found, the loop exits, and the mProcess variable is populated. If the process is not found, the thread sleeps for a half second before attempting to find the process again. This loop has the effect of blocking the current thread.

If asynchronous notification is required, a new thread, referenced as the private class level variable mtWait, is started using the PollForProcess private method with a priority of Lowest.

The PollForProcess method runs the same WaitForProc method (although on a separate thread) and when the process is found, raises the ProcessStarted event. Finally, the CancelWait method is used to destroy the background thread if the client chooses to wait for a process to start and then changes its mind. In the event that the client does not call CancelWait, the Finalize method contains a call to CancelWait. CancelWait suppresses finalization as discussed in Chapter 4. In the event that the client subsequently uses WaitForStart, the ReRegisterForFinalize method is called on the object to make sure that finalization will again run.

For a client to use ProcessNotify, it simply has to instantiate the object and, if asynchronous notification is required, add event handlers for the ProcessCompleted and ProcessStarted events. The following sample code uses the class to be notified when the notepad.exe application starts and stops:

```
Dim objNotify As ProcessNotify

objNotify = New ProcessNotify()   ' Assume local machine

' Add event handler
AddHandler objNotify.ProcessComplete, AddressOf Completed
AddHandler objNotify.ProcessStarted, AddressOf Started

' Wait synchronously
objNotify.WaitForStart(False, "notepad")

' Its now running
Console.WriteLine(objNotify.HasExited) ' Should be false
Console.WriteLine(objNotify.ProcessID)

' Wait for asynchronous completion
objNotify.WaitForCompletion(True)

' Do other work
```

Although this example shows how to add the handler for both events, only the Completed event is used because the WaitForStart method is invoked synchronously. The events handling procedures then would look as follows:

```
Private Sub Completed(ByVal ProcessName As String)
   Console.WriteLine(ProcessName & " completed!")
End Sub

Private Sub Started(ByVal ProcessName As String)
   Console.WriteLine(ProcessName & " started! ")
End Sub
```

Using Cryptography

As mentioned in Chapter 1, "The Microsoft .NET Architecture," modern distributed applications have different requirements than the previous generation of applications. Nowhere is this more true than in the area of security. VB .NET and the Services Framework support this need for increased functionality by providing cryptographic services in the `System.Security.Cryptograpy` namespace.

Simply put, this namespace allows programmatic access to a variety of cryptographic algorithms that you can incorporate into your applications to encrypt and decrypt data. Although a complete discussion of this namespace is beyond the scope of this book, a brief overview followed by a code example is warranted.

The classes in the `Cryptography` namespace can be broken into roughly three primary divisions based on the type of algorithm you want to implement. Each type of algorithm contains a base class that represents the type of algorithm and from which specific implementations are derived.

The first type is a *symmetric cryptographic algorithm*. Symmetric algorithms derive their name from the fact that they have a single secret key used for both encryption and decryption. Obviously, both the sender and receiver must keep the key secret for the encryption to remain secure. In addition, symmetric algorithms require an initialization vector (IV), a non-secret binary value used to initialize the algorithm and introduce additional cryptographic variance. The `SymmetricAlgorithm` class is an abstract base class from which other algorithm-specific classes are derived. The supported symmetric algorithms include Data Encryption Standard (DES), RC2, Rijndael, and Triple Data Encryption Standard (TripleDES). Each of the implementations of the algorithms contain a base class derived from `SymmetricAlgorithm`, such as `DES`, and a service provider class used in your code derived from the base class, such as `DESCryptoServiceProvider`. The latter class contains the methods used to encrypt and decrypt data.

The second type of algorithm is known as an *asymmetric algorithm*, or *public-key*, and derives from the class `AsymmetricAlgorithm`. These algorithms include well-known algorithms such as Digital Signature Algorithm (DSA) and RSA. Asymmetric algorithms rely on a pair of keys, one private and the other public. The public key is made available to anyone and is used by a sender to encrypt data, whereas the private key remains secure and is used to decrypt data encrypted with the public key. The implementation of these algorithms also contains a base class derived from `AsymmetricAlgorithm`, in addition to a service provider class derived from the base class. In addition, the more complex nature of the algorithms might also require additional helper classes.

The final type of algorithm exposed by the `Cryptography` namespace is a *hash algorithm*. This type of algorithm computes a fixed-size unique string of binary values based on a longer string of bytes. Different types of hash algorithms are used to compute digital signatures and to ensure data integrity. The `Cryptography` namespace contains a base class called `HashAlgorithm` and derived classes that support the MD5, SHA1, SHA256, SHA384, and SHA512.

In addition to the three types of algorithms, the `Cryptography` namespace contains helper classes, such as the `RandomNumberGenerator` class and the `CryptoStream` class. The `CryptoStream` class is particularly important because it is derived from `Stream` and is used to provide a stream-based model to cryptographic transformations. In other words, data can be encrypted and decrypted with any of the algorithms by streaming it through the `CryptoStream` class.

To illustrate how to use the basic cryptographic functionality provided by this namespace, the `TextFileCrypto` class has been created and is shown in Listing 12.11. This class can be used to symmetrically encrypt and decrypt a file using DES with a key generated by the class and saved to a file.

12

ACCESSING SYSTEM SERVICES

LISTING 12.11   Basic Cryptography. This class uses the DES algorithm to encrypt and decrypt text files.

```
Option Strict On

Imports System.IO
Imports System.Security.Cryptography
Imports System.Threading

Public Class TextFileCrypto
  ' Encrypts and decrypts text file given a key

  Private mstrFile As String ' File to decrypt
  Private mstrKey As String ' Key file
  Private mKey(7) As Byte   ' DES key
  Private mDES As DESCryptoServiceProvider
  Private mIV(7) As Byte ' Initialization Vector

  Public Sub New()
    mDES = New DESCryptoServiceProvider()
  End Sub

  Public Property KeyFile() As String
    Get
      Return mstrKey
    End Get
    Set(ByVal Value As String)
      If File.Exists(Value) Then
        mstrKey = Value
```

LISTING 12.11   Continued

```
      OpenKeyFile() ' Open the key file and read its contents
    Else
      Throw New Exception(Value & " file does not exist.")
    End If
  End Set
End Property

Public Property FileName() As String
  Get
    Return mstrFile
  End Get
  Set(ByVal Value As String)
    If File.Exists(Value) Then
      mstrFile = Value
    Else
      Throw New Exception(Value & " does not exist.")
    End If
  End Set
End Property

Private Sub OpenKeyFile()
  Dim fsKey As New FileStream(mstrKey, _
    FileMode.Open, FileAccess.Read)

  ' Open the key file and read the key from it
  fsKey.Read(mKey, 0, 8)
  fsKey.Read(mIV, 0, 8)
  fsKey.Close()

  mDES.Key = mKey
  mDES.IV = mIV
End Sub

Public Function SaveKeyFile(ByVal FilePath As String) As Boolean
  Dim fsKey As New FileStream(FilePath, _
    FileMode.OpenOrCreate, FileAccess.Write)

  ' Generate a new random key and IV and save it to the file
  ' Note these will be generated randomly automatically
  ' if you don't do it
  mDES.GenerateKey()
  mDES.GenerateIV()

  mKey = mDES.Key
  mIV = mDES.IV
```

LISTING 12.11   Continued

```
  fsKey.Write(mKey, 0, mKey.Length)
  fsKey.Write(mIV, 0, mKey.Length)
  fsKey.Close()

  mstrKey = FilePath
End Function

Public Function EncryptFile() As Boolean
  ' Encrypt the given file

  ' Check the key
  If mKey Is Nothing Then
    Throw New Exception("You must have a key in place first.")
    Return False
  End If

  Dim fsInput As New FileStream(mstrFile, _
    FileMode.Open, FileAccess.Read)
  Dim fsOutput As New FileStream("temp.dat", _
    FileMode.Create, FileAccess.Write)
  fsOutput.SetLength(0)

  Dim arInput() As Byte

  ' Create DES Encryptor from this instance
  Dim desEncrypt As ICryptoTransform = mDES.CreateEncryptor()
  ' Create Crypto Stream that transforms file stream using DES encryption
  Dim sCrypto As New CryptoStream(fsOutput, desEncrypt, _
    CryptoStreamMode.Write)

  ReDim arInput(Convert.ToInt32(fsInput.Length - 1))
  fsInput.Read(arInput, 0, Convert.ToInt32(fsInput.Length))
  fsInput.Close()

  ' Write out DES encrypted file
  sCrypto.Write(arInput, 0, arInput.Length)
  sCrypto.Close()

  ' Delete and rename
  File.Copy("temp.dat", mstrFile, True)
  File.Delete("temp.dat")

End Function

Public Function DecryptFile() As Boolean
```

LISTING 12.11   Continued

```
    ' Decrypt the given file

    ' Check the key
    If mKey Is Nothing Then
      Throw New Exception("You must have a key in place first.")
      Return False
    End If

    ' Create file stream to read encrypted file back
    Dim fsRead As New FileStream(mstrFile, FileMode.Open, _
      FileAccess.Read)
    Dim fsOutput As New FileStream("temp.dat", _
      FileMode.Create, FileAccess.Write)
    ' Create DES Decryptor from our des instance
    Dim desDecrypt As ICryptoTransform = mDES.CreateDecryptor()
    ' Create crypto stream set to read and do a des decryption
    ' transform on incoming bytes
    Dim sCrypto As New CryptoStream(fsRead, desDecrypt, _
      CryptoStreamMode.Read)
    Dim swWriter As New StreamWriter(fsOutput)
    Dim srReader As New StreamReader(sCrypto)

    ' Write out the decrypted file
    swWriter.Write(srReader.ReadToEnd)

    ' Close and clean up
    swWriter.Close()
    fsOutput.Close()
    fsRead.Close()

    ' Delete and rename
    WaitForExclusiveAccess(mstrFile)
    File.Copy("temp.dat", mstrFile, True)
    File.Delete("temp.dat")
  End Function

  Private Sub WaitForExclusiveAccess(ByVal fullPath As String)
    While (True)
      Try
        Dim file As FileStream
        file = New FileStream(fullPath, FileMode.Append, _
          FileAccess.Write, FileShare.None)
        file.Close()
        Exit Sub
      Catch e As Exception
```

LISTING 12.11   Continued

```
        Thread.Sleep(100)
      End Try
    End While
  End Sub

End Class
```

As shown in Listing 12.11, the constructor of the class instantiates a class level `DESCryptoServiceProvider` class that exposes the methods that return encryptor and decryptor objects used to encrypt and decrypt data. The public `KeyFile` and `FileName` properties are used to open an existing file that contains the key and initialization vector (IV) and to set the name of the file to encrypt or decrypt. If the key file exists, the file is opened using the private `OpenKeyFile` method, and the key and IV are read into `Byte` arrays. The `SaveKeyFile` method calls the `GenerateKey` and `GenerateIV` methods of the underlying `DES` class to generate a random key and IV. These values are then saved to the file passed in as an argument. At this point, the key file should be kept secret and can be transmitted to someone who will use it to decrypt the data.

> **TIP**
>
> The DES algorithm uses a 64-bit (8 byte) key. Although DES supports only a single key size, the valid key sizes for other algorithms can be found by calling the `LegalKeySizes` property, which returns an array of `KeySize` objects that represent the legal sizes. For stronger encryption, a new size can be set using the `KeySize` property.

The core of the `TextFileCrypto` class is the `EncryptFile` and `DecryptFile` methods. The `EncryptFile` method opens the file to encrypt along with a temporary file used to store the encrypted data. To encrypt the file, the method creates an encryptor object using the `CreateEncryptor` method of the service provider, in this case `DESCryptoServiceProvider`. This object implements the `ICryptoTransform` interface and therefore can be passed to the constructor of `CryptoStream` that transforms the data as it is written out to a file backed by a `FileStream`—in this case, `fsOutput`. The original file is then overwritten with the temporary file. The result is an encrypted file that can be safely FTP'd or sent as an attachment over the Internet.

The `DecryptFile` method does the reverse of `EncryptFile` by creating a decryptor using the `CreateDecryptor` method of the `DESCryptoServiceProvider`. This object is likewise passed to the constructor of the `CryptoStream` to decrypt the file as it is read from the `FileStream` fsRead. Finally, the decrypted data is saved to a text file by the StreamWriter class using the ReadToEnd method of the StreamReader class.

A client can use the TextFileCrypto class to encrypt data as follows:

```
Dim objCrypt As New TextFileCrypto()

objCrypt.FileName = "students.txt"

' Generate and save the key
objCrypt.SaveKeyFile("mykey.dat")

' Encrypt the file
objCrypt.EncryptFile()
```

On the other side, when a client receives the file, he can decrypt it like so:

```
Dim objCrypt As New TextFileCrypto()

objCrypt.FileName = "students.txt"

' Read in the key
objCrypt.KeyFile = "mykey.dat"

' Decrypt the file
objCrypt.DecryptFile()
```

Summary

Building distributed applications often involves more than simply constructing dynamic Web pages and data access logic. In some cases, you need to rely on system services, such as file I/O, threading, interacting with other processes, and cryptography. In this chapter, I've tried to give you a good feel for how these topics can be addressed in a straightforward manner in VB .NET and the Services Framework.

In a similar way, the next chapter will address a common development challenge that is elegantly solved by the Services Framework—implementing Windows services.

Implementing Services

IN THIS CHAPTER

One of the components of many distributed solutions, and a task that most corporate VB developers have faced at one time or another, is the challenge of creating a VB application that runs as a Windows Service. However, as most of you have probably discovered, this could be somewhat tricky without including a bevy of Win32 API calls or resorting to third-party ActiveX controls. The problems were multiplied when the service also needed to support multiple threads of execution; for example, in cases when the service supported connections from several clients or needed to perform some background processing. Although some techniques existed (see Chapter 19 of my book *Pure Visual Basic* for one), none of them were particularly elegant. In the .NET world, this changes because VB .NET is a first-class citizen and can take advantage of the Services Framework support for service applications.

> **NOTE**
>
> A Windows Service application is simply one that runs in the background under the Windows NT/2000/XP operating systems, has no user interface (UI), and is controlled through a set of Win32 APIs and the Windows service controller (also referred to as the *Service Control Manager* or *SCM*). Put simply, the SCM is comprised of the operating system components responsible for configuring and running an executable as a service. These background processes can be started, stopped, paused, and continued through the services console and can run under the context of a specific account.

In this chapter, we'll take a look at how to build an executable that includes a Windows service and how it can take advantage of the system services that typical services use. The approach used in the chapter is to build a service incrementally starting with the minimum amount of code required, and building on it by adding various features. As a general rule, the code listings are added to the service template in order to build the entire service.

> **NOTE**
>
> All code listings and supplemental material for this chapter can be found on the book's Web site at samspublishing.com.

Creating Service Applications

All the functionality required to create a service, install it, and control it from an external application is exposed through the System.ServiceProcess namespace located in the assembly of the same name. This namespace contains the major classes shown in Table 13.1 to support service applications.

TABLE 13.1 Classes in the `System.ServiceProcess` namespace used to implement, install, and control a service.

Class	Description
ServiceBase	Acts as the base class for the service. Each executable can contain many classes derived from `ServiceBase`.
ServiceInstaller	Class called by the installer utility to install services and set their configuration parameters as derived from `ServiceBase`.
ServiceProcessInstaller	Class called by the installer utility to install the executable in which the service classes derived from `ServiceBase` live.
ServiceController	Used to control the execution of a service programmatically. Analogous to using the Services applet in the Microsoft Management Console (MMC).

Essentially, the classes listed in Table 13.1 abstract the interaction with the SCM and the Win32 API from your VB .NET application, thereby making the task of manipulating services fairly simple. As a result, to create a service, you simply need to set a reference to the `System.ServiceProcess` assembly, derive a class from `ServiceBase`, override some methods and add your custom functionality, and create an installer class so that the installation utility will be able to install the service.

In the remainder of the chapter, we'll build a sample service that Quilogy might use to monitor a directory for the presence of XML files that are produced to send out to a vendor. As new files enter the directory, the service processes them, logs the results to both a text log and the Event Log subsystem, increments a performance monitor counter, FTPs the file to a destination location, and finally moves the file to an archive directory.

Building a Service

To begin creating the service, you first need to pick the Windows Service Application template from the New Project dialog in VS .NET. The template produces a single file that contains a class derived from `ServiceProcess.ServiceBase`. Because the executable can contain multiple services, you can create more than one class derived from `ServiceBase` within the application. In this case, the class will be renamed to `QXMLTransfer`. However, you'll note that because the template produces only a single service, the only code file includes a shared procedure called `Main`, which in the class acts as the entry point for the executable in much the same way as a console application. Obviously, you should rename the default .vb file to something more appropriate for your application.

NOTE

As with most projects created in VS .NET, the Component Designer also creates a region that initializes the Component Designer so that you can drag and drop items from the toolbox and Server Explorer onto the Designer's surface. This code will not be discussed here. This is possible because ServiceBase is derived from System.ComponentModel.Component as discussed in Chapter 8.

TIP

In applications that expose multiple services, you'll probably want to change the StartupObject property (found in the Project Properties dialog box invoked by right-clicking on the project in the Solution Explorer window) to a module and place the Sub Main in that module for readability and ease of maintenance.

Within the Sub Main, you must instantiate a class for each of the services that this executable creates and pass them to the shared Run method of the ServiceBase class. This will load the service and make it available to receive start and stop events from the SCM. For example, assume that the application contains a single service called QXMLTransfer. The following code would instantiate the object and load it into memory:

```
Imports System.ServiceProcess

Public Class QXMLTransfer :     Inherits ServiceBase
    ' Class code goes here
End Class

Public Sub Main()
    Dim svcXML As New QXMLTransfer()

    ServiceBase.Run(svcXML)
End Sub
```

If the application contains multiple services, you can optionally pass an array of ServiceBase objects into the overloaded Run method like so:

```
Public Sub Main()
    Dim servicesToRun() As ServiceBase

    servicesToRun = New ServiceBase() {New QXMLTransfer(), _
      New QXMLReceive()}
      ServiceBase.Run(servicesToRun)
End Sub
```

At this point, the services in the application are loaded into memory and are ready to run. However, in order for a service to respond to events from the SCM, you'll first need to override several of the methods of `ServiceBase` in your derived class; in this case, `QXMLTransfer`. First, you'll want to create your own constructor for the class that calls the constructor of the base class `ServiceBase`. Your constructor should set various properties that indicate to the SCM that your service will respond to events.

The code in Listing 13.1 shows the constructor for the `QXMLTransfer` service. Note that it sets the `CanShutdown`, `CanStop`, and `CanPauseAndContinue` properties inherited from `ServiceBase` to indicate to which events it will respond. In addition, it sets the `ServiceName` and `AutoLog` properties to set the name of the service and whether to report start, stop, continue, and pause events in the Application event log, respectively. Setting the `ServiceName` is the only required code in the constructor.

LISTING 13.1   Service constructor. The constructor of service class calls the base class constructor before setting the properties particular to this service, such as `ServiceName`.

```
Public Sub New()
    ' Called only when first loaded not with each start and stop
    MyBase.New()

    ' Set the properties for the service
    With Me
        .ServiceName = "QXMLTransfer"
        .CanShutdown = True
        .CanStop = True
        .CanPauseAndContinue = True
        .AutoLog = True
    End With

    ' Static Initialization
    ' Set the log file name
    mLogFile = "QXMLTransfer.log"
    mCriteria = "*.xml"
End Sub
```

13

Keep in mind that the constructor of your class will be called only at load-time when the object is instantiated, and not each time the service is started and stopped. As a result, you'll want to initialize variables within the constructor that will persist from the time the service is first started until the machine is rebooted. Notice that in Listing 13.1 several private class variables are initialized including `mLogFile`, which is used to store the name of the text file containing the log.

> If your application contains multiple services, the constructors for all service classes will be called when the first service is started. However, the other services will not be started. Therefore, you want to avoid initializing variables that require large amounts of memory or performing initialization that is time consuming. A better place to perform such activities is in the OnStart method of the individual service class.

The other methods that you'll need to implement are the methods called by the SCM in response to the start, stop, pause, continue, and shutdown events. Each of these is implemented in the base class as a protected method that you must override. For example, to respond to the start event from the SCM, you'll implement the OnStart method as shown in Listing 13.2. Note that an implementation of OnStart is included in the project template that you can fill out.

LISTING 13.2 The OnStart event. You must override the OnStart event to start your service in motion.

```
Imports System.ServiceProcess
Imports System.Timers
Protected Overrides Sub OnStart(ByVal args() As String)
    ' Read from the registry
    If Not GetRegValues() Then
        Throw New Exception( _
          "The service could not be started. See the event log for details.")
        Return
    End If

    ' Start the timer
    mProcess = New Timer(mInterval)
    AddHandler mProcess.Tick, AddressOf OnTimer
    mProcess.Start()

    ' Log the fact that it started in the text log
    LogText("QXMLTransfer Service Started.", mLogFile, False, False)
End Sub
```

Note that the OnStart method needs to contain code that allows a service to do its work. In other words, the service will not perform any action unless code in the OnStart method gets the ball rolling. In this case, the service first calls a private procedure to read some initialization data from the registry. If successful, it sets up a system timer using a class-level variable so that the service can poll the file system for changes to the directory. Finally, if everything goes well, a private LogText procedure is called to log the fact that the service was started to both a text file and an application log. Because reading from the registry, using timers, and logging are common activities for service applications, they will be discussed later in the chapter.

TIP

You'll notice that the OnStart method can accept command-line arguments. Although not typically done, you can set these arguments in the property dialog for the service in the Service snap-in or when you start the service programmatically using the ServiceController class as discussed later in the chapter.

In a similar fashion, the OnStop method should take steps to release any resources held by the service, such as database connections and file handles. Note that your service does not have to respond to pause, continue, and shutdown events and so you are not required to override those methods. Although pause and continue are fairly obvious, if your service supports shutdown, the SCM will notify the service when the operating system is shutting down. This allows you to clean up any resources acquired in the class constructor as well.

TIP

A common question that arises when discussing SCM events regards the differences between pause and continue versus stop and start. Basically, you implement pause and continue when your service can stop its processing without deallocating all its resources or otherwise being reset to a newly initialized state. For example, if your service must scan a large number of directories, you might allow it to be paused on the current directory and later continue so that it can resume processing at the point at which it was paused. By stopping and restarting a service, you are implicitly indicating the service will not remember its state at the time it was stopped.

At this point, the service is ready to respond to the start event from the SCM as initiated through the Services MMC snap-in or the ServiceController class.

> **TIP**
>
> Note that just as in other VB .NET applications, you can debug a service application using the VS .NET debugger. When this occurs, the SCM attempts to start your service by calling the OnStart method. The SCM will then wait 30 seconds for the method to complete before returning an error. As a result, you'll want to make sure that you step through the code in OnStart (if you placed a breakpoint there) within 30 seconds or else the SCM will not start your service.

Installing Services

Of course, getting to a place where a Windows service is ready to run is more complex than installing and configuring a standard executable. This is primarily the case because the service must be registered with the SCM. In addition, the service is configured with its own properties, which include the security context it will run under and how the service will be started (automatic, manual, or disabled). All this information is typically specified at installation and can be easily implemented using the ServiceProcessInstaller and ServiceInstaller classes of the ServiceProcess namespace.

To install the service, as discussed in Chapter 5, "Packaging, Deployment, and Security," your project can include a class derived from System.Configuration.Install.Installer. This class will in turn be called by the installation utility and its constructor used to add items to install (referred to as "installers" and derived from ComponentInstaller) to the list of components to install. Eventually, the Install method of the base class will be executed to install the service and any associated components such as performance monitor counters or application-specific event logs. In the case of services, you'll need to include a minimum of two installers: one for the service process and one for the service class. For example, consider the code in Listing 13.3 that shows the installer class called QXMLInstall derived from Installer.

LISTING 13.3   Installer class. This class is used by the installation utility to install the service executable and its associated services.

```
Imports System.ComponentModel
Imports System.Configuration.Install
Imports System.ServiceProcess

Public Class <RunInstaller(True)> QXMLInstall : Inherits Installer

    ' For each service
    Private WithEvents mServiceInstaller As ServiceInstaller
    ' For the entire executable
    Private mProcessInstaller As ServiceProcessInstaller
```

LISTING 13.3 Continued

```
Public Sub New()
        MyBase.New
        ' Instantiate installers for process and services.
        mProcessInstaller = New ServiceProcessInstaller()
        mServiceInstaller = New ServiceInstaller()

        ' The services will run under the system account.
        mProcessInstaller.Account = ServiceAccount.LocalSystem

        ' The services will be started manually.
        mServiceInstaller.StartType = ServiceStartMode.Manual

        ' ServiceName must equal those on ServiceBase derived classes.
        mServiceInstaller.ServiceName = "QXMLTransfer"
        mServiceInstaller.DisplayName = "Quilogy XML Transfer"

        ' Add installers to collection. Order is not important.
        ' here is where you add performance monitor
        ' installers or event log installers
        Installers.Add(mServiceInstaller)
        Installers.Add(mProcessInstaller)
    End Sub

    ' Catch the events
    Public Sub mServiceInstaller_AfterInstall(ByVal sender As Object, _
        ByVal e As System.Configuration.Install.InstallEventArgs) _
            Handles mServiceInstaller.AfterInstall
        WriteLog("The service was installed successfully.", False)
    End Sub

    Public Sub mServiceInstaller_AfterUninstall(ByVal sender As Object, _
        ByVal e As System.Configuration.Install.InstallEventArgs) _
            Handles mServiceInstaller.AfterUninstall
        WriteLog("The service was uninstalled successfully.", False)
    End Sub
End Class
```

First, you'll see that the class is decorated with the RunInstaller attribute set to True to indicate to the installation utility that it should indeed process the class. In addition, instances of the ServiceProcessInstaller and ServiceInstaller classes are declared and then created in the constructor. After it is instantiated, you use the ServiceProcessInstaller to set properties for the executable as a whole. These include the account to use to run the process. In this case, the Account property is set to ServiceAccount.LocalSystem to indicate that the system account will be used. Note that the system account does not have permission to perform network operations and so when a different account is required, you can set the UserName and Password properties of the ServiceProcessInstaller class.

Second, you'll set the properties of the ServiceInstaller class as shown in Listing 13.3. These include the method for starting the service exposed through the StartType property and both the short name and description of the service. The short name must be the same as the ServiceName property specified in the service class constructor. Although not shown in the listing, the ServiceInstaller class also supports a ServicesDependedOn property defined as an array of strings that you can set to the service names of all services that must be running in order for this service to start. If one of the enumerated services is not started, the SCM will attempt to do so. However, if one or more of the services fails to start, your service will not be started either and an entry will be written to the Application event log. This property can come in handy when you must write multiple services that work together or when your service depends on a standard Windows 2000/XP/NT service. For example, a service that looks for files sent through FTP to a path on the server might require that the FTP service is running in order to start. In that case, the following code snippet would be added to the constructor of the QXMLInstall class:

```
Dim arServices() As String

ReDim arServices(1)
arServices(0) = "FTP"
mServiceInstaller.ServicesDependedOn = arServices
```

> **TIP**
>
> You can verify that the ServicesDependedOn information is set correctly by viewing the Dependencies tab on the service property dialog in the Services snap-in.

Finally, you must add the installers to the Installers collection of the QXMLInstall class using the Add method. At this point, the service can be installed using the InstallUtil.exe in a transacted way.

When the installation occurs, you can also tap into events fired by the installer to capture when the service is installed or uninstalled, for example. In this case, Listing 13.3 shows how to catch the AfterInstall and AfterUninstall events in order to write the fact that the service was manipulated to the Application event log using the private procedure WriteLog (discussed later in the chapter). As a whole, the ServiceInstaller supports After and Before events on the install, uninstall, commit, and rollback activities of the installer.

To install the service, simply run the InstallUtil.exe utility and pass it the executable that contains your service. If everything goes smoothly, you can then view your service in the Services MMC snap-in found in the Administrative Tools group as shown in Figure 13.1.

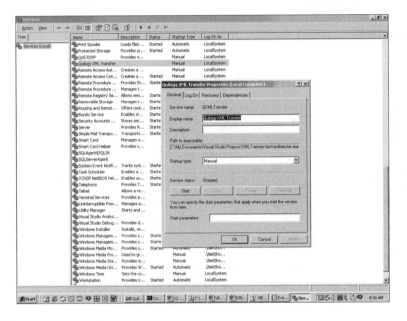

FIGURE 13.1
The Services snap-in. This figure shows the snap-in used to configure and control services on the local machine. The property dialog can be accessed by right-clicking on the service.

Handling Custom Actions

As with the installers discussed in Chapter 5, you can also add your own custom actions to the installation by overriding the `Install` and `Uninstall` methods of the base class and including custom code. In this case, a service such as `QXMLTransfer` might want to create registry entries or read configuration information from a file, such as the interval at which to poll the file system, the directory paths to search, and the FTP site to send the files to when the service is started. To provide default values, the installer can create registry keys when the service is installed. The code in Listing 13.4 shows the overridden `Install` and `Uninstall` methods for the `QXMLInstall` class.

LISTING 13.4 Custom actions. These methods of the `QXMLInstall` class include custom installation and uninstallation actions.

```
Imports Microsoft.Win32

Public Overrides Sub Install(ByVal state As IDictionary)
```

LISTING 13.4 Continued

```
' Write default values to the registry
Dim objKey As RegistryKey
Dim objRun As RegistryKey

MyBase.Install(state)

Try
    objKey = Registry.LocalMachine.OpenSubKey( _
      "System\CurrentControlSet\Services\QXMLTransfer", True)
    objRun = objKey.CreateSubKey("RunningValues")
    objRun.SetValue("Timer", 15000)
    objRun.SetValue("Path", "c:\")
    objRun.SetValue("FTPTo", "ftp.ssosa.com")
Catch e As Exception
    WriteLog("Default parameters were not created.", False)
End Try

End Sub

Public Overrides Sub UnInstall(ByVal state As IDictionary)
    ' Write default values to the registry
    Dim objKey As RegistryKey

    Try
        objKey = Registry.LocalMachine.OpenSubKey( _
          "System\CurrentControlSet\Services\QXMLTransfer", True)
        objKey.DeleteSubKey("RunningValues")
    Catch e As Exception
        WriteLog("Default parameters were not uninstalled.", False)
    Finally
        MyBase.UnInstall(state)
    End Try
End Sub
```

Note that after calling the base class `Install` method passing in the state information, this listing uses classes from the `Microsoft.Win32` namespace to manipulate the registry. In particular, the shared `OpenSubKey` method of the `Registry.LocalMachine` field is used to point to the subkey to open. In this case, because services are installed in the HKEY_LOCAL_MACHINE\ System\CurrentControlSet\Services key, the code attempts to open a subkey called `QXMLTransfer` and make it writable (as specified by the final argument to the method). After the subkey is opened, a new key called RunningValues is created using the `CreateSubKey` method. At this point, the key can be populated with values by calling the `SetValue` method.

> **NOTE**
>
> Note that using the `Registry` class in the `Microsoft.Win32` namespace to manipulate the registry for services is preferred over using the `SaveSetting`, `GetSetting`, `DeleteSetting`, and `GetAllSettings` functions included in VB .NET. This is because this method is more flexible and powerful. The aforementioned functions save their settings into only the VB and VBA Program Settings key under the `HKEY_USERS` subkey for the account that executes the code. As a result, if the service logs on as a different account, it does not have access to the registry settings.

As shown in Listing 13.2, the `OnStart` method of the `QXMLTransfer` class calls the private procedure `GetRegValues` shown in Listing 13.5. This procedure also uses the `RegistryKey` class to open the subkey in read-only mode when the service starts and places the values into private class variables. Note that when reading the key values using `GetValue`, they are returned as objects and must be converted to the appropriate type.

LISTING 13.5   Reading the registry. This private procedure reads the registry on service startup to initialize parameters for the service.

```
Imports Microsoft.Win32
Private Function GetRegValues() As Boolean
    Dim objKey As RegistryKey

    Try
        objKey = Registry.LocalMachine.OpenSubKey( _
         "System\CurrentControlSet\Services\QXMLTransfer\RunningValues", False)
        mInterval = CInt(objKey.GetValue("Timer", 30000))
        mPath = objKey.GetValue("Path").ToString
        mFTP = objKey.GetValue("FTPTo").ToString
    Catch e As Exception
        LogText("Could not get registry parameters.", mLogFile, True, False)
        Return False
    End Try

    Return True

End Function
```

All the activity in the `Install` method is included in a `Try` block so that if it fails, an exception can be caught and reported to the Application log using the private `WriteLog` procedure.

13

Because the installer is transacted, you could optionally call the MyBase.Rollback method, being sure to pass in the state object passed into the Install method in the Catch clause of the Try block. Doing so would ensure that the registry entries were actually created and if not, the entire installation would be undone (rolled back). However, in this case, failing to write the registry entries is not deemed severe enough to cause the service not to install.

The Uninstall method shown in Listing 13.4 performs the opposite operation to the Install by first deleting the registry entries for this application and then calling the Uninstall method of the base class. In this case, however, overriding Uninstall is not strictly necessary because the act of uninstalling the service would delete all registry entries associated with the service, including those created in Install (because they are subkeys).

Controlling Services

In addition to being able to easily create and install a service, the Services Framework also includes the ServiceController class to make it trivial to programmatically inspect and control a service both locally and remotely.

The ServiceController class is relatively simple and includes methods to both query the services on a machine as well as manipulate a single service. The code in Listing 13.6 illustrates the use of ServiceController in a simple console application. Note that it is, of course, possible to use the ServiceController class from inside a service for example, to start a service that your service depends on. However, it can also be used in other types of applications such as the one shown in Listing 13.6.

LISTING 13.6 Using ServiceController. This procedure illustrates using the ServiceController class to find and manipulate a service.

```
Imports System
Imports System.ServiceProcess

Sub Main()

' First get a look at all services
Dim arServices() As ServiceController
Dim objService As ServiceController
Dim tsTime As New TimeSpan(0, 0, 30)

' Replace  "ssosa" with your machine name, or don't
' pass any parameters to use the local machine
arServices = ServiceController.GetServices("ssosa")

For Each objService In arServices
    ' Print the name of all services
    Console.writeline(objService.DisplayName())
```

LISTING 13.6   Continued

```
' Get the service we want to interrogate
If objService.ServiceName = "QXMLTransfer" Then

    Console.WriteLine(objService.CanPauseAndContinue)
    Console.WriteLine(objService.CanShutdown)
    Console.WriteLine(objService.CanStop)

    If objservice.ServiceType = ServiceType.Win32OwnProcess Then
        Console.Writeline("Running in its own process")
    End If

    ' Get the most recent values
    objService.Refresh()

    Try
        ' Test for status values to make sure the
        ' service is running when we leave
        Select Case objService.Status
            Case ServiceControllerStatus.Stopped, _
              ServiceControllerStatus.StopPending
                objService.WaitForStatus(ServiceControllerStatus.Stopped, _
                  tsTime)
                objService.Refresh()
                If objService.Status = ServiceControllerStatus.Stopped Then
                    objService.Start()
                Else
                    Throw New Exception( _
                        "Could not get the service stopped.")
                End If

            Case ServiceControllerStatus.Paused, _
              ServiceControllerStatus.PausePending
                objService.WaitForStatus(ServiceControllerStatus.Paused, _
                  tsTime)
                objService.Refresh()
                If objService.Status = ServiceControllerStatus.Paused Then
                    objService.Continue()
                Else
                    Throw New Exception("Could not get the service paused.")
                End If
        End Select

        ' Make sure the service is running
        objService.WaitForStatus(ServiceControllerStatus.Running, tsTime)

        ' If not then raise an error
```

LISTING 13.6 Continued

```
                If objService.Status <> ServiceControllerStatus.Running Then
                    Throw New Exception("Could not get the service started.")
                End If

            Catch e As Exception
                Console.Writeline("Caught exception of : " & e.ToString())
            Finally
                ' Release the handle
                objService.Close()
            End Try

        End If

        objService.Close()
    Next

End Sub
```

After reviewing the code in Listing 13.6, you'll notice that the procedure first calls the shared GetServices method of the ServiceController class in order to return an array of ServiceController objects. The constructor is overloaded and, in this case, the procedure is simply passing in the name of the machine on which to enumerate the services. If no machine is passed, the method will assume the local machine.

After the services have been placed into the arServices array, they can be enumerated using a For...Each loop. On each pass through the loop, the objService variable is populated with a reference to a service. As you would expect, you can then interrogate its properties such as ServiceName, MachineName, CanPauseAndContinue, CanShutdown, and ServicesDependedOn, among others. In this case, the loop simply prints the DisplayName and then looks for the service called QXMLTransfer. When found, additional properties are printed to the console and the ServiceType is tested using the included enumerated type.

TIP

You can also refer to a service without going through a loop by simply instantiating a ServiceController object and passing into the overloaded constructor the service name and machine name to reference.

After looking at the properties, the procedure refreshes them using the Refresh method to ensure that the procedure has the latest information before entering the Select Case statement.

The Select Case statement checks the service status, which indicates the running status of the service, with the goal of ensuring that the service is started before the procedure ends. However, before starting the service, you must be certain that it is stopped. Note that the case statement first checks to see whether the service is either stopped or is in the process of being stopped. In either case, it uses the WaitForStatus method to block the current thread until the service either reaches the status indicated in the argument (in this case, stopped) or until the timeout period is exhausted.

> **TIP**
>
> You specify the timeout period using the System.Timespan class. You'll note that the tsTime object was instantiated at the top of the procedure with the arguments to the constructor representing 0 hours, 0 minutes, and 30 seconds.

When the WaitForStatus method returns, you can be assured that the service has stopped or the timeout has expired. To check for the latter case, the Refresh method is run once again and then the status is rechecked. If the status is not stopped, an exception is thrown. If the service has been successfully stopped, the procedure attempts to start it using the Start method. An analogous operation takes place in the second case when it checks for a paused status.

After the case statement executes the procedure, it waits for a running status using the WaitForStatus method. Again, if the timeout period expires, an exception is thrown. Finally, as indicated in both the Finally block of the Try statement and before the Next statement of the loop, the Close method of the service is called to release the connection to the service from the ServiceController class.

Scheduling the Service

Because a service is by default a passive process, you must add code to the service in order for it to periodically perform its work. There are several techniques you can use to do this that involve scheduling the service to run at predefined intervals using a timer provided in the System.Timers namespace found in the system assembly.

Using a Simple Timer

To use a simple system timer implemented by the operating system, you can use the Timer class in the System.Timers namespace. As is shown in Listing 13.2, the OnStart method of the QXMLTransfer class first instantiates the mProcess private variable as Timer and passes into its constructor the interval in milliseconds at which to fire the timer event (setting the Interval

13

property). In this case, the interval was retrieved from a registry setting and also stored as a private variable. The relevant code is shown in the following snippet:

```
Imports System.Timer
' At the class level
Private mProcess As Timer

' Within the OnStart method
mProcess = New Timer(mInterval)
```

The OnStart method then hooks up the timer using a dynamic event handler as described in Chapter 4, "Object-Oriented Features," using the AddHandler method as follows:

```
AddHandler mProcess.Tick, AddressOf OnTimer
```

In this case, it passes the address of a private procedure called OnTimer, the result being that at each interval, the OnTimer procedure will be executed. To kick off the timer, the Start method of the Timer is then invoked. The timer also includes an Enabled property, which by default is set to True and is the equivalent of using the Start and Stop methods. Alternatively, you could also declare the mProcess variable using the WithEvents keyword to hook up the event handler automatically. Because the OnTimer procedure handles an event, it must accept the standard arguments for an event procedure, as shown in Listing 13.7.

LISTING 13.7   Handling a simple timer. This procedure shows how to handle the event raised when a simple timer interval expires.

```
Private Sub OnTimer(ByVal source As Object, ByVal e As EventArgs)
    ' Timer has gone off

    mProcess.Stop()
    LogText("QXMLTransfer Waking up", mLogFile, False, True)

    ' Now process the rest
    ProcessFiles()

    mProcess.Start()
End Sub
```

As a standard practice in service applications, you'll want to first stop the timer using the Stop method before doing any other work. In Listing 13.7 you can see that the service logs the fact that it is waking up and then carries out its work using the private ProcessFiles procedure (discussed later in the chapter). After the work has completed, the Start method can again be invoked so that the OnTimer event will fire at the next interval. As an alternative, you can also set the AutoReset property to False, which raises the Tick event only once. By default, AutoReset is set to True so that the event is raised at each interval.

TIP

As shown in Chapter 12, "Accessing System Services," perhaps a more efficient method of looking for files in a particular directory path would be to use the FileSystemWatcher class found in the System.IO namespace. In this way, your service could be notified immediately when a new file is added to the directory rather than having to wait for the next interval of the timer.

Using Event Logging

In service applications, it is especially important to handle and track error conditions. This is for the obvious reason that the service runs without user interaction and is therefore responsible for taking corrective action, or at least recording detailed error information so that an administrator or the service itself can determine how to proceed. One of the features that makes tracking the activities of a service easier is the integration of the Services Framework with the Windows Event Logging service.

By default, the Windows NT, Windows 2000, and Windows XP operating systems support three types of event logs accessible through the Event Viewer MMC snap-in found in the Administrative Tools program group. The System and Security logs are typically used by the OS and other system software such as the TCP/IP software, DHCP server, IIS, and the Service Control Manager itself. The Application log, on the other hand, can be used by any application running in the OS in order to log messages. As you'll see, the Services Framework also allows applications to install their own event logs to further provide customized reporting.

Internally, the Event Logging system receives messages through what are called *event sources*. Your application can register one or more event sources with various logs and then write to them using the event logging classes found in the System.Diagnostics namespace. However, each unique event source (identified by a string) can be mapped to only a single log at a particular point in time. In the QXMLTransfer service, we'll use these classes to log messages both to the Application and a custom event log.

NOTE

As discussed in Chapter 6, "Error Handling and Debugging," you can also gain access to the event logs through classes derived from TraceListener that your program instantiates. In this way you could simply use the Trace class to log messages to an event log although this chapter logs messages explicitly through custom methods.

Writing to the Event Log

When a service application is installed using an `Installer` class, it automatically registers an event source in the Application log using the name as the service. It then initializes an object of the `System.Diagnostics.EventLog` class with the source and log name and uses it to populate the `EventLog` field of the service class derived from the `ServiceBase` class. This `EventLog` field can then be used to write new entries to the log using the `WriteEntry` method. For example, the following line of code can be executed from within the service class to write the message "Files Processed" to the Application event log:

```
Me.EventLog.WriteEntry("Files Processed", EventLogEntryType.Information)
```

Note that if the `AutoLog` property of the service class is set to `True`, the `Start`, `Stop`, `Pause`, and `Continue` events will automatically be written to the Application event log.

Alternatively, entries can be written using other sources by taking advantage of the overridden `WriteEntry` methods that allow you to specify the source and optional event IDs and category identifiers.

Maybe Next Time

Event IDs and Categories are two concepts supported by the event logging Win32 APIs that the Service Framework supports only nominally. Simply put, a developer can create a DLL that includes a series of Event IDs and associated string values (with substitution placeholders) that represent the messages. When an entry is written to the log, it can be specified with its ID rather than the full text of the message. The end result is that less data needs to be stored in the event log because the message string is read from the DLL when it is presented to the user. This technique is also used for localization, because a DLL for each language can be used instead of having to localize the message strings inside the application using a resource file. Categories are simply a means of grouping Event IDs. In this version of the Services Framework, developers must build their own DLLs and associate them with the event log through the Win32 API although as mentioned earlier, the Event IDs can be specified in the `WriteEntry` method.

The `EventLog` class also supports `Log` and `Source` properties that can be used to change which log the `EventLog` property of the service class uses. (`MachineName` is also supported, but is defaulted to "." to represent the local machine.) Keep in mind, though, that before calling the `WriteEntry` method, the `Source` specified must be registered with the `Log` or an exception will be generated. To avoid having to manually synchronize these properties, after the `Source` is set, you can simply set the `Log` property to an empty string and it will be set appropriately as long as the source is valid.

Rather than changing the `EventLog` field of the service class, your application might simply create a new instance of the `EventLog` class to write or manipulate messages directly in a specific event log. In the sample service application, a public procedure called `WriteLog` is used by the `QXMLInstall` class shown in Listing 13.3 to log events to the Application log during the install process, as shown in Listing 13.8.

LISTING 13.8 Writing event log entries. This procedure connects to the Application log on the local machine and writes an entry to it.

```
Imports System.Diagnostics
Public Const QUILOGY_APPLOG_SOURCE As String = "QXMLTransfer"

Friend Sub WriteLog(ByVal pMessage As String, ByVal pError As Boolean)
  ' Write to the application log (MachineName defaulted)
  Dim objLog As New EventLog("Application")

  objLog.Source = QUILOGY_APPLOG_SOURCE

  Try
    ' Make sure the source is registered, it should be
    If (Not EventLog.SourceExists(objLog.Source)) Then
      EventLog.CreateEventSource(objLog.Source, "Application")
    End If

    ' Write the message to the log
    If pError Then
      objLog.WriteEntry(pMessage, EventLogEntryType.Error)
    Else
      objLog.WriteEntry(pMessage, EventLogEntryType.Information)
    End If
  Catch e As Exception
    ' Not so important so skip it
  Finally
    objLog.Dispose()
  End Try

End Sub
```

Note that the `EventLog` class constructor can be used to set the `Log`, `Source`, and even machine name during initialization. To avoid exceptions, you can use the `SourceExists` and `CreateEventSource` static methods to make sure that the source exists or to create it if it does not exist.

In addition to the `EventLog` class, the `System.Diagnostics` namespace contains several helper classes that are used to perform tasks such as enumerating logs and events, as well as responding to notification as events are written to a specific log, as discussed later in the chapter. You

13

IMPLEMENTING SERVICES

can use the classes, for example, to check the log for the last message written by the service so that it can resume processing at a specific point using data within the entry. To do so, you would use the `Entries` property to enumerate through the entries using the `EventLogEntry` class as follows:

```
Dim evLog As New EventLog("Application")
Dim obj, objLast As EventLogEntry

For Each obj In evLog.Entries
  If obj.Source = "QXMLTransfer" Then
    objLast = obj
  End If
Next

Console.Writeline("The last entry for QXMLTranfer was [" _
  & objLast.Message & "] at " & objLast.TimeWritten)
```

As you would expect, the `EventLogEntry` class exposes all the data for the event as properties, including the `Message`, `Source`, `TimeGenerated`, `EntryType`, and `TimeWritten` properties. Note, however, that this technique does not allow you to filter, sort (the entries are always returned starting with the oldest), or search the event log in any but a brute force manner. You cannot, in other words, set the `Source` property to a specific source and only enumerate events for that source. As a result, you'll want to make sure that, if your application normally reads an event log, the log settings controlled from the Event Viewer MMC snap-in are set to control the number of entries.

Using a Custom Log

Although your service can use the Application log to log all its messages, it is sometimes more efficient and convenient to log detailed information to an event log owned by your application. To do this, you can simply install a custom log in the installer class with a different source name and then write to it within your service using that source.

To install a new event log, you can use the `EventLogInstaller` class with a class derived from `Installer` such as `QXMLInstall`, shown in Listing 13.3. As with other installers, the procedure for using it is simply to instantiate it within the constructor of the installer, set its properties, and add it to the collection of installers. The additional code in Listing 13.3 to support the installation of a custom log called "Quilogy Applications" is the following:

```
mELogInstaller = New EventLogInstaller()

' Set up the event log
mELogInstaller.Log = "Quilogy Applications"
mELogInstaller.Source = QUILOGY_CUSTLOG_SOURCE

Installers.Add(mELogInstaller)
```

This code should be placed in the constructor—`Public Sub New()`—in the `QXMLInstall` class. You will also need to declare a variable `mELogInstaller` of type `EventLogInstaller` that is private to the class.

Note that in this case, the constant `QUILOGY_CUSTLOG_SOURCE` is used to specify the event source for the new log, which must be different than the name of the service class and any other event sources that will be used on this computer. Although you can also create new event logs directly through the `EventLog` class, by allowing the installer to create the log you ensure that it will be uninstalled when the service is uninstalled. If you do not use the installer, you'll need to remove the log using your own code because there is no easy way to remove it through the Windows UI.

To use the new log within your service, you can simply use the source name specified in the installer within the `WriteEntry` event. Listing 13.9 shows a procedure within the service application that is used to log events to both a text file and the custom log.

LISTING 13.9 Logging errors. This procedure shows one technique for writing messages to both a text log and a custom event log.

```
Imports System.IO
Imports System.Diagnostics

Public Sub LogText(ByVal messageText As String, ByVal fileName As String, _
  ByVal isError As Boolean, ByVal isFileOnly As Boolean)
  ' Write to both the text file and the Quilogy log

  Try
    ' Create or open the log file
    Dim objFs As FileStream = New FileStream(fileName, _
      FileMode.OpenOrCreate, FileAccess.Write)
    Dim objSw As StreamWriter = New StreamWriter(objFs) 'create a stream writer
    objSw.BaseStream.Seek(0, SeekOrigin.End) ' set the file pointer to the end

    objSw.Write("Log Entry : ")
    objSw.Write("{0} {1}", DateTime.Now.ToShortTimeString(), _
      DateTime.Now.ToShortDateString())
    objSw.WriteLine(":" & messageText)
    objSw.Flush()  ' update underlying file
    objSw.Close()
  Catch e As Exception
    WriteLog("Could not create or open " & fileName & ": " & e.Message, True)
  Finally
    If Not isFileOnly Then
      Try
        If isError Then
          EventLog.WriteEntry(QUILOGY_CUSTLOG_SOURCE, messageText, _
```

LISTING 13.9   Continued

```
            EventLogEntryType.Error)
        Else
          EventLog.WriteEntry(QUILOGY_CUSTLOG_SOURCE, messageText, _
            EventLogEntryType.Information)
        End If
      Catch e As Exception
        WriteLog("Could not write to Quilogy log.", True)
      End Try
    End If
  End Try

End Sub
```

The custom log with its entries can be viewed through the Event Viewer, as shown in Figure 13.2.

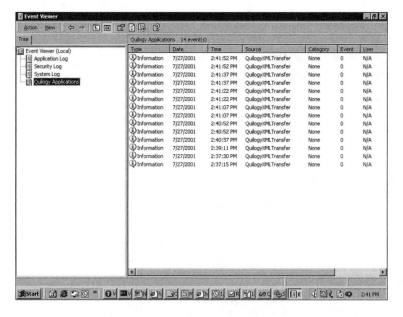

FIGURE 13.2

A custom event log. This screen shot shows the Event Viewer and a custom event log with messages logged from the QXMLTransfer *service.*

One reason you might want to employ the technique shown in Listing 13.9 is precisely because the log will be deleted when the service is uninstalled, but the log file will remain. It should be noted that it is a simple task to enumerate the entries in a log and write them to disk using the Save method of the EventLogEntryType.

Receiving Notification

In addition to writing to and reading from an event log, you can also use the EventLog class to receive notifications as events enter a log. This can be very useful when your service relies on another service such as SQL Server and needs to know if it is stopped or paused. The great thing for developers is that monitoring a log is as simple as catching events from the class. For example, the code in Listing 13.10 could be used by the QXMLTransfer service to monitor SQL Server events.

LISTING 13.10   Monitoring an event log. This code sets up an event handler to monitor the Application log for SQL Server events.

```vb
Imports System.Diagnostics
' In the OnStart event
Dim evLog As EventLog

evLog = New EventLog("Application")

AddHandler evLog.EntryWritten, AddressOf NewAppLogEvent
evLog.EnableRaisingEvents = True

Private Sub NewAppLogEvent(ByVal sender As Object, _
  ByVal e As EntryWrittenEventArgs)
  ' Check the Source
  If e.Entry.Source = "MSSQLServer" Then
    ' Look for specific messages
    If Instr(1, "terminating", e.Entry.Message, CompareMethod.Text) > 0 Then
      ' Stopping
      Me.OnStop()
      Return
    End If

    If Instr(1, "pause", e.Entry.Message, CompareMethod.Text) > 0 Then
      ' Pausing
      Me.OnPause()
      Return
    End If
  End If
End Sub
```

Note that the code at the beginning of the listing should be added to the OnStart event of the service and that the private class-level EventLog object (evLog) points to the Application event log. It then uses the AddHandler statement to dynamically hook the EntryWritten event to the NewAppLogEvent procedure. In order for the monitoring to begin, it sets the EnableRaising

Events property to True. The NewAppLogEvent procedure then uses the EntryWrittenEventArgs object's Entry property to inspect the event. If the source identifies it as a SQL Server event, the message can be parsed to determine whether the event is of interest. If so, the appropriate action can be taken; in this case the service is stopped or paused.

TIP

Remember that you'll also want to include the appropriate cleanup code to set the EnableRaisingEvents property to False so that events are not fired when the service is stopped. In addition, the Dispose method of evLog should be executed in the OnStop method.

Monitoring Performance

Another feature of many Windows services is that they often log information to performance counters visible through the Performance Monitor utility found in the Administrative Tools group. In the past, accessing or creating this information required detailed knowledge of the relevant Win32 APIs. Fortunately, the Services Framework provides classes under the System.Diagnostics namespace not only to read built-in counters provided by the OS, but also to read and write to user-defined counters.

NOTE

Performance counters are set up in a hierarchical system with the machine at the highest level and proceeding through category or object, counter, and finally instance. Categories are simply used to group counters together and typically refer to an OS subsystem or an application such as a service. A counter represents what is actually being measured and is the level at which data is recorded. Counters can optionally include multiple instances that are discrete (for example, a CPU utilization counter can include an instance for each running process). The Services Framework allows you to work with all four levels.

The primary class used to manipulate performance counter information is, not surprisingly, called PerformanceCounter. With it, you can connect to an existing counter and read its values through sampling or create a new counter and set its value by either incrementing it or setting its raw or underlying value. However, before manipulating a user-defined performance counter, it must be installed on the system.

Installing Custom Performance Counters

To make sure that a performance counter is present when the application runs and is cleaned up when uninstalled, you should use the `PerformanceCounterInstaller` class within the `Installer` class in your service. In the example of the `QXMLTransfer` service, the service will report on two counters: total files processed since the service was restarted and the number of files processed in the most recent interval.

To create these counters, the code in Listing 13.11 would be added to the constructor of the `QXMLInstall` class shown in Listing 13.3.

LISTING 13.11 Installing performance counters. This code snippet installs two performance counters for the `QXMLTransfer` service.

```
Imports System.Diagnostics
mPerfCounterInstaller = New PerformanceCounterInstaller()

' Set up the perf counter
Dim objCounter As New CounterCreationData("Total Files", _
    "The total number of files processed by this " & _
    "service since it was restarted.", _
    PerformanceCounterType.NumberOfItems32)

Dim objCounter1 As New CounterCreationData("Files", _
    "The number of files processed in the last interval.", _
    PerformanceCounterType.NumberOfItems32)

mPerfCounterInstaller.CategoryName = "Quilogy XML Transfer"
mPerfCounterInstaller.Counters.Add(objCounter1)
mPerfCounterInstaller.Counters.Add(objCounter)

Installers.Add(mPerfCounterInstaller)
```

The class-level private variable `mPerfCounterInstaller` is first instantiated as the installer. Each counter is represented by a `CounterCreationData` object that is instantiated with a constructor that accepts arguments for the name of the counter (in this case, Total Files and Files), the help description available in the Performance utility, and the type of the counter. The Services Framework supports 28 different types of counters ranging from percentages to elapsed time to rate of change. In this example, both counters are simple raw numbers and so the `NumberOfItems32` member of the `PerformanceCounterType` enumerated type is used.

After the counters have been created, the `CategoryName` property of the `PerformanceCounter Installer` class is used to set the unique category name before the counters are added to the

Counters collection using the Add method. Finally, as with other installers, the Performance CounterInstaller is added to the Installers collection and will subsequently be processed at install time.

NOTE

Performance counters can also be created and deleted directly in an application using the Exists, Create, and Delete shared methods of the PerformanceCounterCategory class.

Using Performance Counters

After the counters have been installed, it is simple to use them to report data from the service. In this example, the QXMLTransfer service is reporting on the number of files processed. The logical place to put the code to manipulate the performance counters is in the private ProcessFiles method that is run whenever the service is awakened by the timer as shown in Listing 13.7.

The ProcessFiles method is designed to search for all files in the target directory that meet a specific criteria and process them using a For...Each loop. As each file is processed, a local counter variable is incremented that will be reported as the most recent value to the Files counter. The Total Files counter will use this value to increment the current value. The skeleton code for the ProcessFiles method is shown in Listing 13.12.

LISTING 13.12 Processing files. This incomplete code of the ProcessFiles methods shows the flow of code within the QXMLTransfer service as it searches for and processes files.

```
Imports System.Diagnostics
Imports System.IO
Private Sub ProcessFiles()
  Dim objFile As FileInfo
  Dim strFile As String
  Dim intCount As Integer
  Dim objCounter As PerformanceCounter
  Dim objDir As Directory

  Try
    'Go get each file
    For Each strFile In objDir.GetFileSystemEntries (mPath, mCriteria)
      objFile = New FileInfo(strFile)
      ' Process it in some way
      intCount = intCount + 1
    Next
```

Listing 13.12   Continued

```
Catch e As Exception
  ' Log the fact that an error occurred

Finally
  ' Write the number processed to the log

  ' Increment Perf Counter
  If PerformanceCounterCategory.Exists("Quilogy XML Transfer") Then
    objCounter = New PerformanceCounter("Quilogy XML Transfer", _
      "Files", False)
    objCounter.RawValue = intCount

    objCounter = New PerformanceCounter("Quilogy XML Transfer", _
      "Total Files", False)
    objCounter.IncrementBy(intCount)
    objCounter.Dispose()
  End If
End Try

End Sub
```

Note that the code used to write the performance data is placed in the `Finally` block because it should run regardless of whether an error occurred during the processing. In addition, note that the shared `Exists` method of `PerformanceCounterCategory` is called to make sure that the category or object (as it is called in the Performance utility) actually exists before writing to it. If so, the Files counter is set by directly manipulating the underlying `RawValue` property and setting it to the number of files processed in the invocation of `ProcessFiles`. Because the Total Files counter keeps a running total of the number of files, the `IncrementBy` method is used to add to the total. Note that the third argument to the overloaded constructor of `PerformanceCounter` is set to `False` to indicate that the counter is not read-only. There is also a `ReadOnly` property that can be queried before attempting to change the value to prevent exceptions caused when writing to a read-only counter.

> **Note**
>
> The `PerformanceCounter` class also exposes `Increment` and `Decrement` methods that add or subtract one from the counter.

When finished, the method allows the runtime to deallocate resources using the `Dispose` method.

13

IMPLEMENTING
SERVICES

When the QXMLTransfer service stops, it must also clean up the counters to ensure that they are reset when the service is restarted. To do this, a private TearDown procedure is called from the OnStop and OnShutdown methods to release resources. In this method, the following code resets the counters to 0:

```
Private Sub TearDown()
  Dim objCounter As PerformanceCounter

  objCounter = New PerformanceCounter("Quilogy XML Transfer", "Total Files")
  objCounter.RawValue = 0

  objCounter = New PerformanceCounter("Quilogy XML Transfer", "Files")
  objCounter.RawValue = 0

  objCounter.Dispose()
  ' Other deallocation

End Sub
```

As mentioned in Chapter 4, the pattern you can use to implement methods that deallocate resources calls for the inclusion of a Dispose method. Other resource deallocation tasks can be accomplished from the TearDown procedure, such as stopping timers and stopping the monitoring of event logs.

The Performance utility showing the counters for the QXMLTransfer class can be seen in Figure 13.3. You can see from the graph that the service has processed 19 files in four consecutive 15-second intervals. Note that the Files counter (the red horizontal line) remained constant at 19 while the Total Files (the green line) continued to increment each time the service responded to the timer.

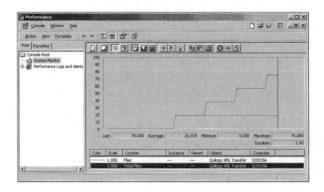

FIGURE 13.3

The Performance utility. This screen shot shows the performance counters for the QXMLTransfer *utility.*

Sampling Performance Counters

Although not required by the QXMLTransfer service, the PerformanceCounter class can also be used to read from existing counters using the NextValue and NextSample methods, whereas the PerformanceCounterCategory class can read from all counters in a category using the ReadCategory method.

The simplest technique to read from a counter is to instantiate a new PerformanceCounter object and simply call the NextValue method, which returns Single, reflecting the calculated value for the most recent interval. The following snippet reads the processor utilization for the entire machine:

```
Dim sngProcPct As Single
Dim objCounter As New PerformanceCounter("Processor", _
  "% Processor Time", "_Total")

sngProcPct = objCounter.NextValue()
```

To obtain more detailed information, you can alternatively call the NextSample method, which returns a CounterSample structure containing eight fields including the RawValue, CounterFrequency, and TimeStamp data. In addition, the structure supports a Calculate method to return the equivalent of NextValue, as shown in the following code:

```
Dim sngProcPct As Single
Dim objCounter As New PerformanceCounter("Processor", _
  "% Processor Time", "_Total")
Dim objSample As CounterSample

objSample = objCounter.NextSample
sngProcPct = objSample.Calculate(objSample)
```

Finally, the ReadCategory method can be used to return a collection of data for all instances in the category returned through the InstanceDataCollectionCollection class. Although it might not appear so, if you must read values from more than one counter, it is more efficient to call ReadCategory and then traverse the collections.

Communicating over the .NET

If you've followed the discussion in this chapter up to this point, you've noticed that the QXMLTransfer service that has been created has several significant features such as event logging and writing to performance counters, but does not yet actually perform any useful work. The final section of this chapter details using the System.Net namespace to add the transfer functionality to the service to enable FTP transfer of the processed files over the Internet.

Using `System.Net`

The `System.Net` classes can be used to add networking functionality to any managed application. In this respect, they take the place of the WinInet Win32 APIs, but also provide enhanced support for HTTP, TCP, and UDP in addition to a mechanism to create and register "pluggable" protocols for use as the Internet evolves. These classes were also designed for a high-stress environment where they are used by middle-tier components in ASP.NET applications to communicate across the Internet. In addition to being used in middle-tier components the `System.Net` classes can be used in a wide variety of application scenarios, from creating rich client applications along the vein of Napster to satisfying low-level machine to machine communication like that found in a manufacturing environment.

The `System.Net` namespace is technically factored into two namespaces, `System.Net` and `System.Net.Sockets`, which comprise three layers of communication:

- A request/response layer, which defines the model for communication
- Application protocols, which implement specific protocols such as HTTP
- The transport layer, where the TCP and UDP communication takes place

For example, at the request/response level, the `System.Net` namespace is built on a model where clients initiate requests over the network and in turn receive responses either synchronously or asynchronously. To implement this model, the `System.Net` namespace includes `WebRequest` and `WebResponse` classes that serve as base classes for specific application protocol classes such as `HttpWebRequest` and `HttpWebResponse`. In turn, the application protocol classes use classes from `System.Net.Sockets` such as the `Socket` and `NetworkStream` classes to transport the data across the Web. This model can be seen in Figure 13.4.

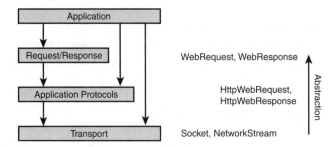

FIGURE 13.4

The `System.Net` *architecture. The* `System.Net` *classes are comprised of three layers, each of which abstracts details from the underlying layer.*

As an example of using this model, consider the code in Listing 13.13. In this example, the VB .NET application is using the `WebRequest` and `WebResponse` classes to call a URL on a Web server to return data. In this case, the URL might return an HTML document that the application wants to cache on the file system for later use.

LISTING 13.13 Using WebRequest and WebResponse. This listing shows how a client application can download a Web page using the HTTP protocol and save the results to a file.

```
Dim wReq As WebRequest
Dim wResp As WebResponse
Dim srData As StreamReader
Dim fsDest As FileStream
Dim wrStream As StreamWriter
Dim buffer(1024) As Char
Dim intBytes As Integer
Dim strData As String

' Create the file to hold the results
fsDest = New FileStream("c:\newsdoc.htm", _
  IO.FileMode.OpenOrCreate, IO.FileAccess.Write)
wrStream = New StreamWriter(fsDest)

' Make the request and get the response
wReq = WebRequest.Create("http://my.quilogy.com/news/news.asp?s=1224")
wResp = wReq.GetResponse()

' Retrieve the data
srData = New StreamReader(WResp.GetResponseStream(), Encoding.ASCII)
intBytes = srData.Read(buffer, 0, 1024)

Do While (intBytes > 0)
  wrStream.Write(Buffer, 0, intBytes)
  intBytes = srData.Read(Buffer, 0, 1024)
Loop

' Clean up
wrStream.Close()
srData.Close()
fsDest.Close()
```

13

Notice that in Listing 13.13, the file is opened and readied for writing using the standard FileStream and StreamWriter classes discussed in Chapter 12. Next, the code sets up the call to the URL using the shared Create method of the WebRequest class. Because the System.Net classes support multiple protocols, the URI passed to the Create method is parsed to determine which underlying protocol to use (in this case, "http"). The request is actually sent when the GetResponse method is invoked, and because this is a synchronous call, the method blocks until the result is returned. Note that if the URL doesn't exist, a WebException will be thrown in response to the GetResponse method.

> **TIP**
>
> Even though the example shown in Listing 13.13 uses a synchronous call, asynchronous calls can also be created using the BeginResponse and EndResponse methods of WebRequest. Note that these require the use of the asynchronous design pattern in the Services Framework and delegates as discussed in Chapter 4.

After the request has successfully returned, the results must be read from the WebResponse. This can be done using a StreamReader object; in this case, instantiated as srData. You'll notice that the Read method of srData is called in a loop, each time reading 1KB of data before writing the data to a file using the FileStream class from the System.IO namespace. The paradigm of using streams (literally a sequence of bytes) to access data is a common pattern that you'll find recurring throughout the Services Framework.

The WebRequest and WebResponse classes can also be used to send data to a Web server in the same way as shown in Listing 13.13. However, before calling GetResponse, you must set properties such as Method (POST in this case), ContentType, and ContentLength and then load the data to the Web server in a stream exposed using the GetRequestStream property of WebRequest.

Although the request/response model as discussed here is not difficult to comprehend, the System.Net namespace also contains the WebClient class that abstracts the interaction with the WebRequest and WebResponse classes into a single class with simple methods. For example, the same functionality as shown in Listing 13.13 can be accomplished with the WebClient class in two lines of code:

```
Dim wClient As New WebClient()

wClient.DownloadFile( _
 "http://my.quilogy.com/news/news.asp?s=1224", _
 "c:\newsdoc.htm")
```

Alternatively, the URL can be set using the combination of the BaseAddress and QueryString properties. In the event you want to access the stream returned from the URL rather than simply saving it to a file, you can use the OpenRead method. As you might expect, the WebClient class can be used to send data to a web server using the UploadFile and OpenWrite methods as well.

While the request/response model works well for most applications, there might be times where you need to work at a lower level. In these cases, you can use the classes in System.Net.Sockets directly to work at the socket level. However, while this low-level functionality is exposed, the Sockets namespace, modeled after the Berkely sockets implementation, also includes TCP and UDP classes that provide higher-level abstractions when building TCP clients and listeners. For example, the TcpClient class can be used to create a TCP connection to a remote server using a given port and return the response stream as follows:

```
Dim timeStream As Stream
Dim timeClient As New TcpClient("time.quilogy.com",13);

timeStream = timeClient.GetStream()
```

On the server side the TcpListener class can be used to listen for incoming connections, create the current date and time as a byte array, and send it back to the client.

```
Dim listener As New TcpListener(13)
Dim strDate As String
Dim byteDate As Byte()
Dim dataSocket As Socket

listener.Start()

Do While True
  dataSocket = listener.AcceptSocket()

  strDate = DateTime.Now.ToShortDateString & " " _
    & DateTime.Now.ToLongTimeString()

  byteDate = Encoding.ASCII.GetBytes(strDate.ToCharArray())
  dataSocket.Send(byteDate, byteDate.Length, SocketFlags.None)
Loop

listener.Stop()
```

Note that the constructor of the TcpListener class is called with the port, 13 in this case, that will be used to listen on. The Start method is then called to start listening for connections on the port although the thread the program runs on is not blocked until the AcceptSocket method is called. Additionally, TcpListener supports an AcceptTcpClient method that returns the TcpClient instance for the current request. The current date and time is used to populate a byte array using the ToCharArray method and the data sent back to the client with the Send method of the Socket class.

The code shown here would ostensibly be placed in a Windows service application or other host application that would be running in the background waiting to handle incoming requests. You'll also note that the listener is placed in a loop so that it can continue to process requests while the host application is executing.

NOTE

In more sophisticated applications the code shown here could also be enhanced to support multiple threads through the System.Threading namespace as discussed in Chapter 12, "Accessing System Services."

UdpClient is a second higher level class used to both send and receive UDP datagrams from a remote host and remote client.

In addition to sending and receiving data the System.Net namespace contains helper classes such as Dns and Cookie that provide simple domain name resolution functionality and manage the client-side cookies respectively. An example of the Dns class can be used retrieve the IP addresses associated with the current machine as follows.

```
Dim myMachine As String
Dim ip As IPHostEntry
Dim addressList() As IPAddress
Dim add As IPAddress

myMachine = Dns.GetHostName
ip = Dns.Resolve(myMachine)
addressList = ip.AddressList()

For Each add In addressList
  Console.WriteLine(Dns.IpToString(add.Address))
Next
```

In this snippet note that the shared GetHostName method returns the DNS host name of the current machine and then the IP addresses are found by calling the Resolve method, which accepts either the host name or an IP address formatted as a String (referred to as "dotted-quad notation"). The Dns class also exposes GetHostByAddress and GetHostByName methods to explicitly use either the host name or IP address. The IP addresses associated with the host name are returned in an array of IPAddress objects, which can be enumerated and converted to dotted-quad notation using the IpToString method.

Handling Security

The System.Net classes also support the ability to use authentication mechanisms such as basic, digest, NTLM, and Kerberos. They also support proxy servers.

> **TIP**
>
> Secure Sockets Layer (SSL) is supported transparently in `System.Net`. When the https prefix is detected, the underlying classes use SSL automatically.

To support sending credentials to a Web server, the `WebRequest` class exposes the `Credentials` property, which can accept objects that implement the `ICredentials` interface such as `NetworkCredential` or `CredentialCache`. The former maps to a single set of credentials while the latter encapsulates multiple sets of credentials of different types.

For example, suppose that the my.quilogy.com Web site was protected by basic authentication on the Web server. As expected, without sending credentials, a `WebException` would be generated on the invocation of `GetResponse` with a HTTP 401 status code. To supply the username and password, the `Credentials` properties can be set to a new instance of `NetworkCredential` initialized with the account information as follows:

```
wReq = WebRequest.Create("http://my.quilogy.com/news/news.asp?s=1224")
wReq.Credentials = New NetworkCredential("dlfox", "notmypassword")
```

When using NTLM authentication, the static `DefaultCredentials` property of `CredentialCache` is automatically populated with the operating system account information so that accessing a site using NTLM is transparent, as follows:

```
wReq = WebRequest.Create("http://my.quilogy.com/news/news.asp?s=1224")
wReq.Credentials = CredentialCache.DefaultCredentials
```

To mix and match credentials, you can also build your own `CredentialCache` and add new credentials to it using the `NetworkCredential` class, as follows:

```
Dim netCred As New NetworkCredential("dlfox", "notmypassword")
Dim netCred1 As New NetworkCredential("dlfox", "notmypassword ", "KCPDC")
Dim netCache As New CredentialCache()

netCache.Add("http://my.quilogy.com", "Basic", netCred)
netCache.Add("http://kc.quilogy.com", "NTLM", netCred1)
```

The `netCache` object can then be set to the `Credentials` property of any `WebRequest` and if the URIs match, the appropriate authentication will be used. Note that when using NTLM, the domain name is also passed in the constructor of `NetworkCredential`.

By default, the proxy information on the local machine is automatically used by the `System.Net` classes, although it can also be overridden globally for all requests or on a

13

IMPLEMENTING
SERVICES

request-by-request basis. To override the global settings, you can use the shared Select method of the `GlobalProxySelection` class to specify a new `WebProxy` object like so:

```
Dim objProxy As Uri

objProxy = New Uri("http://kdpdc:80")
GlobalProxySelection.Select = New WebProxy(objProxy)
```

To specify different proxy servers for a single request, you can set the `Proxy` property of `WebRequest` for each request. The following code snippet shows how to override the global proxy setting for a particular request:

```
Dim wReq As WebRequest
Dim objProxy As New WebProxy

objProxy.Address = New Uri("http://kcpdc:80")
objProxy.BypassProxyOnLocal = True

wReq = WebRequest.Create("http://my.quilogy.com/news/news.asp?s=1224")
wReq.Proxy = objProxy
```

Notice that the `WebProxy` object is used to specify the new settings and that the `BypassProxyOnLocal` property can be set to `True` in order to skip using the proxy server for addresses within the Intranet. Authenticated proxies are also supported through the inclusion of a `Credentials` property on the `WebProxy` object.

Using FTP

As mentioned earlier, the `System.Net` classes support the idea of "pluggable" protocols. In other words, as Internet protocols are enhanced and as new ones are developed, the `System.Net` classes can be extended to support them.

As an example of this architecture, the Services Framework does not ship with support for FTP in this version. As a result, you can implement the FTP protocol by creating derived `FtpWebRequest`, `FtpWebResponse`, and `FtpRequestCreator` from `WebRequest`, `WebResponse`, and `IWebRequestCreate`, respectively. These classes would then override members in the base class, such as `GetResponse`, `GetResponseStream`, and `GetRequestStream`, in order to implement the particulars of the protocol. For example, the `FtpWebRequest` class would be responsible for creating the sockets used to perform the communication while its overridden `GetResponse` method actually sends and receives data through the sockets.

Although all of this might be interesting, most corporate developers would rather not spend their time implementing the FTP protocol. Luckily, Microsoft has made available an unsupported sample that "plugs in" the FTP protocol in `System.Net`. This assembly is written in VC# and is provided on the companion Web site. Not surprisingly, this assembly exposes

FtpWebRequest, FtpWebResponse, and FtpRequestCreator classes as mentioned earlier. To use these classes effectively, you can create a reusable class that encapsulates the primary operations in FTP. Listing 13.14 shows just such a class that includes an Upload File method used to place a file on an FTP site.

LISTING 13.14   FTPClient class. This class uses the pluggable FTP protocol that ships with the Services Framework to expose common FTP functionality.

```
Public Class FtpClient
  ' Simple FtpClient

  Public LastMessage As String
  Public UserName As String
  Public Password As String

  Private ftpUri As Uri

  Public Sub New(ByVal ftpSite As Uri)
    ftpUri = ftpSite
    InitClass()
  End Sub

  Public Sub New(ByVal ftpSite As String)
    ftpUri = New Uri(ftpSite)
    InitClass()
  End Sub

  Private Sub InitClass()
    ' Register the prefix
    Dim creator As FtpRequestCreator = New FtpRequestCreator()
    WebRequest.RegisterPrefix("ftp:", creator)
  End Sub

  Public Function UploadFile(ByVal source As String, ByVal dest As String) As
Boolean
    Dim ftpReq As FtpWebRequest
    Dim ftpResp As FtpWebResponse

    ' Setup the request
    ftpReq = CType(WebRequest.Create(ftpUri), FtpWebRequest)
    ftpReq.Method = "PUT"

    ' Set the destination file
    ftpReq.m_szCmdParameter = dest
```

Listing 13.14   Continued

```vb
    ' Login if necessary
    If UserName.Length > 0 Then
      ftpReq.Credentials = New NetworkCredential(UserName, Password)
    End If

    Try
      LoadStream(source, ftpReq.GetRequestStream)
      ftpResp = CType(ftpReq.GetResponse, FtpWebResponse)

      ' See if it worked
      LastMessage = ftpResp.StatusDescription
      If ftpResp.Status = 226 Then
        Return True
      Else
        Throw New Exception("File Upload Failed [" _
          & source & "]:" & LastMessage)
        Return False
      End If

    Catch e As Exception
      LastMessage = e.Message
      Throw New Exception("File Upload Failed [" _
        & source & "]:" & LastMessage)
      Return False

    Finally
      ftpReq.CloseDataConnection()
      ftpReq = Nothing
      ftpResp = Nothing
    End Try

  End Function

  Private Function LoadStream(ByVal pSrcFile As String, ByRef s As Stream) As
String
    Dim fsSrc As FileStream
    Dim BytesRead As Integer = 0
    Dim ReadBuffer() As Byte
    Dim ftpResp As FtpWebResponse

    Const SIZETOREAD As Integer = 1024

    ' Open the stream for Reading
    Try
```

```
    fsSrc = New FileStream(pSrcFile, FileMode.Open, FileAccess.Read)
  Catch e As Exception
    Throw New Exception(e.Message & _
        " [Unable to open local file " + pSrcFile + " to upload]")
  End Try

  Try
    ' If openend successfully and not empty
    If fsSrc.Length > 0 Then
      Do ' Loop through the file and write it to the stream
        ReDim ReadBuffer(SIZETOREAD)
        BytesRead = fsSrc.Read(ReadBuffer, 0, SIZETOREAD)
        s.Write(ReadBuffer, 0, BytesRead)
      Loop Until BytesRead = 0
    End If
    fsSrc.Close()
    s.Close()

  Catch e As Exception
    Throw New Exception(e.Message & _
        " [Unable to upload file " + pSrcFile & "]")
  End Try
  End Function

End Class
```

Because the QXMLTransfer service needs to upload files to an FTP site specified in the registry as the files are processed, the FtpClient class implements only the UploadFile method. Note that the overloaded constructor makes the appropriate initializations by registering the FTP prefix and accepting the FTP site that the client will connect to.

As shown in Listing 13.14 the UploadFile method first registers the URI to be contacted using the Create method of the WebRequest object in order to return an FtpWebRequest object. The FtpWebRequest object then exposes the Method property, which is set to PUT in this case to indicate that a file transfer is about to occur. The field m_szCmdParameter is used to specify particulars of the command about to executed[md]here, the name of the destination file. As with the WebClient class the FtpClient exposes the Credentials property which can accept credentials passed to the public fields of the FtpClient object.

Finally, the private LoadStream method opens the file passed to it and reads it into the Stream to be sent with the request using the GetRequestStream method of the FtpWebRequest object. If no exceptions are raised the actual uploading occurs when the GetResponse method is subsequently called.

The FtpWebRequest object also exposes both Status and StatusDescription properties that return 226 and Transfer Complete messages from the FTP server, if everything worked ok. If not, the return value from UploadFile is set to False, an exception is thrown, and the message is used to populate the LastMessage field that the client can inspect.

For the QXML Transfer service to use Ftp Client, it would simply need to set a reference to the assembly and add the code shown in Listing 13.15 to the Process Files method.

LISTING 13.15   Client-side FTP. The following code snippet can be used by the QXMLTransfer service to FTP files that it processes.

```
Dim ftpMyClient As FtpClient
Dim objDir As Directory
Dim objFile As FileInfo
Dim intCount As Integer
Dim strFile As String

  ' Set up the FTP call
  ftpMyClient = New FtpClient(mFTP)
  ftpMyClient.UserName = mUser
  ftpMyClient.Password = mPwd

  'Go get each file
  For Each strFile In objDir.GetFileSystemEntries(mPath, mCriteria)
  objFile = New FileInfo(strFile)
   Try
     ' FTP it out
     ftpMyClient.UploadFile(objFile.FullName, objFile.Name)
     ' Archive it
     objFile.MoveTo(mArchivePath & "\" & objFile.Name)
   Catch e As Exception
     ' Log the fact that an error occurred
     LogText("An error occurred processing file: " & __
       e.Message, mLogFile, True, False)
   Finally
     LogText("Processed " & objFile.FullName, mLogFile, False, True)
     intCount = intCount + 1
   End Try
  Next

' Clean up the FTP
ftpMyClient = Nothing
```

First, the constructor of `FtpClient` is passed the address of the FTP server stored in the registry to initialize the `FtpWebRequest`. The application then logs on using private variables also stored in the registry. If the login succeeds, the directory is traversed, and is searched for files that match the criteria. As each file is found, it is uploaded to the FTP site using the `UploadFile` method. Note that if an exception is generated for the file, the next file is attempted.

Obviously, this service could be enhanced to include properties that support retrying files, a maximum error count before aborting, and support for uploading to a specific directory on the FTP site.

Summary

This chapter has focused on the Services Framework classes required to create a robust service application that utilizes the registry, event logging, performance counters, timers, and communicating over the Internet. Anyone who has developed services in previous versions of VB will vouch for the fact that the combination of these services provided by .NET makes this process much simpler and less error prone.

The final chapter will extend the reach of distributed applications developed in VB .NET by discussing integration with the enterprise using XML and messaging.

13

IMPLEMENTING
SERVICES

Integrating with the Enterprise

IN THIS CHAPTER

To create distributed applications that take advantage of all the resources in an enterprise, it is often necessary to go beyond accessing relational databases. This chapter focuses on three additional sources of data that often require integration. Although not an exhaustive reference for these topics, this chapter provides an overview of how to manipulate XML documents, Microsoft Message Queue server, and Active Directory using the classes provided in the Services Framework.

NOTE

All code listings and supplemental material for this chapter can be found on the book's Web site at www.samspublishing.com.

Using the XML Classes

As is obvious by now, XML is ingrained in .NET from configuration files, to the protocol for Web Services, to acting as the data store for ADO.NET `DataSet` objects. Of course, these particular uses of XML highlight its self-describing and flexible nature. As a result, many organizations use XML to pass documents and data both within the organization and between trading partners and vendors. The ubiquitous nature of these exchanges means that sooner or later, developers will need to read and write XML documents, transform them with XSL, and validate them using XML schemas. This section discusses the support in the Services Framework for working with XML in these ways.

At the highest level, the classes used to manipulate XML in the Services Framework are included in the `System.Xml` namespaces shown in Table 14.1.

TABLE 14.1 XML Namespaces and Their Uses

Namespace	Description
System.Xml	Contains the core XML classes to read and write XML documents and map the document to the Document Object Model (DOM).
System.Xml.Schema	Contains classes to work with XSD schemas and validate documents.
System.Xml.Serialization	Contains objects that enable classes to be serialized to XML.
System.Xml.XPath	Contains classes that allow you to navigate XML documents using XPath.
System.Xml.Xsl	Contains classes that allow you to transform documents using XSL style sheets.

As you can tell from the descriptions of the namespaces, the System.Xml namespace collectively supports the W3C standards, XML 1.0 and Document Type Definitions (DTDs), XML namespaces (http://www.w3.org/TR/REC-xml-names/), XML schemas (http://www.w3.org/TR/xmlschema-1/), XPath expressions (http://www.w3.org/TR/xpath), XSL transformations (http://www.w3.org/TR/xslt), DOM Level 2 Core (http://www.w3.org/TR/DOM-Level-2), and SOAP 1.1.

XML in COM

Developers familiar with working with XML documents in the COM world no doubt will have used the MSXML parser to programmatically manipulate documents. For those developers, the System.Xml classes will seem familiar because they map to the DOM, and because System.Xml was modeled after MSXML. However, the Services Framework implementation includes better standards compliance and a simpler programming model (especially for streamed access) that should make life easier.

That being said, you can continue to use MSXML through COM Interop, although I think you'll find that porting code that works with the DOM is relatively simple, whereas rewriting code that uses SAX, the Simple API for XML introduced in MSXML 3.0, makes for a more straightforward and efficient application.

To give you an overview of how the System.Xml namespace provides standards-based support for working with XML, this discussion includes dealing with streamed access to XML documents, manipulating XML documents with the DOM, handling XML schemas, and using XML serialization.

Streaming XML

Perhaps the biggest innovation in the System.Xml namespace, and the way in which you'll typically interact with XML documents, is through the use of a stream-based API analogous to the stream reading and writing performed on files discussed in Chapter 12, "Accessing System Services." At the core of this API are the XmlReader and XmlWriter classes, which provide read-only, forward-only cursor access to XML documents and an interface for writing out XML documents, respectively. Because these classes implement a stream-based approach, they do not require that the XML document be parsed into a tree structure and cached in memory as happens when working with the document through the DOM.

Using XML Readers

When the DOM was first published and vendors such as Microsoft began writing parsers such as MSXML to read those documents, it became immediately apparent that the programming model was not ideal for all applications. This was particularly the case when the XML

14

INTEGRATING WITH THE ENTERPRISE

document was large because by definition the DOM represents the entire document in an in-memory tree structure. Not only did performance suffer using the DOM because you had to wait for the document to be parsed and loaded, but also the application processing the document tended to eat up significant amounts of memory. As a result, Microsoft included the SAX APIs in MSXML 3.0 to provide an event-driven programming model for XML documents. Although this alleviated the performance and memory constraints of the DOM, it did so at the cost of complexity.

The XmlReader implementation is in many ways a melding of the DOM and SAX, and provides a simplified programming model like the DOM, but in a stream-based architecture. The programming model is simplified because it is a pull rather than a push model. In other words, developers pull data from the document using a familiar cursor-style looping construct, rather than simply being pushed data by responding to events fired from the parser.

The XmlReader class is actually an abstract base class for the XmlTextReader, XmlValidatingReader, and XmlNodeReader classes. The XmlReader often is used as the input or output arguments for other methods in the Services Framework. A typical use of the XmlReader is to read XML produced from the FOR XML statement in SQL Server 2000, and then load a DataSet object as shown in the following code:

```
Imports System.Xml
Imports System.Data.SqlClient
Imports System.Data
Dim cn As New SqlConnection("server=ssosa;database=enrollment;uid=sa")
Dim cm As New SqlCommand( _
   "SELECT FName, LName, Company FROM Student FOR XML AUTO, XMLDATA", cn)
Dim xmlr As XmlReader
Dim ds As New DataSet()

cn.Open()
cm.CommandType = CommandType.Text
xmlr = cm.ExecuteXmlReader
ds.ReadXml(xmlr, XmlReadMode.Fragment)
```

The ExecuteXmlReader method of the SqlCommand object returns an XmlReader, which is then accepted as an argument to one of the overloaded ReadXml methods of the DataSet object. As discussed in Chapter 7, "Accessing Data with ADO.NET," the second argument to the ReadXml method specifies how the XML is parsed using one of the XmlReadMode constants.

Navigating a Document

As implied by the names, XmlTextReader simply provides a reader that checks for well-formedness of an XML document and any inline DTDs, but does not perform validation using an associated DTD or schema as does XmlValidatingReader. As a result, XmlTextReader is the fastest way to parse an XML document using a file, Stream, or TextReader as input. XmlNodeReader, on the other hand, can parse XmlNode objects from an XML DOM subtree, as will be discussed later. To give you a feel for the readers, Table 14.2 lists the important members of the XmlTextReader class.

TABLE 14.2 Important XmlTextReader Members

Member	Description
AttributeCount	Returns the number of attributes on the current node.
BaseURI	Returns the base URI used to resolve external references to the current node.
Close	Closes the document and changes the ReadState to Closed.
Depth	Returns the depth of the current node within the XML document.
EOF	Returns True if the XmlReader is positioned at the end of the stream.
GetAttribute	Returns the value of the attribute given the index or name. If it does not exist, returns an empty string.
GetRemainder	Returns that part of the document still in the buffer as a TextReader object.
HasAttributes, HasValue	Returns True if the current node has attributes or a value.
IsDefault	Returns True if the attribute of the current node was generated from the default specified in the DTD or schema.
IsEmptyElement	Returns True if the current node is an empty element.
IsStartElement	Returns True if the current node is a start tag. Also overloaded to accept an element name that first navigates to the next content element using MoveToContent.
Item	Indexed property that returns an attribute from the current node.
LineNumber, LinePosition	Returns current location information.

14

INTEGRATING
WITH THE
ENTERPRISE

TABLE 14.2 Continued

Member	Description
LocalName, Name	Returns the name of the current node without the namespace prefix and the qualified name, respectively.
MoveToAttribute, MoveToContent, MoveToElement, MoveToFirstAttribute, MoveToNextAttribute	Methods that navigate through the document to find the specified data.
NamespaceURI	Specifies the namespace of the current node.
NodeType	Returns the XmlNodeType for the current node.
ReadState	Returns the state of the XmlReader using one of the ReadState constants (Closed, EndOfFile, Error, Initial, Interactive).
Read	Reads the next node from the stream and makes it the current node.
ReadString, ReadChars, ReadBase64, ReadBinHex	Reads the value of the text of the current node and returns it in the appropriate data type.
ReadInnerXml, ReadOuterXml	Reads the current node and its markup as a String and also includes its children, respectively.
Skip	Skips the current element and positions the reader on the next element.
Value	Returns the value of the current node as a String.
WhitespaceHandling	Specifies how to parse whitespace encountered in the document.

To illustrate the use of XmlTextReader, consider the ExtractStudents method shown in Listing 14.1.

LISTING 14.1   Using XmlTextReader. This method uses the XmlTextReader to read the contents of an XML document and extract student names to save in a database.

```
Imports System.Xml
Imports System.IO
Imports System.Data.SqlClient
Imports System.Data
Public Sub ExtractStudents(ByVal FileName As String)
```

LISTING 14.1   Continued

```
Dim oRead As XmlTextReader

Try
  Dim strFName, strLName, strOrg As String
  oRead = New XmlTextReader(FileName)
  oRead.NameTable.Add("Student")

  Do While oRead.Read
    oRead.MoveToContent()
    If oRead.Name.Equals("Student") And oRead.Depth = 1 Then
      strFName = oRead.GetAttribute("FName")
      strLName = oRead.GetAttribute("LName")

      If oRead.AttributeCount = 3 Then
        strOrg = oRead.GetAttribute("Company")
      Else
        strOrg = ""
      End If

      Call SaveStudent(strFName, strLName, strOrg)
    End If
  Loop

Catch e As XmlException
  LogMessage(FileName, e.Message, _
    e.LineNumber, e.LinePosition, oRead.Name)
Finally
  oRead.Close()
End Try

End Sub
```

In this example, the ExtractStudents method uses the overloaded constructor of the
XmlTextReader class to pass in the name of a file. In addition, the XmlReader exposes an
XmlNameTable in the NameTable property that is used to store frequently used strings. By using
a name table, the XML parser can reuse the strings in the table when returning element names
and can use more efficient object pointer comparisons when doing comparisons. An existing
XmlNameTable also can be passed into the constructor so that comparisons across readers will
also be more efficient.

If the file can be opened, a Do Loop is used to iterate through the contents of the document
using the Read method, which returns False upon reaching the end of the stream.

14

One of the interesting aspects of an XmlReader is that the Read method not only returns each tag (begin and end elements, processing instructions, CDATA sections, comments, and document type definitions) but also whitespace. And as you might imagine, it does so in a recursive way such that an entire element including all its children is processed before moving on to a sibling element. The type of the current node can be checked using the NodeType property.

To more efficiently move through the document, you can use the move methods such as MoveToContent, as in this example. MoveToContent skips over any processing instructions, DTDs, comments, and whitespace and moves to the next CDATA section, beginning or ending element, or entity reference.

As mentioned previously, the XmlTextReader only makes sure that the document is well-formed and otherwise throws an XmlException. In this example, both the Read method and the MoveToContent methods might generate the exception because both perform navigation. Note also that when a well-formedness error is encountered, the ReadState of the XmlTextReader is set to Error, and no more processing on the document can be performed.

> **TIP**
>
> By logging the LinePosition of the error, as is done here, the method could be easily altered to reprocess the document starting with the appropriate line.

> **TIP**
>
> You also can skip only the whitespace by setting the WhiteSpaceHandling property to the None constant of the WhiteSpaceHandling enumeration.

The element name can then be checked using the Name property before proceeding to read the value of the element using the Value property or one of the read methods shown in Table 14.2.

> **TIP**
>
> In Listing 14.1, the Depth property is used to ensure that the method only processes top-level Student elements by checking for a depth of 1.

However, you'll notice in this case that the data for the student actually is contained in attributes of the Student element. Attributes are not represented as separate nodes by XmlReader, but rather as a collection associated with the node. As a result, attributes typically are accessed using the `Item` property or the `GetAttribute` method. Alternatively, the `MoveToAttribute` method can be used to position the cursor over the attribute passed to the method, and the `Name` and `Value` properties are set to the name of the attribute and its value. The collection also can be navigated in this way using the `MoveToFirstAttribute` and `MoveToNextAttribute` methods.

The values then are extracted from the attributes and passed to a method that saves them in the database.

An advanced technique that `XmlReader` supports, not shown in Listing 14.1, is the optional expansion of entity references. Simply put, an entity reference allows an XML document to be compressed by defining an entity once in a document and referencing it multiple times like so:

```
<!DOCTYPE Classes [
 <!ENTITY 2073 "<CourseNum>2073</CourseNum>
   <CourseDesc>Programming Microsoft SQL Server 2000</CourseDesc>">
]>
<Class>
<Course>&2073;</Course>
</Class>
```

When the `XmlReader` encounters the expression `&2073`, the `NodeType` is set to `EntityReference`. By invoking `ResolveEntity`, the substitution occurs and processing continues with the `CourseNum` and `CourseDesc` elements. Note that `XmlTextReader`, however, does not support entity referencing (an `InvalidOperationException` will be thrown), and the `CanResolveEntity` property can be used to determine whether entities can be resolved.

Validating a Document

To perform validation against an XML document, you can associate an `XmlValidatingReader` object with an `XmlTextReader`. The `XmlValidatingReader` exposes a `Schemas` collection (`XmlSchemaCollection`) that contains one or more schemas (DTDs, XSD, XDR) represented as `XmlSchema` objects that can be used to validate the document. Validation errors then are reported through a `ValidationEventHandler`. The `Validate` method in Listing 14.2 shows the basics of validating a document using an XDR schema.

LISTING 14.2 Validating XML. This method shows how to validate a document against a schema.

```
Imports System.Xml
Imports System.Xml.Schema
Public Sub Validate(ByVal FileName As String, ByVal SchemaName As String, _
   ByVal xmlns As String)

   Dim oRead As XmlTextReader
```

14

INTEGRATING
WITH THE
ENTERPRISE

LISTING 14.2 Continued

```
Dim oValid As XmlValidatingReader

Try
  oRead = New XmlTextReader(FileName)
  oValid = New XmlValidatingReader(oRead)

  AddHandler oValid.ValidationEventHandler, _
    New ValidationEventHandler(AddressOf ValidationError)

  oValid.Schemas.Add(xmlns, SchemaName)
  oValid.ValidationType = ValidationType.Auto

  Do While oValid.Read
    ' Read through the document here
  Loop

Catch e As Exception
  LogMessage(pFileName, e.Message, e.LineNumber, _
    e.LinePosition, oRead.Name)
Finally
  oValid.Close()
End Try

End Sub

Public Sub ValidationError(ByVal o As Object, _
  ByVal args As ValidationEventArgs)
  ' Validation error occurred
  LogValidationError(args)
End Sub
```

The XmlValidating reader is initialized with the XmlTextReader and the schema added
through the Add method of the XmlSchemaCollection. The arguments represent the namespace
URI (as it is referred to in the document to be validated) and the URL of the schema to load.
The event handler where errors will be reported is created using the AddHandler statement, in
this case pointing to the ValidationError method. The schemas must be added to the collection before the Read method is called. The ValidationType property is set to the Auto constant
of the ValidationType enumeration so that the schema type will be auto-detected. In addition,
it can be set to DTD, None, XDR, or Schema.

> **TIP**
>
> By setting the ValidationType property to None, validation will be bypassed. However, it is more efficient to simply use the XmlTextReader if validation is not required.

A client can then call the Validate method in Listing 14.2 as follows.

```
Validate("regdata.xml", "regdata.xsd", "http://www.quilogy.com/education")
```

As an alternative to creating the XmlSchemaCollection on-the-fly, as shown in Listing 14.2, you can create a standalone XmlSchemaCollecton object and, when needed, pass it to the Add method of the Schemas property. In this way, the schemas are loaded only once. This allows multiple documents to be loaded without reloading and reparsing the schemas.

Using XML Writers

Not only does System.Xml provide streamed access for reading documents, it also includes the XmlWriter class for high-performance output. Once again, the XmlWriter class is the base class, whereas you typically work with the XmlTextWriter derived class.

Basically, the XmlTextWriter includes properties that allow you to control how the XML will be written in terms of its formatting and namespace usage, methods analogous to other stream writers discussed in Chapter 12, such as Flush and Close, and a bevy of Write methods that add text to the output stream. Table 14.3 shows the important members for the XmlTextWriter class.

TABLE 14.3 Important XmlTextWriter Members

Member	Description
Close	Closes the XmlTextWriter and the underlying stream.
Flush	Flushes whatever is in the buffer for the XmlTextWriter and the underlying stream.
Formatting	When set to Formatting.Indented, specifies that output will be formatted according to the Indentation and IndentChars properties.
Indentation	Specifies how many IndentChar characters to write out for each level in the hierarchy. Default is 2.
IndentChar	Specifies which character to use for indentation.

14

INTEGRATING WITH THE ENTERPRISE

TABLE 14.3   Continued

Member	Description
LookupPrefix	Returns the closest prefix defined in the current namespace scope.
Namespaces	When set to True, namespaces are supported.
QuoteChar	Specifies which character to use to quote attribute values.
WriteState	Set to one of the WriteState enumeration constants (Attribute, Closed, Content, Element, Prolog, Start).
WriteAttributes	Writes out all the attributes found at the current position in the XmlReader.
WriteAttributeString	Writes an attribute with the specified value.
WriteBase64, WriteBinHex, WriteChars, WriteString	Write the given argument to the underlying stream using the appropriate data type.
WriteCData, WriteComment, WriteDocType, WriteEntityRef, WriteProcessingInstruction, WriteWhitespace, WriteStartDocument, WriteEndDocument	Write out particular XML elements as implied by their names.
WriteStartAttribute, WriteEndAttribute, WriteStartElement, WriteEndElement,	Write an attribute to the document.
WriteFullEndElement	Write an element to the document.
WriteRaw	Writes the given string or character array to the underlying stream.

The interesting aspect of the XmlTextWriter class is that it abstracts all the formulation and writing of tags that typically would have to be done if you were creating an XML document manually. In fact, the XmlTextWriter is smart in that it keeps track of the hierarchy of the document to automatically provide ending tags through methods such as WriteEndElement and WriteEndDocument. The result is a programming model that not only performs well, but also is simple to use.

To illustrate the use of the XmlTextWriter class, consider the WriteXml method shown in Listing 14.3.

LISTING 14.3 Writing XML. This simple method accepts a text file as an argument and writes it out as an XML document.

```
Imports System.Xml
Imports System.IO
Public Sub WriteXml(ByVal FileName As String)
  Dim fs As FileStream
  Dim sReader As StreamReader
  Dim strLine As String
  Dim strStudentID, strFName, strLName, strOrg As String
  Dim tw As XmlTextWriter

  Try
    fs = New FileStream(FileName, FileMode.Open, FileAccess.Read)
    sReader = New StreamReader(fs)
    tw = New XmlTextWriter(FileName & ".xml", _
      New System.Text.UTF8Encoding())

    tw.Formatting = Formatting.Indented
    tw.Indentation = 4

    ' Write out the header information
    tw.WriteStartDocument()
    tw.WriteComment("Produced from " & FileName & " on " & Now.ToString)
    tw.WriteStartElement("stud", "Students", "www.quilogy.com/education")

    ' Loop through the input file
    strLine = sReader.ReadLine
    Do While Not strLine Is Nothing
      strStudentID = Trim(Mid(strLine, 1, 5))
      strFName = Trim(Mid(strLine, 13, 25))
      strLName = Trim(Mid(strLine, 64, 25))
      strOrg = Trim(Mid(strLine, 115, 25))

      ' Now write the Xml
      tw.WriteStartElement("Student")
      tw.WriteAttributeString("StudentID", strStudentID)
      tw.WriteStartElement("Name")
      tw.WriteAttributeString("First", strFName)
      tw.WriteAttributeString("Last", strLName)

      ' Close the Name tag
      tw.WriteEndElement()

      If strOrg.Length = 0 Or strOrg.Equals("NULL") Then
```

14

INTEGRATING
WITH THE
ENTERPRISE

Listing 14.3   Continued

```
      ' Skip
    Else
      tw.WriteElementString("Organization", strOrg)
    End If

    ' Close the Student tag
    tw.WriteEndElement()

    strLine = sReader.ReadLine
  Loop

  ' Finish off the document
  ' Close the Students tag
  tw.WriteEndDocument()

  ' Close the files
  tw.Flush()
  tw.Close()
  sReader.Close()

Catch e As IOException
  ' Catch initial io errors
  LogMessage(FileName, e.Message)
Catch e As XmlException
  LogMessage(FileName & ".xml", e.Message, e.LineNumber, e.LinePosition)
End Try
End Sub
```

In this example, a text file containing student information is passed into the WriteXml method and is opened using a standard FileStream object. The XmlTextWriter is initialized with the name of the XML document to write to in addition to the encoding to use. The overload constructor also accepts Stream or TextWriter objects.

As indicated in Table 14.3, the formatting for the document is specified using the Formatting and Indentation properties. The header of the document, along with a comment, then is written using the WriteStartDocument and WriteComment methods. The WriteStartElement method writes out the Students element and includes a namespace declaration. As implied by the name, this method writes out the beginning of the tag, but does not yet close it.

The Do Loop reads through each line of the text file (which in this case is a fixed-format file) and parses its contents into four variables that include the student's ID, name, and organization. To write out the meat of the data, a Student element is created using WriteStartElement, and its attribute using `WriteAttributeString`. Both these methods also can accept namespace and prefix information. A child element to contain the name then is created by invoking `WriteStartElement` again. Its attributes are then also created. At this point, two elements have been created, but have not been closed. The `WriteEndElement` method determines the current context and writes the appropriate ending tag (either a "/>" or a full ending tag that includes the element name). In this case, it simply closes the `Name` tag because it does not contain a value.

If the organization is present, the `WriteElementString` method is used to write a complete element including its closing tag along with the value passed to the method. The `Student` tag then is closed once again using the `WriteEndElement` method.

After the input file has been exhausted, the XML document is finished off by writing the ending tag for the `Students` element using `WriteEndDocument`. This method also tracks the current context and closes any open elements. The file is closed by calling `Flush` followed by `Close`, as is typical of stream writers. A small portion of the resulting XML document is shown here:

```
<?xml version="1.0" ?>
<?xml-stylesheet type="text/xsl" href="test.xsl"?>
<!--Produced from C:\My Documents\Visual Studio Projects\VB.NET Book\
13Enterprise\ReadandWrite\students.txt on 5/19/2001 7:39:27 AM-->
<qed:Students xmlns:qed="http://www.quilogy.com/education">
    <Student StudentID="1">
        <Name First="Derrick" Last="Whelply" />
    </Student>
    <Student StudentID="2">
        <Name First="Jeanne" Last="Derry" />
    </Student>
    <Student StudentID="3">
        <Name First="Michael" Last="Spence" />
        <Organization>Quilogy</Organization>
    </Student>
</qed:Students>
```

Accessing Data With the DOM

In addition to providing streamed access to XML documents, the `System.Xml` namespace also includes the familiar DOM programming model. The primary class that supports the DOM is `XmlDocument`, which, as mentioned earlier, implements the W3C DOM Level 1 Core and the Core DOM Level 2 specifications using an in-memory tree representation of the document. Many developers already will be familiar with the DOM from working with the MSXML parser, and, in fact, the `XmlDocument` class is analogous to the `DOMDocument` class found in MSXML, with some minor exceptions.

14

NOTE

For example, asynchronous loading is not directly supported because a developer can control this using the XmlReader.

First, as you might expect, the XmlDocument class uses the XmlReader and XmlWriter classes behind the scenes when reading documents (from a file, Stream, TextReader, or XmlTextReader) and serializing the output (to a file, Stream, TextWriter, or XmlTextWriter), respectively. In addition, the XmlDocument class is actually a base class used by the XmlDataDocument, as discussed in Chapter 7. In this way, DataSet objects can be accessed either as a DataSet or as an XmlDocument depending on the need. In addition, the XmlDocument class uses a number of helper classes that represent nodes within the document. In fact, all these and XmlDocument itself are derived from XmlNode, which contains most of the standard members to perform navigation (SelectNodes, SelectSingleNode, NextSibling, PreviousSibling, FirstChild, LastChild), modify the document (AppendChild, Clone, InsertAfter, InsertBefore, RemoveChild, ReplaceChild), and return information about the node (InnerText, InnerXml, NodeType, Value, HasChildNodes) among others.

To illustrate the use of the XmlDocument class, assume that Quilogy collects class registrations from external sources in XML documents like that shown in Listing 14.4. This information is then processed by Quilogy using the PreprocessDoc method shown in Listing 14.5. This method accepts a filename that refers to an XML document containing external registration information.

LISTING 14.4   Enrollment XML. This XML document can be processed by the method shown in Listing 14.5.

```
<QuilogyRegistration xmlns="http://www.quilogy.com/education">
 <Enrollment ClassID="1234" WebEnroll="N" PaymentType="BL">
  <Cost>1745</Cost>
  <Student>
   <FName>Sammy</FName>
   <LName>Sosa</LName>
   <Organization>Chicago Cubs</Organization>
   <ContactInfo>
    <AddressLine>3345 North Shore Drive</AddressLine>
    <City>Chicago</City>
    <State>IL</State>
    <Zip>43211</Zip>
    <Phone>3145551212</Phone>
    <Email>ssosa@cubs.com</Email>
```

LISTING 14.4   Continued

```
  </ContactInfo>
  <Comments>Make sure to have hot coffee available</Comments>
  </Student>
 </Enrollment>
</QuilogyRegistration>
```

LISTING 14.5   Using `XmlDocument`. This listing illustrates the use of `XmlDocument` to process an existing XML document.

```vb
Imports System.Xml
Imports Quilogy.Education.Schedule
Public Sub PreprocessDoc(ByVal FileName As String)

  Dim oDoc As New XmlDocument()
  Dim oList As XmlNodeList
  Dim oStudent, oEmail As XmlNode
  Dim oStud As New Students(mstrConnect)
  Dim strEmail, strLName As String
  Dim intStudentID As Integer
  Dim atExisting, atStudentID As XmlAttribute

  Try
    ' Load the document and save the processing time
    oDoc.PreserveWhitespace = True
    oDoc.Load(FileName)
    oDoc.DocumentElement.InsertBefore(oDoc.CreateComment( _
      "Processed on " & Now.ToString), oDoc.DocumentElement.FirstChild)

    ' Loop through all of the students
    oList = oDoc.GetElementsByTagName("Student")
    For Each oStudent In oList
      ' Gather info on each student
      Try
        strLName = oStudent.Item("LName").FirstChild.Value
        oEmail = oStudent.Item("ContactInfo").Item("Email")
        strEmail = oEmail.FirstChild.Value

        ' Check if the student already exists
        intStudentID = oStud.CheckIfExists(strEmail, strLName)
        atExisting = oDoc.CreateAttribute("Existing")
        If intStudentID > 0 Then
          atExisting.Value = "Y"
          atStudentID = oDoc.CreateAttribute("StudentID")
```

14

LISTING 14.5   Continued

```
              atStudentID.Value = intStudentID.ToString
              oStudent.Attributes.Append(atStudentID)
          Else
              atExisting.Value = "N"
          End If
          ' Add the existing attribute
          oStudent.Attributes.Append(atExisting)
        Catch e As Exception
          ' Not enough information or an error so skip it
          LogMessage(pFileName, e.Message)
        End Try

    Next

    ' Save the document
    oDoc.DocumentElement.AppendChild(oDoc.CreateComment( _
      "Finished Processing on " & Now.ToString))
    oDoc.Save(FileName & ".new.xml")

      ' Send it to a method for processing
      Call AddEnrollments(oDoc.InnerXml)
    Catch e As Exception
      LogMessage(FileName, e.Message)
    Finally
      oDoc = Nothing
    End Try

End Sub
```

Although Listing 14.4 shows only a single enrollment, typically, the document would contain multiple Student elements. The role of the PreprocessDoc method in Listing 14.5 is to open and iterate through the document to determine whether the student already exists in the database. In either case, the "Existing" attribute will be added to the Student element and set appropriately. If the student exists, his StudentID also will be captured in an attribute. The document then is saved under a new name, and the XML passed to an AddEnrollments method (not shown) for further processing.

The document is loaded using the Load method, although the XmlDocument class also supports the LoadXml method that accepts a String containing the XML fragment. As with the XmlTextReader, the document must be well-formed, although in this case, the XmlException will be thrown during the Load method and not as the content is navigated to. Before the Load method is called, the PreserveWhitespace property is set to True to keep any whitespace that exists. Even if the property is set to `False`, standard indentation is used when the document is serialized with the `Save`, `WriteTo`, or `WriteContentTo` methods.

As with `DOMDocument`, the `DocumentElement` property returns the root `XmlElement` object of the document. As with any node, the `InsertBefore` method can be used to add new content to the document. In Listing 14.5, an `XmlComment` object is created using the `CreateComment` method and inserted before the next element (`Enrollment`) in the document, as referenced by the `FirstChild` property of the root element.

NOTE

The `XmlDocument` class also exposes class factories to create elements (`CreateElement`), attributes (`CreateAttribute`), CDATA (`CreateCDataSection`), entity references (`CreateEntityReference`), document types (`CreateDocumentType`), processing instructions (`CreateProcessingInstruction`), XML declarations (`CreateXmlDeclaration`), whitespace (`CreateWhitespace` and `CreateSignificantWhitespace`), document fragments (`CreateDocumentFragment`), text nodes (`CreateTextNode`), and generic nodes (`CreateNode`). All these methods return objects derived from `XmlNode`.

After the root element is referenced, the `GetElementsByTagName` method is used to return a node list (`XmlNodeList`) containing all the `Student` elements. The `XmlNodeList` is a collection of `XmlNode` objects that implement the `IEnumerable` interface, and a `For Each` loop can be used to iterate through the students. In addition to using the navigation methods, `SelectNodes` and `SelectSingleNode`, that accept XPath queries and return either a node list or a single node, the child nodes can be accessed directly using the `Item` property. In this case, the `LName` element is referenced using the collection and its text returned by accessing the `Value` property of the `FirstChild` property, which points to the text node (`XmlText`) containing the name. Similarly, the `Email` element is referenced by first navigating to the `ContactInfo` element in the collection, and then to its child `Email` element. Once again, the actual text of the `Email` element is returned using the `Value` property of `FirstChild`.

TIP

Keep in mind that an alternative way to navigate through particular nodes in an `XmlDocument` is to use the `XmlNodeReader` class. By passing the `XmlNode` to navigate through to the constructor of the `XmlNodeReader` object, you can use a cursor model as shown in Listing 14.1 to iterate through the node.

14

After the values have been collected, the CheckIfExists method of the Students data access class is invoked to check the database to determine whether the student exists given the e-mail address and last name. In either case, the Existing XmlAttribute object is created using the CreateAttribute method and eventually added to the Student element with the Append method of the Attributes collection. If the student was found, the Existing attribute is set to "Y", and an attribute containing the StudentID is created and appended to the Student element (oStudent).

Finally, a second comment is written at the end of the document to indicate when the document processing was completed, and the documented is written out using the Save method. Alternatively, you could use the WriteTo or WriteContentTo to write all or just the children of the XmlDocument node to an XmlWriter object. The document is serialized to a string and passed to the AddEnrollments method (not shown) using the InnerXml property.

NOTE

Note that this property (and OuterXml) replaces the Xml property of the DOMDocument object in MSXML. However, InnerXml is also writable, allowing you to insert a simple string containing XML into the document. XmlDocument also supports the InnerText property to return the concatenated values of all the children of the node.

Transforming a Document

As shown in Table 14.1, the System.Xml namespace includes the Xsl namespace that exposes classes that enable the programmatic use of XSLT (Extensible Stylesheet Language Transformations) 1.0. Simply put, XSLT allows you to transform an XML document into an XML, HTML, or text document using a set of rules (templates) defined in a third XML document known as a style sheet.

NOTE

The transformation rules used to map one document to another are beyond the scope of this book, suffice it to say that XSLT contains many of the constructs developers are familiar with, including variables, functions, iteration, and conditional statements. For more information, see msdn.microsoft.com/xml and http://www.w3.org/TR/1999/PR-xslt-19991008.html.

Not surprisingly, the capability to transform a document is contained in the XslTransform class. In its most basic form, all that is required is to use the Load method to load the XSL style sheet into the XslTransform object and then call the Transform method to perform the translation.

> **TIP**
>
> The XSL style sheet must include the namespace declaration xmlns:xsl=http://www.w3c.org/1999/XSL/Transform for the transformation to work.

Typically, XSL transforms are used to transform an XML document from one schema to another. However, they also can be used to transform an XML document into an HTML document or an alternative text output. As an example of the latter, consider the following XSL style sheet:

```
<xsl:stylesheet version='1.0' xmlns:xsl='http://www.w3.org/1999/XSL/Transform'
  xmlns:qed='http://www.quilogy.com/education'>
<xsl:output method="text" />
<xsl:template match="/">StudentID,FName,LName,Company
  <xsl:for-each select="qed:Students/Student">
<xsl:value-of select="@StudentID" />,"<xsl:value-of select="Name/@First" />",
 "<xsl:value-of select="Name/@Last"/>","<xsl:value-of select="Organization"/>"
  </xsl:for-each>
</xsl:template>
</xsl:stylesheet>
```

In this example, the style sheet processes the XML document produced in Listing 14.4 containing basic information about students. Note that the style sheet contains the xsl:output element, whose method attribute is set to "text" to instruct XSLT to produce text, rather than XML or HTML output. The document then contains a single set of rules (a template) that prints out a header row with the column names and loops through each Student element and prints out the student ID, first name, last name, and organization in a comma-delimited row. The end result is a comma-delimited text file that can be used by a legacy process to insert or update a database, for example. This process can be carried out by a method like that shown in Listing 14.6.

LISTING 14.6 Programmatic XSLT. This listing shows how to programmatically transform a document using the XslTransform class.

```
Imports System.Xml
Imports System.IO
Imports system.Xml.XPath
Imports System.Xml.Xsl
```

14

INTEGRATING WITH THE ENTERPRISE

LISTING 14.6 Continued

```
Public Sub TransformDoc(ByVal FileName As String, ByVal XslDoc As String, _
  ByVal s As Stream)

  Try
    Dim oDoc As New XPathDocument(FileName)
    Dim oXsl As New XslTransform()

    oXsl.Load(XslDoc)
    oXsl.Transform(oDoc, Nothing, s)

  Catch e As XsltException
    LogMessage(pFileName, e.Message & e.InnerException.Message)
  Catch e As Exception
    LogMessage(pFileName, e.Message)
  Finally
    ' Close the stream
    s.Flush()
    s.Close()
  End Try

End Sub
```

The `TransformDoc` method shown in Listing 14.6 accepts the XML document to transform, the XSL style sheet to use for the transformation, and a `Stream` object that catches the output. In this example, the XML document to be transformed (`FileName`) first is loaded using an `XPathDocument` object. The `XPathDocument` object is a lightweight and fast-performing cache designed specifically for XSLT processing. For example, it does not cache node properties as the document is traversed, as evidenced by its lack of members; nor does it perform all the rule checking performed in the `XmlDocument` class. Note that the constructor to `XPathDocument` is overloaded and can accept an `XmlReader`, `TextReader`, or `Stream`, in addition to a URI, as in this case.

The `XslTransform` object then is instantiated and the style sheet loaded using the overloaded `Load` method. Once again, the `Load` method accepts `XmlReader`, `XPathNavigator`, and objects that expose the `IXPathNavigable` interface.

> **NOTE**
>
> `XPathNavigator` is an abstract base class used by the `XslTransform` class to perform the transformations. Basically, it provides a cursorlike interface for reading data from a document and the XPath methods to query the document. For example, it supports

the Compile method that compiles an XPath expression to an XPathExpression object so that it can be reused in later queries. Although it is possible to construct your own XPathNavigator object, it typically is not required unless you want to perform your own XPath queries on the document.

The IXPathNavigable interface is implemented by the XmlNode and XPathDocument classes; so, for example, because XmlDocument is derived from XmlNode, you can use polymorphism to pass an instance of XmlDocument populated with the style sheet to the Load method.

The transformation then occurs by invoking the Transform method where the first argument is the XML document to process as either a filename, an XPathNavigator object, or an object that exposes the IXPathNavigable interface. The second argument, set to Nothing in this case, can be set to an XsltArgument object. The XsltArgument object can simply contain parameters passed into the style sheet. In this way, the transformation can include dynamic elements. For example, in the style sheet used to write out student data shown previously, the delimiter is hard-coded to a comma. However, this could be changed by adding an xsl:param element in the style sheet and populating the parameter like so:

```
Dim oArgs As New XsltArgumentList()
oArgs.AddParam("delimiter", _
  "http://www.w3.org/1999/XSL/Transform ", strDelimiter)
oXsl.Transform(oDoc, oArgs, pOut)
```

The final argument to Transform is the Stream, XmlWriter, or TextWriter used to handle the output. In addition, Transform can act as a function and return an XmlReader so that the results of the transformation can be immediately traversed.

If errors occur, the Transform method throws an XsltException object, which exposes the InnerException property from which you can extract the message. However, the Load method simply throws a generic exception if the style sheet cannot be loaded. In this case, both are handled in the Try block and the output stream flushed and closed in the Finally block.

Handling XML Schemas

As mentioned previously in the discussion on validation, XML documents can be validated by the XmlValidatingReader class using either an XDR, DTD, or XSD schema. However, because the XML schema (XSD) grammar was approved as a W3C recommendation on May 2, 2001 (see http://www.w3.org/XML/Schema for more details), the Services Framework supports it more fully than the other means of validating the content of an XML document.

The support for XSD can be found in the System.Xml.Schema namespace and particularly the XmlSchema class. In addition, the namespace contains myriad helper classes to represent the components of an XSD schema.

A typical use of the XmlSchema class is to precompile a schema for use in validating XML documents. For example, the AddSchema method shown in Listing 14.7 can be used to compile an XSD schema and add it to a collection of schemas that can subsequently be used with an XmlValidatingReader object.

LISTING 14.7 Compiling an XSD Schema. This method loads and compiles an XSD schema using the XmlSchema class.

```
Imports System.Xml
Imports system.Xml.Schema
Public Sub AddSchema(ByVal SchemaFile As String, _
 ByRef Schemas As XmlSchemaCollection)

  Dim oSchema As New XmlSchema()
  Dim oReader As New XmlTextReader(SchemaFile)
  Dim oErrorEvent As New ValidationEventHandler(AddressOf ValidationCallback)

    Try
    ' Read it in and compile it
    oSchema = XmlSchema.Read(oReader, oErrorEvent)
    oSchema.Compile(oErrorEvent)
    If oSchema.IsCompiled Then
      ' Add to the collection
      Schemas.Add(oSchema)
    Else
      LogMessage(SchemaFile & " not compiled")
    End If

  Catch e As Exception
    If e.InnerException Is Nothing Then
      LogMessage(SchemaFile, e.Message)
    Else
      LogMessage(SchemaFile, e.Message & ":" & e.InnerException.Message)
    End If
  End Try

End Sub

Public Sub ValidationCallback(ByVal sender As Object, _
  ByVal args As ValidationEventArgs)
    LogMessage("Validation error", _
      args.ErrorCode.ToString & ":" & args.Message)
End Sub
```

In Listing 14.7, the schema file passed into the method is loaded using an XmlTextReader. The shared Read method is passed the XmlTextReader object along with a ValidationEventHandler delegate to call if the schema cannot be parsed. If no exceptions occur, the Compile method is invoked to compile the schema and ensure that it can be used for validation. Note that the same ValidationEventHandler delegate pointing to the address of the ValidationCallback method is used. Each validation error fires the method and passes it the ValidationEventArgs object that can be used to record the error.

If the schema is compiled successfully, as indicated by the IsCompiled method, the schema is added to the XmlSchemaCollection passed into the method. The collection of schemas then can be used to populate the Schemas property of an XmlValidatingReader object.

Of course, in addition to simply loading prebuilt schemas, VS .NET and the Services Framework support creating schemas both graphically and programmatically. To graphically create the schema, you can use the XML Designer discussed briefly in Chapter 7. To programmatically create the schema, you can use the helper classes found in the System.Xml.Schemas namespace.

To illustrate creating a simple schema, consider the WriteSchema method shown in Listing 14.8.

LISTING 14.8   Building an XSD Schema. This method builds an XSD schema using the schema helper classes.

```vb
Imports System.Xml
Imports system.Xml.Schema
Public Function WriteSchema() As XmlSchema

  Dim oSchema As New XmlSchema()

  ' <xsd:element name="Organization" type="string">
  Dim elOrg As New XmlSchemaElement()
  oSchema.Items.Add(elOrg)
  elOrg.Name = "Organization"
  elOrg.SchemaTypeName = _
    New XmlQualifiedName("string", "http://www.w3.org/2001/XMLSchema")

  ' <xsd:element name="Name">
  Dim elName As New XmlSchemaElement()
  oSchema.Items.Add(elName)
  elName.Name = "Name"

  ' <xsd:complexType>
  Dim complexType As New XmlSchemaComplexType()
  elName.SchemaType = complexType
```

Listing 14.8 Continued

```
' <xsd:attribute name="First" type="xsd:string" />
Dim atFirst As New XmlSchemaAttribute()
atFirst.Name = "First"
atFirst.SchemaTypeName = _
  New XmlQualifiedName("string", "http://www.w3.org/2001/XMLSchema")
complexType.Attributes.Add(atFirst)


' <xsd:attribute name="Last" type="xsd:string" />
Dim atLast As New XmlSchemaAttribute()
atLast.Name = "Last"
atLast.SchemaTypeName = _
  New XmlQualifiedName("string", "http://www.w3.org/2001/XMLSchema")
complexType.Attributes.Add(atLast)


' <xsd:element name="Student">
Dim elStud As New XmlSchemaElement()
oSchema.Items.Add(elStud)
elStud.Name = "Student"


' <xsd:complexType>
Dim complexType1 As New XmlSchemaComplexType()
elStud.SchemaType = complexType1


' <xsd:attribute name="StudentID" type="xsd:string" />
Dim atID As New XmlSchemaAttribute()
atID.Name = "StudentID"
atID.SchemaTypeName = _
  New XmlQualifiedName("integer", "http://www.w3.org/2001/XMLSchema")
complexType1.Attributes.Add(atID)


' <xsd:all minOccurs="0" maxOccurs="1">
Dim allStud As New XmlSchemaAll()
complexType1.Particle = allStud
allStud.MinOccurs = 0
allStud.MaxOccurs = 1


' <xsd:element ref="Name"/>
Dim refName As New XmlSchemaElement()
allStud.Items.Add(refName)
refName.RefName = New XmlQualifiedName("Name")


' <xsd:element ref="Organization"/>
Dim refOrg As New XmlSchemaElement()
allStud.Items.Add(refOrg)
refOrg.RefName = New XmlQualifiedName("Organization")
```

LISTING 14.8   Continued

```
' <xsd:element name="Students">
Dim elStuds As New XmlSchemaElement()
oSchema.Items.Add(elStuds)
elStuds.Name = "Students"

' <xsd:complexType>
Dim complexType2 As New XmlSchemaComplexType()
elStuds.SchemaType = complexType2

' <xsd:all minOccurs="0" maxOccurs="unbounded">
Dim allStuds As New XmlSchemaAll()
complexType2.Particle = allStuds
allStuds.MinOccurs = 0

' <xsd:element ref="Student"/>
Dim refStud As New XmlSchemaElement()
allStuds.Items.Add(refStud)
refStud.RefName = New XmlQualifiedName("Student")

Return oSchema

End Function
```

The WriteSchema method is straightforward in that it builds an XSD schema to represent student information in an XML document. At the highest level, the XmlSchemaElement object is used to define each element, and items are added to the schema using the Add method of the Items collection. In fact, the classes that represent components of the XSD schema used here, such as XmlSchemaAttribute, XmlSchemaAll, XmlSchemaComplexType, and XmlSchemaElement, are all ultimately derived from XmlSchemaObject.

The general approach used to build the schema is to define the appropriate XmlSchemaObjects and then add them to the appropriate Items collection. For example, the allStud variable is of type XmlSchemaAll, which represents the all compositor element in the W3C specification. This element allows the elements in the group to appear in any order within the containing element. To add elements to the group, you then simply define the elements, in this case refName and refOrg, and add them to the Items collection of allStud.

The result of the schema built here can be seen as follows:

```
<?xml version="1.0" encoding="IBM437"?>
<schema xmlns="http://www.w3.org/2001/XMLSchema">
  <element name="Organization" type="string" />
  <element name="Name">
```

14

```
        <complexType>
          <attribute name="First" type="string" />
          <attribute name="Last" type="string" />
        </complexType>
      </element>
      <element name="Student">
        <complexType>
          <all minOccurs="0" maxOccurs="1">
            <element ref="Name" />
            <element ref="Organization" />
          </all>
          <attribute name="StudentID" type="integer" />
        </complexType>
      </element>
      <element name="Students">
        <complexType>
          <all minOccurs="0">
            <element ref="Student" />
          </all>
        </complexType>
      </element>
    </schema>
```

In this case, the XmlSchema object is returned from the function for later use.

Serializating to XML

One of the most interesting features of the XML classes in the Services Framework is the support for XML serialization found in the System.Xml.Serialization namespace. This namespace contains attributes that are typically used to decorate your custom classes so that they can be translated between a strong type and an XML representation. This process is referred to as *serialization* and was discussed briefly in Chapter 8, "Building Components." In addition, the main class in the namespace is XmlSerializer, which exposes the Serialize and Deserialize methods that implement the functionality.

> **NOTE**
>
> The Serialization namespace also contains attributes that you use to decorate a WebService class, such as SoapElementAttribute and SoapAttributeAttribute, among others, as discussed in Chapter 11, "Building Web Services."

To illustrate the use of serialization, Listing 14.9 shows the QStudents, Student, and Name classes.

LISTING 14.9 XML Serialization. This listing shows how a class can be decorated with attributes and can serialize and deserialize to XML using the XmlSerializer class.

```vb
Imports System.Xml.Serialization
Imports System.Xml
Imports System.IO
<XmlRoot([Namespace]:="www.quilogy.com/education", IsNullable:=False, _
  ElementName:="Students")> _
Public Class QStudents

  <XmlElementAttribute(IsNullable:=False)> _
  Public Students() As Student

  Shared Sub SaveXml(ByVal q As QStudents, _
    ByRef xmlWrite As XmlTextWriter)

    Try
      Dim s As New XmlSerializer(q.GetType)
      ' Write out the XML
      s.Serialize(xmlWrite, q)
    Catch e As Exception
      Throw New Exception("Could not serialize.", e)
    End Try

  End Sub

  Public Shared Function HydrateXml( _
    ByRef xmlRead As XmlTextReader) As QStudents

    Dim o As New QStudents()

    Try
      Dim s As New XmlSerializer(o.GetType)
      If s.CanDeserialize(xmlRead) Then
        o = CType(s.Deserialize(xmlRead), QStudents)
        Return o
      Else
        Return Nothing
      End If
    Catch e As Exception
      Throw New Exception("Could not deserialize.", e)
    End Try

  End Function
```

14

INTEGRATING WITH THE ENTERPRISE

LISTING 14.9   Continued

```vb
  Public Sub AddStudent(ByVal first As String, ByVal last As String, _
    ByVal studentID As Integer, ByVal organization As String)

    Dim s As Student

    s = New Student()
    s.StudentID = studentID
    s.Name.First = first
    s.Name.Last = last
    s.Organization = organization

    ' Add the student object to the array
    Try
      ReDim Preserve Students(Students.GetUpperBound(0) + 1)
    Catch e As NullReferenceException
      ' First time through redim the array
      ReDim Students(0)
    Finally
      Students(Students.GetUpperBound(0)) = s
    End Try
  End Sub

End Class

<XmlRoot([Namespace]:="", IsNullable:=False)> _
Public Class Student

  Public Sub New()
    Name = New Name()
  End Sub

  <XmlElement(IsNullable:=False)> _
  Public Name As Name

  <XmlElementAttribute(IsNullable:=True)> _
  Public Organization As String

  <XmlAttributeAttribute(DataType:="int")> _
  Public StudentID As Integer

End Class

<XmlRoot([Namespace]:="", IsNullable:=False)> _
Public Class Name
```

LISTING 14.9 Continued

```
  Private mLast As String

  <XmlAttributeAttribute()> _
  Public First As String

  <XmlAttributeAttribute()> _
  Public Property Last() As String
    Get
      Return mLast
    End Get
    Set(ByVal Value As String)
      If Not Value Is Nothing Then
        mLast = Value
      Else
        Throw New ArgumentException("Last must contain a non-empty string")
      End If
    End Set
  End Property
End Class
```

To begin, as you might expect, the role of the attributes contained in the serialization namespace is to customize how the members of the class are represented in the XML document. In Listing 14.9, the QStudents, Student, and Name classes contain various attributes that indicate how the classes will be serialized to XML. For example, the XmlRootAttribute declaration on the QStudents class signature indicates that QStudents acts as the root element in the XML document and specifies the Namespace and ElementName as they appear in the document. The XmlElementAttribute that decorates the Students array of Student objects indicates that each Student object in the array will be represented as an element. Similarly, the Organization field and the Name property of the Student class are mapped to elements, whereas the StudentID field of the Student class and the First and Last properties of the Name class are mapped to attributes using XmlAttributeAttribute. Note that the XmlAttributeAttribute associated with the StudentID field also includes the DataType property and sets it to "int" in the document.

14

> **NOTE**
>
> To populate this simple object model, the AddStudent method creates a new Student object and its associated Name object and populates them with the arguments passed into the method. It does this using simple array manipulation. Obviously, you could also use the various collection classes discussed in Chapter 3.

However, the most interesting aspect of the QStudent class is the shared SaveXml and HydrateXml methods that use the XmlSerializer class to serialize and deserialize the object. The SaveXml method first creates a new XmlSerializer object by passing the type the serializer will work with in the constructor. In this case, the method uses the instance of QStudents passed into it as a parameter. Next, the overloaded Serialize method is called with the XmlTextWriter passed into the method as the destination object along with the object to serialize. The Serialize method also can accept TextWriter and Stream objects to serialize the output to.

The Serialize method only converts the public fields and read/write properties of an object to XML. It does not convert methods, indexers, private fields, or read-only properties. In addition, those public fields and read/write properties marked with the XmlIgnoreAttribute are also obviously ignored. However, as in this case, if the public fields or properties refer to other classes, they too will be serialized.

> **NOTE**
>
> As discussed in Chapter 8, to serialize all of an object's fields and properties, both public and private, you must use the BinaryFormatter.

The HydrateXml method performs the opposite function by first creating an XmlSerializer for the QStudents object and then testing whether the document passed in the XmlTextReader can be deserialized using the CanDeserialize method. To actually create a strongly typed object from the document, the return value from the Deserialize method is cast to the appropriate type using the CType function.

> **TIP**
>
> Both the SaveXml and HydrateXml methods are shared so that they are accessible without first creating an instance of the QStudents class.

For a client to take advantage of the functionality, he can simply instantiate a QStudents object and populate it using the AddStudent method like so:

```
Dim o As New QStudents()

o.AddStudent("Sammy", "Sosa", 1233, "Cubs")
o.AddStudent("Kerry", "Wood", 232, "Cubs")
```

After the object is populated, it can be serialized by invoking the `SaveXml` method with an `XmlTextWriter` as the argument as follows:

```
Dim xmlWriter As New XmlTextWriter("c:\students.xml", _
  New System.Text.ASCIIEncoding())
xmlWriter.Formatting = Formatting.Indented
QStudents.SaveXml(o, xmlWriter)
xmlWriter.Flush()
xmlWriter.Close()
```

The resulting XML can be seen as follows:

```
<?xml version="1.0" encoding="us-ascii" ?>
<Students xmlns:xsi="http://www.w3.org/2001/XMLSchema-instance"
  xmlns:xsd="http://www.w3.org/2001/XMLSchema"
  xmlns="www.quilogy.com/education">
  <Student StudentID="1233">
    <Name First="Sammy" Last="Sosa" />
    <Organization>Cubs</Organization>
  </Student>
  <Student StudentID="232">
    <Name First="Kerry" Last="Wood" />
    <Organization>Cubs</Organization>
  </Student>
</Students>
```

In an analogous fashion, the `student.xml` document can be deserialized into a new `QStudents` object as follows:

```
Dim g As QStudents
Dim myReader As New XmlTextReader("c:\students.xml")

g = QStudents.HydrateXml(myReader)
myReader.Close()
```

Obviously, the technique shown here is in many ways analogous to creating a derived `DataSet` class. In both cases, the end result is a strongly typed class that can also be easily represented as XML to be passed between tiers in a distributed application or saved to a file. However, for developers who have existing object models that need to be ported to VB .NET, or who simply want to not use the `DataSet` class, XML serialization provides a powerful mechanism to easily persist objects to XML. Although this provides the ultimate flexibility, it also can require more coding because you must write custom code to populate the objects from sources other than XML, whereas the `DataSet` object can be populated using a `DataAdapter`.

> **Tip**
>
> XML serialization comes in particularly handy for developers who, in VB 6.0, followed an object model architecture or who used the LSet statement to serialize User-Defined Types (UDTs) to strings. The big difference of course is that the CLR was built to handle objects and serialization and so there is no penalty for creating many small objects as in VB 6.0 and no need to resort to compiler tricks.

Also note that classes containing the XML serialization attributes can be generated automatically from an XSD schema using the XSD utility discussed in Chapter 7. For example, given an XSD schema in a file called students.xsd, the following command line generates the file students.vb that includes a class to represent it:

```
xsd.exe students.xsd /c /l:vb
```

The output from XSD often is useful as a starting point for developing classes that must be serialized or to create a proxy class when loading XML documents for which you have the schema.

Integrating Messaging

One particularly effective way to increase the scalability and reliability of a distributed application is to move from a model where application requests are processed synchronously to one where some or all of the requests are processed asynchronously. As discussed in Chapter 8, Microsoft includes the Microsoft Message Queue (MSMQ) product as a service in its server operating systems to provide the queueing infrastructure for applications to create and manipulate queues, in addition to sending to and receiving messages from those queues.

> **Note**
>
> MSMQ is not installed by default in Windows 2000 Server. You can do so by using the Configure Your Server utility found in the Administrative Tools group and looking under the Advanced option.

Not surprisingly, the Services Framework provides a namespace, System.Messaging, that encapsulates the functionality of MSMQ. This section examines the System.Messaging namespace, first in how queues are programmatically referenced and administered, and second in how messages are serialized, sent, and received by application programs.

Administering Queues

Although the `System.Messaging` namespace contains more than 20 classes, the central class is `MessageQueue`. This class contains both shared and instance methods to allow you to query for queues contained on a particular machine or across the network, in addition to manipulating individual queues.

At the most basic level, the set of shared members includes `Create`, `Delete`, `Exists`, and several methods prefixed by `Get` that allow you to query for queues. For example, the following code uses the `Exists` method to determine whether a queue identified by the `mstrPath` variable exists and, if not, creates it. In either case, the queue then is referenced by creating an instance of `MessageQueue` and passing in the identifier of the queue:

```
If Not MessageQueue.Exists(mstrPath) Then
  MessageQueue.Create(mstrPath, False)
End If

Dim oQueue As MessageQueue
oQueue = New MessageQueue(mstrPath, False)
```

In the `Create` method, the second argument indicates whether the queue should be transactional, in other words, use the Microsoft Distributed Transaction Coordinator (MSDTC) service to ensure message delivery. And, in the constructor of the `MessageQueue` object, the second argument specifies whether the first application to access the queue receives exclusive access to it. Creating a new `MessageQueue` object using the `New` keyword does not create a new queue; it simply references one that already exists.

The path passed into these methods is simply a string that identifies the queue. In fact, the string can take one of three forms:

- The path to the queue as returned by the `Path` property of the `MessageQueue` object. This is the typical approach in the form *MachineName\QueueName*. For private queues, it is *MachineName\private$\QueueName*. System queues, such as `Deadletter$` and `Journal$`, also can be accessed this way.

- The format name returned by the `FormatName` property prefixed with `"FormatName:"`. This is typically used for offline access to queues.

- The label of the queue as returned by the `Label` property prefixed with `"Label:"`. The `Label` property can be set for a queue to provide a description. Using the `Label` is not recommended because labels are not required to be unique and can thus cause exceptions to be thrown when sending messages or referencing a queue.

In addition to creating and deleting queues, the `MessageQueue` class also provides query and enumeration methods to list the queues on a machine and the message within the queue. To illustrate these capabilities, review the `SetupQueues` method shown in Listing 14.10.

14

INTEGRATING
WITH THE
ENTERPRISE

LISTING 14.10   Manipulating Queues. This method manipulates the private queues on the given machine.

```vb
Imports System.Messaging

Public Sub SetupQueues(ByVal machine As String)
  Dim oQueue As MessageQueue
  Dim arQueues() As MessageQueue

  ' Enable the connection cache
  MessageQueue.EnableConnectionCache = True

  Try
    ' List the private queues on the machine
    arQueues = MessageQueue.GetPrivateQueuesByMachine(machine)
    For Each oQueue In arQueues
      If Right(oQueue.Path, 1) <> "$" Then
        With oQueue
          .MaximumQueueSize = 2048
          .MaximumJournalSize = 4192
          .UseJournalQueue = True
          .EncryptionRequired = EncryptionRequired.None
        End With

        ' Purge the journals
        Dim oJournal As MessageQueue
        If MessageQueue.Exists(oQueue.Path & "\Journal$") Then
          oJournal = New MessageQueue(oQueue.Path & "\Journal$")
          oJournal.Purge()
        End If

        ' Delete acknowledgement messages
        Dim enMessages As MessageEnumerator
        enMessages = CType(oQueue.GetEnumerator(), MessageEnumerator)
        While (enMessages.MoveNext())
          If enMessages.Current.MessageType = MessageType.Acknowledgment Then
            enMessages.RemoveCurrent()
          End If
        End While
      End If
    Next
  Catch e As MessageQueueException
    ' Log a message
  End Try

End Sub
```

First, the SetupQueues method uses the EnableConnectionCache shared property to enable the MessageQueue class to reuse read and write handles to queues, thereby increasing performance. You can clear the cache using the ClearConnection cache shared method.

Next, the GetPrivateQueuesByMachine method is invoked with the name of the computer on which to retrieve the queues. The result is an array of MessageQueue objects stored in the arQueues object. The array can then be iterated over. Note that the Path property is parsed to determine whether the queue is a system queue (denoted with a $ at the end). If not, various properties that put storage limits on the queue, ensure that copies of all messages are saved to a journal queue, and that turn off encryption are set. These changes take effect immediately and throw exceptions if the code does not have permissions.

> **NOTE**
>
> Each queue has a set of permissions—for example, Set Properties, and Get Properties permissions—that can be set in the MSMQ UI by right-clicking on the queue and selecting Properties. MSMQ can be administered in the Computer Management MMC console under Services and Applications. These administrative permissions also can be programmatically manipulated using the SetPermissions and ResetPermissions methods of the MessageQueue class.
>
> Of course, the code calling these methods and manipulating message queues must also have permissions to do so. As mentioned in Chapter 5, "Packaging, Deployment, and Security," the System.Messaging namespace includes the code access permission classes MessageQueuePermission and MessageQueuePermissionAttribute that can be used both imperatively and declaratively, and can be set using the .NET Admin Tool.

Using the Path of the current queue, the journal queue, if it exists, is then referenced using its pathname by the oJournal object. The entire collection of messages in the queue is then deleted using the Purge method.

Finally, the messages in a particular queue are traversed using a MessageEnumerator object. Simply put, the MessageEnumerator exposes a forward-only cursor of messages populated by one of several Get methods in the MessageQueue class. In this case, the GetEnumerator instance method simply returns an enumerator that traverses all the messages in the queue. The MessageEnumerator itself returns the current message (Message object) in the Current property and exposes methods, such as MoveNext and RemoveCurrent, to manipulate the list. In this case, the MessageType of each message is checked; if it is an acknowledgement message, it is deleted.

A Little Recognition Please?

Acknowledgement messages are special types of messages where the body of the message is empty. Acknowledgements can be sent automatically when the message reaches its destination queue or is successfully retrieved from the queue. MSMQ can send both positive and negative acknowledgement—for example, to send a message if the message is not retrieved in a set amount of time.

To enable acknowledgement, you must reference the queue you want to send acknowledgement to in the AdministrationQueue property of the Message object and then set the AcknowledgeType property to one of the AcknowledgeTypes enumeration constants. You then check the AdministrationQueue as you would any other queue. We will discuss this later in the chapter.

The interesting aspect of the enumerator is that it is dynamic. In other words, if new messages with a lower priority than the Current message are added to the queue, they will be included in the cursor. To retrieve a static list of messages, you can use the GetAllMessages method.

Querying Public Queues

Not only does the MessageQueue class support querying for private queues, it can also query for publicly available queues. The GetPublicQueues, GetPublicQueuesByCategory, GetPublicQueuesByLabel, and the GetPublicQueuesByMachine all return an array of MessageQueue objects. However, the first method in this list also is overloaded to accept a MessageQueueCriteria object in which you can specify multiple criteria like those exposed by the other methods (Category, Label, and MachineName), in addition to when the queue was created (CreatedAfter, CreatedBefore) and last modified (ModifiedAfter, ModifiedBefore).

Alternatively, rather than return a static array of queues, the GetMessageQueueEnumerator can be used to create a dynamic cursor that can query the public queues based on criteria specified in a MessageQueueCriteria object. For example, the following code queries the network for queues that match the given category and adds the Path and CreateTime properties to a list to display to the user:

```
Dim enQueues As MessageQueueEnumerator
Dim crMessage As MessageQueueCriteria

crMessage.Category = New Guid("00000000-0000-0000-0000-000000000002")
enQueues = MessageQueue.GetMessageQueueEnumerator(crMessage)

While enQueues.MoveNext
    AddToList(enQueues.Current.Path(), enQueues.Current.CreateTime)
End While
```

Note that the `Category` is simply a `Guid` that needn't be unique. As the name implies, you can use this property to categorize your queues.

Installing Queues

As shown in the previous discussion, the `MessageQueue` class can be used to create and delete queues programmatically. However, as with event logs, performance counters, and other system resources, the recommended technique is to install the resource, if needed, along with the application that uses it. Not surprisingly, the `System.Messaging` namespace contains the `MessageQueueInstaller` class to do just that.

The `MessageQueueInstaller` class works like the installer classes discussed in Chapter 13, "Implementing Services." To use it, you first need to derive a class from `Installer` that will be run by the `Installutil.exe` utility when its `RunInstaller` attribute is set to `True`. Next, you can declare a variable to hold an instance of the `MessageQueueInstaller` class and use it in the constructor of the derived `Installer` class to specify how the queue will be installed. For example, the following code would be contained in the `New` method of the derived `Installer` class:

```
Imports System.Configuration.Install
Imports System.Messaging
mMSMQInstaller = New MessageQueueInstaller()

With mMSMQInstaller
    .Label = "QuilgoyDocQueue"
    .UninstallAction = UninstallAction.Remove
    .UseJournalQueue = True
    .Transactional = True
    .Path = ".\Private$\QuilogyDocs"
End With

Installers().Add(mMSMQInstaller)
```

In this example, the variable `mMSMQInstaller` is instantiated, and its properties are set to those required for this queue. Note that only the `Path` property is required, and here uses the "." to indicate that the queue will be installed on the local machine. In addition, the `UninstallAction` property is used to make sure that the queue is removed from the system when this application is uninstalled. As with other installers, you must add it to the `Installers` collection using the `Add` method as shown here.

14

INTEGRATING WITH THE ENTERPRISE

TIP

Rather than setting all the properties manually as is done in this case, you also have the option of passing a `MessageQueue` object to the overloaded constructor of

> `MessageQueueInstaller`. Doing so copies the queue properties to the newly created queue.

Sending and Receiving Messages

After a queue has been referenced, applications use the `MessageQueue` object to place (send) messages on the queue and read (receive) messages from the queue.

Sending Messages

To send a message, all you need to do is call the overloaded `Send` instance method, passing it the object to place on the queue. The object is then automatically serialized to either XML or a binary representation, and placed in the `Body` of the `Message` object. How the serialization takes place is determined by the `Formatter` property of either the `MessageQueue` object or the `Message` being sent to the queue.

The `System.Messaging` namespace supports three types of formatters: `XmlMessageFormatter` (the default), `ActiveXMessageFormatter`, and `BinaryMessageFormatter`. By default, an instance of `XmlMessageFormatter` is created with the `MessageQueue` object and is assigned to the `Formatter` property. It then is used to serialize the message to a `Stream` and place it in the `Body` property of the `Message` object when the message is sent and again to deserialize it when the message is read from the queue. The `ActiveXMessageFormatter` can be used to serialize COM objects and allows interoperability with VB 6.0, whereas the `BinaryMessageFormatter` can be used to serialize a more compact (and complete) binary representation of the type.

By using this approach, the `Send` method simply can accept the `System.Object` data type and, as long as the object can be serialized (either to a binary format by marking the class and its child classes with the `Serializable` attribute, or to XML), it can be saved in the message body. For example, an instance of the `QStudents` class shown in Listing 14.10 can be sent to queue like so:

```
Dim o As New QStudents()

o.AddStudent("Sammy", "Sossa", 1233, "Cubs")
o.AddStudent("Kerry", "Wood", 232, "Cubs")

Dim oQueue As New MessageQueue(".\private$\Registrations")
oQueue.Formatter = New BinaryMessageFormatter()
oQueue.Send(o)
```

In this case, the default `XmlMessageFormatter` is replaced with a `BinaryMessageFormatter`. Similarly, by omitting the explicit population of the `Formatter` property, the `QStudents` object will be serialized to XML. The message body, as viewed from the MSMQ snap-in, can be seen in Figure 14.1.

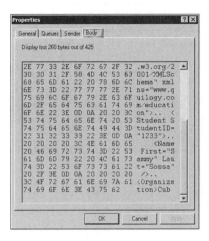

FIGURE 14.1
A MSMQ message in XML format. This dialog is accessed from the MSMQ administrative console by navigating to the appropriate queue and message and selecting Properties from the context menu.

> **NOTE**
>
> For the QStudents object to be serialized using the binary formatter, the QStudents, Student, and Name classes each must have the Serializable attribute set, which is not shown in Listing 14.10.

Although using the automatic serialization provided by the formatters is the easiest way to place objects into a message, you also can directly populate the Body or BodyStream properties of the Message object itself. This is useful when you are placing data from files or other sources into the queue. To illustrate how this works, review the ProcessDocs method shown in Listing 14.11.

LISTING 14.11   Writing to a Message. This method opens files and writes their contents directly to the Body of a Message object using the BodyStream property.

```
Imports System.IO
Imports System.Messaging

Public Sub ProcessDocs(ByVal path As String, ByVal queue As String)

    ' Loop through all docs in a directory
    Dim oFile As FileInfo
    Dim strFile As String
```

LISTING 14.11   Continued

```
Dim oQueue As MessageQueue
Dim fs As FileStream

Try
  ' Ensure queue exists
  If Not MessageQueue.Exists(queue) Then
    Throw New ArgumentException("Queue " & queue & " does not exist.")
    Return
  End If

  ' Reference the queue
  oQueue = New MessageQueue(queue)

  'Go get each file
  For Each strFile In Directory.GetFileSystemEntries(path, "*.xml")
    ' Open the file
    oFile = New FileInfo(strFile)
    fs = oFile.OpenRead

    ' Send the contents to the queue
    Dim oMessage As New Message()
    With oMessage
      .BodyStream = fs
      .Label = oFile.FullName
      .UseDeadLetterQueue = True
      .TimeToBeReceived = New TimeSpan(1, 0, 0, 0)
      .Priority = MessagePriority.Normal
    End With
    oQueue.Send(oMessage)
    fs.Close()
  Next

Catch e As MessageQueueException
  ' Log the fact that an error occurred
Catch e As Exception
  ' Log the fact that an error occurred
End Try

End Sub
```

In Listing 14.11, the method accepts a file path and the path to a queue. After determining that the queue is available and referencing it as oQueue, the directory is traversed for files with the .xml extension. As each file is encountered, it is opened for reading using the OpenRead method of the FileInfo object. This method returns a FileStream that can then be placed directly into the BodyStream property of the Message object. In addition, this method sets some of the properties of the Message, including the Priority and Label, the latter of which can be used as a description and a property to query on.

> **NOTE**
>
> The Message object also supports the AppSpecific and Extension properties that can be used to store application-specific data along with the message. A typical use for these properties is the storage of properties that describe the Body of the message but that are separate from it.

The UseDeadLetterQueue and TimeToBeReceived properties work together to ensure that if the message is not read by another application before the time elapses as specified by the TimeSpan object (in this case 1 day), the message will be sent to the dead letter queue (*MachineName*\Deadletter$).

When the Send method is invoked, the Stream (in this case the FileStream) is read, and the Body property of the Message is populated.

Receiving Messages

The MessageQueue class also supports several methods for receiving messages from a queue. These methods fall into two categories: "peek" methods and "receive" methods.

The peek methods include Peek, PeekByCorrelationId, PeekById, BeginPeek, and EndPeek. In the first three cases, the method returns a Message object from the queue without removing it. In this way, an application can read a message before determining whether it needs to be processed. Whereas Peek returns the first message in the queue, PeekByCorrelationId and PeekById search the queue to find the first message whose CorrelationId and Id properties match the given criteria, respectively.

> **NOTE**
>
> The CorrelationId property is used by acknowledgement, response, and report messages to reference the original message. In other words, it allows you to link an originating message with messages created in response.

All three methods are synchronous, so they block the current thread until a message is received. To avoid blocking indefinitely, they also are overloaded to accept a TimeSpan argument that releases the thread and throws a MessageQueueException when the time expires. The

BeginPeek and EndPeek methods allow asynchronous access to the first message in the queue so that the current thread is not blocked.

The collection of "receive" methods includes analogous Receive, ReceiveByCorrelationId, ReceiveById, BeginReceive, and EndReceive. As you might imagine, the first three in this list behave analogously to the peek methods but have the effect of removing the message from the queue after it is read. The latter two methods are used to read messages asynchronously.

Although reading simple messages synchronously is straightforward, when receiving serialized objects as messages, you must be aware of the type you want to deserialize to. For example, in an earlier code example, an instance of QStudents was serialized to a Message using the BinaryMessageFormatter. To read this message, your code needs to set the Formatter property appropriately and then cast the Body of the Message to the appropriate type like so:

```
Dim oQueue As New MessageQueue(".\private$\Registrations")
Dim oNew As QStudents

oQueue.Formatter = New BinaryMessageFormatter()
oNew = CType(oQueue.Receive.Body, QStudents)
```

The oNew variable now contains the deserialized QStudents object.

TIP

To improve performance, you can set properties of the MessagePropertyFilter object exposed in the MessageReadPropertyFilter property of the MessageQueue instance you are reading from. Each property represents one of the message properties and can be set to True or False to specify whether the property is returned. By default, only nine of the approximately 40 properties are returned.

Although the previous code example used the BinaryMessageFormatter to serialize the object, using the XmlMessageFormatter is more flexible. The reason is that when using the BinaryMessageFormatter, the object is serialized using the type definition (including the version) of the class. This implies that when the object is deserialized, it must be cast to exactly the same type. In other words, the QStudents class must be publicly available in the Global Assembly Cache (GAC) or included as a private assembly and referenced by the receiving application.

By using the XmlMessageFormatter, the receiving application can create its own proxy class to handle the deserialized object. This class can be manually created or generated from XSD. However, when using this approach, the TargetTypes or TargetTypeNames property must be populated before receiving the message. This is required so that the XmlMessageFormatter knows into which object to deserialize the message body. For example, if the QStudents object was serialized to XML, as shown in Figure 14.1, it could be deserialized using the code

```
Dim oNew As QStudentsNew
```

```
oQueue.Formatter = New XmlMessageFormatter(New String() {"QStudentsNew"})
oNew = CType(oQueue.Receive.Body, QStudentsNew)
```

where QStudentsNew is a new class built from the same schema. In this case, the TargetTypeNames property (an array of Strings) is populated in the constructor. The overloaded constructor also can accept an array of Type objects.

One of the subtle advantages to serializing objects directly to the queue is that the objects can encapsulate required behavior. For example, the QStudents class can expose a SaveToDatabase method that knows how to persist the contents of the object to SQL Server using the System.Data.SqlClient namespace. This makes working with the object simple for the receiving application, which can simply deserialize the object and invoke the SaveToDatabase method. In this way, the receiving application needn't understand the internal structure of the QStudents object.

However, in other scenarios, you might want to parse the message yourself—for example, if it contains an XML document. To that end, just as the BodyStream property of the Message object can be populated with a Stream, it also can be used to access the Body of the message. For example, the RetrieveDocs method, shown in Listing 14.12, drains the given queue of its messages and passes the BodyStream of the Message to the ExtractStudents method.

LISTING 14.12   Draining the Queue. This method drains the given queue by calling the Receive method and then passes the BodyStream to a method that processes it.

```
Imports System.Messaging

Public Sub RetrieveDocs(ByVal queue As String)
  Dim oQueue As MessageQueue
  Dim oMessage As Message
  Dim flDone As Boolean = False

  Try
    ' Ensure queue exists
    If Not MessageQueue.Exists(queue) Then
      Throw New ArgumentException("Queue " & queue & " does not exist.")
      Return
    End If

    ' Reference the queue
    oQueue = New MessageQueue(queue)
```

LISTING 14.12 Continued

```
    ' Drain the queue
    While Not flDone
      Try
        oMessage = oQueue.Receive(New TimeSpan(0, 0, 5))
        Call ExtractStudents(oMessage.BodyStream)
      Catch e As MessageQueueException
        flDone = True
      End Try
    End While

  Catch e As MessageQueueException
    ' Log the fact that an error occurred
  Catch e As Exception
    ' Log the fact that an error occurred
  End Try
End Sub
```

The Receive method is called with a timeout value of 5 seconds, so that as soon as no new messages are received in a 5-second interval, the loop is exited. The ExtractStudents method is similar to that shown in Listing 14.1, with the exception that it has been modified to accept a Stream object, rather than a file name like so:

```
Public Sub ExtractStudents(ByVal msgStream As Stream)
```

In this way, you can easily take advantage of the many classes in the Services Framework that rely on streams.

Finally, the MessageQueue class follows the Services Framework pattern for asynchronous operations by exposing BeginPeek, BeginReceive and EndPeek, EndReceive methods. The Begin methods are overloaded and as expected do not block the current thread and return immediately. The methods spawn a background thread that waits until a message is found. When found, the application is notified through either the PeekCompleted and ReceiveCompleted events, or an explicit AsyncCallback object passed to the method.

For example, to add the event handler for the ReceiveCompleted event and initiate the asynchronous process, the following code could be used:

```
oQueue = New MessageQueue(queue)
AddHandler oQueue.ReceiveCompleted, AddressOf MessageFound
oQueue.BeginReceive(New TimeSpan(0, 0, 5))
```

Notice that the BeginReceive method also can be passed a TimeSpan object that fires the ReceiveCompleted event if the time expires before a message is found. Although not shown here, an Object can be passed to the Begin method that contains state information returned in the AsyncState property of the AsyncResult object.

Within the event handlers, the MessageQueue from which the message is returned is populated in the first argument, whereas the arguments are encapsulated in the ReceiveCompletedEventArgs object. The actual Message object can then be accessed by calling the EndReceive method, as illustrated by the template code that follows:

```
Public Sub MessageFound(ByVal s As Object, _
  ByVal args As ReceiveCompletedEventArgs)

    Dim oQueue As MessageQueue
    Dim oMessage As Message
    Dim oState As Object

    ' Retrieve the state if needed
    oState = args.AsyncResult.AsyncState()

    ' Retrieve the queue from which the message originated
    oQueue = CType(s, MessageQueue)

    Try
      oMessage = oQueue.EndReceive(args.AsyncResult)
      ' Process the message here
    Catch e As MessageQueueException
      ' Timeout expired
    End Try

End Sub
```

When using the asynchronous peek methods, there is an analogous PeekCompletedEventArgs object for use in the PeekCompleted event handler.

> **TIP**
>
> If you want to continue receiving documents in the background, you can call BeginReceive at the end of the event handler.

Integrating Active Directory

The final topic in this chapter deals with programmatically accessing directories using the System.DirectoryServices namespace. This is important because developers of distributed applications often have to query and synchronize information from one or more directories including Active Directory, Windows NT, and Novell NetWare.

Simply put, the classes in this namespace allow you to seamlessly interact with these directories by abstracting the directory-specific features in service providers (analogous to OLE DB providers or ODBC drivers).

> **NOTE**
>
> This should sound familiar to some readers because the `DirectoryServices` namespace simply provides a wrapper around the Active Directory Services Interface (ADSI) components you might have used in VB 6.0.

Although the underlying ADSI technology is not new, the `DirectoryServices` namespace simplifies the programming model by exposing all objects in a directory as `DirectoryEntry` objects, rather than exposing specific classes for each type of object as in the COM object model. By passing a path to the constructor of the `DirectoryEntry` object, the appropriate service provider is notified and the object returned. To invoke a service provider, you need to prefix the path with the type of provider you want to access, as shown in Table 14.4. As a result, you can access the same directories using the service providers in .NET as in VB 6.0.

TABLE 14.4 Services Providers and Their Path Strings

Service Provider	Path Format
Windows NT or Windows 2000	`WinNT://path`
Internet Information Server	`IIS://path`
Lightweight Directory Access Protocol	`LDAP://path`
Novell NetWare Directory Service	`NDS://path`

After the object is returned, you can query and change its properties using the `Properties` collection in addition to dynamically calling its methods using the `Invoke` method. However, for most developers, the primary task is simply to query the directory and return some information. For example, one of the tasks that Web developers often are faced with is determining the full name of the Windows user authenticated using Windows Integrated or NTLM authentication. This can be done fairly easily using a method like the following:

```
Imports System.DirectoryServices
Public Function GetFullName(ByVal webPage As Page) As String
    ' Extract the domain and user name
    Try
        Dim strUserName As String = webPage.User.Identity.Name
        strUserName = strUserName.Replace("\", "/")
```

```
        Dim oEntry As New DirectoryEntry("WinNT://" & strUserName)
        Return oEntry.Properties("Fullname")(0)
    Catch e As Exception
        Return Nothing
    End Try
End Function
```

The GetFullName method accepts a Page object (from the System.Web.UI namespace) as a parameter, which exposes the currently authenticated user from IIS in the User property. The Name property returns the domain and user account of the logged-on user, which then is modified and used as input to the constructor of the DirectoryEntry object. If the user account is found (it might not be, for example, if the domain controller is offline), the Fullname property is accessed from the Properties collection and returned.

Querying the Directory

In addition to simply accessing a single entry in the directory, you can perform searches on the directory and return multiple entries using the DirectorySearcher class. Although space prohibits a more complete discussion, the class exposes the FindOne and FindAll methods, which return SearchResult and SearchResultCollection objects, respectively. The search criteria is specified using the Filter property.

> **NOTE**
>
> At this time, only the LDAP service provider supports searching.

To illustrate querying Active Directory on a Windows 2000 network, Listing 14.13 provides the ADUser class. ADUser should be thought of as a utility class that can be used in conjunction with a Web- or form-based application to query the Active Directory for information about a user. This information then can be used to modify the user interface or restrict access to what the user can see.

> **NOTE**
>
> For a good overview of Active Directory, see *Active Directory Programming* by Gil Kirkpatrick, ISBN: 0672315874.

14

INTEGRATING
WITH THE
ENTERPRISE

LISTING 14.13   Querying Active Directory. This listing shows the ADUser class used to query Active Directory and return information on a user.

```vb
Imports System.DirectoryServices
Imports System.Collections.Specialized

Public Class ADUser

  Public ReadOnly UserName As String
  Public ReadOnly Name As String
  Public ReadOnly Department As String
  Public ReadOnly Email As String
  Public ReadOnly Groups As StringCollection

  Public Sub New(ByVal logonName As String)
    ' Parse the NT Account path (DOMAIN\USER)
    Dim strUserName As String = _
      logonName.Substring(logonName.IndexOf("\") + 1)
    ' Populate the fields in the class
    Call PopulateUser(strUserName, UserName, Name, _
      Department, Email, Groups)
  End Sub

  Private Sub PopulateUser(ByVal user As String, _
   ByRef userName As String, ByRef name As String, _
   ByRef dept As String, ByRef email As String, _
   ByRef groups As StringCollection)

    'Find the path to the user
    Dim oSearcher As New DirectorySearcher()
    Dim oResult As SearchResult
    Dim dirEntry As DirectoryEntry
    Dim obj As Object
    Dim strGroupPathName As String
    Dim strFilter As String

    Try
      'Set the LDAP search filter
      strFilter = String.Format("(&(objectCategory=person)" & _
        "(objectClass=user)(sAMAccountName= {0}))", user)
      oSearcher.Filter = strFilter

      'Search for the user entry
      oResult = oSearcher.FindOne()
      If oResult Is Nothing Then
        Return
```

LISTING 14.13 Continued

```
      End If

      ' Found so get the directory entry
      dirEntry = oResult.GetDirectoryEntry

      ' Get the properties
      With dirEntry
        userName = .Properties("sAMAccountName")(0).ToString
        name = .Properties("name")(0).ToString
        dept = .Properties("department")(0).ToString
        email = .Properties("mail")(0).ToString
      End With

      For Each obj In dirEntry.Properties("memberOf")
        strGroupPathName = obj.ToString()
        groups.Add(strGroupPathName)
      Next

    Catch e As Exception
      Throw New Exception("Could not populate the ADUser: " & e.Message)
    End Try

  End Sub

End Class
```

In Listing 14.13, the constructor is passed the Windows logon account of the user as returned by the Name property of the WindowsIdentity object. This string then is parsed to return only the username portion, which then is passed to the private PopulateUser method where all the work takes place.

> **TIP**
>
> Because the fields that PopulateUser will populate are read-only, they can be modified only in the constructor and must be passed as ByRef arguments to the method.

In the PopulateUser method, a new DirectorySearcher object is instantiated and its filter set using an LDAP query string. Although the structure of Active Directory is beyond the scope of this book, you can see that the class of the objects to be returned is set to "user" and is passed the Security Accounts Manager (SAM) account name. To execute the query, the FindOne

14

method is called, which returns a `SearchResult` object. If more than one entry is found, only the first is returned. If no entry is found, the result object is set to `Nothing`.

If the query returns an object, its `DirectoryEntry` can be returned using the `GetDirectoryEntry` method of the `SearchResult` object. Using this technique, the directory is queried again using the `Path` property of the `SearchResult` object. To bypass this round-trip, the `PropertiesToLoad` property of the `SearchResult` object can be populated ahead of time with the names of properties you want to return with the `SearchResult`. By default, only the `Name` and `Path` properties are returned.

Properties are returned for a `DirectoryEntry` in a `PropertyCollection`, which, in addition to standard collection members, exposes both `PropertyNames` and `Values` properties that themselves return collections of the properties for the object. In addition, properties can be multivalued, and each property is actually a `PropertyValueCollection` object. This is why to access simple properties, such as the department, name, and mail, you must use the index of 0 on the property.

Populating a collection of the groups the user belongs to in the `memberOf` property is an example of accessing a multivalued property. In this case, the property itself can be traversed with a `For Each` loop and the path to the group added to the `StringCollection`.

From the client's perspective, he simply needs to instantiate the `ADUser` class and pass it the Windows logon name and subsequently change the UI accordingly like so:

```
Dim objUser As New ADUser(Page.User.Identity.Name)

If objUser.Department = "Sales" Then
    ' Show the sales graph
End If
```

Summary

As applications become more connected, it is increasingly important to be able to access data from a variety of sources. This chapter focused on three of those sources: using classes in the Services Framework to work with XML data (`System.Xml`), message queuing (`System.Messaging`), and directory services (`System.DirectoryServices`).

This completes Part III on integrating with the enterprise, in addition to serving as the finale of this book. My aim in this book was to provide corporate developers with a mental map of VB .NET and how it can be used to build distributed applications. To that end, I hope that you found it not only interesting, but useful as you work with VB .NET to build your own solutions.

INDEX

A